Programming Microsoft® ASP.NET MVC

Dino Esposito

PUBLISHED BY
Microsoft Press
A Division of Microsoft Corporation
One Microsoft Way
Redmond, Washington 98052-6399

Library of Congress Control Number: 2010925900

Printed and bound in the United States of America.

1 2 3 4 5 6 7 8 9   WCT   5 4 3 2 1 0

Distributed in Canada by H.B. Fenn and Company Ltd.

A CIP catalogue record for this book is available from the British Library.

Microsoft Press books are available through booksellers and distributors worldwide. For further information about international editions, contact your local Microsoft Corporation office or contact Microsoft Press International directly at fax (425) 936-7329. Visit our Web site at www.microsoft.com/mspress. Send comments to mspinput@microsoft.com.

Acquisitions Editor: Ben Ryan
Developmental Editor: Lynn Finnel
Project Editors: Lynn Finnel and Carol Vu
Editorial Production: Ashley Schneider, S4Carlisle Publishing Services
Technical Reviewer: Kenn Scribner; Technical Review services provided by Content Master, a member of CM Group, Ltd
Cover: Tom Draper Design

Body Part No. X16-88503

To Silvia, Francesco, and Michela, who wait for me and keep me busy.
But I'm happy only when I'm busy.

—Dino

Contents at a Glance

Table of Contents

What do you think of this book? We want to hear from you!

Microsoft is interested in hearing your feedback so we can continually improve our books and learning resources for you. To participate in a brief online survey, please visit:

www.microsoft.com/learning/booksurvey/

Acknowledgments

The man who doesn't read good books has no advantage over the man who can't read them.

—Mark Twain

We started discussing this book around the release of ASP.NET MVC 1.0, in the late spring of 2009. It was not exactly an ideal time for making plans, even though business had to go on in spite of the world financial crisis and severe downturn in the economy. Now that the book is finished, we seem to live in slightly better times, and we all sincerely hope that the worst of it is behind us. However, as I look at this book project now that it's finished, I realize I'm deeply missing one special person—**Lynn Finnel**.

Lynn was laid off in the middle of the project as a result of one of the many restructurings that a lot of companies went through in the past year. Lynn and I have done so many books together, and we always shared a mutual high level of satisfaction with the outcome. Not sending chapters and reviews to Lynn any more was a big change in this part of my professional life. And, who knows, one day I might have Lynn, at the height of her new career as a physical therapist, just take care of my poor back, stressed by its unnatural posture and too many hours of tennis.

Changing the project editor in the middle of a book project can sometimes be a tough experience, but as arranged by **Carol Vu** the transition was seamless. Despite the difficulties in replacing an editor of Lynn's caliber, I really didn't notice any difference.

In the past few months, **Ben Ryan** got a bunch of e-mails from me asking, with different tones, always the same question: "Are you still there?" Yes, fortunately, he's still there with prompt and insightful suggestions. Cheap and valuable—only two cents each! But I've never valued any advice more than Ben's two-cent propositions.

And, fortunately, **Kenn Scribner** is still part of the team and a rock-solid pillar. The degree to which Kenn can be helpful is just beyond human imagination. Now Kenn, let me challenge you: I wrote this same sentence about you in another book. Which one? Hey, you have only a few days to answer as another project is in sight! :)

Many editors say that my written English is more than acceptable for it not being my first language. Readers don't actually know much about my (real) English because **Roger LeBlanc** has a pass on every thought that I happen to put down in words. I would like a wireless version of Roger that could intercept my thoughts at the source and fix them in correct English right away.

I owe you all the usual, but heart-felt, monumental "Thank You" for being so kind, patient, and accurate. (Don't worry, Roger will have fixed this too.)

Like millions of other Italian students, I spent many hours of my teenage years trying to catch the spirit of *The Divine Comedy*. As you may know, the whole poem develops around a journey that Dante undertakes through the three realms of the dead, guided by the Roman poet Virgilio. With due distance, I similarly spent many hours of my past months trying to catch and express the gist of ASP.NET MVC. I began a journey through controllers, views, models, and filters, guided by a top-notch developer, trainer, and friend—**Hadi Hariri**.

At times during the project, I searched for advice on a few specific architectural aspects of ASP.NET MVC and found that

1. The number of matching responses was surprisingly low.

2. And the first significant post reported was from Hadi.

This combination of results happened only a couple of times, but a couple of times is a huge quantity given the very specific questions I was trying to find out more.

After advocating **ReSharper** for many years, Hadi now works for **JetBrains** and reinforced the strongly positive feeling I always had for the product. Of course, he helped me a lot with the appendix at the end of the book.

Loyal readers of my books may know about my (insane) passion for tennis. My wife, Silvia, asked me once, *"OK, you like tennis so much, but is there any chance that you can make some money from it?"* I never dared ask whether she meant "make money playing and winning tournaments" or "make money through software applied to tennis." To be on the safe side, I covered both possibilities and decided to train and play a lot more, while spending many hours helping out **Giorgio Garcia** and the entire team at **Crionet** and **e-tennis.tv** to serve better services to tennis tournaments and their related fans.

Finally, I must mention my kids, Francesco (12) and Michela (9). In different ways, they seem to feel comfortable on stage, be it on Wimbledon's Centre Court with Roger Federer in the background or in a nice theater in Rome.

Till the next one!

Dino Esposito

Introduction

Get your facts first, and then you can distort them as much as you please.

—*Mark Twain*

In the spring of 2006, I had the privilege of taking a very early look at what would eventually become ASP.NET MVC. Scott Guthrie of Microsoft arranged a personal demo just for me backstage at the DevConnections conference in balmy Nice, France. At the time, I had just started playing with ASP.NET Web Forms and the Model-View-Presenter (MVP) pattern. I expected to see the usual great set of designers to automatically define models, controllers, and views. Instead, I was surprised to see a brand-new application model being worked out on top of the same ASP.NET runtime. (Note that what I saw at that time was at best a distant relative to what you know today as ASP.NET MVC, but the key facts were already visible.)

Not that getting rid of the postback model looked like a bad thing to me, but frankly the idea of changing the programming model quite significantly didn't impress me that much. The combination of ASP.NET Web Forms and MVP seemed to me a more natural and less disruptive way to achieve separation of concerns and overall better quality code. Scott pointed me to a couple of team members that I pinged a few times during the summer for more information and newer builds. But nothing happened. Instead, in the summer of 2006 all the excitement being generated was for the upcoming ASP.NET AJAX Extensions (remember Atlas?). Overwhelmed by the AJAX bandwagon, I gravitated to this clear sentiment: that funky ASP.NET MVC thing was just a proof of concept, a *good-for-fun* project. So I removed it from my mind.

In October 2007, I was in Malaga, Spain, to make a presentation to a local user group. During a break, my friend Hadi Hariri asked my opinion about the just-released, first preview of ASP.NET MVC.

ASP.NET what?

I had a look at the bits, and a few weeks later I even wrote one of the very first articles about ASP.NET MVC for the DotNetSlackers Web site. The article is still there (and mostly valid) at *http://www.dotnetslackers.com/articles/aspnet/AnArchitecturalViewOfTheASPNETMVCFramework .aspx*. The taste of ASP.NET MVC was bittersweet for me. Overall, ASP.NET MVC seemed like an entire step backwards and I couldn't see the point of it. And I asked the same question so many times:

When is this going to be really (and tangibly) better than ASP.NET Web Forms?

This is the fundamental question. And it is still largely unanswered, to the point that I suspect that it can't really have an answer.

Although it's based on the same runtime environment, ASP.NET MVC is significantly different from ASP.NET Web Forms. It supports a radically different pattern—MVC (actually the special flavor of MVC known as Model2) rather than a pure Page Controller—and was designed with a radically different set of goals—testability, extensibility, and closeness-to-the-metal of both the Web and ASP.NET runtime.

It doesn't matter what kind of software professional you are, when it comes to choosing the platform for a new .NET Web application you feel like you are at a crossroads. You know you have to choose, and you look around for guidance. You see pros and cons on both sides, and you can hardly see—clearly and tangibly—what's the right way to go. For this reason, the core question—should we use ASP.NET Web Forms or ASP.NET MVC—often ends up being an endless and pointless religious discussion where all parties push their own vision and scream louder with the gathering force of their conviction.

In the end, the correct answer is that it depends. In the end, the choice is really like Microsoft describes it: car vs. motorcycle or automatic vs. manual.

This leads to a new and largely unspoken question: *Did we really need a second option?* Wouldn't it have been better for us if Microsoft detected the signs of age of Web Forms and worked as hard as they worked on ASP.NET MVC to improve that, sticking to just *one* framework?

Aren't two options always better than one? Sure, but two options imply a choice. And a choice implies information, education, and responsibility. Here's where this book hopefully fits in.

ASP.NET MVC and Web Forms

Until late 2008, I was happy enough with Web Forms. I did recognize its weak points and was able to work around them nicely with discipline and systematic application of design principles. In the beginning, ASP.NET MVC was enthusiastically received by a relatively small segment of the community, but one that was screaming loudly and posting a lot. Even though I've never been a member of the ALT.NET community, I'm still constantly keeping an eye out for any better ways of doing my tasks. So I started to explore the ASP.NET MVC architecture and tried to understand its potential, while constantly trying to envision concrete business scenarios in which to employ it. I did this for about a year.

What did I learn?

Technically speaking, ASP.NET MVC is *far superior* to Web Forms. This is because it's newer and was designed around an alternate and more modern set of principles and patterns. Is this sufficient reason for you to switch to it? In my opinion, it isn't. ASP.NET MVC is an excellent choice from the perspective of developers, but that fact alone doesn't automatically translate into a tangible benefit for the customer and the project. Moreover, ASP.NET MVC is much less forgiving than Web Forms and requires training, or at least self-training.

In 10 years of using Web Forms, I've seen many professionals with limited programming skills produce effective Web front ends using data-bound controls and a bit of Microsoft Visual Basic. This will not happen with ASP.NET MVC. Worse yet, if you start writing ASP.NET MVC code taking the learn-as-you-go approach that worked for many with Web Forms, you will surely cook up great examples of much hated spaghetti code.

So learning ASP.NET MVC makes you a better developer, but it has a cost. Who's supposed to pay for that? Your customer? Your company? You, yourself? How would you justify to a project manager the extra training costs for just using ASP.NET MVC? You can try, but the natural objection is this: "OK, but where's my return? Can't we take this project home by simply using Web Forms, which we already know through and through?"

In the end, picking ASP.NET MVC over Web Forms is a matter of preference and attitude, or it's a matter of dealing with some *nonfunctional* requirements. In the first case, you don't have extra costs because it can be assumed you know your stuff very well. The second case, instead, introduces the *only scenario* I can think of where ASP.NET MVC is a clear winner.

How can you fulfill requirements such as strict accessibility, adherence to Web standards, XHTML, theme-ability, cross-browser experience, and rich AJAX capabilities?

These requirements lead to the necessity of exercising strict control over the markup emitted for each page. This is an area where ASP.NET MVC is incomparably better than Web Forms, even when you take into consideration Microsoft's latest improvements to the ASP.NET 4 framework and your own programming self-discipline.

Every other argument being presented as a plus of ASP.NET MVC—such as testability, separation of concerns, extensibility, and the like—is just a plus of the framework, not a breakthrough for the project. By the way, even though in the .NET space we seem to have discovered testability only a few years ago, it has been listed as a fundamental attribute of software in the ISO/IEC 9126 paper since 1991. (For more information, have a look at *http://en.wikipedia.org/wiki/ISO_9126*.)

Who Is This Book For?

As explained in great detail in Chapter 1, "Goal of ASP.NET MVC and Motivation for Its Development," ASP.NET Web Forms is showing the signs of age. And ASP.NET MVC is an excellent (although still incomplete) replacement. My guess—my humble, two-cent guess—is that in a couple of years (and in a couple of versions) ASP.NET MVC will offer the same level of productivity as Web Forms—either because of framework enhancements or because of even more powerful tooling. At that point, you will have two options that are equivalent functionally and in terms of productivity. But one of them (ASP.NET MVC) can help you write better code, faster. This may not be the case today with ASP.NET MVC 2, but it likely will be the case with ASP.NET MVC 3 or 4.

I don't think that ASP.NET Web Forms will be dismissed very soon. For example, rumors suggest that ASP.NET Web Forms will move decidedly toward increasing testability in version 5 through the introduction of some MVP support. We'll see, but as I see things ASP.NET MVC is and will remain far superior technically.

Although pushing a team to use ASP.NET MVC today on a project might be an arguable choice, pushing it within a software company isn't an arguable choice at all. Having a deep understanding of ASP.NET MVC makes you a better developer. ASP.NET MVC is easy to pick up for junior developers who are just out of school, even though it could be harder for experienced Web Forms developers to learn. This book assumes you have knowledge of Web Forms programming as it explains how ASP.NET MVC works and how to use it effectively.

My experience shows that too many Web Forms developers built their expertise by trial and error. ASP.NET MVC requires a sort of reset, and you know that after you reboot your machine it normally runs faster. But this personal reboot may take a bit of effort. Start today with ASP.NET MVC, even in parallel with current Web Forms projects. You'll see the difference, understand the basic facts of Web development, and soon be ready for writing better code with both Web Forms and ASP.NET MVC.

Companion Content

This book features a companion Web site that makes available to you all the code used in the book. This code is organized by chapter, and you can download it from the companion site at this address: *http://go.microsoft.com/fwlink/?LinkId=189142*.

Hardware and Software Requirements

You'll need the following hardware and software to work with the companion content included with this book:

- Microsoft Windows Vista Home Premium Edition, Windows Vista Business Edition, or Windows Vista Ultimate Edition, Microsoft Windows 7 Home Premium Edition, Windows 7 Business Edition, or Windows 7 Ultimate Edition, Windows Server 2008, SP1.

- Microsoft Visual Studio 2008 Standard Edition, Visual Studio 2008 Enterprise Edition, or Microsoft Visual C# 2008 Express Edition and Microsoft Visual Web Developer 2008 Express Edition, Visual Studio 2010 Professional Edition, Visual Studio 2010 Premium Edition, Visual Studio 2010 Ultimate Edition.

- Microsoft SQL Server 2008 Express Edition, Service Pack 1.

- 1.6 GHz Pentium III+ processor, or faster.

- 1 GB of available, physical RAM.

- Video (800 × 600 or higher resolution) monitor with at least 256 colors.

- CD-ROM or DVD-ROM drive.

- Microsoft mouse or compatible pointing device.

Support for This Book

Every effort has been made to ensure the accuracy of this book. As corrections or changes are collected, they will be added to a Microsoft Knowledge Base article accessible via the Microsoft Help and Support site. Microsoft Press provides support for books, including instructions for finding Knowledge Base articles, at the following Web site: *http://www.microsoft.com/learning/support/books/.*

If you have questions regarding the book that are not answered by visiting the site above or viewing a Knowledge Base article, send them to Microsoft Press via e-mail to *mspinput@microsoft.com.*

Please note that Microsoft software product support is not offered through these addresses.

We Want to Hear from You

We welcome your feedback about this book. Please share your comments and ideas via the following short survey: *http://www.microsoft.com/learning/booksurvey*

Your participation will help Microsoft Press create books that better meet your needs and your standards.

Note We hope that you will give us detailed feedback via our survey. If you have questions about our publishing program, upcoming titles, or Microsoft Press in general, we encourage you to interact with us via Twitter at *http://twitter.com/MicrosoftPress*. For support issues, use only the e-mail address shown above.

Part I
The Programming Paradigm

Chapter 1
Goals of ASP.NET MVC and Motivation for Its Development

You affect the world by what you browse.

—*Tim Berners-Lee*

The open era of the World Wide Web (WWW) began on April 30, 1993. That day, the European Organization for Nuclear Research (CERN, from the French original name of *Conseil Européen pour la Recherche Nucléaire*) announced publicly that the World Wide Web would be free for anyone to browse and build within.

As a Web professional, you should keep this date in mind, carefully track it in your calendar and, perhaps, celebrate it regularly with friends and family. It is a significant day in history. After all, it's *the* date on which your profession was officially born. Without this date in history, you might have found yourself a car mechanic or store salesperson!

As Tim Berners-Lee—the inventor of the World Wide Web—noted once, the development of the Web was very quick compared to other media and mass devices such as the telephone or TV. A number of ancillary factors contributed to the rapid growth of the WWW. One was certainly the decision, adopted only a few weeks before the CERN announcement, by the University of Minnesota to charge a fee for use of its Gopher server. At the time, Gopher—a TCP/IP layer for retrieving documents over the Internet—was an even better established and more credible alternative to the World Wide Web. The fee announced by the University of Minnesota was only for the use of one particular server, but people saw in it the threat of an incoming charge to be imposed on any Gopher server worldwide.

That's just one example of an early catalyst to the growth of the WWW. You've lived and personally experienced the rest of the story.

By the end of the 1990s, Gopher was in full stagnation while the WWW was expanding and, among other things, fueling the notorious Internet bubble. (If you're curious about Gopher, you can dig further into the topic by visiting the reference on Wikipedia at the following address: *http://en.wikipedia.org/wiki/Gopher_(protocol).*)

The first significant Web sites and applications appeared shortly after CERN waived any copyrights on the WWW. In general terms, a Web application is a kind of client/server application that consists of a set of individually addressable pages. Pages form the user interface of the application and are accessed via a general-purpose client application—the Web browser. Pages work over the network whether it is the Internet or an intranet.

What is a Web page? How is a Web page coded?

The answers to these questions are precisely what this book covers from the perspective of ASP.NET MVC, which is a framework for building Web applications using the Microsoft ASP.NET platform. ASP.NET MVC (for *Model View Controller*) marks a significant change in how developers code Web pages within the ASP.NET platform.

Abstractly speaking, a Web page can be seen as a dual container where a public interface is backed by a number of technologies on a variety of hardware/software platforms. Publicly, a Web page produces a standard *markup mix* made of HTML, cascading style sheets (CSS), and JavaScript that Web browsers know how to render. Internally, a Web page can employ a number of technologies, frameworks, languages, and patterns to process a Web request to an acceptable markup mix.

Microsoft scored a remarkable victory in the Web industry with the introduction of the ASP.NET platform back in 2001. ASP.NET opened the doors of Web development to a huge number of professionals and contributed to changing the development model of Web applications. ASP.NET wasn't alone in producing this effort. ASP.NET followed up the progress made by at least a couple of earlier technologies: classic Active Server Pages (ASP) and Java Server Pages (JSP).

In its early years, the Web pushed an unusual programming model and a set of programming tools and languages that were unknown or unfamiliar to the majority of programmers. Anybody who tried to build even a trivial Web site in the 1990s had to come to grips with the HTML syntax and at least the simplest JavaScript commands and objects. The public interface of Web pages—the aforementioned markup mix—had to be written manually in the past decade. And this created a sort of trench separating *die-hard* C/C++ programmers from *freaky* Web developers.

Whereas classic ASP introduced the concept of dynamic content generation and laid the groundwork for rapid application development (RAD) tools, JSP explored a more structured approach to Web development based on the reassessment of some popular (and effective) design patterns.

Classic ASP was a blast to work with because developers really liked the idea of designing Web pages as HTML-based templates interspersed with some code blocks to be interpreted and executed at run time and generating dynamic content on the fly. However, there's a strong, underlying assumption in this model.

Any Web requests that come along are processed to generate an HTML page. All server efforts to process the request are aimed at getting an HTML page, from the opening *<html>* tag to the closing *</html>* tag. Any code and processing required along the way are overshadowed by the necessity of producing detailed HTML. The link between the Web request and some server-side operation is surely not lost, but it doesn't always show up clearly at the developer level.

For years, this remained the major difference between classic ASP (and, later, ASP.NET) and JSP. This gap is covered today with the release of an alternative programming model for the ASP.NET platform. Welcome, ASP.NET MVC!

Note You might have noticed that I didn't mention Personal Home Page (PHP) language when I listed some of the technologies that influenced Web development models. When it comes to Web development technologies, PHP can't just be ignored.

According to Netcraft's January 2010 Web server survey (which you can find at *http://news .netcraft.com/archives/2010/01/07/january_2010_web_server_survey.html*), Apache is firmly the market leader serving around 50 percent of monitored sites. And because Apache is part of the open-source LAMP (Linux + Apache + MySQL + PHP) stack—with Linux as the operating system, Apache as the Web server, MySQL as the database server, and PHP (or Python or Perl) as the programming language—you can easily conclude that PHP is an extremely popular Web development framework. PHP and ASP.NET together have the lion's share of the development market.

However, PHP and ASP.NET developed along independent paths and thus have quite different characteristics. ASP.NET was devised to be the successor of classic ASP; in the newer flavor of ASP.NET MVC, some of the ideas originally developed for JSP have been reworked. That's why you didn't find PHP mentioned earlier.

The Deep Impact of ASP.NET

Classic ASP had two main merits. First, it made dynamic HTML generation really easy for many developers. Second, it was one of the first programming environments to host the logic of Web applications within the Web server with a subsequent marked performance gain.

Based on script code and interpreted by a runtime engine, ASP pages were upgraded to the rank of compiled code with the advent of the .NET platform. Totally superseded by ASP.NET, classic ASP is today a dead end and survives only in legacy Web sites.

ASP.NET pages are based on compiled code written using first-class programming languages such as Microsoft C# and Visual Basic. What was easy and effective to do with classic ASP turned out to be even easier and smoother with ASP.NET.

Productivity Is King

The advent of ASP.NET represented a turning point for the Web industry as a whole. ASP.NET was built on top of classic ASP and added a lot of new features. The quest for productivity was the primary driving force behind the innovations introduced with ASP.NET.

The Fast-Growing Web Industry

Scott Guthrie of Microsoft notes in an interview on MSDN's Channel 9 that in the late 1990s his team was called to devise the next generation of Web applications. That happened at the time when classic ASP, COM, and Microsoft Transaction Server (MTS) represented the cutting edge of Web and multitier applications. The team started gathering feedback from customers writing real-world Web applications and quickly learned that there was a heck of a lot to do to make their task easier and quicker.

The feature set of classic ASP was too small for scaling up the technology. In addition, there was a strong demand for rapid application development (RAD) and administration tools capable of speeding up all tasks that usually accompany the building of an application—deployment, back-office tasks, visual feedback.

> **Note** You can find the full transcript of Scott Guthrie's Channel 9 interview at *http://channel9 .msdn.com/shows/ARCast+with+Ron+Jacobs/ARCast-Scott-Guthrie-the-man-the-myth-the-legend*. Currently Microsoft Corporate VP of the .NET Developer Platform, Scott was a member of the team that originally devised and built ASP.NET.

ASP.NET was devised in the late 1990s at a time when many companies in various industry sectors were rapidly discovering the new media called the Internet. For companies, the Internet was a real breakthrough, making possible innovations in software infrastructure, marketing, distribution, and communications that were impractical or impossible before.

A ton of old-fashioned, mainframe-based enterprise applications were redesigned around a Web-based front-end topping a bunch of .NET-based tiers. In addition, the advent of e-commerce, intranets, portals, and new publishing opportunities pushed growth in industries based specifically on the Web at an incredible pace. A fast-growing Web industry spurred rapid growth in the number of Web sites. And this was possible only with robust and reliable Web development technologies that could generate unprecedented productivity.

ASP.NET was the right technology at the right time.

Adapting the RAD Model to the Web

Before ASP.NET was developed, in Microsoft's space the RAD, event-driven model of Visual Basic was the best (and most envied) practice. Visual Basic made it quick and easy to prototype an application driven by the needs of the user interface. So you could start by putting a few buttons on a form, double-click on them to have a stub of code added, and then edit that code with some database commands.

Results could be tested in a matter of seconds, and users could share feedback on graphics pretty soon afterward. In a word, development became inherently more agile; the attention to detailed blueprints inevitably decreased.

The RAD model was created for smart-client desktop applications. The challenge for the ASP.NET team was figuring out how to expand the RAD model to the Web.

The original Visual Basic RAD model evolved into the Windows Forms model with the introduction of the Microsoft .NET Framework. With the Windows Forms model, no matter what connectivity exists between the client and server components, the server always works in reaction to the client's input. The server is aware of the overall application state and operates in a two-tier, connected manner. This model was easy to implement in a smart-client scenario, but it required some extra machinery to get it to work over the Web. Figure 1-1 compares the smart-client Windows Forms model with ASP.NET's Web Forms model.

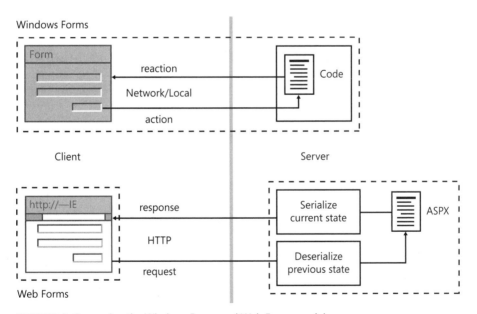

FIGURE 1-1 Comparing the Windows Forms and Web Forms models

Because the Web is based on a stateless protocol, implementing an event model over the Web requires any data related to the client-side user's activity to be forwarded to the server for corresponding and stateful processing. The server processes the output of client actions and triggers reactions.

The state of the application contains two types of information: the state of the client and the state of the session. The needed machinery is represented by the state deserialization that occurs when the Web page is requested, and the state serialization is performed when the HTML response is being generated.

> **Note** I can't emphasize enough the importance of understanding the concepts involved with *stateless* programming when developing Web applications. As mentioned, HTTP is a stateless protocol, which means two successive requests across the same session have no knowledge of each other. On the server side, they are resolved by newly instantiated environments in which no session-specific information is automatically maintained, except all the information the application itself might have stored in some of its own global objects.
>
> The ASP.NET runtime carries the page state back and forth across page requests. When generating HTML code for a given page, ASP.NET encodes and stuffs the state of server-side objects into a few hidden, and transparently created, fields. When the page is requested, the same ASP.NET runtime engine checks for embedded state information—the hidden fields—and uses any decoded information to set up newly created instances of server-side objects. The net effect of such a mechanism is not unlike the Windows Forms model on the desktop and is summarized in Figure 1-1.

Engineering Current Best Practices

In addition to re-creating an overall environment similar to a desktop's Windows Forms model, the ASP.NET team managed to select a number of ASP best development practices and engineered them into the new ASP.NET framework and runtime environment. Let's briefly review a few examples.

To start off, it was common for ASP developers to place a common bunch of code on top of every page that had to be protected from unauthorized access. Typically, such code checked the content of an aptly named cookie on the user's machine and used that information as the credentials. ASP.NET doesn't require you to include this code on top of the page; instead, you configure a runtime module that runs before every page request and does the same thing for you.

In classic ASP, the content of HTML input fields in a form was often bound to posted values, as shown here:

```
<input name="TextBox1" type="text" value='<% Request.Form["TextBox1"] %>' />
```

In this way, the input field retains the value the user typed in case the form posts to itself. This is a useful practice to show input values that failed validation or to arrange a wizard-like input process. In ASP.NET, every page is allowed to have just one all-encompassing HTML form, and the runtime machinery automatically restores the posted values on the input fields.

In classic ASP, every page is a sort of HTML template with some placeholders here and there for *dynamically generated* markup. In ASP.NET, such placeholders are engineered into server controls, which are configurable and programmable blocks of server code that, as a result, produce well-formed and data-bound HTML markup.

Finally, in ASP.NET the page HTML template is abstracted to a page class, thus creating the conditions to set up hierarchies of pages in homage to object-oriented programming best practices.

In the final analysis, some of the main traits of the ASP.NET platform result from engineering popular ASP best practices. The resulting programming model is known as *Web Forms*.

A deeper look at the Web Forms model is useful to gain an understanding of its current-day limitations and, subsequently, the need for an alternative model such as ASP.NET MVC.

The Web Forms Model

The best-selling point of ASP.NET is that it opens the world of Web programming to many developers with limited or no skills at all in HTML and JavaScript. Because of its abstraction layer over HTTP and HTML, ASP.NET attracted Visual Basic, Delphi, C/C++, and even Java programmers.

For years, in fact, programming the Web meant developing a completely different skill set. ASP.NET, instead, combined the productivity of a visual and RAD environment backed by powerful tools with a component-based programming model.

Nicely enough, the ASP.NET programming model could be approached effectively from both perspectives. It was the next step for both *freaky* HTML/JavaScript professionals and for *die-hard* C++ professionals.

With that introduction in mind, let's now begin to look at what makes Web Forms tick. There are three pillars to the Web Forms model: page postbacks, view state, and server controls.

Page Postbacks

An ASP.NET page is based on a single form component that contains all of the input elements the user can interact with. The form can also contain submission elements such as buttons or links.

A form submission sends the content of the current form to a server URL—by default, the same URL of the current page. This is known as the *postback*. In ASP.NET, the page submits any content of its unique form to itself. In other words, the page is a constituent block of the application and contains both a visual interface and some logic to process user gestures.

The similarity between the ASP.NET page and a Windows form is readily apparent. Another aspect, though, is much less obvious.

Suppose the user clicks on a button hosted in a page that is displayed within the client browser. The click instructs the browser to request a new instance of the same page from the Web server. In doing so, the browser also uploads any content available in the (single) page's form. On the server, the ASP.NET runtime engine processes the request and ends up executing some code. The following code shows the link between the button component and the handler code to run:

```
<asp:Button runat="server" ID="Button1" OnClick="Button1_Click" />
```

The running code is the server-side handler of the original client-side event. From within the handler, the developer can update the user interface by modifying the state of the server controls, as shown next:

```
public void Button1_Click(object sender, EventArgs args)
{
    // Sets the label to display the content of the text box
    Label1.Text = "The textbox contains: " + TextBox1.Text;
}
```

At the time the handler code runs, any server controls on the page have been updated to hold exactly the state they had during the last request to the page, plus any modifications resulting from posted data. Such stateful behavior is largely expected in a desktop scenario; in ASP.NET, however, it requires the magic of page postbacks.

That Controversial Big Thing Named View State

The view state is a dictionary that ASP.NET pages use to persist the state of their child controls across two consecutive postbacks. The view state plays an essential role in the implementation of the postback model. No *statefulness* would be possible in ASP.NET without the view state.

To summarize: The view state is the result of engineering a common solution in classic ASP pages. In classic ASP, developers frequently used hidden fields to track critical values across two successive requests. This was necessary when multiple HTML forms were used in the page. Posting from one would, in fact, reset any values in the fields within the other. To make up for this behavior, the values to track were stored in a hidden field and employed to programmatically initialize fields during the rendering of the page.

The view state is just an engineered and extended version of this common trick. The view state is a unique (and encoded) hidden field that stores a dictionary of values for all controls in the (unique) form of an ASP.NET page.

By default, each page control saves its entire state—all of its property values—to the view state. In an average-sized page, the view state takes up a few dozen KBs of extra data. This data is downloaded to the client and uploaded to the server with every request for the page. However, it is never used (and should not be used) on the client.

Because of its size, and also because of its not-so-obvious role, the view state is often considered to be just a huge weight on the shoulders of an ASP.NET page, or just a smart way to waste some bandwidth.

It is definitely possible to write pages that minimize the use of the view state for a shorter download, but the view state remains a fundamental piece of the ASP.NET Web Forms architecture. To eliminate the view state from ASP.NET, a significant redesign of the platform would be required.

> **Note** The view state's bad reputation is more a result of the default way of (ab)using it than any effective architectural limitations. Very few controls in very few scenarios really require the use of the view state but it's way too alluring to just stuff things into the view state that shouldn't be there, such as complex object graphs. The view state is delicate, and minor code changes sometimes result in a much larger view state if you don't know exactly what you're doing.
>
> The most effective approach is to disable it for all controls that don't need it. This can be done programmatically through the *EnableViewState* property or, better yet, in ASP.NET 4 via the new *ViewStateMode* property.

Server Controls

Server controls are central to the ASP.NET Web Forms model. The output of an ASP.NET page is defined using a mix of HTML literals and markup for ASP.NET server controls. A server control is a component with a public interface that can be configured using markup tags, child tags, and attributes. Each server control is characterized by a unique ID and is fully identified by that.

In the ASP.NET page markup, the difference between a server control and a plain HTML literal string is the presence of the *runat* attribute. Anything in the source devoid of the *runat* attribute is treated as literal HTML and is emitted to the output response stream as is. Anything else flagged with the *runat* attribute is identified as a server control. An instance of the corresponding server control class is created to process the content in the markup. The control, in turn, is responsible for emitting proper HTML for the output stream.

Server controls shield developers from the actual generation of HTML and JavaScript code. Programming a server control is as easy as setting properties on a reusable component. When processed, though, the server control emits HTML. In the end, programming server controls is a way of writing HTML markup without knowing much (if any) of its unique syntax and feature set.

The "Page Controller" Pattern

In an ASP.NET page, any user action (such as clicking or changing the current selection) originates a postback. The output of any postback is a new HTML string that the browser replaces on the currently displayed page. The HTML string is generated based on the markup found in the source code of the requested ASP.NET page.

Ultimately, a postback is a client request for some server action. For an ASP.NET developer, handling the postback is a matter of writing a method in the class that represents the page. For the Web server, handling the postback is a matter of serving an incoming HTTP request.

The Web server serves an ASP.NET request by dispatching it to the ASP.NET runtime engine. Internally, the request is resolved by finding a special component named the *HTTP handler*. The HTTP handler gets input from the HTTP packet, performs some tasks, and prepares a return HTTP packet.

A Web programming model is all about *how* an incoming request is resolved. The ASP.NET Web Forms model resolves an incoming request by dispatching the request to an HTTP handler component. According to the ASP.NET Web Forms model, the HTTP handler is expected to return HTML for the browser.

As we'll see later in this chapter, and in the remainder of the book, an alternate model such as ASP.NET MVC can take a different approach.

The HTTP Handler

An HTTP handler component is an instance of a class that implements the *IHttpHandler* interface. This component is a pillar of the ASP.NET runtime architecture. Here's the definition of the interface:

```
public interface IHttpHandler
{
    public void ProcessRequest(HttpContext context);
    public bool IsReusable;
}
```

The name of the method *ProcessRequest* says it all about the intended semantics. It takes the context of the request as the input and ensures that the request is serviced. In the case of synchronous handlers, when *ProcessRequest* returns, the output is ready for forwarding to the client. (It is not of primary importance here, but HTTP handlers can also work asynchronously according to the methods in the *IHttpAsyncHandler* interface.)

In Visual Studio, you build an ASP.NET application as a collection of Web Forms pages. Each page consists of two files: an *.aspx* markup file describing the expected HTML template and a C# (or Visual Basic) class file that contains postback handlers and any ancillary methods.

Where's the HTTP handler, then? Who writes the HTTP handler for each and every ASP.NET request that originates within an application? Is the Web Forms model really centered on the concept of an HTTP handler?

The answer is in the underlying design pattern used to implement the Web Forms model. Known as *Page Controller,* the pattern suggests that you arrange the processing of an HTTP request around the concept of the page. Processing the request is a task that goes through a number of steps, such as instantiating the page, initializing the page, restoring the page's state, updating the page, rendering the page, and unloading the page.

In the implementation of the pattern, you start from a base page class and define a strategy to process the request—the *page life cycle.* In the implementation of the page life cycle, you come up with an interface of virtual methods and events that derived pages will have to override and handle. Derived page classes are known as *code-behind classes* in ASP.NET jargon.

In ASP.NET, the base page class is *System.Web.UI.Page* and, guess what, most of what it does is implement the *IHttpHandler* interface. (See Figure 1-2.)

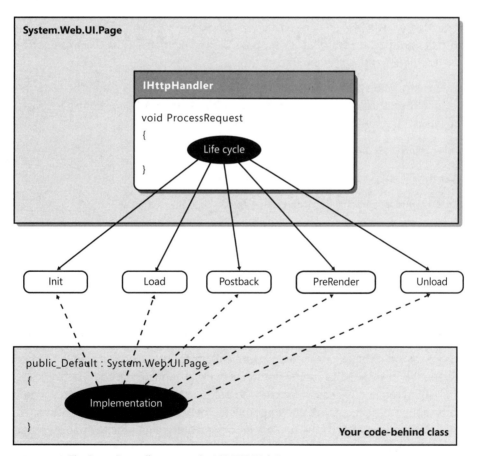

FIGURE 1-2 The Page Controller pattern in ASP.NET Web Forms

The Code-Behind Class

The underlying page controller class—the *System.Web.UI.Page* class—implements the *IHttpHandler* interface and provides the glue code invoked by the ASP.NET runtime to start the processing. As a page developer, you are not required to implement *IHttpHandler* yourself and you do not participate actively in the processing of the request. All you do is handle some public events and, at most, override some protected virtual methods that are left there so that you can customize some steps of the overall request life cycle. The Page Controller pattern is about centralizing the process and yielding to user code only at specific stages and sharing specific pieces of information.

ASP.NET developers are allowed to do only a couple of things: describe the user interface they want via HTML literals and ASP.NET markup, and express the desired behavior via specific life cycle events and overridable processing methods exposed through the *Page* class.

Events are well-known page events such as *Init, Load, PreRender,* and *Unload.* Overridable page methods are *LoadViewState* and *SaveViewState.* Further customization is possible through overrides on specific controls, such as those allowed by methods on the *IPostBackDataHandler* and *IPostBackEventHandler* interfaces.

Any customization is possible only in the code-behind class of a page. The code-behind class is a user-specific class that is required to inherit from the root page controller class. Here's the typical structure of a user-defined page class:

```
public class _Default : System.Web.UI.Page
{
    public void Page_Load(object sender, System.EventArgs e)
    {
        // Predefined handler for Load event

            .
            .
            .
    }

        .
        .
        .

}
```

The code-behind class contains only the behavior of the page. What about the list of child controls to be instantiated for the page in order to build the desired user interface?

The actual list of child controls and visual elements for the page is stored in the *.aspx* markup file. The ASP.NET runtime doesn't actually instantiate the code-behind class to process the request. Instead, it looks for a class built from the *.aspx* markup that knows both about the child controls and the expected behavior. This helper class is not written by developers; it is created by the runtime environment the first time the page is requested in the application.

Such a dynamically created class inherits from the code-behind class (thus grabbing the desired behavior), and all it does in the constructor is parse the associated markup file for *runat*-flagged elements and populate the *Controls* collection of the parent *Page* class with instances of server controls.

> **Note** A detailed explanation of the ASP.NET page life cycle can be found in Chapter 3 of my previous ASP.NET book, *Programming ASP.NET 3.5* (Microsoft Press, 2008). However, what's important here is to note that Web Forms page processing is fairly rigid and difficult to customize to any great extent. From a Web programmer's point of view, the significant portions of the HTML processing are abstracted into pages and server controls that you manipulate at an object level rather than at an HTML level.

Page Hierarchies

The Page Controller pattern builds a small hierarchy of classes in which the code-behind class derives from the page controller class and then the dynamically generated page class, in turn, inherits from the code-behind class. (See Figure 1-3.)

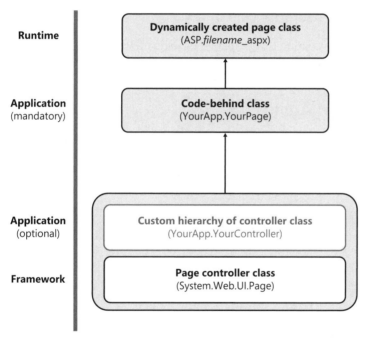

FIGURE 1-3 The hierarchy of ASP.NET pages. The word "controller" here is related to the Page Controller pattern and should not be interpreted in the MVC sense.

Developers can extend the hierarchy shown in the figure at will. Especially in large applications, it can be useful to create intermediate page classes to model complex views and to fulfill sophisticated navigation rules.

Building a custom hierarchy of page classes means placing custom classes in between the page controller and the actual code-behind class. The ultimate reason for having a custom page hierarchy is to customize the page controller, with the purpose of exposing a tailor-made life cycle to developers. An intermediate class, in fact, will incorporate portions of common application behavior and expose specific new events and overridable methods to developers.

The ASP.NET Age of Reason

So ASP.NET was a success and, more importantly, it has been adopted for nearly any new Web project that has been started in the past six or seven years when targeting the Microsoft platform. Today, ASP.NET is unanimously considered a stable, mature, and highly productive platform for Web development.

Five years of a software technology constitute a huge amount of time, however. Any software technology inevitably shows the first signs of age after that amount of time. ASP.NET is no exception.

Microsoft significantly improved and refined ASP.NET along the way. Today ASP.NET includes a number of extensibility points that weren't part of it in the beginning. Today, ASP.NET offers a rich platform for AJAX development, and built-in controls have been adapted to better support CSS and XHTML requirements.

Is ASP.NET still an excellent option for companies developing Web applications? Is the Web Forms model the best model possible? Should we look around for an alternative approach?

ASP.NET's Signs of Aging

The primary goal of ASP.NET was to enable developers to build applications quickly and effectively without having to deal with low-level details such as HTTP, HTML, and JavaScript intricacies. That was what the community loudly demanded in the late 1990s. And ASP.NET is what Microsoft delivered, exceeding expectations by a large extent.

But people's requirements change over time.

As more and more companies upgrade existing sites to ASP.NET, or port corporate applications to the Web, the complexity of the average Web application grows. After five years, expectations have probably passed the critical threshold that makes the Web Forms model not necessarily the best option.

Productivity is a great thing, but not if it forces you to sacrifice some other aspects of a good model, such as maintainability, readability, design, testability, and control of HTML. For a long time, the trade-off was beneficial. Today, more and more people are pointing out less-than-optimal aspects of the ASP.NET Web Forms model.

What are the new features the community of developers is loudly demanding for ASP.NET? What would be good to redesign in ASP.NET? Three main aspects are considered insufficient today: the average application of the separation of concerns (SoC) principle, testability, and control over HTML.

Limited SoC

High cohesion and low coupling are the two pillars of a *neat* software design. A neater software design increases maintainability and readability of code and helps you deal with complexity.

This said, you should also consider that a neat design is always desirable but is not always an absolute necessity. If you're only arranging a few pages to put some pictures online, or if you're taking care of a friend's personal site, you probably don't want to invest too much time carefully designing code-behind pages.

SoC is a general principle that, properly applied, is helpful in achieving high cohesion and low coupling in your software design. SoC was introduced back in 1974 by Edsger W. Dijkstra in the paper, "On the Role of Scientific Thought." If you're interested, you can download the full paper from *http://www.cs.utexas.edu/users/EWD/ewd04xx/EWD447.PDF*.

SoC is all about breaking the system into distinct and possibly nonoverlapping features. Each feature you want in the system represents a *concern* and an *aspect* of the system. Terms such as *feature, concern,* and *aspect* are generally considered synonyms. Concerns are mapped to software modules (that is, classes) and, to the extent that it is possible, there's no duplication of functionalities.

SoC suggests that you focus on one particular concern at a time. It doesn't mean, of course, that you ignore all other concerns of the system. More simply, after you've assigned a concern to a software module, you focus on building that module. And from the perspective of that module, any other concerns are irrelevant.

How much SoC can you get out of ASP.NET?

ASP.NET made the Web really simple to work with and every developer a lot more productive. To achieve this result, ASP.NET was designed around the concept of Web Forms; and Web Forms are UI focused. All you do is author pages and the code that runs behind the page. The page gets input; the page posts back; the page determines the output for the browser. The model leads you to perceive any request simply as a way to generate HTML. The code required to obtain that HTML executes in the background and abstracts HTML production.

It would be terribly incorrect to say that ASP.NET doesn't support or allow SoC. At the same time, it is safe to say that ASP.NET was not designed to lead adopters to apply best-design practices. In the end, ASP.NET certainly doesn't prevent SoC, but the application of any good design practices is entirely on the developers' shoulders. Conversely, the Web Forms model and available RAD tools make it particularly seductive to create page code that *just* works. Within Visual Studio, you can quickly drag a control from the toolbox onto the form, edit content, and have some stub code generated for you to extend with database commands and any required logic. More advanced design patterns such as Model-View-Presenter (MVP) are certainly neither prohibited nor blasphemous, but for one reason or another very few developers apply it.

> **Note** Best intentions don't always go hand in hand with the realities of schedules and budgets. Applying good design practices to ASP.NET Web Forms requires you to break the existing cycle a bit and provide your own framework. Often, though, it turns out to be too much work. "We'll fix it later" is the mantra. "Just get it working now" is what we're told by stakeholders more often than not.

Limited Testability

In software, testability is defined as the ease of performing testing. Testing, in turn, is the process of checking software to ensure that it behaves as expected, contains no errors, and satisfies its requirements. A software test verifies that a component returns the correct output in response to given input and a given internal state. Having control over the input and the state and being able to *observe* the output is therefore essential for a successful and reliable test. If you could even automate the process to a tailor-made application, that would be ideal. This is exactly what *unit testing* is all about.

What about the testability of ASP.NET Web Forms applications?

First and foremost, ASP.NET doesn't prevent unit testing and thus is an inherently testable platform. The point is, how much and how easy?

Because an ASP.NET Web Forms application is based on pages, to test such an application you should arrange ad hoc HTTP requests to be sent to each page. And next you should observe the response and ensure that it matches your expectations. But the output of a page is HTML—that is, a potentially long string and having multiple possible equally valid representations. In addition, to test an ASP.NET page you need to spin up all of the ASP.NET runtime. Testing is not easy in these conditions.

A testable page has an internal architecture that deeply applies SoC and lives in a runtime environment that allows mimicking some of its components for testing purposes. This is doable but not facilitated in ASP.NET Web Forms. For this reason, many developers end up testing their sites by simply poking around.

> **Note** A couple of popular antipatterns relate to testing practices. One is the *Test-By-Release* antipattern. It refers to releasing a software product without paying much attention to time-consuming chores such as unit and integration testing. Because users are the final recipients of the product, the pattern consists of leaving them the last word on whether the software works or not. Another testing antipattern is *Test-By-Poking-Around*. It consists of taking a tour around the feature set of the product and tracking and fixing any errors or misbehaviors that show up along the way. At a minimum, these (common) antipatterns are based on nonrepeatable sequences, which makes it hard to catch regression failures.

Limited Control over HTML

ASP.NET pages produce their HTML via server controls or perhaps via static HTML literals. Server controls have been one of the main reasons for the success and rapid adoption of ASP.NET. A server control is a black-box component that, when declaratively or programmatically configured, ends up outputting HTML and JavaScript for the browser.

In the beginning of the ASP.NET era, this black-box nature was the best-selling point of server controls. Things change, however. Today, more and more Web developers demand increasing control over the HTML markup the page serves to the browser.

Can the markup of server controls be adjusted to some extent? Can the final markup be generated from other sources, such as XAML or XSLT?

The developer can hardly control the markup emitted by a server control. The set of public configurable properties leaves you the final word on some aspects of the resulting markup. You can't intervene, however, on the underlying HTML template. A few years ago, Microsoft released a free toolkit to enable a few built-in controls to output CSS-friendly markup where, for example, the *<table>* tag is not used or used much less and in accordance with XHTML rules. The CSS Control Adapter Toolkit is based on the ASP.NET control adapter architecture, meaning that you can still use the same approach to make the list of supported controls longer or edit the way in which existing controls render themselves through CSS. For more information about the control adapter logic and internal architecture, pay a visit to *http://www.asp.net/CSSAdapters/WhitePaper.aspx*.

This kind of control over the HTML generated by server controls is a good thing to have, but it is not sufficient to always give developers all the freedom they may need. At the end of the day, to build a rich and highly interactive interface with multibrowser support, accessibility, script, and styles, you need to control every single HTML element.

In ASP.NET, you have no alternatives other than using server controls or perhaps static HTML. The generation of the user's view is strictly intertwined with the request processing. As you proceed with the logic, you configure server controls and, at the end of the processing, you build the HTML page. Processing and HTML generation are not distinct steps. Using server controls makes it quick and effective. Not using server controls is certainly possible, but it requires you to build your own framework to move data from processing components to the view. ASP.NET Web Forms is just not optimized for this scenario.

Alternative Models Grow Up

Over the years, alternative ASP.NET models have been developed to do more effective ASP.NET development. The most popular is certainly MonoRail. (For more details, check out *http://www.castleproject.org/monorail*.)

MonoRail is a variation of the classic Web Forms model; it has you build the page user interface and logic in terms of *controllers* and *views*. The output being generated by a page is the view and is made of plain HTML. The view is taken care of by an ad hoc engine. The engine gets a source template and input data, and it produces HTML. The view engine is part of the system and is triggered by controllers associated with pages. The controller wraps up any code to be executed in response to the user's activity.

When MonoRail is used, as a developer you don't mainly focus on pages as you would in Web Forms. You focus, instead, on the actions being taken from the page (methods on a controller class) and its user interface (markup and data placeholders in the view).

MonoRail is different from Web Forms and not completely similar to Web Forms in terms of skills required. MonoRail has you build pages by focusing on what you need to do and the response to generate. It also comes with a number of helper frameworks (that is, the Castle ActiveRecord scaffolding) to further speed up development. Properly handled, it offers an alternative model to Web Forms that might turn out to be even faster to adopt and more enjoyable to use.

The success gained by MonoRail definitely accelerated the process of finding ways to improve the ASP.NET Web Forms model.

The Turning Point

In our imperfect world, requirements change over time. So some of the major original strengths of ASP.NET Web Forms turned up to be sort of weakness five years later. Can the Web Forms model be revised to address its signs of age?

Is a Better ASP.NET Really Possible?

The level of SoC and testability in an ASP.NET solution can be raised, even significantly, by handcrafting the content of code-behind classes. By extensively using the MVP pattern, you can take a large share of the page logic out of the code-behind class. When the logic lives in its own *presenter* class (flying high, you can also use the term *controller* here), it can be tested in isolation with no dependencies on the runtime environment.

As for testability, it should also be noted that the ASP.NET runtime environment is not designed with testability in mind. The HTTP context can't be easily mocked up to a custom object. To automate tests on an ASP.NET page, you likely need a made-to-measure tool (either commercial or handmade) that prepares in the background HTTP requests and determines a way to check returned values or markup.

As for control over HTML, there's not much else that can be done in ASP.NET Web Forms to augment the range of options available to create the user interface. What the platform can offer remains limited to server controls or HTML literals.

In the end, it is definitely possible to produce better ASP.NET Web Forms pages with an increased level of testability and separation of concerns. For more ambitious things, it should be noted that the runtime environment is not designed with extensibility in mind and that the Page Controller pattern used for processing requests naturally leads to black-box solutions that limit the freedom of developers. Have a look at Figure 1-4.

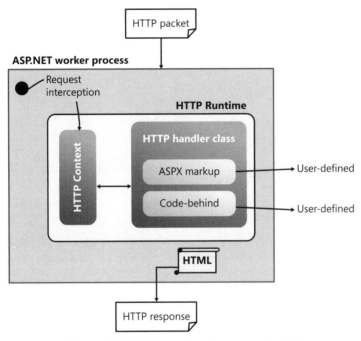

FIGURE 1-4 The overall ASP.NET procedure that generates HTML

The ASP.NET runtime environment and the Page Controller pattern centralize the request processing. Everything takes place in a hard-coded way, and only two customization points are left to developers: the ASPX markup and the code-behind class.

This is by design. Subsequently, for a radical change a new ASP.NET platform is needed.

However, before we take the plunge into such a new platform—ASP.NET MVC—it would be interesting to have a quick look at other options for improving the design of ASP.NET applications, such as a manual implementation of the MVP pattern.

The Model-View-Presenter Pattern in ASP.NET Web Forms

Today, the Model-View-Presenter (MVP) pattern is considered the best practice for organizing the presentation layer of complex, mostly enterprise-class applications. Developed at Taligent in the early 1990s, MVP was designed to improve on another very popular design pattern—the Model-View-Controller (MVC) pattern.

In Chapter 3, "The MVC Pattern and Beyond," I'll return to both patterns and discuss them in detail in the context of the ASP.NET MVC framework architecture. For now, let's briefly explore what it means to you as a developer to implement the MVP pattern in an ASP.NET Web Forms solution. Figure 1-5 shows the overall schema of the MVP pattern.

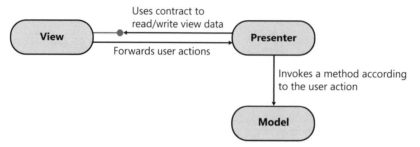

FIGURE 1-5 The actors of the MVP pattern

An MVP solution separates the concerns for a given problem into three elements, referred to as *actors*: the model, view, and presenter. The presenter sits in between the view and the model; it receives input from the view and issues commands to the model. It then gets results and updates the view through the contracted view interface. The model represents the data the application works with, and it can be identified with the public interface of the application's middle tier. Finally, the view is responsible for producing the user interface.

Any communication between the view and presenter takes place through a contracted interface. In this way, the presenter is independent from the actual technology used to implement the view. It would be possible, for example, to reuse the same presenter class for an equivalent view developed in an ASP.NET Web Forms and Windows Forms front end. (This is not simply abstract theory, but it might not be easy to apply in some real scenarios.)

The presenter is an inherently testable class because it has no tight dependencies on the view. If you also abstract the model to an interface, the presenter becomes an isolated class, ideal for testing. The view can be devised to be as simple as possible or to incorporate some presentation logic. A humble and mostly passive view is uniquely responsible for displaying values. Testing the view, therefore, is simply a matter of ensuring that visual elements are properly laid out and that the presenter passes expected values. In other words, you don't need to automate tests on an MVP passive view.

How would you code MVP in ASP.NET Web Forms?

First, you define an interface for each ASPX page (view) you have in the application. For example, for *default.aspx* you define an *IDefaultView* interface. The interface contains members that abstract the expected content and behavior of the view. We'll return to this topic in Chapter 3, but for now Figure 1-6 gives you an idea of what is intended.

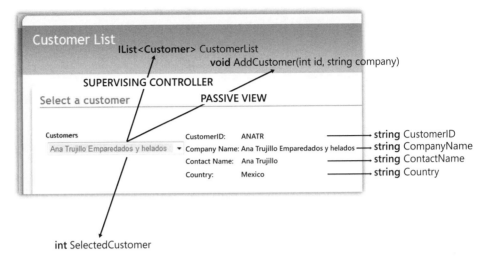

FIGURE 1-6 Abstracting a view to an interface

You implement the interface in the code-behind class of the page. Each member of the interface is implemented in terms of the actual controls in the user interface. Here's an example:

```
public partial class _Default : Page, IDefaultView
{
    private DefaultViewPresenter presenter;

    protected void Page_Load(object sender, EventArgs e)
    {
        presenter = new DefaultViewPresenter(this);
        if (!IsPostBack)
            presenter.InitializeView();
    }

    #region IDefaultView
    public string CustomerID
    {
        get { return custID.Text; }
        set { custID.Text = value; }
    }

    public string CustomerName
    {
        get { return custName.Text; }
        set { custName.Text = value; }
    }

    :
    :

    #endregion
```

```
protected void Button1_Click(object sender, EventArgs e)
{
    presenter.ExpandCustomer();
}
    .
    .
    .

}
```

As you can see, the *CustomerName* property is a wrapper around the *Text* property of the server control (that is, a *TextBox*) that renders the customer name in the user interface.

The typical presenter also features one method for each action the user can take from within the displayed user interface. If, say, the user can click a button, the presenter is expected to have a corresponding method to handle the event. No data is passed to the method; the presenter retrieves any necessary data from the view interface.

Implementing the MVP pattern is not free of charge and might not be worth the effort in just any ASP.NET page. However, especially in the context of enterprise applications, it can help you deal with the surrounding complexity and make the whole solution much more testable and easy to maintain. We'll return to the topic of viable ASP.NET design patterns in Chapter 3.

The Web Client Software Factory Experience

An MVP implementation requires sweat and blood to write if you do so entirely on your own, and that's why a few developers do it. At some point, the Patterns & Practices group at Microsoft released a helper framework for building Web clients that relied on the MVP pattern for the generation of the user interface. This framework is the Web Client Software Factory (WCSF).

WCSF is a software factory made of a collection of reusable components and libraries to apply proven practices and patterns to ASP.NET development. WCSF comes with a bunch of Visual Studio templates, automated tests, and wizards with the clear purpose of speeding up development. For more information, see *http://msdn.microsoft.com/en-us/library/cc304793.aspx*.

The software factory is built on top of the Windows Workflow Foundation and the Enterprise Library. As mentioned, WCSF supports MVP and comes with Visual Studio templates and extensions (shown in Figure 1-7) that help you to get an MVP implementation without needing to write all the code (view interfaces and presenters) yourself.

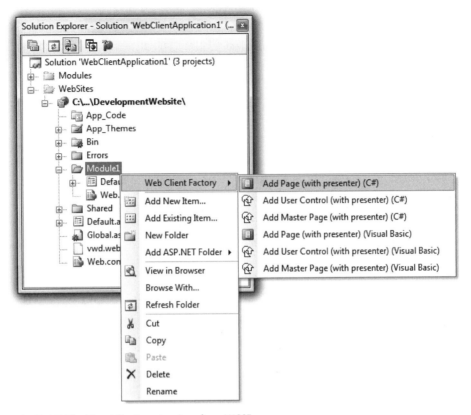

FIGURE 1-7 The Visual Studio extensions from WCSF

Why should you consider using WCSF in your upcoming projects?

Because WCSF is built on the MVP pattern, it gives you neat separation of concerns between the view and presenter. At the same time, it isn't a radical paradigm shift from the Web Forms model and the Page Controller pattern. In other words, you need to get acquainted with the new API of WCSF, but you'll be able to reuse all of your existing ASP.NET and control skills. Internally, the WCSF framework uses inversion of controls extensively, which gives you a nice way to do unit testing and mock objects in the ASP.NET runtime environment.

That said, WCSF is not for just any applications. WCSF is not a productivity tool *tout-court*. More precisely, it is a productivity tool for complex (mostly enterprise-class) applications. All in all, WCSF hasn't captured the heart of too many developers; this is mostly because it's rather complex to learn and use, and it carries the full weight of the Enterprise Library with it, which in itself is complex and requires dedication to learn and use. Because WCSF is designed for enterprise-scale applications, it cannot be seen as a general way of adding testability and SoC to the ASP.NET Web Forms model for all applications.

ASP.NET MVC at a Glance

ASP.NET MVC is a new platform for building ASP.NET applications. Based on the same run-time environment as classic ASP.NET Web Forms, ASP.NET MVC makes developing Web applications a significantly different experience than the Web Forms model.

ASP.NET MVC was designed to focus on the actions a user can take when browsing a page. It has a different view engine and allows much more control over the generated markup. In a way, ASP.NET MVC is action-centric and close to the metal. ASP.NET MVC disregards the Page Controller pattern and opts for a different pattern that can be considered a Web-oriented variation of the classic Model-View-Controller (MVC) pattern.

Atop the standard ASP.NET runtime environment, ASP.NET MVC built its own shell of functionalities. On one end, the ASP.NET MVC shell connects to effective ASP.NET run-time objects (for example, *Request* and *HttpContext*). On the other end, it exposes a set of *intrinsic objects* to internal components. The most interesting aspect, though, is that such intrinsic objects are actually *injected* into the ASP.NET MVC runtime shell. This makes for an inherently higher level of testability and is a pillar for building applications with a strong SoC.

ASP.NET MVC Highlights

If you look at the programming model made available to developers, you find that ASP.NET MVC offers a completely new paradigm.

When you write an ASP.NET MVC application, you think in terms of controllers and views. Your decisions are about how to expose your controllers to the users and how to pass data to the view. Each request is resolved by invoking a method on a controller class. No postbacks are ever required to service a user request, and no view state is ever required to persist the state of the page. Finally, no server controls exist to produce HTML for the browser.

However, if you look a bit further under the hood of ASP.NET MVC, it's clear that its way of working is still based on handling HTTP requests, except that the URL string is treated differently and any resulting action is expressed by developers using methods on controller classes instead of postbacks.

Overall, the ASP.NET MVC programming model poses new challenges to developers. We'll be delving into all of them in the rest of the book. For now, let's briefly summarize some facts about the ASP.NET MVC programming model.

Underlying Pattern

The working machinery of ASP.NET MVC is based on the combination of two patterns: the *Front Controller* pattern and the *Model2* pattern. Together, these two patterns propound a programming model significantly different from ASP.NET Web Forms and, to a great extent, require a different skill set.

The *Front Controller* pattern involves using a centralized component that handles all incoming requests and dispatches them to another component down the pipeline for actually servicing the request. How is this different from the Page Controller approach?

In the Page Controller pattern, there's a different handler for each request, the specific handler for which is determined on a URL by URL basis. The Page Controller pattern suggests you build a hierarchy of pages to reuse some code across pages. Years of experience have proven that, in Web applications, pages in a hierarchy often grow over time with code that is not common to all pages in the hierarchy.

In the Front Controller approach, all incoming requests are channeled through a single component. In ASP.NET MVC, this component is the MVC HTTP handler. This common class contains the logic that parses the URL and decides which controller is due to service the request and which view component is due to produce the resulting HTML. The controller is a plain class with public methods, and each method executes an action following the user gestures. Figure 1-8 illustrates the difference between the Front Controller and Page Controller approaches in an ASP.NET scenario.

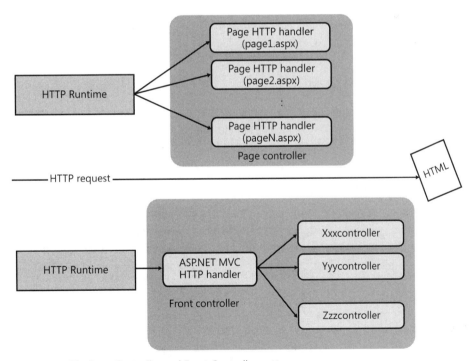

FIGURE 1-8 The Page Controller and Front Controller patterns

In ASP.NET MVC, the interaction between the front controller and action-specific controllers and views is ruled by the Model2 pattern. Figure 1-9 presents the sequence diagram for a request serviced according to the Front Controller+Model2 pattern.

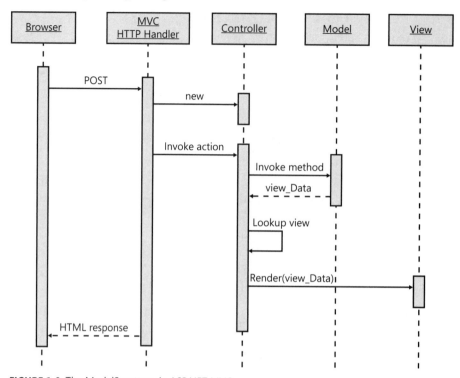

FIGURE 1-9 The Model2 pattern in ASP.NET MVC

The front controller figures out the controller to use and invokes one of its methods. The controller's method runs, gets some data, and figures out the view to use. Finally, the view generates the markup for the browser and writes it in the output response stream.

A RESTful Flavor

An architectural style, REST stands for *REpresentational State Transfer*. It is based on the idea that the caller receives the representation of the requested resource and can manipulate the underlying resource via its representation. Callers use addresses to reach resources. REST is not strictly limited to HTTP, but the Web as a whole works according to the REST style.

Beyond the formal definition of REST you can find in Chapter 5 of Roy Fielding's doctoral dissertation (available at *http://www.ics.uci.edu/~fielding/pubs/dissertation/rest_arch_style.htm*), REST is an attribute most commonly applied to Web services. A RESTful Web service is a Web service that can be seen as a collection of addressable resources. Each addressable resource can be operated on using a set of methods and returns any of a known set of types. Over the Web, this means that a RESTful service works over HTTP and allows you to address resources via URIs and exchange MIME types such as JSON or XML.

ASP.NET MVC is an excellent example of a RESTful framework.

ASP.NET MVC works by sending requests to resources. Each resource is identified with a URL. The addressable set of resources is the collection of controller objects. Any request corresponds to an action executed on an addressable resource. Any request returns HTML. ASP.NET MVC is plain, simple, and very close to the metal, with no hidden machinery such as postback events and view state. In a word, it is just RESTful.

Taking Action

ASP.NET MVC leads Web developers to reason in a different way than they do when using Web Forms. Whereas in Web Forms you focus on the page to render, in ASP.NET MVC you focus on the action to take and, subsequently, the markup to generate.

You organize the application around a few controller classes, each with a set of methods. Each URL contains routing information for the front controller to use to identify the target controller. Action and production of the response are distinct steps taken care of by distinct subsystems—controllers and the view engine.

In ASP.NET MVC, postback events fired by user interface elements are no longer the way to add life to pages. Each user action should be mapped instead to a controller method. Likewise, the classic Web Forms page life cycle and view state are no longer essential to the processing of the request. Server controls are just one possible way of generating the markup for the view. You can live without server controls and be much happier than you were with Web Forms because you have helpers to generate simple pieces of HTML.

Finally, in ASP.NET MVC there's no URL-to-file direct association. In other words, you usually do not request the content of an *.aspx* server file. Instead, you request a URL that maps to a server action that, in turn, generates markup.

> **Note** One of the arguments often made when comparing ASP.NET MVC and Web Forms is that the former gains you much more control over the generated HTML markup. It is hard to prove this statement wrong, but some considerations are in order for further clarification. Really, nothing prevents you from writing classic ASP.NET pages using plain HTML elements and code blocks. However, if you do so you lose the benefits (and niceties) of server controls and postback events. In classic ASP.NET, programming without server controls and postback events means hitting the metal, not simply getting closer to it. On the other hand, if you use server controls, programming is easier and more productive but you don't get full control over the generated HTML.

Testability

The internal, extremely modular architecture of ASP.NET MVC makes it an inherently more testable framework. The developer's code is articulated in controller classes. Each controller class can be designed in a testable way. This can be done either by forcing every controller method to take input data from its signature or using an injected intrinsic object to wrap the ongoing HTTP request. When testing is done in this way, the controller class can easily be tested in isolation with proper mock objects to replace internal dependencies.

In addition, the ASP.NET MVC framework is isolated from the ASP.NET run-time machinery and uses abstractions of intrinsic objects to process the request. The ASP.NET MVC runtime infrastructure uses a number of wrapper objects for common ASP.NET intrinsic objects, including *HttpSessionState*, *HttpRequest*, and *HttpContext*. In this way, a controller designed to work against ASP.NET MVC wrappers can receive mock objects and be tested without spinning up the whole ASP.NET worker process.

Finally, the generation of the markup is a process that belongs to the *view engine*. The view engine, as well as many other subsystems around ASP.NET MVC, is abstracted to an interface and can be replaced declaratively or programmatically. Extensibility and, subsequently, testability are two key attributes of the whole ASP.NET MVC framework.

Let's compare it now to classic ASP.NET Web Forms.

Web Forms vs. ASP.NET MVC

As clearly stated by Microsoft, ASP.NET MVC is *not* the successor to Web Forms. It is rather a fully fledged and fully qualified alternative to Web Forms. Each framework has its own set of peculiarities. Ultimately, it's hard, and also kind of pointless, to try to decide which one is objectively better.

Choosing between ASP.NET Web Forms and ASP.NET MVC is essentially a matter of personal attitude, skills, and of course, customer requirements. As an architect or developer, however, you definitely need to understand the structural differences between the frameworks so that you can make a thoughtful decision.

Let's start our analysis with a look at the recognized pros and cons of each framework.

 Note Although I can't guarantee the following list of pros and cons is exhaustive, I do believe that it nails down the most important facts about ASP.NET MVC and ASP.NET Web Forms. This said, placing a given fact in the *pro* or *con* column, well, that is often a matter of your personal perspective.

Pros and Cons of Web Forms

ASP.NET Web Forms is a stable and mature platform fully supported by heaps of third-party controls and tools. The Web Forms model provides a simulated stateful model for Web developers, effectively mimicking the desktop point-and-click metaphor that gained so much success in the past with Visual Basic and RAD tools. As a result, you don't have to be a Web expert with a lot of HTML and JavaScript knowledge to write effective Web applications.

To simulate a stateful programming model over the Web, ASP.NET Web Forms introduces features such as view state, postbacks, and an overall event-driven paradigm. To write an ASP.NET application, as a developer you need to know the basics of .NET development, the programming interface of some ad hoc components (such as server controls), plus of course, quite a bit about the underlying programming postback-based paradigm. Server controls that generate HTML programmatically contribute significantly to a fast development cycle.

Productivity and rapid development of data-driven, line-of-business applications have been the selling points of ASP.NET Web Forms.

Years of experience prove beyond any reasonable doubt that separation of concerns has not been integral to the Web Forms paradigm. Although ASP.NET Web Forms certainly doesn't prevent SoC, it doesn't make it the natural choice either. Manual MVP implementation and WCSF are valid solutions, but they fail to deliver the simplicity of use that is key to rapid and widespread adoption. Likewise, automated testing of a Web Forms application is difficult, and not just because of a lack of SoC. ASP.NET Web Forms is based on a monolithic runtime environment that can be extended, to some extent, but it is not a pluggable and flexible system. It's nearly impossible to test an ASP.NET application without spinning up the whole runtime.

ASP.NET Web Forms was perfect for its time. A few years later, though, we find ourselves facing a different set of challenges, and some features that were originally clear strengths of ASP.NET now turn out to be weaknesses.

For modern Web pages, abstraction from HTML is a serious issue because it hinders accessibility, browser compatibility, and integration with popular JavaScript frameworks such as jQuery, Dojo, and PrototypeJS. The postback model that defaults to each page posting to itself makes it harder for search engines to rank ASP.NET pages very high. Search engines and spiders work better with links that have parameters, and even better if they're rationalized to human-readable strings.

The ASP.NET Web Forms postback model, on the other hand, goes in the opposite direction. Also, an excessively large view state is problematic because the keyword the search engine might rank could be located past the view state, and therefore far from the top of the document. Some engines return a lower rank in this case.

Therefore, for a number of good reasons, a new ASP.NET platform was designed.

Note Some of the issues related to Web Forms have been smoothed out in ASP.NET Web Forms 4. For example, you have much more control over the view state and HTML. You also have a richer URL rewriting engine—the same one you find in ASP.NET MVC. This doesn't change the overall outlook, however. The design of ASP.NET Web Forms reflects a different set of priorities than the ones that exist today. Using ASP.NET Web Forms is still an excellent option for building applications, but something different is being demanded loudly. And with good reason.

Pros and Cons of ASP.NET MVC

ASP.NET MVC is a completely new framework for building ASP.NET applications, designed from the ground up with SoC and testability in mind. With ASP.NET MVC, you rediscover the good, old taste of the Web—stateless behavior, full control over every single bit of HTML, and total script and CSS freedom.

Processing the request and generating the HTML for the browser are distinct steps and involve distinct components. Each of these components—controllers and views—has its own interface and can be replaced if necessary.

In ASP.NET MVC, there's no dependency on ASPX physical server files. ASPX files can still be part of your project, but they now serve as plain HTML templates, along with their code-behind classes. The default view engine is based on the Web Forms rendering engine, but you can use other pluggable engines such as *NVelocity* or XSLT. (I'll cover controllers and the view engine in full detail in Chapter 4, "Inside Controllers," and Chapter 5, "Inside Views.")

The runtime environment is largely the same as in ASP.NET Web Forms, but the request cycle is simpler and more direct. An essential part of the Web Forms model, the page life cycle, is now just an optional implementation detail in ASP.NET MVC. Figure 1-10 compares the run-time stack for Web Forms and ASP.NET MVC.

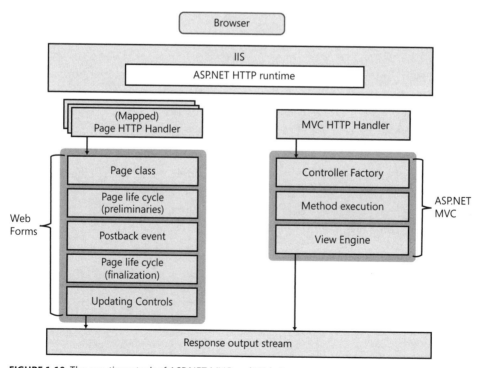

FIGURE 1-10 The run-time stack of ASP.NET MVC and Web Forms

As you can see, the run-time stack of ASP.NET MVC is simpler and the difference is because of the lack of a page life cycle. However, this makes it problematic to maintain the state of visual elements across page requests.

As mentioned, ASP.NET MVC is closer to the metal, and this has its own side effects. If you need to maintain state, how to do that is up to you. For example, you can store it in *Session* or *Cache* or you can even create, guess what, your own tailor-made, view state–like infrastructure. In the end, the simplicity of ASP.NET MVC is rather the result of different architectural choices than some overhead in the design of the Web Forms model.

So ASP.NET MVC brings to the table a clean design with a neat separation of concerns, a leaner run-time stack, full control over HTML, an unparalleled level of extensibility, and a working environment that enables, rather than penalizes, test-driven development (TDD).

Is ASP.NET MVC, therefore, a true paradise for Web developers? Just like with Web Forms, what some perceive as a clear strength of ASP.NET MVC, others may see as a weakness.

To gain full control over HTML, JavaScript, and CSS, ASP.NET MVC requires that you write Web elements manually, one byte after the next. This means that, for the most part, you are responsible for writing every single *<li>* or *<table>* tag you need. In ASP.NET MVC, there's no sort of component model to help you with the generation of HTML. As of today, HTML helpers and perhaps user controls are the only tools you can leverage to write HTML more quickly. Overall, some developers may see ASP.NET MVC as taking an entire step backward in terms of usability and productivity.

> **Note** Because ASP.NET MVC supports pluggable view engines, you are not forced to express your desired presentation using HTML. You can consider adopting a non-HTML view engine to express the view you want and then have it converted to plain HTML. In both cases, though, you can rely on JavaScript libraries to help you create markup programmatically.

Another point to be made, regarding the impact of ASP.NET MVC on everyday development, is that it requires some up-front familiarity with the MVC pattern. You need to know how controllers and views work together in the ASP.NET implementation. In other words, ASP.NET MVC is not something you can easily learn as you go. In my experience, this can be the source of decreased productivity for the average developer, especially for the average developer with some years of experience with Web Forms.

Overall, the possible initial decrease of productivity is nothing dramatic and likely nothing to be seriously worried about, because it can be recovered in a matter of days with study and application. Likewise, it is something that shouldn't be ignored in order to prevent more serious worries and concerns. ASP.NET MVC requires full awareness of its features. Although it can sometimes look dangerously similar to Web Forms, it is (architecturally speaking) significantly different. In Chapter 5, I'll focus on this point while demonstrating how tricky it can prove to be using server controls in ASP.NET MVC.

This consideration leads us straight to another important point—the skills and attitude of the development team.

Do Not Overlook a Team's Skills and Attitude

All in all, ASP.NET Web Forms and ASP.NET MVC are functionally equivalent in the sense that a skilled team can successfully use either to build any Web solution. The skills, education, and attitude of the team, though, are the key points to bear in mind.

Full control over HTML, for example, can be a lifesaver to one person but a nightmare to another. I was shocked the first time I saw the content of a nontrivial view page in ASP.NET MVC. But when I showed the same page to a customer whose application was still using a significant number of ASP pages, well, he was relieved.

If you have accessibility as a strict requirement, you probably want to take full control over the HTML being displayed. And this is not always entirely possible with Web Forms. On the other hand, if you're building a heavy data-driven application, you'll welcome the set of data-bound controls and statefulness offered by Web Forms.

Correctly, Microsoft has not positioned ASP.NET MVC as a replacement for ASP.NET Web Forms. Web Forms is definitely a paradigm that works for Web applications. At the same time, a non-Microsoft, MVC-based Web programming framework, Ruby-on-Rails, has proved that MVC can also be a successful pattern for Web applications; and the enthusiastic welcome received by ASP.NET MVC just confirms this.

Indisputable Facts

After using Web Forms for years, I recognize a number of its drawbacks that ASP.NET MVC addresses quite well: testability, HTML control, and separation of concerns. But though I see ASP.NET MVC as an equally valid option at this time, I don't believe it to be a silver-bullet solution for every Web application.

In my opinion, ASP.NET MVC in its first version lacks some level of abstraction for creating standard pieces of HTML. HTML helpers (discussed later, in Chapter 5) are an interesting attempt to speed up HTML creation. I hope to see in the near future a new generation of MVC-specific server controls that are as easy to learn and use as Web Forms server controls but that are totally unbound from the postback and view-state model.

ASP.NET Web Forms and ASP.NET MVC are not in competition in the sense that one is supposed to replace the other. You have to choose one, but different applications might force you to make different choices. In the end, it's really like many Microsoft presenters often observed: It's like choosing between driving a car or a motorcycle when taking a trip. Each trip requires a choice, and having both vehicles available should be seen as an opportunity, not as a curse.

To summarize, here is my top-ten list of hard-to-deny facts about both frameworks:

1. Web Forms is hard to test.

2. ASP.NET MVC requires or allows you to specify every little bit of HTML. (However, it also offers to plug in an alternative view engine that might support a non-HTML syntax to express the view.)

3. ASP.NET MVC is not the only way to get separation of concerns in ASP.NET.

4. Web Forms allows you to learn as you go.

5. The size of the view state can be largely controlled (because there are better tools in ASP.NET 4), and the view state can even be disabled.

6. Web Forms was designed to abstract the full Web machinery.

7. ASP.NET MVC was designed to surface the underlying architecture of the Web instead of hiding it. This is what makes it a RESTful framework.

8. ASP.NET MVC was designed with testability and Dependency Injection (DI) in mind.

9. ASP.NET MVC guides you toward better design of code.

10. ASP.NET MVC currently lacks a component model. But it is just at the beginning of a presumably very long path.

ASP.NET MVC was not created to replace Web Forms but to partner with it and deliver a richer set of options to architects. ASP.NET MVC turns some of the weaker elements of Web Forms into its own internal strengths. However, problems such as lack of testability, SoC, limited search engine optimization (SEO), and HTML control can be avoided or reduced in Web Forms with some discipline and good design, though the framework itself doesn't provide enough guidance.

Summary

I first saw Microsoft ASP.NET in action in 1999, when it was tentatively named ASP+. At that time, building a Web application on the Microsoft platform was a matter of assembling a bunch of ASP pages.

ASP.NET received a very warm welcome from the community of developers. It simplified a number of everyday tasks and, more importantly, enabled developers to work at a higher level of abstraction. This allowed them to focus more on the core functions of the Web application rather than on common tasks related to Web page design.

Based on server controls, ASP.NET allows developers to build real-world Web sites and applications with minimal HTML and JavaScript skills. The whole point of ASP.NET is productivity, achieved through powerful tools integrated in the runtime as well as the provision of development facilities, such as server controls, user controls, postback events, view state, forms authentication, and intrinsic objects. The model behind ASP.NET is called Web Forms, and it was clearly inspired by the desktop Windows Forms model (which, in turn, was deeply inspired by the Visual Basic RAD philosophy).

So why did Microsoft release another ASP.NET framework, called ASP.NET MVC?

The simple answer is that this "other" ASP.NET framework better responds to the needs of today's Web developers. Web Forms moves toward an abstraction of the Web that simulates a stateful environment, whereas ASP.NET MVC leverages the natural statelessness of the Web and guides you toward building applications that are loosely coupled and inherently testable, search-engine friendly, and have full control of HTML. In any case, keep in mind that there's nothing you can do in ASP.NET MVC that can't be done in Web Forms and vice versa. The *how* may be different, but the *what* is not.

As a Web developer or architect, you should know exactly what each framework has to offer and how it lets you approach every task related to Web development. Beyond that, feel free to choose the tool that you reckon is right for the job and for the people you have in your organization. You don't have to go with ASP.NET MVC because it's cool and modern. Likewise, you don't have to stick to ASP.NET Web Forms because that's all you've been doing for the past five years. Making a choice is an extra step, but two options are better than one.

Today, ASP.NET Web Forms and ASP.NET MVC are two distinct and functionally equivalent models for ASP.NET development. Could these two models merge in some near or even remote future? If this were to happen, my guess is that it would be ASP.NET MVC that would get enhanced with some more abstract component model, rather than Web Forms moving toward testability and SoC. But, again, this is half my guess and half my hope. On that point, we'll just have to wait and see.

Chapter 2
The Runtime Environment

Part of the inhumanity of the computer is that, once it is competently programmed and working smoothly, it is completely honest.

—Isaac Asimov

From the developer's perspective, ASP.NET Web Forms and ASP.NET MVC look like two different and largely incompatible frameworks. Under the hood, though, they have a lot in common. In particular, both frameworks are built on top of the same runtime environment—the standard ASP.NET runtime environment.

Generally speaking, the runtime environment is the collection of components that, hosted within the Web server, contribute to processing an incoming HTTP request to some response for the client browser. This runtime machinery is the same for both ASP.NET Web Forms and ASP.NET MVC. Among other things, this means that classic ASP.NET pages and ASP.NET MVC resources can be hosted side by side in the same application.

Even though the underlying machinery is the same, the steps taken to process an ASP.NET MVC request and a Web Forms request are quite different. In particular, ASP.NET MVC installs a sort of personalized run-time shell atop the standard ASP.NET runtime and implements a different pipeline for any requests that it picks up.

In this chapter, I'll first briefly review the pillars of the ASP.NET runtime environment and then explore the characteristics of the ASP.NET MVC run-time shell and explain the work it does to support the new MVC programming model.

The ASP.NET Runtime Machinery

Any Web application is hosted within a Web server; for ASP.NET applications, the Web server is typically Microsoft Internet Information Services (IIS). A Web server is primarily a server application that can be contacted using a bunch of Internet protocols, such as HTTP, File Transfer Protocol (FTP), Network News Transfer Protocol (NNTP), and Simple Mail Transfer Protocol (SMTP). IIS—the Web server included with the Microsoft Windows operating system—is no exception.

The Web server—say, IIS—spends most of its time listening to a variety of ports, including port 80, which is where HTTP packets are usually forwarded. The details of what happens next depend on the programming interface of the Web server and the functionalities of the external modules bound to the Web server.

Note When it comes to ASP.NET, frankly it doesn't make much sense to look around for a Web server other than Microsoft's IIS. Nevertheless, with the proper set of add-on modules you can make ASP.NET run on other Web servers, such as Apache. In particular, for Apache the *mod_mono* module is used to run ASP.NET applications. The *mod_mono* module runs within an Apache process and forwards all ASP.NET requests to an external Mono process that actually hosts your ASP.NET application. For more information, pay a visit to *http://www.mono-project.com/Mod_mono*.

ASP.NET and the IIS Web Server

When the request for a resource arrives, IIS first verifies the type of the resource. Static resources such as images, text files, HTML pages, and scriptless ASP pages are typically resolved directly by IIS without the involvement of any external modules. IIS accesses the file on the local Web server machine and flushes its contents to the output console so that the requesting browser can receive it.

Resources that require server-side elaboration are passed on to any tailor-made modules that are registered to handle those resources. Requested resources are mapped to registered modules based on their file extension.

The details of how a request is being processed depend on the process model in use within IIS and ultimately on the internal architecture of the Web server. The internal architecture of IIS has changed quite a bit since the introduction of ASP.NET 1.0 back in 2002. Figure 2-1 shows at a relatively high level of abstraction how the IIS architecture evolved from IIS 5.0 up to IIS 7.0.

Note The only purpose of Figure 2-1 is to show the overall evolution of the IIS architecture in relation to ASP.NET, so I tried to keep the figure clear and straight to the point. This said, I do recognize that the figure lacks or simplifies a number of significant details, including the host process of the WWW service, the role of the Web Administration Service (WAS) and what it takes for a request to be served by IIS natively or forwarded to the worker process. If you need to delve deeper into the IIS architecture, I recommend getting a copy of *Internet Information Services 7.0 Resource Kit* (Microsoft Press, 2008).

As you can see from the figure, a significant innovation over the years has been the introduction of *application pools* to group multiple Web applications under the same instance of a worker process. In parallel, IIS gained many more built-in functionalities to implement earlier in the process chain and, for any type of resource, many of the powerful features of the ASP.NET runtime, such as process recycling, output caching, and form-based authentication. This is known as the *Integrated* IIS and ASP.NET request-processing pipeline, and it has been up and running since IIS 7.0 in Windows Server 2008.

Let's expand on some architectural elements of IIS, focusing on the most recent version (IIS 7.0) available with Windows 2008 Server and, in a shrink-wrapped version, also on Windows Vista.

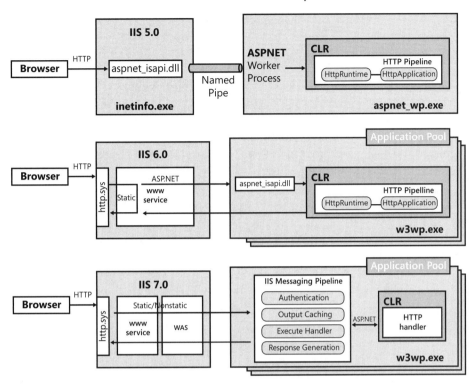

FIGURE 2-1 Architectural changes to IIS over the years

Note Windows 7 comes with a version of IIS that is superior to the version you find in Windows Vista. However, the version of IIS that ships with desktop operating systems is not particularly relevant here in the context of an ASP.NET book. Although you can certainly develop part of your Web site on a Windows Vista or Windows 7 machine, using Windows Vista or Windows 7 as a Web server to host a site is simply out of the question. Although it's fully functional, the IIS version that ships with Windows Vista and Windows 7 can be seen as a live tool to experiment and test. The "real" IIS for Web developers and administrators is currently the one available with Windows 2008 Server.

Handling the Request

In both IIS 6.0 and IIS 7.0, any incoming HTTP request is captured by an HTTP listener (the *http.sys* driver) that operates as a kernel-level module. A kernel-level module lives in its own protected environment and is never exposed to any third-party code. Among other things, this means that no user-mode crashes can ever affect the stability of IIS.

Any request the driver intercepts is posted to the request queue of the appropriate *application pool*. An *application pool* is a blanket term that identifies a worker process and a virtual directory. A module, called the Web Administration Service (WAS, not to be confused with the Windows Activation Service, which also uses the same acronym), reads from the IIS metabase and instructs the *http.sys* driver to create as many request queues as there are application pools registered in the metabase.

So when a request arrives, the driver looks at the URL and queues the request to the corresponding application pool. The WAS module is also responsible for creating and administering the worker processes for the various pools. The IIS worker process is an executable named *w3wp.exe*, whose main purpose is extracting HTTP requests from the kernel-mode queue and processing them. The behavior of the worker process actually depends on the working mode of IIS.

> **Note** In IIS 6.0 and later, the worker process that serves up the request is not specific to a particular server technology or request type. In other words, the same worker process can serve an ASP.NET Web Forms request, an ASP.NET MVC request, or even a classic ASP request. Part of the IIS platform, the *w3wp.exe* worker process hosts a core application handler dynamic-link library (DLL) to actually process the request and load request-specific components to produce the response.

ISAPI Extensions

A Web server generally knows how to serve a few types of resources (static HTML pages, text files, images) and forwards other requests to ad hoc modules that basically exist to extend the Web server's core capabilities.

For this to happen, the Web server provides a documented application programming interface (API) for enhancing and customizing the server's capabilities. Historically speaking, the first of these extension APIs was the Common Gateway Interface (CGI). A CGI module is a new application that is spawned from the Web server to service a request.

As you can easily understand, the CGI approach is rather inadequate for modern, high-volume Web sites because it creates severe scalability issues. IIS supports CGI applications, but you will seldom use this feature unless you have serious backward-compatibility issues. In the past decade, Web servers started supplying an alternative and more efficient model to extend the capabilities of the server. In IIS, this alternative model takes the form of the Internet Server Application Programming Interface (ISAPI).

An ISAPI extension is a Win32 DLL that gets loaded into the IIS worker process that's in charge for any given Web application. In IIS 6.0 and later, this worker process is *w3wp.exe*. The DLL communicates with the host process by exposing a well-known set of entry-point functions—the Win32 ancestor of modern service contracts. To start servicing a request, the worker process just ensures the ISAPI extension DLL is loaded in memory and then calls a well-known entry point in its public interface.

In Figure 2-1, you recognize the ISAPI extension for ASP.NET requests in the *aspnet_isapi.dll* component. Figure 2-2 offers a view of the IIS 7.0 metabase configuration tool where the mapping between *.aspx* resources and *aspnet_isapi.dll* is established.

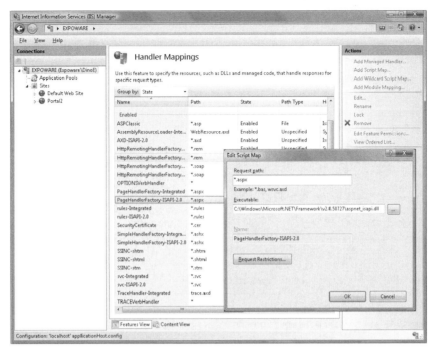

FIGURE 2-2 Setting the handler for ASPX resources in IIS 7.0

Depending on how IIS is configured to work, the *w3wp.exe* process might load the *aspnet_isapi.dll* extension. In turn, the ISAPI extension will load the CLR in the worker process and launch the ASP.NET runtime pipeline to actually process the request. (I'll return to the discussion of IIS working mode in just a moment.)

In the IIS jargon, ISAPI extensions are plain Win32 DLLs designated to do some server-side processing and return a response. The extensibility model of IIS, though, includes another flavor of component as well—*ISAPI filters*.

ISAPI Filters

ISAPI filters are components that intercept specific server events before the server itself handles them. Upon loading, the filter indicates what event notifications it will handle. If any of these events occur, the filter can process them or pass them on to other filters.

ISAPI filters can accomplish tasks such as implementing custom authentication schemes, compression, encryption, logging, and request analysis. The ability to examine, and if necessary modify, both incoming and outgoing streams of data makes ISAPI filters powerful and flexible.

Filters are also a delicate gear in the IIS machinery. They can facilitate applications and let them take control of customizable aspects of the engine. For this same reason, though, ISAPI filters can also degrade performance if they're not written carefully or if they're used when not strictly necessary. Filters, in fact, can run only in-process.

Extensions and Filters in IIS 7.0

ISAPI extensions and ISAPI filters are specific members of the IIS ecosystem. In any version of IIS older than version 7.0, you have no choice other than writing such ISAPI components as a C or C++ DLL, using either Microsoft Foundation Classes (MFC) or perhaps the ActiveX Template Library (ATL).

For years, ASP.NET offered capabilities largely equivalent to ISAPI extensions and filters within its own runtime environment. HTTP handlers are the ASP.NET counterpart to ISAPI extensions, whereas HTTP modules are the ASP.NET version of filters. The big difference is that ASP.NET HTTP handlers and modules are written using managed code and, as such, they are significantly easier to write than ISAPI extensions and filters.

Note Before IIS 7.0, you had essentially two distinct runtime environments: one within the IIS process and one within the application pool of any hosted ASP.NET application. The two runtime environments had different capabilities and programming models. Only resources mapped to the ASP.NET ISAPI extension were subjected to the ASP.NET runtime environment; all the others were processed within the simpler IIS machinery. IIS 7.0 offers a new runtime environment nearly identical to that of ASP.NET. When this runtime environment is enabled, ASP.NET requests use the managed ASP.NET runtime environment only to produce the response.

IIS 7.0 represents the unification of the ASP.NET and IIS platforms. In IIS 7.0, HTTP handlers and modules, the runtime pipeline, and configuration files become constituent elements of a common environment. The whole IIS 7.0 internal pipeline has been componentized to originate a distinct and individually configurable component—the IIS Messaging Pipeline box that was shown in Figure 2-1. In addition, a new section has been added to the *web.config* schema of ASP.NET applications to configure the surrounding IIS environment.

In a certain way, it's as if the ASP.NET runtime expanded to incorporate and replace the surrounding Web server environment. It's hard to say whether things really went this way or whether it was the other way around. The result is that the same concepts and instruments you know from ASP.NET are available in IIS 7.0 at the Web server level.

This means that in IIS 7.0 you can write HTTP handlers and modules to filter *any* requests and implement any additional features using .NET code for whatever resources the Web server can serve. More precisely, you'll continue writing HTTP handlers and modules as you do today for ASP.NET, except that you will be given the opportunity to register them for any file type, even those not natively mapped to ASP.NET such as images and HTML files.

Note Obviously, old-style ISAPI extensions and filters are still fully supported in IIS 7.0. However, it's easy to predict that unmanaged extensions and filters will soon become a thing of the past. Looking back at Figure 2-1, you should note that the IIS Messaging Pipeline can work with unmanaged ISAPI filters as well as load a common language runtime (CLR) instance and trigger managed HTTP modules. At the same time, executing the handler might mean invoking an unmanaged ISAPI extension as well as yielding to the CLR and the HTTP runtime environment.

Application Pools

As in Figure 2-1, ASP.NET was originally built as a stand-alone runtime environment to be hosted in IIS 5.0 running on Windows 2000 Server. The ASP.NET runtime environment was governed by a made-to-measure worker process. The advent of IIS 6.0 and Windows Server 2003 marked the introduction of *application pools* and led developers to choose one of these pools to deploy their own application.

An application pool is a group of one or more URLs that are served by an instance of the IIS worker process. An application pool represents the boundary that contained Web applications cannot cross. Applications in one pool are isolated from applications in other pools and cannot affect them in any way.

Through the IIS Manager console, you can give a pool a friendly name, set the version of the Microsoft .NET Framework to be loaded, select the security account under which the application pool's worker process will run, and edit recycling conditions for hosted applications.

Another parameter you can configure for all applications in a given IIS 7.0 pool is the pipeline working mode: Integrated or Classic mode. You choose Integrated if you want IIS to process requests through its own managed pipeline before handing them over to ASP.NET for generating any response. If you want, or more likely need, IIS to yield to the ASP.NET runtime the whole burden of processing any ASP.NET request (authentication, caching, and the like), you stick to Classic mode. Classic mode is the standard way of working for versions of IIS earlier than 7.0.

Figure 2-3 shows the dialog box through which you configure the application pool for a given Web application.

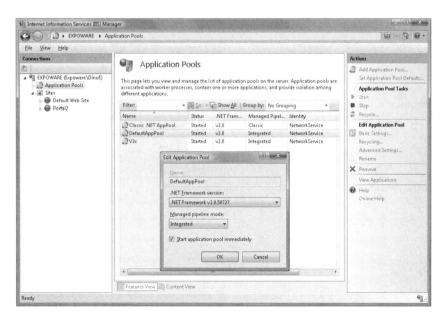

FIGURE 2-3 Configuring the application pool

ASP.NET Runtime Components

A typical ASP.NET request has the form of a URL that ends with the *.aspx* extension. And typically such a request is resolved by loading the content of the corresponding *.aspx* file and parsing it to HTML.

Does it mean that the ASP.NET runtime doesn't let you place a request for an action or, more in general, for anything else different from a server disk file? Well, not exactly. And the existence of the ASP.NET MVC framework itself proves this!

The actual behavior of the ASP.NET runtime machinery can be affected by some runtime pluggable components that intercept the request at various prefixed stages and alter the regular processing flow. These runtime components are *HTTP handlers* and *HTTP modules*. Using these special components, you can do a number of interesting things such as rewriting the URL or redirecting the request to a specific HTTP handler to service it.

An HTTP handler is a special managed class that implements a contracted interface for the ASP.NET runtime environment (or the IIS messaging pipeline) to invoke. The overall behavior of an HTTP handler is fairly simple: all it does is get the HTTP context of the pending request and processes it, performing any necessary calculation and writing any response down to the output stream.

An HTTP module is also a managed class that implements another contracted interface. The interface lets the HTTP module intervene at any or all prefixed stages a request goes through during processing. After the interface is registered with the application (or the IIS messaging pipeline), an HTTP module is automatically invoked for any incoming request when the request processing reaches the hooked stage. Depending on the stages it is designed to handle, an HTTP module can even alter the context and content of the request. Prefixed stages for an HTTP module to intervene exist both before and after the HTTP handler generates the response for the request.

> **Important** I should make this point clear here in the early stages of the book. In a nutshell, ASP.NET MVC is based on a collection of ad hoc HTTP modules and HTTP handlers that altogether transform ASP.NET into a RESTful platform and bypass the classic Web Forms pipeline and define and support a brand new programming model.

Before we delve deeper into the intricacies of the bolted-on ASP.NET MVC runtime environment, let's recap the important actions that take place within the native ASP.NET runtime environment.

Life Cycle of an ASP.NET Request

Any HTTP requests that knock at the IIS door that are directed at a hosted ASP.NET application are handed over to the instance of the IIS worker process in charge of the pool that the application belongs to.

The details of what happens next depends on the IIS pipeline mode—Classic or Integrated.

> **Note** For an *.aspx* request, it makes no significant difference whether the application pool operates in Integrated or Classic mode under IIS 7.0. That request is always handed over to the ASP.NET ISAPI for actual response generation.
>
> The Integrated mode affects ASP.NET applications in the sense that developers can now exercise stricter control (HTTP handlers and HTTP modules) over any requested resources, even those (for example, image files) not mapped to an ASP.NET application.
>
> From the IIS perspective, the Integrated mode sets up a different architecture for processing any requests—including, but not limited to, ASP.NET requests.

Figure 2-4 illustrates the life cycle of an ASP.NET request in Classic pipeline mode. This is the way ASP.NET requests are processed in IIS 6.0 and IIS 7.0 Classic.

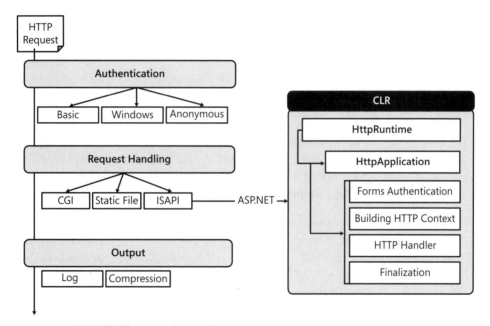

FIGURE 2-4 IIS 6.0/7.0 Classic pipeline mode

The request first goes through the IIS authentication stage, and then it's examined to determine what the right handler is. If the handler turns out to be an ISAPI extension, the request is handed over to that extension. In particular, if it's an ASP.NET request, the ASP.NET ISAPI makes it flow through the standard ASP.NET runtime pipeline, where steps such as forms authentication, authorization, session state acquisition, output caching, and mapping of the HTTP handler follow one another until the response is generated. ASP.NET returns the response to IIS, which logs the response, optionally compresses the response, and sends it back to the browser.

Figure 2-5, on the other hand, illustrates what happens in the case of an Integrated pipeline.

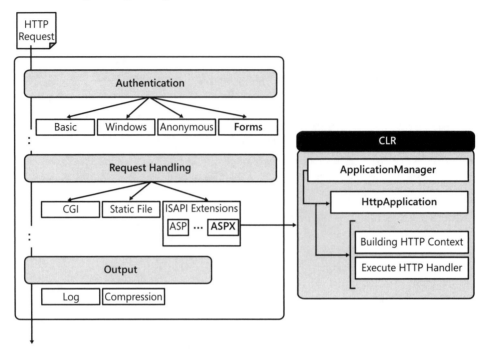

FIGURE 2-5 IIS 7.0 Integrated pipeline mode

The most evident difference is that the ASP.NET pipeline is greatly simplified and most of its steps have been moved to (actually, integrated in) the IIS pipeline. For an ASP.NET request, it might not be a huge change; it is, though, a big change for any other types of requests and it's good news for ASP.NET developers, who can now attain more programming power.

In Integrated mode, IIS makes the request flow through a greater number of steps in its messaging pipeline than in earlier versions. At the end of the day, the overall pipeline looks a lot like the ASP.NET HTTP pipeline. In this pipeline, you can register your own HTTP modules (both managed and unmanaged) to handle any resources. Forms authentication is still supported, but the HTTP module responsible for that is now invoked from IIS rather than from the ASP.NET runtime environment.

In an integrated pipeline, an ASP.NET request is like any other request except that, at some point, it yields to a sort of simplified ASP.NET runtime environment that now just prepares the HTTP context, maps the HTTP handler, and generates the response.

When the application pool that contains an ASP.NET application running in Integrated mode is initialized, it hosts ASP.NET in the worker process and gives ASP.NET a chance to register a set of built-in HTTP modules and handlers for the IIS pipeline events. This guarantees, for example, that Forms authentication, session state, and output caching work as expected in ASP.NET. At the same time, the ASP.NET runtime also subscribes to receive notification of when an ASP.NET request needs processing.

Let's expand on the specific events that form the life cycle of an ASP.NET request.

> **Important** The sequence of events in Classic and Integrated mode is the same. However, because in Integrated mode ASP.NET modules execute in the IIS messaging pipeline, they can subscribe to certain events (for example, authentication, begin-request) earlier than in plain ASP.NET processing. This fact makes possible previously unavailable functionality and increases the power made available to ASP.NET developers.
>
> In particular, in Integrated mode your HTTP modules are allowed to intercept the request before any processing has taken place (for example, for URL rewriting). Likewise, you can write HTTP modules to replace built-in authentication modes, modify the headers of an incoming request, or filter outgoing responses for any content type and not just for ASP.NET requests.

Events in the Request Life Cycle

The following list of events are fired within the IIS messaging pipeline and, as such, they are available for HTTP modules to subscribe to. Events are fired in the following sequence:

1. *BeginRequest*   The ASP.NET HTTP pipeline begins to work on the request. This event reaches the application after *Application_Start*.

2. *AuthenticateRequest*   The request is being authenticated. ASP.NET and IIS integrated authentication modules subscribe to this event and attempt to produce an identity. If no authentication module produced an authenticated user, an internal default authentication module is invoked to produce an identity for the unauthenticated user. This is done for the sake of consistency so that code doesn't need to worry about null identities.

3. *PostAuthenticateRequest*   The request has been authenticated. All the information available is stored in the *HttpContext*'s *User* property at this time.

4. *AuthorizeRequest*   The request authorization is about to occur. This event is commonly handled by application code to perform custom authorization based on business logic or other application requirements.

5. *PostAuthorizeRequest*   The request has been authorized.

6. *ResolveRequestCache*   The runtime environment verifies whether returning a previously cached page can resolve the request. If a valid cached representation is found, the request is served from the cache and the request is short-circuited, calling only any registered *EndRequest* handlers. Both ASP.NET Output Cache and the new IIS 7.0 Output Cache feature "execute now" capabilities.

7. *PostResolveRequestCache*   The request can't be served from the cache, and the procedure continues. An HTTP handler corresponding to the requested URL is created at this point. If the requested resource is an *.aspx* page, an instance of a page class is created.

8. *MapRequestHandler*   The event is fired to determine the request handler.

9. *PostMapRequestHandler*   The event fires when the HTTP handler corresponding to the requested URL has been successfully created.

10. *AcquireRequestState*   The module that hooks up this event is willing to retrieve any state information for the request. A number of factors are relevant here: the handler must support session state in some form, and there must be a valid session ID.

11. *PostAcquireRequestState*   The state information (such as *Application* or *Session*) has been acquired. The state information is stored in the *HttpContext*'s related properties at this time.

12. *PreRequestHandlerExecute*   This event is fired immediately prior to executing the handler for a given request.

13. *ExecuteRequestHandler*   At this point, the handler does its job and generates the output for the client.

14. *PostRequestHandlerExecute*   When this event fires, the selected HTTP handler has completed and generated the response text.

15. *ReleaseRequestState*   This event is raised when the handler releases its state information and prepares to shut down. This event is used by the session state module to update the dirty session state if necessary.

16. *PostReleaseRequestState*   The state, as modified by the page execution, has been persisted.

17. *UpdateRequestCache*   The runtime environment determines whether the generated output, now also properly filtered by registered modules, should be cached to be reused with upcoming identical requests.

18. *PostUpdateRequestCache*   The page has been saved to the output cache if it was configured to do so.

19. *LogRequest*   The event indicates that the runtime is ready to log the results of the request. Logging is guaranteed to execute even if errors occur.

20. *PostLogRequest*   The request has been logged.

21. *EndRequest*   This event fires as the final step of the pipeline. At this point, the response is known and made available to other modules that might add compression or encryption, or perform any other manipulation.

Another pair of events can occur during the request, but in a nondeterministic order. They are *PreSendRequestHeaders* and *PreSendRequestContent*. The *PreSendRequestHeaders* event informs the *HttpApplication* object in charge of the request that HTTP headers are about to be sent. The *PreSendRequestContent* event tells the *HttpApplication* object in charge of the request that the response body is about to be sent. Both of these events normally fire after *EndRequest*, but not always. For example, if buffering is turned off, the event gets fired as soon as some content is going to be sent to the client.

Speaking of nondeterministic application events, it must be said that a third nondeterministic event is, of course, *Error*.

Let's delve deeper into the mechanics of ASP.NET request processing.

> **Note** Technically, most of the IIS pipeline events are exposed as events of the ASP.NET *HttpApplication* class. A significant exception is *ExecuteRequestHandler*. You find this event in the IIS messaging pipeline, but you won't find an easy way to subscribe to it from within ASP.NET code. Internally, the ASP.NET runtime subscribes to this event to receive notification of when an ASP.NET request needs to produce its output. This happens using unmanaged code that is not publicly available to developers. If you want to control how an incoming request is executed by IIS, you have to resort to Win32 ISAPI filters. If you want to control how an ASP.NET request is executed, you don't need the IIS *ExecuteRequestHandler* event, because a simpler HTTP handler will do the job.

ASP.NET Request Processing in Classic Pipeline Mode

As shown in Figure 2-4, in Classic pipeline mode an ASP.NET request is handed over to an ISAPI extension right after IIS has obtained an authentication token for the sender. The request life cycle is governed by a static instance of the *HttpRuntime* class. A single instance of the *HttpRuntime* class exists per application, and it's created when the first request for the application comes in.

When the *HttpRuntime* object is commanded to process a request, it performs a number of initialization tasks, the first of which is the creation of the HTTP context object. As its second step, the *HttpRuntime* object sets up an ASP.NET application object to carry out the request. An ASP.NET application object consists of an instance of a dynamically created class that inherits from the system's *HttpApplication* class. The *HttpApplication*-derived class is built based on the content of the *global.asax* file.

The HTTP runtime attempts to pick up an *HttpApplication* object from a pool. If no *HttpApplication* object is available, either because the application has not been started yet or all valid objects are busy, a new *HttpApplication* is created and added to the pool. The selected *HttpApplication* object is responsible for managing the entire lifetime of the request it is assigned to. That instance of *HttpApplication* can be reused only after the request has been completed.

The *HttpRuntime* object uses a contracted interface—the *IHttpHandler* interface—to drive the behavior of the *HttpApplication* object. When the request has been processed, the HTTP runtime finalizes the request and returns control to its ISAPI caller.

ASP.NET Request Processing in Integrated Pipeline Mode

In IIS 7.0 running in Integrated pipeline mode, no explicit handoff of the request from IIS to ASP.NET ever occurs.

Any managed HTTP modules registered to handle early stages of the request can execute without first routing the request to the managed runtime of ASP.NET. A managed HTTP module can be added through the IIS manager and can operate on both managed and native requests. Similarly, a managed HTTP handler can be mapped to any resource types directly from the IIS manager or via the *web.config* file of the ASP.NET application. Mappings set directly within the IIS manager are stored in the *applicationHost.config* file.

In Integrated pipeline mode, all the request life-cycle events I just described are fired within the IIS space and are in no way specific to an ASP.NET request. In between the *PreRequestHandlerExecute* and *PostRequestHandlerExecute* events, IIS hands an ASP.NET request to some code in the ASP.NET runtime environment for actual processing.

Hosted in the IIS worker process, the ASP.NET environment is governed by a new class—the *ApplicationManager* class. This class is responsible for creating and managing any needed AppDomains to run the various ASP.NET applications located in the same pool. During the initialization, the *ApplicationManager* class invokes a specific *PipelineRuntime* object, which ultimately registers a handler for the *ExecuteRequestHandler*.

This ASP.NET internal handler is called back by IIS whenever an ASP.NET request needs be processed. The handler invokes a new static method on the *HttpRuntime* object that kicks in to take care of the request notification. The method retrieves the HTTP handler in charge for the request, prepares the HTTP context for the request, and invokes the HTTP handler's public interface.

What Executes the ASP.NET Request?

Each ASP.NET request is mapped to a special component known as the *HTTP handler*. The ASP.NET runtime uses a built-in algorithm to figure out the HTTP handler in charge of a given ASP.NET request.

In Web Forms, this algorithm is based on the URL of the requested page. You have a different HTTP handler for each page requested. If you requested, say, *page.aspx*, the HTTP handler is a class named *ASP.page_aspx* that inherits from the code-behind class you specified in your source code. The first time the request is made this class doesn't exist in the AppDomain. If the class does not exist, the source code for the class is obtained by parsing the ASPX markup and then it's compiled in memory and loaded directly into the AppDomain. Successive requests then can be served by the existing instance. (ASP.NET site precompilation is all about running this process in advance for all pages in a site.)

An HTTP handler is a managed class that implements the *IHttpHandler* interface, as shown in the following code snippet. The body of the *ProcessRequest* method ultimately determines the response for the request.

```
public interface IHttpHandler
{
    void ProcessRequest(HttpContext context);
    bool IsReusable { get; }
}
```

The well-known *System.Web.UI.Page* class—the base class for Web Forms pages—is simply a class that provides a sophisticated implementation of the *IHttpHandler* interface, which basically turns out to be a full implementation of the Page Controller pattern.

For individual requests, or for a logically defined group of requests, within an application you can define an alternate handler that employs different logic to generate the response. Ultimately, this is just what ASP.NET MVC does.

As we'll see later, in ASP.NET MVC the HTTP handler is unique for all requests and decides the action to take by looking at the characteristics of the request URL.

What's an HTTP Handler, Anyway?

As mentioned earlier, an HTTP handler is just a managed class that implements the *IHttpHandler* interface. More specifically, a synchronous HTTP handler implements the *IHttpHandler* interface; an asynchronous HTTP handler, on the other hand, implements the *IHttpAsyncHandler* interface. Because this section is not supposed to provide in-depth coverage of HTTP handlers, I'll limit the discussion to tackling synchronous handlers.

If you feel you need richer and more advanced information on HTTP handlers, you can have a look at Chapter 18 of my earlier book *Programming Microsoft ASP.NET 3.5* (Microsoft Press, 2008).

The *IHttpHandler* Interface

The *IHttpHandler* interface defines only two members: *ProcessRequest* and *IsReusable*, as shown in Table 2-1. *ProcessRequest* is a method, whereas *IsReusable* is a Boolean property.

TABLE 2-1 Members of the *IHttpHandler* interface

Member	Description
IsReusable	This property provides a Boolean value indicating whether the HTTP runtime can reuse the current instance of the HTTP handler while serving another request.
ProcessRequest	This method processes the HTTP request.

The *IsReusable* property on the *System.Web.UI.Page* class—the most common HTTP handler in ASP.NET—returns *false*, meaning that a new instance of the HTTP request is needed to serve each new page request. You typically make *IsReusable* return *false* in all situations where some significant processing is required that depends on the payload of the request. Handlers used as simple barriers to filter special requests can set *IsReusable* to *true* to save some CPU cycles.

The *ProcessRequest* method takes the context of the request as the input and ensures that the request is serviced. In the case of synchronous handlers, when *ProcessRequest* returns, the output is ready for forwarding to the client.

A Simple but Effective HTTP Handler

If anything significant is ever going to happen around an HTTP handler, that will surely take place in the *ProcessRequest* method. In light of this, the following code is more than enough to demonstrate the true power of HTTP handlers:

```
using System.Web;

namespace Samples.Components
{
    public class SimpleHandler : IHttpHandler
    {
        // Override the ProcessRequest method
        public void ProcessRequest(HttpContext context)
        {
            context.Response.Write("<h1>Hello, I'm an HTTP handler</h1>");
        }

        // Override the IsReusable property
        public bool IsReusable
        {
            get { return false; }
        }
    }
}
```

The difference between this admittedly trivial handler and a much more complex one is all in the amount of code you put in *ProcessRequest* and in how you consume the HTTP context.

Registering the HTTP Handler

You need an entry point to be able to call the handler. In this context, an entry point into the handler's code is nothing more than an HTTP endpoint—that is, a public URL. The URL must be a unique name that IIS and the ASP.NET runtime can map to this code. When registered, the mapping between an HTTP handler and a Web server resource is established through the *web.config* file:

```
<configuration>
    <system.web>
        <httpHandlers>
            <add verb="*"
                 path="hello.axd"
                 type="Samples.Components.SimpleHandler" />
        </httpHandlers>
    </system.web>
</configuration>
```

The *<httpHandlers>* section lists the handlers available for the current application. These settings indicate that *SimpleHandler* is in charge of handling any incoming requests for an endpoint named *hello.axd*.

Note that the endpoint is simply a public resource identifier and doesn't have to be a physical resource on the server, such as a file. It doesn't have to end with the *.axd* extension, either, although for this example it does. The endpoint can be any string that the target handler knows how to process. (This feature of HTTP handlers is another point that helps explain how it's possible for ASP.NET Web Forms and ASP.NET MVC to share the same runtime environment.)

The *type* attribute in the configuration schema references the class and assembly that contains the handler. Its canonical format is *type[,assembly]*. You omit the assembly information if the component is assumed to be in one of the application's dynamically compiled assemblies.

If you invoke the *hello.axd* URL, you obtain the results shown in Figure 2-6.

FIGURE 2-6 A sample HTTP handler that answers requests for *hello.axd*

Note If you're using a custom extension or a URL format that doesn't match any of the predefined mappings in IIS, you need to edit the metabase manually to map the resource type to ASP.NET. In IIS 7, with the Integrated pipeline, you don't need to edit the metabase but can simply register the handler in the application's *web.config* file under the *<system.webServer>* section, right below the root *<configuration>* node. Also note that for applications running under IIS 7 Integrated mode, the section *<httpHandlers>* under *<system.web>* is not used. You should move settings under *<handlers>* in *<system.webServer>*.

HTTP Handlers as ASHX Resources

HTTP handlers are not a tool for everybody. They serve a specific purpose: determining the way a particular resource, or set of resources, is served to the user. You can use handlers to filter out resources based on run-time conditions. You can use handlers to apply any form of additional logic to the retrieval of traditional resources, such as pages and images. Finally, you can use HTTP handlers to apply routing policies and even to serve certain resources in an asynchronous manner.

For HTTP handlers, the registration step is key.

Registration enables ASP.NET to know about your handler and its purpose. Registration is required for two practical reasons. First, it serves to ensure that IIS forwards the call to the correct ASP.NET application. Second, it serves to direct your ASP.NET application to the class to "handle" the request. To register an HTTP handler, though, you need to modify the *web.config* file of the application.

An alternative way to define an HTTP handler is through an *.ashx* file. The file contains a special directive, named *@WebHandler*, that expresses the association between the HTTP handler endpoint and the class used to implement the functionality. All *.ashx* files must begin with a directive like the following one:

```
<%@ WebHandler Class="Samples.Components.SimpleHandler" %>
```

When an *.ashx* endpoint is invoked, ASP.NET parses the source code of the file and figures out the HTTP handler class to use from the *@WebHandler* directive. This automation removes the need to update the *web.config* file. The actual code for the handler can be found in the specified class or inline in the *.ashx* file. If the code is placed inline, you must add a *Language* attribute to the *@WebHandler* directive to instruct the ASP.NET runtime environment about which compiler to use to generate the dynamic assembly:

```
<%@ WebHandler Language="C#" Class="Samples.Components.SimpleHandler" %>
namespace Samples.Components
{
    public class SimpleHandler : IHttpHandler
    {
        .
        .
        .
    }
}
```

When *.ashx* resources are used to implement an HTTP handler, you just deploy the source file and you're done.

> **Note** In a nutshell, exposing an HTTP handler via either an AXD or ASHX endpoint doesn't have any significant impact on aspects such as performance, usability, and code readability. In both cases, you need to write an HTTP handler class. If you opt for an ASHX endpoint, you write an ASHX endpoint file and the handler is automatically visible to the application. If you opt for any other endpoint (AXD, ASPX, or custom extensions), you also need to tweak the *web.config* file to make the handler visible.

HTTP Handlers in an ASP.NET MVC Application

Note that in a Web Forms application you can easily use any extensions to characterize the HTTP endpoint for the handler, including the well-known .*aspx* extension. This doesn't work in an ASP.NET MVC application, at least not with the default routing configuration. Try using the following script to register an HTTP handler:

```
<httpHandlers>
    <add verb="*"
        path="hello.aspx"
        type="Samples.Components.SimpleHandler" />
</httpHandlers>
```

It will work as expected in a Web Forms application; on the other hand, it will return a nasty HTTP 404 error code in the context of an ASP.NET MVC application. Why is this so? And why is it that handlers registered to .*axd* and .*ashx* extensions work just fine?

As we'll see later in the chapter, ASP.NET MVC applications live behind a routing module that, when properly instructed by the application configuration, redirects certain ASP.NET requests to the ASP.NET MVC run-time shell. After it is routed to the ASP.NET MVC run-time shell, the request must have all the expected characteristics of an ASP.NET MVC request and, in particular, it must be bindable to a controller class.

By default, the ASP.NET MVC routing module handles all requests that don't match an existing physical file. It ignores any ASP.NET requests that don't match an existing server file. This means that because an ASHX request matches a physical file—the .*ashx* file you are required to write, anyway—that request is handed over to the standard ASP.NET runtime and served as expected.

When the HTTP handler is bound to an .*aspx* endpoint, how things go depends on whether a physical file exists with that name. With regard to the previous example, if a file named hello.aspx can be located, ASP.NET MVC yields to classic ASP.NET and the request is served as expected and routed to the HTTP handler. It's amazing that the content of *hello.aspx* can be anything—even empty content. All that matters is whether a physical file exists that matches the name in the requested endpoint.

If no *hello.aspx* file can be found on the server, the request for *hello.aspx* within ASP.NET MVC fails with HTTP 404, regardless of the accuracy of the *web.config* script. Because no file match is found, ASP.NET MVC intercepts the request and attempts to serve it via a controller. In doing so, ASP.NET MVC completely bypasses any settings in the *web.config* file. Unless proper route information is entered, the ASP.NET MVC run-time shell can't figure out what controller is valid and fails. A detailed explanation of what happened can be found in the source of the error's HTML page, as shown in Figure 2-7.

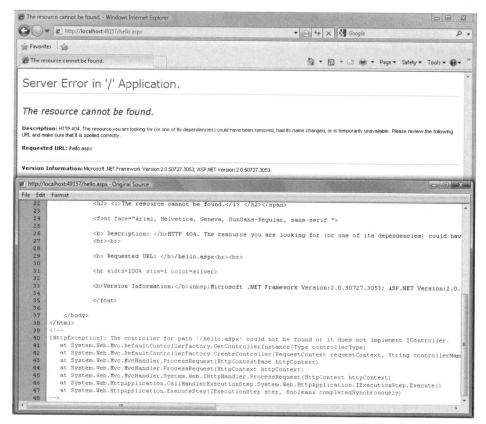

FIGURE 2-7 ASP.NET MVC fails to serve *hello.aspx* if no such server file exists.

The inner HTTP exception just says, *"The controller for path '/hello.aspx' could not be found or it does not implement* IController." It couldn't be clearer, could it?

So everything's clear? Well, not entirely. It still remains to be explained why on earth a request for an *.axd* endpoint works just fine even when there's no such server file. This is because of the following code, which is located by default in the *global.asax.cs* file of an ASP.NET MVC application:

```
public static void RegisterRoutes(RouteCollection routes)
{
    routes.IgnoreRoute("{resource}.axd/{*pathInfo}");
    .
    .
    .
}
```

The code just tells the ASP.NET MVC router to ignore any requests for an AXD resource.

In summary, to successfully define HTTP handlers in an ASP.NET MVC application, you either register them with an AXD or ASHX endpoint. If you can't avoid using an ASPX endpoint, just make sure you deploy a server file with the same name as the endpoint. Such a file can have any content and can even be empty.

What's an HTTP Module, Anyway?

As we've just seen, the processing of an ASP.NET request consists of various steps aimed at identifying the HTTP handler that will actually serve the request. A bunch of ad hoc components can hook up the request at any of the prefixed stages and read and write its content. Such components are *HTTP modules*.

An HTTP module is a .NET Framework class that implements the *IHttpModule* interface. The HTTP modules that filter the raw data within the request are configured on a per-application basis within the *web.config* file. All ASP.NET applications, though, inherit a bunch of system HTTP modules configured in the global *web.config* file.

Generally speaking, an HTTP module can pre-process and post-process a request, and it intercepts and handles system events as well as events raised by other modules. The highly configurable nature of ASP.NET makes it possible for you to also write and register your own HTTP modules and make them plug into the ASP.NET runtime pipeline, handle system events, and fire their own events.

The *IHttpModule* Interface

The *IHttpModule* interface defines only two methods: *Init* and *Dispose*. The *Init* method initializes a module and prepares it to handle requests. At this time, you subscribe to receive notifications for the events of interest. The *Dispose* method disposes of the resources (all but memory!) used by the module. Typical tasks you perform within the *Dispose* method are closing database connections or file handles.

The *IHttpModule* interface has the following signature:

```
public interface IHttpModule
{
    void Dispose();
    void Init(HttpApplication context);
}
```

The *Init* method receives a reference to the *HttpApplication* object that is serving the request. You can use this reference to wire up to system events. The *HttpApplication* object also features a property named *Context* that provides access to the intrinsic properties of the ASP.NET application. In this way, you gain access to *Response*, *Request*, *Session*, and the like.

Table 2-2 lists the events that HTTP modules can listen to and handle.

TABLE 2-2 *HttpApplication* **events**

Event	Description
AcquireRequestState, PostAcquireRequestState	Occurs when the handler that will actually serve the request acquires the state information associated with the request.
AuthenticateRequest, PostAuthenticateRequest	Occurs when a security module has established the identity of the user.
AuthorizeRequest, PostAuthorizeRequest	Occurs when a security module has verified user authorization.
BeginRequest	Occurs as soon as the HTTP pipeline begins to process the request.
Disposed	Occurs when the *HttpApplication* object is disposed of as a result of a call to *Dispose*.
EndRequest	Occurs as the last event in the HTTP pipeline chain of execution.
Error	Occurs when an unhandled exception is thrown.
LogRequest, PostLogRequest	Occurs when the response has been generated and logging modules can do their work. *These events are fired only to applications that run in Integrated pipeline mode under IIS 7.*
MapRequestHandler	Occurs when it is about time to set the handler to serve the request. *This event is fired only to applications that run in Integrated pipeline mode under IIS 7.*
PostMapRequestHandler	Occurs when the HTTP handler to serve the request has been found.
PostRequestHandlerExecute	Occurs when the HTTP handler of choice finishes execution. The response text has been generated at this point.
PreRequestHandlerExecute	Occurs just before the HTTP handler of choice begins to work.
PreSendRequestContent	Occurs just before the ASP.NET runtime sends the response text to the client.
PreSendRequestHeaders	Occurs just before the ASP.NET runtime sends HTTP headers to the client.
ReleaseRequestState, PostReleaseRequestState	Occurs when the handler releases the state information associated with the current request.
ResolveRequestCache, PostResolveRequestCache	Occurs when the ASP.NET runtime resolves the request through the output cache.
UpdateRequestCache, PostUpdateRequestCache	Occurs when the ASP.NET runtime stores the response of the current request in the output cache to be used to serve subsequent requests.

All these events are exposed by the *HttpApplication* object that an HTTP module receives as an argument to the *Init* method.

Wiring Up Events

In a typical HTTP module, most of the business takes place in the *Init* method and revolves around wiring up application events. In the *Init* method, you normally don't need to do more than simply register your own event handlers. The *Dispose* method is, more often than not, empty. Subsequently, the behavior of the HTTP module is really expressed by the event handlers you define.

The following listing shows the implementation of the *Init* and *Dispose* methods for a sample module that adds a signature at the top and bottom of each served piece of HTML:

```
public class MarkerModule : IHttpModule
{
    public void Init(HttpApplication app)
    {
        // Register for pipeline events
        app.BeginRequest += new EventHandler(OnBeginRequest);
        app.EndRequest += new EventHandler(OnEndRequest);
    }

    public void Dispose()
    {
    }

    // Event handlers go here
    :
    :

}
```

The *BeginRequest* and *EndRequest* event handlers have a similar structure. They obtain a reference to the current *HttpApplication* object from the sender and get the HTTP context from there. Next, they work with the *Response* object to append text or a custom header:

```
public void OnBeginRequest(object sender, EventArgs e)
{
    HttpApplication app = (HttpApplication) sender;
    HttpContext ctx = app.Context;

    // Possibly more code here
    :
    :

    // Add custom header to the HTTP response
    ctx.Response.AppendHeader("Author", "DinoE");

    // PageHeaderText is a constant string defined elsewhere
    ctx.Response.Write(PageHeaderText);
}

public void OnEndRequest(object sender, EventArgs e)
{
    // Get access to the HTTP context
    HttpApplication app = (HttpApplication) sender;
    HttpContext ctx = app.Context;

    // Possibly more code here
    :
    :

    // Append some custom text
    // PageFooterText is a constant string defined elsewhere
    ctx.Response.Write(PageFooterText);
}
```

OnBeginRequest writes specified page header text and also adds a custom HTTP header. *OnEndRequest* simply appends the page footer. The effect of this HTTP module is visible in Figure 2-8.

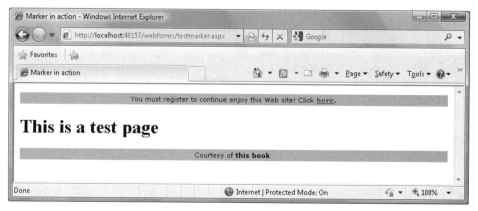

FIGURE 2-8 A sample HTTP module in action

> **Important** The registered HTTP modules are called to process every incoming request for the application. However, nothing prevents you from using some logic in any of your event handlers to skip work for requests you're not interested in.

Registering HTTP Modules

You register a new HTTP module by adding an entry to the *<httpModules>* section of the configuration file. The overall syntax of the *<httpModules>* section closely resembles that of HTTP handlers. To add a new module, you use the *<add>* node and specify the *name* and *type* attributes. The *name* attribute contains the public name of the module. If the module fires custom events, this name is also used as the prefix for building automatic event handlers in the *global.asax* file:

```
<system.web>
  <httpModules>
    <add name="Marker"
         type="Samples.Components.MarkerModule,Samples" />
  </httpModules>
</system.web>
```

The *type* attribute is the usual comma-separated string that contains the name of the class and the related assembly. The configuration settings can be entered into the application's configuration file as well as into the global *web.config* file. In the former case, only requests within the application are affected; in the latter case, all requests within all applications in the Web server are processed by the specified module.

The order in which modules are applied depends on the physical order of the modules in the configuration list. You can also remove a system module and replace it with your own that provides similar functionality. In this case, in the application's *web.config* file you use the *<remove>* node to drop the default module and then use *<add>* to insert your own. If you want to completely redefine the order of HTTP modules for your application, you can clear all the default modules by using the *<clear>* node and then re-register them all in the order you prefer.

These settings apply to applications working under IIS 6 or IIS 7 Classic mode. For applications working in IIS 7 Integrated mode, you need to move entries under the *<modules>* section within *<system.webServer>*. In Integrated mode, in fact, settings stored under the *<httpModules>* section under *<system.web>* are not used.

URL Routing

The whole ASP.NET platform originally developed around the idea of serving requests for physical pages. It turns out that most URLs used within an ASP.NET application are made of two parts: the path to the physical Web page that contains the logic, and some data stuffed in the query string to provide parameters. Here's a typical URL:

```
http://northwind.com/news.aspx?id=1234
```

The *news.aspx* page incorporates any logic required to retrieve, format, and display any given piece of news. The ID for the specific news to retrieve is provided via a parameter on the query string.

This approach has worked for a few years, and still works today. The content of the news is displayed correctly, and everybody is generally happy. In addition, you have just one page to maintain and you still have a way to identify a particular piece of news via the URL.

Are there any possible issues around the corner?

A possible drawback of this approach is that the real intent of the page might not be clear to users and, possibly, to search engines as well. To fix this, you need to make the entire URL friendlier and more readable. But you don't want to add new Web pages to the application or a bunch of made-to-measure HTTP handlers.

Original URL Rewriting API

To address the problem, ASP.NET has supported a feature called *URL rewriting* since its inception. At its core, URL rewriting consists of an HTTP module (or a *global.asax* event handler) that hooks up a given request, parses its original URL, and instructs the HTTP runtime environment to serve a "possibly related but different" URL. Here's a quick example:

```
protected void Application_BeginRequest(object sender, EventArgs e)
{
    // Get the current request context
    HttpContext context = HttpContext.Current;
```

```
    // Get the URL to the handler that will physically handle the request
    string newURL = ParseOriginalUrl(context);

    // Overwrite the target URL of the current request
    context.RewritePath(newURL);
}
```

The *RewritePath* method of *HttpContext* lets you change the URL of the current request on the fly, thus performing a sort of internal redirect. As a result, the user is provided the content generated for the URL you set through *RewritePath*. At the same time, the URL shown in the address bar remains the originally requested one.

URL rewriting helps you in two ways. It makes it possible for you to use a generic front-end page such as *news.aspx* and then redirect to a specific page whose actual URL is read from a database or any other container. In addition, it also enables you to request user-friendly URLs to be programmatically mapped to less intuitive, but easier to manage, URLs.

In a nutshell, URL rewriting exists to let you decouple the URL from the physical Web form that serves the requests.

> **Note** The change of the final URL takes place on the server and, more importantly, within the context of the same call. *RewritePath* should be used carefully and mainly from within the *global.asax* file. In Web Forms, for example, if you use *RewritePath* in the context of a postback event, you can experience some view-state problems.

URL Routing Engine

URL rewriting is a powerful feature, but it's not free of issues.

The first drawback is that as the API changes the target URL of the request, any postbacks are directed at the rewritten URL. For example, if you rewrite *news.aspx?id=1234* to *1234.aspx*, any postbacks from *1234.aspx* are targeted to the same *1234.aspx* instead of to the original URL.

This might or might not be a problem for you. For sure, it doesn't break any page behavior. At the same time, you'll likely always want to use the same, original URL as the front end. In this case, URL rewriting just creates problems.

In addition, the URL rewriting logic is intrinsically monodirectional because it doesn't offer any built-in mechanism to go from the original URL to the rewritten URL and then back.

In ASP.NET 3.5 Service Pack 1, Microsoft introduced a new and more effective API for URL rewriting. Because of its capabilities, the new API got a better name—*URL routing*. URL routing is built on top of the URL rewriting API, but it offers a richer and higher-level programming model.

The URL routing engine is a system-provided HTTP module that wires up the *PostResolveRequestCache* event. Essentially, the HTTP module matches the requested URL to one of the user-defined rewriting rules (known as *routes*) and finds the HTTP handler that is due to serve that route. If any HTTP handler is found, it becomes the actual handler for the current request.

The URL routing maps URLs to HTTP handlers based on some input you provide through routes and route handlers.

URL Patterns and Routes

The big difference between plain URL rewriting and ASP.NET routing is that with ASP.NET routing, the URL is not changed when the system begins processing the request but later in the life cycle. In this way, the runtime environment can perform most of its usual tasks on the original URL, which maintains a consistent and robust solution.

In addition, a late intervention on the URL also gives developers the big chance of extracting values from the URL and the request context. In this way, the routing mechanism can be driven by a set of rewriting rules or patterns. If the original URL matches a particular pattern, you rewrite it to the associated URL. URL patterns are an external resource and are kept in one place, which makes the solution more maintainable overall.

The URL patterns that you define are known as *routes*.

A route contains placeholders that can be filled up with values extracted from the requested URL. Often referred to as a *URL parameter*, a placeholder is a name enclosed in curly brackets { }. You can have multiple placeholders in a route as long as they are separated by a constant or delimiter. The forward slash (/) character acts as a delimiter between the various parts of the route. Here's the default route for an ASP.NET MVC application:

```
{controller}/{action}/{id}
```

In this case, the sample route contains three placeholders separated by the delimiter. The route is made of three parts that coincide with the placeholder because no constant text is used. A URL that matches the preceding route is the following:

```
/Customers/Edit/ALFKI
```

The route barely defines a set of rules according to which the routing module decides whether or not the incoming request URL should be rewritten. The component that ultimately decides *how* to rewrite the requested URL is another one entirely. Precisely, it is the *route handler*.

Route Handlers

The route handler is the object that processes any requests that match a given route. Its sole purpose in life is returning the HTTP handler that will actually serve any matching request.

Technically speaking, a route handler is a class that implements the *IRouteHandler* interface. The interface is defined as shown here:

```
public interface IRouteHandler
{
    IHttpHandler GetHttpHandler(RequestContext requestContext);
}
```

Defined in the *System.Web.Routing* namespace, the *RequestContext* class encapsulates some information about an HTTP request that matches a route:

```
public class RequestContext
{
    public RequestContext(HttpContextBase httpContext, RouteData routeData);

    // Properties
    public HttpContextBase HttpContext { get; set; }
    public RouteData RouteData { get; set; }
}
```

In particular, the *RequestContext* class encapsulates the HTTP context of the request plus any route-specific information such as the *Route* object itself, URL parameters, and constraints. Note that the *HttpContextBase* class is the ASP.NET MVC abstraction of ASP.NET's *HttpContext* class. I'll return to the topic of ASP.NET MVC abstractions later in the chapter.

In its *GetHttpHandler* method, a route handler typically looks at route data to figure out if any of the information available needs to be passed down to the HTTP handler (for example, an ASP.NET page) that will handle the request. If this is the case, the route handler adds this information to the *Items* collection of the HTTP context. Finally, the route handler obtains an instance of a class that implements the *IHttpHandler* interface and returns that.

Mapping URLs to Routes

The ASP.NET URL routing module employs a number of rules when trying to match an incoming requested URL to a defined route. The most important rule is that routes are checked in the order they were registered in *global.asax*. To ensure they are processed in the right order, you must list them from the most specific to the least specific. In any case, keep in mind that the search for a matching route always ends at the first match. This means that just adding a new route at the bottom of the list might not work and might also cause you a bit of trouble. In addition, be aware that placing a pattern made of a single catch-all placeholder (for example, *{*any}*) at the top of the list will make any other patterns—no matter how specific—pass unnoticed. Beyond order of appearance, other factors affect the process of matching URLs to routes. One is the set of default values that you might have provided for a route. Default values are simply values that are automatically assigned to defined placeholders in case the URL doesn't provide specific values. Consider the following two routes:

```
{Orders}/{Year}/{Month}
{Orders}/{Year}
```

If you assign the first route's default values for both *{Year}* and *{Month}*, the second route will never be evaluated because, thanks to the default values, the first route is always a match regardless of whether the URL specifies a year and a month.

A trailing forward slash (/) is also a pitfall. For example, *"{Orders}/{Year}"* and *"{Orders}/{Year}/"* are two very different things. One won't match the other, even though logically, at least from a user's perspective, you'd expect them to.

Another factor that influences the selection of the URL-to-route match is the list of constraints that you optionally define for a route. A route constraint is a condition that a given URL parameter must fulfill to make the URL match the route. A constraint is defined via either regular expressions or objects that implement the *IRouteConstraint* interface. Here's how to add a route in *global.asax* that specifies default values and constraints:

```
public static void RegisterRoutes(RouteCollection routes)
{
    :
    :

    // Add a new route with default values and constraints
    routes.MapRoute(
        "NewDefault",
        "{controller}/{action}/{id}",
        new { controller = "Home", action = "Index", id = "" },
        new MyConstraint()
    );
}
```

The first argument to the *MapRoute* method indicates the name of the route. It's followed by the URL pattern and two objects. The former object indicates the default values for the various URL parameters. The latter specifies the route constraint object. A route constraint object might look like the one shown in the following code:

```
public class MyConstraint : IRouteConstraint
{
    public bool Match(HttpContextBase httpContext,
                      Route route,
                      string parameterName,
                      RouteValueDictionary values,
                      RouteDirection routeDirection)
    {
        bool result = true;

        if(routeDirection != RouteDirection.IncomingRequest)
            return result;
```

```
              if (String.Equals(parameterName, "id", StringComparison.OrdinalIgnoreCase))
              {
                  object o = values[parameterName];

                  // Apply your logic here
                  :
                  :

              }

          return result;
     }
}
```

The *IRouteConstraint* interface counts on a single method—*Match*—which returns a Boolean value. The return value indicates whether the request matches the route or not. In the body of a route constraint object, you first ensure that the parameter being checked is one you have constraints on, and then you apply any validation logic you have defined.

> **Note** Among the information passed down to the route constraint object, you find a *RouteDirection* parameter. It takes values from the *RouteDirection* enumeration. Feasible values are *IncomingRequest* and *UrlGeneration*. The *RouteDirection* parameter indicates whether the constraint check is required because the routing system is processing a request from a client or because it's generating a URL from a route definition.
>
> The ASP.NET routing system, in fact, also works bidirectionally and can match an incoming URL to a route as well as getting you a URL based on a route definition. To generate a URL from a route definition, you use the *GetVirtualPath* method on the *RouteCollection* class and pass it the request context and route data. More likely, though, you'll be using the static member *RouteCollection.Routes* instead of getting an ad hoc new instance of the *RouteCollection* class for invoking only *GetVirtualData*.

Handling Requests for Physical Files

Another configurable aspect of the routing system that contributes to a successful URL-to-route matching is whether or not the routing system has to handle requests that match a physical file.

By default, the ASP.NET routing system ignores requests whose URL can be mapped to a file that physically exists on the server. Note that if the server file exists, the routing system ignores the request even if the request matches a route.

If you need to, you can force the routing system to handle *all* requests by setting the *RouteExistingFiles* property of the *RouteCollection* object to *true*, as shown here:

```
// In global.asax.cs
public static void RegisterRoutes(RouteCollection routes)
{
    routes.RouteExistingFiles = true;
    :
    :
}
```

Note that having all requests handled via routing can create some issues in an ASP.NET MVC application. For example, if you add the preceding code to the *global.asax.cs* file of a sample ASP.NET MVC application and run it, you'll immediately face an HTTP 404 error when accessing *default.aspx*.

Preventing Routing for Defined URLs

The ASP.NET URL routing module gives you maximum freedom to keep certain URLs off the routing mechanism. You can prevent the routing system from handling certain URLs in two steps. First, you define a pattern for those URLs and save it to a route. Second, you link that route to a special route handler—the *StopRoutingHandler* class.

Any request that belongs to a route managed by a *StopRoutingHandler* object is processed as a plain ASP.NET Web Forms endpoint. The following code instructs the routing system to ignore any *.axd* requests:

```
// In global.asax.cs
public static void RegisterRoutes(RouteCollection routes)
{
  routes.IgnoreRoute("{resource}.axd/{*pathInfo}");
     .
     .
     .
}
```

The *IgnoreRoute* method, as well as the *MapRoute* method we encountered a moment ago, are extension methods for the *RouteCollection* class defined in *System.Web.Mvc*. All that *IgnoreRoute* does is associate a *StopRoutingHandler* route handler to the route built around the specified URL pattern.

Finally, a little explanation is required for the *{*pathInfo}* placeholder in the URL. The token *pathInfo* simply represents a placeholder for any content following the *.axd* URL. The asterisk (*), though, indicates that the last parameter should match the rest of the URL. In other words, anything that follows the *.axd* extension goes into the *pathInfo* parameter. Such parameters are referred to as *catch-all parameters*.

The ASP.NET MVC Run-Time Shell

As you learned in Chapter 1, "Goals of ASP.NET MVC and Motivation for Its Development," ASP.NET Web Forms and ASP.NET MVC put forth two significantly different programming models inspired by two distinct patterns—the *Page Controller* pattern for Web Forms and the *Model2* pattern for ASP.NET MVC. In spite of the different underlying philosophies, though, the two ASP.NET frameworks share the same runtime environment—the original runtime environment of ASP.NET Web Forms, which has been around since ASP.NET 1.0, was released back in 2002.

The inherently extensible and customizable nature of the ASP.NET runtime environment made it possible to adapt the existing infrastructure to create a new platform that even supports a radically different programming model.

The Big Picture

You can customize the ASP.NET runtime environment using made-to-measure HTTP modules and HTTP handlers that intercept incoming requests at various stages and process specific requests as appropriate.

ASP.NET MVC is based on an HTTP module that acts as a front controller and forwards any requests that matches certain criteria to a tailor-made HTTP handler. The MVC HTTP handler then serves the request by invoking a particular method on a particular controller class. The return values of the controller are forwarded to the view engine to generate the actual response for the client. Figure 2-9 offers an interior view of the ASP.NET runtime environment for both ASP.NET Web Forms and ASP.NET MVC.

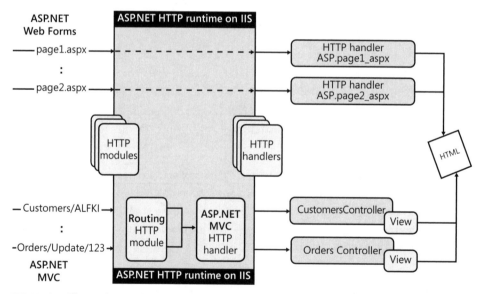

FIGURE 2-9 The runtime environments in Web Forms and ASP.NET MVC

As you can see, the runtime environment of ASP.NET MVC is simply a customized version of the original ASP.NET runtime environment.

How do you customize the runtime environment? There's just one possible way of doing that: using special sections of the *web.config* file. Let's then have a look at the *web.config* file of a typical ASP.NET MVC application.

Default Configuration

When Visual Studio creates a new ASP.NET MVC project, it gives you a ready-made *web.config* file. The file contains some boilerplate script to link assemblies and namespaces; reference compilers for dynamically created code; register default providers for membership, user profiles, and role management; and configure forms authentication.

The following listing illustrates the parts of the *web.config* file that are, instead, specific to ASP.NET MVC. The listing refers to Visual Studio 2010 and ASP.NET MVC 2. Compared to ASP.NET MVC 1, it looks slimmer because it mostly differs in terms of version numbers:

```
<configuration>
    .
    .
    .
    <system.web>
        .
        .
        .
        <compilation>
            <assemblies>
                .
                .
                .
                <add assembly="System.Web.Abstractions, Version=4.0.0.0, ..." />
                <add assembly="System.Web.Routing, Version=4.0.0.0,  ..." />
                <add assembly="System.Web.Mvc, Version=2.0.0.0,  ..." />
            </assemblies>
        </compilation>

        <httpHandlers>
            .
            .
            .
            <add verb="*"
                 path="*.mvc"
                 validate="false"
                 type="System.Web.Mvc.MvcHttpHandler" />
        </httpHandlers>


    </system.web>

    <system.webServer>
        <validation validateIntegratedModeConfiguration="false"/>
        <modules runAllManagedModulesForAllRequests="true"/>
        <handlers>
            <remove name="MvcHttpHandler"/>
            <add name="MvcHttpHandler"
                 preCondition="integratedMode"
                 verb="*"
                 path="*.mvc"
                 type="System.Web.Mvc.MvcHttpHandler"/>
        </handlers>
    </system.webServer>
</configuration>
```

The first aspect that catches the eye is that the ASP.NET MVC framework is articulated on three assemblies, referenced in the *<compilation>* section and detailed in Table 2-3.

TABLE 2-3 ASP.NET MVC assemblies

Assembly	Version	Description
System.Web.Abstractions	4.0	Defines base classes for most ASP.NET intrinsic objects so that fake objects can be created from them for testing purposes
System.Web.Mvc	2.0	Defines the core classes that make up the ASP.NET MVC framework
System.Web.Routing	4.0	Defines the classes for the routing module

In addition, you find an HTTP handler for **.mvc* requests. Compared to the *web.config* file created by Visual Studio 2008, in Visual Studio 2010 and ASP.NET MVC 2 you will no longer find an explicit reference to the URL routing the HTTP module. It is no longer in the application's configuration file, but it has not disappeared. Instead, it has been moved to the Web-server-level *web.config* file that you find in the following folder:

```
%Windows%\Microsoft.NET\Framework\[version]\Config
```

Also note that in the .NET Framework 4, the *UrlRoutingModule* class has been moved to *system.web* from *system.web.routing* as a way to demonstrate that it is part of the whole ASP.NET platform and not specific to ASP.NET MVC.

The handler for **.mvc* requests is added to the default *web.config* file for convenience and might be removed in some cases. In particular, you need this handler definition in case you're running your application on IIS 6.0 or on a version of IIS 7.0 but it's configured to run in Classic pipeline mode. If you're hosting on IIS 7.0 configured in the default way (that is, in Integrated pipeline mode), you can remove the **.mvc* HTTP handler from anywhere in *web.config*.

Let's summarize the configuration changes required for ASP.NET MVC (and ASP.NET URL routing) to fully support various versions of the IIS Web server.

ASP.NET MVC and Web Server Compatibility

The default configuration of the runtime environment you get out of the Visual Studio project template is optimized for IIS 7.0 and an application hosted using the Integrated pipeline mode. In all other cases, some changes are required.

Some of these changes are already taken care of in the *web.config* file you get from Visual Studio. (To keep your files clean, however, you might want to ensure that every configuration setting you have is necessary.)

Note IIS 7.0 comes with Windows Server 2008, but it can also be installed on client machines equipped with Windows Vista, except the Home Basic edition. Windows Server 2003 includes IIS 6.0, but it doesn't support upgrading IIS 6.0 to IIS 7.0. Finally, Windows Server 2000 comes with IIS 5.0.

When running ASP.NET MVC on IIS 6.0, IIS 5.0, or IIS 7.0 in Classic mode, you end up sending requests to the server for URLs that don't have an extension. What happens is that IIS assumes you are making a request for a virtual directory within the application. As a result, the request never reaches the routing system and it can't be served by IIS as well because no such virtual path exists. An HTTP 404 error is inevitable.

There are basically two ways to solve the routing issue. You can modify the route table to use file extensions, or you can use a wildcard script map.

The easiest way to get ASP.NET routing to work with older versions and legacy configurations of IIS is to modify the route table in *global.asax*. This is a typical approach for hosted scenarios. Here are the details:

```
public static void RegisterRoutes(RouteCollection routes)
{
    routes.IgnoreRoute("{resource}.axd/{*pathInfo}");

    // Added an .mvc extension to the URL
    routes.MapRoute(
        "Default",
        "{controller}.mvc/{action}/{id}",
        new { action = "Index", id = "" }
    );

    // You also need this new route to handle requests
    // made against the root of the application. For this reason,
    // the URL pattern is just the empty string.
    routes.MapRoute(
        "Root",
        "",
        new { controller = "Home", action = "Index", id = "" }
    );
}
```

With these changes in place, the application will be able to handle URLs such as */customers .mvc/edit/alfki* instead of */customers/edit/alfki*. The URL is a bit less clean and elegant because of the *.mvc* extension, but at least IIS is now able to route it correctly to ASP.NET MVC. To make the *.mvc* extension known to IIS, though, you need to register it. You can do that manually through the IIS Manager or programmatically via a script named *RegisterMvc.wsf*, which is available under the following folder:

```
C:\Program Files\Microsoft ASP.NET\ASP.NET MVC 2\Scripts
```

The script is copied when you install ASP.NET MVC 2 or simply when you install Visual Studio 2010.

Obviously, you need access to the IIS environment to register a new extension such as *.mvc. If you don't have access to IIS (for example, you operate in an Internet Service Provider scenario), you can replace *.mvc with an existing extension already mapped to ASP.NET—for example, *.aspx or *.axd.

> **Note** As obvious as it might sound, I should point out that you should also make sure that adding an extension to route URL patterns doesn't break any links within the application. Checking all of the URLs to verify they now incorporate the extension (whether *.mvc or *.aspx) is up to you. However, if your links are generated using the HTML helper method *Html.ActionLink*, you should not need to make any changes.

Adding a URL extension in some ways makes the magical world of ASP.NET MVC a bit less magical because URLs are not as clean and human-readable as they can be under IIS 7.0. If you don't want to modify the URLs for your ASP.NET MVC application but you still have access to the IIS manager, you might want to consider the wildcard script map alternative.

A wildcard script map (shown in Figure 2-10) instructs IIS to route *all* requests to a given module—in this case, the ASP.NET ISAPI module. In this way, the URL routing system can intercept any requests—including, of course, extensionless requests.

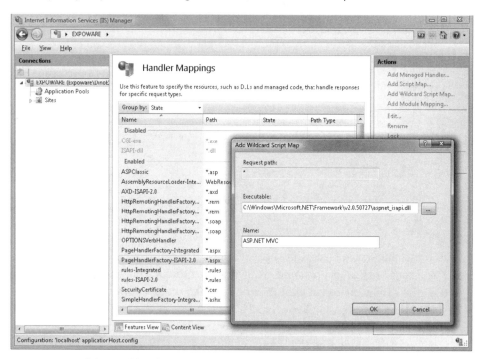

FIGURE 2-10 Defining a wildcard script map

Setting a wildcard script map causes IIS to intercept every request made to the Web server, including images, classic ASP, and HTML pages. Make sure you choose this option thoughtfully because it might have an impact on the overall performance of the site.

Special Settings for HTTP Handlers and HTTP Modules

ASP.NET MVC needs the services of the ASP.NET URL routing module we discussed earlier in the chapter. Note that, although originally developed for ASP.NET MVC, the URL routing engine reached the rank of an official member of the ASP.NET platform as of ASP.NET 3.5 SP1. Today, you can use URL routing with both ASP.NET MVC and ASP.NET Web Forms applications, and the reference to the HTTP routing module has been conveniently moved up to the machine-level configuration script. This said, you should consider that in ASP.NET Web Forms the routing module is an optional element; in ASP.NET MVC, on the other hand, it's an essential component of the framework.

You might find it necessary also to replicate any settings for HTTP modules and HTTP handlers under the *<system.webServer>* section of the configuration file. This is mandatory if you are running the application under IIS 7.0 hosted in an application pool configured for the Integrated pipeline. However, if your application runs under IIS 6.0 or, even though it's hosted in IIS 7.0 it uses the Classic pipeline mode, you don't need a *<system.webServer>* section in the *web.config* file. In this case, you're better off dropping the section entirely from the configuration file. (Visual Studio just adds it for your convenience.)

The settings in the *<system.webServer>* section are the same ones you find in the *<system.web>* section as far as HTTP handlers and HTTP modules are concerned.

> **Note** In the configuration script for ASP.NET MVC 1 applications created under Visual Studio 2008, you might notice a special HTTP handler mapped to the *UrlRouting.axd* resource. This line is required to work around a bug in IIS 7.0 Integrated mode that shows up when routing is active and an extensionless URL is requested. The bug is fixed in the .NET Framework 4, and the need for the special URL has disappeared.

Routing the Request

Given the default configuration of the ASP.NET MVC runtime environment, what happens exactly when a request knocks at the IIS gate? Figure 2-11 gives you an overall picture of the various steps involved and how things work differently for different URLs.

In the beginning, all requests directed to an ASP.NET application are, and look, the same— they are, in the end, plain HTTP packets. In a way, the URL routing module is like the bouncer at a disco club. Based on received instructions, the bouncer decides who's let in and who's not. The disco club, in this case, is the ASP.NET MVC special processing environment.

The URL routing module intercepts any requests for the application that could not be served otherwise by IIS. If the URL refers to a physical file, the routing module ignores the request, unless otherwise configured. The request then falls down to the classic ASP.NET machinery to be processed as usual in terms of a page handler.

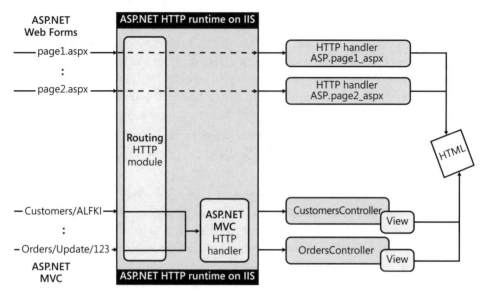

FIGURE 2-11 The role of the routing module in ASP.NET MVC

Otherwise, the URL routing module attempts to match the URL of the request to any of the defined routes. If no match is found, the request will be served by the standard ASP.NET runtime.

In the end, only requests that the routing module selects based on route data are allowed to enjoy the ASP.NET MVC run-time shell. As shown in Figure 2-11, all such requests are routed to a common HTTP handler that instantiates a controller class and invokes a defined method on it. Next, the controller method, in turn, selects a view object to generate the actual response.

This is just the big picture of how the ASP.NET MVC runtime works. I'll cover request processing in more detail in the upcoming "Processing an ASP.NET MVC Request" section. Before I get there, though, let me tackle a couple of other side topics: mixing Web Forms and ASP.NET MVC pages in the same application.

Mixing Web Forms and MVC Pages

Because ASP.NET MVC takes advantage of the same runtime environment as classic ASP.NET Web Forms, mixing together Web Forms pages and ASP.NET MVC pages is definitely possible.

Because ASP.NET Web Forms pages are clearly based on disk files, the URL routing system lets them pass and doesn't route them to the ASP.NET MVC runtime environment. This ensures that an ASP.NET MVC application can serve both types of resources.

I recommend you create a folder in your project and group your *.aspx* pages below it. In a way, it's like having a separate Web Forms project within the root ASP.NET MVC project. (See Figure 2-12.)

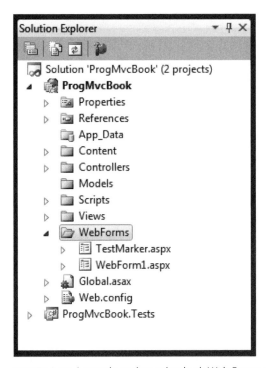

FIGURE 2-12 A sample project using both Web Forms and MVC pages

Hosting Web Forms pages in an ASP.NET MVC application is possible, but the opposite doesn't work. To process ASP.NET MVC extensionless URLs and resolve them in terms of controllers and views, you need to tweak the runtime environment and the folder structure to make the whole application just become a new ASP.NET MVC application!

So you're back to square one; you can mix Web Forms and MVC pages in an ASP.NET MVC project, but nothing else.

Processing an ASP.NET MVC Request

After the routing module has matched the incoming requested URL to one of the defined routes, the ball passes to the *route handler* component in charge of that route. Each route can have its own route handler; the default route handler, though, is the *MvcRouteHandler* class defined in the *System.Web.Mvc* namespace.

The *MvcRouteHandler* Class

As discussed earlier in the chapter, the purpose of a route handler is to determine the HTTP handler object that will serve the request whose URL matched the route. The *MvcRouteHandler* class has a surprisingly neat and clear implementation, as shown here:

```
public class MvcRouteHandler : IRouteHandler
{
    // Implementation of the IRouteHandler interface
    IHttpHandler IRouteHandler.GetHttpHandler(RequestContext requestContext)
    {
        return this.GetHttpHandler(requestContext);
    }

    // Helper method
    protected virtual IHttpHandler GetHttpHandler(RequestContext requestContext)
    {
        return new MvcHandler(requestContext);
    }
}
```

It's straightforward to see that, given the preceding code, any ASP.NET MVC request—that is, any request that matches an existing route—is served by the same HTTP handler. Let's dig out more detail about this handler.

The *MvcHandler* Class

MvcHandler is ultimately responsible for generating the response for the request being processed. The *MvcHandler* class receives information about the ongoing request from the constructor, as you can see in the implementation of the *GetHttpHandler* method in the *MvcRouteHandler* source code just shown.

Let's have a look at how the class implements *IHttpHandler*:

```
void IHttpHandler.ProcessRequest(HttpContext context)
{
    this.ProcessRequest(context);
}
protected virtual void ProcessRequest(HttpContext context)
{
    // HttpContextWrapper inherits from HttpContextBase
    HttpContextBase ctxBase = new HttpContextWrapper(context);
    this.ProcessRequest(ctxBase);
}
protected internal virtual void ProcessRequest(HttpContextBase ctxBase)
{
        .
        .
        .
}
```

The original HTTP context of the request, as prepared by IIS or the ASP.NET runtime environment, is flushed into a more generic container—the *HttpContextWrapper* class.

The wrapper HTTP context is then passed to the actual processor of the request—the internal *ProcessRequest* method you see in the preceding listing.

> **Important** *HttpContextWrapper* actually inherits from *HttpContextBase,* which serves as the base class for classes that contain HTTP-specific information about an individual HTTP request. *HttpContextBase* (and derived classes) plays a key role in ASP.NET MVC. It decouples the ASP.NET MVC HTTP handler—and more importantly, any invoked controllers—from the ASP.NET native *HttpContext* class. Controllers can still receive the same context information, except that now they get it using a generic container instead of an object whose creation is handled internally by the ASP.NET runtime environment.

Processing an ASP.NET MVC request consists of parsing the URL to figure out the name of the controller class to use and creating an instance of it. Here's some code that illustrates the behavior:

```
protected internal virtual void ProcessRequest(HttpContextBase context)
{
    // Add a version header to the response
    AddVersionHeader(context);

    // Get the name of the controller class to use to serve the request
    string name = RequestContext.RouteData.GetRequiredString("controller");

    // Get the currently selected controller factory object
    IControllerFactory factory = ControllerBuilder.GetControllerFactory();

    // Get an instance of the controller class
    IController controller = factory.CreateController(RequestContext, name);
    if (controller == null)
    {
        throw new InvalidOperationException();
    }

    // Order the controller to process the request
    try
    {
        controller.Execute(this.RequestContext);
    }
    finally
    {
        factory.ReleaseController(controller);
    }
}
```

The controller factory is responsible for the creation of instances of any controller class. The controller factory is a replaceable system component that implements the *IControllerFactory* interface. The default factory is the *DefaultControllerFactory* class. All this class is using is a bit of reflection to create an instance of the specified controller type:

```
controller = (IController) Activator.CreateInstance(controllerType);
```

The default controller factory uses the default parameterless constructor of the controller class. To specify extra parameters through the constructor, you need to replace the controller factory.

After getting the controller instance, the *MvcHandler* class yields to it by calling the *Execute* method. As a result, the controller executes the requested action. In Chapter 4, "Inside Controllers," I'll return to the topic of controllers and actions with many more details.

ASP.NET MVC Wrapper Objects

ASP.NET MVC takes testability very seriously, and it shows in a number of ways. For example, ASP.NET MVC supplies abstract classes for the various ASP.NET intrinsic objects, including *HttpContext*, *HttpRequest*, and *HttpResponse*.

Abstract classes come in two forms: a base class and a wrapper class. The base class (that is, *HttpRequestBase*) exposes the same interface as the intrinsic object it abstracts. It exposes only virtual members whose implementation invariably throws an exception. The corresponding wrapper class (that is, *HttpRequestWrapper*), instead, provides a concrete implementation of the base class. Such an implementation basically defines a thin layer around a wrapped object that can be the ASP.NET intrinsic object or, for testing purposes, a mock object. Here's an excerpt from the source code of the *HttpRequestWrapper* class:

```
public class HttpRequestWrapper : HttpRequestBase
{
    // Fields
    private HttpRequest _httpRequest;

    // Ctor
    public HttpRequestWrapper(HttpRequest httpRequest)
    {
        if (httpRequest == null)
            throw new ArgumentNullException("httpRequest");
        this._httpRequest = httpRequest;
    }

    // Public methods
    public override byte[] BinaryRead(int count)
    {
        return this._httpRequest.BinaryRead(count);
    }
    :
    :
}
```

As you can see, any methods in the wrapper class end up invoking the same method on an underlying object injected via the constructor.

Base and wrapper classes live in the *System.Web.Abstractions* namespace. Table 2-4 lists all classes in ASP.NET MVC that abstract native ASP.NET system objects.

TABLE 2-4 *System.Web.Abstractions* **classes**

Class	Description
HttpApplicationStateBase, HttpApplicationStateWrapper	Abstracts the intrinsic *Application* object
HttpBrowserCapabilitiesBase, HttpBrowserCapabilitiesWrapper	Abstracts the *HttpBrowserCapabilities* class that gathers information about the capabilities of the browser that has made the current request
HttpCachePolicyBase, HttpCachePolicyWrapper	Abstracts the *HttpCachePolicy* class that sets cache-specific HTTP headers and controls page output caching
HttpContextBase, HttpContextWrapper	Abstracts the intrinsic *HttpContext* object
HttpFileCollectionBase, HttpFileCollectionWrapper	Abstracts the *HttpFileCollection* class that controls files uploaded by a client
HttpPostedFileBase, HttpPostedFileWrapper	Abstracts the *HttpPostedFile* class that controls individual files uploaded by a client
HttpRequestBase, HttpRequestWrapper	Abstracts the intrinsic *Request* object
HttpResponseBase, HttpResponseWrapper	Abstracts the intrinsic *Response* object
HttpServerUtilityBase, HttpServerUtilityWrapper	Abstracts the intrinsic *Server* object
HttpSessionStateBase, HttpSessionStateWrapper	Abstracts the intrinsic *Session* object
HttpStaticObjectsCollectionBase, HttpStaticObjectsCollectionWrapper	Abstracts the *HttpStaticObjectsCollection* class that provides a collection of application-scoped objects

As of ASP.NET 3.5 SP1, these base classes are new classes added to serve the needs of ASP.NET MVC 1.0. These base classes are completely unknown to ASP.NET, and none of the ASP.NET intrinsic objects actually inherits from such classes. It wouldn't be a bad idea, however. And I'm fairly sure that this might happen in the near future. A clue is the fact that the *System.Web.Abstractions* assembly also shipped with ASP.NET 3.5 SP1; so it is no longer just an ASP.NET MVC assembly.

For testing purposes, you can easily create a mock object that can be used in lieu of any of the intrinsic ASP.NET objects referenced in Table 2-4. All you need to do is derive a new class, as shown next, and use it wherever the base class is accepted:

```
public class MockHttpContext : HttpContextBase
{
    :
    :
}
```

I'll return to the topics of testing and mock objects in Chapter 11, "Testability and Unit Testing."

Summary

ASP.NET MVC was not built entirely from scratch. More precisely, it is a new run-time shell within the existing ASP.NET run-time machinery. In the new run-time shell, you find a routing system, a collection of routes, route handlers, and just one standard HTTP handler responsible for the processing of any intercepted requests.

The routing system is the key component because it interacts with, and to some extent depends on, the host Web server. The routing system ultimately determines whether a given request has to be processed via ASP.NET MVC or classic ASP.NET. In other words, the routing system determines whether a given request will enter the new run-time shell of ASP.NET MVC or live its life outside of it.

The standard project template you get from Visual Studio is configured to make the application work just fine in the default scenario (IIS 7.0, Integrated mode), while limiting the number of required changes in a few critical secondary scenarios, including IIS 6.0 and IIS 7.0 Classic mode.

In this chapter, we dug deep into the runtime environment of ASP.NET and ASP.NET MVC and unveiled most of the intricacies and architecture. In the next chapter, we'll shift the focus back to applications and the programming model in particular. What exactly is the MVC in the name of the framework? And what does an ASP.NET MVC project look like? Read on!

Chapter 3
The MVC Pattern and Beyond

In mathematics you don't understand things. You just get used to them.

—*John Von Neumann*

Aside from a number of technical details in the API, the biggest difference between ASP.NET Web Forms and ASP.NET MVC is the underlying pattern of the resulting applications. As we discussed in Chapter 1, "Goals of ASP.NET MVC and Motivation for Its Development," a classic ASP.NET application is based on the concept of the page and all that developers do is create pages by defining their markup and code. The runtime maps a typical *.aspx* request to a special component that produces an HTML page. This pattern is known as the *Page Controller* pattern.

In ASP.NET MVC, on the other hand, the focus is on the action that follows a request. Every request is therefore mapped to another breed of component that just executes an action and obtains results. Processing the request and generating the response for the client are two distinct steps that involve distinct parts of the runtime environment. The inspiring principle of this approach is the association of concerns with at least two distinct actors: one performing the action and one taking care of the view. The underlying pattern is known as *Model-View-Controller* (MVC).

Introduced about 30 years ago, the MVC pattern was not really designed for the special world of the Web that was still to come. However, given the flexibility of the model, it was not a big deal to adapt it to the Web only a few years later.

What's MVC exactly? How does an MVC application behave in detail? How strictly defined is the pattern?

Born as a relatively loosely defined pattern, MVC has been associated with a number of different implementations over years. As a result, there's some confusion today about what the real mechanics are that are suggested by the pattern. This chapter starts from the original formulation of MVC and compares that to the actual (and somewhat different) pattern implemented by ASP.NET MVC.

Along the way, I'll also briefly touch on a couple of other patterns, including *Model-View-Presenter* (MVP) and *Presentation Model* (PM), with the purpose of offering a complete overview and helping you gain a better understanding of the ASP.NET MVC design. Finally, a look at the structure and content of the ASP.NET MVC template project tops off the chapter.

Note A portion of this chapter contains information about patterns that have been around for quite a few decades. So if you know enough about MVC and MVP, you might find it bothersome to read through any further description of them, regardless of the added value a different perspective on a known topic can produce. The purpose of this chapter's tour around the most popular presentation patterns is just to provide a perspective on the evolution that has taken place over the years. I'll be examining the past to discern possible future developments. If you have no interest in MVC, MVP, Model2, MVVM, and the like, feel free to jump directly to the "ASP.NET MVC Project Template" section. It's there where the hot stuff about ASP.NET MVC begins.

The Original MVC Pattern

Regardless of how you design it, any application is driven by the use-cases recognized in the analysis phase. A use-case describes one scenario in which the user is expected to interact with the system. For the user to interact with the system, some sort of presentation layer is required.

The MVC pattern is still a milestone today—30 years after its introduction—because it addresses the organization of the whole application and establishes a preferred flow of information within the system. In this regard, MVC is an application pattern. However, because nearly all applications (with very few exceptions) are driven by users, an application pattern inevitably has a deep impact on the presentation layer. It's not surprising, therefore, that MVC is often sold as a presentation pattern—and with some justification, indeed. As you'll see in a moment, in fact, all of the MVC implementation lives in just one layer—the presentation layer.

MVC Interaction Model

In the earliest software, the presentation layer was made of monolithic, *autonomous views* (AVs) displayed to the user. The user interacted with the view and generated some input. The view captured the input, processed it internally, and updated itself or moved to another view.

An AV is a class that contains display and state information for the view, as well as the full logic to handle any user actions from start to finish. With such monolithic components, you have a presentation layer that is hard (if not impossible) to test and that has no separation of concerns between the user interface (graphics) and presentation logic (code behind).

Note By using the rapid application development (RAD) facilities of a powerful development environment such as Microsoft Visual Studio 2010 to their fullest, you can quickly, comfortably, and even inadvertently fall back into the bygone era of autonomous views. In fact, you might end up having a Web form with a code-behind class that contains almost everything you need—presentation logic, business logic, and even data access logic. This resulting lack of separation of concerns, although not inherent in the ASP.NET Web Forms Page Controller pattern, is so common and easy to achieve that it prompted the ASP.NET team to offer an alternative, and inherently structured, model—the ASP.NET MVC model.

To achieve testability and separation of concerns in the user interface of a generic software application, the MVC pattern was introduced back in 1979. A more contemporary paper can be found here: *http://st-www.cs.uiuc.edu/users/smarch/st-docs/mvc.html*.

The Original Idea

Let's look at an excerpt from the paper I just referenced:

> *In the MVC paradigm the user input, the modeling of the external world, and the visual feedback to the user are explicitly separated and handled by three types of objects, each specialized for its task.*

As you can see, the word *paradigm* is used in the original paper. Today, instead, we refer to MVC as a pattern. Is it a pattern or paradigm? Is there really any difference?

The Oxford English Dictionary indicates three synonyms for the word *paradigm*: pattern, model, and exemplar. In software terms, though, a pattern is a particular concrete and proven solution, whereas a paradigm indicates a family of similar patterns. Or, put another way, a paradigm indicates the base class from which a variety of concrete design patterns derive.

In my vision, the original use of the word *paradigm* means that MVC is a (deliberately?) loosely defined pattern. It just shows the way to go, but it leaves the architect a lot of freedom when it comes to implementation details. This is probably the reason why so many variations of MVC exist. This is probably also the reason why different people might give you different definitions of MVC—sometimes, also slightly incompatible definitions.

The primary goal of MVC is to split the application into distinct pieces—the model, the view, and the controller. The *model* refers to the state of the application, wraps the application's functionalities, and notifies the view of state changes. The *view* refers to the generation of any graphical elements displayed to the user, and it captures and handles any user gestures. The *controller* maps user gestures to actions on the model and selects the next view. These three actors are often referred to as the *MVC triad*.

Switching to an MVC design brings several benefits.

In the first place, testing the user interface gets significantly simpler and more affordable. Taking code out of the view makes it easier to change the graphics without altering the behavior of the user interface. Taking as much code as possible out of the view also encourages code structuring and logical layers. Splitting the presentation layer into distinct objects lays the groundwork for various teams to work on different parts of the application simultaneously—for example, designers taking care of the view and developers coding actual actions.

> **Note** Taking code out of the view? Wasn't this exactly the main purpose of the code-behind model in ASP.NET Web Forms? Sure, but as it too often happens, the devil is in the details. Looking at the preceding text, the keyword to focus on is "encourages." The classic ASP.NET code-behind model *encourages* code structuring and logical layers. It *doesn't force* developers to do just that. In the long run, code-behind classes dangerously started looking a lot like old-fashioned autonomous views.
>
> I guess that a significant share of this book's readership is too young to preserve important memories of the pre-MVC and pre-OOP era, but it was all another programming experience and all another type of job.
>
> Well, to many of us, it didn't look like a job either; instead, it looked alluringly like crazy fun. But at some point, "fun" became established and solidified into a "job." And the complexity that came later required new and more powerful tools.

Presenting the Actors

The introduction of MVC represented a quantum leap. The benefits of MVC on software architecture have been so deep and profound that they still influence development 30 years later. (And consider that five years in software constitute a significant era.)

Figure 3-1 summarizes the new age in software architecture that started with the introduction of the MVC pattern.

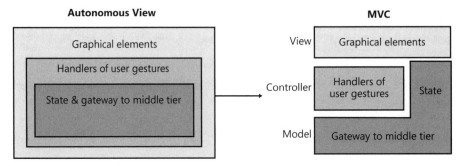

FIGURE 3-1 The evolution from autonomous views to MVC

In the 1980s, applications of any complexity were essentially based on a monolithic block of code that structured programming was just trying to break down into more usable and reusable pieces. The user interface was therefore a collection of autonomous views, each managing the screen real estate, capturing user-generated events, and deciding what to do after. Before MVC, the code was basically developed by nesting calls from the user interface down to the core of the system.

View, model, and controller are a group of strongly related objects that together participate in the life of a logical view. A logical view is essentially a sequence of forms displayed to the user in the context of a use-case.

In my opinion, of the three actors the *model* is the trickiest to put into perspective.

In the original formulation of MVC, the model is an object designed to hold state and contain any data being worked on in the physical view. This was a comprehensive definition for the applications of 20 and more years ago. Today, it deserves a deeper look.

Modern, multitier applications have a presentation layer made of multiple views, each paired with a controller and likely with a view-specific model object. But there's more than this to consider. In a multitier system, you have a business layer where server-side data is *modeled* in some way (typically, by using an entity-relationship model), created from memory in that format, or loaded in that format from some storage. Is this server-side *model* the same as the view-specific model? It depends on the architecture.

Today, in the context of MVC the model is essentially a client-side model of data that is tightly related (if not coupled) with the view. Triggered by the *view*, the *controller* performs some server tasks and, in doing so, it might touch on the middle tier and the server-side entity model. Changes induced on the server-side model and the storage must be, at some point, transferred to the client to be notified to the user. This likely requires either a transfer of data from the server-side model to the view-specific model or sharing the model between the presentation and business layers. If the entity model is being shared between the presentation and business layers, you might find that the view-specific model and entity model coincide. Otherwise, they are distinct objects. (See Figure 3-2.)

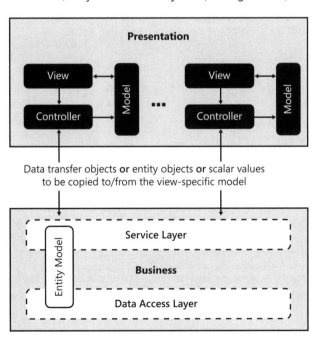

FIGURE 3-2 The MVC triad works in the presentation layer.

In MVC, the view is made of interactive controls (such as input fields, buttons, and lists), and it waits for any user actions. When the user places a command that requires some further work, the view forwards the input to the controller.

The controller *fulfills* the request, whatever that means in the application. In a multitier system (including Web applications), this means interacting with the middle tier, exchanging data, and loading data into the view-specific model. Next, the view and model talk, and changes flow into the user interface.

Let's review in more detail the expectations set for the view and controller.

The View Actor on the Stage

In MVC, the view is as *dumb, humble,* and *passive* as possible. (*Dumb, humble,* and *passive* are terms commonly used to describe the role of the view in an MVC scenario.) Translated as instructions for developing code, it means that the view should care only about painting the interface to display to users.

Ideally, the view is so simple and logic free as to need virtually no testing. Users (and developers before users) can reasonably test the view by simply looking at the pixels on the screen. Anything else beyond pure graphical rendering should *ideally* be taken out of the view and placed in the controller. This includes, for example, the logic that determines whether a certain button should be enabled or grayed out at some point.

What are the responsibilities of the view in MVC?

As mentioned, the view is responsible for forwarding the call to the controller. How this happens largely depends on platform, languages, and development tools. In general, in a .NET application the view handles its events in the code-behind class and invokes a particular method on the associated controller class.

As you saw in Chapter 2, "The Runtime Environment," the forwarding of the user action to the controller happens automatically, by means of some run-time machinery in the ASP.NET MVC framework. The view displayed in the browser basically posts to a URL. A server-side module captures the requests, examines the URL, and figures out which action to execute.

Another key responsibility of the view is rendering.

In an MVC implementation, the controller updates the view-specific model by executing the triggered action. The model then notifies the view about pending changes on its state that the view might want to reflect in the user interface. The view reads the model and provides an updated interface.

The view and the model are bound to the rules of the *Observer* pattern. In the Observer pattern, the subject (in this case, the model) notifies the observer (in this case, the view) about changes that have occurred. As a result, the view requests the current state from the model and works with it.

Note The Observer pattern is the pattern behind events and event-driven programming. The pattern refers to a class that has the ability to notify registered observers of some internal states. Whenever a particular state is reached, the class loops through the list of registered observers and notifies each observer of the event. It does that using a contracted observer interface. In languages such as Microsoft C# or Visual Basic .NET, the Observer pattern is natively implemented and exposed through ad hoc keywords and programming facilities. Consider the following code:

```
Button1.Click += new EventHandler(Button1_Click);
```

When it runs, a new "observer for the *Click* event" is added to the list maintained by object *Button1*. The observer in this case is a delegate—a special class wrapping a class method. The interface through which the observer and object communicate is the signature of the method wrapped by the delegate.

The Controller Actor on the Stage

The controller interacts with the middle tier (typically, the service layer) in a way that is coherent with the user action. The controller scripts the endpoints exposed by the middle tier to achieve the results expected from the user action. The interaction can be as simple as invoking just one method, or it can require a series of calls and some flow logic.

The controller has no idea of the changes to be imposed on the view by its interaction with the middle tier. According to the original MVC pattern, the controller is simply *not* responsible for updating the view. The controller doesn't exist in MVC to separate the view and model. The controller is not a mediator between the view and the model; rather, it's the mediator between the user and the application.

In MVC, the view knows the model directly and the model knows the view through the Observer relationship. The controller gets input from the view, operates on the middle tier, and updates the model. Figure 3-3 shows the overall interaction between the three actors.

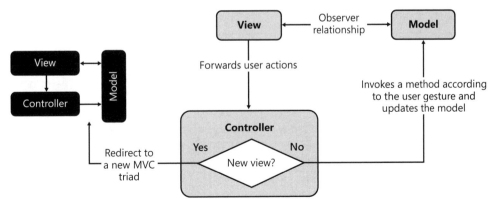

FIGURE 3-3 The MVC triad in action

The controller, however, has some responsibilities with regard to the view. In particular, the controller is responsible for selecting the next view to display to the user. If the user action doesn't require a switch to a different view, the controller simply proceeds with any interaction with the model that is required. Otherwise, it just creates a new triad for the new user interface—new view, new model, and new controller.

Figure 3-4 offers an alternate view of the interaction that takes place between the MVC actors. It illustrates the sequence of steps as they occur on a timeline. The notation used, in fact, is just that of UML sequence diagrams.

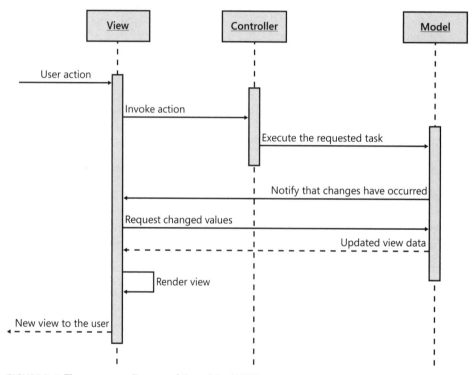

FIGURE 3-4 The sequence diagram of the *original* MVC pattern

The word *original* used in the caption of the figure says it all. It should be noted that the diagram in Figure 3-4, as well as most of the discussion here, pertains to the original formulation of the MVC pattern.

Today, MVC is mostly associated with Web development and, in particular, with a revisited and reworked version tailor-made for the Web interaction model. For desktop development (and to a large extent for rich Internet development too), the original MVC turned out to be insufficient because of some structural limitations. These limitations led, over time, to improving the pattern to the Model-View-Presenter model and the Presentation Model (implemented as MVVM in WPF and Silverlight circles, as noted earlier). Let's look at the required improvements.

Limitations of the MVC Pattern

The advent of MVC made it clear that applications should be designed with separation of concerns (SoC) in mind. SoC was already a known principle, but MVC put it into practice. MVC was not perfect, though.

Classic MVC has two big drawbacks. One is that the model needs to communicate to the view changes of the state—typically, through an Observer relationship. The other is that the view has intimate knowledge of the model. The view, in fact, refreshes when it gets a notification that changes have occurred in the model.

Insufficient Testability

In MVC, the controller is a distinct class that gets input through method signatures and passes any return values down to the model. Overall, the controller is testable. You create an instance of it, call methods with fake values, and check the return values either from methods or from the modified state of the model object.

The model has no logic except for the Observer relationship it has with the view. What about the view? Is it testable?

The view can't just be completely passive and dumb in MVC. At a minimum, it has to contain logic for retrieving changes from the model. The view basically reads from the model any information it needs and displays it through its UI elements. There's no explicit contract that states which data the view needs precisely. As a result, the view needs to have its own logic to select data from the big model and massage it into UI elements. This code can hardly be taken out of the view—the view is not as passive as it should be. And also, the view depends to some extent on the underlying platform or UI toolkit being used.

These conditions hinder testability.

Insufficiently Clean Design

The core problem of MVC is the two-way connection established between the view and the model: view knows model, and model knows view. This two-way connection is necessary because the controller has not been given enough power and control over the flow of data. In MVC, the controller is a mediator between the user and the application; its role would be more effective if it acted as a mediator between the view and model. With the controller getting input from the view and returning values back to the view, you separate the view and model and reduce the number of arrows that were shown in Figure 3-3.

Figure 3-5 shows a new possible design of MVC that improves on and cleans up the overall design by using the controller as a true *mediator*. You'll be surprised to see that the schema in the figure looks nearly the same as what you get in ASP.NET MVC, MVP, and PM.

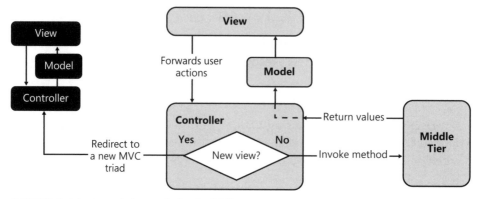

FIGURE 3-5 A better and cleaner design for MVC

The controller gets the ball from the view, interacts with the middle tier, and then massages updates for the view into the model. The model gets passed to the view. MVP, PM, MVVM, and even Model2 are based on this overall schema and differ only in terms of implementation and design details.

> **Note** In MVP, the model doesn't really exist unless you want to recognize it in the topmost layer of the middle tier. As you'll see later, in MVP the view exposes an interface and that controller uses that interface to read and write values from and to the view. In PM and MVVM, instead, the model is incorporated in the controller and the view is tied to it via data-binding. Finally, the Model2 pattern, and therefore ASP.NET MVC, works nearly the same as what is shown in Figure 3-5.

The Model2 Pattern

When MVC was formulated, there was no worldwide Web in sight as yet. Later on, in the mid-1990s, adapting the MVC pattern to the Web interaction model required some extra work. From this adaptation work, a new MVC-based pattern emerged that is technically known as Model2 or WebMVC. This pattern inspired the internal architecture of the ASP.NET MVC framework. The overall schema of Model2 is similar to Figure 3-5.

MVC and the Web

When someone seriously attempted to use MVC to build Web applications, it was clear beyond any reasonable doubt that MVC was not designed for the Web. At the same time, though, another key fact emerged: the loose definition of MVC left room for frameworks to customize MVC to particular areas.

This is exactly the case for Model2.

Model2 is an extremely popular Web-oriented variation of MVC created by Sun Microsystems to support the building of Web applications using Java Server Pages (JSP).

A Brief History of Model2

In the 1990s, following up on the success of Microsoft Active Server Pages (ASP), Sun decided to extend its *servlet* API to fill the gap existing between Java server programming and the production of dynamic content for the Web. The effort originated Java Server Pages (JSP).

In a way, Java servlets are similar to Internet Server Application Programming Interface (ISAPI) extensions, meaning that a servlet programmer must use the standard output console to send out some HTML markup. Done from within a servlet component, the generation of HTML can't rely on templates, dynamic scripting, and other facilities like in ASP. JSP made it possible to embed servlet components and Java code into a surrounding HTML template.

Blueprints for JSP applications suggest two design models. Originally referred to as Model1 and Model2, these models have never been given a more significant name and are still referred to that way in literature.

Model1 is a relatively simple model and is mostly recommended for small applications. Model2, instead, works for applications of any size of and is the preferred choice for enterprise-class applications. The difference between the two models can be reduced to the following. In Model1, the request processing (including rendering) takes place entirely within the boundaries of the JSP page. In Model2, separate components take care of processing the request and rendering results to markup.

Overall, Model1 is fairly similar to classic ASP.NET, where the output is largely determined by the logic in the page template and external components (ad hoc beans in Java, data source controls in ASP.NET) take care of downloading data.

In Model2, a servlet component is in charge of the request processing and acts as a *controller*. This servlet is responsible for the creation of any objects used by the page (mostly Java beans) and for redirecting to other JSP pages following the user's actions. In Model2, there is no processing logic within the JSP page itself. All the JSP page does is extract dynamic content from the servlet and insert that within static templates.

In the end, Model2 is a concrete implementation of the MVC pattern that works over the Web. The overall diagram is shown in Figure 3-6.

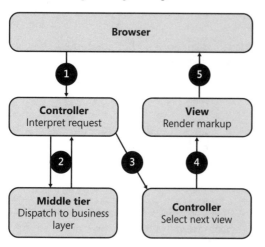

FIGURE 3-6 A step-by-step diagram for the Model2 pattern

The Model2 pattern owes a lot of its popularity to the Struts framework, part of the open-source Jakarta project. (See *http://struts.apache.org*.) The framework extends the JSP framework and implements the MVC pattern in full accordance with the Model2 architecture.

 Note A good introduction to Model2 can be found on the Java Web site at the following URL: *http://java.sun.com/blueprints/guidelines/designing_enterprise_applications_2e/web-tier/web-tier5.html*.

The Controller Actor over the Web

There are two remarkable differences between the diagram that describes the classic MVC and the diagram for Model2. Let's tackle the first difference.

As Figure 3-6 reveals, the first MVC actor that is called on stage is the controller, not the view. This difference is entirely due to the differences between the desktop platform and the Web platform. In a Web scenario, the user interface displayed to the end user is plain HTML displayed through a client browser. The *view* for the user doesn't coincide with the view for the application.

So the user interacts with his view of the application and triggers commands. The browser posts these commands to the Web server in the form of HTTP requests. Within the Web server, an *ad hoc* module intercepts the request, parses the URL, and decides which controller to instantiate. The ad hoc module is often referred to as the *front controller*.

The front controller is a *servlet* component in a Java Web application and an HTTP module in ASP.NET MVC. Typically, this component is provided out of the box by some tailor-made framework, such as Struts in the Java space and MonoRail or ASP.NET MVC in the .NET space.

From the perspective of a Model2 application, the entry point in the triad is the *controller*. The controller connects to the middle tier, performs tasks, gets updated data, and loads it into the model—that is, a representation of the data being worked on in the view.

The View Actor over the Web

The view actor is a simple markup generator. It acts as an engine that gets templates and fresh data as its input and produces markup for the browser. In the most common scenario, the view is based on static HTML templates to be filled in with data obtained from the controller. In other cases, the view might be based on XML templates and might not return plain HTML but something else—for example, XAML.

The view is typically based on a rendering engine and is neatly separated from the controller. The view no longer triggers the controller as it did in classic MVC. Quite the reverse; the view receives input from the controller, generates the markup, and forwards it directly to the output stream toward the browser.

The Model Actor over the Web

Overall, the model actor plays a secondary role in MVC over the Web. The model is simply the object that the controller uses to pass fresh data to the view. It can be a general-purpose dictionary of name/value pairs, or it can be a strongly typed object.

The controller works on the model by stuffing values in it that the rendering engine needs to retrieve. The rendering engine consumes any data in the model object and uses it to fill its own templates and produce Web content dynamically.

Model2 and ASP.NET MVC

Let's see how the inspiring principles of Model2 set the groundwork for ASP.NET MVC. First and foremost, in ASP.NET MVC, you have a front controller that looks at the URL and dispatches the request to a controller object. This component is the MVC HTTP handler you met in Chapter 2. It works for any requests mapped to ASP.NET MVC and triggered by the route handler.

In ASP.NET MVC, the first member of the MVC triad involved in the processing of a request is the controller. The view is just a rendering engine, and the model is a plain data container populated by the controller and consumed by the view.

Figure 3-7 shows a sequence diagram that illustrates the life cycle of an ASP.NET MVC request.

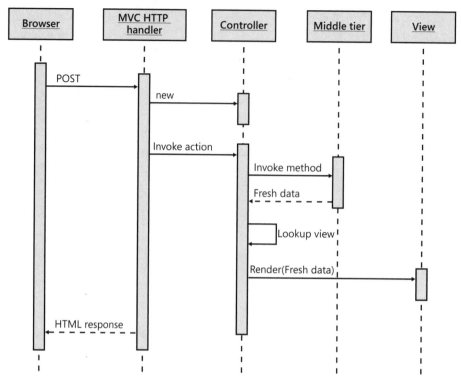

FIGURE 3-7 The sequence diagram for the ASP.NET MVC architecture

You won't see any model actor in the figure. However, the model is essentially the container for the data labeled "Fresh data." It represents the return values of any method invoked by the controller on the middle tier. This content is then forwarded to the view engine for the actual rendering of the HTML response.

In ASP.NET MVC, the model actor might have a fixed and system-provided form—a dictionary—or it might become a strongly typed graph of objects under the total control of the developer.

Implementation of the Controller Actor

In ASP.NET MVC, you generally don't think in terms of pages to build, but rather in terms of actions to perform and subsequent views to create. The controller is a .NET class that exposes a bunch of public methods for the MVC HTTP handler to invoke in response to a request.

Arguments for the controller's method are figured out from the request in a pure REST fashion. As you'll see in great detail in Chapter 4, "Inside Controllers," the framework does a good job of guessing your intention and extracting values from either the query string or the body of the request to match any declared formal parameter on the selected method. Otherwise, the author of the controller's method can always extract input data directly from ASP.NET intrinsic collections such as *Request.QueryString* and *Request.Form*.

Any action method on a controller's method has three responsibilities: performing the action, populating the model with the results, and triggering the view engine.

Typically, the controller invokes one endpoint in the service layer (the front of the middle tier) and gets some data back. Next, it massages this data into the model. This could be as easy as packing objects into a name/value dictionary or mapping values and instances to the properties of made-to-measure objects. Finally, the controller selects the next view for the user and orders the view engine to render it using the information stored in the model. Here's a quick but illustrative example of a controller method:

```
public ActionResult About()
{
    // Populate the model
    this.LoadLocalizableInformationIntoModel();

    // Next view
    string viewName = this.GetNextView("About");

    // Trigger the next view
    return View(viewName);
}

private void LoadLocalizableInformationIntoModel()
{
    // Load data into the built-in model actor.
    // Data is read from a global resource file named globals.resx. The item
    // read in this case is labeled WelcomeMessage.
    ViewData["WelcomeMessage"] = this.HttpContext.GetGlobalResourceObject(
            "globals", "WelcomeMessage");
    :
    :
    :
}

private string GetNextView (string currentViewName)
{
    // Possible workflow implemented here to select next view
    // and assign its name to the returned view name variable...
    :
    :

    // Return next view name
    return currentViewName;
}
```

The *About* method in the example doesn't really invoke any endpoint on the service layer. It's limited to extracting some information from the application's resource file and stuffing that into the model—the *ViewData* collection. In addition, the controller selects the next view to render and orders its rendering via the *View* method.

Implementation of the View Actor

In this regard, a view is ultimately the response sent to the client browser. A view is identified by name and has content that, processed by a view engine, produces the response for the browser.

As you've seen, a controller method returns an object of type *ActionResult*. The *ActionResult* type is an internal framework type that encapsulates the result of an action method and represents the following step after the controller has completed its job. To be precise, the *View* method doesn't actually return *ActionResult* but a derived type—*ViewResult*. Here's the complete type hierarchy:

```
public class ViewResult : ViewResultBase
{
    :
    :
}
public abstract class ViewResultBase : ActionResult
{
    :
    :
}
```

ViewResultBase is the base class used to supply the model to the view and contains most of the code to trigger the rendering of the view to get some response for the browser. The *ViewResult* type customizes its base class by providing the logic to find the view content to pass to the selected engine.

As it turns out, *ViewResult* isn't a simple container of data. Instead, it encapsulates all the logic necessary to produce a response for the user. The logic can be broken down into various steps.

First, the *ViewResult* object retrieves the currently selected view engine. Next, it locates the source for a particular view and passes it to the engine. The view engine mixes the source code (for example, an HTML template) with any content in the model (for example, the *ViewData* collection) and returns a response.

A default view engine is preregistered with any ASP.NET MVC application; however, you can create your own engines and add them programmatically to the application handling the *Application_Start* event in *global.asax*. If you want to use different view engines for different controller actions, you then set the view engine directly in the body of the controller method just before invoking the *View* method. (I'll return to the details of this in Chapter 5, "Inside Views.")

Note The default view engine is a class named *WebFormViewEngine*, and it inherits from an abstract base class—*VirtualPathProviderViewEngine*. The base class provides a basic implementation of the *IViewEngine* interface that characterizes a view engine. You can use the *VirtualPathProviderViewEngine* class as a starting point for building your own view engine, especially if your view engine needs to access disk files to read the source of the view. In fact, the *VirtualPathProviderViewEngine* class relies on the ASP.NET *VirtualPathProvider* class to access disk files on the server. The *VirtualPathProviderViewEngine* won't create a view object, but it delegates that work to any derived class—currently, the sole *WebFormViewEngine*. As you might guess, this class retrieves and processes view sources in the form of ASPX and ASCX markup files.

Implementation of the Model Actor

In ASP.NET MVC, the view receives data directly from the controller in a format that can vary quite a bit. Data can flow into the view through a general-purpose dictionary or through a strongly typed object model.

In the former case, the *ViewData* collection is used that is defined on the base controller class:

```
public abstract class ControllerBase : MarshalByRefObject, IController
{
    :
    :
    public ViewDataDictionary ViewData { get; set; }
}
```

The *ViewData* property represents a built-in container used for passing data between a controller and a view. The property is of type *ViewDataDictionary*. It's a plain .NET class that implements the *IDictionary* interface and looks and behaves like a classic name/value pair, enumerable dictionary:

```
public class ViewDataDictionary : IDictionary<string, object>,
                                  ICollection<KeyValuePair<string, object>>,
                                  IEnumerable<KeyValuePair<string, object>>,
                                  IEnumerable
{
    :
    :
}
```

The *ViewData* property is defined on the *ControllerBase* class to make it available to any custom controllers you might have. The idea is that once the controller has executed a given action, it packs any significant values into the *ViewData* container to make it flow all the way through the view.

```
public class HomeController : Controller
{
    public ActionResult Index()
    {
        this.ViewData["Message"] = "Welcome to ASP.NET MVC!";
        return this.View();
    }
}
```

A dictionary is a plain collection of name/value pairs with some additional capabilities, such as sorting and filtering. Any data you store in a dictionary is treated as an object and requires casting, boxing, or both to be worked on. A dictionary is definitely not something you would call strongly typed but, at the same time, a dictionary is straightforward to use and works just fine.

With all the stock dictionary classes available in the .NET Framework, why did the ASP.NET MVC team assemble yet another dictionary class? The *ViewDataDictionary* is kind of unique because it also features a *Model* property, as shown here:

```
public class ViewDataDictionary : IDictionary<string, object>,
                                  ICollection<KeyValuePair<string, object>>,
                                  IEnumerable<KeyValuePair<string, object>>,
                                  IEnumerable
{
    public object Model { get; set; }
    :
    :
}
```

The *Model* property is an alternative and object-oriented way of passing data to the view object. Instead of fitting flat data into a dictionary, you can shape up a custom object that faithfully represents the data the view expects. In other words, the *Model* property represents your chance of creating an object model that is unique for each view. I'll return to the model actor in the context of ASP.NET MVC in Chapter 6, "Inside Models."

Presentation-Oriented Variations of MVC

The Model2 pattern that inspired the design of ASP.NET MVC and other popular .NET Web frameworks such as Castle MonoRail is an evolution of the original MVC pattern. As you've seen, the view and model are no longer in touch with one another and the controller is a mediator between the model and the view. In addition, the view can be represented using a user-defined object model.

Separating the view from the model is a facet found in another well-known design pattern—the Model View Presenter (MVP) pattern. Using a strongly typed representation of the view that is, in some way, incorporated in the controller is the key aspect of yet another pattern that is gaining recognition these days—the Presentation Model, also known as Model-View-View Model (MVVM).

Although these two patterns have little to do with the ASP.NET MVC framework, I believe that a brief summary of what they offer is valuable, if for no other reason than to see the ASP.NET MVC design from a wider perspective.

If you have no interest in such background topics, you can quickly jump to the next major section, "The ASP.NET MVC Project Template." I warmly invite you to read on, though.

The MVP Pattern

MVP is a derivative of MVC aimed at providing a cleaner separation between the view, the model, and the controller. The pattern was originally developed at Taligent in the 1990s. The paper you find at *http://www.wildcrest.com/Potel/Portfolio/mvp.pdf* offers an introduction to MVP that describes how and why the pattern has been devised.

Starting from the MVC triad, creators of MVP neatly separated the model from the view/controller pair, which they called *presentation*. The core of MVP is the strictly regulated interaction taking place between the view and the controller. To reinforce the idea of the controller being the central console of the presentation machinery, in MVP the controller is renamed to *presenter*.

MVP Actors at a Glance

Figure 3-8 offers a graphical overview of the MVP pattern. Two fundamental differences between MVP and classic MVC stare you in the face.

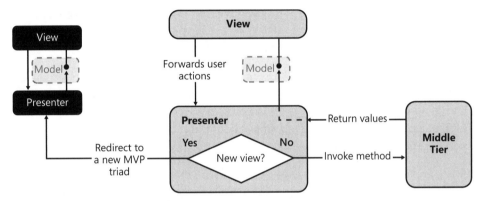

FIGURE 3-8 Actors at a glance in MVP

In MVP, the model has a much less relevant role. There's neither an explicit model object that the view connects to (as in classic MVC), nor is there a container that is being explicitly filled by the presenter.

I like to say that there's no model at all in MVP; or, if you want to find a place for it, the model is implicit in the presenter or, better yet, it's *fused* to the view.

The key aspect of MVP is that the view exposes a contract through which the presenter accesses the portion of the user interface that needs updates after an action. This interface is technically part of the view implementation—it's actually an interface implemented by the view class. However, that interface can also be seen as the background model used to flow data into and out of the view. Figure 3-8 just reflects this idea.

In MVP, the presenter ignores any UI technology behind the view. All the presenter knows is the contract exposed by the view. Whether the view is implemented on top of a Web or desktop application is completely irrelevant from the presenter's perspective. This makes it possible to reuse the presenter logic across different applications. It's possible, therefore, that the same presenter class for a given view is shared by an ASP.NET Web Forms and Windows Forms or WPF application.

Note Reusing the presenter logic is definitely possible, but it doesn't always happen and it doesn't always happen for free. It's a pleasant side effect when you build multiple front ends on top of the same core application—for example, a Web presentation, a Windows presentation, and perhaps a mobile presentation. Clearly, "reusing" here means reusing the same assembly. This reuse can be hindered by binary incompatibilities between involved platforms. For example, no reuse is possible between a full .NET platform (up to 4.0) and Silverlight (up to version 3.0).

Implementation of the View Actor

With the model playing a secondary role, the core of MVP is the interaction between the view and the presenter. In MVP, the view is devised to be as thin and passive as possible. This is the theory, anyway. In the real world, a really passive view can be quite cumbersome to write and maintain and can add a lot of complexity to the presenter.

If you opt for a passive view, you have an inherently more testable system because the logic in the view is reduced to an absolute minimum. Subsequently, you run no serious risk at all by not automating testing on the view. Any piece of code can contain mistakes, but in the case of a passive view the extreme simplicity of the code allows for only gross and patently obvious mistakes that can be easily caught without any automated procedure.

The complexity taken out of the view moves to another layer—in this case, the presenter. A passive view is inevitably coupled with a more complex presenter. Opting for a passive view is a trade-off between high testability and complexity in the presenter classes. This approach goes under the name of *Passive View* (PV). For more information, see *http://martinfowler.com/eaaDev/PassiveScreen.html*.

Note Although the driving force for PV remains maximum testability, there's another benefit in it that you might want to consider. In a Passive View approach, the view is a raw sequence of UI elements with no additional data-binding or formatting. The presenter acts directly on the UI elements and works simply by loading data into them. There's nothing that happens in the UI that you can't spot easily. If there's something wrong in the UI, it's right before your eyes. Your eyes are your test harness.

You can also opt for a more active view that contains some logic as far as data-binding and data formatting is concerned. Developing a richer view is easier, and it distributes the required complexity between the view and the presenter. The view needs to take care of some synchronization and adaptation work to make input data usable by user-interface elements. This approach goes by the name *Supervising Controller* (SVC). For more information, see *http://martinfowler.com/eaaDev/SupervisingPresenter.html*.

In an SVC scenario, the model actor is back on duty. In this case, the presenter might need to pass aggregated data to the view using the members of the interface. The structure of the view interface can range from a collection of scalar values that bind directly to UI elements to a single member that accepts a complex type. The complex type defines an object model for the view, and the view caches and massages those values into UI elements.

Opting for an SVC view entails making a trade-off between testability and ease (and speed) of development. Testing an SVC view means testing a piece of user interface with logic and graphics—not exactly a walk in the park.

How do you test a user interface?

The general idea is to force the view to generate nonvisual output that can be asserted in the unit test to verify the soundness of the UI. Some tools exist to help with this. For ASP.NET, an interesting tool is WatiN (which you can see at *http://watin.sourceforge.net*), which you might want to consider along with the toolkit unit testing in the Visual Studio 2008 Team Tester edition. Another non-ASP.NET-specific automatic test tool for applications is IBM's Rational Robot. For more information, visit *http://www-306.ibm.com/software/awdtools/tester/robot*.

Passive View and Supervising Controller are both reasonable approaches to building the view in an MVP scenario. According to Fowler, you never use MVP; rather, you use either Passive View or Supervising Controller. Or you use a mix of the two.

Implementation of the Presenter Actor

A common question is, why change the name? Why is it a *presenter* and not a *controller*? The name *presenter* better conveys the sense of a component that is responsible for handling user actions; the presenter presents user requests to the back-end system; after that, it presents a response to the user.

The presenter sits in between the view and the back-end system; it receives input from the view and passes commands down to the back-end system. It then gets results and updates the view through the contracted view interface, optionally stuffing data into a strongly typed model object.

MVP and Enterprise-Class Applications

MVP is not a pattern that can be implemented quickly. It requires you to define an interface and a presenter for nearly every view in the application—each Web form in ASP.NET and each form in Windows.

MVP provides guidance on how to manage heaps of views and, quite obviously, comes at a cost—the cost of increased complexity in the application code. As you can imagine, these costs are easier to absorb in large applications than in simple programs. MVP, therefore, is not just for any application.

In MVP, the view is defined through an interface, and this interface is the only point of contact between the system and the view. As an architect, after you've abstracted a view with an interface, you can give developers the green light to start developing presentation logic without waiting for designers to produce the graphics. After developers have interfaces, they can start coding and interfaces can be extracted from user stories, if not from full specifications.

MVP is an important presentation pattern that can be a bit expensive to implement in relatively simple applications. On the other hand, MVP shines in enterprise-class applications, where you really need to reuse as much presentation logic as possible, across multiple platforms, and in Software-As-A-Service (SaaS) scenarios.

Cardinality of MVP Triads

In an MVP implementation, is it OK to have one interface and one presenter for each supported view? How many application controllers should you have? Just one? Well, it depends.

Logically speaking, each view is represented by an interface and managed by a presenter. Take a moderately complex application with dozens of views, and you'll start feeling the burden of MVP on your shoulders quite soon. Microsoft released an ad hoc application block (the Web Client Software Factory) to smooth out some of these issues at least in the realm of ASP.NET Web Forms applications. There's no magic, though—just some designer tools to create ready-made stubs with views and presenters and a workflow to handle the navigation logic. MVP is inherently complex and targeted to enterprise applications and to other scenarios where complexity is large enough to require precise patterns and policies.

So to get back to the original question about cardinality, most of the time you do have a one-to-one correspondence between logical views, interfaces, and presenters. A wise use of base classes and inheritance can certainly lessen the coding burden and save you some code in certain presenters. On the other hand, a presenter is the presentation logic for a particular view: if you need two different views, why should you have only one or maybe three presenters?

As far as application controllers are concerned, things can be a little bit different. An application controller is the machinery that decides about the next view based on some input, such as the view name (as in our example) or just a collection of values that denote the state of a view. If you have a large application with hundreds of views, the application controller that takes care of all possible transitions for all views can become quite a complex one. For this reason, you might want to split the navigation logic across multiple controllers at the granularity that you feel works best for you. You might even want to use an application controller for each use-case, if use-cases involve several views and complex navigation sequences. Needless to say, in a presentation layer with multiple navigation controllers, each presenter must receive a reference to its navigation controller upon instantiation.

Important Although a significant design difference exists between MVP and the original MVC, MVP and Model2 have a lot in common. The biggest difference remains the interaction between view and controller—it's strictly based on a contract in MVP, and it's kind of free form in Model2. This said, you can find particular implementations of the patterns that blur this difference significantly. In ASP.NET MVC, for instance, you don't have an interface for the view, but using the *Model* property of the *ViewData* dictionary, you can define an equally strongly typed model for each view.

Another difference between MVP and Model2 is the driver of the action. In MVP, the action is triggered by the view; in Model2, the entry point is the controller. Precisely for this reason, in Model2 (unlike MVP) the runtime environment is responsible for instantiating the controller.

All in all, if you employ Model2 as your definition of MVC, you can hardly see the difference between it and MVP. But the difference does exist; and it's not even small. To grasp it, though, you must read the full story.

Presentation Model Pattern (Also Known as MVVM)

Developed by Martin Fowler, the Presentation Model (PM) pattern is fully described here: *http://martinfowler.com/eaaDev/PresentationModel.html*.

How does PM differ from MVP? Ultimately, it's not an entirely different type of animal. It's correct to consider it yet another variation of MVP that is particularly suited to supporting a rich and complex user interface. On the Windows platforms, PM works well with user interfaces built with Windows Presentation Foundation and Silverlight.

Microsoft recommends it here: *http://msdn.microsoft.com/en-us/library/cc707885.aspx*. However, Microsoft also developed a WPF-specific version of PM that goes under the name of *Model-View-ViewModel* (MVVM). As I see things, PM and MVVM are not different things—MVVM is just a WPF-specific implementation of PM. In this book, I'll consider PM and MVVM to be the same thing.

PM, like MVP, is based on three actors: the view, the model, and the presenter.

PM Actors at a Glance

In MVP, the view exposes a contract to the presenter and the presenter talks back to the view through that interface. Binding of the data occurs through the implementation of the interface in the view class—the *Page* class in ASP.NET, the *Form* class in Windows Forms, and the *Window* class in WPF. The code that does the binding belongs to the view and can be as simple as a property assignment or as sophisticated as data-binding.

In PM, the view doesn't expose any interface, but a data model for the view is incorporated in the presenter. The view elements are directly bound to properties on the model. In summary, in PM the view is passive and doesn't implement any interface. The interface is transformed into a model class and incorporated in the presenter. See Figure 3-9.

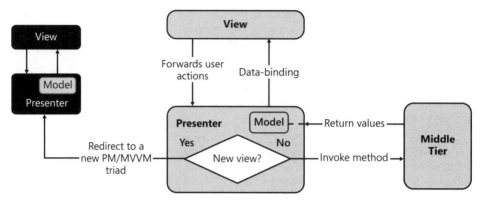

FIGURE 3-9 The triad in the Presentation Model pattern

Let's examine the role played by the actors in a bit more detail.

Implementation of the Model Actor

In PM, the model plays the same role it played in the original formulation of MVC: a container for any data being worked on in the view. Unlike MVC, though, there's no bidirectional link between the view and model in the form of an Observer relationship.

The view is bound to the model and uses any stored information to generate the response. The actual form of the binding is an implementation detail, but it's always something close to data-binding.

The innovative point of PM is that the presenter doesn't operate on the view. The presenter, instead, exposes an object model tailor-made for the view and takes care of populating it with fresh data. The view, in turn, gains access to the presenter's object model in some way. In the .NET space, data-binding is a common way in which this is achieved.

Implementation of the View Actor

The view is utterly simple. It's nothing more than a bunch of UI elements bound to properties in the model. Any events raised by the user are transmitted to the presenter, handled, and end up updating the model.

When the user action requires an interaction with the middle tier, the presenter updates the model with the results it gets. The view is generally owned by the presenter so that the presenter, after updating the model, just orders the view to render.

No information is passed to the view. The view holds a reference to the presenter and uses this reference to gain direct access to the model that is exposed out of the presenter class. The most boring part of the Presentation Model pattern is writing the synchronization code that keeps the elements in the view and the properties in the model in sync. Thankfully, in the .NET Framework data-binding helps a lot.

Note that view/model synchronization is bidirectional. When the user selects an item in a list, for example, the model should be updated; when an action occurs that modifies the selection, the model is updated. PM has become a popular pattern, especially in the WPF community, because of the great support the WPF platform offers for two-way data-binding.

Implementation of the Presenter Actor

The presenter in the PM pattern accomplishes nearly the same tasks as in MVP and MVC. It receives events from the view and processes them against the presentation layer, business logic, or both. In PM, though, the presenter holds a model object and is responsible for filling it up with any state changes resulting from back-end operations. Finally, the presenter calls the view to refresh. Figure 3-10 illustrates the sequence.

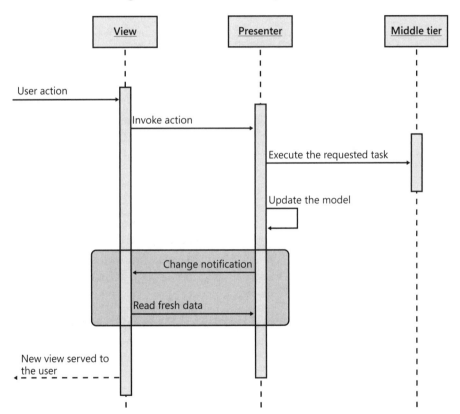

FIGURE 3-10 The Presentation Model diagram

In the PM jargon, the presenter is often referred to as the *PresentationModel* and exposes public methods as well as all the public properties that form the data model for the view. The gray area in Figure 3-10 that surrounds a bidirectional exchange between the view and the presenter is where view/model synchronization code lives. In frameworks that offer great support for native two-way data-binding, that part of the diagram is implemented according to the data-binding idiom of the framework. This has led to the creation of a slight variation of PM for the WPF/Silverlight platform that is known as MVVM.

MVVM in Rich User Interfaces

MVVM is the target pattern for any .NET system with a significant amount of logic (domain logic, formatting, UI validation) on the presentation layer. The MVVM pattern allows you to define a specific view model object that contains formatting and UI validation instructions. At the same time, you place in this "view" object any extra presentation logic and keep data-binding code as clean as possible.

MVVM is particularly effective in user-interfaces built using WPF and Silverlight because these platforms provide superb support for (two-way) data-binding. Figure 3-11 illustrates the idea behind the MVVM pattern in a WPF context.

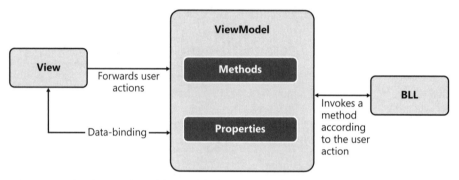

FIGURE 3-11 An abstract view of the Model-View-View Model pattern

Using MVVM means that you place your binding stuff in the XAML markup (the view). The data context of the binding elements is the *ViewModel* object (the presenter).

User actions are forwarded to the presenter by invoking methods. In WPF, by using ad hoc XAML features (for example, triggers and commands) you can keep the code-behind class empty. In Silverlight 3.0 where the support for triggers and commands is insufficient, you'll use the code-behind class of the XAML file to handle user actions and invoke methods on the presenter.

The MVVM pattern is particularly suited to WPF and Silverlight development because of the extremely powerful support for data-binding. Figure 3-12 shows in more detail an MVVM application in WPF and Silverlight.

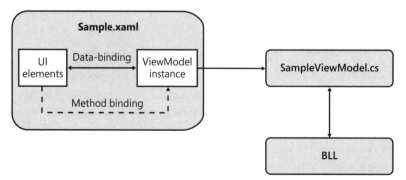

FIGURE 3-12 Practical schema of an MVVM implementation in WPF and Silverlight

The markup in the XAML file defines all the details of the data-binding. The data context is an instance of the presenter (*ViewModel*) class. The code-behind class is extremely thin when it's not just empty. Typically, you set the data context to an instance of the view model class directly in the markup as shown here:

```
<UserControl x:Class="Samples.MainPage"
            xmlns="http://schemas.microsoft.com/winfx/2006/xaml/presentation"
            xmlns:x="http://schemas.microsoft.com/winfx/2006/xaml"
            xmlns:data="clr-namespace:MyModel;assembly=MyModel">
  <UserControl.Resources>
    <data:SampleViewModel x:Key="SampleViewModel1" />
  </UserControl.Resources>
  <Grid x:Name="LayoutRoot"
       DataContext="{Binding Source={StaticResource SampleViewModel1}}">
    ⋮
  </Grid>
</UserControl>
```

The code sets a binding between UI elements and properties on the presenter object. A method binding can be set directly in XAML using commands and triggers. In this case, the code-behind class is just empty. In Silverlight, this might require adding some code in the code-behind class to dispatch events to methods on the view model class. The logic to interact with the middle tier is buried in the folds of the presenter class.

Important Here at the end of our exploration of patterns for the presentation layer, you can't help but notice that the design of ASP.NET MVC doesn't have much to do with the original idea of MVC. The overall design is much closer to the Model2 pattern. The tag "MVC" in the framework's name still makes sense, but you'll soon be off track if you use the behavior of ASP.NET MVC as your definition and understanding of the MVC pattern.

The ASP.NET MVC Project Template

Visual Studio 2008 and newer versions (for example, Visual Studio 2010) come with a specific template to create an ASP.NET MVC project. In the end, an ASP.NET MVC application is an ASP.NET application with some special settings. Some of these tailor-made settings are stored in the *web.config* file; others are implicitly assumed from the location of certain resources and their names.

Note ASP.NET MVC was introduced as an add-on framework to ASP.NET 3.5 SP1 in March 2009. Visual Studio 2010 ships with ASP.NET MVC 2, which includes new programming features, an enhanced project template, and an improved design experience.

Peculiarities of an ASP.NET MVC Project

As you saw in Chapter 2, ASP.NET MVC and classic ASP.NET share the same run-time environment, only configured in a slightly different manner. Configuring the run-time environment means adding or removing HTTP handlers and modules, registering ad hoc providers, and linking assemblies and namespaces. Let's start by briefly summarizing what you're required to have in the *web.config* file. (You saw this in more detail in Chapter 2.)

The *web.config* File

The beating heart of an ASP.NET MVC application is the URL-routing HTTP module. The module is registered under the *<httpModules>* section of the *web.config* file:

```
<httpModules>
    <add name="ScriptModule" type="System.Web.Handlers.ScriptModule,
            System.Web.Extensions, Version=3.5.0.0, ..." />
    <add name="UrlRoutingModule" type="System.Web.Routing.UrlRoutingModule,
            System.Web.Routing, Version=3.5.0.0, ..." />
</httpModules>
```

The *ScriptModule* node, conversely, is not strictly related to any ASP.NET MVC–specific functionalities. It has to do with the implementation of AJAX functionalities.

> **Note** The latest version of the *ScriptModule* component is defined with the *System.Web.Extensions* assembly. The version released with ASP.NET 3.5 Service Pack 1 has a dependency on *System.Web .Abstractions*—an assembly originally developed for ASP.NET MVC and then incorporated in the full ASP.NET platform with Service Pack 1. This means that *ScriptModule* version 3.5 is compatible with AJAX functionalities in both ASP.NET Web Forms and ASP.NET MVC.

The *<httpHandlers>* section also contains a setting that relates to ASP.NET MVC, as shown here:

```
<httpHandlers>
    :
    :
    <add verb="*" path="*.mvc" validate="false"
        type="System.Web.Mvc.MvcHttpHandler, System.Web.Mvc, Version=1.0.0.0, ..." />
</httpHandlers>
```

Other settings you encounter in the section are common to any ASP.NET application with AJAX features enabled.

Both HTTP handlers and HTTP modules settings are replicated in the *<system.webServer>* section so that a single *web.config* file can serve the application whether it's running in Integrated Pipeline mode under IIS 7 and in classic mode under either IIS 6 or IIS 7.

An ASP.NET MVC application is also dependent on three specific assemblies: *System.Web .Abstractions*, *System.Web.Routing*, and *System.Web.Mvc*. A few namespaces are also automatically registered to save you from adding a bunch of <@*Import ...%*> directives in each ASPX view.

```
<pages>
    :
    :
    <namespaces>
        <add namespace="System.Web.Mvc" />
        <add namespace="System.Web.Mvc.Ajax" />
        <add namespace="System.Web.Mvc.Html" />
        <add namespace="System.Web.Routing" />
        :
        :
    </namespaces>
</pages>
```

Unlike modules, handlers, and assemblies, though, namespaces are not essential content for the *web.config* file and might not even be required if you switch to a custom view engine. However, if you switch to a custom view engine (or a custom controller factory), you might want to edit the *web.config* file to register your custom assemblies.

The *global.asax* File

In general, the *global.asax* file serves a number of purposes as far the initialization and configuration of the application is concerned (for example, the definition of handlers for global events such as HTTP module events and application events).

For an ASP.NET MVC application, the *global.asax* file also serves an additional purpose: defining the format of the URLs being recognized. In summary, at a minimum the *global.asax* file of an ASP.NET MVC application configures the URL routing mechanism for the application:

```
protected void Application_Start()
{
    // Specific to ASP.NET MVC 2
    AreaRegistration.RegisterAllAreas();

    RegisterRoutes(RouteTable.Routes);
}

public static void RegisterRoutes(RouteCollection routes)
{
    // Register your routes here
    routes.MapRoute( ... );
    :
    :
}
```

You can register routes at any time by simply calling the *MapRoute* method on the *RouteTable.Routes* static collection. However, most of the time you just want to have all of the routes enabled when the application starts. For this to happen, you need to configure routing in the *Application_Start* method of the *global.asax* class.

> **Note** You might have noticed that in the standard *global.asax* file the routes are defined in a public static method named *RegisterRoutes,* which is then called from within *Application_Start.* Why not simply fill up the route table in the body of *Application_Start?* The obvious answer is testability. A public static method on the application's global class makes it possible to test certain features of the application with a different route table:
>
> ```
> YourMvcApplication.RegisterRoutes(yourTestRoutes);
> ```
>
> Probably not a feature you use every day, but one that is good to have.

The *default.aspx* File

As you go through the default ASP.NET MVC project, you run across an old acquaintance: the *default.aspx* file. In a typical Web Forms application, this file represents the common entry point in the application and the URL to the home page. Because of this, the file is often a content page (based on a master page) and shows off the main capabilities of the application. In other words, you expect to find a lot of content in it. Here, instead, is the content of the typical *default.aspx* file of an ASP.NET MVC application:

```
<%@ Page Language="C#"
         AutoEventWireup="true"
         CodeBehind="Default.aspx.cs"
         Inherits="MvcApplication1._Default" %>
```

To add even more thrills, a comment in the ASPX markup strongly recommends that you don't delete the file. What about the code-behind class? Here's what it looks like:

```
using System.Web;
using System.Web.Mvc;
using System.Web.UI;

namespace MvcApplication1
{
    public partial class _Default : Page
    {
        public void Page_Load(object sender, System.EventArgs e)
        {
            string originalPath = Request.Path;
            HttpContext.Current.RewritePath(Request.ApplicationPath, false);
            IHttpHandler httpHandler = new MvcHttpHandler();
```

```
            httpHandler.ProcessRequest(HttpContext.Current);
            HttpContext.Current.RewritePath(originalPath, false);
        }
    }
}
```

What's the real purpose of the *default.aspx* file and its code-behind file?

The role of the file depends on the version of the IIS Web server you're using. If you are running the application under IIS 7 in Integrated Pipeline mode, you don't need *default.aspx*. In this case, you can remove that file, and all of its subfiles, from the project. In IIS 7 Integrated Pipeline mode, a request for the application root (for example, *http://yourserver/*) is automatically captured by the routing system and processed in terms of the predefined routes. The same thing happens if you test the application with the embedded Web server (also known as Cassini) that comes with Visual Studio 2008 Service Pack 1 and newer versions.

If you're using an older version of Visual Studio, or if you're hosting the ASP.NET MVC application under IIS 6 or IIS 7 Classic mode, *default.aspx* is required. In all these cases, a request for the application root (for example, *http://yourserver/*) is resolved in terms of a startup document—*default.aspx*. In other words, a request for the application root is not recognized as an ASP.NET MVC request under older versions of IIS.

For this reason, you need to have a *default.aspx* in your ASP.NET MVC application to capture the request. In addition, this default.aspx doesn't need to be a controller or a view. It just needs to perform the trick of forcing the ASP.NET MVC runtime to process the request. The code in the *Page_Load* event of the *default.aspx* code-behind class first rewrites the requested path to the application root "/" and then explicitly processes the request using the *MvcHttpHandler* class:

```
// Save the path of the current request (default.aspx)
string originalPath = Request.Path;

// Rewrites the path back to the application root ("/")
HttpContext.Current.RewritePath(Request.ApplicationPath, false);

// Explicitly processes the current request via ASP.NET MVC
IHttpHandler httpHandler = new MvcHttpHandler();
httpHandler.ProcessRequest(HttpContext.Current);

// At this point, the request has been fully processed.
```

The MVC HTTP handler uses routing information to send the request to the mapped controller and view. When *ProcessRequest* returns, the request has been fully served, but the control is still in the *Page_Load* event of *default.aspx*. The Web Forms life cycle triggered for *default.aspx* continues to its natural end without producing any further updates to the output stream. (Nothing more happens because the *default.aspx* file is ultimately an empty file with no controls and no postback code.)

In the end, the user receives any HTML produced by the MVC HTTP handler.
(See Figure 3-13.)

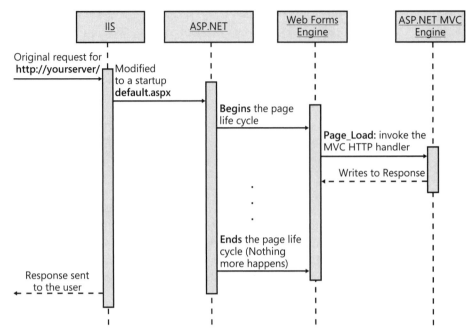

FIGURE 3-13 The sequence diagram for an application root request in IIS 6.

After processing the request, the code in *Page_Load* restores the original path so that the
output caching module (if enabled) can correctly process the response.

```
// Restore the originally requested path for the sake of output caching
HttpContext.Current.RewritePath(originalPath, false);
```

If your system is running under IIS 7 Integrated Pipeline mode (hold on, this is the default
configuration), you can remove *default.aspx* from the project. If you keep the file in the
project, the two following URLs produce the same result:

```
http://yourserver/
http://yourserver/default.aspx
```

Obviously, if you remove the *default.aspx* file from the project, a request for the second URL
will fail.

Convention-over-Configuration

Convention-over-Configuration (CoC) is a development paradigm designed to reduce
the number of decisions made during a project. The paradigm is not a sort of philosophy
that inspires architectural decisions. It's all about increasing all-around simplicity without
sacrificing flexibility.

That *convention* is used over *configuration* doesn't mean that you end up getting no configuration settings. More simply, you use conventions to indicate a given (and well-defined) configuration.

A convention is a group of assumptions made about the code. If you follow the convention, you don't need to write any configuration information anywhere. If you don't go by convention, you write only what differs in some external file.

CoC is a very helpful paradigm when writing a framework or when used in the context of a large project that integrates multiple applications.

In ASP.NET MVC, a convention says that any controller class has a trailing "Controller" word. If you call a controller, say, *Home*, by convention, the resulting class is *HomeController*.

For more information about CoC, go to the following Web site: *http://softwareengineering .vazexqi.com/files/pattern.html*.

ASP.NET MVC Special Folders

All in all, an ASP.NET MVC application is made of controller classes and views.

A *controller* class is a container of logically related actions that can be invoked from the user interface. The signature of a controller class must meet a given standard; however, this standard can be modified on a per-application (or even on a per-request) basis by registering a custom controller factory.

A *view* is any content that the currently registered *view engine* can use to produce a response. By default, the view is an ASPX file that is passed as input to the view engine to generate HTML. The default view engine is adapted from the Web Forms rendering engine and, just for this reason, it recognizes and supports the ASPX markup of classic ASP.NET. By selecting a custom view engine, you no longer need ASPX files and can replace them with any content that represents valid input for the view engine—for example, XML or XAML documents.

An ASP.NET MVC project is articulated in a bunch of folders with predefined content. The Views folder, for instance, contains the source file used by the selected view engine to generate views. The Controllers folder contains classes for controller components.

Figure 3-14 shows a freshly created ASP.NET MVC project that contains only sample controllers and views. Let's examine the structure of the project template and explore the content and intended role of each folder.

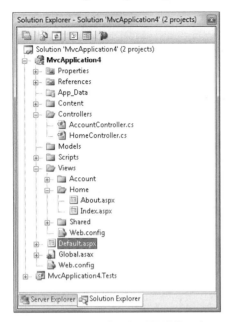

FIGURE 3-14 A sample ASP.NET MVC project

The Controllers Folder

As shown in the figure, the Controllers folder contains all the controller classes needed by the application. In the routes, a controller is identified with a moniker such as *Home*, *Account*, or perhaps *Customer*. The moniker for a controller is up to you and is definitely part of the naming convention rules you decide to employ.

As mentioned, the real class behind a controller moniker follows an established convention: the word *Controller* trails the moniker, as shown in Figure 3-14. Such a convention is used by the MVC HTTP handler to resolve an incoming request. From the matching routes, the handler figures out the controller's moniker, builds the real class name, and instantiates that. Here's the structure of a controller class:

```
public class HomeController : Controller
{
    public ActionResult Index()
    {
        :
        :
    }

    public ActionResult About()
    {
        :
        :
    }
}
```

If you want or need the actual controller class name to deviate from the standard convention, you install a custom controller factory, as you'll see in the next chapter.

The number of controller classes that form an ASP.NET MVC application is up to you. Generally speaking, it results from a number of factors, including the design of URLs, the logical split of functionalities to implement, your programming preferences, and your sense of cohesion. In Chapter 4, I'll explore the intricacies of controller classes in much greater detail.

The Views Folder

The Views folder is designed to contain any files used to produce a response for the browser. A view is always associated with a controller action. For this reason, the Views folder contains one subfolder for each supported controller. In turn, each controller-specific view folder contains any files the currently selected view engine requires to generate the view.

The default view engine is the Web Forms view engine. It works by producing HTML based on some ASPX templates. In Figure 3-14, under the folder Views/Home you see a couple of *.aspx* files: *index.aspx* and *about.aspx*.

Those files are never requested directly by the user. However, by convention the ASP.NET MVC runtime knows that when the *Home* controller method returns the *Index* view, the content of *views/home/index.aspx* must be used as a template for generating the actual markup for the browser.

The name of the view is one of the parameters you pass when you create a view, as shown here:

```
public class HomeController : Controller
{
    public ActionResult Index()
    {
        // Perform the action
        :
        :

        // Create the view (default name)
        return View();
    }

    public ActionResult About()
    {
        // Perform the action
        :
        :

        // Create the view (explicit name)
        return View("About");
    }
}
```

The conventional name of the view, if not otherwise specified, is the name of the method. Visual Studio 2008 provides some facilities to deal with views. Figure 3-15 shows the dialog box displayed when you right-click on the Views node and choose to add a new view.

FIGURE 3-15 Adding a new view from Visual Studio 2008

The Views folder also contain a subfolder named Shared. The Shared folder conventionally contains views not specific to a given controller, such as views for error pages, master pages, and user controls.

The Areas Folder

ASP.NET, although clearly inspired by MonoRail, doesn't offer in its first version a handy functionality that MonoRail developers use fruitfully—*areas*. So what's an area in this regard? Quite simply, it's a logical container of controllers. Although areas can be simulated in ASP. NET MVC 1 and in Visual Studio 2008, they are an out-of-the-box feature in ASP.NET MVC 2 and Visual Studio 2010. (See Figure 3-16.)

Each controller must belong to an area, and any application must contain at least one area. If custom areas are not defined, a global and unnamed area is conventionally assumed.

An *area* represents a section of the application and is a feature particularly suited to large Web applications developed using the MVC approach. Ultimately, each area is a sort of subapplication within the same global project. Each area, in fact, has its own set of controllers, views, shared content, models, and so forth and, more importantly, is developed in isolation.

FIGURE 3-16 Grouping controllers and views in areas in ASP.NET MVC 2

Looking at the actual implementation, each area is a distinct project. All area projects are then merged together in the main solution as the application is deployed.

Note The ability to group controllers in areas has been added to version 2 of ASP.NET MVC by popular demand. However, it's possible to simulate the same feature in ASP.NET MVC 1 by following the instructions (and avoiding the related pitfalls) in the following post: *http://haacked .com/archive/2008/11/04/areas-in-aspnetmvc.aspx*.

Other Folders in the Project

A typical ASP.NET MVC project contains a bunch of other folders, as detailed in Table 3-1.

TABLE 3-1 Additional folders of an ASP.NET MVC project

Folder	Description
Content	Contains global files used in the project, including cascading style sheets (CSS).
Models	Contains the various models required by the application, whatever those happen to be. (More on this in a moment.)
Scripts	Contains any script files required within the project.

In addition, you can create additional folders to add more script files and keep them separate from others. You can add an Image folder or a WebForms folder if you're mixing Web Forms and ASP.NET MVC in a single application. The folders discussed in this section are those that play a particular role in the framework. Other folders can be added as long as you find a role for them in the application.

What's the intended content for the Models folder?

ASP.NET MVC doesn't mandate (or deny) any specific model and framework for representing your data. You can use Entity Framework, LINQ-to-SQL, or a true Active Record framework such as Castle ActiveRecord, or you can draw your domain model using NHibernate or another commercial Object/Relational Mapper (O/RM) tool.

In any of these cases (likely in 100 percent of the scenarios, though), you end up linking the model as a separate assembly. And you don't need a Models folder. As stated earlier in this chapter, the model in MVC is not necessarily the object model that represents data being worked on by the application. That was probably true when MVC was introduced, but today the model is more about the data worked on in the *view*.

The ideal content for the *Models* folder, therefore, is any class file that you use to render the data being passed in and out of a given view—the view-model. I'll return to this in Chapter 6.

Summary

In spite of the MVC in the name, the ASP.NET MVC framework is about MVC but it's not a precise implementation of it. In the end, the ultimate reason for writing this chapter was to share a bit of knowledge about what MVC really is, how it was devised, and how it evolved.

If asked to share your definition of the MVC pattern, don't look at how ASP.NET MVC works to make your points. The behavior of ASP.NET MVC is certainly based on the MVC philosophy, but a lot of details are omitted. Why? Because, MVC was designed at a time when there was no Web around; and the Web is quite a different beast.

Model2 is the variation of the original MVC that works best for the Web, providing at the same time an alternative paradigm to a classic page controller. If you're looking for a pattern that closely describes the behavior of ASP.NET MVC, Model2 is what you're looking for.

Be honest—when considering an ASP.NET MVC application, all that you take into account are controllers and views. Where's the model? The model intended as the application's object model or domain model is elsewhere, in a distinct assembly modeled and persisted typically using ad hoc O/RM tools. The model of MVC is how you read input data from the view and how you pass updated data back.

ASP.NET MVC today supports the *ViewData* dictionary and a strongly typed object to pass data to a view. And more and more, developers are finding *ViewData* to be obsolete, inadequate, and a working-but-dirty solution. However, when you opt for a strongly typed model, you slowly move toward an MVVM pattern—the same pattern that is getting rave reviews in Silverlight and WPF circles.

There's definitely more than just MVC in ASP.NET MVC.

With the upcoming chapters, I'll take the plunge into the internal mechanics of the ASP.NET MVC framework and examine its pillars, one after the next. The next chapter is about controllers.

Part II
The Core of ASP.NET MVC

Chapter 4
Inside Controllers

They always say time changes things, but you actually have to change them yourself.

—Andy Warhol

The primary goal of the Model-View-Controller (MVC) pattern is to separate as neatly as possible the code that generates the graphical interface displayed to users from the code that manages any user actions. For years, taking code and presentation logic out of the view has been a task that developers faced on a daily basis.

Nearly every developer and engineer would agree in principle that separation between a graphical interface and any code behind it is a key design achievement. Everybody sees the value in it. But recognizing a general principle is one thing; it is quite another to apply it systematically in everyday work.

For this reason, ASP.NET MVC is a fundamental milestone for ASP.NET developers. It is the framework now that forces you toward more accurate design. It is the framework now that mandates separation of concerns, at least between controllers and views.

In this chapter, I'll review the role of controllers in the economy of an ASP.NET MVC application and delve deep into the mechanics of such components while reviewing many development aspects of them.

> **Important** Before digging deep into the structure, behavior, and design of ASP.NET MVC controllers, I'll take you through a tour of components that play the role of the "controller" in an ASP.NET MVC scenario. The idea is to demonstrate that adding controller-like components to ASP.NET Web Forms is not impossible, and a new framework makes it easier to do and especially smooth and seamless. If you've already made up your mind to use ASP.NET MVC and want to go straight to the point of learning about ASP.NET MVC controllers, feel free to skip this part and go directly to the section "Anatomy of an ASP.NET MVC Controller" later in the chapter.

The Role of Controllers and the Motivation for Using Them

When you open up a Web project in Microsoft Visual Studio and add a new Web page, you are presented with a blank designer that needs to be filled with HTML elements and server controls. In the development of a classic ASP.NET Web Forms page, therefore, you initially focus on the expected user interface and author an .ASPX markup file by composing a bunch of related server controls and literals. Next, you focus on the events raised by any components in the user interface, and for each event (for example, button clicks, changes of selection, and so forth) you code the expected behavior.

Abstractly speaking, a user interface exists to implement a *use-case*. The term *use-case* is generally used to refer to a specific interaction between the user and the system. More precisely, a use-case is one of the numerous Unified Modeling Language (UML) diagrams and describes the interaction taking place between two actors, including users and the system itself. From a design perspective, a unique action corresponds to every interaction between the system and user.

The trigger of this unique action is an event fired by any of the user interface visual elements. For example, when the user clicks a button, an event is fired to trigger the expected use-case. How would you handle this in an ASP.NET Web Forms page?

You just write an event handler in the code-behind class for the ASP.NET form. Invoked over a postback request, this event handler ends up acting as the orchestrator of any logic required for the use-case.

At the very end of the day, you keep the user interface definition distinct from any attached presentation logic. Even better, code for the user interface and for the presentation logic live in distinct, but related, files. Could you ask for anything more? Well, you should.

Beyond the Code-Behind Approach

In the beginning of ASP.NET, the code-behind approach seemed to be a very well-architected solution because it guarantees physical separation between user-interface elements and the presentation logic. The physical separation of the user-interface definition and related code was definitely a step forward from the Active Server Pages, script-driven programming environment.

However, the code-behind approach is only a good first step. Other, and more important, steps are left to savvy developers.

So what are these steps? And, subsequently, what are the main drawbacks of the code-behind model?

Limited Code Visibility and Control

In a code-behind class, you basically write handlers only for user-interface events such as button clicks, selection changes, and text editing. All these event handlers are methods buried in the code-behind class. They are invoked in response to user-interface events, which in turn result from the ASP.NET run-time processing of postback HTTP requests.

Any method in a code-behind class is hardly visible to surrounding application code. Let's consider a sample code-behind class with a button click event handler:

```
public partial class WebForm1 : System.Web.UI.Page
{
    protected void Page_Load(object sender, EventArgs e)
    {
    }

    protected void Button1_Click(object sender, EventArgs e)
    {
        Label1.Text = "Clicked today at " + DateTime.Now.ToString();
    }
}
```

By default, any event handler in the class is marked as a *protected* member, which clearly means that only derived classes can call it. This is not the point, however. Let's suppose you edit the source code just shown to make the *Button1_Click* method public. I would still say what I did earlier: the method is *hardly visible* outside the class. As it is implemented in the preceding code snippet, you can simply call it from outside the class using the following code:

```
Button1_Click(null, EventArgs.Empty);
```

In more realistic scenarios, you might have to exercise some control over the method invocation. For this to happen, it would be nice if the method could provide a simple signature that doesn't force you to package arguments into a particular data structure.

Passing ad hoc parameters to *Button1_Click* is not impossible, but it's not immediate and not especially slick, either.

In addition, the ability to observe the state of the page class from outside is not something you get out of the box. You can write your event handlers in a way that favors visibility, but that's just not what the ASP.NET programming model spurs you on to do.

But what would be an external environment from which you might want to call such a method? Well, it could be, for instance, a unit test.

Limited Testability

When it comes to testability, two attributes of the code assume special importance: *visibility* and *control*. They are defined as follows.

The attribute of *visibility* indicates the ability to observe the current state of the method under test and any output it can produce. The attribute of *control*, on the other hand, refers to the degree to which the code allows testers to apply fixed input data to the method under test.

If testers have a way to programmatically observe a given behavior, they can easily test it against expected and incorrect values. That's why visibility does matter. Furthermore, any piece of software runs according to a virtual contract that includes preconditions. The easier you can configure preconditions, the easier you can write effective tests.

Testability can hardly apply to event handlers as written by default in a code-behind class. As a result, with the code-behind model you get some minimal separation between user-interface visuals and presentation logic. This separation is mostly physical as code is spread over two distinct files—markup and code.

You won't really get the much expected separation of concerns (SoC) between the process of calculating output values from input data and the process of generating a new HTML view based on freshly calculated data. The process is kind of hard-coded and based on an overall rendering algorithm with some placeholders interspersed for processing logic (for example, postbacks). The inherent level of testability of an ASP.NET Web Forms–based page is not really very high. And, moreover, it's not as high as today's applications generally require.

Tightly Coupled to Event Handlers

The code-behind model mandates that you have a *Page*-derived class to act as the outermost container of any presentation code you might have. Such a code-behind class consists of a collection of event handlers that reply to page and control events. Each event handler has its own fixed signature and is invoked according to a protocol that you, as a developer, do not control.

In ASP.NET Web Forms, an event handler is invoked during the processing of a postback request. When a postback request arrives, the ASP.NET runtime environment determines the ID of the HTML element that originated the postback. If a server control exists with a matching ID, the runtime checks whether the control is equipped for handling postback events. In particular, the runtime checks whether the control class implements the *IPostBackEventHandler* interface:

```
public interface IPostBackEventHandler
{
    void RaisePostBackEvent(string eventArgument);
}
```

If this is the case, the runtime invokes the *RaisePostBackEvent* method as defined on the posting control. Take a look at the following pseudo-code that closely follows the behavior of the *RaisePostBackEvent* method on the ASP.NET *Button* class:

```
protected virtual void RaisePostBackEvent(string eventArgument)
{
    :
    :

    this.OnClick(EventArgs.Empty);

    :
    :
}
```

```
protected virtual void OnClick(EventArgs e)
{
    // Retrieve the handler for the Click event
    EventHandler handler = FindHandlerForEventClick();

    // Call it
    if (handler != null)
    {
        handler(this, e);
    }
}
```

In Web Forms, the code in the handler of the postback event is ultimately the code responsible for processing the request. This central piece of code is always invoked through an event-based mechanism that naturally leads developers toward stuffing all the code in the handler without further (and often due) layering and without even thinking of SoC.

Further Layering Is Up to You

If you take it literally, the code-behind model doesn't really preclude SoC and the building of multiple layers of code in your ASP.NET Web Forms pages. Nothing prevents you from splitting any code that logically belongs to a postback handler across multiple user-defined layers. Your click event handler and the surrounding class, for instance, might look like this:

```
public partial class WebForm1 : System.Web.UI.Page, IWebForm1_View
{
    WebForm1_Controller _controller;

    protected void Page_Load(object sender, EventArgs e)
    {
        _controller = new WebForm1_Controller(this);
    }

    protected void Button1_Click(object sender, EventArgs e)
    {
        _controller.SetLabel();
    }

    public string IWebForm1_View.LabelText
    {
        get { return Label1.Text; }
        set { Label1.Text = value; }
    }
}

public class WebForm1_Controller : SomeBaseController
{
    IWebForm1_View _view;

    public WebForm1_Controller(IWebForm1_View view)
    {
        _view = view;
    }
```

```
    public void SetLabel()
    {
        _view.LabelText = "Clicked today at " + DateTime.Now.ToString();
    }
}
```

The controller class is loosely coupled to the host Web page through an interface. Nothing in the controller class requires ASP.NET to be tested. The controller class is fully reusable, as long as there's a scenario where you can really reuse it. Finally, the controller class can undergo a reasonable number of changes without any serious risks of breaking related code.

As you can see, you can add as many layers as you need and want in a Web Forms solution. And this is possible because of the open characteristics of the code-behind model.

However, you must be a disciplined (often, a self-disciplined) developer to get to this point. And, let's face it, this assumes you're not in a hurry.

Introducing Controllers

As you saw in Chapter 3, "The MVC Pattern and Beyond," separation of concerns is an old principle of software development that sets the foundation of well-designed and easy-to-test software. In a Web scenario, there are two primary concerns that a developer would ideally keep separate: how to *process* the request and how to *generate* the subsequent view.

A third concern is how to achieve both previous results in a way that smoothes out the testing process or, at a minimum, doesn't further hinder it.

Controllers in ASP.NET Web Forms

Abstractly speaking, the controller is a component that deals with the performance of any business-related tasks triggered within the page. A controller is invoked in response to some user action and likely needs some input data to do its job. Which other components will take care of passing data down to the controller?

In an ASP.NET Web Forms scenario, only the event handler can collect input data from the server controls and package it for the controller to proceed.

```
protected void Button1_Click(object sender, EventArgs e)
{
    // Collect input data for the controller.
    // Establish direct access to the properties of server controls.
    object param1 = ...;
    object param2 = ...;

    // Pass data down to the controller explicitly
    object results = _controller.PerformTask(param1, param2);

    // Use return values to refresh the view
    Label1.Text = results.NewTextForLabel1;
    :
}
```

The controller receives plain data that the code-behind class retrieves. In this scenario, the code-behind class ends up being tightly coupled to the details of the user interface. This is acceptable as long as it allows you to move much of the code out to a distinct class.

Views in ASP.NET Web Forms

What about any return values you might get from the pseudo-method *PerformTask* that was just shown? Those values, which result from any calculation triggered by the request, serve to refresh the view. Again, the code-behind class takes care of that.

Although a controller component can be quickly segregated from the host page, isolating the view subsystem from the rest of the code-behind page is quite a different matter. In Web Forms, the HTML in the view is mostly generated by server controls. Server controls, in turn, are easily controlled from the code-behind class.

How can you take the code that updates the view out of the code-behind class?

The simple answer is that there's no simple way to do that. A possible approach entails you wrapping the code that accesses server controls in a distinct command class and invoking a method on it, as shown here:

```
protected void Button1_Click(object sender, EventArgs e)
{
    // Collect input data for the controller.
    // Establish direct access to the properties of server controls.
    object param1 = ...;
    object param2 = ...;

    // Pass data down to the controller explicitly
    object results = _controller.PerformTask(param1, param2);

    // Use return values to refresh the view
    WebForm1_ViewEngine generator = new WebForm1_ViewEngine();
    generator.Render(results);
    :
}
```

To gain access to server controls, the pseudo-class *WebForm1_ViewEngine* must either inherit from the code-behind class or receive a pointer to that class. The benefits deriving from the former approach are fairly limited. You still have a dependency between the code-behind class and a new class—the bottom line is that you just add some overhead.

Injecting a reference to the code-behind class is a much better option. However, to gain enough separation from the context, it must be based on an interface that abstracts away the details of the Web page. I just showed the skeleton of this solution earlier in the "Further Layering Is Up to You" section.

> **Note** Patternwise, the solution hinted at in the "Further Layering Is Up to You" section is a simple but effective implementation of the popular Model-View-Presenter (MVP) pattern that we covered in Chapter 3.

Web Forms Views and Controllers Are Mostly About Overhead

The key consideration is that ASP.NET Web Forms certainly does let you add layers to segregate the logic behind a given request and the logic required to refresh the current view. The cleanest and most effective approach to achieve this goal is to use the Model-View-Presenter (MVP) pattern.

However, because of the overall architecture of Web Forms request processing, any form of separation of concerns results in extra work and overhead. Most of the time, this overhead is something you would happily trade for increased maintainability and testability. Even if extra overhead is clearly required, the side benefits are much more valuable in the context of complex, line-of-business applications.

Figure 4-1 shows where the overhead lies.

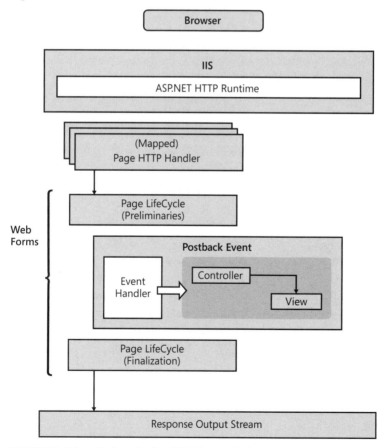

FIGURE 4-1 Where SoC applies in a Web Forms solution

Web Forms is built around a model that proceeds, step by step, from the parsing of the incoming request to the generation of HTML based on an ASPX page template. To change this way of working, you have two options, one of which is quite radical.

You can simply add SoC within the handler of the postback event, as shown in the figure and discussed in earlier code snippets. Using this approach, you don't cut off any of the built-in infrastructure, and instead just buy extra layers of code for the purpose of testability and maintainability. The approach delivers you a better solution from a design perspective, but it doesn't create any new architectural points.

You fix things nicely; you don't rationalize the architecture of your Web pages. This is why the second, more radical option—ASP.NET MVC—is here.

Testing in ASP.NET Web Forms

Just as with SoC, automated testing is definitely a feature you can choose to add on top of Web Forms pages, but it's not especially easy to attain.

Testing a Web page means being able to send it a *controlled* set of values and observe its state during the processing. You determine whether the test passed by looking at the output.

The final output of a Web page is pure HTML—that is, a potentially long string and not necessarily one with a unique representation of content. Testing is easier if you can define in a more formal way the expected output of the page.

A successful approach consists of abstracting the view to a set of values that the controller is responsible for producing. You then make the (reasonable) assumption that if the view data is correct, the view will render as expected. (See Figure 4-2.)

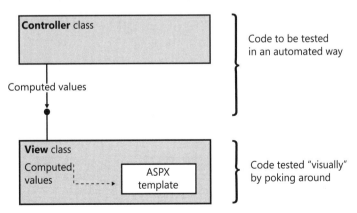

FIGURE 4-2 A testing scenario for Web Forms pages

You visually test the ASPX page and ensure that any given server controls are correctly bound to a specific member of the externally received collection of values. This code is not hard to test—either it works or it contains bugs that can be fixed quickly. From here, you make the assumption that if the view class receives correct data, it will produce the expected HTML.

You then use automated tests to check the controller class and verify it returns expected values based on received input.

The great news is that you no longer need to check HTML. The bad news, conversely, is that to get to this point you need to architect an MVP-like solution for each Web Forms page.

The bottom line is that if you're looking for SoC and testability, Web Forms is not necessarily the optimal solution. It can certainly be bent to achieve SoC and testability, but that doesn't spring naturally out of the architecture. Hence, be ready to make trade-offs between design improvements and overhead.

ASP.NET MVC is a different thing. Let's briefly review the mechanics of controllers and views in ASP.NET MVC, before taking the plunge into the implementation of controllers.

> **Note** In Figure 4-2, the box labeled "View class" symbolizes a traditional code-behind class that implements a user-defined interface. The interface is page specific and contains the list of values the page depends on for rendering. The simplification of the relationships between abstract entities such as controllers and views is a big advantage of using the ASP.NET MVC framework.

Mechanics of Controllers in ASP.NET MVC

In Chapter 2, "The Runtime Environment," I covered in detail the internal architecture of the runtime environment of ASP.NET MVC applications. However, I'm sure you'll find it useful to briefly revisit those details to see the different perspective of SoC and testability that you get when using ASP.NET MVC instead of Web Forms.

Processing HTTP Requests

In an ASP.NET MVC application, any request that hits the Web server is intercepted by the routing module and dispatched to a centralized HTTP handler—the MVC HTTP handler. The handler, in turn, looks at the content of the request (specifically, the URL format) and figures out the controller to use. This sequence is exemplified in Figure 4-3.

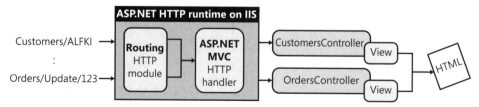

FIGURE 4-3 A request's path to its controller

It turns out that in ASP.NET MVC there's no page life cycle at all. The HTTP handler that takes care of the request is unique and not page specific. The overall scheme looks more like that of a desktop application where the user triggers some action, some action is performed, and then the user interface is updated.

You'll certainly agree that such a model has two huge advantages over Web Forms. First, it more naturally fulfills the need for SoC and testability. Second, it's significantly more straightforward and agile—and also faster.

The Central Role of Controllers

The adoption of an action-centric view of the request (vs. the page-centric vision of Web Forms) neatly separates the process of handling the request and the process of generating the next HTML view. In a way, the generation of the view becomes a task for a sort of black-box component—the view engine. You can even say that the generation of the view is a process outsourced to an external (and replaceable) provider.

When it comes to designing an ASP.NET MVC application, you don't reason much in terms of pages to author and code. Rather, you focus on the actions that a user might trigger from the displayed user interface. In other words, you focus on the use-case the Web page is called to implement.

A controller is a plain class with some public methods. Each method usually has a one-to-one link with a possible user action, such as changing a list selection or clicking a button.

From all this, it turns out that the role of controllers is central to the architecture of an ASP.NET MVC application.

Actions and Controllers

Although the controller's role in ASP.NET MVC is simple to understand overall and extremely attractive, former Web Forms developers can't help but raise some objections.

It's fine to have the ability to directly call a class to obtain a fixed behavior, but not at the price of giving away some much-needed capabilities of Web Forms, such as server controls, free data binding, authorization, error pages, and output cache. So in ASP.NET MVC, how do you deal with some common scenarios such as handling exceptions or caching the response generated by a request? Additionally, how do you handle authentication and authorization?

Each ASP.NET MVC request is ultimately directed at executing a method on a selected controller class. The controller's method runs, processes input data, executes some application logic, and figures out the view to use.

An ad hoc mechanism is required to functionally equalize a controller's method to a Web Forms event handler. This is exactly the role of *action filters* in ASP.NET MVC. An action filter is ultimately an attribute that decorates a controller's method to declaratively provide it with a pre-action and post-action behavior. As we'll see later in this chapter, some predefined action filters exist to specifically handle the display of error views, output caching, and authorization.

A Typical Controller Class

It's key to note that the responsibilities of the controller end with the identification of the view to show next. The view is responsible for generating the markup for the browser and for writing it in the output stream.

Here's the structure of a typical controller class with a couple of methods:

```
public class HomeController : Controller
{
    public ActionResult Index()
    {
        // Execute some application logic
        :
        :

        // Yield to the view engine. The name of the view
        // in this case defaults to the name of the method.
        return this.View();
    }

    public ActionResult About()
    {
        // Execute some application logic
        :
        :

         // Yield to the view engine. The name of the view
        // is explicitly specified.
        return this.View("About");
    }
}
```

A controller's method is expected to return an *ActionResult* object or any object that inherits from *ActionResult*. Most of the time, though, a controller's method doesn't directly instantiate an *ActionResult* object. It uses, instead, an action helper—that is, an object that internally instantiates and returns an *ActionResult* object. The method *View* in the preceding example provides an excellent example of an action helper. (More on this later.)

Controller Methods and Input Parameters

What about any input data that must be passed on to a controller's method? Any accessible input data is any data posted with the HTTP request. The ASP.NET MVC runtime groups any input data in a single container—the parameters dictionary. The dictionary is made available to any controller instance through a public property.

When writing the body of an action method, you can certainly access any available input through the familiar *Request* object and any of its child collections, such as *Form*, *Cookies*, *ServerVariables*, and *QueryString*.

However, the ASP.NET MVC runtime environment also offers another interesting feature—automatic parameter resolution. If you specify a parameter list in the signature of the action method, ASP.NET MVC attempts to match those parameter names to members of the parameters dictionary.

I'll return to input parameters for action methods later as we delve deeper into the anatomy of controllers.

> **Note** Automatic parameter resolution is free of charge as long as you adhere to the Convention-over-Configuration (CoC) paradigm. In practical terms, parameter resolution works automatically only if you can guarantee that the name of each formal parameter in an action method matches any of the element names in the parameters dictionary. The match is case insensitive. When you violate the convention, parameter resolution—more often referred to as *model binding*—is still possible but requires you to do some work on your own. Precisely, it requires you to write a custom model binder component. (I'll cover model binding in detail in Chapter 6, "Inside Models.")

Anatomy of an ASP.NET MVC Controller

The role of the controller is central to the architecture of ASP.NET MVC. For this reason, a controller class is expected to have a fixed structure and provide some well-defined characteristics. As a developer, though, when you write a new controller class you are actually absolved from fulfilling many of these requirements yourself.

Developers writing a controller class are simply required to define a public class with a few public methods. This controller class, however, must derive from a mandatory base class—the *Controller* class. In turn, the *Controller* class derives from a base class that implements a given interface.

Let's take the plunge into the internal structure of ASP.NET MVC controllers.

Inside the Structure of a Controller

The primary responsibility of a controller is executing any task associated with the incoming request. Around this key responsibility, a number of other features are built. In the end, a controller has quite a layered structure, as illustrated in Figure 4-4.

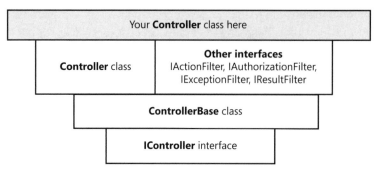

FIGURE 4-4 An interior view of a controller class

Let's start with the *IController* interface.

The *IController* Interface

The *IController* interface has a precise, single responsibility: executing the specified request context. A request context is the ASP.NET MVC abstraction that encapsulates information about the HTTP request that matches a defined route.

Admittedly, the purpose of the interface couldn't be clearer. A controller is expected to receive an HTTP request that matches any of the routes your application supports and execute it. Here's the definition of the interface as it appears in the *System.Web.Mvc* assembly. (The namespace of the interface is also *System.Web.Mvc*.)

```
public interface IController
{
    void Execute(RequestContext requestContext);
}
```

The *RequestContext* object is defined in the *System.Web.Routing* assembly as follows:

```
public class RequestContext
{
    public RequestContext(HttpContextBase httpContext, RouteData routeData);
    public HttpContextBase HttpContext { get; internal set; }
    public RouteData RouteData { get; internal set; }
}
```

As you can see, the context of an HTTP request is identified by the ASP.NET *HttpContext* object, and any data (controller name, method name, and optionally parameters) is extracted from the route.

> **Important** You should note the use of the ASP.NET MVC *HttpContextBase* class instead of the ASP.NET native *HttpContext* class. This is done to decouple the controller from the ASP.NET infrastructure for testing purposes. Essentially, *HttpContextBase* serves as the base class for classes that contain HTTP-specific information about an individual HTTP request.

The *ControllerBase* Class

The implementation of the *IController* interface is buried in the *ControllerBase* class, which is also defined in the *System.Web.Mvc* assembly. The class *ControllerBase* represents the base class for all ASP.NET MVC controllers. The structure of the class is shown here:

```
public abstract class ControllerBase : IController
{
    // Fields
    :
    :

    // Methods
    protected ControllerBase();
    protected virtual void Execute(RequestContext requestContext);
    protected abstract void ExecuteCore();
    protected virtual void Initialize(RequestContext requestContext);
    void IController.Execute(RequestContext requestContext);

    // Properties
    public ControllerContext ControllerContext { get; set; }
    public TempDataDictionary TempData { get; set; }
    public bool ValidateRequest { get; set; }
    public IDictionary<string, ValueProviderResult> ValueProvider { get; set; }
    public ViewDataDictionary ViewData { get; set; }
}
```

The role of each public property is explained in Table 4-1. These are properties that you may be using quite often in the development of your own controllers and, probably even more often, in the writing of unit tests for your controllers. So grabbing a solid understanding of their intended meaning and the information they carry out is an important achievement.

TABLE 4-1 Properties of the *ControllerBase* class

Property	Description
ControllerContext	Gets and sets an object that encapsulates the operational context of the controller. The controller context consists of the request context plus a reference to the controller itself. (More on this in a moment.)
TempData	Gets and sets a dictionary of data that persists across only two successive requests. Any data stored in the dictionary is accessible in the context of the next request, but it is then automatically discarded.
ValidateRequest	Indicates whether the request is valid. The constructor of the class sets it to *True*. The property is read/write.
ValueProvider	Gets and sets the parameters dictionary, which is a collection of values available to the controller that include the following, in this order: form values, route values, and query string values.
ViewData	Gets and sets a dictionary of values that the view object will receive to produce a new user interface following the controller's action.

What does the *ControllerBase* do in its implementation of the *IController* interface? Here's an illustrative code snippet:

```
void IController.Execute(RequestContext requestContext)
{
    this.Execute(requestContext);
}
protected virtual void Execute(RequestContext requestContext)
{
    if (requestContext == null)
    {
        throw new ArgumentNullException("requestContext");
    }
    this.VerifyExecuteCalledOnce();
    this.Initialize(requestContext);
    this.ExecuteCore();
}
```

In *ControllerBase*, the *Execute* method does some initialization work and then yields to another method for actual execution. The *ExecuteCore* method is marked as abstract and will be defined by inheritors, such as the class *Controller*.

The initialization of the controller is a simple task, as this code snippet shows:

```
protected virtual void Initialize(RequestContext requestContext)
{
    this.ControllerContext = new ControllerContext(requestContext, this);
}
```

All it consists of is the instantiation of the *ControllerContext* property. The *ControllerContext* type encapsulates information about the ongoing HTTP request and the controller. Even though *ControllerContext* doesn't have any parent class, it can be considered an extension of *RequestContext* that just adds a reference to the controller object in addition to route data and HTTP context.

```
public class ControllerContext
{
  // Fields
   :
   :

  // Methods
  public ControllerContext();
  protected ControllerContext(ControllerContext controllerContext);
  public ControllerContext(RequestContext requestContext, ControllerBase controller);
  public ControllerContext(HttpContextBase httpContext, RouteData routeData,
                         ControllerBase controller);

  // Properties
  public virtual ControllerBase Controller { get; set; }
  public virtual HttpContextBase HttpContext { get; set; }
  public RequestContext RequestContext { get; set; }
  public virtual RouteData RouteData { get; set; }
```

```
    // Properties available only in ASP.NET MVC 2
    public bool IsChildAction { get; }
    public ViewContext ParentActionViewContext { get; }
}
```

Aside from constructors, the *ControllerContext* class features a few additional properties. However, two of them—*HttpContext* and *RouteData*—exist mostly for convenience because the information they deliver is accessible through the *RequestContext* property. The additional piece of data you find in *ControllerContext* is just a reference to the underlying controller instance. In ASP.NET MVC 2, the new support for *render actions* led to introducing the concept of child actions, and subsequently two extra properties were added to the *ControllerContext* class. I'll return to child actions later in the chapter.

> **Note** Considering that the *ControllerContext* property is exposed by the controller class itself, what's the purpose of having a member of type *Controller* in the *ControllerContext* class? The operational context of the controller is being exchanged with the view engine and with the provider of temporary data that survives the current request and the next. In addition, it's used by the action invoker component to execute the action following a request. The action invoker needs a reference back to the controller to retrieve input parameters. For testability reasons, the action invoker class (usually, the *ControllerActionInvoker* class) needs to get an explicit reference to the controller. This is where *ControllerContext* fits in.

The *Controller* Class

The *Controller* class inherits from *ControllerBase* and adds a bunch of new methods and properties. All public and protected members of this class should interest you because your application's controllers ultimately inherit from *Controller*. In addition, the *Controller* class provides an override for the sole method on *ControllerBase* that remained abstract—*ExecuteCore*. Here's the signature of the *Controller* class:

```
public abstract class Controller : ControllerBase,
                                   IActionFilter,
                                   IAuthorizationFilter,
                                   IDisposable,
                                   IExceptionFilter,
                                   IResultFilter
{
    ⋮
}
```

We'll take a look at implemented interfaces in the next section. Table 4-2, instead, describes the behavior of prominent *Controller* methods. All methods in the table are protected, and most of them are internal. Only a few are virtual and can be overridden in your controller classes.

TABLE 4-2 Methods of the *Controller* class

Method	Description
Content	Internal and overloaded method. It gets some raw data (primitive data, custom objects) and returns a *ContentResult* object to render it to the browser.
CreateActionInvoker	Virtual method. It creates an action invoker to be used to govern the execution of action requests.
CreateTempDataProvider	Virtual method. It creates the actual container for data accessible through the *TempData* dictionary. By default, the temp data provider is an instance of the *SessionStateTempDataProvider* class.
Dispose	Virtual method. It performs application-specific tasks associated with freeing, releasing, or resetting unmanaged resources used by the controller.
ExecuteCore	Takes care of executing the action method as specified in the route data associated with the current request.
File	Internal and overloaded method. It returns a *FileResult* object used to render the content of a file. Content to render can be expressed in a variety of formats: file name, byte array, or stream.
HandleUnknownAction	Virtual method. It is called whenever a request matches the controller, but not an action method of the controller. The default implementation just throws an exception.
Initialize	Performs another step of initialization on the controller class. It first calls the base *Initialize* method (described earlier) and then instantiates a helper object for URL manipulation.
JavaScript	Internal and overloaded method. It returns a *JavaScriptResult* object that encapsulates a piece of script code to be written to the response stream.
Json	Internal and overloaded method. It returns a *JsonResult* object that encapsulates a JSON string resulting from the serialization of a given object.
PartialView	Internal and overloaded method. It gets a view name and returns a *PartialViewResult* object that renders a partial (that is, incomplete) view to the response stream. A partial view is much like a user control in Web Forms.
Redirect	Virtual method. It returns a *RedirectResult* object that contains information about the URL to redirect to.
RedirectToAction	Internal and overloaded method. It gets the controller name, action name, and route values. The method returns a *RedirectToRouteResult* object to redirect to the URL identified by the specified controller, action, and route parameters.
RedirectToRoute	Internal and overloaded method. It gets route name and route values. The method returns a *RedirectToRouteResult* object to redirect to the URL identified by the specified route and related parameters.

Method	Description
TryUpdateModel	Internal and overloaded method. It updates the specified model instance using values currently stored in the parameters dictionary exposed via the *ValueProvider* property. The method returns a Boolean value to indicate success or failure of the update.
UpdateModel	Internal and overloaded method. It works like *TryUpdateModel* except that it throws an exception if the update fails.
View	Internal and overloaded method. It returns a *ViewResult* object that renders a view (that is, a new page) to the response stream.

I'll cover the return values of controller methods later in the chapter. I'll take care of model updates in great detail in Chapter 6. Views, on the other hand, will be the main topic of Chapter 5, "Inside Views."

Before we go any further, it's worth spending a few more words to explain the differences between three apparently similar methods: *Redirect*, *RedirectToAction*, and *RedirectToRoute*. All three methods actually move the control to another view. In raw MVC terms, we would say that all redirect methods move to another MVC triad. The way in which you specify the next triad is different for each considered method.

The *Redirect* method is the simplest—it just redirects to the view represented by the specified URL. The *RedirectToAction* method, on the other hand, requires that you indicate the next view through the action (and, optionally, the controller and parameters) that renders it. You can also use *RedirectToAction* to switch from one controller to another. The method *RedirectToAction* assumes that you intend to redirect to the same route, perhaps changing the controller, action, and parameters.

The *RedirectToRoute* method works in much the same way as *RedirectToAction*, but it offers a bit more flexibility. *RedirectToRoute* explicitly requires that you specify the route name and, optionally, all of its parameters. In doing so, you can switch from one route to another. In light of their similarity, it's not coincidental that *RedirectToAction* and *RedirectToRoute* return an object of the same type—*RedirectToRouteResult*.

In spite of the surface difference, essentially all redirect methods work the same way—they collect parameters, build a URL, and then invoke the method *Redirect* on the *HttpResponse* object.

Tip If no method match is found, an override of *HandleUnknownAction* gives you the last chance to decide what to do. At a minimum, you can also use an override of *HandleUnknownAction* as a custom exception handler for unknown actions.

Table 4-3 details the properties of the *Controller* class.

TABLE 4-3 Properties of the *Controller* class

Property	Description
ActionInvoker	Gets and sets an *IActionInvoker* object for the controller. An action invoker defines the contract for invoking an action in response to an HTTP request. This object is responsible for the actual execution of the action.
Binders	Gets and sets the collection of model binders available for the application. A model binder is a sort of serializer for complex types that need to be passed around across requests. (More on this later.)
HttpContext	Gets all HTTP-specific information about the ongoing request.
ModelState	Gets a *ModelStateDictionary* dictionary object that represents the current state of the model object. The model object, if defined for a view, is populated with posted data. The *ModelState* dictionary contains information about anything that is wrong with the posted values. The property mirrors the *ModelState* property of the *ViewData* collection. Its primary use is to carry message errors to the view after the action method executed and validated posted data. (I'll return to *ModelState* in Chapter 6 and Chapter 7, "Data Entry in ASP.NET MVC.")
Request	Gets the ASP.NET MVC abstraction of the ASP.NET native *Request* object. It returns an instance of the *HttpRequestBase* class.
Response	Gets the ASP.NET MVC abstraction of the ASP.NET native *Response* object. It returns an instance of the *HttpResponseBase* class.
RouteCollection	Internal property. Gets and sets the collection of routes for the application.
RouteData	Gets the *RouteData* object for the current request. The *RouteData* object encapsulates information about a route, such as tokens and the route handler. The *RouteData* class also offers methods to read tokens with ease.
Server	Gets the ASP.NET MVC abstraction of the ASP.NET native *Server* object. It returns an instance of the *HttpServerUtilityBase* class.
Session	Gets the ASP.NET MVC abstraction of the ASP.NET native *Session* object. It returns an instance of the *HttpSessionStateBase* class.
TempDataProvider	Gets and sets the *ITempDataProvider* object responsible for storing data for the next request. The default provider stores data in the session state. The class is named *SessionStateTempDataProvider*.
Url	Gets and sets the helper object used to generate URLs using specified ASP.NET routes. The helper object is of type *System.Web.Mvc.UrlHelper*.
User	Gets the ASP.NET MVC abstraction of the ASP.NET native *User* object. It returns an object that implements the *IPrincipal* interface.

As you can see, the base class of the user-defined controller makes available several properties that provide handy access to request-specific information. Such information includes intrinsic ASP.NET objects such as *Session*, *Request*, and *Response*, and it also includes *User* for security information, route information, and the whole *HttpContext* object.

Note that intrinsic objects in ASP.NET MVC are wrappers for native ASP.NET intrinsic objects such as *Request* and *Response*. In addition, the *Controller* class exposes an ad hoc object for executing the action associated with the request. This object is the action invoker. Let's find out more.

Execution of a Request

Any requests that hit an ASP.NET MVC application are destined to be resolved with the invocation of an action method within a controller class. Defined on the *Controller* class, the *ExecuteCore* method is where the action method is actually invoked. Here's the source code of the method:

```
protected override void ExecuteCore()
{
    // Load temp data (if any) to be used in this request
    // (Nothing happens if this is a child action.)
    PossiblyLoadTempData();
    try
    {
        // Execute the action
        string actionName = this.RouteData.GetRequiredString("action");
        if (!this.ActionInvoker.InvokeAction(base.ControllerContext, actionName))
        {
            this.HandleUnknownAction(actionName);
        }
    }
    finally
    {
        // Save temp data (if any) for the next request
        // (Nothing happens if this is a child action.)
        PossiblySaveTempData();
    }
}
```

Essentially, the *ExecuteCore* method first attempts to populate the current instance of the *TempData* collection with any data that was previously stored for this request to consume. Next, it figures out from route data the name of the action method to execute and passes it to the action invoker.

The action invoker simply uses .NET reflection to execute the method and returns a Boolean value to denote success or failure. The action invoker obtains any input parameters required by the action method from the controller context.

The *ActionInvoker* property on *Controller* references an instance of the *ControllerActionInvoker* class. This class is architected to take into account action filters such as those for authorization and exception handling.

Filter Interfaces for a Controller

The *Controller* class implements a bunch of extra interfaces, as detailed in Table 4-4.

TABLE 4-4 Additional interfaces for class *Controller*

Interface	Description
IActionFilter	Defines methods for an action filter. An action filter defines actions to be taken before and after the execution of an action method.
IAuthorizationFilter	Defines methods for an authorization filter. An authorization filter checks whether the user that is attempting to execute the action method has enough rights to do it.
IExceptionFilter	Defines methods for an exception filter. An exception filter hooks up any exceptions that might occur during an action method.
IResultFilter	Defines methods for a result filter. A result filter defines actions to be taken before and after the execution of the result of an action method. For example, if you want to run your own code before and after the generation of the next view, you can take advantage of the methods of the *IResultFilter* interface.

The implementation of all the interfaces in Table 4-4 results in a few additional methods on the *Controller* class. Table 4-5 lists them and comments on them all.

TABLE 4-5 Filter methods in the class *Controller*

Method	Description
OnActionExecuting	Invoked just before an action method is executed.
OnActionExecuted	Invoked right after the execution of an action method is completed.
OnAuthorization	Invoked when authorizing the execution of an action method.
OnException	Invoked when an exception occurs in an action method.
OnResultExecuting	Invoked just before an action result is executed.
OnResultExecuted	Invoked right after the execution of an action result is completed.

All these methods are protected and virtual and can therefore be overridden in your controller classes to achieve more specialized behavior.

Behavior of a Controller

The typical behavior of a controller can be summarized in four main steps: getting input data, executing the request-related action method, preparing data for the view, and triggering the refresh of the view.

Input Parameters of an Action Method

Because an action method is invoked in response to an HTTP request, any input parameters it might need can be only data posted with the request. This includes query string values, form data, and cookies. Here's a quick example:

```
public class HomeController : Controller
{
    public ActionResult Index()
    {
        // Retrieve input parameters from the request. (Assuming there is a
        // value named Param1 in the posted data.)
        object param1 = Request["Param1"];
        // Execute some application logic
        :
        :


        // Prepare data for the view. This step may include some validation
        // on the data generated by the processing logic.
        :
        :


        // Yield to the view
        return this.View();
    }

    :
    :

}
```

The MVC HTTP handler in charge of the incoming HTTP request extracts any content from the HTTP packet and stores that in the *Request* property of the controller's instance being used. This *Request* property of controllers offers a programming interface nearly identical to that of the ASP.NET's *Request* intrinsic object. (Once more, bear in mind that the *Request* object used in the preceding snippet is *not* the ASP.NET intrinsic object but an ASP.NET MVC ad hoc wrapper object.)

To be precise, in the preceding code snippet we actually use the *Item* property on the *Request* object through its popular default syntax *Request[...]*. Note that when you use the default property on the *Request* object, it automatically searches for a matching variable name in up to four collections: *Form*, *Cookies*, *ServerVariables*, and *QueryString*.

If you need to retrieve an input value specified in the URL as a route value, you must resort to the parameters dictionary—precisely, the *ValueProvider* collection on the *Controller* class. This collection groups together route values with the content of the *Form* and *QueryString* collections.

Although perfectly functional, this approach is one you hardly use in any real-world code. Interestingly, in fact, the ASP.NET MVC framework can automatically map segments of the URL to parameters for an action method. This is another nice side effect of the Convention-over-Configuration paradigm so widely employed in ASP.NET MVC. This feature is known as *model binding*. To enable this behavior, all you need to do is change the signature of the action method to accommodate input parameters, as shown in the following example:

```
public class HomeController : Controller
{
    public ActionResult Index(int tabID)
    {
        // The value of tabID comes from a possible element named tabID
        // in the Form and QueryString collections or route data. The
        // parameter is undefined if no such match can be found.

        // Execute some application logic
        :
        :

        // Yield to the view
        return this.View();
    }
    :
    :

}
```

If the HTTP request contains posted values whose names match the names of any formal parameters of the method, those values are automatically passed to the action method. The match is case insensitive and results in an exception if any of the method parameters cannot be resolved.

If you mark input parameters in the method as nullable, you can avoid exceptions—provided, of course, that your code is ready to handle *null* parameters:

```
public class HomeController : Controller
{
    // Arguments in the signature are both nullable, so no exceptions are
    // thrown during the preliminaries of the method execution.
    public ActionResult Index(int? tabID, string topic)
    {
        // If you try to use parameter tabID without first
        // checking it against nullness, you are exposed to a
        // NullReference exception.
        int id = 0;
        if (tabID.HasValue)
            id = tabID.Value;

        :
        :

    }
    :
    :

}
```

Using automatic parameter resolution is a convenient and effective feature. However, it's a rather advanced framework feature and should be used only if you, as a developer, are fully aware of what it means and how it works. Otherwise, it might look like a fantastic piece of magic. And there should be no magic in software.

Using Complex Data Types in an Action Method

Automatic parameter resolution is not limited to situations in which you use primitive data types such as numbers and strings. Look at the following sample:

```
public class CustomerController : Controller
{
    // You expect the action method to receive a complex data type
    public ActionResult Detail(Customer customerID)
    {
        // ASP.NET MVC ensures that, under proper conditions,
        // the Customer object is built for you from posted data.
        :
        :
    }
    :
    :
}
```

As a matter of fact, an instance of the *Customer* class is rebuilt on the server and then passed on to the action method. However, any pieces of data that form the *Customer* instance have to be sent off to you over the HTTP request. A built-in component of the ASP.NET MVC framework—the model binder—makes an attempt to bind posted data to public members of the specified type—*Customer* in this case.

A default algorithm is applied that is hard-coded in the *DefaultModelBinder* class. The default algorithm entails that a public property on the target type is matched by name to an element of the form data collection. For example, property *CustomerID* on *Customer* gets a non-null value if a *CustomerID* item is found in the posted data—typically, because of a nondisabled *CustomerID* input field in the posting HTML form.

You can change the binding algorithm on a per-type basis by defining a model binder class. I'll show how to create custom model binders in Chapter 6.

> **Note** Design-by-contract is an old approach to software development that has been pushed aside in the Windows platform for too many years. Today, design-by-contract is gaining popularity also thanks to the Microsoft .NET Framework 4 and its Code Contract API. Simply put, design-by-contract recommends that you define for each method a sort of software contract where you clearly indicate what preconditions exist for the method to execute, what postconditions are expected at the end of execution, and what conditions never change before and after execution. In particular, preconditions provide a formal way of ensuring that all required parameters are available, their values are in the right range, and so forth.

Does it make sense to use preconditions in the development of action methods? You bet. Action methods are plain methods, and input validation is always a must. Preconditions are just an effective way to validate input for a method.

Action Methods

An action method is simply a public method defined on a class that inherits (either directly or indirectly) from *Controller*. By default, any public method on the controller class is considered an action method and is therefore callable from the browser via the default route or any other routes you might have.

Important You must be fully aware of the potential security issues that could result from the definition of a public method on a controller class. Because any public method is automatically an action method potentially callable over the Internet, you should make sure that any public methods of yours are OK to call for any users. Otherwise, you should either drop the *public* modifier for the method or secure the method so that only authenticated and authorized users can call it. Later on, in the "Attributes of a Controller" section, we'll explore security attributes for an action method.

Nonpublic methods are not recognized as action methods. If users place a request to a protected, private, or internal method on a controller class, the request fails with an HTTP 404 status code. (This, at least, is the default behavior that can be changed by overriding the *HandleUnknownAction* method on a controller class.)

A controller class, however, can also have public methods that are not exposed as action methods. To achieve this, you just decorate the method with the *NonAction* attribute, as shown here:

```
public class HomeController : Controller
{
    [NonAction]
    public void ConfigureControllerForTesting()
    {
        :
        :
    }

    public ActionResult Index()
    {
        :
        :
    }

    :
    :
}
```

Needless to say, a nonaction method is not bound to returning an *ActionResult* object. The signature of a nonaction method is entirely up to you.

When would it be desirable to have a public method that is not intended to be an action method?

A controller class can certainly have internal methods that action methods invoke to do their job. These nonaction methods, though, don't need to be public. A method that exists only for design and abstraction purposes is better modified to be a *protected* or perhaps *private* method.

So, again, when would it be useful to have public nonaction methods? Definitely, testing-specific methods configure a possible scenario. As in the code snippet just shown, you can have a public nonaction method that performs some configuration work to prepare the controller for testing. You might decide this is the way to avoid the burden of having to repeat that configuration code over and over again in your unit tests.

> **Note** As far as testing is concerned, you can also mark a test-only method as internal. In this way, the method would not be publicly visible but can still be used in unit tests if you declare the unit test assembly as a "friend" of the controller's assembly. This is achieved by adding a special attribute to the AssemblyInfo.cs file of the controller's assembly. The attribute to add is an assembly-level attribute named *InternalsVisibleTo*. The attribute takes a string parameter that bears the name of the friend assembly. In this way, all internals around the controller class are visible from within the unit test assembly.

Behavior of an Action Method

The purpose of an action method is to execute any business logic that is associated with the ongoing request and represented by the current URL. Most of the time, an action method will interact with the middle tier of the Web application. In other, less frequent, situations it's possible that the method performs some calculation internally and uses any results to prepare the view.

Essentially, an action method might need to hold (or acquire) a reference to some application-specific object that represents the gateway to the middle tier. Depending on how you have devised your business layer, this gateway might be a reference to an object in the *service layer*, a user-defined *repository* object for data access operations or, more directly, the entry point to an object model such as those encapsulated by Object/Relational Mapper (O/RM) tools such as NHibernate, Entity Framework, or even LINQ-to-SQL.

The action method is definitely responsible for creating, or obtaining, an instance of whatever gateway object it needs. Although some coupling between action methods and gateways is unavoidable and necessary, you should consider how to keep it to the lowest possible level.

Coupling can impact the testability of the controller. It's always desirable that you test controllers (and components in general) in full isolation from dependencies. This means that in real-world applications you might need to architect the controller class in a way that makes it easy and effective to inject any external dependencies, such as that to the middle-tier gateway, to the file system, or perhaps to the ASP.NET runtime environment. I'll return to this topic later when discussing design and testability issues for a controller.

Patterns for the Gateway to the Middle Tier

In the special flavor of MVC you get from the ASP.NET MVC framework, the controller is a sort of mediator between the user interface and the application's middle tier.

The controller is ultimately responsible for interacting with the topmost layer you have in the business logic. The shape and color of your business logic depend on the pattern you used to design it, and also on the required level of abstraction. The Service Layer pattern suggests that you define on top of your business logic a bunch of coarse-grained methods that map one-to-one to use-cases. Methods in the service layer essentially implement the application logic.

Instead of adding yet another layer, can you simply store all the orchestration logic required for processing a use-case in the action method itself? Sure, you can. And this is exactly the scenario that requires your action methods to hold a reference to components in the Data Access Layer (DAL) or directly to an O/RM root object such as the *DataContext* object in LINQ-to-SQL, the *ObjectContext* object in Entity Framework, and the *Session* object in NHibernate.

The Service Layer pattern serves the purpose of allowing you to use a cleaner design, and all it does is add another layer, which ultimately contributes to decoupling controllers from the middle tier.

There is, however, a sort of middle ground between using a Service Layer and creating direct DAL access—an implementation of the *Repository* pattern. A repository layer essentially groups data access operations in a way that abstracts DAL details away from the controller. A repository layer is a wrapper around O/RM or ADO.NET direct calls. As such, it might look dangerously similar to the Service Layer. So what's the difference?

The Service Layer is a collection of classes that belong to the business layer. The Repository is a collection of classes that belong to the data access layer. The Repository, therefore, is not supposed to include any orchestration logic, beyond that necessary to perform query and Create, Read, Update, Delete (CRUD) operations against the data model. If you opt solely for Repository, you should place any orchestration-specific and application-specific logic in the action method. A combination of the Service Layer and Repository patterns is not just possible but, moreover, welcome. However, consider that any new layer adds some overhead and turns out to be overkill in simple scenarios. On the other hand, never forget that layering is the most powerful tool you have to fight complexity.

I'll touch on business layer design issues again in Chapter 6. Anyway, a good reference for this kind of patterns is "*Microsoft .NET: Architecting Applications for the Enterprise,*" by Dino Esposito and Andrea Saltarello (Microsoft Press, 2008).

Passing Data to a View

After the action method has executed any tasks associated with the request, it likely holds some fresh data to be integrated in the next view to be displayed. In ASP.NET MVC, the generation of the view is delegated to a distinct layer of code—the view engine. Figure 4-5 shows the whole life cycle of an action method—from processing the input data to delivery of view data to the rendering engine.

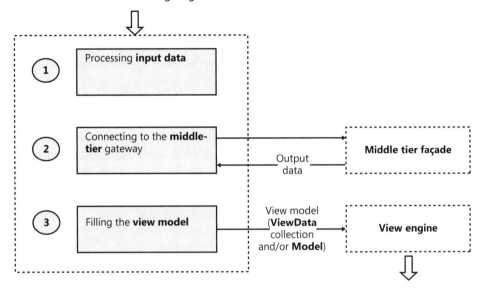

FIGURE 4-5 The life cycle of an action method

Because the view engine is distinct from the controller, it needs to receive any data required to generate the next browser view. Earlier in the chapter, while discussing the *ControllerBase* class (see Table 4-1), you briefly met a property named *ViewData* that is defined as follows:

```
public abstract class ControllerBase : IController
{
    :
    :

    public ViewDataDictionary ViewData { get; set; }
}
```

The *ViewData* property represents a built-in container used for passing data between a controller and a view. The property is of type *ViewDataDictionary*. The idea is that once the controller has executed a given action, it packs it into the *ViewData* container and gets any significant results to be shown to the user. The following code snippet, which is an extremely simple depiction, shows you what you get with any ASP.NET MVC project template:

```
public class HomeController : Controller
{
    public ActionResult Index()
    {
        // Pack data for the view
        this.ViewData["Message"] = "Welcome to ASP.NET MVC!";
```

```
            // Tell the view to render
            return this.View();
    }

        :
        :

}
```

The *ViewData* dictionary is definitely the object that contains a valid representation of the view-model—that is, any data being worked on in the view. You can add as many entries to the *ViewData* dictionary as you plan to consume from within the view class.

From within a view class, you then retrieve the content of the *ViewData* dictionary using the same syntax as just shown. Here's an example:

```
<!-- Snippet taken from an ASPX template in the Views folder -->
<%@ Page Language="C#" Inherits="System.Web.Mvc.ViewPage" %>
<h2><%= Html.Encode(this.ViewData["Message"]) %></h2>
```

What's different in the two snippets, of course, is the type of the *this* object, which exposes the *ViewData* property. It is a *Controller*-derived class in the first snippet; it is a *ViewPage*-derived class in the snippet just shown.

It's useful now to have a closer look at the type of the *ViewData* property—the *ViewDataDictionary* type.

The View-Model Container

As noted in Chapter 3, the *ViewDataDictionary* type is a class that implements the *IDictionary* interface, and it looks and behaves like a classic name/value pair, enumerable dictionary. Any data you store in a dictionary is treated as a plain *object* and requires casting, boxing, or both to be worked on. (This is nothing new for ASP.NET developers because it is the same model that you still use for managing the global ASP.NET cache or the session state.)

A dictionary is definitely not something you would call a *strongly typed* container. At the same time, though, a dictionary is straightforward to use and works just fine.

The *ViewDataDictionary* class is special because it also features a *Model* property, as shown here:

```
public class ViewDataDictionary : IDictionary<string, object>,
                                  ICollection<KeyValuePair<string, object>>,
                                  IEnumerable<KeyValuePair<string, object>>,
                                  IEnumerable
{
    public object Model { get; set; }
    :
    :
}
```

The *Model* property is an alternative and object-oriented way of passing data to the view object. Instead of fitting flat data into a dictionary, you can shape up a custom object that faithfully represents the data the view expects. In other words, the *Model* property just represents your chance of creating a *view-model* object that is unique for each view.

A view class that supports a strongly typed view-model must inherit from the generic version of *ViewPage*, as shown here:

```
<!-- Snippet taken from an ASPX template in the Views folder -->
<%@ Page Language="C#" Inherits="System.Web.Mvc.ViewPage< YourViewModel>" %>
<h2><%= Html.Encode(this.ViewData.Model.Message) %></h2>
```

Inheritance from *ViewPage<T>* ensures that the *Model* object is not null if data for it is received from the controller. In the view template, you refer to any properties in the view-model using the *ViewData.Model* path. As a developer, you are responsible for defining the structure of the view-model class—for example, the *YourViewModel* class in the preceding example.

I'll have much more to say about views and view-models in Chapters 5 and 6.

Note The term *view-model* is relatively new and is not mentioned in the original MVC formulation. However, today it should be considered a more precise term to refer to the object model that describes the data being worked on in the view. In a way, the expression *View Model* replaces what MVC originally called the *Model*. The reason for this change is that today with the advent of domain-related object models in the business layer, the term *Model* has become a bit overloaded and therefore unclear.

What do you mean exactly when you say "model"? Are you referring to the model used to represent data in the business layer? Or are you referring to the data as represented in the view? Additionally, are the two models the same?

When MVC was originally devised, the two models coincided. Today, this is no longer true. In addition, it's becoming false for more and more applications every day. That's why it's important to use the expression *view-model* to refer to the description of data worked on in the view. Other terms, such as *business data model* or *entity model*, work better to describe business data.

Finally, what about *object model* and *domain model*? The former term is fine to use but is a bit too generic. The latter, conversely, is too specific because it refers to an entity model with some very specific characteristics.

Return Value of an Action Method

An action method typically returns an object of type *ActionResult*. The type *ActionResult* is not a data container, though. More precisely, it is an abstract class that offers a common programming interface to execute some further operations on behalf of the action method. Here's the definition of *ActionResult*:

```
public abstract class ActionResult
{
    protected ActionResult()
    {
    }

    public abstract void ExecuteResult(ControllerContext context);
}
```

By overriding the *ExecuteResult* method, a derived class gains access to any data produced by the execution of the action method and triggers some subsequent action. Generally, this subsequent action is related to the generation of some response for the browser.

Because *ActionResult* is an abstract type, every action method is actually required to return an instance of a more specific type. Table 4-6 lists all predefined action result types.

TABLE 4-6 Predefined *ActionResult* types in ASP.NET MVC

Type	Description
ContentResult	Sends raw content (not necessarily HTML) to the browser. The *ExecuteResult* method of this class serializes any content it receives.
EmptyResult	Sends no content to the browser. The *ExecuteResult* method of this class just does nothing.
FileContentResult	Sends the content of a file to the browser. The content of the file is expressed as a byte array. The *ExecuteResult* method simply writes the array of bytes to the output stream.
FilePathResult	Sends the content of a file to the browser. The file is identified via its path and content type. The *ExecuteResult* method calls the *TransmitFile* method on *HttpResponse*.
FileStreamResult	Sends the content of a file to the browser. The content of the file is represented through a *Stream* object. The *ExecuteResult* method copies from the provided file stream to the output stream.
HttpUnauthorizedResult	Sends an HTTP 401 response code to the browser. The HTTP status code identifies an unauthorized request.
JavaScriptResult	Sends JavaScript text to the browser. The *ExecuteResult* method of this class writes out the script and sets the content type accordingly.
JsonResult	Sends a JSON string to the browser. The *ExecuteResult* method of this class sets the content type to the application or JSON and invokes the *JavaScriptSerializer* class to serialize any provided managed object to JSON.
PartialViewResult	Sends HTML content to the browser that represents a fragment of the whole page view. As mentioned, a partial view in ASP.NET MVC is a concept very close to a user control in Web Forms.
RedirectResult	Sends an HTTP 302 response code to the browser to redirect the browser to the specified URL. The *ExecuteResult* method of this class just invokes *Response.Redirect*.
RedirectToRouteResult	Like *RedirectResult*, it sends an HTTP 302 code to the browser and the new URL to navigate to. The difference is in the logic and input data employed to determine the target URL. In this case, the URL is built based on action/controller pairs or route names.
ViewResult	Sends HTML content to the browser that represents a full page view.

Note that *FileContentResult*, *FilePathResult*, and *FileStreamResult* derive from the same base class, *FileResult*. You use any of these action result objects if you want to reply to a request with the download of some file content or even some plain binary content expressed as a byte array.

PartialViewResult and *ViewResult* inherit from *ViewResultBase* and return HTML content. *ViewResult* is by far the most frequently used action result object in an ASP.NET MVC application. A view result object is also significantly more complex than any other action result. A view result object, in fact, deals with the currently registered view engine—a replaceable component—and accesses the view-model. As we'll see in more detail in Chapter 5, a view engine gets an input template and the view-model and produces HTML. The input template, however, doesn't have to be an ASPX file. Whether it is ASPX markup, XAML, or plain XML depends exclusively on the capabilities of the selected view engine.

> **Note** What if your controller action method doesn't return *ActionResult*? First and foremost, no exceptions are raised. Quite simply, ASP.NET MVC encapsulates any return value from the action method (numbers, strings, or custom objects) into a *ContentResult* object. The execution of a *ContentResult* object causes the plain serialization of the value to the browser. For example, an action that returns an integer or a string will get you a browser page that displays data as is. On the other hand, returning a custom object displays any string resulting from the implementation of the object's *ToString* method. If the method returns an HTML string, any markup will not be automatically encoded and the browser will likely not properly parse it. Finally, a *void* return value is actually mapped to an *EmptyResult* object whose execution just causes a no-op.

More often than not, an action method doesn't directly create and return an *ActionResult* object. As shown in Table 4-2, the base *Controller* class features a bunch of helper methods that you internally create and that return an appropriate *ActionResult* object. The most popular of these helper methods is *View*. Here's the list of overloads for the method:

```
ViewResult View();
ViewResult View(object model);
ViewResult View(string viewName);
ViewResult View(IView view);
ViewResult View(string viewName, object model);
ViewResult View(string viewName, string masterName);
virtual ViewResult View(IView view, object model);
virtual ViewResult View(string viewName, string masterName, object model);
```

The method can accept the view name, the master page name, and the view-model. All parameters are optional and, if not specified, are resolved in some way internally. In some cases, the *View* method might also accept an *IView* object that points it directly to an internal object ready for rendering. (I'll say more about the rendering mechanism in Chapter 5.)

Attributes of Controllers and Action Methods

In .NET, attributes are a declarative way of attaching some specific behavior to a class or a method. The behavior of both the controller class and its methods can be further specialized using a number of attributes.

There are three categories of attributes that affect a controller class and its methods: filters, invocation attributes, and action selectors.

Filter Attributes

A *filter* is a piece of code that can be attached to a few predefined stages during the execution of an action method. Table 4-7 lists the built-in filters available in ASP.NET MVC.

TABLE 4-7 **Predefined filters in ASP.NET MVC**

Filter	Description
AsyncTimeout	Marks an action method as one that will execute asynchronously and terminate in the specified number of seconds. A companion attribute also exists for asynchronous methods that do not set a timeout. This companion attribute is *NoAsyncTimeout*. *This is available only in ASP.NET MVC 2.*
Authorize	Marks an action method as one that can be accessed only by specified users, roles, or both.
ChildActionOnly	Marks an action method as one that can be executed only as a child action during a render-action operation. *This is available only in ASP.NET MVC 2.*
HandleError	Marks an action method as one that requires automatic handling of any exceptions thrown during its execution.
OutputCache	Marks an action method as one whose output needs to be cached.
RequireHttps	Marks an action method as one that requires a secure request. If the method is invoked over HTTP, the attribute forces a redirect to the same URL but over a HTTPS connection, if that's ever possible. *This is available only in ASP.NET MVC 2.*
ValidateAntiForgeryToken	Marks an action method as one that requires validation against the antiforgery token in the page for each POST request.
ValidateInput	Marks an action method as one whose posted input data might (or might not) need validation.

If filters are applied to the controller class instead of individual methods, they will have an effect on all action methods exposed by the controller.

All the attributes listed in Table 4-7 derive from base class *FilterAttribute*, which defines a base property—*Order*. The *Order* property indicates the order in which multiple attributes will be applied. Note that by default the *Order* property is assigned a value of –1, which means that the order is unspecified. However, any filter with an unspecified order is always executed before a filter with a fixed order.

An important attribute is not listed in Table 4-7 because it is an abstract class—the *ActionFilter* attribute. This class represents the base class for all action filter attributes—that is, those attributes that allow you to execute custom code before and after the execution of the action method and before and after the generation of the result. The *ActionFilter* attribute class is defined as follows:

```
public abstract class ActionFilterAttribute : FilterAttribute,
                                              IActionFilter,
                                              IResultFilter
{
    protected ActionFilterAttribute();
    public virtual void OnActionExecuted(ActionExecutedContext filterContext);
    public virtual void OnActionExecuting(ActionExecutingContext filterContext);
    public virtual void OnResultExecuted(ResultExecutedContext filterContext);
    public virtual void OnResultExecuting(ResultExecutingContext filterContext);
}
```

Of all the attributes listed in Table 4-7, only *OutputCache* and *AsyncTimeout* derive directly from *ActionFilter*. So what's the ultimate purpose of the *ActionFilter* attribute? It is the base class from which you can create your own custom action filters. Examples of custom action filters are a component that logs the method's execution and, perhaps, a component that applies GZIP compression to any response sent out by a given action method. I'll cover customizable components of ASP.NET MVC–like action filters in Chapter 11, "Customizing ASP.NET MVC."

Figure 4-6 diagrams the steps performed during the execution of an action method, taking into account action filters.

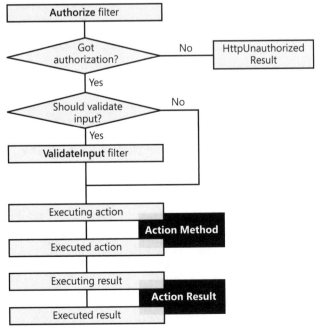

FIGURE 4-6 Invoking an action method with filters

Any exceptions resulting from the execution of the action method will be trapped by the filter installed with the *HandleError* attribute, if any.

The *Authorize* Attribute

You use the *Authorize* attribute when you want to make sure that only authorized users can gain access to a particular method or to any action methods in a given controller. Here's an example:

```
[Authorize]
public ActionResult Index()
{
     .
     .
     .
}
```

In this way, the method executes only if the current user is authenticated. No check is made against the user name or role. To enforce only certain users or roles, you simply add more named parameters to the attribute, as shown here:

```
[Authorize(Roles="admin, poweruser", Users="DinoE, FrancescoE")]
public ActionResult Index()
{
     .
     .
     .
}
```

If a user is not authenticated or doesn't have the required user name or role, the authorization filter returns an HTTP 401 status code. Interestingly enough, this status code is never displayed to the user. Let's find out why.

By default, any ASP.NET MVC application has the FormsAuthentication HTTP module in place. This HTTP module registers its own handler for the *EndRequest* application event. As expected, the FormsAuthentication HTTP module then captures the end of the failed request that returns an HTTP 401 code. The FormsAuthentication HTTP module is programmed to automatically redirect to the login page if an HTTP 401 status code is detected.

As a result, if you attempt to invoke an action method without being authenticated and authorized, you are redirected to the login page. (See Figure 4-7.)

Note that the *Authorize* attribute doesn't distinguish between users who are not logged in and logged-in users that do not have the rights to invoke a given action method. In both cases, the attempt to call the action method fails and the user is redirected to the login page.

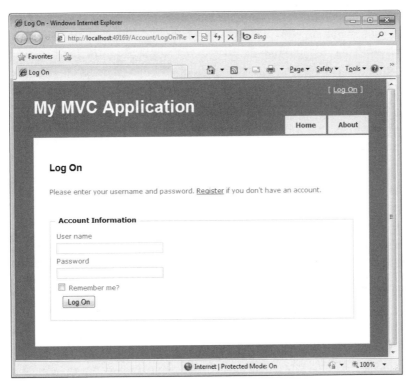

FIGURE 4-7 An unauthorized user is redirected to the login page.

You might or might not like this behavior. If you do not, one thing you can do is create an enhanced attribute class, as shown here:

```
public class AuthorizeExAttribute : AuthorizeAttribute
{
    public override void OnAuthorization(AuthorizationContext filterContext)
    {
        base.OnAuthorization(filterContext);
        CheckIfUserIsAuthenticated(filterContext);
    }

    private void CheckIfUserIsAuthenticated(AuthorizationContext filterContext)
    {
        // If Result is null, we're OK
        if (filterContext.Result == null)
            return;

        // If here, you're getting an HTTP 401 status code
        if (filterContext.HttpContext.User.Identity.IsAuthenticated)
        {
            ViewResult result = new ViewResult();
            result.ViewName = "Error";
            filterContext.Result = result;
        }
    }
}
```

In the new class, you override the *OnAuthorization* method and run some extra code to check whether you're getting HTTP 401. If this is the case, you then check whether the current user is authenticated and redirect to your own error page. The net effect is that if you're getting HTTP 401 because the user is not logged in, you'll go to the log-in page. Otherwise, if the request failed because of authorization permissions, the user will receive a friendly error page. Using the new attribute couldn't be easier:

```
[AuthorizeEx(Roles="admin", Users="DinoE")]
public ActionResult Index()
{
    .
    .
    .
}
```

Note This said, however, I wonder whether a more radical solution wouldn't be even better. What if you prevent users from accessing protected resources prior to the users attempting to access them by simply disabling or hiding links and buttons? In this case, there would be no need to worry about why the request failed.

The *HandleError* Attribute

You use the *HandleError* attribute when you want to set up a safety net to protect your controller (or just a particular method) from run-time exceptions. The *HandlerError* attribute tells the ASP.NET MVC framework that a custom error page should be displayed in lieu of the standard yellow screen of death if an unhandled exception occurs.

The default custom error page is *error.aspx*, which is defined under the Views\Shared folder. Note, though, that you can override this error page by defining another *error.aspx* page in the controller-specific folder under the Views folder.

When you attach the *HandleError* attribute to a method (or, more likely, to the whole controller class), you won't notice any special behavior on your development machine until you modify the *web.config* file, as shown next. Note that you must modify the global *web.config* file, not the *web.config* file you might find under the Views folder:

```
<customErrors mode="On">
</customErrors>
```

With the default settings for the *customErrors* section, only remote users will see a generic error page. Local users (for example, developers) will be deliberately shown the classic error page with detailed information about the stack trace.

By default, the *HandleError* attribute catches any exceptions both during the execution of the action method and the subsequent rendering of the view. You can, however, restrict your control over only a few exceptions, as shown here:

```
[HandleError(ExceptionType=typeof(NullReferenceException), View="SyntaxError")]
[HandleError(ExceptionType=typeof(InvalidOperationException), View="InternalError")]
public ActionResult Index()
{
    :
    :
}
```

The preceding code won't be able to trap unhandled exceptions beyond the two exception types explicitly listed. If you want to handle all exceptions in a default way and just provide two personalized views for certain exceptions, you add a parameterless *HandleError* attribute to the action method.

In Chapter 8, "The ASP.NET Infrastructure," I'll return to the topic of exception handling in ASP.NET MVC applications to put it in a wider perspective that includes search-engine optimization and redirection.

 Note Any views you specify for error handling will be first sought in the controller-specific folder under the Views folder and then in the Shared folder under Views.

The *OutputCache* Attribute

The *OutputCache* attribute integrates ASP.NET MVC with the output-caching feature of classic ASP.NET. Using the attribute is trivial:

```
[OutputCache(Duration=10, VaryByParam="None")]
public ActionResult Index()
{
    :
    :
}
```

The *Duration* parameter indicates in seconds how long the method's response should stay cached in memory. The *VaryByParam* attribute, on the other hand, indicates how many distinct versions of the response you should cache—one for each distinct value of the specified property. If you use *None*, you tell the system you don't want multiple versions of the same method's response.

The *ValidateAntiForgeryToken* Attribute

A Cross-Site Request Forgery (CSRF) attack is easy to prepare, and it can be as disruptive as the notorious cross-site scripting (XSS) attack. A CSRF attack consists of finding a victim who loads a fake page into his browser on his computer. The fake page contains some hidden script code and markup that posts some data to a server. OK, where's the problem?

Because the post occurs from the victim's computer, any authentication cookies on the machine are uploaded. If successful, a CSRF attack enables the hacker to upload his own data through the victim's account with the remote server and also makes him capable of gaining full control over the victim's credentials.

How can you avoid all of this?

ASP.NET MVC makes available a couple of tools—a helper method to generate some ad hoc HTML markup and the *ValidateAntiForgeryToken* attribute.

You might want to apply the *ValidateAntiForgeryToken* attribute to any action methods that work over the HTTP POST verb:

```
[AcceptVerbs(HttpVerbs.Post)]
[ValidateAntiForgeryToken]
public ActionResult Edit(Customer customer)
{
    :
    :
}
```

The attribute contains some code that kicks in during the authorization phase of an action method request. At this time, the attribute code ensures the posted request contains a cookie and a form field with a common fixed name. If any of these items are missing, an exception is thrown. Otherwise, the attribute ensures that the content of both the cookie and the input field match. Figure 4-8 shows an antiforgery exception.

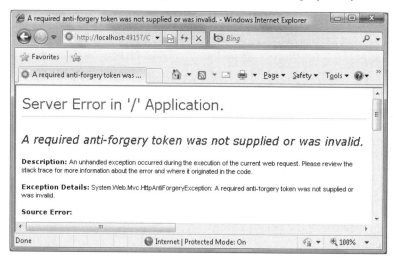

FIGURE 4-8 An antiforgery exception

Who's responsible for adding the security cookie and input field? That's where the HTML helper method comes into play. In any view that might post some critical data to the server, add the following within a *<form>* tag:

```
<%= Html.AntiForgeryToken() %>
```

The *Html.AntiForgeryToken* method creates a cookie on your machine and adds a hidden field to the form, as shown here:

```
<input name="__RequestVerificationToken"
       type="hidden"
       value="O87cIVi274xnacCCSZfy+wPRwzwW4wNMRtPJFISV8EJtOEm7MsfUc7GCN2MZyN7k" />
```

If the action method target of the form is decorated with the *ValidateAntiForgeryToken* attribute, the content of the cookie and input field are checked before the action method is authorized.

> **Note** Two questions arise quite naturally. Why is CSRF so dangerous? Why is the ASP.NET MVC antiforgery barrier so safe? CSRF is dangerous because of the nature of the Web. An action method can be publicly invoked because it's there on the Internet. Sure, you can require that the caller be authenticated, but there's not much you can do if the hacker uses a legitimate user to post malicious data on her behalf. This is just what CSRF does.
>
> The two-fold antiforgery token added by ASP.NET MVC prevents a hacker from forging an ad hoc form. The hacker can't create a valid cookie because she doesn't know the content to put in it. And even if the victim's machine already contains an antiforgery cookie (because of a previous legitimate operation against the site), the content of the cookie can't be read via script to arrange a form input field on the fly. An antiforgery cookie is *HttpOnly* and can't be accessed via script.
>
> Is this enough to protect your sites from CSRF attacks? This mechanism protects only POST action methods and requires cookies to be enabled on the client machine. In addition, be aware that this barrier can be easily circumvented if other parts of your application are vulnerable to cross-site scripts. In this case, in fact, external scripting is possible, so it is possible to read the content of the antiforgery cookie.

The *ValidateInput* Attribute

In ASP.NET, any data you post is automatically validated to check whether it contains potentially dangerous characters. The check spans the data in the posted form, the query string, and cookies. As an example, if you attempt to enter HTML tags in a form field, when submitting it you will inevitably incur a request validation exception. The same occurs in ASP.NET MVC.

In classic ASP.NET, this feature is controlled via the *ValidateRequest* Boolean property that you can set on a per-page basis via the *@Page* directive. Alternately, you can set the property for all pages in the application by tweaking the *web.config* file.

The built-in validation layer for the requested content certainly is not a silver bullet, and many times it becomes more of an issue than a lifesaver. It's not uncommon for developers to just disable automatic request input validation and replace it with a made-to-measure custom validation layer.

In ASP.NET MVC, though, the techniques in classic ASP.NET that disable request validation do not work. Alternately, you are given the *ValidateInput* attribute:

```
[AcceptVerbs(HttpVerbs.Post)]
[ValidateInput(false)]
public ActionResult Edit(Customer customer)
{
    .
    .
    .
}
```

The preceding code disables any built-in input validation on the content being posted to the *Edit* action method. Rest assured that it's safe to disable automatic input validation only if you add your own validation layer for input data. Failure to do so properly and you're inviting disaster, however.

Invocation Attributes

All the attributes we considered so far can be applied to both controllers and individual methods. A couple of other attributes—specifically, *AcceptVerbs* and *ActionName*—are useful only if applied to action methods.

The *AcceptVerbs* attribute allows you to specify which HTTP verb is required to execute a given method. Let's consider the following example:

```
[AcceptVerbs(HttpVerbs.Post)]
public ActionResult Edit(Customer customer)
{
    .
    .
    .
}
```

Given that code, it turns out that the *Edit* method can't be invoked using a GET. If no *AcceptVerbs* attribute is specified, the controller default action is to process the request as GET. Note that multiple *AcceptVerbs* on a single method are not allowed. Your code won't compile if you add multiple *AcceptVerbs* attributes to an action method. The *AcceptVerbs* attribute takes any value from the *HttpVerbs enum* type.

```
public enum HttpVerbs
{
    Get = 1,
    Post = 2,
    Put = 4,
    Delete = 8,
    Head = 0x10
}
```

In ASP.NET MVC 2, GET, POST, and PUT verbs can be associated with methods using simpler attributes: *HttpGet*, *HttpPost*, and *HttpPut*, respectively.

You perform an HTTP GET command when you follow a link or type the URL to the address bar. You perform an HTTP POST when you submit the content of an HTML form. Any other HTTP command can be performed only via AJAX or perhaps from a Windows client that sends requests to the ASP.NET MVC application.

The ability to assign a specific verb to a given action method naturally leads to duplicate method names. Two methods with the same name are acceptable in a controller class as long as they accept distinct HTTP verbs. Otherwise, an exception will be thrown, because ASP.NET MVC doesn't know how to resolve the ambiguity.

The *ActionName* attribute allows you to decouple the method name from the action name. The following code is perfectly valid:

```
[ActionName("Edit")]
[AcceptVerbs(HttpVerbs.Post)]
public ActionResult EditViaPost(string id)
{
    string customerID = id;
    return RedirectToAction("Edit",
            new RouteValueDictionary(new { id = customerID }));
}

[ActionName("Edit")]
[AcceptVerbs(HttpVerbs.Get)]
public ActionResult EditViaGet(string id)
{
    :
    :

    return View("Edit");
}
```

The code features a controller class with two methods that have different names but share the same *ActionName* attribute. The code works as long as the two methods accept different HTTP verbs. In particular, note that the *EditViaPost* method redirects to the action method named *Edit*. Because a redirect is actually a GET, the *EditViaGet* method will be invoked next.

Another scenario where the *ActionName* attribute is useful is when you have overloaded methods in a controller class. In this case, the attribute helps you to disambiguate the references. Here's an example:

```
[ActionName("Refresh")]
[AcceptVerbs(HttpVerbs.Post)]
public ActionResult Update(string id)
{
    // Refreshes the entire record
    :
    :

}
```

```
[ActionName("Update")]
[AcceptVerbs(HttpVerbs.Post)]
public ActionResult Update(string id, string company, Contact contact)
{
    // Selectively updates only company and contact
     :
     :
}
```

Action Selector Attributes

The *AcceptVerbs* attribute as well as the aforementioned *NonAction* attribute have the base class in common. In particular, both attributes are action selector attributes in that they decide when and how an action method is invoked. Starting from the base class *ActionMethodSelectorAttribute*, you can create your own action selector attributes.

The *ActionMethodSelectorAttribute* class is a simple abstract class and contains just one method to override:

```
public abstract class ActionMethodSelectorAttribute : Attribute
{
    protected ActionMethodSelectorAttribute()
    {
    }

    public abstract bool IsValidForRequest(
            ControllerContext context,
            MethodInfo methodInfo);
}
```

The implementation of the *IsValidForRequest* method is entirely up to you. All that matters is which Boolean value you return from the method. *True* means that the method can be executed; *false* indicates that the method is not a good match for the request.

The following code shows a selector attribute that enables any tagged method to run only on a particular day of the week. (Admittedly, this is not a piece of code you can likely reuse, but it's certainly an amusing and illustrative example.)

```
public class DayMethodAttribute : ActionMethodSelectorAttribute
{
    private DayOfWeek _dayOfWeek = DayOfWeek.Sunday;

    public DayMethodAttribute(DayOfWeek day)
    {
        _dayOfWeek = day;
    }

    public override bool IsValidForRequest(
            ControllerContext controllerContext,
            MethodInfo methodInfo)
    {
        return IsToday();
    }
```

```
    private bool IsToday()
    {
        return (DateTime.Now.DayOfWeek == _dayOfWeek);
    }
}
```

The *IsValidForRequest* method simply checks whether the current day of the week matches the expected day of the week associated with the method. Here's how you attach the attribute to a method:

```
[DayMethod(DayOfWeek.Tuesday)]
public ActionResult Index()
{
    // This method runs only on Tuesdays
    :
    :
}
```

More serious and useful examples of action selector attributes are attributes that enable a method to execute only if it has been invoked through an AJAX call, if it has been invoked from a particular IP address, or if the request contains a given header.

Writing a Controller

Even though *IController* and *ControllerBase* are defined and publicly documented, it's not recommended that you build your controllers from the ground up. Inheriting from *Controller* saves you a lot of preparatory work without limiting your programming power.

The writing of a controller class can be summarized in two simple steps: creating a class that derives from *Controller* and adding a bunch of public methods.

The definition of the range of methods that belong to a particular controller, instead, is a very delicate art and deserves a bit of preliminary analysis. Another point that deserves some attention is to decide whether or not you actually need to create your own application-specific base controller class.

Design of a Controller Class

Visual Studio makes it easy to create your own application-specific base controller class. It tells you to right-click on the Controllers folder in the open ASP.NET MVC project and choose to add a new controller class, as shown in Figure 4-9.

Visual Studio also offers to create a bunch of action methods for you that address common CRUD scenarios. Is that really all that you need?

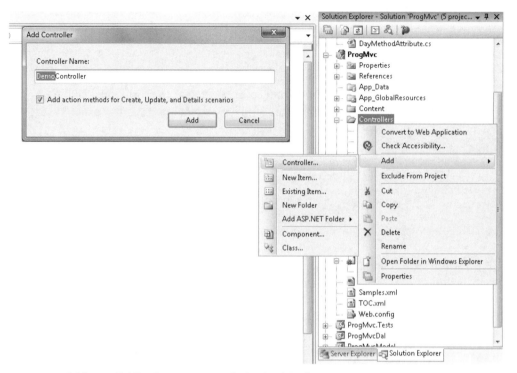

FIGURE 4-9 Adding scaffolding for a new controller in Visual Studio

Honestly, the Visual Studio facilities are good at making sense of ASP.NET MVC and its controller objects, but they're of little help when it comes to designing a real-world application.

You devise your controller classes based on two factors: granularity and responsibilities. The final set of controller classes should effectively meet the needs of the presentation layer, be easy to test, be easy to maintain and evolve, and map nicely to any URL scheme you might have in mind for the application.

Mapping Functions to Controllers

In an ASP.NET MVC application, controllers exist to respond to any requests a user makes from within the user interface. Any possible interaction between the user and the application is typically described by a use-case. As an architect, you start from use-cases to form a clear idea of the functions that a user should be able to perform through the application.

Your next task will *simply* be mapping functions to controller classes.

There are no fixed rules as far as the granularity of controller classes is concerned. No technical reasons prevent you from having a single all-encompassing controller class;

likewise, there are no technical hurdles blocking you from having one controller class for each possible request.

You're now at the point of partitioning off the set of functions in a *balanced* number of controller classes. How you do that depends on the functions and, more importantly, on the *vision* of the application that emerges from use-cases. As a rule of thumb, you should endeavor to have one controller class for each significant entity in the domain of the problem your application is called to solve.

In a commercial site, it's likely that you face use-cases that require CRUD operations on customers, orders, and invoices. You can then start with an *OrderController* to let customers create a new order as well as update or delete existing orders. In doing so, you must stay focused on the needs of the presentation layer and put aside, as momentarily irrelevant, the needs of the entity model for the business layer.

If you deal with orders, you likely need to deal with order details and products. However, although *Order*, *OrderDetail*, and *Product* are all good candidates to become a member of the entity model (or domain model if you apply the domain-driven design methodology), only *Order* makes sense as the inspirer of a controller class. From the user-interface perspective, in fact, a user will place commands only to create, update, or delete an order. If that's the case, it's then OK to have an *OrderController*, but it's not OK to have an *OrderDetailController*. A quick rule is the following:

Have a controller for each business entity that is directly exposed to the presentation layer.

This might be only the first pass, though.

Suppose that one of the use-cases require you to let users view invoices. An *InvoiceController* class will then be in order to serve the users' needs. In a commercial site, though, you'll likely provide a back-office section for administrative work, such as processing orders and invoices. In this case, it might be useful to have a distinct controller to support back-office operations on orders and invoices. Another quick rule is the following:

Have a controller for each business entity that is directly exposed to the presentation layer *and for each operational context.*

In the end, the mapping of functions to controllers, and the subsequent mapping of methods to controllers, is certainly not an exact science. However, with the correct and systematic application of a key design principle, you can really achieve a design that's acceptable to all stakeholders in the project. The principle is the *Single Responsibility Principle* (SRP). The two quick rules outlined earlier descend from SRP as applied to controllers in an MVC scenario.

The Single Responsibility Principle

The essence of SRP is that any software module—whether a class, a service, a component or even a procedure—should have just one reason to change. What, then, is a "reason to change"?

A class that focuses on doing just *one thing* needs to be changed only if requirements change for that single feature. Hence, a class that focuses on doing just *one thing* has just one reason to change.

The principle stresses the need to have highly cohesive classes that expose a set of strongly and logically related methods. All methods in a class contribute to serve just one purpose—the single responsibility of the class. SRP is about cohesion, and in software, cohesion measures the distance between the logic expressed by the various methods of a class. To get a better grasp of software cohesion, think for a moment about what cohesion means in another field—chemistry. In chemistry, cohesion is a physical property of a substance that indicates the attraction existing between like molecules within a body. Methods in the body of a class should be similar to like molecules in the body of a substance.

So SRP is about having classes with just *a few* methods. But how few? The concept of "a few" here is rather vague and relates to the actual single responsibility. It's impossible to set a physical boundary for "a few" and say, for example, that it can never exceed 10 or 30. A class should have only the methods that logically participate in the implementation of a single purpose.

This said, it's hard to imagine an SRP-compliant class with 30 or more methods. If this is the case, well, you're probably giving a class a single responsibility—but too big of one! (A quick rule of thumb is keeping an eye on the vertical scrollbar when you edit the file in Visual Studio. Ideally, the scrolling area is kept to a minimum.)

Mapping Behavior to Methods

All in all, the trickiest part of the design process is mapping functions to controllers. After you have established a comprehensive list of controllers, it should be clear which methods belong to each controller. A controller's methods are known as *action methods*—and the name couldn't be more appropriate. In a controller class, you're going to have one method per user action that falls under the (single) responsibility of the controller.

How do you code an action method? Earlier in the chapter, I identified some common steps that all action methods should implement. The template of an action method can be summarized as follows:

- **Get input data**   An action method can get input arguments from a couple of sources—route values and collections exposed by the *Request* object. ASP.NET MVC doesn't mandate a particular signature for action methods. For testability reasons, it's preferable that any input parameter is received through the signature. Avoid, if you can, methods that retrieve input data programmatically from *Request*. Preconditions also help to ensure that no incorrect values are passed down the layers of the system.

- **Perform the task**   At this point, the method does its job based on input arguments and expected results. Most of the time, the method needs to interact with the middle tier and any interaction takes places through ad hoc dedicated services. Validation of calculated values occurs at this stage.

- **Fill the view model**   At the end of the task, any (computed or referenced) values that should be incorporated in the response are added to the view model. The view model can be a plain dictionary of name/value pairs or a view-specific, strongly typed object.

- **Prepare the result object**   In ASP.NET MVC, a controller's method is not responsible for producing the response itself. It is, however, responsible for triggering the process that will use a distinct *View* object to render content to the output stream. The method identifies the type of response (file, plain data, HTML, JavaScript, or JSON) and sets up an *ActionResult* object as appropriate.

Does this sound easy overall? Well, another tricky aspect is how you devise the code that performs the task.

Action Methods and Stereotypes

Generally speaking, an action method has two possible roles. It can play the role of a *controller* or it can be a *coordinator*. For completeness, I should say that the method can also be a *service provider*; however, this won't likely happen in real-world applications.

Where do words like *controller*, *coordinator*, and *service provider* come from? Needless to say, in this context the word *controller* has nothing to do with an ASP.NET MVC controller class.

These words refer to *object stereotypes*, a concept that comes from a methodology known as Responsibility-Driven Design (RDD). Normally, RDD applies to the design of an object model, but some of its concepts also apply neatly to the relatively simpler problem of modeling the behavior of an action method.

 Note   For more information about RDD, check out *Object Design: Roles, Responsibilities, and Collaborations*, by Rebecca Wirfs-Brock and Alan McKean (Addison-Wesley, 2002).

A *stereotype* refers to a set of traits that characterizes the behavior of an object or, as in this case, a method. Table 4-8 details the RDD stereotypes that might apply to an action method.

TABLE 4-8 Stereotypes that might apply to an action method

Stereotype	Description
Controller	Refers to a behavior in which the method directs activities and makes most of the important decisions regarding its assigned task.
Coordinator	Refers to a behavior in which the method delegates work to other components and is limited to orchestrating the various steps of its assigned task.
Service provider	Refers to a behavior in which the method just performs a particular operation with no interaction with the outside world.
	This role doesn't realistically apply to an action method because it implies an overall, one-step, simple task that doesn't require connections to other layers or tiers. It would be good for quick demos, but not for a real-world application. In RDD, a service provider is commonly a component that controllers and coordinators work with.

So should an action method play the role of a *controller* or *coordinator*?

That mostly depends on the architecture of your business layer. An ASP.NET MVC controller class belongs to the presentation layer and needs to get in touch with other layers to perform any significant task. Figure 4-10 provides a graphical view of a classic layered architecture focused on ASP.NET MVC on the presentation layer.

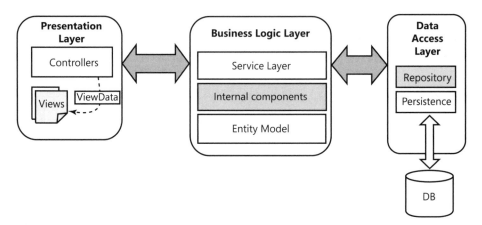

FIGURE 4-10 A typical layered architecture that is common to many ASP.NET applications

If you implement the Service Layer pattern in the Business Logic Layer (BLL), your action methods simply delegate the performance of their task to a method on the service layer:

```
[AcceptVerbs(HttpVerbs.Post)]
public ActionResult Update(Customer customer)
{
    // The code below determines a tight relationship between the controller
    // and service layer. The service instance should be injected into the
    // controller class instead of being created.
```

```
    CustomerServiceLayer service = new CustomerServiceLayer();
    service.UpdateCustomer(customer);

    // Back to the Edit view
    return View("Edit");
}
```

By design, a service layer is made of coarse-grained methods that map to UI functions. This is to say that from an action method you can easily find a matching method to call on the service layer. In this case, your action method clearly plays the role of the *coordinator*—which is the most desirable option from a testing and maintenance perspective.

If you implement the Repository pattern, or if you just expose the native persistence interface (for example, Entity Framework's *ObjectContext* object), you end up with an action method that plays the role of the *controller*. It incorporates all the logic necessary to perform the task. Here's a code snippet if you have direct access to the persistence layer:

```
[AcceptVerbs(HttpVerbs.Post)]
public ActionResult Update(Customer customer)
{
    // Get the entity model handle
    MyAppEntities context = new MyAppEntities();

    // Apply changes
    // This pseudo-syntax is based on features in Entity Framework 4
    context.Customers.ApplyChanges(customer, ...);

    // Save to storage
    context.SaveChanges();

    // Back to the Edit view
    return View("Edit");
}
```

A solution in which the action method gains direct access to the persistence layer results in intrinsically more coupled code that can get even worse as the complexity grows. You clearly see that, in this case, the action method is directing activities and making any decisions required for the task to perform its duties.

Let's consider the Repository pattern using an update scenario. If you have implemented the Repository pattern, your update action code will look like this:

```
[AcceptVerbs(HttpVerbs.Post)]
public ActionResult Update(Customer customer)
{
    // Tight coupling between controller class and repositories. The
    // instance of the repository should ideally be injected into the controller.
    CustomerRepository rep = new CustomerRepository();
    rep.UpdateCustomer(customer);

    // Back to the Edit view
    return View("Edit");
}
```

So what's the difference between this approach and the Service Layer pattern? Why is it that using a repository configures a *controller* role, whereas using the service layer upgrades the action method to the rank of a *coordinator*? Is a coordinator role always preferable?

Action Methods: Coordinator vs. Controller

Admittedly, you might not see the difference between a coordinator and a controller from the preceding trivial code. It's exactly the complexity of the code, however, that constitutes the difference. A service layer refers to a much higher level of abstraction than a plain repository. As mentioned earlier, the service layer belongs to the BLL, whereas the repository is part of the DAL. The repository encapsulates only data access operations; the service layer encapsulates all operations in the use-case being implemented.

In a more complex scenario, the performance of a UI-invoked task likely spans multiple entities and repositories and requires multiple database operations. If this is the case, you end up filling the action method with multiple calls to repositories and perhaps internal BLL components. The overall code then slowly leads the action method into a controller role.

But it doesn't end there. Giving an action method the role of the coordinator gets you a couple of nontrivial benefits.

First, testing the controller in isolation is much easier because you have to mock up only one dependency—the service layer class—which is a class of yours. If the controller depends on, say, Entity Framework, you will have a much harder time testing in isolation.

Second, think about deployment and scalability. The controller lives on the Web server within the boundaries of the ASP.NET worker process. What about the DAL? Ideally, the DAL lives on the same machine as the database. If you have a distinct database server, either you end up placing a bunch of remote database calls (when the DAL is in the same tier as controllers) or, worse, you place a number of cross-tier calls to the DAL (when the DAL is on the database server). With a service layer, you make just one cross-tier call from the presentation per action. In addition, you have an extra layer to scale out if you have scalability issues.

> **Note** If you're considering the use of a simpler Repository layer in the DAL and then decide to place it on a tier distinct from controllers, you have the problem of remoting the Repository interface. In practice, this means creating a Windows Communication Foundation (WCF) service around your repository classes. At this point, you probably want to make the WCF service interface a bit chunky to avoid the RPC-like communication antipattern. In doing so, you simply move from a Repository pattern to a Service Layer pattern. Think of it in advance then!

Design Is Design, Regardless of Whether or Not It's for the Web

Although ASP.NET MVC gently leads you down the right path for software design, it doesn't really have the superhuman power of stopping you from screwing things up. Even in the strongly object-oriented world of ASP.NET MVC, you can end up writing bad code.

As I see things, one of the biggest differences between Web Forms and ASP.NET MVC from the developer's standpoint is that ASP.NET MVC requires you to possess some design skills before you can effectively start and to have a clear architectural vision of what you're building. Put another way, ASP.NET MVC is not as forgiving as Web Forms can be and makes learning as you go significantly harder. Trial and error can really be a dangerous approach in ASP.NET MVC.

Want practical advice? Don't mistake ASP.NET MVC views and Web Forms pages. They're actually the same thing as far as display is concerned. However, they are radically different entities as far as design is concerned. When you design a Web Forms application, you focus on pages and you map functionalities to pages. In ASP.NET MVC, you should focus on functions instead and map them to controllers and methods. A view in ASP.NET MVC, therefore, is simply a piece of the infrastructure that merges a template for the page with some input data. No code at all belongs to the view.

To complete the parallel, in Web Forms a page mixes a template with code and the code is responsible for generating data and for mapping data to elements in the template. It is a much more entangled graph of relationships that forms a (perfectly working) black box.

The way you approach the design of functionalities in ASP.NET MVC is different and requires preparation, skills, and possibly an unbiased mind. If you are still stuck finding the best way to render a "page" as a "view," the best thing you can do is add a plain Web Forms page to an ASP.NET MVC application.

The right way to approach ASP.NET MVC is by the classic rules of analysis and design. You identify the functions that need to be implemented and find the right component that can take care of that. This component will return some output values to you. You pass these values to a component that will merge them into a template to produce HTML. In ASP.NET MVC, design is plain design; it's not different from the design of a Windows or Windows Presentation Foundation (WPF) application or a service. Gone are the days when a Web application has to be devised (if not implemented) using a made-to-measure set of principles and design guidelines.

Should You Use Your Own Base Class?

An aspect you might want to seriously consider when writing a controller class is adding an extra layer of common functionality in an intermediate controller class. You define your application-specific base controller class and inherit your working controllers from there. In this way, you can have available in all of your working controllers an additional set of properties.

The question mark in the title of the section suggests that there might be situations in which an application-specific base controller class is not required. Frankly, I believe you should always have your own base class for any application of some complexity.

How should you measure complexity here? The number of requirements? The frequency of requirements changes? Complexity is a nebulous concept and, overall, something that is hard to describe but easy to recognize when you see it.

As far as ASP.NET MVC is concerned, I'd say that when you start having quite a few controllers, you might find it useful and more productive to move some common functionalities out to a superclass.

Signature of a Controller SuperClass

A firm point about the new superclass is that it will inherit from *Controller*. The following class definition doesn't really move any code around, but it creates an extra layer that adds flexibility to the whole solution:

```
public class MyControllerSuperClass : Controller
{
}
```

The next question is also the most critical—what kind of functions would you add to the superclass?

The *MyControllerSuperClass* class creates a safe and clean environment for overriding some of the *Controller* virtual methods without mixing action methods and internal features. For example, you can override the *ExecuteCore* method of *Controller* to add logging capabilities:

```
public class MyControllerSuperClass : Controller
{
    // We should make the setter internal and provide for it during the construction
    // of the controller. However, this is not possible unless we set up a custom
    // controller factory. We'll see how to do that in Chapter 11.
    public ILogger Logger { get; set; }

    protected override void ExecuteCore()
    {
        // Capture the name of the action being executed.
        string action = this.RouteData.GetRequiredString("action");
```

```
        // Log before executing
        if (Logger != null)
        {
            Logger.Log("Executing [{0}] action at {1}",
                        action, DateTime.Now.ToString());
        }
        // Execute as usual
        base.ExecuteCore();

        // Log after execution
        if (Logger != null)
        {
            Logger.Log("Executed [{0}] action at {1}",
                        action, DateTime.Now.ToString());
        }
    }
}
```

The *MyControllerSuperClass* superclass now features an additional member—*Logger* of a custom type *ILogger*:

```
public interface ILogger
{
    void Log(string format, params object[] args);
}
```

MyControllerSuperClass now has a dependency on the *ILogger* type, which is a good thing. It would have been much worse if *MyControllerSuperClass* retained a dependency on an actual implementation of *ILogger*. In the preceding code, *MyControllerSuperClass* injected a member of type *ILogger* as an external dependency. This is a great achievement for testability.

The preceding code doesn't show how the *Logger* property initialized and when. I briefly hinted at dependency injection, but dependency injection is the means. It doesn't say much about the time at which injection can occur. I'll get back to this point in a moment. Let's see a couple of other features you can easily stuff in a controller superclass, such as exception handling and your own policy for unknown actions.

> **Note** Dependency injection (DI) is simply a pattern according to which a class exposes injection points for external callers to pass it references to specific objects. Common injection points are the constructor of the class, a public property, or perhaps the signature of a method. This is what dependency injection is all about. It turns out that any code required to retrieve and instantiate external objects pertains to the caller. And it is fairly repetitive code. This is where Inversion of Control (IoC) frameworks kick in. They essentially automate the implementation of the DI pattern. We could even say that IoC frameworks are an idiom of DI.
>
> As you might have figured out already, some really powerful code results from the integration of an IoC framework and a controller superclass.

Centralized Exception Handling

The aforementioned *HandleError* attribute enables centralized exception handling for a single action method or all methods in a controller. Filter attributes are inheritable, so if you add *HandleError* to the superclass, all derived controllers automatically gain the ability to trap exceptions:

```
[HandleError]
public class MyControllerSuperClass : Controller
{
    :
    :
}
```

The preceding code doesn't prevent you from adding a more specific version of the *HandleError* attribute in your actual controllers to trap a particular exception and redirect to an ad hoc view.

In addition, you can still override the *OnException* method in the *MyControllerSuperClass* class to set up your own exception-handling mechanism:

```
protected override void OnException(ExceptionContext filterContext)
{
    // Your exception handling logic here
    :
    :
}
```

The *OnException* method is guaranteed to be invoked whenever an unhandled exception occurs in the execution of the action.

Handling Unknown Actions

The controller superclass is also an excellent place to store any common logic you want to employ to handle the invocation of an unknown action. All you do is override the method *HandleUnknownAction,* as shown here:

```
protected override void HandleUnknownAction(string actionName)
{
    // Your logic here to handle unknown actions
    :
    :
}
```

The logic for unknown actions is good to have to avoid nasty HTTP 404 failures and possibly a generic error view. Specifying the wrong action is logically a different error than HTTP 404. For this reason, you might want to employ your own logic and display a nice error message to the user while making it clear to search engines that the requested URL is not valid. Furthermore, you don't want to reiterate the same fairly vanilla logic over and over again for each controller you write. A superclass comes to the rescue, as shown here:

```
protected override void HandleUnknownAction(string actionName)
{
    // Your logic here to handle unknown actions
    :
    :

    // Fill in the view model
    string format = "Action <b>[{0}].[{1}]</b> is not supported.";
    this.ViewData["Message"] = String.Format(format,
            this.ControllerMoniker, actionName);

    // Set the status code for search engines
    this.Response.StatusCode = 404;

    // Switch to a nice user-specific view from here
    this.View("CustomError").ExecuteResult(this.ControllerContext);
}
```

After you have caught the unknown action and performed any related tasks (for example, logging), you are ready to display a message to the user. Typically, you want to show both controller and action name in the message. The action name can be obtained from the argument list; the controller name must be obtained programmatically. The new *MyControllerSuperClass.ControllerMoniker* property does that by reading the controller name from the route data:

```
private string _controllerMoniker = String.Empty;
public string ControllerMoniker
{
    get
    {
        if (String.IsNullOrEmpty(_controllerMoniker))
            _controllerMoniker = this.RouteData.GetRequiredString("controller");
        return _controllerMoniker;
    }
}
```

To inform the user that an unknown command has been sent, the simplest thing to do is invoke the *View* method on the controller class to get a *ViewResult* object. Next, you call *ExecuteResult* to render the view:

```
this.View("CustomError").ExecuteResult(this.ControllerContext);
```

Here's some sample code that shows the *CustomError* view. (I'll cover views in the next chapter.)

```
<h2>
<%
    string msg = "Sorry, an error occurred while processing your request.";
    if (this.ViewData.ContainsKey("Message"))
        msg = this.ViewData["Message"] as string;
%>
<% = msg %>
</h2>
```

Figure 4-11 shows the effect of having a handler for unknown actions.

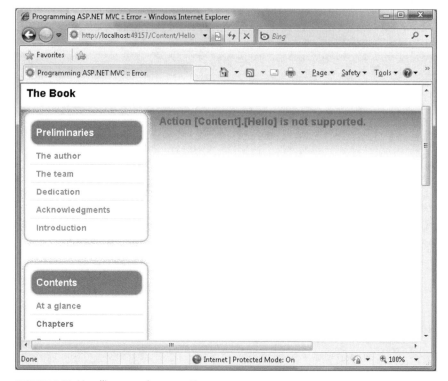

FIGURE 4-11 Handling an unknown action

Displaying a view is more effective than redirecting to an action or to an error page. In the example, the HTML view based on the *CustomError* template is just the response to invoking an unknown action—no extra work and no extra roundtrips.

Managing Dependencies

In ASP.NET MVC, a controller class is not simply a class with a bunch of public methods. It is responsible, for example, for connecting to a number of external components, not the least of which is the gateway to the middle tier. In addition, the controller is responsible for supporting a number of cross-cutting concerns (for example, logging, security, localized information to pass on to the view, or caching).

Each of these concerns might require an external dependency—that is, an object that must either be instantiated by the controller or created outside the controller and passed to it. A controller superclass is perfect for providing this infrastructure.

A way to approach the task is to define an application-wide context class that groups all dependencies shared by all controllers. Here's an example:

```
public class ApplicationContext
{
    // Constructors
    public ApplicationContext()
    {
        Initialize(null, null);
    }
    public ApplicationContext(ServiceLayerContext context)
    {
        Initialize(context, null);
    }
    public ApplicationContext(ServiceLayerContext context, ILogger logger)
    {
        Initialize(context, logger);
    }

    // Properties
    public ServiceLayerContext ServiceLayerContext { get; private set; }
    public ILogger Logger { get; private set; }

    // Methods
    private void Initialize(ServiceLayerContext context, ILogger logger)
    {
        .
        .
        .
    }
}
```

In *ApplicationContext*, you group objects that need to be instantiated and then injected in the controller for execution and testing purposes. You won't place properties (or methods) here, such as *ControllerMoniker*, that are resolved in terms of the members of the internal context of the controller itself.

The method *Initialize* is responsible for resolving any dependencies for which an explicit value is not provided as an argument:

```
private void Initialize(ServiceLayerContext context, ILogger logger)
{
    // Ensures that ServiceLayerContext member and its child members are instantiated
    this.ServiceLayerContext = (context ?? new ServiceLayerContext());
    if (this.ServiceLayerContext.ContentServiceLayer == null)
        this.ServiceLayerContext.ContentServiceLayer = new ContentServices();

    // Repeat for any members in the service layer context
    .
    .
    .
```

```
        // Ensures that Logger is instantiated
        this.Logger = (logger ?? new FileLogger(...));
    }
```

Let's skip over the details of the *ServiceLayerContext* class for a moment. For now, suffice it to say that it represents the gateway to the middle tier.

At this point, you have a unique object that groups all dependencies required by a nontrivial controller. How would you pass this object down to the controller? Here's some code:

```
public class MyControllerSuperClass : Controller
{
    public MyControllerSuperClass() : base()
    {
    }
    public MyControllerSuperClass(ApplicationContext appContext) :
    this()
    {
        _appContext = (appContext ?? new ApplicationContext());
    }

    // Fields
    private ApplicationContext _appContext = null;
    :
    :

    // Properties
    public ApplicationContext ApplicationContext
    {
        get
        {
            if (_appContext == null)
                _appContext = new ApplicationContext();
            return _appContext;
        }
        set
        {
            _appContext = value;
        }
    }

    :
    :
}
```

The best deal is if you can provide a double constructor—the default parameterless constructor plus one that receives an *ApplicationContext* object as an argument. The ASP.NET MVC framework will use the default constructor to create instances of any derived class.

The second constructor is provided for testability reasons. In a unit test, in fact, you might want to inject an instance of *ApplicationContext* that points to fake objects. An ad hoc constructor greatly simplifies this task.

When the default constructor is used, however, you need to provide a built-in code path that instantiates *ApplicationContext*. The *getter* method of the property seems to be the ideal place.

The Controller's Factory

The instantiation of a controller class is an operation that takes place outside the reach of your code. A made-to-measure factory class takes care of that. The ASP.NET MVC framework provides such a class in the form of *DefaultControllerFactory*.

The *DefaultControllerFactory* class defaults to using the parameterless constructor and fails if it doesn't exist. If you want to change something in the process of creating a controller instance, you have no other choice than to write and register your own controller factory. I'll discuss this in greater detail in Chapter 11, which is dedicated to customizing the various pieces of the ASP.NET MVC puzzle.

A nice feature you can easily implement in the factory (and exactly the feature I'll be demonstrating in Chapter 11) is the use of an IoC container to resolve automatically all dependencies at the same time in which a new instance of the controller is created.

> **Note** In ASP.NET MVC, it's mandatory that the name of the controller class is made of two tokens—a moniker and the suffix *Controller*. For example, valid names for classes are *HomeController*, *CustomerController*, *MenuController*, and the like. However, when a method requires you to specify a controller name (for example, one of the overloads to the *Controller*'s *RedirectToAction* method), you should indicate only the moniker without the *Controller* suffix. If you fail to do so, ASP.NET MVC won't be able to recognize the controller class and an exception will be thrown.
>
> There's just one place in the full framework where the moniker is matched to an actual controller type—in the factory class and, specifically, in the *GetControllerType* method. By overriding that method, you can circumvent the default convention of having a trailing *"Controller"* string in every controller class name. However, I'm not saying that you have to break the convention; nonetheless, the extreme flexibility of the ASP.NET MVC framework also makes that possible.

Special Capabilities

As you have seen, the primary purpose of a controller is serving the needs of the user interface. Any server-side functions you need to implement should be mapped to a controller method and triggered from the user interface. After performing its own task, a controller's method selects the next view, packs some data, and orders it to render.

This is the essence of the controller's behavior. However, other characteristics are often required in a controller, especially when controllers are employed in large and complex applications with particular needs, such as frequent updates to the user interface, numerous commands to deal with, or long-running requests.

The following section covers additional capabilities you can take advantage of when working with controllers.

Grouping Controllers

How many controllers do you expect to have in your application? The answer mostly depends on the complexity of the application. Suppose you have 50 controllers (and assume that you've balanced the responsibilities well among controllers). Typically, you end up with all of these 50 classes packaged within the single *Controllers* folder of the project. And what about views?

Under the single Views folder, you will find up to 50 subfolders, each with a bunch of view templates such as ASPX files. In a nutshell, your project is quite messy and hard to manage. Most of the time, a single *Controllers* folder is enough for many—maybe most—applications written with ASP.NET MVC, but sometimes it's not enough.

As of ASP.NET MVC 1.0, there is not much you can do to split the project, or just controllers, into distinct folders. A few attempts have been made by prominent members of the ASP.NET community to find an effective way to partition controllers into groups without breaking the routing capabilities of ASP.NET MVC.

In ASP.NET MVC 2, however, a new feature has been added that addresses exactly this point.

The Rationale Behind Areas

Areas provides a means of partitioning large applications into multiple blocks (named *areas*), each of which can be developed independently. From the perspective of developers, an *area* provides a way to group controllers (and related views) in smaller and more manageable collections.

The whole idea of areas is nothing new, as it was a feature originally offered by Castle MonoRail—an open-source Model2-based framework for building Web applications on the .NET platform. (See *http://www.castleproject.org/monorail*.) According to MonoRail, all controllers always belong to an area and any project consists of at least one default and unnamed area.

> **Note** One could even cynically say that the whole idea of ASP.NET MVC is also nothing new. On the other hand, isn't this what I repeatedly pointed out in Chapter 1 and Chapter 3? ASP.NET MVC builds on top of the Model2 pattern created some 15 years ago for Java Server Pages and more recently revamped for the .NET platform by Castle MonoRail. But it does add some nice goodies of its own.
>
> Software, like science, has an inherent cumulative nature: what you do today can possibly inspire someone else tomorrow to build a similar-but-improved product which, in turn, might inspire you and so forth in what is hopefully an endless chain. A graduate instructor of mine summed it up when he said, "As for software reuse, steal everything you can."

The ability to group controllers in areas is beneficial also because it leads you to partition your application into discrete functionalities. If you feel the need to go beyond the default single group of controllers, you are forced to think in terms of logical functionalities that emerge out of your requirements. When areas are used, an application grows up as a collection of distinct applets managed under the umbrella of a single solution.

This said, I feel the need to reinforce the key statement about areas. Areas are not for just any application. Areas come to the rescue when you are having a hard time taming dozens of controllers and views. If your application deals with blogs, forums, and news logical sections, you might want to dedicate an area to each in such a way that each area can be architected and developed in relative isolation with no naming conflicts between controller classes and view templates.

Defining Areas in Your Project

Visual Studio tooling for ASP.NET MVC 2 makes it easy adding areas to a project. You start with a classic ASP.NET MVC project and then add as many areas as you need. By default, a new ASP.NET MVC comes with the default area. By right-clicking on the project node, you can start adding new areas. At this stage, an area is identified by its name. Figure 4-12 shows a sample Visual Studio project with two additional areas defined—*Account* and *Store*.

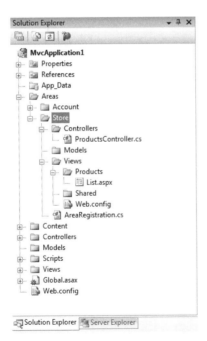

FIGURE 4-12 Areas in an ASP.NET MVC 2 project

Each area looks like a small subproject and owns its collection of controllers, views, and view-model classes. As in the figure, each *Views* folder contains its own copy of the *web.config* file. In addition, a new *AreaRegistration.cs* class file is added for each area.

The next step for you as a developer is adding controller classes and views to the area. Doing this within an area is in no way different from doing the same in the context of the main application.

Two other programming aspects make areas a little bit special—adding the area token to routes and linking views across different areas.

Registering Routes to Areas

The use of areas is not transparent to the ASP.NET MVC machinery. Because areas are a way to group controllers, the routing subsystem must receive an additional piece of information that identifies the area the controller belongs to.

Imagine a URL that points to a generic *Home* controller you've created to support your application. In a scenario where you have no explicit areas, that controller can be resolved only within a single environment. So if two controller classes with the same name and different namespaces are found, you just get an exception. When areas are used, instead, you can have the same *Home* controller class defined in different namespaces and in different areas. As a result, the routing system definitely needs the area name along with the controller name and the action name.

This means that any helpers that produce URLs for the view must be extended to include area names—for example, the *Html.ActionLink* helper that we'll meet in person later in the book. It also means that you must define routes that send requests to the appropriate area based on the requested URL.

Each area comes with a system-provided registration file that defines the routes supported by the area. Here's an example:

```
public class StoreAreaRegistration : AreaRegistration
{
    public override string AreaName
    {
        get
        {
            return "Store";
        }
    }

    public override void RegisterArea(AreaRegistrationContext context)
    {
        context.MapRoute(
            "Store_default",
            "Store/{controller}/{action}/{id}",
            new { action = "Index", id = "" }
        );
    }
}
```

As you can see, the default route registered in *RegisterArea* includes an extra data token that matches the name of the area. The route, however, is fully customizable. In *global.asax*, you use a new helper method to register routes for all areas in the project. Here's the revised startup method in *global.asax*:

```
protected void Application_Start()
{
    AreaRegistration.RegisterAllAreas();
    RegisterRoutes(RouteTable.Routes);
}
```

The *RegisterAllAreas* method loops through all available areas and invokes *RegisterArea* for each of them.

Linking to Areas

As long as you navigate within the same area, no special measures are required to ensure that the link is followed correctly. However, to support cross-area links, you need to resort to an updated version of some HTML helpers, such as *Html.ActionLink*. As we'll see later in Chapter 5, an HTML helper is a method that helps you produce plain HTML literals without writing any angle brackets.

In particular, the *ActionLink* helper method generates an anchor *<a>* tag with the correct URL. The method is smart enough to generate a URL also from route values. Here's how to use the helper with areas:

```
<ul id="menu">
    <li><%= Html.ActionLink("Home", "Index", "Home",
                         new { area = "" }, null)%></li>
    <li><%= Html.ActionLink("Store", "List", "Products",
                         new { area = "Store" }, null)%></li>
</ul>
```

The first link displays "Home" as its text and points to the *Index* action on the *Home* controller within the default area. The second link displays "Store" as its text and links the *List* method on the *Products* controller within the *Store* area.

The area token is optional as long as you don't cross the boundaries of the current area. Note that you indicate the area token using the *routeValues* dictionary parameter in the *ActionLink* list of overloads. However, to ensure that the proper overload is picked up, you also need to add a subsequent *null* argument. The trailing *null* argument, therefore, is required only to drive the compiler to using the right overload of the *ActionLink* method.

Asynchronous Controllers

Especially for server-based applications, asynchronous operations are a fundamental asset on the way to scalability. In ASP.NET, asynchronous requests take advantage of asynchronous

HTTP handlers, which are a feature of the ASP.NET platform since the first version. However, both ASP.NET Web Forms and ASP.NET MVC provide their own facilities to make it simpler for developers to implement asynchronous actions. In particular, ASP.NET MVC 2 provides asynchronous controllers.

> **Important** In ASP.NET, asynchronous pages are commonly associated with the idea of improving the performance of a given page that is about to perform a potentially lengthy operation. Although this can't be denied, a couple of additional points should be cleared up. First, from the user's perspective synchronous and asynchronous requests look nearly the same. If the requested operation is expected to take, say, 30 seconds to complete, the user will wait at least 30 seconds to get the new page back. This happens regardless of the synchronous or asynchronous implementation of the page. Furthermore, don't be too surprised if an asynchronous page ends up taking a bit more time to complete on the single request. So what's the benefit of asynchronous pages?
>
> The benefit that asynchronous pages bring to the table is that they require much less work for the threads in ASP.NET pool. This doesn't make lengthy requests run faster, but it does help the system to serve non-lengthy requests as usual—that is, without special delays resulting from ongoing slow requests. Scalability is not quite the same as performance. Or, at least, scalability is about performance but as it applies to a different scale—that is, it applies to the whole application instead of the single request.

Mechanics of Asynchronous Actions

In ASP.NET MVC 1, any controller actions can run only synchronously. In ASP.NET MVC 2, however, a new *AsyncController* class makes its debut, thus enabling you to define controller actions that run asynchronously.

The overall programming model doesn't change when you define an asynchronous action: you still create a public method optionally using a set of attributes. These methods don't need to be bound to special routes and return standard action result objects. Compared to a classic synchronous method, an async action is made of only a pair of methods—*xxxAsync* and *xxxCompleted*, where *xxx* indicates the action name. I'll get into details in a moment. Let's focus on the mechanics of an async action first.

In general, an async ASP.NET request is served in two distinct steps, each requiring a thread from the ASP.NET pool. In the first step, half of the request proceeds from the beginning to the async point. The second half resumes from the async point and completes the processing. The two steps do not form a continuous sequence, and there's no guarantee that the same thread will be serving both steps. The first half (which I'll refer to as the *trigger*) prepares the execution of the request and stops when the lengthy operation begins. The second half begins once the lengthy operation has terminated and finalizes the request. (I'll refer to the final step as the *finalizer.*)

What's the async point, exactly?

The Async Point

The *async point* is the point in the execution flow when you release the thread in charge of the trigger to the ASP.NET pool. This means that the initial ASP.NET thread is now free to serve other incoming requests, and it is no longer bound to wait for the lengthy operation to complete. This is where the benefit of async operations lies.

What happens between the async point and the moment in which the request resumes and completes? Which thread is taking care of the lengthy operation? (You do need a thread—any thread, but a thread—to take care of any operations in Windows.)

The final step of the trigger method is to return an *IAsyncResult* object. An object that supports the *IAsyncResult* interface stores state information for an asynchronous operation and provides a synchronization object to allow threads to be signaled when the operation completes. In the Microsoft .NET Framework, there are a few common ways to get an *IAsyncResult* object. A typical example is invoking a *BeginXXX* method such as *BeginRead* on the *FileStream* class. Another great example is invoking the *BeginXXX* method on a service proxy. Another common scenario for asynchronous operations is when you explicitly start a custom thread or post your work item to a pooled thread through the *ThreadPool* class. You can even provide your own implementation, but do so carefully and test it well.

In any case, the ultimate purpose of a trigger method is finding another thread (from outside ASP.NET) to take care of the lengthy operation and post the work item to it. When the post occurs, that is the async point.

After the potentially lengthy task has been started, what happens with the ASP.NET thread that took the request up to the async point? That thread has only to wait, in an idle state, until the operation completes elsewhere. Asynchronous HTTP handlers in ASP.NET manage to use an operating system thread, instead of an ASP.NET thread, to wait until the operation completes. This system thread is obtained through a Windows-specific mechanism known as *I/O completion ports*.

When the async point is reached, ASP.NET binds the pending request to an I/O completion port and registers a callback to get a notification when the request has terminated. The operating system will use one of its own dedicated threads to monitor the termination of the operation, thus freeing the ASP.NET thread from the need to wait in full idle. When the operation terminates, the operating system places a message in the completion queue. A message in the completion queue will trigger the ASP.NET callback, which will then pick up one of its own threads to resume and finalize the original request.

This is the general explanation of asynchronous request processing in ASP.NET. In ASP.NET MVC 2, the various steps are a bit abstracted to hide details such as the async point, HTTP handlers, and I/O completion ports. Let's review the mechanics of asynchronous requests in the context of ASP.NET MVC.

Async Actions in ASP.NET MVC

As Figure 4-13 shows, in an ASP.NET MVC request the async point is placed between the *ActionExecuting* and *ActionExecuted* events. The action invoker is responsible for orchestrating the various steps.

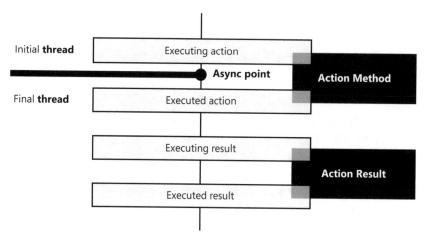

FIGURE 4-13 Mechanics of an asynchronous action

When the action invoker sends a notification that it is about to execute the action, the thread engaged is still the original ASP.NET thread that picked up the request from the Web server queue. The code running at this point is the trigger method, usually in the form of an *xxxAsync* method, as the following code shows:

```
public void PerformLengthTaskAsync(SomeData data)
{
    // Process input
    :
    :

    // Post a work item to a component that can result
    // in a lengthy operation (for example, invoke a Web service)
    :
    :

    // That's all for now—the action is being executed elsewhere.
    // All that remains to be done is wait for it to terminate;
    // for this task, we don't want to squander an ASP.NET thread.
    return;
}
```

When the trigger method returns, the lengthy action is running in the care of some other thread, possibly on some other process. The asynchronous action invoker manages to sync up with the ASP.NET runtime so that a completion port is used to monitor the completion of the operation. When this happens, the ASP.NET runtime puts the requests back in circulation with a special flag that indicates it only needs to complete its second half. The first available ASP.NET thread picks up the request and begins processing it.

In ASP.NET MVC, this means that the action is executed and the finalizer method is invoked. Here's the typical structure of a finalizer:

```
public ActionResult PerformLengthTaskCompleted(SomeResponse data)
{
    // Manage the model state (if any)
    :
    :

    // Prepare and render the view
    :
    :

}
```

The finalizer receives a custom object (or a multitude of parameters) that contains the data it is expected to process and pass on to the view object. However, the signature of the finalizer must be known in some way to the trigger. Let's find out the details.

Designing Asynchronous Action Methods

Is there any difference between synchronous and asynchronous routes? In ASP.NET MVC 2, no distinction exists at the route level. You still use the *MapRoute* method to define both. (I'll cover routes in detail in Chapter 8.)

```
routes.MapRoute(
    "Default",
    "{controller}/{action}/{id}",
    new { controller = "Home", action = "Index", id = "" }
);
```

The URL of the request is therefore processed as usual to find out the name of the controller class. A controller that exposes asynchronous methods is expected to derive from the new *AsyncController* class.

```
public class ServerFacadeController : AsyncController
{
    :
    :

}
```

Note that an *AsyncController* class can serve both synchronous and asynchronous requests. The name of the method conventionally indicates how the method has to be processed. You must be careful to avoid any ambiguity when you name your methods in an *AsyncController* class. Let's consider the following example that has a synchronous method and an asynchronous method:

```
public class ServerFacadeController : AsyncController
{
  public ActionResult PerformTask(SomeData data)
  {
      :
      :

  }
```

```
public void PerformTaskAsync(SomeData data)
{
    .
    .
    .
}
public ActionResult PerformTaskCompleted(SomeResponse data)
{
    .
    .
    .
}

}
```

The preceding code will throw an exception, as shown in Figure 4-14.

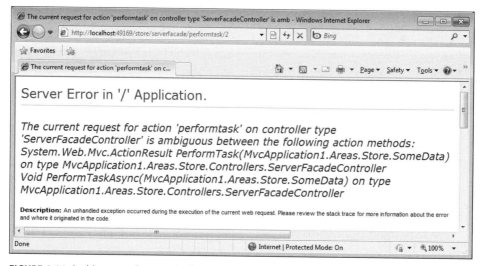

FIGURE 4-14 Ambiguous references in the name of the action

An async action is identified by name, and the expected pattern is *xxxAsync* where *xxx* indicates the default name of the action to execute. Clearly, if another method named *xxx* exists and is not disambiguated using attributes, an exception is thrown.

The word *Async* is considered as a suffix and the URL required to invoke the *PerformTaskAsync* method will contain only the prefix *PerformTask*. For example, the following URL will invoke the method *PerformTaskAsync* passing a value of *2* as a route parameter:

```
http://myserver/serverfacade/performtask/2
```

Whether it will be resolved as a synchronous or asynchronous action depends on the methods you actually have in the *AsyncController* class: for a given action name, you can only have either a synchronous or an asynchronous method match.

As mentioned, the *xxxAsync* method identifies the trigger of the operation. The finalizer of the request is another method in the controller class named *xxxCompleted*. You'll get another exception if a proper *xxxCompleted* method cannot be found.

Note the different signature of the two methods defining the asynchronous action. The trigger is expected to be a void method. If you define it to return any value, the return value will be simply ignored. The input parameters of the *xxxAsync* method are subject to model binding as usual. The finalizer method returns an *ActionResult* object as usual, and it receives a custom object that contains the data it is expected to process and pass on to the view object. A special protocol is necessary for matching the values calculated by the trigger to the parameters declared by the finalizer.

Coding Asynchronous Action Methods

In an asynchronous controller class, each asynchronous method is actually a pair of methods and an ad hoc invoker will call each at the right time. In particular, the invoker needs a counter to track the number of individual operations that compose the action so that it can synchronize results before declaring the overall action terminated. In light of this, here's the typical structure of the internal code of a pair of trigger/finalizer methods:

```
public void PerformTaskAsync(SomeData data)
{
    AsyncManager.OutstandingOperations.Increment();

    var response = new SomeResponse();
    :
    :

    // Do some remote work (for example, invoke a service)
    :
    :

    // Terminate operations, and prepare data for the finalizer
    AsyncManager.Parameters["data"] = response;
    AsyncManager.OutstandingOperations.Decrement();
}

public ActionResult PerformTaskCompleted(SomeResponse data)
{
    // Prepare the view (for example, massage received data into a view model class)
    var model = new PerformTaskViewModel(data);
    :
    :

    return View(model);
}
```

The *OutstandingOperations* member on the *AsyncManager* class provides a container that maintains a count of pending asynchronous operations. The *OutstandingOperations* member is an instance of the *OperationCounter* helper class and supplies an ad hoc API to increment and decrement. The *Increment* method is not limited to unary increments, as the following code demonstrates:

```
AsyncManager.OutstandingOperations.Increment(2);
service1.GetData(...);
AsyncManager.OutstandingOperations.Decrement();
service2.GetData(...);
AsyncManager.OutstandingOperations.Decrement();
```

The *Parameters* dictionary on the *AsyncManager* class is used to group values to be passed as arguments to the finalizer method of the asynchronous call. The *Parameters* dictionary will contain an entry for each parameter to be passed to the finalizer. If a match can't be found between entries in the dictionary and parameter names, a default value is assumed for the parameter. The default value results from the evaluation of the *default(T)* expression on the parameter's type. No exception is raised unless an attempt is made to access a null object.

Attributes of Asynchronous Action Methods

Any applicable filter attributes for an asynchronous method must be placed on the trigger method *xxxAsync*. Any attributes applied to the finalizer will be ignored. If an *ActionName* attribute is placed on *xxxAsync* to alias it, the finalizer must be named after the trigger method, not the action name. Consider the following code:

```
[ActionName("Test")]
public void PerformTaskAsync(SomeData data)
{
    :
    :
}
public ActionResult PerformTaskCompleted(SomeResponse data)
{
    :
    :
}
```

You need to use the name *Test* in the URL, but you don't need to change anything in the names of trigger and finalizer methods. Also, note that the view name, instead, is being resolved in terms of the action. So, in this case, the default name of the view is *Test*, not *PerformTask*.

In addition, you can set a timeout on a per-controller or per-action basis by using the *AsyncTimeout* attribute:

```
[AsyncTimeout(3000)]
```

The attribute is invoked by ASP.NET MVC before the asynchronous action method executes. The duration is expressed in milliseconds and defaults to 30 seconds. By default, all methods are subject to this timeout. If you don't want any timeout, you set that preference explicitly by using the *NoAsyncTimeout* attribute. No timeout is equivalent to setting the timeout to the value of *System.Threading.Timeout.Infinite*.

By setting the *Timeout* property of the *AsyncManager* object, on the other hand, you can set a new global timeout value that applies to any call unless it's overridden by attributes at the controller or action level.

Candidates for Asynchronous Actions

Not all actions should be considered for an asynchronous behavior. Only I/O-bound operations are, in fact, good candidates to become asynchronous action methods on an asynchronous controller class.

An I/O-bound operation is an operation that doesn't depend on the local CPU for completion. When an I/O-bound operation is going on, the CPU just waits for data to be processed (for example, downloaded) from external storage such as a database or a remote Web service. Operations in which the completion of the task depends on the activity of the CPU are, instead, referred to as CPU-bound.

The typical example of an I/O-bound operation is the invocation of a remote Web service. In this case, the real work is being done remotely by another machine and another CPU. The ASP.NET thread would be stuck waiting and be idle all the time. Releasing that idle thread from the duty of waiting, and making it available to serve other incoming requests, is the performance gain you can achieve by using asynchronous actions or pages.

It turns out that not all lengthy operations give you a concrete benefit if they're implemented asynchronously. A lengthy in-memory calculation, for example, doesn't provide you with any significant benefit if they're implemented asynchronously because the same CPU both serves the ASP.NET request and performs the calculation.

On the other hand, if remote resources are involved (or even multiple resources), using asynchronous methods can really boost the performance of the application, if not the performance of the individual request.

> **Note** How does this relate to the situation where the controller is operating as a coordinator, as we examined earlier? In this case, the controller will probably be limited to invoking just one method on the service layer. If the service layer is remote, almost any action can be considered for an asynchronous implementation.

Render Actions

Controller methods exist to be mapped to routes and execute some action in response to a request. All the logic you need to run to serve a request belongs to the selected controller method, and the view is as passive as possible—no logic in the view and no data to be rendered by the view are received from the controller.

This is good in theory, but is it also good in practice?

Well, there's a common scenario whose optimal implementation is controversial in ASP.NET MVC—rendering parts of the view that are global and shared by multiple views. On the way to simplifying the implementation of this common scenario, ASP.NET MVC 2 offers developers of controller classes the possibility of defining *render actions*.

The *RenderAction* Helper

A render action is a controller method that is specifically designed to be called from within a view. A render action is therefore a regular method on the controller class that you invoke from the view using one of the following HTML helpers: *Action* or *RenderAction*.

```
public static MvcHtmlString Action(this HtmlHelper htmlHelper, string actionName);
public static MvcHtmlString RenderAction(this HtmlHelper htmlHelper, string actionName);
```

I'll cover HTML helpers in detail in the next chapter. For now, suffice it to say that a helper method is a special method callable from the view that produces markup. A helper method is usually defined as an extension method for the *HtmlHelper* system class.

Action and *RenderAction* behave mostly in the same way; the only difference is that *Action* returns the markup as a string, whereas *RenderAction* writes directly to the output stream. Both methods support a variety of overloads through which you can specify multiple parameters, including route values, HTML attributes and, of course, the controller's name.

So when are *Action* and *RenderAction* really helpful to justify sacrificing the design on the altar of implementation?

Simply put, *Action* and *RenderAction* offer a simple but effective solution to populating parts of a view that are shared with other views and that are not directly related to the current request. For example, suppose you have a menu to render in many of your views. Whatever action you take in relation to your application, the menu has to be rendered. Rendering the menu, therefore, is an action not directly related to the current ongoing request. How would you handle that? In the next chapter, I'll dig out the details of this aspect of ASP.NET MVC programming. For now, I just want to present a possible solution—render actions.

In one of your controller classes, you define a method intended to be the renderer of some view-related action. This method doesn't need any special signature or attribute in order to be visible from the view:

```
public ActionResult Menu()
{
    var options = new MenuOptions();
    options.Items.Add("File");
    options.Items.Add("Edit");
    options.Items.Add("Help");
    return PartialView("menu", options);
}
```

The content of the *menu.ascx* file is not relevant here; all it does is get the model object and render an appropriate piece of markup. Let's see the view source code for one of the pages you might have in the application:

```
<asp:Content ID="Content1" ContentPlaceHolderID="MainContent" runat="server">
    <h2>Perform Some Task</h2>
    <% Html.RenderAction("Menu"); %>
    <hr />

    <!-- Remainder of the view here -->
      .
      .
      .
</asp:Content>
```

The *RenderAction* helper method calls the *Menu* method on the specified controller (or on the controller that ordered the current view to be rendered) and directs any response to the output stream. In this way, the view incorporates some logic and calls back the controller. At the same time, your controller doesn't need to worry about passing the view information that is not strictly relevant to the current request it is handling.

> **Note** As you'll see in more detail in Chapter 5, this point is controversial and it is mostly a matter of preference. If your gut feeling says you like render actions, don't hesitate to use them. On the other hand, feel free to explore other solutions if you don't want to trade design for implementation. Whatever your final decision is, I suggest that you make it for yourself, your application, and your team and avoid making it a dogmatic matter. It is an open point, and it will probably remain open.

Child Actions

The *Action* and *RenderAction* helper methods can call into any public method of the controller class. Note that the attributes take into account the *ActionName* attribute if specified. The execution of a render action, however, is not simply a call made to a method via reflection. A lot more of this happens under the hood.

In particular, a render action is a child request that originates within the boundaries of the main user request. The *RenderAction* method builds a new request context that contains the same HTTP context of the parent request and a different set of route values. This child request is forwarded to a specific HTTP handler—the *ChildActionMvcHandler* class—and is executed as if it came from the browser. The overall operation is similar to what happens when you call *Server.Execute* in general ASP.NET programming. There's no redirect and no roundtrip, but the child request goes through the usual pipeline of a regular ASP.NET MVC request and has all filters honored.

Not all filter attributes, however, should re-execute in the case of a child action. The most illustrious example is *AuthorizeRequest*. In ASP.NET MVC 2, such critical filters have been updated to check a new property on the *ControllerContext* class that you met earlier in the chapter—*IsChildAction*. The *IsChildAction* property is a Boolean value that indicates whether the filter is being invoked as the result of render action or a URL action.

Another filter that needs to distinguish between regular and child requests is *OutputCache*. The *OutputCache* filter will honor its contract and cache the output of a request only if the request has been sent via a URL. The *OutputCache* filter, therefore, will ignore child requests. What if you want to cache the output of the child action, then? The trick consists of placing the call to *RenderAction* in a partial view—a user control—and setting the *@OutputCache* directive on it.

By default, any action method can be invoked from a URL and via a render action. However, any action methods marked with the *ChildActionOnly* attribute won't be available to public callers, and its usage is limited to render actions and child requests. An exception will be thrown otherwise.

RenderAction vs. RenderPartial

Two HTML helpers exist in ASP.NET MVC 2 with similar names and overall similar behaviors: *RenderAction* and *RenderPartial*. Both are able to load some commonly used content into the view being rendered. When do you use which?

RenderPartial is designed to render a user control—namely, a partial view. You can have it render only whatever is saved as an ASCX resource. This limitation doesn't exist with *RenderAction*. *RenderAction*, in fact, can render anything that derives from *ActionResult*. However, the most significant difference—the one that determines when to use which—is this: *RenderPartial* can work only with data that is available within the calling view. In a view, if you have all the data you need and want to create a child view, *RenderPartial* is the way to go. In this context, it represents a better option for performance reasons.

RenderAction, on the other hand, is preferable when you need some logic to retrieve all the data you need for rendering. The retrieval logic, in this case, belongs to the controller. When the data has to be retrieved—whether from the cache or through a query— *RenderAction* is the way to go. A render action can be parameterless, or it can accept parameters as shown here:

```
<% Html.RenderAction("OrderList", "Order", new {CustomerId = Model.CustomerId}); %>
```

A common situation is when you want to display order information within a view focused on the demographics of a customer. The preceding code snippet passes the customer ID, as available to the view, to a method that uses that information to query for the orders.

Controllers and Testability

A trivial controller class with no external dependencies is ready to test and doesn't need any special treatment. A less trivial controller with some dependencies (perhaps on the DAL) can still be tested as is, but it requires that you have access to the DAL and the underlying database anytime you run the test.

The perfect controller is not the one without dependencies. Dependencies are an absolute must for any realistic controller. The ideal controller is the one that effectively manages all of its dependencies by providing a way for you to inject them smoothly both for regular execution and during automated testing.

Making Controllers Easy to Test

A while back in the chapter, I started addressing effective ways to manage dependencies within a controller class. Now I'm ready to finalize the discussion and demonstrate the benefits of a modular design for testability.

> **Note** The whole point of testability is, in the final analysis, a false problem. I challenge anybody to find a difference between a testable piece of code that works and an untestable piece of code that works. All that matters is that the code just works. Does all the emphasis on testability still make sense, then? In the end, the focus on testability is an excellent excuse to focus on better design. Code designed for testability is inherently much better designed code. Testability and design are strictly related, whatever way you look at them.

Basics of Testability

A broadly accepted measure for software testability is the ease with which testing can be performed. And testing is the process of checking software to ensure that it behaves as expected, contains no errors, and satisfies its requirements.

Testing happens at various levels. *Unit tests* determine whether individual components of the software meet functional requirements. *Integration tests* determine whether the software fits in the environment and works well with other components. Finally, *acceptance tests* determine whether the completed system meets customer requirements.

Unit tests and integration tests pertain to the development team and serve the purpose of making the team confident about the quality of the software they're building. Unit tests, in particular, can also serve to prevent regression failures after significant changes are entered into the classes.

A software test verifies that a method returns the correct output in response to a given input and a given internal state. Having control over the input and the state, and being able to observe the output, is therefore essential for testing. Your responsibility is to ensure that all methods (and classes) that need to be tested meet these requirements. If not, you should endeavor to refactor your code for testability.

Dealing with Dependencies

When you test a method, you want to focus only on the code within that method. All that you want to know is whether that code provides the expected results in the tested scenarios. To get this answer, you need to get rid of all dependencies the method might have. If the method, say, invokes another class, you assume that the invoked class will always return correct results. In this way, you eliminate at the root the risk that the method fails under test because a failure occurred down the call stack. If you test method A and it fails, the reason has to be found exclusively in the source code of method A and not in any of its dependencies.

How can you neutralize dependencies when testing a method? You do so by designing the method (and its surrounding class) to properly make use of forms of dependency injection.

Dependency injection really comes in handy here and is a pattern that has a huge impact on testability. A class is inherently more testable if it depends on interfaces and uses dependency injection to receive from the outside world any objects it needs to do its own work. Establishing these characteristics has to be the aim when you're creating your controllers and related classes.

Tightly Coupled Controllers

As you saw earlier, a controller class typically invokes a class on the application's service layer. The application's service layer is responsible for implementing the application logic and is ultimately in charge of any orchestration required that involves other components in other layers, such as BLL and DAL.

Note that the controller belongs to the presentation layer. Hence, in observance of the principle of layering, it can talk only to its closest layer—the business layer. The service layer is just part of it. Here's a typical method on a controller:

```
public ActionResult Find(int customerId)
{
    // Some simple forms of validation might take place here. Classic server-side
    // validation against business rules will occur in the service layer class.
    :
    :

    // Invoke the business logic
    var service = new CustomerServices();
    var customer = service.FindById(id);
```

```
    // Deal with possibly wrong return values caused by server exceptions
    :
    :
    // Fill the view model container
    this.ViewData["Customer"] = customer;

    // Trigger the view
    return this.View();
}
```

The method uses a service layer class to get information about the specified customer.
In turn, the service layer class *CustomerServices* uses a specific repository object to wrap any
data access code:

```
public class CustomertServices
{
    public IList<Customer> FindAll()
    {
        // Get any necessary data from the DAL
        var rep = new CustomerRepository();
        var customer = rep.GetAll();

        // Return data
        return customers;
    }

    public Customer FindById(int id)
    {
        // Get any necessary data from the DAL
        var rep = new CustomerRepository();
        var customer = rep.GetByID(id);

        // Return data
        return customer;
    }
}
```

This code works just fine. But both the *CustomerController* and *CustomerServices* classes hold
references to explicit objects and use the *new* operator to get instances. This code is not ideal
from a testing perspective because dependencies are hard-coded.

You need to find a way to inject in the controller class any dependencies it might have on
the service layer. Furthermore, you also need to refactor the service layer to be injected with
dependencies on repositories.

ServiceLayerContext Class

The simplest way to inject a reference to the service layer in a controller class is to add an ad
hoc property. Instead of repeating this property for each new controller class, you might
want to add it to a tailor-made superclass.

As discussed earlier, the *ApplicationContext* class does the trick. This class is a container of all dependencies a controller might have. In particular, it exposes a reference to a *ServiceLayerContext* object, as shown here:

```
public class ApplicationContext
{
    public ApplicationContext(ServiceLayerContext context)
    {
        Initialize(context, null);
    }
    .
    .
    .

    // Properties
    public ServiceLayerContext ServiceLayerContext { get; private set; }

    .
    .
    .
}
```

The service layer is not made of a single class. Generally, you'll likely have a service layer class for each controller that needs to invoke the middle tier. The *ServiceLayerContext* object is, then, another global container for all service layer classes you happen to have:

```
public class ServiceLayerContext
{
    public ICustomerServices CustomerService { get; private set; }
    .
    .
    .
}
```

As you might have noticed, the *ServiceLayerContext* class uses an abstraction of the content service class—the *ICustomerServices* interface. That's precisely the trick. Here's how the aforementioned *Find* method on the *CustomerController* class looks now:

```
// ApplicationContext is inherited from custom controller superclass
public ActionResult Find(int customerId)
{
    // Some simple forms of validation might take place here. Classic server-side
    // validation against business rules will occur in the service layer class.
    .
    .
    .

    // Invoke the business logic
    var service = ApplicationContext.ServiceLayerContext.CustomerService;

    var customer = service.FindById(id);
    this.ViewData["Customer"] = customer;


    // Fill the view model container and trigger the view
    .
    .
    .
}
```

If you design the controller to work against an abstraction and manage to provide a concrete object that implements that abstraction, you end up with an extensible and maintainable design and gain a lot in terms of testability.

Propagating Testability Changes to the Service Layer

The chain of changes doesn't end here. Methods on a typical service layer class will likely have dependencies on the DAL. To test service layer classes effectively and in full isolation, you also need to decouple them from DAL references. Here's a revamped version of the *CustomerServices* class:

```
public class CustomerServices : ICustomerServices
{
    // Constructors
    public CustomerServices()
    {
        Initialize(null, null);
    }
    public CustomerServices(ICustomerRepository custRepo,
                        IOrderRepository orderRepo)
    {
        Initialize(custRepo, orderRepo);
    }

    // Properties
    ICustomerRepository CustomerRepository { get; private set; }
    IOrderRepository OrderRepository { get; private set; }

    // Methods
    public Customer FindById(int customerId)
    {
        // Get any necessary data from the DAL
        var customer = CustomerRepository.FindById(customerId);
        return customer;
    }
    .
    .
    .

    // Internal members
    private void Initialize(ICustomerRepository custRepo,
                        IOrderRepository orderRepo)
    {
        CustomerRepository = (custRepo ?? new CodeSampleRepository());
        OrderRepository = (orderRepo ?? new ChapterRepository());
    }
}
```

Also in this case, the behavior of the DAL components the service layer class depends upon has been abstracted to an interface and a parameter-based constructor has been added to the service layer class primarily for testability reasons. Let's see how to write unit tests.

Writing Unit Tests

A *unit* is the smallest part of an application that is testable—typically, a method. Unit testing consists of writing and running a small program (referred to as a *test harness*) that instantiates classes and invokes methods in an automatic way. In the end, running a battery of tests is much like compiling. You click a button, you run the test harness and, at the end of it, you know what went wrong, if anything.

The most effective way to conduct unit testing passes through the use of an automated test framework. An automated test framework is a developer tool that normally includes a run-time engine and a framework of classes for simplifying the creation of test programs. Choosing a framework is up to you, and quite a few excellent options exist in the open-source arena. A popular framework is NUnit. (See *http://www.nunit.org*.)

A testing framework, MSTest, is also integrated with Visual Studio. As shown in Figure 4-15, ASP.NET MVC asks you whether you want to add a test project to your solution.

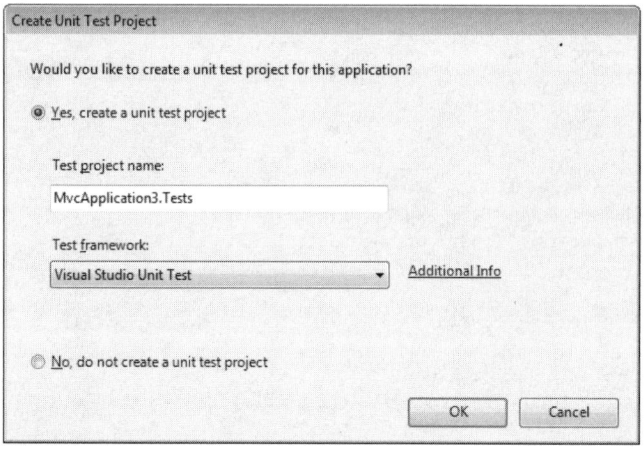

FIGURE 4-15 Creating a unit test project

Basics of Unit Testing with MSTest

You start by grouping related tests in a text fixture. Text fixtures are just test-specific classes where methods typically represent tests to run. In a text fixture, you might also have code that executes at the start and end of the test run. Here's the skeleton of a text fixture with MSTest:

```
using Microsoft.VisualStudio.TestTools.UnitTesting;
:
:

[TestClass]
public class CustomerTest
{
    private Customer customer;
```

```
    [TestInitialize]
    public void SetUp()
    {
      customer = new Customer();
    }

    [TestCleanup]
    public void TearDown()
    {
      customer = null;
    }

    // Your tests go here
    [TestMethod]
    public void ShouldAssignCompanyNameToCustomer()
    {
       .
       .
       .
    }
    .
    .
    .
}
```

You need to have tests for each significant class. A good practice is to have an *XxxTest* class for each *Xxx* class in a given assembly.

With MSTest, you transform a plain .NET class into a test fixture by simply adding the *TestClass* attribute. You turn a method of this class into a test method by using the *TestMethod* attribute instead. Attributes such as *TestInitialize* and *TestCleanup* have a special meaning and indicate code to execute at the start and end of each and every test so that no two tests are dependent.

Let's write out a test for a sample *ContentController* class that uses a service layer infrastructure to retrieve information about chapters. The *ContentController* class derives from our base class and thus gains access to the *ApplicationContext* class.

Writing a Sample Unit Test

The test we're going to write verifies that the *ContentController* class will successfully retrieve information about Chapter 1 when a value of *1* is passed to its *LoadChapters* method. Here's the code of the test fixture:

```
[TestClass]
public class ContentControllerTest
{
    private ApplicationContext appContext;

    [TestInitialize]
    public void Setup()
    {
        appContext = new ApplicationContext();
        appContext.Logger = new FakeLogger();
```

```
        appContext.ServiceLayerContext = new ServiceLayerContext();
        ICodeSampleRepository sampleRepo = new FakeCodeSampleRepository();
        IChapterRepository chapRepo = new FakeChapterRepository();
        appContext.ServiceLayerContext.ContentService =
                        new ContentServices(sampleRepo, chapRepo);
    }

    [TestMethod]
    public void ShouldFindOneChapterByItsId()
    {
        // Arrange
        var controller = new ContentController(appContext);

        // Act: try to get information on Chapter #1
        var result = controller.Chapters(1) as ViewResult;

        // Assert
        ViewDataDictionary viewData = result.ViewData;
        var chapter = viewData["Chapter"] as Chapter;
        Assert.AreEqual(1, chapter.ID);
    }

    [TestMethod]
    public void FailIfNegativeChapterIdIsPassed()
    {
        // Arrange
        var controller = new ContentController(appContext);

        // Act: try to get information on Chapter # -1
        var result = controller.Chapters(-1) as ViewResult;

        // Assert
        ViewDataDictionary viewData = result.ViewData;
        object data_chapter = viewData["Chapter"];
        Assert.IsNull(data_chapter);
    }

        .
        .
        .

}
```

The method *ShouldFindOneChapterByItsId* gets an instance of the controller class under test and calls its *Chapters* method. Next, armed with full knowledge of the method's output, it goes through a number of assertions. If all is fine, the test passes.

The constructor of the controller class gets an *ApplicationContext* object that delivers all of the much needed dependencies. An ad hoc version of the *ApplicationContext* object is created in the initialization step of the fixture.

As you can see in the preceding code, references to repositories have been replaced with fake objects that just return canned values and never fail or throw. Here's a sample fake repository:

```
public class FakeChapterRepository : IChapterRepository
{
    public IList<Chapter> GetAll()
    {
        List<Chapter> chapters = new List<Chapter>();
        for (int i = 1; i <= 12; i++)
            chapters.Add(CreateFakeChapter(i));
        return chapters;
    }

    public Chapter GetByID(int chapterID)
    {
        return CreateFakeChapter(chapterID);
    }

    private Chapter CreateFakeChapter(int chapterID)
    {
        var chapter = new Chapter();
        chapter.ID = chapterID;
        chapter.Title = String.Format("Chapter #{0}", chapterID);
        chapter.Abstract = String.Format("This is chapter #{0}", chapterID);
        return chapter;
    }
}
```

Figure 4-16 shows the results of these tests.

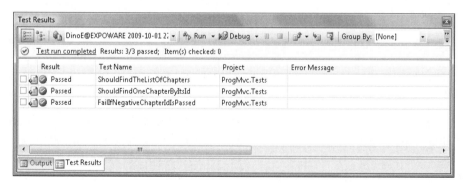

FIGURE 4-16 The test run completed successfully.

Ultimately, with proper abstractions in place, the controller and the service layer classes can work with both a real repository that performs data access and with a fake one that just returns canned values. Power to dependency injection!

> **Note** Recall that dependency injection is a simple pattern that provides guidance on how to inject objects into a class. Raw dependency injection is just what we did here. There's another, more spectacular, way of implementing dependency injection—via IoC containers. In Chapter 11, in the context of ASP.NET MVC customization, I'll discuss controller factories and rework this example to use dependency injection via an IoC container.
>
> In case you can't make the connection right now and are momentarily left wondering why you need to mix up controller factories with IoC containers, let me give you a bit of quick relief. To keep the controller's code free of any initialization burden, you want to resolve all dependencies when the controller is instantiated. For this to happen, you need to rewrite the factory and let the factory deal with the setup of the IoC container first and resolve dependencies next.

From Fakes to Mocks

In testing, a *fake* object is a relatively simple clone of an object that offers the same interface as the original object but returns hard-coded or computed values. The fake object has no state and no significant behavior. From the fake object's perspective, it makes no difference how many times you invoke a fake method and when in the flow the call occurs.

A *mock* object is a more sophisticated version of a fake. A mock does all that a fake does, plus something more. In a way, a mock is an object with its own personality that mimics the behavior and interface of another object. What more does a mock provide to testers?

When you use fakes, you're mostly interested in verifying that some expected output derives from a given input. You are interested in the state that a fake object might represent; you are not interested in interacting with it.

You use a mock instead of a fake only when you need to interact with dependent objects during tests. For example, you might want to know whether the mock has been invoked or not, and you might decide within the test what the mock object has to return for a given method.

Writing mocks manually is hardly an option: the code is generally too complex and often changes frequently. Alternatively, you might come up with a generic mock class that works in the guise of any object you specify. This generic mock class also exposes a general-purpose interface through which you set your expectations for the mocked object. This is exactly what mocking frameworks do for you. In the end, you never write mock objects manually; you generate them on the fly using some mocking framework, such as TypeMock, Moq, RhinoMocks, or NMock2, to name a few of the more popular ones. (No mocking framework is currently shipped with any version of Visual Studio.)

Summary

Controllers are the heart of an ASP.NET MVC application. They are linked to user-interface actions and are in touch with the middle tier. Controllers mediate between the user requests and the capabilities of the server system. Controllers, however, simply implement pieces of functionality. They order the rendering of the page, but they don't include the rendering of any response for the user.

This is a key difference with ASP.NET Web Forms. In a controller, the processing of the request is neatly separated from the display. In Web Forms, instead, the page processing phase incorporates both execution of some tasks and rendering of the response.

What does it mean to you as a developer?

You have to start with a clear design of the functions required for the system and map them to a set of executors—the controller classes. Controllers, in turn, control a number of possible views and switch among them following the needs of use-cases. The number of controllers can grow significantly in large applications, and this is where areas fit in. An area is a clear way to partition large applications into smaller and more manageable sets.

In the end, with ASP.NET MVC—and with controllers in particular—the importance of design shows up. Maybe for the first time in the .NET space, the design of a Web application follows the same canonical rules of software design. Design is design, regardless of whether or not it's for the Web. As a final piece of advice, I suggest you keep in mind the mantra that I learned through my own trials and tribulations in the early days of object-oriented design: *we all know the good, sane principles, but then we all make the same mistakes over and over again*.

Finally, you might have noticed a lot of forward references in this chapter—specifically to Chapter 5. This is mostly because the activity of a controller inevitably intersects with the activity of views and models. The next chapter is just about views.

Chapter 5
Inside Views

Design is not just what it looks like and feels like. Design is how it works.

—Steve Jobs

The rave reviews that ASP.NET MVC has received from the development community since its first appearance in October 2007 convinced many developers to give it at least a quick try. When one approaches ASP.NET MVC without the strong commitment that derives from an impending project or deadline, there's one particular aspect of it that the newcomer often has difficulty making sense of—the generation of the HTML for the browser.

In ASP.NET Web Forms, you don't even think of an action—you think of pages. And you tend to map to a page any functional needs your application might have. As a Web Forms developer, you see the implementation of a functional need as the page that generates the response you expect for it. Imagine you're working on the use-case for a user who registers with a given site. If the process completes successfully, you then want to display a thank-you screen. How do you design this behavior?

In a Web Forms scenario, you typically arrange a form to collect the user's data and then submit this data through a postback. Next, you might have a server-to-server redirection from *register.aspx* to *thankyou.aspx* or maybe a plain message displayed in the body of the same *register.aspx* page.

In ASP.NET MVC, you instead think of the effects of the *Register* action and the subsequent view to display. This is neither more nor less of what you do in a non-Web scenario. In ASP.NET MVC, you might not even have a *thankyou.aspx* page—you simply need to have a component within your application with the ability to generate the expected thank-you screen. This component is the *view*.

In this chapter, I'll attempt to dissect the internal structure of the view component—one of the key actors in the Model-View-Controller (MVC) pattern (and all of its derivatives). I'll explore the properties and behavior of the various classes that form the hierarchy and touch on the architecture of the underlying view engine. Finally, I'll focus on practical aspects of writing a view in an ASP.NET MVC application.

To start off, though, I'll briefly examine the points of contact between controllers and views, such as which item triggers what, and how data is being exchanged.

Views and Controllers

In ASP.NET MVC, a *view* is a class that gets a template and some data and then produces a response for the browser. The controller selects the next view and asks it to render out the response. The controller won't get anything back from the view. The controller's responsibilities end when it yields to the view. Subsequently, the view is in charge of writing to the output stream any content for the browser.

From Controllers to Views

The view doesn't have a real autonomous life in ASP.NET MVC. A view exists only to be invoked at the end of certain controller actions to produce a response. One of the biggest changes in ASP.NET MVC is the role of the view—it's simply a black box. You put something in it, and something else comes out at the other end.

Views and Action Results

After the controller instance has completed its job, there might be some computed data to display to the user. Most of the time, this data is fused to an HTML template and written to the output stream. However, controller actions don't always require displaying some HTML to the browser. In some situations, in fact, the user doesn't receive any HTML; instead, the user receives a JavaScript file or maybe a JSON string.

In Chapter 4, "Inside Controllers," Table 4-6 details all possible action result types in ASP.NET MVC. In the same chapter, you also learned that any controller action always ends up returning an *ActionResult* object. The type *ActionResult* is not really a data container. It is, instead, an abstract class that offers a unified programming interface to execute any operations that have the system produce a result for the browser.

The particular action result that returns HTML to the browser is known as a *ViewResult* object. This chapter is mostly about these view results.

Passing Data to the View

In ASP.NET MVC, the controller packages data and actions according to its design, and the view receives whatever the controller provides. It's the interpretation of the data that is under the view's jurisdiction. Maybe it outputs a table, maybe it outputs a menu, maybe something else. The view does not dictate how the data is provided, even though controllers and related views aren't written in a vacuum. However, the point is that one controller could provide the same or similar data to several views.

The view might be written to accept content from the *ViewData* dictionary, or it might be written to expect a strongly typed object.

You met the *ViewData* dictionary already in Chapter 4. It's defined on the *Controller* as a container for data to be consumed by the selected view. You can add as many entries to the *ViewData* dictionary as you plan to consume from within the view class. The *ViewData* dictionary is only the default option for the controller and view to exchange data. (See Figure 5-1.)

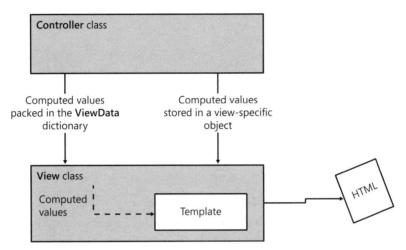

FIGURE 5-1 The controller passes data down to the view.

Building the Response for the Browser

The view component is the class the developer writes to complete the puzzle that results in the runtime environment delivering an HTML response to the browser. If you look under the hood of the view object, however, you find quite complex machinery centered on the *view engine* object.

The View Engine

The view engine is the component that physically builds the output for the browser. It gets an engine-specific template file and mixes its content with any context information it receives from the controller.

As mentioned, the final output generated by a view engine is expected to be mostly HTML, but it can be anything the Web engine decides it should be. However, if you expect to return a special content type, you're probably better off using an ad hoc action result type. ASP.NET MVC defines action results for JSON strings, files, and JavaScript code. (See Chapter 4.) The mechanism is so easy to extend that you can create a custom action result type in a few lines of code. I'll cover this in detail in Chapter 11, "Customizing ASP.NET MVC"

The view engine is a pluggable element of the ASP.NET MVC architecture. The framework comes with a built-in engine that leverages the display infrastructure of ASP.NET Web Forms. A view engine is merely a class that implements the *IViewEngine* interface, which is shown here:

```
public interface IViewEngine
{
    // Methods
    void RenderView(ViewContext viewContext);
}
```

You can definitely consider replacing this default view engine with one of your own. Although this is definitely an interesting possibility, it's a step you might not want to undertake with a light heart. A few alternative engines have been made available by the development community, and you can find them listed here: *http://mvccontrib.codeplex.com/documentation.*

We'll have a look at a simple override of the default view engine later in the chapter.

> **Note** If you're somehow unsatisfied with the default view engine (based on the Web Forms rendering model), the first alternate view engine you might want to look at is the Spark view engine you can get at *http://sparkviewengine.com*. Spark works with ASP.NET MVC as well as Castle MonoRail. What differentiates it from the default engine is the dominance of the HTML markup in the template. There's nothing like server controls or HTML helpers in the resulting template; everything is HTML, and pieces of additional logic (loops, data binding) fit nicely in the HTML through ad hoc attributes. The Spark view engine is gaining popularity, but it is not necessarily better than all the others. What's better depends on your attitude, preference, needs and, why not, gut feeling.

A Template for the View

Any nontrivial view engine must be based on a template file that describes the output you expect. Typically, a template also includes some placeholders for data computed by the invoking controller. The template file, however, can be made of any text that the selected view engine is able to understand and process.

ASP.NET MVC operates with a default view engine that leverages Web Forms for the actual rendering of HTML. For this reason, you are allowed to write a view using an ASPX-based template. This trick preserves for you the ability to use server controls, user controls, and master pages even in an ASP.NET MVC view.

As you'll see later in the chapter, although you're allowed to use server controls in the building of ASP.NET MVC views, you should be aware that not all the features of a typical server control (especially rich server controls) can be successfully leveraged in

ASP.NET MVC. The best you can do is accept that using server controls can be a nice and possibly effective shortcut, but it's hardly the preferred way to go. I suggest that you still consider server controls to be part of your tool set, but resort to them only when you have a strong reason to do so. HTML helpers are a lightweight counterpart of server controls supported by the default view engine. They kind of preserve the Web Forms programming style without forcing view-state, postbacks, as well as the classic page life cycle.

On the other hand, my experience reveals that when you have a team with strong Web Forms skills you might still want to consider the default engine first. For sure, using server controls in ASP.NET MVC requires a delicate balancing of features and practices, but probably learning slightly different ways of using server controls combined with HTML helpers is quicker than training a bunch of people on using a completely different template language.

Important Even though you still end up defining the expected user interface through the familiar ASPX markup, the role of the ASPX files you write is radically different in Web Forms and ASP.NET MVC. In Web Forms, the user points the browser to the ASPX file that is considered to be the *resource* to access. Access to the resource causes the system to perform some tasks and generate some response. In ASP.NET MVC, the user points the browser to an action to execute, and the ASPX file is merely the template used internally to generate the HTML layout to contain the response the action has computed. For this reason, you need to plan your ASP.NET MVC application around required functions instead of required pages.

Anatomy of an ASP.NET MVC View

The process that has ASP.NET MVC render the view is fairly sophisticated, although it's hidden to developers for the most part. Developers are primarily responsible for preparing a bunch of view templates and for selecting the right view from the controller. That said, the whole view process can be observed and controlled step by step; however, this is not a primary need for developers in most scenarios.

Selecting the View

After the invoked controller's method has accomplished the given task, it selects the next view and triggers the process that ultimately results in building the response for the browser.

The logic the controller employs to select the next view can be as complex as necessary. In simple cases, it consists of the plain invocation of a particular view. In other situations, the logic can be more sophisticated, ranging from a few *if* branches to a true workflow. A controller method usually calls into the *View* method to generate a view result for the action invoker. Let's find out more about the *View* method and the action invoker.

The Controller's *View* Method

The *View* method on a controller class assembles and returns an instance of the
ViewResult class. The *ViewResult* class is packed with any computed data that the view needs
to know about. The *View* method has a number of overloads, but all of them refer to the
following two:

```
virtual ViewResult View(IView view, object model);
virtual ViewResult View(string viewName, string masterName, object model);
```

The source code of these two methods is nearly identical and essentially aimed at creating
a *ViewResult* object to return:

```
protected virtual ViewResult View(IView view, object model)
{
    // You provided a strongly typed object for the data in the view.
    // Let's store it properly.
    if (model != null)
    {
        base.ViewData.Model = model;
    }

    // Arrange a view result object
    ViewResult result = new ViewResult();

    // Put some data into it.
    result.View = view;

    // Pass ViewData and TempData dictionaries down to the view
    result.ViewData = this.ViewData;
    result.TempData = this.TempData;

    // Return
    return result;
}
```

Instead of receiving a ready-to-use *IView* object, the method can get the name of the view to
create, and optionally its master view. The structure of the method doesn't really change that
much, as you can see here:

```
protected virtual ViewResult View(string viewName, string masterName, object model)
{
    :
    :

    // Put some data into it.
    result.ViewName = viewName;
    result.MasterName = masterName;

    :
    :
}
```

Instead of the *IView* object, the view name and master name are stored into the newly created instance of *ViewResult*. In the end, the *ViewResult* object contains an *IView* object or any data required by the view engine to create an *IView* object. The *IView* object will actually generate the response for the browser. The action invoker is then responsible for processing the *ViewResult* object.

The Action Invoker

As you saw in Chapter 4, the execution of any controller method is monitored by a special component known as the *action invoker*. The following listing serves as a reminder of the code that governs the execution of an action method:

```
// This virtual method on the Controller class controls the
// execution of the selected action method
protected override void ExecuteCore()
{
    :
    :

    try
    {
        string requiredString = this.RouteData.GetRequiredString("action");
        if (!this.ActionInvoker.InvokeAction(
                base.ControllerContext, requiredString))
        {
            this.HandleUnknownAction(requiredString);
        }
    }
    finally
    {

        :
        :

    }
}
```

The action invoker is a customizable component of the controller's scaffolding. From a developer's perspective, it's simply a class that implements the *IActionInvoker* interface. The action invoker is exposed through the public property *ActionInvoker*. The default action invoker is an instance of the class *ControllerActionInvoker*. The following listing shows the implementation of the *ActionInvoker* property in the *Controller* base class:

```
private IActionInvoker _actionInvoker;
public IActionInvoker ActionInvoker
{
    get
    {
        if (this._actionInvoker == null)
            this._actionInvoker = new ControllerActionInvoker();
        return this._actionInvoker;
    }
```

```
    set
    {
        this._actionInvoker = value;
    }
}
```

The *IActionInvoker* interface defines the policy according to which a controller can invoke an action in response to an HTTP request:

```
public interface IActionInvoker
{
    bool InvokeAction(ControllerContext controllerContext, string actionName);
}
```

The action invoker does two key things. First, it executes the controller's method and saves the action result. Next, it processes the action result. Here's the relevant section of code:

```
protected virtual void InvokeActionResult(
    ControllerContext controllerContext, ActionResult actionResult)
{
    actionResult.ExecuteResult(controllerContext);
}
```

As you can see, processing the action result ends up in a call being made to the *ExecuteResult* method of the action result object. For an HTML view, executing the result just renders the markup to the response stream. This operation is orchestrated by the *ExecuteResult* method on the *ViewResult* class.

The *ViewResult* Class

The *ViewResult* class basically supplies the model to the view object and then renders it to the response. The class inherits from *ViewResultBase*, whose properties are listed in Table 5-1.

TABLE 5-1 Properties of the *ViewResultBase* class

Member	Description
TempData	Initially set with the content of the *TempData* dictionary as defined on the controller class.
View	Contains the *IView* object to be rendered to the response.
ViewData	Initially set with the content of the *ViewData* dictionary as defined on the controller class.
ViewEngineCollection	Refers to the collection of view engines available to the application.
ViewName	Contains the name of the view to be rendered. If the value of this property is null, the name will be resolved when processing the view result.

The *ViewResultBase* class also features a couple of methods. In particular, the class overrides the *ExecuteResult* method and defines an additional abstract method—the *FindView* method.

The *ExecuteResult* method contains the entire logic employed to orchestrate the rendering of the view:

```
public override void ExecuteResult(ControllerContext context)
{
    // Make sure we have a context to work with
    if (context == null)
        throw new ArgumentNullException("context");

    // Resolve the view name (if left unspecified by the developer)
    if (string.IsNullOrEmpty(this.ViewName))
        this.ViewName = context.RouteData.GetRequiredString("action");

    // Ask the view engine to return an IView object (if not specified)
    ViewEngineResult result = null;
    if (this.View == null)
    {
        // Method FindView must be overridden by derived classes such as ViewResult
        result = this.FindView(context);
        this.View = result.View;

        // Note that the FindView method on derived classes would throw an
        // exception if the view could not be created.
    }

    // Prepare a view context container object, and render the view
    ViewContext viewContext = new ViewContext(
                context, this.View, this.ViewData, this.TempData);
    this.View.Render(viewContext, context.HttpContext.Response.Output);

    // Release the IView object
    if (result != null)
            result.ViewEngine.ReleaseView(context, this.View);
}
```

First, assuming there is a context to work with, the *ExecuteResult* method resolves the view name. If the developer left it unspecified (for example, the developer invokes the parameterless overload of the *View* method on the controller class), the view name defaults to the name of the current action method.

If no valid *IView* object has been passed, the method leverages the *FindView* method to locate the current view engine and have it return a valid *IView* object. Note that *FindView* is abstract on *ViewResultBase* and must be overridden in *ViewResult* and other derived classes.

The *ViewResult* class extends *ViewResultBase* by simply adding a *MasterName* property to indicate the name of the master view (if any) and overriding *FindView*.

Finally, the *ExecuteResult* method prepares the view context container and passes that to the *Render* method on the *IView* object for writing markup to the output stream.

> **Note** The *FindView* method leverages the capabilities of the view engine to retrieve and instantiate the view object. If the view engine is unable to create and return a valid view object, the *FindView* method on the *ViewResult* class bundles up information and throws an exception. The view engine will not throw any exception itself, but it provides information about the searched locations. Note that getting a view object is only a preliminary step and no rendering has happened as yet at this point.

The *ViewContext* Class

The *ViewContext* class extends *ControllerContext* by adding some view-related properties. Specifically, it adds *TempData*, *ViewData*, and *View*. All in all, the *ViewContext* class has no other purpose than grouping any information that is functional to rendering the view.

Creating the View

As mentioned earlier, you need an *IView* object in order to render the response to the browser. The *IView* object can be created, or obtained, by the controller and passed along using the overload of method *View* that accepts an *IView*. More often, though, the *IView* object is created internally through the services of the view engine.

The View Engine

The view engine is a replaceable component that receives all the information packed in the *ViewResult* container. The view engine is expected to create and return an object that knows how to render the response to the output stream.

ASP.NET MVC defines the interface for the view engine plus a small hierarchy of concrete view engine classes. The interface is *IViewEngine*, and it's defined as follows:

```
public interface IViewEngine
{
    ViewEngineResult FindPartialView(
        ControllerContext controllerContext,
        string partialViewName,
        bool useCache);
    ViewEngineResult FindView(
        ControllerContext controllerContext,
        string viewName,
        string masterName,
        bool useCache);
    void ReleaseView(
        ControllerContext controllerContext,
        IView view);
}
```

The role of each method is relatively straightforward and is detailed in Table 5-2.

TABLE 5-2 Methods of the *IViewEngine* interface

Method	Description
FindPartialView	Creates and returns an *IView* object based on the specified controller information plus the name of a partial view
FindView	Creates and returns an *IView* object based on the specified controller information plus the name of a view and its master
ReleaseView	Releases the specified *IView* object

Both *FindPartialView* and *FindView* return a *ViewEngineResult* object, which represents the results of locating a view engine. The type is a plain container and, despite the "Result" suffix in the name, doesn't inherit from *ActionResult*.

```
public class ViewEngineResult
{
    public ViewEngineResult(IEnumerable<String> searchedLocations);
    public ViewEngineResult(IView view, IViewEngine viewEngine);

    public IEnumerable<String> SearchedLocations { get; private set; }
    public IView View { get; private set; }
    public IViewEngine ViewEngine { get; private set; }
}
```

The *ViewEngineResult* type just aggregates the *IView* object, the view engine object used to create it, and the list of locations searched to create the view. The content of the *SearchedLocations* property depends on the structure and behavior of the selected view engine. The *ReleaseView* method is intended to dispose of any reference that the *IView* object has in use. Obviously, the implementation of the *ReleaseView* method also can vary—even significantly—depending on the view engine.

ASP.NET MVC includes one default view engine that I'll examine in a moment.

The View Object

The *IView* interface is an abstraction for a dedicated object that builds on the view context and writes a response to a text writer. The interface is shown here:

```
public interface IView
{
    void Render(ViewContext viewContext, TextWriter writer);
}
```

As you saw earlier, the text writer is provided by the *ViewResult* object—the final consumer of the *IView* object. Any view object has a relatively simple structure—a generic renderer of markup—but its internal structure and logic are tightly coupled to the mechanics of the view engine.

Partial Views

In ASP.NET MVC, you can distinguish between views and partial views. There's no great difference between a view and a partial view. Quite simply, a partial view is a small and reusable piece of a view. The difference between views and partial views in ASP.NET MVC is nearly the same as between Web Forms and user controls.

Both types of a view get the same input and produce the same output; both are represented by the *IView* interface. A partial view, however, has no concept of a master view and is therefore simply a fraction of the total rendering necessary for the request. The total view can result from multiple partial independent views.

A partial view can be driven by a different view engine than the parent view. As the *IViewEngine* interface shows, a view engine is expected to support both partial views and global views.

The Default View Engine

ASP.NET MVC comes with a default view engine that is extensively based on a subset of the Web Forms machinery. Note that ASP.NET MVC leverages the existing Web Forms scaffolding only for rendering and largely ignores the postback capabilities of it.

The *VirtualPathProvider* View Engine

In ASP.NET Web Forms, the generation of the response is based on the processing of a template file expressed using the ASPX markup. The Web Forms machinery is responsible for locating the ASPX source file and compiling it dynamically into an HTTP handler class. Next, the dynamically created class is processed, goes through the ASP.NET page life cycle, and writes any response out at the end of it all.

To locate the ASPX source file, Web Forms relies on the services of a special component—the *VirtualPathProvider* class, defined in the *System.Web.Hosting* namespace within the *system.web* assembly. The *VirtualPathProvider* class implements a virtual file system for a Web application and returns content in response to a file name request. More details about the role of a virtual path provider in ASP.NET can be found in the sidebar "What's a Virtual Path Provider, Anyway?".

ASP.NET MVC builds its default view engine around the services of the *VirtualPathProvider* class. Basically, the default view engine leverages the path provider to locate the ASPX templates and process them into markup. In doing so, most of the processing logic of Web Forms is reused.

ASP.NET MVC defines a small hierarchy of view engine classes. The abstract class *VirtualPathProviderViewEngine* provides the set of core services. The derived class *WebFormsViewEngine*, on the other hand, fills in any behavior that the parent class left unspecified.

What's a Virtual Path Provider, Anyway?

Introduced with ASP.NET 2.0 to serve the needs of the Microsoft Office SharePoint Server development team, the virtual path provider mechanism in ASP.NET is a way to virtualize a bunch of files and even a structure of directories. Up to the latest version (4.0), ASP.NET doesn't read the content of any requested resources directly from disk; instead, ASP.NET gets it through the services of the built-in *VirtualPathProvider* class. This class assumes a one-to-one correspondence between *.aspx* resources and disk files and serves ASP.NET with just the expected content. So nothing really works differently for the end developer even though significant architectural refactoring work was performed.

By deriving your own class from the system-provided *VirtualPathProvider* class, you can implement a virtual file system for your Web application. In such a virtual file system, you essentially abstract Web content away from the physical structure of the file system. As an example, you might serve incoming page requests based on the source code you have stored in a Microsoft SQL Server database. A virtual path provider takes a file name, directory name, or both and returns the content for it (or them). Where the content really comes from is a detail hidden in the implementation of the provider.

Most of the files involved with the processing of an ASP.NET request can be stored in a virtual file system. The list includes ASP.NET pages, themes, master pages, user controls, custom resources mapped to a build provider, and static Web resources such as HTML pages and images. A virtual path provider, however, can't serve global resources (such as *global.asax* and *web.config*) and the contents of reserved folders (such as *Bin*, *App_Data*, *App_GlobalResources*, *App_Browsers*, *App_Code*) and any *App_LocalResources*.

Core Services of a Path-Based View Engine

The *VirtualPathProviderViewEngine* class is essentially an implementation of the *IViewEngine* interface. Most of what it does relates to the methods in the interface—resolving views, resolving partial views, and releasing views.

The implementation of an interface's *FindPartialView* and *FindView* methods is nearly identical and differs only in terms of an extra name that has to be resolved for views—the location of the file where the content of the master view is stored. So without getting too specific, let's examine the implementation of the sole *FindView* method.

The method attempts to resolve the view name and the master view name in terms of some physical *.aspx* and *.master* files on the server. If the search is successful, the method attempts to create an *IView* object and packs that into a *ViewEngineResult* object.

The *VirtualPathProviderViewEngine* class doesn't personally take care of the creation of the *IView* object; instead, it delegates that task to derived classes. The method *CreateView* used in the following listing is, in fact, marked as abstract on the *VirtualPathProviderViewEngine* class:

```
public virtual ViewEngineResult FindView(
    ControllerContext context, string viewName, string masterName, bool useCache)
{
    string[] searchedViewLocations;
    string[] searchedMasterLocations;

    :
    :

    // Get the controller name for the current action
    String requiredString = context.RouteData.GetRequiredString("controller");

    // Get the physical path for the ASPX template to use for the specified view
    String viewTemplatePath = this.GetPath(context,
            this.ViewLocationFormats,
            "ViewLocationFormats",
            viewName,
            requiredString,
            "View",
            useCache,
            out searchedViewLocations);

    // Get the physical path for the MASTER template to use for the specified master
    String masterTemplatePath = this.GetPath(context,
            this.MasterLocationFormats,
            "MasterLocationFormats",
            masterName,
            requiredString,
            "Master",
            useCache,
            out searchedMasterLocations);

    // Check physical paths
    if (!String.IsNullOrEmpty(viewTemplatePath) &&
       (!String.IsNullOrEmpty(masterTemplatePath) || String.IsNullOrEmpty(masterName)))
    {
        // Create the view object, and pack it into a ViewEngineResult container
        return new ViewEngineResult(
                this.CreateView(context, viewTemplatePath, masterTemplatePath), this);

    }
    // If here, then view or master couldn't be resolved. The ViewEngineResult
    // being returned then contains only the list of locations unsuccessfully
    // searched. This information is used to arrange the exception message.
    return new ViewEngineResult(
        searchedViewLocations.Union<String>(searchedMasterLocations));
}
```

GetPath is a private member of the *VirtualPathProviderViewEngine* class, which contains the logic for resolving names to files. Ultimately, the method loops through a predefined list of location names and attempts to see whether a match can be found according to naming convention rules currently set. For example, this method is responsible for implementing the rule that says the view *Bar* invoked by controller *XXX* must be a *bar.aspx* file located under the *Views\XXX* folder. The list of locations to search for views, partial views, and master views is stored in ad hoc public properties on the *VirtualPathProviderViewEngine* class.

These properties—named *ViewLocationFormats*, *PartialViewLocationFormats*, and *MasterLocationFormats*, respectively—are string arrays left unassigned in the *VirtualPathProviderViewEngine* class. They are set, instead, by the actual view engine class doing the real job of creating *IView* objects.

The *GetPath* method also uses a cache to speed up the search. Any view name that is successfully resolved is stored in a location view cache. The cache is then checked first on any subsequent access. The view cache is abstracted by the *IViewLocationCache* interface and is exposed as a public read/write property named *ViewLocationCache*. The class that provides view location cache services by default is *DefaultViewLocationCache*. It stores any resolved view names in the ASP.NET *Cache* object.

> **Note** Just like any other class in ASP.NET MVC, the *DefaultViewLocationCache* class doesn't use any ASP.NET intrinsic objects directly. Instead, it uses the *HttpContextBase* class as an intermediary, which gains you isolation from the ASP.NET runtime during testing.

When the View Name Can't Be Resolved

It's interesting to notice that the view engine doesn't throw any exception when the view name can't be resolved. As you might have noticed, the *GetPath* method provides an output argument at the bottom of the signature. This argument is expected to be an array of strings containing the searched locations.

```
private string GetPath(
    ControllerContext controllerContext,
    string[] locations,
    string locationsPropertyName,
    string name,
    string controllerName,
    string cacheKeyPrefix,
    bool useCache,
    string[] searchedLocations)
```

The argument is filled with any locations on the Web server where the *GetPath* method attempts to find a match between existing files and any provided view name.

If the view engine detects that it doesn't hold enough information to create the view, it performs a set union operation between the paths that were searched for view and master view and packs that information into the returned *ViewEngineResult* container. That information is then displayed in the subsequent exception, as illustrated in Figure 5-2.

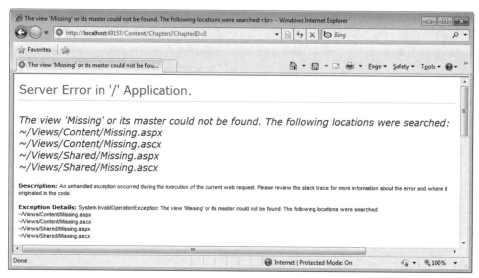

FIGURE 5-2 Message and stack trace of the exception shown when a view can't be created.

The Web Forms View Engine

As mentioned, the *VirtualPathProviderViewEngine* class provides only the core services of a file-based view engine. The details are filled in by the *WebFormsViewEngine* class, which is the class that provides the *IView* objects for any ASP.NET MVC application that doesn't use its own view engine.

The *WebFormsViewEngine* Class

The *WebFormsViewEngine* class derives from *VirtualPathProviderViewEngine* and extends it by overriding *CreatePartialView*, *CreateView*, and *FileExists*. The signature of the class is shown here:

```
public class WebFormViewEngine : VirtualPathProviderViewEngine
{
    // Fields
    private IBuildManager _buildManager;

    // Methods
    public WebFormViewEngine();
    protected override IView CreatePartialView(
        ControllerContext context, string partialPath);
    protected override IView CreateView(
        ControllerContext context, string viewPath, string masterPath);
    protected override bool FileExists(
        ControllerContext context, string virtualPath);

    // Properties
    internal IBuildManager BuildManager { get; set; }
}
```

Setting Location Formats

The constructor of *WebFormsViewEngine* sets the paths to be searched when resolving views, partial views, and master views:

```
public WebFormViewEngine()
{
    // Set the locations to search to resolve master views
    base.MasterLocationFormats = new string[] {
            "~/Views/{1}/{0}.master",
            "~/Views/Shared/{0}.master" };
    // Set the locations to search to resolve master views if areas are used
    base.AreaMasterLocationFormats = new string[] {
            "~/Areas/{2}/Views/{1}/{0}.master",
            "~/Areas/{2}/Views/Shared/{0}.master" };

    // Set the locations to search to resolve views
    base.ViewLocationFormats = new string[] {
            "~/Views/{1}/{0}.aspx",
            "~/Views/{1}/{0}.ascx",
            "~/Views/Shared/{0}.aspx",
            "~/Views/Shared/{0}.ascx" };
    // Set the locations to search to resolve views if areas are used
    base.AreaViewLocationFormats = new string[] {
            "~/Areas/{2}/Views/{1}/{0}.aspx",
            "~/Areas/{2}/Views/{1}/{0}.ascx",
            "~/Areas/{2}/Views/Shared/{0}.aspx",
            "~/Areas/{2}/Views/Shared/{0}.ascx" };

    // Same locations for views and partial views
    base.PartialViewLocationFormats = base.ViewLocationFormats;
    // Same locations for views and partial views if areas are used
    base.AreaPartialViewLocationFormats = base.AreaViewLocationFormats;
}
```

From here, it should be clear that if you have reasons for using a different directory schema for some of your views, all you need to do is derive a simple class as shown here:

```
public class MyWebFormsViewEngine : WebFormViewEngine
{
    public MyWebFormsViewEngine()
    {
        // Ignoring areas in this example

        this.MasterLocationFormats = base.MasterLocationFormats;
        this.ViewLocationFormats = new string[]
                                    {
                                        "~/Views/{1}/{0}.aspx"
                                    };

        // Customize the location for partial views
        this.PartialViewLocationFormats = new string[]
                                    {
                                        "~/PartialViews/{1}/{0}.aspx",
                                        "~/PartialViews/{1}/{0}.ascx"
                                    };
    }
}
```

To use this class in lieu of the default view engine, you enter the following code in *global.asax*:

```
protected void Application_Start()
{
    RegisterRoutes(RouteTable.Routes);

    // Removes the default engine and adds the new one
    ViewEngines.Engines.Clear();
    ViewEngines.Engines.Add(new MyWebFormsViewEngine());
}
```

From now on, your application will fail if any of the partial views is located outside a *PartialViews* subfolder. (See Figure 5-3.)

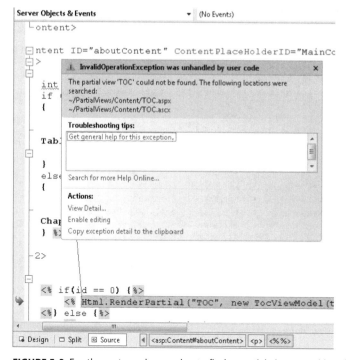

FIGURE 5-3 For the custom view engine to find a partial view, an ad hoc folder is required.

There's more to say about registration of custom view engines, so I'll return to this topic in Chapter 11.

The *WebFormView* Class

The main purpose of the *WebFormsViewEngine* class is to create *IView* objects for views and partial views. The parent class of *WebFormsViewEngine* does most of the orchestration but leaves the derived class with the burden of physically creating the object. As you can see from the implementation of the *CreateView* and *CreatePartialView* methods, the default view object is an instance of the *WebFormView* class:

```
protected override IView CreatePartialView(
        ControllerContext context, string partialPath)
{
    return new WebFormView(partialPath, null);
}
protected override IView CreateView(
        ControllerContext context, string viewPath, string masterPath)
{
    return new WebFormView(viewPath, masterPath);
}
```

WebFormView is a class that contains the information needed to build a Web Forms page in ASP.NET MVC and the behavior to render it. The class constructor doesn't really do much other than store the view and master paths internally.

The *WebFormView* class implements the *IView* interface, so it's no surprise that most of the job the class performs is concentrated in the *IView.Render* method.

The method *Render* relies extensively on the ASP.NET Web Forms infrastructure to produce a response for the browser. First, the method resorts to the ASP.NET *BuildManager* object to ensure that the ASPX (or ASCX) source files are properly compiled to the canonical dynamic page class. Next, it gets from the build manager a reference to the page object to render. The behavior is summarized in the following code snippet:

```
public virtual void Render(ViewContext viewContext, TextWriter writer)
{
    :
    :

    // Gets the ASP.NET dynamic page object
    object obj = this.BuildManager.CreateInstanceFromVirtualPath(
                                        this.ViewPath, typeof(object));

    :
    :

    // In ASP.NET MVC, the dynamic page object derives from ViewPage, not Page
    ViewPage page = obj as ViewPage;
    if (page != null)
    {
        this.RenderViewPage(viewContext, page);
    }
    else
    {
        // If not a ViewPage, it might be a ViewUserControl
        ViewUserControl control = obj as ViewUserControl;
        if (control != null)
            this.RenderViewUserControl(viewContext, control);
    }
}
```

In ASP.NET MVC, when the Web Forms–based view engine is used, it's assumed that the code-behind class inherits from *ViewPage* for plain views and *ViewUserControl* for partial views. You can use any custom class on top of those in your actual code. However, at the very minimum, page and user control classes need to have the extended set of members that characterize *ViewPage* and *ViewUserControl* rather than *Page* and *UserControl*, which are available in plain Web Forms.

The *ViewPage* and *ViewUserControl* Classes

These classes extend ASP.NET's canonical *Page* and *UserControl* classes by adding a variety of properties that collect the view context for the request. Table 5-3 lists extra properties for *ViewPage*.

TABLE 5-3 Properties of the *ViewPage* class

Property	Description
Ajax	Helper object of type *AjaxHelper* that groups a number of methods useful for rendering HTML in AJAX scenarios.
Html	Helper object of type *HtmlHelper* that groups a number of methods useful for HTML rendering.
MasterLocation	Gets and sets the master location.
Model	Convenience property used to access the *Model* property on *ViewData*.
TempData	Convenience property used to access the *TempData* property on *ViewContext*.
Url	Helper object of type *UrlHelper* that groups a number of methods useful for working with ASP.NET MVC routes.
ViewContext	Gets and sets the view context for the request.
ViewData	Gets or sets a dictionary that contains data to pass between the controller and the view.
Writer	Gets and sets the HTML writer object used to render any response.

As you saw earlier, the *ViewContext* class is a container for a bunch of view-related properties, including *Model*, *TempData*, and *ViewData*. In *ViewPage*, you find both a *ViewContext* property and individual properties for some of its exposed members. As far as *Model* and *TempData* are concerned, the redundant properties exist simply for your own convenience:

```
// References the object in the Model property of the ViewData object
public object Model
{
    get { return this.ViewData.Model; }
}

// References the object in the TempData property of the ViewContext object
public TempDataDictionary TempData
{
    get { return this.ViewContext.TempData; }
}
```

```
public ViewDataDictionary ViewData
{
    get
    {
        if (this._viewData == null)
            this.SetViewData(new ViewDataDictionary());
        return this._viewData;
    }
    set { this.SetViewData(value); }
}
```

The implementation of *ViewData*, on the other hand, is that of a plain *get/set* property in both *ViewPage* and *ViewUserControl*. Weird, isn't it? So, are *ViewData* and *ViewContext. ViewState* really two distinct containers? Yes, of course—they just point to the same object reference. The trick is that *WebFormView* sets the *ViewData* property of *ViewPage* to the object referenced by the *ViewContext* object. Right after that, *WebFormView* orders the *ViewPage* instance to render.

In the end, it seems to be simply a matter of convoluted design or, more likely, a point that was missed during the refactoring process. The documentation for the public *ViewData* property on the *ViewPage* class is not very clear on this point.

You will find that most of these *ViewPage* properties listed in Table 5-3 are also supported by the twin class *ViewUserControl*, with a couple of notable exceptions. The *MasterLocation* property is not supported for user controls. In addition, the *ViewUserControl* class supports an extra string property named *ViewDataKey*.

The use of the *ViewDataKey* property relates to filtering the content being sent to the partial view. Let's find out more.

Filtering *ViewData* Content in Partial Views

A typical view for a realistic ASP.NET MVC application is made of a main view and a variety of partial views, possibly nested. Each (partial) view is expected to rely entirely on the content of the provided *ViewData* dictionary to get any information it needs to render. How does the content of *ViewData* (originally set by the controller) flow into the multiple partial views?

The content of *ViewData* flows unchanged from the main view down to any of its partial views, and from there to any nested views. Note, though, that even when views and partial views share the same *ViewData* content, it's never the same object reference. Each partial view, in fact, receives from the parent its own copy of the *ViewData* container. The parent, of course, can pass down the exact copy of its own *ViewData* object or a modified version.

As you'll see later in the chapter, the parent view creates a new *ViewData* dictionary explicitly when it intends to pass a different set of data items to the partial view. When the parent doesn't care about adjusting the *ViewData* content for a partial view, making a copy of the *ViewData* dictionary is the precise responsibility of the HTML helper used to render the partial view. (I'll say more about this in a moment.)

Because a partial view (including a nested partial view) always receives a copy of the *ViewData* dictionary, it just can't rely on the dictionary to pass data back to its parent. In general, the philosophy of ASP.NET MVC entails that views are completely isolated from one another and never attempt to communicate.

Accepting Only a Section of the *ViewData* Content

So the main view can filter the content of the *ViewData* dictionary being passed on to the partial view. At the same time, the partial view can also be configured to accept only a segment of the parent's *ViewData* dictionary.

By setting the *ViewDataKey* property on a partial view, you instruct the partial view to load only the content of the parent's *ViewData* dictionary that is stored in the specified item, if any. Note that the value stored in *ViewDataKey* is taken into account only if the partial view receives a null *ViewData* dictionary. In this case, if the parent dictionary contains a matching entry, the value is extracted and processed, as in the following pseudo-code:

```
// Get the ViewData for this ViewUserControl
ViewDataDictionary myViewData = ...;
    .
    .
    .

if (!String.IsNullOrEmpty(ViewDataKey))
{
    // Extract the object in the ViewDataKey entry of ViewData
    object target = myViewData.Eval(this.ViewDataKey) as ViewDataDictionary;

    // Take it, if it is another dictionary
    if (target != null)
        myViewData = target as ViewDataDictionary;
    else
        // If it is not another dictionary, store it in Model
        myViewData = new ViewDataDictionary(myViewData) { Model = target };
}
```

If the dictionary value pointed to by *ViewDataKey* is another *ViewDataDictionary* object, it's taken and passed on to the partial view. Otherwise, a new dictionary is created where the *Model* property contains just the object pointed to by the *ViewDataKey* entry in the parent dictionary.

Keep in mind that the effect produced by the *ViewDataKey* property depends on the way in which you reference the partial view. If you do that through the *RenderPartial* HTML helper, the partial view is guaranteed to receive a non-null dictionary, which means that *ViewDataKey* is disregarded.

```
<% Html.RenderPartial("yourpartialview"); %>
```

What else can you do, then, to reference a partial view? You can use the old-fashioned, but still effective, server-side approach:

```
<x:YourPartialView runat="server" ViewDataKey="SampleKey" />
```

If you do so, no view data dictionary gets silently passed to the partial view; subsequently, the value of *ViewDataKey* is processed and a fraction of the main dictionary is passed to the partial view.

Rendering the View

To top off our discussion about the mechanics of view rendering, one more argument is left to cover. So let's briefly examine what happens after the *ViewPage* (or the *ViewUserControl*) object has received control and has been ordered to render the view.

As the following pseudo-code shows, the *WebFormView* class first configures the page object (or user control) and then orders it to render:

```
void RenderViewPage(ViewContext context, ViewPage page)
{
    if (!string.IsNullOrEmpty(this.MasterPath))
        page.MasterLocation = this.MasterPath;

    page.ViewData = context.ViewData;
    page.RenderView(context);
}
```
It's particularly interesting to look at the internal implementation of the *RenderView* method on *ViewPage*.

The method checks what's behind the response stream object—the *Response.Output* property. There are two possibilities: it is the real output stream, or it is a text writer object provided by code in an attempt to capture the output being written by the view. If no custom text writer has been provided, the request is served through *ProcessRequest* as if it were a regular Web Forms call. If a custom text writer has been provided, the request is executed via *Server.Execute*, which offers a chance to pass in a writer where the output could be accumulated.

In the end, the rendering of an ASP.NET MVC view is triggered with either a call to *Server. Execute* or *ProcessRequest* method. It's the same method defined on the *System.Web.UI.Page* class that implements the ASP.NET Web Forms request life cycle.

This fact has a number of implications—for example, it means you can use server controls inside of an ASP.NET MVC view or partial view. In addition, it means that the classic life-cycle events you might have learned from Web Forms (*Init*, *Load*, *PreRender*, as well as control-specific events such as the *GridView*'s *RowDataBound* event) are still there and fully supported.

Writing a View

Writing an ASP.NET MVC view entails writing a source file that represents a template for the response you want to serve to the end user. The template can be written in any syntax that any of the currently registered view engines can understand. The *ViewResult* class resolves the view name by looping through the list of registered view engines and looking for the first engine that can resolve the view into an *IView* object.

To successfully resolve a view, the view engine must be able to find the template associated with the view name and that understand its content. Each view engine can use a different set of rules as far as the view name-to-template association is concerned, and each view engine might be able to recognize a different syntax in the template.

The default view engine—the *WebFormsViewEngine* class—uses the familiar ASPX markup syntax of ASP.NET Web Forms. This means that a number of Web Forms markup features can be reused, including server controls, master pages, themes, data binding expressions, and *$*-prefixed dynamic expressions.

Free HTML for Everybody

I already briefly touched on this topic in Chapter 1, "Goals of ASP.NET MVP and Motivations for Its Development," but it would be useful to restate some points here now that you've become more familiar with ASP.NET MVC and can look at Web Forms from a broader perspective.

When working with Web Forms, you use server controls for almost anything you need to have in the user interface. This approach certainly increases your productivity and also gives you a great design-time experience—you see what a page looks like as you author it. Server controls, however, come with a cost. They're essentially black boxes that get some input through properties and return some HTML. The returned HTML is influenced by the configuration you provide through properties, but very few server controls let you declaratively alter the structure of their output. For example, a server control designed to output a plain HTML table can typically not be configured to build and output a list, or even an XHTML-compliant table.

As a matter of fact, server controls limit the expressiveness of the HTML you can obtain. Is this a problem? This limitation is becoming a bigger problem every day because of the following functional and nonfunctional forces:

- The desire or need to be XHTML-compliant

- The need to provide high degrees of accessibility

- The desire or need to use cascading style sheets (CSS) to style pages

- The desire or need to use AJAX capabilities, and the subsequent need to control element IDs and the structure of any parts of the DOM

- The need to ensure the page will look the same on a number of different Web browsers

For many people, the natural equation seems to be *Web Forms equals server controls*. This equation is largely true, but it's not exactly true. Nothing really prevents you from writing ASPX pages using plain HTML elements that are even devoid of the *runat=server* attribute that adds some server-side capabilities. The point is that if you do so, you then enter into a "do less with more" scenario because you still pay for the view state and the complex infrastructure of Web Forms without gaining any benefit from it.

In ASP.NET MVC, you are forced to take a "close to the metal" approach when it comes to authoring a view and you don't pay extra costs in terms of run-time behavior. In addition, the programming model of ASP.NET MVC leads you toward *passive* and *humble* views that just render the data they get from the outside. All the logic is being moved up to the controller level, where a rich abstraction layer (for example, model binders and Convention-over-Configuration aspects) let you map input data to a strongly typed data model for easier processing. After the work is done, you just attach pieces of data to the view according to the needs of the view layout.

In summary, you can always gain the freedom of using the HTML you want; technologically speaking, there's nothing to stop you from getting this. The conventional Web Forms programming style, however, leads you to using server controls and losing control over the HTML—quite the opposite of what happens with ASP.NET MVC.

The View's Template

When using the default rendering engine, the view is a common ASPX file and can contain virtually any markup expressions you would use in classic ASP.NET. An ASPX file for a view is typically a single *.aspx* file that is limited to declaring the name of its parent view-page class. If required, though, it can have an explicit code-behind class with some logic inside.

Adding a New View

Most of the views you add to an ASP.NET MVC application are bound to a controller and go under the *Views* folder in a subfolder with the name of the controller. However, views shared by multiple controllers (for example, error views or partial views) can be placed under the Views\Shared folder. (See Figure 5-4.)

You can add a new view by simply adding a file in the right location or using the Add View dialog box in Microsoft Visual Studio, which is shown in Figure 5-5. You trigger the dialog box by right-clicking on any item under the Views folder. The right-clicked item determines the actual destination of the view file.

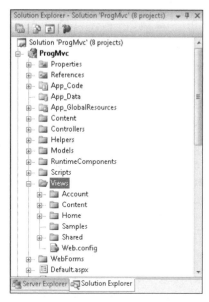

FIGURE 5-4 An interior view of the Views folder in an ASP.NET MVC project.

FIGURE 5-5 Adding a new view to an ASP.NET MVC application.

The dialog box doesn't let you choose the actual destination of the new view file. Its default location is based on where you right-clicked. If the file doesn't show up where you want it to be, it's up to you to move it around in the right folder.

Note As long as you use the default view engine, you're forced to keep all your views in one of two places. They can live only under the controller's folder below the *Views* folder or in the Views\ Shared folder. The default view engine won't be able to resolve views located anywhere else.

The main parameters of a view are the name, whether it's a partial view, whether it's a strongly typed view, and its master page. The name of the view is a plain string and doesn't need any extensions. The file created automatically has the proper extension added to it—either *.aspx* for main views or *.ascx* for partial views. You refer to the view programmatically using the name of the file without extension.

Partial Views

The first key decision to make about a view is whether you want it to be partial or not. A partial view covers a fraction of the total view and is expected to be a small and reusable piece of user interface. A partial view can't be based on a master page, either.

In ASP.NET MVC, a partial view is analogous to a user control in Web Forms. The syntax for a partial view is also the same syntax for a user control in Web Forms. This includes special features such as output caching. Under the hood, rendering a partial view entails rendering a user control, at least when using the default view engine.

A partial view in ASP.NET MVC is rendered through the *ViewUserControl* class, which derives from ASP.NET's *UserControl* class. The *ViewUserControl* class adds some extra properties (which are listed in Table 5-3) and implements the *IViewDataContainer* interface. Note that this interface exists only to abstract the *ViewData* property.

```
public interface IViewDataContainer
{
    ViewDataDictionary ViewData { get; set; }
}
```

It's interesting to look at the heading of a partial view:

```
<%@ Control Language="C#" Inherits="System.Web.Mvc.ViewUserControl" %>
```

The heading doesn't mention any code-behind class file and is limited to declaring that the dynamic class created by the ASP.NET runtime on the fly will derive from *ViewUserControl*. This also means that no code-behind class is required for the partial view. Most of the time, in fact, you just don't need it. But I'll return to this point in the next section when discussing how to fill up a view.

The typical location for a partial view is the Shared folder under Views. However, you can also store a partial view under the controller-specific folder. This location is searched earlier in the rendering process, too. A partial view usually gets the *.ascx* extension, but it can also have the *.aspx* extension. Other extensions are not recognized by the default view engine.

Master Pages

If the view is not a partial view, it can have a master page. The master page in this context is exactly the same as the master page in Web Forms. It's a standard *.master* file, but it's located under the *Views\Shared* folder.

In ASP.NET MVC, a master page is implemented through the services of *ViewMasterPage*, which is defined as follows:

```
public class ViewMasterPage : MasterPage
{
    public ViewMasterPage();

    // Properties
    public AjaxHelper Ajax { get; }
    public HtmlHelper Html { get; }
    public object Model { get; }
    public TempDataDictionary TempData { get; }
    public UrlHelper Url { get; }
    public ViewContext ViewContext { get; }
    public ViewDataDictionary ViewData { get; }
    internal ViewPage ViewPage { get; }
    public HtmlTextWriter Writer { get; }
}
```

As you can see, it extends the ASP.NET *MasterPage* class with the typical helpers and properties of ASP.NET MVC views, such as *Html*, *Model*, and *ViewContext*.

By default, a master page in ASP.NET MVC doesn't require a code-behind class. However, if you need to expose your own programming model out of the master, you can use a *<script>* server-side tag (which is the recommended approach) or manually create code-behind classes. Here's a brief example:

```
public partial class SiteMasterExtended : System.Web.Mvc.ViewMasterPage
{
    public string PageHeading
    {
        get { return this.__PageHeading.Text; }
        set { this.__PageHeading.Text = value; }
    }
}
```

The sample master page class inherits from *ViewMasterPage* and just adds some properties. Most of the time, extra properties are mere wrappers around some of the controls embedded in the master page template, as shown in the following example:

```
<div>
    <asp:Literal runat="server" ID="__PageHeading">The Book</asp:Literal>
</div>
```

Note that if you decide to add a code-behind class manually, you should ensure that Visual Studio also creates a designer class file (*xxx.master.designer.cs*) that includes references to server controls in the markup:

```
public partial class SiteMasterExtended
{
    protected global::System.Web.UI.WebControls.Literal __PageHeading;
    .
    .
    .
}
```

To set properties exposed by the master view, you need to write a handler for the *PreInit* event in the page life cycle, as shown here:

```
<%@ Page MasterPageFile="~/Views/Shared/Site.Master"
        Inherits="System.Web.Mvc.ViewPage" %>
<%@ MasterType TypeName="ProgMvc.Views.Shared.SiteMasterExtended" %>

<script runat="server" Language="C#">
    protected void Page_PreInit(object sender, EventArgs e)
    {
        this.Master.PageHeading = "Chapters";
    }
</script>

<asp:Content ...>
    .
    .
    .
</asp:Content>
```

In Web Forms, through a *PreInit* handler you could also switch master pages on the fly, as shown below.

```
protected void Page_PreInit(object sender, EventArgs e)
{
    this.MasterPageFile = "~/Views/Shared/VertLayout.Master";
}
```

In ASP:NET MVC, you don't need this if you want to be able to switch master pages on the fly and based on runtime conditions. Because the generation of the view is distinct process in ASP.NET MVC, all you need to do is tell the view engine which master page it has to use.

```
public ActionResult Index()
{
    .
    .
    .
    return View("Index", "SiteMaster");
}
```

You do that simply using a different overload of the controller's *View* method.

Strongly Typed Views

In ASP.NET MVC, any view is expected to be isolated from the controller code. The view should receive from the outside world any data it has to process. Data can be passed in two nonexclusive ways: via the *ViewData* dictionary and via an object model.

As mentioned, *ViewData* is an object of type *ViewDataDictionary*. Any data you store in a dictionary is treated as an object and requires casting, boxing, or both in order to be worked on. A dictionary is definitely not something you would call *strongly* typed. At the same time, a dictionary is straightforward to use and works just fine.

ViewDataDictionary is kind of unique because it also features a few ASP.NET MVC–specific properties such as the *Model*, *ModelState*, and *ModelMetadata* properties, as shown here:

```
public class ViewDataDictionary : IDictionary<string, object>,
                                  ICollection<KeyValuePair<string, object>>,
                                  IEnumerable<KeyValuePair<string, object>>,
                                  IEnumerable
{
   public object Model { get; set; }
   public ModelStateDictionary ModelState { get; }
   public virtual ModelMetadata ModelMetadata { get; set; }
   :
   :
}
```

The *ModelState* property gets information about the state of the model. It typically contains entries describing what's wrong, if anything, in the data being worked on in the view. The *ModelMetadata* property, instead, stores information about the data being processed by the view—the model. Metadata includes display and edit information about properties of the model. Metadata information is obtained from a metadata provider. The default provider is based on the Data Annotations library. (See Chapter 6, "Inside Models," and Chapter 7, "Data Entry in ASP.NET MVC," for more details.)

The *Model* property is an alternative and object-oriented way of passing data to the view object. Instead of fitting flat data into a dictionary, you can shape a custom object to faithfully represent the data the view expects. The *Model* property just gives you a chance to create a view-model object that is unique for each view. If you intend to use the *Model* property to pass data to the view, you have to make it explicit, as shown here:

```
public partial class YourPage : ViewPage<YourViewModel>
{
   :
   :
}
```

The view page class derives from *ViewPage<T>* instead of *ViewPage*. If you don't use a code-behind class, you achieve the same goal with the following page directive in the view file:

```
<%@ Page MasterPageFile="~/Views/Shared/Site.Master"
        Inherits="System.Web.Mvc.ViewPage<YourViewModel>" %>
```

The *ViewData* dictionary is good enough for quick-and-dirty or short-lived sites. However, it becomes inadequate as the complexity of the view (and the number of views) grows beyond a certain threshold. So what should you do?

ViewData vs. *Model*

When you start having dozens of distinct values to pass on to a view, the same flexibility that allows you to quickly add a new entry, or rename an existing one, becomes your worst enemy. You are left on your own to track item names and values; you get no help from Microsoft IntelliSense and compilers.

The only proven way to deal with complexity in software is through appropriate design. So defining an object model for each view helps you track what that view really needs. I suggest you define a view model class for each view you add to the application.

Having a view-model class for each view also creates the problem of choosing an appropriate class name. You could decide to use a combination of controller and view names. For example, the view-model object for a view named *Index* invoked from the *Home* controller might be named *HomeIndexViewModel*.

When you use a view-model class, the template for a controller method becomes the following:

```
public ActionResult Index()
{
    // Perform the requested task, and get any necessary data
    object data = ...;

    // Pack data for the view
    HomeIndexViewModel model = new HomeIndexViewModel();
    PopulateModel(model, data);

    // Stores the view-model object in the transfer dictionary
    ViewData.Model = model;

    // Trigger the view
    return View();
}
```

You pass data to the view in one of two ways. Typically, you copy the view-model instance into the *Model* property of the *ViewData* dictionary. As an alternative, you can pass the view-model object as an argument to the *View* function, as shown here:

```
return View("index", model);
```

In the view markup, you retrieve the view-model object using the *Model* property that is conveniently exposed by the *ViewPage* class or the same *Model* property that is exposed by the *ViewData* dictionary.

> **Note** The *ViewData* dictionary is being pushed to the side in favor of view model objects because of its weakly typed programming model and because, as it is often remarked, the *ViewData* dictionary forces you to use magic strings to refer to stored data. All of this is absolutely correct and can hardly be argued. However, the *ViewData* programming model is exactly the same model we still use for *Session* or *Cache* in *any* flavor of ASP.NET.

Filling Up the View

An ASP.NET MVC view is made of ASPX markup, including HTML literals and server controls, plus some code. What code, exactly? And how much code, exactly?

ASPX Markup

Here's a sample view that renders a list of chapters. The view contains some HTML literals and then yields to a partial view for actual rendering of the chapter information. The executable code is wrapped in an ASP-style code block.

```
<asp:Content ContentPlaceHolderID="MainContent" runat="server">
    <h2>Table of Contents </h2>
    <p>
    <%
        Html.RenderPartial("TOC",
                new TocViewModel(this.ViewData["Chapters"] as IList<Chapter>));
    %>
    </p>
</asp:Content>
```

You render a partial view using an HTML helper method—*RenderPartial*. The method takes the name of the view and some input data—the model—and then does its job. Here's the source code of a partial view named *TOC*. It's an *.ascx* file whose user control class is strongly typed and accepts input data through an instance of the class *TocViewModel*.

```
<%@ Control Language="C#" Inherits="System.Web.Mvc.ViewUserControl<TocViewModel>" %>
<%@ Import Namespace="ProgMvc.ObjectModel" %>
<%@ Import Namespace="ProgMvc.Models.ViewModels" %>

<%
    int currentPart = 0;
    foreach (Chapter ch in this.ViewData.Model.Chapters)
    {
        if (ch.PartNo > currentPart)
        {
            if (currentPart > 0)
            {
%>
        </ul>
<%
            }
            currentPart = ch.PartNo;
%>

        <h3>Part <% = ch.PartNo %></h3>
        <hr />
        <ul>
<%
        }
%>
        <li><small>
            <b><% = ch.ID %>   
            <% = Html.ActionLink(ch.Title, "Chapters", new {chapterID = ch.ID}) %>
```

```
        </b>
      </small></li>
<%
    }
%>
```

The source code can be a mix of HTML literals and code blocks that flow sequentially and form a unique meta-programming expression. This code is parsed and compiled dynamically into an ASP.NET page class and then executed like any other Web Forms page.

In code blocks, you can access any data stored in any public members of *ViewPage*, *ViewPage<T>*, or any derived class. Most of the time, this means accessing data in the *ViewData* dictionary or in the view-model object. The code shown earlier demonstrates a strongly typed partial view. The following listing, on the other hand, illustrates a sample view-model object:

```
using System.Collections.Generic;
using ProgMvc.ObjectModel;

public class TocViewModel : ITocViewModel
{
    public TocViewModel(IList<Chapter> chapters)
    {
        Chapters = chapters;
    }

    public IList<Chapter> Chapters { get; set; }
}
```

For completeness, here's the source code of the *Chapter* class:

```
public class Chapter
{
    public int ID { get; set; }
    public string Title { get; set; }
    public string Abstract { get; set; }
    public int PartNo { get; set; }
    public string Status { get; set; }
}
```

In particular, the partial view just shown loops through a collection of *Chapter* objects and writes it out in the form of a table of contents, as shown in Figure 5-6.

As you can see, chapter titles are rendered as hyperlinks. Whose responsibility is it to add the URL? Where in the code is this indicated? It's the trick played by the HTML helper method *ActionLink*. I'll return to the topic of HTML helpers in a moment.

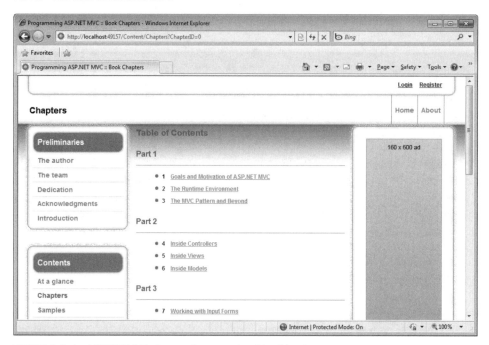

FIGURE 5-6 An ASP.NET MVC view renders out a book's table of contents.

> **Important** Without beating around the bush, the code of a typical ASP.NET MVC view may be quite confusing at first. It's really kind of shocking for the average ASP.NET developer to see. Often, the first (sometimes unconfessed) thought of the developer is that ASP.NET MVC is a huge step backwards from classic ASP.NET. However, I have deliberately chosen to use some messed-up code that I definitely do not recommended that you write. That code works just fine, but it is hard to read and subsequently hard to maintain.
>
> In an ASP.NET MVC view, you should try to keep the logic in code blocks to a minimum and avoid intertwined sequences of code and markup. Some developers say you should never have even an *if* in the view; some others, including myself, say that, well, some simple rendering logic (loops and *if*s) are acceptable.
>
> By keeping the view as passive as possible—one of the goals of the MVC pattern, indeed—you reduce the view to a plain HTML template with some data placeholders and avoid creating code paths in the template. That said, however, more control over HTML means just this—writing plain HTML literals with the necessary amount of logic and data for the purpose you have in mind.
>
> Finally, if you have trouble with the HTML syntax and the way in which ASP.NET intertwines it with code, you can unplug the default view engine and roll your own or use any other publicly available view engine. Spark and NVelocity are two view engines that many developers love. NVelocity, in particular, is the .NET porting of a popular Java template-based tool for view generation. (See *http://www.CodePlex.com/MvcContrib*.)

Code Blocks

Code blocks are fragments of executable code delimited by <% . . . %> tags. Within those tags, you can put virtually everything that the ASP runtime engine can understand and parse, including variable assignments, loop statements, function declarations and, of course, function calls. For compatibility reasons with old ASP, the internal architecture of classic ASP.NET pages always supported this programming model, which appears unstructured, loose, not very rigorous, and inelegant to software purists and to, well, not just them.

This overlooked approach to page construction, however, has been revamped to have new significance in ASP.NET MVC because of its inherent flexibility and because it allows full control over HTML.

Code blocks come in two flavors: inline code and inline expressions. Inline expressions are merely shortcuts for *Response.Write* and preface the expression with an = (equal) symbol:

```
<!-- Sample inline expression -->
<% = ViewData["ChapterID"] %>
```

Inline code is plain code in code block brackets and requires a trailing semi-colon. An inline expression outputs the value of the expression in the output stream; an inline code block simply executes the specified code to create or modify some local state.

Code blocks are compiled into methods added to the page that ASP.NET creates dynamically when processing the view for the first time. Any code block is associated with a server-side parent element that inherits from *Control*. It's associated with the page if no element can be found with the *runat* attribute. (The *Page* class does have the *Control* class in its list of ancestors.)

Why *Control*? Because the *Control* class defines a little-used method named *SetRenderMethodDelegate*. This method takes a delegate method and uses it to render some markup. Here's an excerpt from the render delegate that ASP.NET uses to render the mix of markup and code blocks shown earlier:

```
void __Render__control1(HtmlTextWriter __w, Control parameterContainer)
{
    int currentPart = 0;
    foreach (Chapter ch in this.ViewData.Model.Chapters)
    {
        if (ch.PartNo > currentPart)
        {
            if (currentPart > 0)
            {
                __w.Write("\r\n          </ul>\r\n");
            }
            currentPart = ch.PartNo;
            __w.Write("          \r\n          \r\n          <h3>Part ");
            __w.Write(ch.PartNo );
            __w.Write("</h3>\r\n          <hr />\r\n          <ul>\r\n");
        }

        :
        :
    }
}
```

This code comes directly from the temporary files that ASP.NET creates on the Web server machine during execution. The root directory is located under Temporary ASP.NET Files, which in turn lives under the Windows *Temp* folder. The exact directory for your application is known only at run time and can be detected by watching the content of the *System.Web* *.HttpRuntime.CodegenDir* expression during a debug session. (See Figure 5-7.)

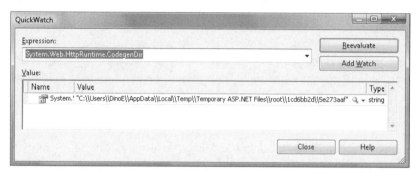

FIGURE 5-7 Detecting the run-time folder to snoop for details about the compilation of code blocks.

Adding Logic to the View

In ASP.NET Web Forms, the view (that is, the page) contains all the logic for both rendering and processing. In ASP.NET MVC, processing logic and rendering logic are distinct and belong to controllers and views. However, there's a gray area of logic that could belong to both processing and rendering. Sometimes it depends on the developer's vision of things; sometimes it's an architectural decision; sometimes it simply happens inadvertently.

Let's recall a couple of guidelines that apply to the design of the view.

The recommended approach when rendering views using ASP.NET MVC is to provide for all view data dependencies *using only data that is explicitly provided* through the view dictionary or, better yet from a design perspective, the view-model object. (You can provide data using both the dictionary and a strongly typed object.)

In addition, the view should contain the *least possible amount of logic that is not strictly related to rendering*. For example, the following excerpt of markup is arguably the best option:

```
< !--  Other markup here  -->
   .
   .
   .
<% int id = (int)ViewData["ChapterID"];
   if (id == 0)
   {
       Html.RenderPartial("TOC", new TocViewModel(ViewData["Chapters"]));
   }
   else
   {
       Html.RenderPartial("SingleChapter", new ChapterViewModel(ViewData["Chapter"]));
   }
%>
```

The code first checks the value of an element in the view dictionary and then decides which partial view to render. This code, in particular, doesn't look bad and still relies only on provided data. However, it attributes some extra power to the view object. The view contains some logic—deciding about the partial view to render—that is not about the physical rendering of the view, such as a *foreach* statement.

You should consider whether the decision about the partial view really belongs to the view. In general, it's preferable to move any logic up to the controller. The controller method that invokes the previous view, then, looks like this:

```
public ActionResult Chapters(int? chapterID)
{
    // Deal with input parameters
    int id = 0;
    if (chapterID.HasValue)
        id = chapterID.Value;

    // Perform any task, and acquire any data
    IContentServices service = ...;

    // Render the entire TOC
    if (id == 0)
    {
        IList<Chapter> chapters chapters = service.LoadChapters();
        return View("TOC", new TocViewModel(chapters));
    }

    // Render details about a single chapter
    Chapter chapter = service.LoadChapter(id);
    return View("SingleChapter", new ChapterViewModel(chapter));
}
```

The net effect is that you now have two simpler views with a minimum amount of logic. If you have reasons to maintain partial views, you can use a view as simple as the one shown here:

```
<!-- Other markup here  -->
    .
    .
    .
Html.RenderPartial("TOC");
```

The partial view automatically receives all the information you passed to the view, dictionary, and model. You can also restrict the information for the partial view if that best suits the needs of your application.

A further optimization to the controller's method can be obtained using an internal method that encapsulates the logic to decide about which view to render:

```
public ActionResult Perform(object data)
{
    // Deal with input parameters
        .
        .
        .
```

```
    // Perform any task, and acquire any data
    .
    .
    .


    // Render the entire TOC
    MyViewModel model = ...;
    return GetMethodView(model);
}

private ActionResult GetViewModel(MyViewModel model)
{
    .
    .
    .

}
```

The View: Passive or Supervising?

The MVC pattern that ASP.NET MVC is based on suggests the view be as thin
and passive as possible. To reinforce the concept, the ASP.NET MVC tools in Visual
Studio don't even add a code-behind file to each view you add. The message couldn't
be clearer—the thinner the better.

This is the theory, however. In the real-world, a really passive view can be quite
cumbersome to write and maintain and would add a lot of complexity to the controller.
A thin view contains nearly no logic and inevitably takes you toward a multiplicity of
smaller and extremely simple views. From here, the possible maintenance required
could be a nightmare.

If you opt for a passive view, you have an inherently more testable system because
the logic in the view is reduced to an absolute minimum. Subsequently, you run no
serious risk at all by not testing the view. Any piece of code can contain mistakes, but
in the case of a passive view the extreme simplicity of the code allows only for gross
and patent mistakes that can be easily caught without any automated procedure.

In software, as well as in physics, a sort of *conservation law* applies. In physics, it's about
the conservation of energy; in software it's about the conservation of complexity.
So the complexity taken out of the view moves to another layer—the controller—
and a passive view is inevitably coupled with a more complex controller. From here,
you encounter the mantra these days as far as ASP.ENT MVC is concerned: *thin view,
fat model*. In the end, opting for a passive view is a tradeoff between high testability
and complexity of the controller classes.

You can also opt for a more active view that contains some logic as far as data binding
and data formatting is concerned. Developing a richer view might be easier, and it
basically distributes the required complexity between the view and the controllers.
The view needs to take care of some synchronization and adaptation work to make any
input data usable by user interface elements. However, this code in an ASP.NET MVC
scenario can only go into a server-side *<script>* tag. (In ASP.NET MVC , code-behind
classes are still supported but kind of banned.)

When do you really need a supervising view? For one thing, you need it if you make use of some ASP.NET server controls. In this case, the code inside of the view lets you configure some of these controls programmatically and, more likely, gives you a chance to handle some internal events, such as those fired by data-bound controls during their rendering. Data binding done through server controls is the specific scenario that a richer, supervising view will address.

View and ASP.NET Intrinsics

From the view, you can certainly access some ASP.NET intrinsic objects, such as *Cache* and *Session*. The issue, though, is whether you should. And, no, you shouldn't.

The view should remain disconnected from the machinery of the runtime environment. If the view needs to consume some data, that data must be passed explicitly to the view, using the view dictionary or the model.

Accessing any ASP.NET intrinsic object is the responsibility of the controller, as shown here:

```
public ActionResult AddToShoppingCart(ShoppingItem item)
{
    ShoppingCart cart = this.Session["CurrentShoppingCart"] as ShoppingCart;
    if (cart == null)
        throw new InvalidOperationException("Invalid shopping cart");

    // Do some work on the shopping cart
    cart.Items.Add(item);
    :
    :

    // Save cart back to the session state
    this.Session["CurrentShoppingCart"] = cart;

    // Show the current content of the cart.
    // The view receives any data it needs to display.
    // It doesn't have to retrieve any of it
    ViewData["CurrentCart"] = cart;
    return View("ShoppingCart");
}
```

To test the controller and simulate action on the session state (or any other intrinsic object), you can create a mock object for the *HttpContextBase* class that contains abstractions for any intrinsic objects. (I'll cover more details on testing in Chapter 10, "Testability and Unit Testing.")

View and Configuration Settings

ASP.NET comes with a bunch of expression types that you can intersperse with HTML literals and server controls. In particular, you can use dynamic expressions such as those in Table 5-4.

TABLE 5-4 ASP.NET dynamic expressions

Syntax	Description
$AppSettings:[Attribute]	Returns the value of the specified attribute from the *<appSettings>* section of the configuration file
$ConnectionStrings:[Entry].[Attribute]	Returns the value of the specified attribute of the given entry in the *<connectionStrings>* section of the configuration file
$Resources:[ResourceFile],[ResourceName]	Returns the value of the specified global resource

You'll seldom find a need to use a connection string from within an ASP.NET MVC view. (If you happen to need to do this, well, make sure you're doing the right thing and, especially, that you're using the right tool.)

It's more likely that you'll need to read directly from the view some application-specific settings, such as those you might have in the *<appSettings>* section of the configuration file. Should you do this?

Again, the guideline is the same—the view should receive any data it needs from the controller. However, in my opinion, using *$AppSettings* expressions in the view is not a deadly sin, and it's acceptable as long as it's really beneficial for the team (as in it really saves you time and increases productivity.) Take a look at the following code:

```
<asp:Literal runat="server" Text="<% $AppSettings:AppVersionNumber %>" />
```

It assigns the *Text* property of the *Literal* control the value associated with the *AppVersionNumber* entry in the *<appSettings>* section:

```
<appSettings>
    <add key="AppVersionNumber" value="8.2.2001" />
</appSettings>
```

Note that any *$* expression requires a server control. You can't use it as a free-floating expression within the ASPX source. The *Literal* is the simplest control you can attach a *$* expression to.

Localizing a View

The scenario for which I would seriously consider using some *Literal* controls and *$* expressions is localization. Here's how you can bind into a view a piece of text coming from the application's resource file:

```
<h2>
    <asp:Literal runat="server" Text="<% $Resources:Globals, WelcomeMessage %>" />
</h2>
```

In the example, *Globals* is the name of one of the *.resx* resource files you might have in the project. *WelcomeMessage* is the name of one of the entries in the dictionary file.

You must be aware that the *$Resources* expression builder doesn't retrieve resources local to a page; it works only with global *.resx* files located in the *App_GlobalResources* folder. Resources local to a view are supported in ASP.NET MVC, but they require you to use server controls extensively.

From a design perspective, the principle of view isolation still holds true. If you follow the principle, you might end up with a controller like the one shown here:

```
public ActionResult Index()
{
    // Load text to populate placeholders in the view
    this.FillViewModel();

    // Trigger the next view
    return View();
}

private void FillViewModel()
{
    // Retrieve localized text from an RESX file
    string msg = HttpContext.GetGlobalResourceObject("globals", "WelcomeMessage");
    ViewData["WelcomeMessage"] = msg;
    :
    :

    // An alternate approach that adds one more layer of abstraction.
    // ApplicationContext is a custom class we discussed in Chapter 4 and
    // represents a global container of common objects such as references to
    // IoC containers, and resolved dependencies such as the resource provider.
    IResourceProvider  resourceProvider = ApplicationContext.ResourceProvider;
    ViewData["WelcomeMessage"] = resourceProvider.GetString("globals", "WelcomeMessage");
    :
    :

}
```

Generally, in ASP.NET MVC the support for localization is limited to adapting what was already available in ASP.NET Web Forms. I'll return on this in Chapter 8. "The ASP.NET MVC Infrastructure."

> **Note** As you might recall, *$* expressions are customizable. To create a custom expression, you have two basic tasks to perform. First, create a new class that inherits from *ExpressionBuilder* and, second, register it in the *<compilation>* section of the configuration file. In doing so, you enable an ASPX file to contain any expression that your code is capable of retrieving. Custom expressions can be used in ASP.NET MVC views without limitations. Keep in mind, however, that the more logic you add, the more you compromise the isolation level of your view.

HTML Helpers

Writing HTML literals in a view can soon become a repetitive and error-prone task. How would you output, say, an HTML input element with some of the attributes set to computed or programmatically passed values?

In classic ASP.NET, you would use a *TextBox* control and set (or have set) corresponding properties programmatically. As you'll see later, a *TextBox* control is a valid option in ASP.NET MVC, too; however, it involves much more of a workaround than a direct, clean solution. ASP.NET MVC is designed to give page authors total control over any generated HTML literals. The *TextBox*, as well as any other server controls, is a black box and its generated HTML cannot be fully controlled.

HTML helpers exist solely to help you with the writing of HTML markup. They are not mandatory and can be happily avoided if that is what you want. As the name suggests, HTML helpers just help you write ASP.NET MVC views more seamlessly.

An *HTML helper* is a method on a system class—the *HtmlHelper* class—that outputs an HTML string based on the provided input data. In a way, an HTML helper method is a simplified and lightweight version of an ASP.NET server control except that it's just tailor-made for ASP.NET MVC. An HTML helper method has no view state, no postbacks, and no page life cycle and events; it consists of a standard HTML template that gets filled with provided data.

The ASP.NET MVC framework supplies a few HTML helpers out of the box, including *CheckBox*, *ActionLink*, and *RenderPartial*. The stock set of HTML helpers is presented in Table 5-5.

TABLE 5-5 Stock set of HTML helper methods

Method	Type	Description
BeginForm, BeginRouteForm	Form	Returns an *MvcForm* object that represents an HTML form
EndForm	Input	Void method, closes the pending </form> tag
CheckBox, CheckBoxFor	Input	Returns the HTML string for a check box input element
Hidden, HiddenFor	Input	Returns the HTML string for a hidden input element
Password, PasswordFor	Input	Returns the HTML string for a password input element
RadioButton, RadioButtonFor	Input	Returns the HTML string for a radio button input element
TextBox, TextBoxFor	Input	Returns the HTML string for a text input element
Label, LabelFor	Label	Returns the HTML string for an HTML label element (Note: requires ASP.NET MVC 2)
ActionLink, RouteLink	Link	Returns the HTML string for an HTML link
DropDownList, DropDownListFor	List	Returns the HTML string for a drop-down list

Method	Type	Description
ListBox, ListBoxFor	List	Returns the HTML string for a list box
TextArea, TextAreaFor	TextArea	Returns the HTML string for a text area
Partial	Partial	Returns the HTML string incorporated in the specified user control *(Note: requires ASP.NET MVC 2)*
RenderPartial	Partial	Writes the HTML string incorporated in the specified user control to the output stream
ValidationMessage, ValidationMessageFor	Validation	Returns the HTML string for a validation message
ValidationSummary	Validation	Returns the HTML string for a validation summary message

Note that *xxxFor* helpers require ASP.NET MVC 2. Any *xxxFor* helper differs from the base version because it accepts a lambda expression, such as shown here:

```
<%= Html.TextBoxFor(model => model.FirstName) %>
<%= Html.ValidationMessageFor(model => model.FirstName) %>
```

The native set of HTML helper methods is definitely a great help, but it's probably insufficient for many real-world applications. Native helpers, in fact, only cover the markup of basic HTML elements. In this regard, HTML helpers are significantly different from server controls because they completely lack abstraction over HTML.

Extending the set of HTML helpers is easy, however. All that is required is an extension method for the *HtmlHelper* class. In Chapter 11, I'll go into the details of a few custom HTML helper methods. For now, let's limit the discussion to examining the native methods in ASP.NET MVC version 1 and version 2.

The *HtmlHelper* Class

You might have noticed the *Html* object being used in some snippets of an ASP.NET MVC view. The *Html* object is a property of the *ViewPage* and *ViewUserControl* classes and points to an instance of the *HtmlHelper* class. The class owes most of its popularity to its numerous extension methods, but it also has a number of useful native methods. Some of them are listed in Table 5-6.

TABLE 5-6 Most popular native methods on *HtmlHelper*

Method	Description
AntiForgeryToken	Returns the HTML string for a hidden input field stored with the antiforgery token. (See Chapter 4 for more details.)
AttributeEncode	Encodes the value of the specified attribute using the rules of HTML encoding.

Method	Description
EnableClientValidation	A Boolean method, gets and sets the internal flag that enables helpers to generate code for client-side validation. (Note: requires ASP.NET MVC 2)
Encode	Encodes the specified value using the rules of HTML encoding.
HttpMethodOverride	Returns the HTML string for a hidden input field used to override the effective HTTP verb to indicate that a PUT or DELETE operation was requested. (Note: requires ASP.NET MVC 2)

In addition, the *HtmlHelper* class provides a number of public methods that are of little use from within a view but offer great support to developers writing custom HTML helper methods. A good example is *GenerateRouteLink*, which returns an anchor tag containing the virtual path for the specified route values.

HTML Encoding

ASP.NET 4 Web Forms and, subsequently, ASP.NET MVC 2 provide a new compact syntax to automatically HTML-encode any text being emitted to the output stream. Consider the following code:

```
<%: ViewData["UserName"] %>
```

It's equivalent to the following:

```
<% Html.Encode(ViewData["UserName"]) %>
```

What if you use the compact syntax on a piece of markup that is already encoded? Without countermeasures, the text will be inevitably double-encoded. Aware of the possibility that developers would be using the new auto-encoding syntax, the development team decided to refactor all HTML helpers in ASP.NET MVC 2 to make them return a new type—*MvcHtmlString*. Here, for example, is the new definition of the *TextBox* helper method:

```
// Returns a text input tag in ASP.NET MVC 2
public static MvcHtmlString TextBox(this HtmlHelper htmlHelper, string name, object value)
{
    :
    :
}
```

The *MvcHtmlString* type is a smart wrapper for a string that contains HTML, and it exposes the *IHtmlString* interface. The auto-encoding feature doesn't apply to any values that implement *IHtmlString*. In this way, double-encoding is avoided and you have an extremely simple and effective way to encode all your output.

Rendering HTML Forms

The unpleasant work of rendering a form in ASP.NET MVC occurs when you have to specify the target URL. The *BeginForm* and *BeginRouteForm* helpers can do the ugliest work for you. The following code snippet shows how to write a simple input form with a couple of fields, *user* and *password*:

```
<% using (Html.BeginForm()) { %>
   <div>
     <fieldset>
        <legend>Account Information</legend>
        <p>
            <label for="userName">User name:</label>
            <%= Html.TextBox("userName") %>
            <%= Html.ValidationMessage("userName") %>
        </p>
        <p>
            <label for="password">Password:</label>
            <%= Html.Password("password") %>
            <%= Html.ValidationMessage("password") %>
        </p>
            .
            .
            .
        <p>
            <input type="submit" value="Change Password" />
        </p>
     </fieldset>
   </div>
<% } %>
```

The *BeginForm* helper takes care of the opening *<form>* tag. The *BeginForm* method, however, doesn't directly emit any markup. It's limited to creating an instance of the *MvcForm* class, which is then added to the control tree for the page and rendered later.

To close the tag, you can use the *EndForm* helper or rely on the *using* statement as in the preceding example. The *using* pattern ends up invoking the *Dispose* method on the *MvcForm* object, which in turn will emit the closing *</form>* tag.

By default, *BeginForm* renders a form that posts back to the same URL and, subsequently, to the same controller action. Other overloads on the *BeginForm* method allow you to specify the target controller's name and action, any route values for the action, HTML attributes, and even whether you want the form to perform a GET or a POST. The following example shows a form that posts to a controller named *Memo* to execute an action named *Update* and passes a collection of route values:

```
<% Html.BeginForm("Update", "Memo", new RouteValueDictionary{ {"MemoID", 100}}); %>
    .
    .
    .
<% Html.EndForm(); %>
```

After you have done this, generating the resulting URL and arranging the final markup is no longer a concern of yours.

BeginRouteForm behaves like *BeginForm* except that it can generate a URL starting from an arbitrary set of route parameters. In other words, *BeginRouteForm* is not limited to the default route based on the controller name and action.

> **Note** In HTML, the *<form>* tag doesn't allow you to use anything other than the GET and POST verbs to submit some content. In ASP.NET MVC 1.0, to use a different verb (such as PUT or DELETE), you have to resort to JavaScript and direct programming via an AJAX framework. In ASP.NET MVC 2, a new HTML helper—*HttpMethodOverride*—comes to the rescue. The helper method emits a hidden field whose name is hard-coded to *X-HTTP-Method-Override* and whose value is PUT, DELETE, or HEAD. The content of the hidden field overrides the method set for the form, thus allowing you to invoke a REST API also from within the browser. The override value can also be specified in an HTTP header with the same *X-HTTP-Method-Override* name or in a query string value as a name/value pair. The override is valid only for POST requests.

Rendering Input Elements

All HTML elements that can be used within a form have an HTML helper to speed up development. Again, there's really no difference from a functional perspective between using helpers and using plain HTML. Here's an example of a check box element, initially set to true, but disabled:

```
<% = Html.CheckBox("ProductDiscontinued", true,
    new Dictionary<string, object>() {{ "disabled", "disabled" }}) ) %>
```

You also have facilities to associate a validation message with an input field. You use the *Html.ValidationMessage* helper to displays a validation message if the specified field contains an error. The message can be indicated explicitly through an additional parameter in the helper, or the method can figure it out by looking at messages in the *ModelState* collection in the *ViewData* object. All validation messages are then aggregated and displayed via the *Html.ValidationSummary* helper.

I'll return to input forms and validation in Chapter 7, "Working with Input Foms."

Action Links

As mentioned, creating URLs programmatically is a boring and error-prone task in ASP.NET MVC. For this reason, helpers are more than welcome, especially in this context. In fact, the *ActionLink* helper is one of the most frequently used in ASP.NET MVC views. Here's an example:

```
<%= Html.ActionLink("Home", "Index", "Home") %>
```

Typically, an action link requires the link text, the action name, and optionally the controller name. The HTML that results from the example is the following:

```
<a href="/Home/Index">Home</a>
```

In addition, you can specify route values, HTML attributes for the anchor tag, and even a protocol (for example, HTTPS), host, and fragment.

The *RouteLink* helper works in much the same way, except it doesn't require you to specify an action. With *RouteLink*, you can use any registered route name to determine the pattern for the resulting URL.

The text emitted by *ActionLink* is automatically encoded. This means you can't use any HTML tag in the link text that the browser will be led to consider as HTML. In particular, you can't use *ActionLink* for image buttons and image links. However, to generate a link based on controllers and actions data, you can use the *UrlHelper* class.

An instance of the *UrlHelper* class is associated with the *Url* property on the *ViewPage* type. The code here shows the *Url* object in action.

```
<a href="<%= Url.Action("Edit") %>">
    <img src="editMemo.jpg" alt="Edit memo" />
</a>
```

The *UrlHelper* class has a couple of methods that behave nearly similar to *ActionLink* and *RouteLink*. Their names are *Action* and *RouteLink*.

Templated HTML Helpers

HTML helpers serve the purpose of letting you write HTML markup faster. What kind of HTML markup do you need to write most of the time? All in all, I'd say that it's lists of custom data objects and input forms.

You render a list by looping over a collection of data items and then building a user interface against each data item. You render an input form by building an editable user interface against a given data item. These two common scenarios share one aspect—rendering a data item in a way that is quick, effective, and especially flexible. To achieve this goal, ASP.NET MVC 2 introduced templated HTML helpers.

Templated HTML helpers aim to make the display and editing of data objects quick to write and independent from too many HTML and CSS details. As you'll see in greater detail in Chapter 6 and Chapter 7, the emerging trend entails building a view-specific object model—the view-model—and having objects in the model drive the rendering of the user interface.

To achieve this, you can decorate your view-model objects with special data annotation attributes that an ad hoc rendering API will recognize and handle properly. The developer still maintains tight control over the user interface, but attributes in the model establish a number of conventions and save the developer from a number of repetitive tasks.

Note Implemented through attributes, data annotations are an emerging cross-platform .NET solution for building a view-specific object model that might or might not coincide with the domain model you have in the business layer. You can use data annotations with Entity Framework classes or with classes in your own handmade data model, and you can have components that understand annotations in Microsoft Silverlight, ASP.NET Dynamic Data, Windows Presentation Foundation (WPF), and ASP.NET MVC. From a design perspective, this means planning a view-model on the presentation layer and possibly having an adapter layer in the business layer to map from view-model objects to domain model objects. The presentation and business data models, though, can coincide if that simplifies your efforts while not compromising the overall design.

Flavors of a Templated Helper

In ASP.NET MVC 2, you have two essential templated helpers: *Editor* and *Display*. They work together to make the code for labeling, displaying, and editing data objects easy to write and maintain. The optimal scenario for using these helpers is that you are writing your lists or input forms around annotated objects. However, the new family of templated helpers can work with both scalar values and composite objects.

Templated helpers actually come with three overloads. Taking the *Display* helper as an example, you have the following more specific helpers—*Display*, *DisplayFor*, and *DisplayForModel*. There's no functional difference between *Display*, *DisplayFor*, and *DisplayForModel*. They differ only by the input parameters they can manage.

The *Display* helper accepts a string indicating the name of the property in the *ViewData* dictionary or on the model to be processed. Note that you don't have to know the exact type of the model in order to use this helper.

```
<%= Html.Display("FirstName") %>
```

The *DisplayFor* helper accepts a model-based expression and subsequently requires that the model type is known within the view. (The *ViewPage* or *ViewUserControl* must be strongly typed.)

```
<%= Html.DisplayFor(model => model.FirstName) %>
```

Finally, *DisplayForModel* is a shortcut for *DisplayFor* getting the expression *model => model*.

```
<%= Html.DisplayForModel() %>
```

You can use *DisplayForModel* even if you don't know the exact type of the model inside of the view context.

I'll be referring to templated editors using the main name that identifies the functionality such as Display or Editor.

All flavors of templated helpers have the special ability to process metadata (if any) and adjust their rendering accordingly—for example, showing labels and adding validation. The display and editing capabilities can be customized using templates, as discussed in a moment. The ability of using custom templates applies to all flavors of a templated helper.

Editing Helpers in Action

The purpose of the *Editor* helper is to let you edit the specified value or object. The editor recognizes the type of the value it gets and picks up a made-to-measure template for editing. Predefined templates exist for *object*, *string*, Boolean, and multiline text, while numbers, dates, and GUIDs fall back to the string editor.

The helper editor works great with complex types. It generically iterates over each public property and builds up a label and an editor for the child value. Nested objects are supported natively.

You can customize the editor by creating a few partial views by convention in the *EditorTemplates* folder of the view. It can be under a controller-specific subfolder or under the Views\Shared folder as well. (See Figure 5-8.)

FIGURE 5-8 Custom templates for editors and visualizers in Visual Studio 2010.

When you invoke an editor for a given type, you can then point the editor to your template. Here's an example that uses the *date.ascx* view to edit a *DateTime* property:

```
<fieldset>
    <legend>Personal Information</legend>
    :
    :
    <p>
        <%= Html.LabelFor(p => person.Birthdate)%>
        <%= Html.EditorFor(p => person.Birthdate, "Date") %>
    </p>
</fieldset>
```

Let's have a look at the internals of the *date.ascx* template:

```
<%@ Control Language="C#" Inherits="System.Web.Mvc.ViewUserControl" %>
<%@ Import Namespace="Samples" %>

<table>
<tr>
    <td><%= Html.Label("Day") %></td>
    <td><%= Html.TextBox("Day", ((DateTime)this.Model).Day)%></td>
</tr>
<tr>
    <td><%= Html.Label("Month")%></td>
    <td><%= Html.TextBox("Month", ((DateTime)this.Model).Month) %></td>
</tr>
<tr>
    <td><%= Html.Label("Year")%></td>
    <td><%= Html.TextBox("Year", ((DateTime)this.Model).Year)%></td>
</tr>
</table>
```

The specified date is edited through three distinct text boxes for day, month, and year, as you can see in Figure 5-9. The *Model* expression the partial view refers to is exactly the value computed by the lambda expression passed as an argument to *EditorFor*.

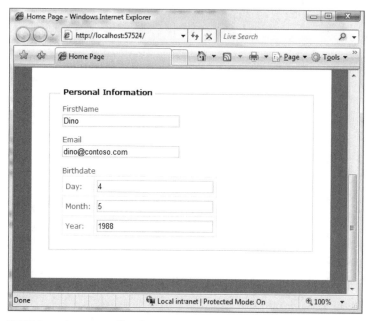

FIGURE 5-9 A custom editor for a *DateTime* value.

You can also force a property to be considered of a given type if that helps the helper to resolve the template. You do that using the *DataType* or *UIHint* annotations:

```
public class Person
{
    :
    :
```

```
    [DataType(DataType.EmailAddress)]
    public String Email {get; set;}

    [UIHint("Date")]
    public DateTime Birthday {get; set;}
}
```

In particular, you use *DataType* to force a string property to use a given template. You use *UIHint* to force any object properties to use a given edit template.

The *Display* Helper in Action

The *Display* helper is the read-only counterpart of *Editor*. It has the same set of capabilities except that it's expected to display read-only templates. The following example shows a possible display template for a *DateTime* value:

```
<%@ Control Language="C#" Inherits="System.Web.Mvc.ViewUserControl" %>
<%= Html.Encode(((DateTime)this.Model).ToString("ddd dd MMM yyyy")) %>
```

Figure 5-10 shows the custom template in action.

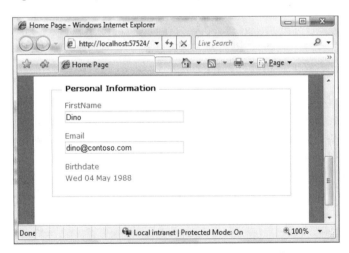

FIGURE 5-10 A custom display template for a *DateTime* value.

Custom display templates go to the *DisplayTemplates* folder under Views. (See Figure 5-8.)

A minor difference between *Editor* and *Display* is that *Display* features a default display template for e-mail addresses, whereas *Editor* supports *MultilineText*. This is in addition to the standard templates for object, Booleans, strings, and numbers.

Datagrids and Paged Views

As long as you use the default view engine, you reuse some of the skills you might have developed on Web Forms. To some extent, in fact, server controls work, master pages work, and data binding work.

However, assuming that authoring an ASP.NET MVC view is the same as authoring a Web Forms view would be a big mistake. The first recommendation for those trying to use server controls in ASP.NET MVC is clear and unambiguous:

Do not use server controls.

Avoiding server controls saves you from a number of potential pitfalls and headaches. If you have a *thorough knowledge* of how both ASP.NET Web Forms and ASP.NET MVC work under the hood, and if you have a *strong* reason to do it, you can take the plunge into server-side programming in ASP.NET MVC. In any other case, avoiding server controls is the best choice.

Important ASP.NET MVC 2 is much less forgiving than ASP.NET MVC 1 as far as server controls are concerned. Using server controls to render a static page that doesn't interact with the user is still doable (even though not necessarily the best option). Using server controls that operate postbacks (i.e., drop-down lists whose selection becomes input for a successive requests or pageable datagrids) is highly problematic in ASP.NET MVC 2. The reason is that due to a change in the way in which the page is rendered, page events like Init and Load are still fired but the IsPostBack property is always false. This fact breaks a number of consolidated Web Forms practices and makes using server controls in MVC just a dangerous trip. So avoid server controls in ASP.NET MVC 2. In ASP.NET MVC 1, you have best chances to arrange a Web Forms like solution in MVC. However, one thing that I've learned about it is the following: if using server controls in MVC works, it is likely a pure stroke of luck.

In the next example, I'll first show how to use a *GridView* server control to render out a table of data. I'm quite sure that what you see won't really scare you. So you might be tempted to go ahead and add, say, a drop-down list to filter the displayed content. As you'll see, operations that are just trivial in Web Forms all of sudden become difficult to accomplish in ASP.NET MVC. Why is that so? It's all about the lack of automatic statefulness you experience in ASP.NET MVC.

Using Server Controls

When it comes to displaying a table of data over the Web, it's hard to find a tool that weds effectiveness and productivity better than a *DataGrid* control or a *GridView* control. While waiting for a component model to come (if one ever does) and to see what third-party vendors have to offer in this regard, for now you need to build a table using your own helper or a mix of HTML literals, data, and maybe the *DisplayFor* helper.

If you try to do it with a *GridView* here's what you end up with:

```
<form runat="server">
    <asp:GridView ID="gridOrders" runat="server"
        AutoGenerateColumns="false"
        OnRowDataBound="gridOrders_RowDataBound">
```

```
        <Columns>
            <asp:BoundField DataField="Id" HeaderText="ID" />
            <asp:BoundField DataField="CustomerName" HeaderText="Customer" />
            <asp:BoundField DataField="DueDate" HeaderText="Due by" />
            <asp:BoundField DataField="OrderDate" HeaderText="Order issued" />
            <asp:BoundField DataField="TotalDue" HeaderText="Amount" />
        </Columns>
    </asp:GridView>
</form>
```

To start, you need a server-side form element. This doesn't interfere with other HTML forms you have around the view. You are restricted to having exactly one server-side form, but you can have, in the same view, as many plain HTML forms as you need.

The *GridView* control can define its own event handlers, such as the handler for the *RowDataBound* event, and it can be configured to display data with the usual extreme freedom. You can use, for example, templated columns and any formatting style you prefer. Here's the *RowDataBound* handler, which offers an even more advanced form of control over the HTML being emitted:

```
<script runat="server">
    protected void gridOrders_RowDataBound(object sender, GridViewRowEventArgs e)
    {
        // Grab a reference to the current data item
        var model = e.Row.DataItem as SalesOrderViewItem;
        if (model == null)
            return;

        // Add a tooltip with the company address
        e.Row.ToolTip = model.Address;
    }
</script>
```

In this example, the *GridView* is bound to a collection of data transfer objects of type *SalesOrderViewItem*.

The key step for using server controls in an ASP.NET MVC view is binding data to the *GridView* control. This can happen only in the *Page_Load* event of the *ViewPage* class.

```
<script runat="server">
protected void Page_Load(object sender, EventArgs e)
{
    var model = ViewData.Model;
    gridOrders.DataSource = model.Orders;
    this.DataBind();
}
</script>
```

At this point, you surely understand what Figure 5-11 illustrates.

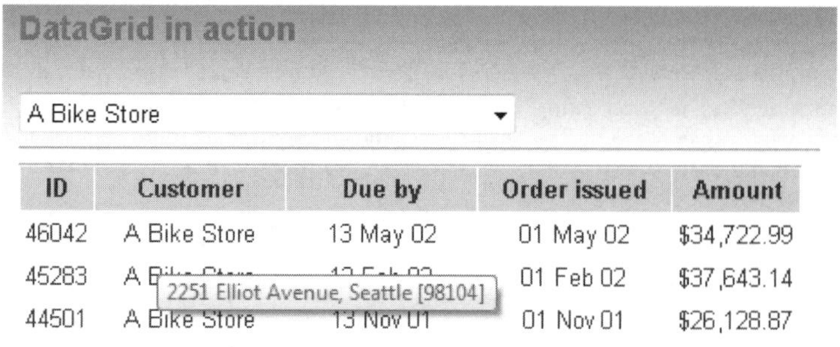

FIGURE 5-11 A table of data rendered using a *GridView* server control.

The view looks nice, and there's really nothing that makes it different in some way because a server control was used. Let's turn our attention now to the drop-down list.

Intricacies of the Postback Model in ASP.NET MVC 2

It's likely that you'll want to add a list to let users filter orders by customer. This means populating a drop-down list and binding the current selection to the grid. Obviously, you can add such a list using plain HTML. But I just want you to experience what it means to use a server control. So here's some markup for the *DropDownList* control:

```
<asp:DropDownList runat="server" ID="ddCustomerList"
    AutoPostBack="true"
    DataTextField="Name"
    DataValueField="Id" />
```

In *Page_Load* now you need to take care of the additional drop-down list control:

```
protected void Page_Load(object sender, EventArgs e)
{
    if (!this.IsPostBack)
    {
        var model = ViewData.Model;
        :
        :
        ddCustomerList.DataSource = model.Customers;
        this.DataBind();
    }
}
```

This code may work in ASP.NET MVC 1, but it won't certainly in ASP.NET MVC 2. Due to changes to the Web Forms view engine occurred in ASP.NET MVC 2, in fact, the postback is never detected. As you may easily guess, this causes a number of issues with server controls. If you know deeply enough ASP.NET Web Forms, you can probably enter some hacks to still have a server-side drop-down list and datagrid work together. Honestly, though, that closely resembles spaghetti-code and is of no utility to embark in such adventures. If the primary benefit of using Web Forms and server controls is productivity, this aspect is the first you say goodbye in the context of ASP.NET MVC.

So what's left? Just using the built-in tools of ASP.NET MVC that are equally effective after an initial startup time.

Building a Grid of Data with HTML Helpers

The key assumption of ASP.NET MVC is that the view receives from the controller all the data it needs to display. So if you plan to display a grid then the collection of data items is being provided via *ViewData* or the view model object. In light of this, the following code is all you need to render a grid of data:

```
<table id="gridOrders">
    <tr>
        <th scope="col">ID</th>
        <th scope="col">Customer</th>
        <th scope="col">Order issued</th>
    </tr>
    <% foreach (Order order in ViewData.Model.Orders)
       {%>
          <tr title="<%= order.Customer.Address %>">
             <td><%= order.OrderID %></td>
             <td><%= order.Customer.CompanyName %></td>
             <td><%= String.Format("{0:dd MMM yy}", order.OrderDate) %></td>
          </tr>
    <% } %>
</table>
```

The final table contains three columns with the order ID, company name, and date of the order. Refreshing the grid based on the selected customer is easy too. You need a classic HTML form and a drop-down list with a static ID, as below:

```
<% using (Html.BeginForm("Index", "Home"))
   {%>
        <%= Html.DropDownList("ddCustomerList",
                new SelectList(ViewData.Model.Customers,
                               "CustomerID",
                               "CompanyName")) %>
        <input type="submit" value="Load" />

        <!-- Data grid goes here -->
        :
        :

        <p>Total orders: <%= ViewData.Model.Orders.Count %></p>
<% } %>
```

The method *Index* on the *HomeController* class will handle the form post and the current selection of the drop-down list will be associated with a matching parameter:

```
public ActionResult Index(string ddCustomerList)
{
    :
    :
}
```

Figure 5-12 shows a grid generated with ASP.NET MVC tools.

ID	Customer	Order issued
11011	Alfreds Futterkiste	09 Apr 98
10952	Alfreds Futterkiste	16 Mar 98
10835	Alfreds Futterkiste	15 Jan 98
10702	Alfreds Futterkiste	13 Oct 97
10692	Alfreds Futterkiste	03 Oct 97
10643	Alfreds Futterkiste	25 Aug 97

Alfreds Futterkiste ▾ Load

Total orders: 6

FIGURE 5-12 A table of data rendered using your own markup and HTML helpers

Note Just giving a drop-down list a predictable ID is a serious issue when you try to use server controls in ASP.NET MVC. You end up handling the post in a controller method, but here you have no reference to the control instance to ask about its unique ID and have no guidance on how to help the default model binder to resolve posted data into method arguments. The model binder can do its job only if the posting control doesn't belong to any naming container including panel controls and master pages. This problem has a practicable workaround in ASP.NET 4 thanks to the new *ClientIDMode* property, but not in ASP.NET 3.5.

Having you designed the grid with your own markup, making it more complex (i.e., hierarchical) is far from impossible. Building a HTML helper for a grid is definitely alluring, but I know so many developers who actually ended up calling it a daunting task instead. My experience is that designing a general grid helper is a hard job because it would invariably result in an intricate sequence of calls and parameters. Here's a possible structure of such a helper. (It was largely inspired by the Telerik's ASP.NET MVC Extensions available at *http://telerikaspnetmvc.codeplex.com*).

```
<%= Html.Grid<Order>(Model)
        .Name("Grid")
        .Columns(columns =>
        {
            columns.Add(o => o.OrderID).Width(100);
            columns.Add(o => o.Customer.ContactName).Width(200);
            columns.Add(o => o.ShipAddress);
            columns.Add(o => o.OrderDate).Format("{0:MM/dd/yyyy}").Width(120);
        })
        .Scrollable(scrolling => scrolling.Enabled((bool) ViewData["scrolling"]))
        .Sortable(sorting => sorting.Enabled((bool) ViewData["sorting"]))
        .Pageable(paging => paging.Enabled((bool) ViewData["paging"]))
        .Filterable(filtering => filtering.Enabled((bool) ViewData["filtering"]))
%>
```

While building a general-purpose grid helper may be an overwhelming task, writing a quick one that serves the need of a module or a project is much easier.

When considering a grid of data to display in a Web view, there's a strictly related aspect that you can hardly avoid: paging.

Adding Paging Support

In Web Forms, you often use rich server controls that provide paging as an embedded feature. It should be noted, though, that paging is standalone functionality. All you need is a piece of UI that provide links for the user to move between pages. When the user clicks, the control just navigates away from the current page to another as referenced in the link. Here's a sample *Pager* HTML helper.

```
public static MvcHtmlString Pager(this HtmlHelper helper,
            string name,
            int count,
            int pageSize,
            string baseUrl,
            int pageIndex,
            object htmlAttributes)
{
    // Convert from object to dictionary
    var dict = (IDictionary<string, object>)new RouteValueDictionary(htmlAttributes);

    // Calculate number of links to render
    int numOfPages = count/pageSize;
    if (count % pageSize > 0)
        numOfPages++;

    // Build the inner part of the pager bar
    var pagerRowBuilder = new StringBuilder("<tr>");
    for (int i = 1; i <= numOfPages; i++)
    {
        var formatNormal = "<a href='{0}?pageIndex={1}'>Page {1}</a>";
        var formatSelected = "<span>Page {0}</span>";
        var content = String.Empty;
        var cssClass = String.Empty;
        if (i==pageIndex)
        {
            content = String.Format(formatSelected, i);
            cssClass = "selectedPage";
        }
        else
        {
            content = String.Format(formatNormal, baseUrl, i);
        }
        pagerRowBuilder.AppendFormat("<td class='{0}'>{1}</td>", cssClass, content);
    }
    pagerRowBuilder.Append("</tr>");
```

```
    // Build the pager bar
    var pager = new TagBuilder("table");
    pager.MergeAttributes(dict);
    pager.MergeAttribute("cellspacing", "0");
    pager.MergeAttribute("cellpadding", "2");
    pager.MergeAttribute("border", "0");
    pager.GenerateId(name);
    pager.InnerHtml = pagerRowBuilder.ToString();
    return MvcHtmlString.Create(pager.ToString());
}
```

The pager is rendered as a single-row table (just an arbitrary choice here) with one cell for each page. (See Figure 5-13.)

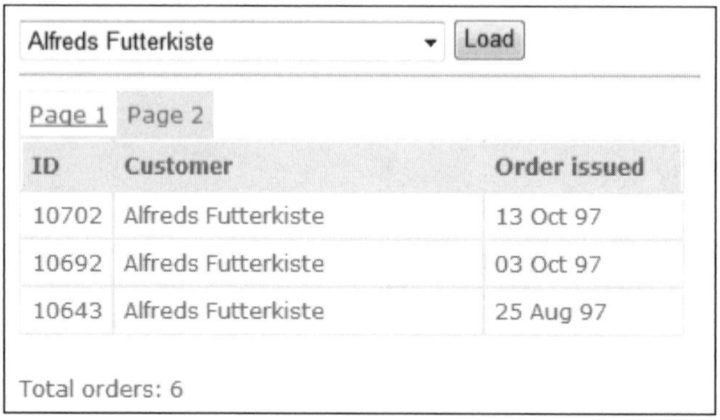

FIGURE 5-13 A pageable grid of data.

In the example, each link in the pager bar points to a URL in the form of *{controller}/{action}/{customer ID}*. To make it easier for the controller method to process the request of a new page (which would be a GET request), it is preferable to distinguish between when the Index action is requested over a POST (such as when you select from the list) and over a GET (such as when you pick up a new page). In addition, the view model object must be enriched with information such as the page size and the current page index.

```
public partial class HomeController : Controller
{
    private const int GridPageSize = 3;

    [HttpPost]
    public ActionResult Index(string ddCustomerList)
    {
        string id = ddCustomerList;

        // Get data from DB or cache
        var model = LoadSalesDataFromCache(id) ?? LoadSalesDataFromSource(id);

        // Complete the view model
        model.PageIndex = 1;
        model.PageSize = GridPageSize;
        return View(model);
    }
```

```
[HttpGet]
public ActionResult Index(string id, int? pageIndex)
{
    var index = pageIndex.HasValue ? pageIndex.Value : 1;
    index = index <1 ?1 :index;

    // Get data from DB or cache
    var model = LoadSalesDataFromCache(id) ?? LoadSalesDataFromSource(id);

    // Complete the view model
    model.PageIndex = index;
    model.PageSize = GridPageSize;
    return View(model);
}
}
```

Writing the pager may take a while but then it is a largely reusable (or easily adaptable) component for any ASP.NET MVC views you may have. The final touch is ensuring that the grid lists an appropriate number of lines:

```
<% foreach (Order order in ViewData.Model.Orders
            .Skip(ViewData.Model.PageSize*(ViewData.Model.PageIndex-1))
            .Take(ViewData.Model.PageSize))
  { %>
    .
    .
    .
<% } %>
```

Adding AJAX Capabilities

The view in Figure 5-13 works perfectly but requires a refresh for each GET or POST. What about some AJAX capabilities? In Chapter 9, we'll get into the details of AJAX in ASP.NET MVC; however, here's a brief preview. In ASP.NET MVC, AJAX is implemented around the *HTML Message* pattern and the final behavior is not much different from the partial rendering you know from Web Forms programming.

The idea is having the form to post its request asynchronously to receive a partial view—that is a chunk of HTML as typically produced by a user control. Likewise, links in the pager bar will place their requests to get similar chunks of markup. In my implementation, I decided to maintain an *Index* method in the controller to allow for a classic landing into the view from other points in the application. A new method—*GetPage*—will handle instead AJAX requests to accommodate for paging and changes of selection. The implementation of *GetPage* is identical to the method Index discussed earlier. (Having two distinct methods makes it easier to distinguish between rendering the page after a landing and refreshing portions of the page subsequent to actions within the page. In this way, we split the necessary complexity over three methods instead of just one.

```
public partial class HomeController : Controller
{
    private const int GridPageSize = 3;

    public ActionResult Index(string ddCustomerList)
    {
        string id = ddCustomerList;
        var model = LoadSalesDataFromCache(id) ?? LoadSalesDataFromSource(id);
        return View(model);
    }

    [HttpPost]
    public ActionResult GetPage(string ddCustomerList)
    {
        string id = ddCustomerList;
        var model = LoadSalesDataFromCache(id) ?? LoadSalesDataFromSource(id);

        // Complete the view model
        model.PageIndex = 1;
        model.PageSize = GridPageSize;
        return PartialView("OrdersViewByPage", model);
    }

    [HttpGet]
    public ActionResult GetPage(string id, int? pageIndex)
    {
        var index = pageIndex.HasValue ? pageIndex.Value : 1;
        index = index <1 ?1 :index;
        var model = LoadSalesDataFromCache(id) ?? LoadSalesDataFromSource(id);

        // Complete the view model
        model.PageIndex = index;
        model.PageSize = GridPageSize;
        return PartialView("OrdersViewByPage", model);
    }
}
```

Now the *PartialView* method renders out a user control named *OrdersViewByPage*. The user controls takes out from the original view the portion that will be refreshed over AJAX actions. Here's the *Index* view and the user control.

```
<!-- Index.aspx -->
<% using (Ajax.BeginForm("GetPage", "Home",
        new AjaxOptions { LoadingElementId = "lblWait", UpdateTargetId = "pnlOrdersView" } ))
   {%>
    <%= Html.DropDownList("ddCustomerList",
            new SelectList(ViewData.Model.Customers, "CustomerID", "CompanyName")) %>
    <input type="submit" value="Load" />
    <span id="lblWait" style="display:none;">Please, wait ...</span>
    <hr />
    <div id="pnlOrdersView" />
<% } %>

<!-- OrdersViewByPage.ascx -->
<div id="pnlOrdersViewByPage">
    <%= Ajax.Pager("pager",
```

```
                        ViewData.Model.Orders.Count,
                        ViewData.Model.PageSize,
                        ViewData.Model.SelectedCustomerId,
                        "GetPage",
                        "Home",
                        "lblWait",
                        "pnlOrdersViewByPage",
                        ViewData.Model.PageIndex) %>
    <table id="gridOrders">
        <tr>
            <th scope="col">ID</th>
            <th scope="col">Customer</th>
            <th scope="col">Order issued</th>
        </tr>
        <% foreach (Order order in ViewData.Model.Orders
                .Skip(ViewData.Model.PageSize*(ViewData.Model.PageIndex-1))
                .Take(ViewData.Model.PageSize))
            {%>
                <tr title="<%= order.Customer.Address %>">
                    <td><%= order.OrderID %></td>
                    <td><%= order.Customer.CompanyName %></td>
                    <td><%= String.Format("{0:dd MMM yy}", order.OrderDate) %></td>
                </tr>
        <% } %>
    </table>
    <p>Total orders: <%= ViewData.Model.Orders.Count %></p>
</div>
```

The pager must be updated too so that it can emit AJAX, script-driven links instead of plain browser-led links. You can certainly use jQuery to emit links that point to an appropriate action. In this example, however, I'm using the *Ajax.ActionLink* helper to generate script-based links. The *ActionLink* helper, though, requires that you specify the target in terms of action and controller. In addition, the pager must receive information about the ID of the customer you're paging through. You can pass the ID of the markup section to use as the progress bar and, of course, the ID of the area to be updated with the results.

```
public static MvcHtmlString Pager(this AjaxHelper helper,
    string name,
    int count,
    int pageSize,
    string itemId,
    string action,
    string controllerName,
    string waitLabel,
    string panelToUpdate,
    int pageIndex,
    object htmlAttributes)
{
    // Convert from object to dictionary
    var dict = (IDictionary<string, object>)new RouteValueDictionary(htmlAttributes);

    // Create a drop-down list with selectable pages
    int numOfPages = count/pageSize;
    if (count % pageSize > 0)
        numOfPages++;
```

```
// Build the inner part of the pager bar
var pagerRowBuilder = new StringBuilder("<tr>");
for (int i = 1; i <= numOfPages; i++)
{
    var formatSelected = "<span>Page {0}</span>";
    var content = String.Empty;
    var cssClass = String.Empty;
    if (i==pageIndex)
    {
        content = String.Format(formatSelected, i);
        cssClass = "selectedPage";
    }
    else
    {
        var temp = helper.ActionLink(
            String.Format("Page {0}", i),
                        action,
                        controllerName,
                        new { pageIndex = i, id = itemId },
                        new AjaxOptions() {
                            HttpMethod = "GET",
                            LoadingElementId = waitLabel,
                            UpdateTargetId = panelToUpdate
                        });
        content = temp.ToHtmlString();
    }

    pagerRowBuilder.AppendFormat("<td class='{0}'>{1}</td>", cssClass, content);
}
pagerRowBuilder.Append("</tr>");

// Build the pager bar
var pager = new TagBuilder("table");
pager.MergeAttributes(dict);
pager.MergeAttribute("cellspacing", "0");
pager.MergeAttribute("cellpadding", "2");
pager.MergeAttribute("border", "0");
pager.GenerateId(name);
pager.InnerHtml = pagerRowBuilder.ToString();
return MvcHtmlString.Create(pager.ToString());
}
```

More details about this example can be found in the source code that comes with the book and that you can download from . . .

Note HTML helpers are the closest you get to server controls in ASP.NET MVC. HTML helpers, however, don't provide a declarative model. Is it possible to write components that are both declarative and tailor-made for the ASP.NET MVC request life cycle? That possibility doesn't exist yet. In ASP.NET MVC 2, you get HTML templated helpers and can consider writing your own templated helpers to express complex logic and layout in a programmatic way. Beyond that, if you still prefer a truly declarative and programmatic approach, you probably need to (try to) build an entirely new family of controls that act as plain renderers of HTML while outputting route-based links and AJAX endpoints. Nothing of the kind from Microsoft or vendors is in sight as yet.

Testing a View

When it comes to testing in the context of ASP.NET MVC, you find out that most examples focus on controllers. So what about views?

In ASP.NET MVC, a good question entails whether you really need to test the view or not. A fundamental trait of automated tests is speed of execution. To be effective, a test has to be simple, quick, and repeatable. Furthermore, it's preferable that the test runs in isolation without bindings to the Web server.

Being a plain class, a controller can certainly be tested in line with all these conditions. The same can't be said for a Web view. This is the primary reason why developers tend to move most code and logic into the controller, keeping the view as simple as possible. An extremely simple view, in fact, might not need automated testing. In this regard, therefore, manual tests aimed at ensuring that bound data displays correctly, and that posted data flow out correctly, should be more than enough.

Testing the view has three different but related aspects: testing the HTML that makes up the view, testing the behavior of the view, and testing form data posted from the view.

Testing the HTML in the View

In ASP.NET MVC, the HTML for the view is generated by the controller when it invokes the *View* method. If you consider the structure of the page trivial or just static, it might suffice that you ensure the correct data is passed on to the view. This can be easily achieved through tests on the controller. (I briefly hinted at this in Chapter 4, and I'll say even more about it in Chapter 10.)

If the structure of the page might differ depending on run-time conditions or parameters, you probably need to look around for some tools that help you test the front end of a Web application.

Testing the Behavior of the View

Testing the front end of a Web application goes beyond classic unit testing and requires ad hoc tools. In this regard, ASP.NET MVC is not much different from ASP.NET Web Forms, or even from Java or PHP Web applications.

You need a tool that allows you to programmatically define a sequence of typical user actions and observe the resulting DOM tree. In other words, you want to test the layout and content of the response when the user performs a given series of actions.

Such tools have recording features, and they keep track of user actions as they are performed and store them as a reusable script to play back. Some tools also offer you the ability to edit test scripts or write them from scratch. Here's a sample test program written for one of the most popular of these front-end test tools—WatiN. The program tests the sample page we discussed earlier with a drop-down list and a grid:

```
public class SampleViewTests
{
    private Process webServer;

    [TestInitialize]
    public void Setup()
    {
        webServer = new Process();
        webServer.StartInfo.FileName = "WebDev.WebServer.exe";
        string path = ...;
        webServer.StartInfo.Arguments = String.Format(
                "/port:8080 /path: {0}", path);

        webServer.Start();
    }

    [TestMethod]
    public void CheckIfNicknameIsNotUsed()
    {
        using (IE ie = new IE("http://localhost:8080/Samples/Datagrid"))
        {
            // Select a particular customer ID
            ie.SelectList("ddCustomerList").Option("1").Select();

            // Check the resulting HTML on first row, second cell
            Assert.AreEqual(
                    "A Bike Store",
                    ie.Table(Find.ById("gridOrders")).TableRow[0].TableCells[1].InnerHtml));
        }
    }

    [TestCleanup]
    public void TearDown()
    {
        webServer.Kill();
    }
}
```

The testing tool triggers the local Web server and points it to the page of choice. Next, it simulates some user actions and checks the resulting HTML.

Different tools might support a different syntax and might integrate with different environments and in different ways. However, the previous example gives you the gist of what it means to test the front end.

Web UI testing tools can be integrated as extensions into browsers (for example, Firefox) but they also offer an API for you to write test applications in C# or test harnesses using MSTest, NUnit, or other test frameworks. Table 5-7 lists a few popular tools.

TABLE 5-7 **Tools for testing a Web front end**

Tools	More information
ArtOfTest	*http://www.artoftest.com/home.aspx*
Selenium	*http://seleniumhq.org*
Visual Studio Team System 2008	*http://msdn.microsoft.com/en-us/library/cc678655.aspx*
WatiN	*http://watin.sourceforge.net*

Testing Posted Data

In ASP.NET MVC, testing controllers is relatively easy. However, each method you test is expected to receive a bunch of parameters, either through the signature or via mocked ASP.NET intrinsic objects. Based on these values, the controller does its job and produces other values to be consumed by the view.

In this way, you can ensure that the controller behaves well based on the data it receives. How can you test that the view really passes in correct data? In other words, how can you test posted data?

Sending automated POST requests to a URL is a feature that all the tools in Table 5-7 support. They all let you fill in and post a form. However, in that case, at least, the local Web server ffmust be up and running. Posting to test pages that do nothing but return a Boolean answer (expected/unexpected) is a possible way to speed up things.

If you want to simply look at what is being transmitted, you can turn your attention to tools such as Fiddler (*http://www.fiddler2.com/fiddler2/*) or HttpWatch (*http://www.httpwatch.com*).

Summary

ASP.NET MVC doesn't include anything that corresponds to a page—at least, as we've come to know pages from ASP.NET Web Forms. ASP.NET MVC doesn't match URLs to disk files; instead, it parses the URL to figure out the next requested action to take. The closest thing to a page in an ASP.NET MVC application is the *view*.

A view is neatly separated from the controller. The controller performs any work, gets fresh data for the next user's view, and then passes the data on to the currently selected view engine. The view engine gets the data and a view name. The view name points to a template whose location and syntax depends on the view engine.

The view as invoked by the controller is, then, a template that is merged with data to produce HTML for the browser. ASP.NET MVC supplies a default view engine that recognizes a syntax that is largely based on the ASPX markup of Web Forms. This allows you to employ server controls in ASP.NET MVC views even though this certainly is not the ideal approach. The development of the view can be made faster by using HTML helper components—static methods that emit HTML based on parameters. Unlike server controls, HTML helpers are simple and don't implement any life cycle.

In this chapter, we first examined in detail what it takes to process a view and then focused on development aspects, including using HTML helpers, templated helpers, localization, server controls and, last but not least, testing a view.

In the next chapter, we'll complete our look at the core of ASP.NET MVC by tackling the third actor of the base MVC pattern—the model.

Chapter 6
Inside Models

It does not matter how slowly you go, so long as you do not stop.

—Confucius

By default, the Microsoft Visual Studio standard project template for ASP.NET MVC applications includes a *Models* folder. If you look around for some guidance on how to use it and information about its intended role, you quickly reach the conclusion that the *Models* folder exists to store model classes. Fine, but which model is it? Or, more precisely, what's the intended definition of a "model"?

I don't much like the *Models* folder. It's not that I don't want to have it around; more simply, I find *Models* to be a misnomer for an otherwise useful folder. As I see things, *ViewModels* would have been a much better name for the folder—and this is how I often rename the folder in my own projects.

What is the point here? The change of a folder name doesn't make an application run faster or make it easier to maintain. However, I've found out in a bunch of real-world projects that less experienced developers—or, regardless of the experience, developers with a not-so-clear understanding of layered systems—tend to confuse view-specific, screen-bound models with business-oriented domain models. The folder named *Models* seems to transmit the message that it is just the place where you need have your application's domain model—the model with business entities such as *Customer*, *Order*, *Invoice*, and so forth.

I agree with anyone who says that not every application needs a neat separation between the object models used in the presentation and business layers. Nonetheless, two distinct models exist, and coexist, in a typical layered Web solution. You might decide that for your own purposes the two models nearly coincide, but you should always recognize the existence of two distinct models that operate in two distinct layers.

In this chapter, I'll first go through the differences between view-models and domain models, and then I'll drill down into how you can effectively design a model for the presentation layer and a model for the business layer. Finally, I'll look into binding posted data into complex and rich data types for the controller to use. In doing so, I'll discuss validation and data member annotations.

What's the Model, Anyway?

As discussed in Chapter 3, "The MVC Pattern and Beyond," the ASP.NET MVC framework is clearly inspired by the Model2 pattern, regardless of the MVC signature in the name. The Model2 pattern had been largely inspired by the original MVC pattern, and it was, in fact, the result of adapting the MVC pattern to the Web scenario.

In the Model2 pattern, most of the work is taken care of by only two actors: the view and the controller. The model is merely a way to represent the data being worked on in the view. The controller orchestrates all operations: it receives posted data, performs any required action, selects the next view, and orders the selected view to render.

Where's the model, then? What's its intended meaning?

As I see things, the model in ASP.NET MVC is simply an abstraction for any data the controller passes down to the view. This definition is perfectly in line with the definition of the "model actor" that you might read about in the original MVC paper. The paper describes the model as "the data being worked on in the view."

With that said, let's forget about the *Models* folder for now and start thinking logically about the various faces of the MVC model you might meet in an ASP.NET MVC application. And, if needed, add new folders to group any new classes and abstractions.

> **Note** The default Visual Studio template for ASP.NET MVC 2 features a non-empty *Models* folder that just contains a file named *AccountModels.cs*. This file relates to the login functionalities of the default template and defines a bunch of helper classes. Unless you find out that the default support for login works for you—it may or may not—you can remove that file from the folder and even rename or remove the folder itself. In a way, however, the content of the *Models* folder in the default ASP.NET MVC 2 project brings up the idea that the folder is expected to contain view-specific data models that span over controllers and views.

How Many Types of Models Do You Know?

In ASP.NET MVC, the term "model" is used to mean three distinct things, as illustrated in Figure 6-1:

- The representation of the data being posted to the controller
- The representation of the data being worked on in the view
- The representation of the domain-specific entities operating in the business tier

In relatively simple scenarios (like many of the Web applications you are commonly asked to write), it might be acceptable that a *single* set of classes—that is, a *unique* model—is employed. However, this is only a *simplified* design that is safe to choose when it doesn't produce any loss of generality.

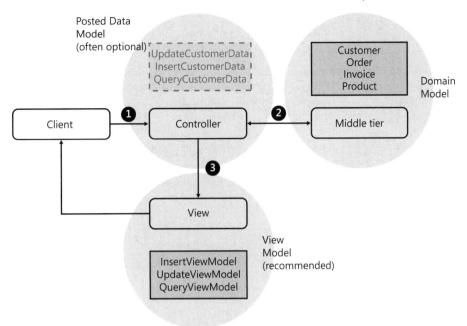

Posted Data
Model
(often optional)

UpdateCustomerData
InsertCustomerData
QueryCustomerData

Customer
Order
Invoice
Product

Domain
Model

Client

Controller

Middle tier

View

InsertViewModel
UpdateViewModel
QueryViewModel

View
Model
(recommended)

FIGURE 6-1 Three flavors of a model in ASP.NET MVC

Data Posted to the Controller

As discussed in Chapter 2, "The Runtime Environment," ASP.NET MVC works on top of the same runtime environment as classic ASP.NET. This means that any requests for an ASP.NET MVC endpoint are routed through the ASP.NET pipeline. Any posted data is packaged into a POST request.

As the preferred ASP.NET MVC endpoint, a controller's method can easily grab any posted data from the collections available through the *Request* object—especially *Form* and *QueryString*.

These collections, though, expose just the raw, string-based data. In classic ASP.NET, the default page HTTP handler forwards this data to target server controls and lets server controls parse and validate the data. The runtime shell of ASP.NET MVC attempts to model any incoming data to strongly typed variables.

In particular, the runtime environment uses some conventions to match the key names of posted values to formal parameters in the target controller's method. If the controller's method declares a complex type, a more sophisticated binding mechanism is triggered:

```
[AcceptVerbs(HttpVerbs.Post)]
public ActionResult Update(Customer customer)
{
    :
    :
}
```

Known as *model binding*, this mechanism attempts to bind posted data to public members of the declared type using the same name-based convention—a public member matched to a posted key value. The mechanism is actually more sophisticated because it allows you to customize the binding process, but that's the basic idea.

In the example, it might happen that posted data is automatically bound to the *Customer* argument.

So what's the *Customer* type? It can definitely be the representation of a business entity as well as an object modeled after the needs of the posting HTML form. More in general, it can be a data container that grabs any incoming data and groups it in a way that is easier for the controller to work with.

To be really picky, data types used as arguments of a controller action method belong to an ad hoc object model—we can call it, the *posted data* object model—distinct from the view-model and the business entity model, as in the following example:

```
[AcceptVerbs(HttpVerbs.Post)]
public ActionResult Update(UpdateCustomerData data)
{
    :
    :
}
```

The *UpdateCustomerData* class is an action-specific class that is used to grab any data posted from the client. You use this class in lieu of the real domain entity—for example, *Customer*—and isolate in it any validation logic and any logic that determines default values for unspecified properties.

Note To avoid an always nefarious proliferation of classes, you will likely decide to ignore this type of model, discard the idea of using any such *UpdateCustomerData* class, and resort to using domain objects (for example, *Customer*) to capture posted data, a sequence of primitive data types, the *FormCollection* object, or even the *Request* object. I'll return to the pros and cons of direct domain object binding later.

Data Worked On in the View

After the controller's method has done its job, it has likely grabbed, or produced, some data to show in the view. To maintain a clean separation of concerns, the controller is expected to calculate and retrieve any data required by the view. In other words, the view is expected to be as passive as possible and just display what it receives.

In doing its work, the controller method typically interacts with the application's middle tier, running queries, executing workflows, or perhaps invoking service methods. Depending on how you design the business layer, the controller—which logically belongs to the presentation layer—receives data in a format that might not be designed for the needs of the next view to display.

Most of the time, some extra work is required before the data can be passed to the view and subsequently served to the end user. Usually, this extra work entails applying ad hoc formatting, fragmenting collections to make them fit into the UI elements, and populating UI list elements with options for the user to choose. This logic doesn't belong to the business tier and subsequently might not be reflected by the objects the controller receives from the middle tier.

It turns out that a new layer of data types must be arranged for the specific needs of the view. These objects are referred to as *view-model classes*, and the controller passes their instances down to the view:

```
[AcceptVerbs(HttpVerbs.Post)]
public ActionResult Index(int? productId)
{
    // Action
    Product product = _service.GetProductById(productId);

    // Prepare for rendering
    var model = new ProductViewModel();
    :
    :

    return View("Product", model);
}
```

In ASP.NET MVC, you often use the word "model" to refer to strongly typed objects you pass to the view, as in the preceding example. The *ProductViewModel* class you see in the listing is a view-bound data type that carries all the values being used by the Product view (and only these values).

Important Do you really need to have an *xxxViewModel* class for each view you happen to have and for each use-case? Yes, in an ideal scenario this is just what you end up with. But we live in an imperfect world. So it is acceptable that you sacrifice the purity of design in the name of pragmatism and, when this is suitable, pass on to the UI the same data objects you have received from the middle tier. This is your own choice though, consciously made for the sake of the project. It should not be sold as, or simply mistaken for, a best practice. Finally, be aware that passing direct entities is hardly what you want, even with moderately complex views. In fact, the needs of the view might require data to be assembled from various entities, which forces you to create ad hoc data transfer classes.

Domain-Specific Entities

In the middle tier, you must have a coherent representation of the data your application processes. This data is expected to describe the entities that populate the domain of the problem your application is called to solve. For example, an application that deals with a trading company will likely have entities such as *Customer, Order,* and *Invoice.*

There might be various ways of implementing domain entities, and they all depend on how you envision the business tier of the application. If you opt for the Domain Model pattern, for instance, you end up with an object model that is completely ignorant of persistence and that focuses on business processes rather than application-specific operations such as database I/O, logging, and security. If you opt for an Active Record pattern, you work with an object model in which entities model closely the underlying tables and each object knows how to load and save itself from and to the database. Finally, if you feel comfortable with the typed DataSets, you opt for the rules of the Table Module pattern and create business objects that encapsulate database tables.

In a Web application, data types defined in the application's business tier typically rise up to the presentation layer, where they can be consumed by controllers. So, for example, if your entity data model relies on a *Customer* object, the same *Customer* object might become visible to the controller; and from there, it can be passed on to the view to arrange a Web page. On the way back, the content of the form might be headed back to a *Customer* object in the context of a controller action method and, from there, down to the business tier to close the circle.

In the end, an ASP.NET MVC application has three different types of models. They all serve a specific and distinct purpose. To a large extent, all these classes can correctly be considered part of the model. But you should be clear about what the real differences are.

With all that said, what should you have in the *Models* folder?

The *Models* Folder

Too many demos of ASP.NET MVC applications have the presenter create a LINQ-to-SQL model or an Entity Framework model to start with. The presenter then frequently refers to these models as the "model" of the application. Some presenters even sometimes copy the DBML or EDMX files into the *Models* folder.

As an architect or developer, you need to understand that, in general, there exist three distinct types of model, each playing a specific role, as you just saw.

Using three distinct sets of classes is the only proven way to deal with particularly complex applications where the needs of the user interface don't match nicely with the representation of the data you have in the middle tier. This model mismatch might result from questionable design choices, from an excessive requirements churn that constrained the design or, more likely, from nonfunctional requirements such as the need to interface with a legacy system.

One-Model-Fits-All: Approach or Antipattern?

Not all applications are so complex as to require three distinct models—for posted data, view data, and business logic. In one common scenario, you have a single model largely inferred from the database and use that everywhere—in the controller as well as in the view. Let's refer to these objects as domain objects or domain entities.

If using a single model everywhere is an approach that works for you, by all means go for it. It's simple and effective. Furthermore, the years of experience captured by Ruby-on-Rails and Castle MonoRail developers prove that this approach is just right for most Web applications. So why not use it in ASP.NET MVC?

On the other hand, as a conscientious developer or architect, you should be aware that by opting for a single model of data you are deliberately simplifying the design. As long as it remains simple and doesn't create issues of any sort, you're OK. Should it, at some point, become simplistic or ineffective, you'll be in serious trouble.

My Model Is the Domain Model

If "model" for you means just the domain model, in any non-toy application you likely don't need the *Models* folder at all. If your model is expected to contain a representation of the domain entities, chances are good that you'll import these classes from an external assembly or service, as in the sample project shown in Figure 6-2.

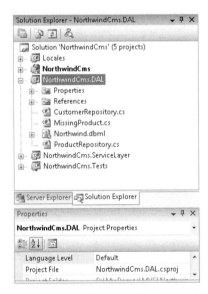

FIGURE 6-2 The data model is imported from an external class library.

In a similar situation, the *Models* folder is just empty and you can safely delete it. The only reason for keeping the *Models* folder is if you are embedding the domain entities in the Web application—it's doable, but not recommended because doing so makes it difficult to keep the project clean and manageable.

Now let's examine the pros and cons of having a single, business-oriented model.

Posting Data to Domain Objects

Every HTTP POST request that hits a Web application brings some data for the application to process. This data travels in the body of the HTTP packet, and the ASP.NET runtime environment then automatically maps this incoming data to a name/value dictionary—usually, the *Form* collection exposed through the *Request* intrinsic object. In ASP.NET MVC, any request—whether it's GET or POST—is mapped to a controller action method. What about the signature of the action method?

As you saw in Chapter 4, "Inside Controllers," an action method is expected to return an *ActionResult* object, but it can accept any sequence of input parameters. If the action method is parameterless, you can resort only to the *Request* object to access posted data. If the action method signature instead contains parameters, the ASP.NET MVC runtime is smart enough to try to match posted values to the names of those formal parameters. For example, consider this controller method:

```
public ActionResult Find(int id)
{
    :
    :
}
```

The *id* parameter gets automatically initialized only if there's a posted value with a matching key name. Otherwise, it remains set to *null* and you can still retrieve any posted value using the *Request* object.

What if the action method declares a complex type as in the following example?

```
public ActionResult Insert(Customer customer)
{
    :
    :
}
```

Who takes care of filling up the properties of the *Customer* parameter? The ASP.NET MVC runtime loops through the public properties of the type specified in the controller method signature and attempts to match the names of those public properties to the key of posted values. For any match found, the corresponding property on the complex type is set.

Issues with Direct Domain Object Binding

This approach is easy to code and it certainly works. However, there's a drawback you might want to consider. *Customer* is *directly* bound to any data being posted over the wire. Any posted value that has a matching key can find its way into the instance of *Customer* being processed by the controller. This approach can even result in a security hole if a made-to-measure, malicious post is prepared and run.

To avoid that, the only serious approach you can take is changing the signature of the controller method and removing the entity object from there. Here are a couple of alternatives for when you have multiple values to move around:

```
public ActionResult Insert(FormCollection formData);
{
    // Similar to using Request.Form but easier to test
}
public ActionResult Insert(string company, string contact, ...);
{
    // List all properties you want to set. Still
    // requires matching between posted values and parameter names.
}
public ActionResult Insert(InsertCustomerData data);
{
    // List all properties you want to set. Still
    // requires matching between posted values and parameter names.
}
```

In addition, it's possible that not all values posted from the view have a match with properties in *Customer*; therefore, some properties might stay unassigned. This possibility has to be verified before the controller proceeds with updates.

Finally, consider that, in any case, you are forced to have matches between property names (or parameter names) and posted values. In other words, the view is not really independent from the model.

> **Note** The way in which posted data is processed by the ASP.NET MVC runtime is controlled by a special type of component—the *model binder*. I'll get to model binders in a moment.
>
> By writing a custom model binder, you can work around some of the issues mentioned. In particular, you can force security checks and avoid arbitrary and malicious data from being passed, and you can ensure that unmatched properties have a default value and even validate data before they are stored in the entity object.

Passing Data to the View

After having processed any input data that comes over the POST command, the controller method is ready to render the view. Because the view is expected to be as simple as possible, the controller will pass it any single piece of data that needs to be displayed.

In a realistic scenario, the data for the view probably won't come from just one entity object. In some simple cases, all you want to do is display (for editing or reporting purposes), say, a *Customer* object. In this case, all is fine and the *View* method just receives a *Customer* instance for a strongly typed view.

However, when the view is not tailor-made for a particular entity, you are left with the problem of aggregating data together. A common situation is when you need to edit a *Customer* object but also need to provide a list of countries for the user to select. You actually have a *Customer* object to pass, plus something else.

You can opt for creating a few entries in the *ViewData* collection, or you can opt for arranging a custom type that represents the model for the view.

Let's now examine more closely the options you have for modeling the domain model and the view-model and how cross-cutting concerns such as error handling and validation apply to both types of models.

Domain Model and View-Model

Nearly all applications, and not just ASP.NET MVC applications, need a domain model that represents, from the application's perspective, the data that the application is supposed to handle. In addition, a view-model is almost as necessary to provide the engine that produces the view with specific information that is just right, in terms of quantity, quality, and formatting.

The two models are hardly disjointed, but their overlapping is hardly total, either. When their overlapping is nearly total, it might make sense that you consider getting rid of the view-model and perhaps resort to the *ViewData* collection for any extra data that is required.

The *Models* folder can be used to contain files related to the domain model (for example, EDMX files if you use Entity Framework, or DBML files if you opted for LINQ-to-SQL), but it can also be used to contain any classes you happen to have in your view-model. The structure of the *Models* folder is a detail that doesn't really affect the design of the application. From a design perspective, the only thing that really matters is your awareness that the domain model and view-model are distinct things.

Business Object Modeling

Regardless of what seems to be implied by the term *Models folder*, ASP.NET MVC doesn't mandate any specific data technology or approach for building a data model. You can use your existing ADO.NET data access layer and be happy. Likewise, you can choose the dazzling approach of LINQ-to-SQL and wed the power of designers and autogenerated code with an object-based vision of your data. If you need more, you can opt for a fully fledged Object/Relational Mapper (O/RM) framework, such as Entity Framework, NHibernate, LLBLGen Pro, Subsonic, or perhaps Castle Active Record.

When it comes to designing a business data model, a lot of pattern names usually show up in discussions—*Domain Model, Active Record, Table Module*, but also *Repository, Unit of Work,* and *Identity Map*. You have to be careful in your analysis to separate the chaff from the wheat and distinguish between patterns for business data modeling and patterns for persistence.

The Model and Persistence

A business data model is a model that an application uses to represent the data it works with. The reference here is to *business* data rather than data used to populate a view or to trigger a controller or service method.

You can organize your business data model according to a number of patterns, but essentially it boils down to choosing between a table-oriented approach and an object-oriented approach. In the final analysis, the point is not whether you use objects or not, but how you model your objects and define their relationship to the database, their expressivity, the fidelity with which they model the problem's domain, and their flexibility in supporting changes. An object model is a collection of classes and often looks similar to the database. On the other hand, it has to act as the database as far as the application is concerned. The patterns listed in Table 6-1 are commonly used to create a business data model.

TABLE 6-1 Patterns for devising a business data model

Pattern	Description
Active Record	Objects are closely modeled after database tables. Usually, you have one object per table and one property per column. Objects are responsible for their own persistence and have very simple domain logic or no domain logic at all.
Domain Model	Objects are aimed at providing a conceptual view of the problem's domain. They have no relationships with the database and focus on the data owned and behavior to offer. Objects have both properties and methods and are not responsible for their own persistence. Objects are uniquely responsible for actions related to their role and domain logic.
Table Module	Each object represents a database table and its entire content. The class has nearly no properties and exposes a method for each operation on the table, whether a query or an update. This is the pattern behind typed DataSets and table adapters in Visual Studio 2005 and later.

For more information on patterns for the business layer, you can refer to my book *Microsoft .NET: Architecting Applications for the Enterprise* (Microsoft Press, 2008).

Once you have the model, though, you need to be able to persist it. With Table Module and Active Record, persistence is embedded in the objects that form the model. More specifically, if you opt for Table Module, your objects expose methods to do classic CRUD operations on the table they represent, as well as any complex query. With Active Record, you have objects that represent a row in a database table, so any CRUD operations recognize the current row.

If you opt for a Domain Model approach instead, the whole theme of persistence is there for you to deal with. Objects in a Domain Model scenario don't know anything about persistence. For this reason, persistence has to be delegated to a distinct layer.

You can write this layer—often referred to as just the Data Access Layer (DAL)—yourself, but it wouldn't be much fun. A well-written DAL for a Domain Model is nearly the same as an O/RM tool. So why not use one of the existing O/RM tools?

O/RM tools such as NHibernate and LLBLGen Pro take your own classes and follow your instructions as to how to map their properties to database columns. Other tools such as Entity Framework force you to create both the model and the mappings through the facilities embedded in Visual Studio.

O/RM tools usually offer a gateway object to orchestrate operations. This object (*Session* in NHibernate, *ObjectContext* in Entity Framework) implements a number of persistence-specific patterns, such as Identity Map and Unit of Work. (So these patterns are of no direct interest when you focus on business data modeling.)

Finally, for testability you should try to wrap access to the DAL via the outermost layer of code that corresponds to the Repository pattern. The Repository pattern is merely a wrapper through which common data access operations are exposed. Often, you have a repository for each (significant) object in the domain model. Here's an example:

```
public interface ICustomerRepository
{
    IList<Customer> GetAll();
    Customer GetById(short id);
    IList<Customer> GetByCriteria(Predicate<Customer> func);
    void Add(Customer customer);
    void Delete(Customer customer);
    void Delete(int id);
    void Save(Customer customer);
    IList<Orders> GetOrdersForCustomer(Customer customer);
}
```

The Repository pattern is not a way to model your data; it is simply a way to model your Data Access Layer.

Abstracting Domain Entities to a Model

For many years, the most natural way to create models was to have them mirror the physical structure of the database. You have a Customers table? Then you need to have a *Customer* object. You have a foreign key to an Orders table? Then you have an *Orders* collection. In this way, the model grows out of the database, offers a thin layer of abstraction from the database details, and remains tightly coupled to the database. Is this wrong?

No, it's not wrong, but this approach might be inappropriate in some cases. It doesn't take you in the wrong direction, but it might make it harder for you to achieve your goals. Let's explore another approach that is not table oriented.

If you consider the creation of an abstract model that includes classes such as the entities you recognize in the problem's domain, you'll realize the model grows out of the domain. The model abstracts your code from database details, and it is loosely coupled to the database. A domain-based model doesn't necessarily take you the right way, but it might make it easier for you to achieve your goals.

The purpose of dealing with an object model that has no direct relationship to the database is to pursue an old dream of many developers and architects: It will let the model evolve independently from the database. It will let you add classes and relationships as needed without having to come to an agreement with the database guys.

(Some companies have very strict IT departments that require you to submit a form for any minimal change made to any table hosted on the company's servers. Imagine how hard it could be to adapt the database for all the changes you might need in development and maintenance.)

The Domain Model pattern applies the model-first approach: it first creates the model and then maps it to the database. Which tools would you use for creating a business data model using the Domain Model pattern?

Entity Framework 4 lets you create the model using a Visual Studio 2010 designer. (See Figure 6-3.)

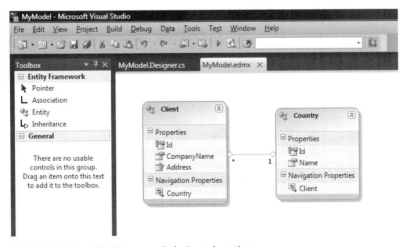

FIGURE 6-3 The Entity Framework designer in action

When you are done with the abstract model, it creates the source code of the classes for you. You can choose among a few different generators—standard, POCO (plain-old C# objects), and self-tracking objects. You should also keep entity classes separated from the data context class. The data context class (inherited from *ObjectContext*) is technically part of the DAL, whereas entities are part of your domain model and, therefore, part of the business layer.

You can also create the model as a class library of plain C# classes and persist them to the database using NHibernate file mappings. In doing so, you also leverage the NHibernate Data Access Layer for any CRUD operations.

> **Note** The expression "Domain Model" has several meanings you should be aware of before you start using the term. Although it can be used to signify an object model created after a specific domain (and not to represent a physical database), it is sometimes assigned a more specific meaning partly taken from the Domain-Driven Design (DDD) methodology. According to this methodology, a domain model is a special flavor of a self-contained object model in which classes have no dependencies on outside types, are not forced to implement interfaces, and feature ad hoc constructors. In this model, everything is a class and primitive types are often replaced with ad hoc value types.

The Active Record Pattern

The Active Record pattern is simpler in some ways than the Domain Model pattern, and it requires much less up-front planning. With Active Record, you get a collection of classes that closely model the tables in an existing database. Most of the time, you have a one-to-one correspondence between classes and tables and between class properties and table columns.

Each class essentially represents a record in a database table: the classes usually have instance methods that act on the represented record and perform common operations such as save and delete. In addition, a class might have some static methods to load an object from a database record and perform some rich queries involving all records.

Classes in an Active Record model have methods, but these methods are mostly doing CRUD operations. There's nearly no domain logic in the classes of an Active Record model, even though nothing prevents you from adding that.

An aspect that makes Active Record so attractive to developers is its extreme simplicity and elegance and, just as significantly, the fact that in spite of its simplicity it works surprisingly well for a many Web applications—even fairly large Web applications. I wouldn't be exaggerating to say that the Active Record model is especially popular among Web developers and less so among Windows developers.

Beyond the simplicity and elegance of the model, available tools contribute significantly to make Active Record such a popular choice. Which tool should you use to implement an Active Record model?

LINQ-to-SQL is definitely an option. Fully integrated in Visual Studio 2008 and later, LINQ-to-SQL allows you to connect to a database and infer a model from there. As a developer, your classes become available in a matter of seconds at the end of a simple wizard. In addition, your classes can be re-created at any time as you make changes, if any, to the database. In terms of persistence, LINQ-to-SQL is not really a canonical Active Record model because it moves persistence to its internal DAL—the data context. LINQ-to-SQL incorporates a persistence engine that makes it look like a simple but effective O/RM tool with full support for advanced persistence patterns such as Identity Map and especially Unit of Work.

Castle Active Record is another framework that has been around for a few years and that offers a canonical implementation of the Active Record pattern. Finally, an emerging framework for Active Record modeling is Subsonic. (See *http://www.subsonicproject.com*.)

Unlike Castle Active Record, Subsonic can generate classes for you but does so in a way that is more flexible than in LINQ-to-SQL: it uses T4 templates. A T4 template is a *.tt* text file that Visual Studio 2008 and later can process and expand to a class. If you add a T4 template to a Visual Studio project, it soon turns it into a working class. This mechanism offers you an unprecedented level of flexibility because you can modify the structure of the class from the inside and not just extend it with partial classes as in LINQ-to-SQL, and it also removes the burden of writing that you must do with Castle Active Record.

The following code shows some simple operations with a Subsonic model:

```
// Find a customer by ID
var customer = Customer.SingleOrDefault(c => c.CustomerID == 'ALFKI');

// Get a list of customers by country
var customers = Customer.Find(c => c.Country == 'USA');

// Delete a customer (fails if data integrity is violated)
Customer c = new Customer('ALFKI');
c.Destroy();

// Update/Insert a customer
Customer c = new Customer('ALFKI');
c.CompanyName = "...";
    ⋮
c.Save();
```

As you can see, queries are accomplished through static methods and lambda expressions, whereas update operations occur via instance methods.

Adding Validation Logic to the Model

In addition to providing a faithful and persistent representation of the entities in the problem's domain, a business data model has to provide a way for developers to validate any instance of data. In other words, there should be a way for the developer to know quickly whether the state of the object is valid or not.

There are various ways to add some validation logic to the model, and which options you have depend on the data access technology you are using more than on the pattern of choice. Let's review a few common scenarios.

A General Approach

Adding validation logic to an object model consists of defining an interface common to all classes in the model that can be queried to check whether a given instance is in a valid state or not. Here's the typical structure of a class that supports a validation layer:

```
public class MyRootDomainObject : ISupportValidation
{
    public virtual bool IsValid
    {
        get
        {
            try
            {
                return new ValidationResults().IsValid;
            }
            catch
            {
                return false;
            }
        }
    }

    ValidationResults ISupportValidation.Validate()
    {
        ValidationResults errors = new ValidationResults();
        :
        :
        return errors;
    }
}
```

Here is what the *ISupportValidation* interface might look like:

```
interface ISupportValidation
{
    bool IsValid { get; }
    ValidationResults Validate();
}
```

ValidationResults is the class in your validation layer responsible for reading and applying validation rules. Validation rules can be defined in a number of ways, including using plain code. However, the approach emerging today as the most popular is to use attributes on properties.

The structure of *MyRootDomainObject* lends itself well to supporting validation attributes. Here's an example of a business entity that inherits from *MyRootDomainObject* and adds some validation attributes:

```
public class Customer : MyRootDomainObject
{
    public Customer()
    {
        ⋮
    }

    [NotNullConstraint(Message="Customer ID cannot be null")]
    [LengthConstraint(5, 5, Message="Customer ID must be exactly 5 chars long")]
    public virtual string ID { get; set; }
    ⋮
}
```

The *Validate* method on the *ISupportValidation* interface simply goes through all attributes for a given instance and checks their expressions against current values. Each attribute expresses a business rule. In the example, the *ID* property of the *Customer* class is set to be non-null and exactly five characters long.

Where would you find these attributes? You can write them yourself (as it is assumed in the preceding code snippet), or you can use analogous attributes defined in Microsoft Enterprise Library.

The Validation Application Block

The Validation Application Block is one of the modules that form Microsoft Enterprise Library. It lets you express business rules using attributes such as *NotNullValidator*, *StringLengthValidator*, *RelativeDateTimeValidator*, *RegexValidator*, and a few others. It also provides various facilities for you to validate the state of a given entity. Here's the code you are required to validate according to the rules set through attributes for the type *Customer*:

```
Validator validator = ValidationFactory.CreateValidator<Customer>();
ValidationResults results = validator.Validate(customer);
```

To incorporate the Validation Application Block in the *MyRootDomainObject* class, you need to rewrite the *Validate* method on the *ISupportValidation* interface as shown here:

```
ValidationResults ISupportValidation.Validate()
{
   Validator validator = ValidationFactory.CreateValidator(this.GetType());
   ValidationResults results = validator.Validate(this);
   return results;
}
```

By using attributes from Enterprise Library and a validation interface, you can endow all classes in the object model with validation capabilities. Additionally, the *ValidationResults* class is a collection of error messages about whatever went wrong. These elements ensure that a business layer performing validation against domain objects will receive the detailed information it needs to take the next steps.

```
public void Update(Customer customer)
{
    if (customer.IsValid())
        _customerRepository.Save(customer);
}
```

An approach based on attributes works if you can freely edit the classes in the model. This is definitely possible if you develop the model yourself or if you can exercise some control on it, as is the case with Subsonic. With LINQ-to-SQL or Entity Framework, instead, this gets a bit problematic because the source code is autogenerated (and maintained) by Visual Studio. It doesn't mean you have to look around for another strategy; more simply you need to make some adjustments.

Note In addition to supporting attributes to be manually added to properties on entity classes, Enterprise Library also supports the concept of a rule set. A rule set is a collection of rules expressed through built-in validators such as *RangeValidator*, *StringLengthValidator*, and the like. A rule set has a name, and one or more rule sets can be applied programmatically to an object. More interestingly, rules and rule sets can be defined in the configuration file without the need to edit source files. This represents a powerful solution to add validation logic to LINQ-to-SQL and Entity Framework models. For some reason, though, this perfectly legitimate and highly effective solution is not achieving the same popularity as other options I'll discuss in a moment.

Validation in an Entity Framework Scenario

To add validation to an Entity Framework object model, you resort to an approach that is specific to the technology. When the object model is autogenerated, each property on an entity class has a pair of extensibility methods, as shown here for a particular *Title* property:

```
public string Title
{
    get
    {
        return this._Title;
    }
    set
    {
        this.OnTitleChanging(value);
        this.ReportPropertyChanging("Title");
        this._Title = value;
        this.ReportPropertyChanged("Title");
        this.OnTitleChanged();
    }
}
```

```
private string _Title;
partial void OnTitleChanging(string value);
partial void OnTitleChanged();
```

Two partial methods are defined: *OnTitleChanging* and *OnTitleChanged*. More in general, you'll have an *OnXxxChanging* method invoked at the beginning of the property setter and an *OnXxxChanged* method invoked at the end. A partial method is defined on a class, but it is initially implemented as an empty method. Unless you give it code in an additional partial class, the method is treated as a non-operation by the compiler and optimized away. If instead you override the base method and provide specific code, that code gets invoked where specified. In other words, for the sample *Title* property, the *OnTitleChanging* and *OnTitleChanged* methods represent the entry and exit points, respectively, in the setter method. These methods, but *OnTitleChanging* in particular, exist just to let you put your own validation code in.

You start by adding a partial class for each entity you intend to validate and then provide an implementation for any *OnXxxChanging* partial method you want. Here's an example:

```
partial void OnTitleChanging(string value)
{
    // Your validation logic for the property here
    string proposedValue = value;
    if (String.IsNullOrEmpty(value))
        throw new ArgumentException();
}
```

If the validation fails, there's not much else you can do other than have the code throw an exception.

> **Important** Overall, the classic approach to validation in Entity Framework is limiting, and it is limiting for two good reasons. First, it forces you to throw an exception if something goes wrong. Second, because it throws an exception, it stops at the first detected error and doesn't offer you a global vision of what's wrong in the current state of the entity. I called this the "classic" approach because it is the only one you can take without adding extra features or linking external libraries. However, after you take the plunge into writing additional code, you can do more and add a collection to each entity where you copy the results of failures and a method to check them programmatically. It's not really a lot of work, but it is probably useless today because with Entity Framework 4 you have even better alternatives.

Implementing partial methods is only the most common strategy to add validation to Entity Framework that works with any version of it. It is not the only option, however.

In the first version of Entity Framework that comes with the .NET Framework 3.5 Service Pack 1, instead of relying on autogenerated classes that inherit from *EntityObject*, you can implement the so-called IPOCO interfaces—*IEntityWithChangeTracker* for tracking changes, *IEntityWithKey* for exposing the entity identity, and *IEntityWithRelationships* for entities with associations. In doing so, you gain total control over the source code of the classes and can decorate them with any attribute you like, including the Microsoft Enterprise Library attributes for validation.

If you stick to the standard code generator, instead, you can add attributes to entities only by overwriting the designer-generated code. In this way, though, you're subjected to the possibility of losing all your changes if the designer is triggered again to update the model. Microsoft Enterprise Library, however, offers the possibility to link validation attributes through a rule set stored in the configuration file. This is a great opportunity that is not advertised as well as it should be. It lets you wed the power of Entity Framework with the flexibility of the Validation Application Block in Enterprise Library. More importantly, it gives you a mechanism to check for the valid state of an object without having to incur an exception to find it out.

Finally, in the newest version of Entity Framework, by choosing the POCO code generator you make yourself entirely responsible for the source code of the classes and can add all attributes and extra code that suits you.

 Note In LINQ-to-SQL, the only approaches are the ones that use partial methods and throw exceptions for invalid states as well as the approach based on the Validation Application Block in Enterprise Library, which requires having all attributes set in the configuration file.

Data Annotations

In the .NET Framework 4, you find a revamped and improved version of the data annotations library in the *System.ComponentModel.DataAnnotations* assembly. Data annotations are a set of attributes you can use to annotate public properties of any .NET class in a way that any interested client code can read and consume.

Attributes fall in various categories: validation, display, and data modeling. Compared to the validators in Enterprise Library, data annotations are definitely richer and more sophisticated. Unfortunately, though, data annotations lack support for settings stored offline in a configuration file. Here's a brief example of some relevant validation attributes:

```
public class Customer
{
    [Required]
    [Range(5, 50)]
    public int CustomerId { get; set; }

    [Required(AllowEmptyStrings=false)]
    [StringLength(5)]
    [RegularExpression(@"^[a-zA-Z''-'\s]{1,40}$",
        ErrorMessage = "Special characters are not allowed in the company name.")]
    public String CompanyName { get; set; }
```

```
    [DataType(DataType.EmailAddress)]
    public String Contact { get; set; }

    [CustomValidation(typeof(SpecialValidation), "ValidateSalesPerson")]
    public String SalesPerson { get; set; }

    [Required]
    [DataType(DataType.Text)]
    public String Country { get; set; }

    [DataType(DataType.PhoneNumber)]
    public String Phone { get; set; }

    [EnumDataType(typeof(Fidelity))]
    [Range(5, 50)]
    public object Fidelity { get; set; }
}
```

The attributes are summarized in Table 6-2.

TABLE 6-2 Data annotation attributes for validation

Attribute	Description
Required	Checks whether a non-null value is assigned to the property. It can be configured to fail if an empty string is assigned.
Range	Checks whether the value falls in the specified range. It defaults to numbers, but it can be configured to consider a range of dates, too.
StringLength	Checks whether the string is longer than the specified value.
RegularExpression	Checks whether the value matches the specified expression.
DataType	Checks whether the value is of the specified type. Note that in this regard the notion of a type is not that of a system type. It refers more to a kind of data, such as text or a date, but it can also refer to something more specific, such as an e-mail address, phone number, or URL.
CustomValidation	Checks the value against the specified custom function.
EnumDataType	Checks whether the value can be matched to any of the values in the specified enumerated type.

Each attribute can accept an error message expressed both as a plain string and as a resource index. The framework provides a base class—*ValidationAttribute*—from which you can create custom attributes to personalize the validation layer. Let's have a look at a sample *EvenNumber* attribute:

```
public class EvenNumberAttribute : ValidationAttribute
{
  // Whether the number is even and also a multiple of 4
  public bool MultipleOf4 { get; set; }

  public override bool IsValid(object value)
  {
    if (value == null)
      return true;
```

```
    if (value % 2 > 0)
      return false;

    return true;
  }
}
```

Checking the state of an annotated object requires a bunch of code nearly identical to validators you've seen in action within Enterprise Library. Here's an example:

```
Customer customer = new Customer { ... };
:
:
var results = new List<ValidationResult>();
var context = new ValidationContext(customer, null, null);
var isValid = Validator.TryValidateObject(customer, context, results);

Console.WriteLine("Results:");
foreach (ValidationResult r in results)
{
    Console.WriteLine("\t{0}", r.ErrorMessage);
}
```

The central object is *Validator*. Its *TryValidateObject* method gets an object and attempts to validate all of its annotations. The results are accumulated into a *ValidationResult* collection. Note that if no collection is provided, validation will stop at the first failure and an exception will be thrown. The *ValidationContext* class describes the context in which a validation check is performed. It groups together the instance to be checked, the service that can be used to perform custom validation, and a dictionary of key/value pairs to make available to the service consumers.

> **Note** In addition to validation attributes, data annotations include display attributes. These attributes decorate the property with meta information for modules living in the presentation layer. A couple of common attributes are *Display* and *UIHint*. The former indicates localizable strings to be used to describe the value; the latter refers to a customized component responsible for rendering the value. Note that the real task of interpreting display attributes is delegated to presentation code that reads values in the attributes and organizes the user interface accordingly. For example, in ASP.NET MVC an HTML helper can read these values and produce an ad hoc HTML block.

Data Annotations and Entity Framework

As discussed earlier, you cannot always decorate properties in an Entity Framework or a LINQ-to-SQL model with your own attributes. Microsoft Enterprise Library offers an interesting way out through its support for validation attributes in the configuration file. What about data annotations, though? Data annotations don't support any configuration file, but offer an alternative mechanism to be bound to autogenerated partial classes—the *MetadataType* attribute.

Let's assume you have in the Entity Framework model a class named *Customer*. The source code of that class has been generated in some way, and you don't want to touch it because you expect to resort to the designer's help files a few more times. To add attribute-based validation without taking the risk of losing all changes at the next update, do as follows:

```
[MetadataType(typeof(CustomerMetaData))]
public partial class Customer
{
    // No code here as the class is already
    // defined in the Entity Framework (or LINQ-to-SQL)
    // designer-generated files.
}
```

The *MetadataType* attribute indicates which type includes the meta information for the type it is attached to. Looking at the preceding code snippet, the class *CustomerMetaData* contains the same public interface as *Customer* except that properties are decorated with data annotation attributes. Here's how:

```
public class CustomerMetaData
{
    [Required]
    [Range(5, 50)]
    public int CustomerId { get; set; }

    [Required(AllowEmptyStrings=false)]
    [StringLength(5)]
    [RegularExpression(@"^[a-zA-Z''-'\s]{1,40}$",
        ErrorMessage = "Special characters are not allowed in the company name.")]
    public String CompanyName { get; set; }

    [DataType(DataType.EmailAddress)]
    public String Contact { get; set; }

        :
        :
}
```

Note that annotations are processed only if an exact match is found between a meta type property and a property on the annotated type.

Data for the View

When architecting ASP.NET MVC, the development team decided to offer two ways for developers to pass data around from the controller to the view. One is the notorious *ViewData* dictionary, and one is the strongly typed view. Ultimately, you can achieve the same results either way. However, this is not a good reason for considering the two approaches to be the same and choosing one based on the flip of a coin.

Is *ViewData* Just for Dummies?

As you saw in Chapter 5, "Inside Views," the *ViewData* dictionary is an untyped dictionary that you use in much the same way as *Session* or *Cache*. So it is easy to use, propounds a familiar programming model, and just works. It's amazing that we sometimes complain about having the option of using an untyped dictionary for passing data to the view when an untyped dictionary is the only option available for caching data. Oddly, the following code might appear in some controllers in one form or another:

```
public ActionResult Index()
{
    :
    :

    // Get data from the ASP.NET Cache
    var data = Cache["MyData"] as IList<Customer>;
    if (data == null)
        data = LoadFromSourceAndCache();

    // Prepare the view
    ViewData["MyData"] = data;

    // Return
    return View();
}
```

Using the *Cache* object (as architects) might send chills down our spine, whereas using the *ViewData* object is more and more a source of outright terror. What's wrong with the *ViewData* dictionary?

In first place, the *ViewData* dictionary is an untyped dictionary that might require you to cast any value to its right type for certain uses. (For data binding, for example, no cast is required.) Second, it requires you to use a string to identify any piece of information you add. Compared to the naming efforts of storing data in the ASP.NET global cache, this is a minimal amount of work. As with *Cache* and *Session*, though, you have to match names in the controller and in the view.

However, also in this case I find that dealing with *ViewData* item naming is easier than solving the same issue with *Cache*. The reason is that the content of *ViewData* is set in the controller to be used only in the invoked view. If you mistype a name, you don't have to look any further to find the problem and fix it.

This said, I prefer to avoid *ViewData* whenever I can and resort to strongly typed views.

Strongly Typed Views

From within a strongly typed view, you can access both the *ViewData* dictionary as a whole and a very specific part of it—the *Model* property. The *ViewData* dictionary is not just a standard .NET dictionary type—it is, instead, a brand-new *ViewDataDictionary* type that extends a standard dictionary type just because of this new property:

```
public object Model {get; set;}
```

You can set this property explicitly from within the controller:

```
ViewData.Model = customers;
return View("Index");
```

You can also set the *Model* property implicitly by passing a data object to the *View* method, as shown here:

```
return View("Index", customers);
```

The view receives a copy of the *ViewData* object created by the controller and accesses its data using the expression *ViewData.Model*. The deal is all sealed in the fact that by creating a strongly typed view—that is, a page class that inherits from *ViewPage<TModel>* instead of *ViewPage*—you specify what is type *TModel* and create the property *Model* of type *TModel* in the page class. Here's an excerpt from the source code of the class *ViewPage<TModel>*:

```
public TModel Model { get; }
public ViewDataDictionary<TModel> ViewData { get; set; }
```

The bottom line is that a strongly typed view class allows you to use a classic property with a verifiable name—*ViewData.Model*—to access the object model for the view. This results in cleaner and less brittle code because no magic strings are still around.

> **Note** If you are simply avoiding magic strings and taking advantage of IntelliSense as much as possible, I suggest you take a look at *http://aspnet.codeplex.com/wikipage?title=T4MVC*. T4MVC is a T4 template for ASP.NET MVC applications that creates strongly typed helpers based on strings found in the controllers' code. By using T4MVC, you can eliminate the use of literal strings when referring to controllers, actions, and views. As a result, your ASP.NET MVC code is easier to maintain and gives you IntelliSense support even in situations where you would never had any otherwise.

The View-Model

What kind of object would you store in the *Model* property of the *ViewData* dictionary? Does it have to be a domain entity object, an aggregate of domain objects, or something completely different? To answer this question, some considerations must be made.

The *Model* property is expected to represent the model for the page—the whole collection of data that the view will work on. This model is not necessarily a single object such as *Customer* or *Product*. More often, you need to incorporate data from various sources and objects. It is advisable that you reason in terms of a new object model—the view-model.

The view-model is a collection of classes, each representing the set of data that a given view will work on. Most likely, a view-model is related to the customer and the view. A possible naming convention is the following: *ControllerViewSuffix*. *Controller* is the controller's name (for example, *Home*); *View* is the view's name (for example, *Index*), and *Suffix* is a common tag you want to add (for example, *ViewModel*). A sample name for a view-model object is *HomeIndexViewModel*. It's just a naming convention, so feel free to change it as it suits you.

In a simple case, here's how you invoke a view using a view-model approach:

```
var model = new CustomerIndexViewModel();
model.Customers = customers;
return View("Index", model);
```

In this case, the view receives a collection of customers. The corresponding type for the view page is *ViewPage<CustomerIndexViewModel>*. An equally valid solution is the following:

```
// The view page is ViewPage<IList<Customer>>
return View("Index", customers);
```

The view-model makes sense especially for pages that have a model. You might have to display pages with a very scanty model—for example, a ThankYou page. In this case, if any data has to be passed from the controller, you probably wouldn't mind using a few simple *ViewData* items.

View-Model Builders

If you follow the view-model approach thoroughly, you end up with a bunch of new classes to create and maintain. Where do you store all these new classes? Here's where that old acquaintance, the *Models* folder, comes back into play.

The *Models* folder is a good container for view-models. Actually, it is the only reason I would keep the folder in an ASP.NET MVC project. And if you have other content that might fit under Models (for example, a DBML or EDMX entity model file), I suggest you consider creating distinct subfolders.

A view-model class is not a bad idea, and it is a particularly good idea when a view starts getting complex. For example, to edit a customer you might need data for the current customer, but you might also need collections for populating drop-down lists and maybe some extra values for UI elements that have to do with the user's preferences. In short, building a view-model can become a really long task. Should you keep this code in the controller?

At the highest level, the responsibility of the controller is ensuring that a response for each request is generated and sent to the browser. This responsibility expands in two main tasks: producing raw data for the response, and ensuring that any raw data is then packaged into a nice view. So any code you need to collect data for the view belongs to the controller; additionally, it's just part of its job.

This said, you might want to consider keeping the controller class as lean as possible for the sake of readability and to minimize the risk of adding extra responsibilities in the long run. In this regard, it can be a good idea to take some code that relates to building a view-model out of the controller and put it into separate helper classes that help build the view-model object to be passed to the view for rendering. It's just a suggestion, but it leads to taking into account another, and a bit subtler, issue—the controller and data shared by multiple views.

> **Note** When you are dealing with view-models, inevitably the need to write some boring code shows up. The "boring" code is the code that simply copies a few properties between two overlapping types. An example is when you create an object that is a subset of *Customer* or another that aggregates data from *Customer* and data from *Order*. Recently, a tool that helps in this regard has emerged. It is AutoMapper, which you can find more information about here: *http://automapper.codeplex.com*. With AutoMapper, you first create a mapping between two types and then you proceed to mapping an instance of one type on the other. The tool works by discovering properties with matching names and copying the value of the source into the target.

Common Data for the Common View

A controller action normally focuses on a particular task and the subsequent view. The granularity of the action and the view, however, might not be the same. It is likely, in fact, that the view refers to the entire page whereas the action affects only a fraction of the rendered page. Typically, this happens when the view incorporates some fixed data that is shared with other views (but not stored in any master pages), such as menus, breadcrumbs, information about the login, user-specific links, ad hoc images, and so forth. In simple scenarios, some (but not all) of this information is static and can be easily incorporated in a master page. In other cases, it is data driven and must be loaded, cached, and made available to the view.

So where's the problem? The problem is that the controller action that triggers the view might have little to do with loading and processing such common data. Imagine a controller action that updates a record that must also be concerned with the rendering of the menus all around.

In my opinion, the controller action is also responsible for ensuring that the view gets its entire data set. So I see no big problems in the controller's action that retrieves data for the menus. On the other hand, I want this code to be as smooth and seamless as possible. An approach that I am inclined to suggest entails the creation of a global class—the registry—that contains properties and methods to be considered global and accessible from any view.

The *Registry* is an application-specific class whose programming interface and therefore depends on the application. Here's a possible example of a global class. Rest assured that if you like the approach you can create many such classes to segregate the interface, perhaps even one registry per controller or one per master page:

```
public interface IRegistry
{
    // Get/Set the list of countries for editing purposes
    void LoadCountries();
    IList<String> GetCountries();

    // Get menu items
    :
    :
}

public class Registry : IRegistry
{
    :
    :
}
```

The *Registry* class is not the only part of the application you might want to move around and have available from various places. As discussed in Chapter 4, you can also store the *Registry* in the *ApplicationContext* class along with other dependencies and global objects. Here's a sample implementation for *ApplicationContext* that makes it work as a singleton:

```
public class ApplicationContext
{
    private readonly IRegistry _registry;

    protected AppContext()
    {
        // Registry
        _registry = new Registry();
    }

    protected static ApplicationContext DefaultInstance = new ApplicationContext();


    public static IRegistry Registry
    {
        get { return DefaultInstance._registry; }
    }
    :
    :
}
```

You can also consider exposing the *IRegistry* explicitly through a setter for the *Registry* property or avoiding the singleton and overloading the *ApplicationContext* constructor to inject an *IRegistry* object. The point here is streamlining the writing of unit tests. Another approach is resolving the dependency on *IRegistry* via an Inversion of Control (IoC) container. (I'll discuss IoC containers in Chapter 10, "Testability and Unit Testing," and Chapter 11, "Customizing ASP.NET MVC.")

You access the registry for reading and writing through the following expression from anywhere:

```
ApplicationContext.Registry
```

A controller method can load data into the view as follows:

```
var model = new CustomerViewModel();
model.CurrentCountry = parameters.Country;
model.Countries = ApplicationContext.Registry.GetCountries();
model.Customers = customers;
```

The loaded code doesn't leak into the view, but it doesn't belong to the controller either. At the same time, the data being passed to the view is clearly visible and readable.

> **Note**   How is it possible that we're having this specific problem only now in ASP.NET MVC? Wasn't it present with Web Forms, too? Well, server controls and view state work together so that this problem never shows up. If you use a server control to display common data, your task is simplified.
>
> With regard to this problem, however, a couple of other solutions have been discussed in the community and are commonly applied. One is based on using action filters to load into the *ViewData* collection any missing piece of data that you don't want the controller action to dirty its hands with. As you saw in Chapter 4, an action filter is an attribute that applies to controller actions and lets you specify what happens before and after each action. When you're using action filters, adding information to *ViewData* instead of any more strongly typed model you might have is almost a necessity because you might not know the actual type of the model from the action filter. If your project targets C# 4, though, you can resort to the new keyword *dynamic* to avoid using *ViewData*.
>
> Another solution available only with ASP.NET MVC 2 is based on render actions. As you saw in Chapter 4, a render action takes a reference to a controller method, executes it, and places the resulting response in the view. In this way, the view calls back some code on some controller to return the partial view for a section of the screen being constructed. The benefit is that you decouple the parts of the controller code that deal with shared data and the response for a specific request.

Model Binding

In ASP.NET MVC as well as in ASP.NET Web Forms, posted data arrives within an HTTP packet and is mapped to a collection on the *Request* object. To offer a nice service to developers, ASP.NET then attempts to expose that content in a more usable way. In ASP.NET Web Forms, the content is parsed and passed on to server controls; in ASP.NET MVC, on the other hand, it is bound to parameters of the selected controller's method. The process of binding posted values to parameters is known as *model binding* and occurs through a registered model binder class.

The Model Binder in Action

The model binder is the system component that knows the rules of parameter binding. The action invoker uses the binder to get parameter values to use in the call to the controller's action. The action of the model binder is governed by the following code executed by the action invoker:

```
// actionDescriptor contains information about the method being executed
// controllerContext contains information about the current controller context
var dictionary = new Dictionary<string, object>();
foreach (ParameterDescriptor pd in actionDescriptor.GetParameters())
{
    dictionary[pd.ParameterName] = GetParameterValue(controllerContext, pd);
}
```

The *GetParameterValue* method is invoked for each expected parameter on the controller's method and uses the model binder internally to see whether any rules exist that can be used to resolve the value for the parameter dynamically.

The *DefaultModelBinder* Class

By default, ASP.NET MVC uses a built-in, preregistered binder object that corresponds to the *DefaultModelBinder* class. The default binder uses convention-based logic to match names of posted values to parameter names in the controller's method. Let's suppose you have a controller method defined as shown here:

```
public ActionResult Index(string country, int maxItems) { ... }
```

If the request contains parameters (route values, query string values, form values) whose names match "country" and "maxItems," binding happens automatically as long as types are compatible. If a conversion cannot be performed, an argument exception is thrown.

The default binder can map primitive types such as string, double, decimal, or *DateTime* and related collections. The *DefaultModelBinder* class also supports binding to complex types and collections of complex types. (Complex types can also be nested.) Here's an example:

```
public ActionResult Edit(Customer customer) { ... }
```

In this case, the model binder looks for posted values whose key names match the pattern *"parameterName.PropertyName"*, such as *customer.ID* or *customer.CompanyName*. The prefix indicating the name of the parameter is not necessary because the default binder also can resolve the parameter without the prefix. Essentially, for each parameter the default binder first looks for a possible match on the *parameterName.PropertyName* expression. If no match is found, it looks for *PropertyName*; otherwise, *null* is returned. However, consider the following race situation:

```
<span>Company Name</span><br />
<input type="text" name="CompanyName" />
<span>Contact Name</span><br />
<input type="text" name="customer.ContactName" />
```

If you are binding to a complex parameter of type *Customer* with *CompanyName* and *ContactName* properties, only the latter will be successfully resolved. Instead, if you remove the "customer" prefix, both properties will be resolved because the empty prefix is assumed. This is to say that all posted values are examined *before* parameters are processed to determine the existence of a prefix.

In functional terms, the use of the default binder is transparent to developers—no action is strictly required on your end—and it keeps the controller code clean.

> **Note** The registered model binder is used explicitly if you define explicit parameters in the signature of the controller methods. Alternately, you can keep the controller methods parameterless but use either *UpdateModel* or *TryUpdateModel* internally to update a variable instance with posted values. Both are helper methods defined on the *Controller* class. Both methods use the registered model binder internally.

Binding to Collection Types

What if that argument that a controller method expects is a collection? For example, can you bind the content of a posted form to an *IList<T>* parameter? The *DefaultModelBinder* class makes it possible, but doing so requires a bit of contrivance of your own. Have a look at Figure 6-4.

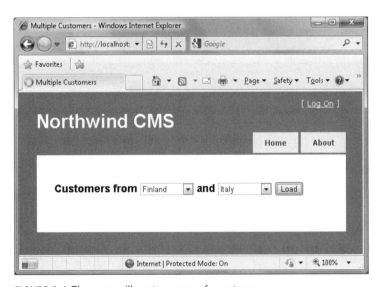

FIGURE 6-4 The page will post an array of country names.

When the user hits the button Load, the form submits its content. Specifically, it sends out the selection on the two drop-down lists. If the lists have different IDs, the posted content takes the following form:

```
DropDownList1=Finland&DropDownList2=Italy
```

In classic ASP.NET, this is the only possible way of working. However, if you manage the HTML yourself, nothing prevents you from assigning the two drop-down lists the same ID. The HTML DOM, in fact, fully supports this scenario, and all it does when you query is return an array of elements. Subsequently, the following markup is entirely legal in ASP.NET MVC and works on nearly all browsers:

```
<% using (Html.BeginForm("Demo", "Customer"))  {%>
<h2>Customers from
    <%= Html.DropDownList("countries",
              new SelectList(ViewData.Model)) %> and
    <%= Html.DropDownList("countries",
              new SelectList(ViewData.Model)) %>
<input type="submit" value="Load" />
</h2>
<% } %>
```

What's the expected signature of a controller method that has to process the two selected countries? Here it is:

```
public virtual ActionResult Demo(IList<String> countries)
{
    :
    :
}
```

Figure 6-5 shows that an array of strings is correctly passed to the method thanks to the default binder class.

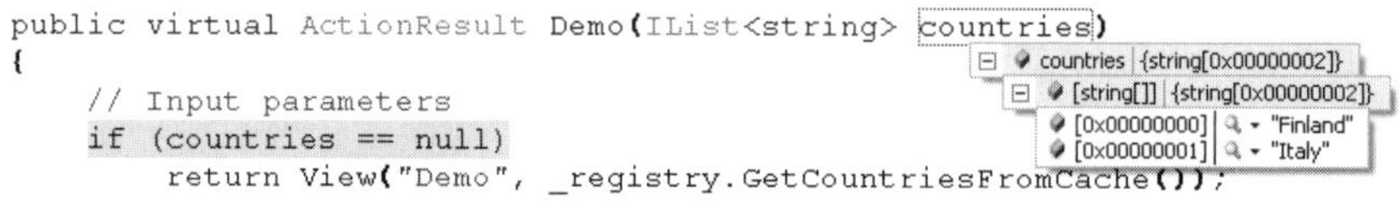

```
public virtual ActionResult Demo(IList<string> countries)
{
    // Input parameters
    if (countries == null)
        return View("Demo", _registry.GetCountriesFromCache());
```

```
□ ● countries {string[0x00000002]}
  □ ● [string[]] {string[0x00000002]}
      ● [0x00000000] 🔍 ▾ "Finland"
      ● [0x00000001] 🔍 ▾ "Italy"
```

FIGURE 6-5 An array of strings has been posted.

In the end, to ensure that a collection of values are passed to a controller method, you need to ensure that elements with the same ID are emitted to the response stream. The ID, then, has to match to the controller method's signature according to the normal rules of the binder.

The default binder can also handle most situations in which the collection contains complex types, nested types, or both:

```
public virtual ActionResult ComplexDemo(IList<CustomerViewModel> customerInfo)
{
    :
    :
}
```

For model binding to occur successfully, all you really need to do is use a progressive index on the IDs in the markup. The resulting pattern is *prefix[index].Property*.

```
<fieldset>
<p>
    <b>Company Name</b><br />
    <input type="text" name="customerInfo[0].CompanyName" />
</p><p>
    <b>Contact Name</b><br />
    <input type="text" name="customerInfo[0].ContactName" />
</p><p>
    <b>Country</b><br />
    <%= Html.DropDownList("customerInfo[0].Country", ViewData.Model.Countries))%>
</p>
</fieldset>
<fieldset>
<p>
    <b>Company Name</b><br />
    <input type="text" name="customerInfo[1].CompanyName" />
</p><p>
    <b>Contact Name</b><br />
    <input type="text" name="customerInfo[1].ContactName" />
</p><p>
    <b>Country</b><br />
    <%= Html.DropDownList("customerInfo[1].Country", ViewData.Model.Countries))%>
</p>
</fieldset>
```

The index is numeric, 0-based, and progressive. Holes in the series (for example, 0 and then 2) seem to stop the parsing.

Rest assured that if you're having trouble mapping posted values to your expected hierarchy of types, it might be wise to consider a custom model binder.

Customizing the Binding Process

Automatic binding stems from a convention-over-configuration approach. Conventions, though, might sometimes harbor bad surprises. If, for some reason, you lose control over the posted data (for example, in the case of data that has been tampered with), it can result in undesired binding—any posted key/value pair will, in fact, be bound. In this regard, you might want to consider using the *Bind* attribute to customize some aspects of the binding process.

The *Bind* attribute comes with three properties, as described in Table 6-3.

TABLE 6-3 Properties for the *BindAttribute* class

Property	Description
Prefix	String property. It indicates the prefix that must be found in the name of the posted value for the binder to resolve it. If specified, the prefix is mandatory and no exceptions are made. The default value is the empty string.
Exclude	Gets or sets a comma-delimited list of property names for which binding is not allowed.
Include	Gets or sets a comma-delimited list of property names for which binding is permitted.

Through the *Exclude* and *Include* properties, you can create black-and-white lists of properties on complex types. This gives you a formidable tool to fight off any attempt to send your controller data that has been tampered with. Here's an example:

```
public ActionResult Insert([Bind(Exclude="Id,CompanyName")] Customer customer)
```

In this case, no matter what is posted to the controller properties *Id* and *CompanyName* on the *Customer* class, it will never be processed by the default model binder.

The *Bind* attribute is often applied to individual parameters on a controller method. However, you can even define it on a class:

```
[Bind(Include="CompanyName,ContactName")]
public class CustomerViewModel
{
    :
    :
}
```

When the class is used as an argument type in a controller method, all of its properties will be bound as indicated by the attribute.

> **Note** Using the *Bind* attribute on a view-model class is totally legitimate and encouraged. Using it on a domain object, on the other hand, will lead you to spoiling the model a bit. A clear sign of this extra coupling is the necessity of linking the *System.Web.Mvc* assembly to the assembly that contains the class. This is yet another good reason to use view-model classes.

Custom Model Binders

The default binder does excellent work, but it is a general-purpose tool aimed at working with most possible types in a way that is not specific to any of them. The *Bind* attribute gives you some more control over the binding process, but some reasonable boundaries still exist. In these cases, all you do is create a custom binder for a specific type.

There are two main reasons you should be willing to create a custom binder. The most important reason is that the default binder is limited to taking into account a one-to-one correspondence between posted values and properties on the model. Sometimes the target model has a different granularity than the one expressed by form fields. The canonical example is when you employ multiple input fields to let users enter content for a single property—for example, distinct input fields for day, month, and year that then map to a single *DateTime* value. The second reason to go beyond the standard model binder is to avoid the use of prefixed IDs in the view.

To create a custom binder, you can implement the *IModelBinder* interface:

```
public interface IModelBinder
{
    object BindModel(
        ControllerContext controllerContext, ModelBindingContext bindingContext);
}
```

Implementing the interface is recommended if you need total control over the binding process. If, say, all you need to do is keep the default behavior and simply force the binder to use a non-default constructor for a given type, inheriting from *DefaultModelBinder* is the best approach. Here's the schema to follow:

```
public CustomerViewModelBinder : DefaultModelBinder
{
    protected override object CreateModel(
        ControllerContext controllerContext,
        ModelBindingContext bindingContext,
        Type modelType)
    {
        :
        :
        return new CustomerViewModel( ... );
    }
}
```

Another common scenario for simply overriding the default binder is when all you want is the ability to validate against a specific type. In this case, you override *OnModelUpdated* and insert your own validation logic, as shown here:

```
protected override void OnModelUpdated(ControllerContext controllerContext,
        ModelBindingContext bindingContext)
{
    var obj = bindingContext.Model as CustomerViewModel;
    if (obj == null) return;
    // Apply validation logic here for the whole model
    if (String.IsNullOrEmpty(obj.CompanyName))
    {
        bindingContext.ModelState.AddModelError("CompanyName", ...);
    }
    :
    :
}
```

You override *OnModelUpdated* if you prefer to keep in a single place all validations for any properties. You resort to *OnPropertyValidating* if you prefer to validate properties individually.

Implementing a Model Binder

Here's an example of a custom binder that implements the *IModelBinder* interface:

```
public class CustomerViewModelBinder : IModelBinder
{
  public object BindModel(ControllerContext controllerContext,
                        ModelBindingContext bindingContext)
  {
    if (bindingContext == null)
        throw new ArgumentNullException("bindingContext");

    // Get the model instance or create one if needed
    var obj = (CustomerViewModel) (bindingContext.Model ?? new CustomerViewModel());
```

```
        //
        obj.CompanyName = FromPostedData<string>(bindingContext, "CompanyName");
        :
        :

        return obj;
}


// Helper routine
private T FromPostedData<T>(ModelBindingContext context, string key)
{
    // Get the value from any of the input collections
    ValueProviderResult result;
    context.ValueProvider.TryGetValue(key, out result);

    // Set the state of the model property resulting from value
    context.ModelState.SetModelValue(key, result);

    // Return the value converted (if possible) to the target type
    return (T) result.ConvertTo(typeof(T));
}
```

Note that when writing a model binder you are in no way restricted to getting information for the model uniquely from the posted data—which represents only the most common scenario. You can grab information from anywhere—for example, from the ASP.NET cache and session state—parse it, and store it in the model.

Registering a Custom Binder

You can associate a model binder with its target type globally or locally. In the former case, any occurrence of model binding for the type will be resolved through the registered custom binder. In the latter case, you apply the binding to just one occurrence of one parameter in a controller method. Global association takes place in the *global.asax* file as follows:

```
void Application_Start()
{
    :
    :

    ModelBinders.Binders[typeof(CustomerViewModelBinder)] =
                    new CustomerViewModelBinder();
}
```

Local association requires the following syntax:

```
public ActionResult Edit(
        [ModelBinder(typeof(CustomerViewModelBinder))]
        CustomerViewModel customerInfo)
{
    :
    :

}
```

As you can tell clearly from the preceding code within *Application_Start*, you can have multiple binders registered. You can also override the default binder if required.

```
ModelBinders.Binders.DefaultBinder = new MyNewDefaultBinder();
```

Finally, note that global binders take precedence over local binders.

Model binding is concerned with reading data from the surrounding environment—most likely the posted data—and stuffing it into controller action parameters. Related to the idea of the model, though, is the idea of validation.

In the next chapter, I'll review various techniques for validating data in the context of input forms that post data and trigger server operations.

Summary

In MVC, the role of the Model actor is to represent the model for any data being worked on in the view. The issue to be decided is which data structures do you use to represent the data flowing in and out of the view.

In simple architectures where everything lives in the Web server tier, except perhaps the database, it might be acceptable that you use just one flavor of the Model actor. In this case, the model represents the data the application works on and the data worked on in the view. In more sophisticated scenarios, where you essentially have multiple layers in the server (if not multiple physical tiers), it is vital that you recognize the difference between the *domain* model and the *view*-model.

The domain model is the representation of data you create for the sake of business processing; the view-model is the representation of data you create for the sake of the view. The controller is responsible for getting domain objects and mapping them to view objects. The view just receives view objects that contain a representation of the data that addresses only the needs of the view. Are these models really different? Actual classes might not be that different in all cases. But the view-model and domain model definitely play different roles in the context of any layered solution.

In this chapter, I also touched upon a third flavor of model that represents the data as it is received by the controller. Model binders provide you with complete control over the deserialization of form-posted values into simple and complex types. By using model binders, you keep your controller's code free of dependencies on ASP.NET intrinsic objects, and thus make it cleaner and more testable.

Model binders also are a nice fit for validation code, and ASP.NET MVC 2 comes with an effective, new built-in binder that weds validation through data annotations with binding to model types. The whole theme of validation doesn't end here, though. In the next chapter, I'll address it from a much more practical perspective as I delve deep into input forms.

Part III
Programming Features

Chapter 7
Data Entry in ASP.NET MVC

Whatever you can do or dream, begin it.

—Wolfgang von Goethe

Classic ASP.NET bases its programming model on the assumption that state is maintained across postbacks. This is not true at all at the HTTP protocol level, but it is brilliantly simulated using the page view state feature and a bit of work in the page life cycle. The view state, which is so often kicked around as a bad thing, represents a great contribution to establishing a stateful programming model in ASP.NET, and that programming model was one of the keys to ASP.NET's success and rapid adoption.

The ASP.NET MVC framework just uses a different pattern, one that is not page-based and relies on a much thinner abstraction layer than Web Forms. As a result, you don't have rich native components such as server controls to quickly arrange a nice user interface where elements can retain their content across postbacks. This fact seems to result in a loss of productivity, at least for certain types of applications, such as applications heavily based on data entry.

Is this really true, though?

If you've grown up with Web Forms and its server controls, you might be shocked when transported into the ASP.NET MVC model. Data entry is a scenario in which server controls really shine and in which their postback and view-state overhead saves you from doing a lot of work. Server controls also give you a powerful infrastructure for input validation. Today, in ASP.NET MVC you have the same functional capabilities as you do with Web Forms, only they're delivered through a different set of tools.

You have some good scaffolding when it comes to creating controllers and views for most common CRUD (Create, Read, Update, Delete) scenarios. You have templated helpers to automatically create simple but effective viewers and editors for any primitive or complex type. You have data annotations to declaratively set your expectations about the content of a field and its display behavior. You have model binders to serialize posted values into more comfortable objects for server-side processing. Finally, you have tools for both server and client validation.

You have the tools, and although they're certainly different than in Web Forms, they're equally effective. This chapter aims to show you how to grab input data through forms, validate it, and process it against a persistence layer.

The Select-Edit-Save Pattern

Many Web applications revolve around the *Select-Edit-Save pattern (SES)*. Essentially, they need to let users select an item of data, place it into edit mode, play with its content, and then save changes back to the storage layer.

In Web Forms, handling that series of actions by the user was made particularly easy by data binding and data source controls. In ASP.NET MVC, you need to take a lower-level approach and stay closer to the Web metal, but you're not left alone to handcraft every little bit of HTML and HTTP needed.

Presenting Data

I'll illustrate the SES pattern through an example that starts by letting users pick a customer from a drop-down list. Next, the record that contains information about the selected customer is rendered into an edit form, where updates can be entered and eventually validated and saved.

For simplicity, but without any loss of generality, the domain model consists of a LINQ-to-SQL model that includes the sole Northwind *Customers* table. Figure 7-1 shows the initial user interface of the sample Customer Management System, an application page I'll use to demonstrate SES concepts with ASP.NET MVC.

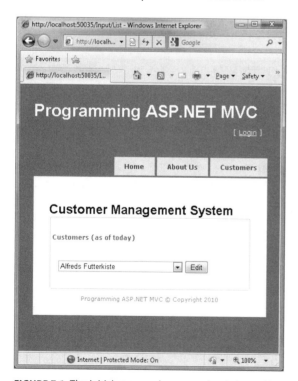

FIGURE 7-1 The initial screen, where users begin by making a selection

Handling Selection

The following listing shows the controller action that is used to populate the drop-down list to offer the initial screen to the user. Note that the structure of the action's code fulfills the patterns I identified in Chapter 4, "Inside Controllers," and Chapter 6, "Inside Models." Note that in this simple case, a plain LINQ-to-SQL query to get data and direct access to the *ViewData* collection would have accomplished the job as well.

```
public ActionResult List()
{
    // Get the data to populate the list of customers. (Data is obtained
    // from the service layer as discussed in Chapter 4)
    var list = _service.GetCustomerListItems();

    // Prepare the view model (See Chapter 6)
    var data = new CustomerIndexViewModel();
    data.Customers = new SelectList(list, "CustomerID", "CompanyName");

    return View("List", data);
}
```

The view that produces the interface in Figure 7-1 is shown here:

```
<fieldset title="Edit customer">
    <p>Customers (as of today)</p>

    <% Html.BeginForm("Edit", "Customer"); %>
        <%= Html.DropDownList("listCustomers", ViewData.Model.Customers) %>
        <input type="submit" id="btnEdit" name="btnEdit" value="Edit" />
    <% Html.EndForm(); %>
</fieldset>
```

After the user has selected a customer from the list, by clicking a submit button he submits a POST request for an *Edit* action on the *CustomerController* class.

URL Formatting

Note that at this point the URL displayed in the browser's address bar looks something like this:

```
http://yourserver/customer/list
```

Unless you take special care when implementing the *Edit* method, after the post has occurred the URL changes to the following:

```
http://yourserver/customer/edit
```

There's nothing particularly bad about this, and the page still works correctly. However, you're cutting off (without any apparently valid reason) a good part of the natural RESTfulness of ASP.NET MVC. In other words, the goal should be to show a URL that identifies the resource being edited. Here's an example:

```
http://yourserver/customer/edit/alfki
```

In addition, you need a mechanism in your controller that allows you to change the customer whose information is being edited by simply changing the last fragment in the browser's address bar—the customer ID. In other words, you need a dual interface to select the customer to edit—one interface for editing via the graphical user interface, and one interface for editing via the browser's address bar. (See Figure 7-2.)

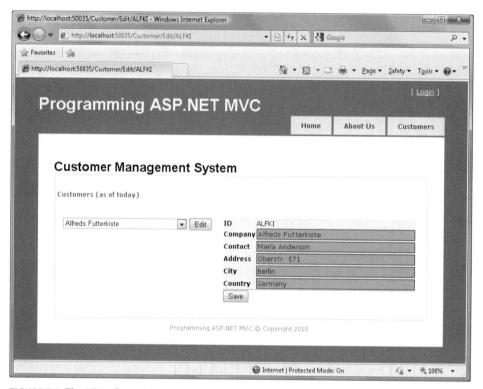

FIGURE 7-2 The URL reflects the customer whose information is currently being edited.

Editing Data

The application enters into edit mode when the user posts from the initially displayed form you saw in Figure 7-1. That form posts to the *Edit* method on the *Customer* controller. What do you expect from the *Edit* method? As you can see in Figure 7-2, you should expect it to retain a drop-down list from which the user can select another customer while displaying a second HTML form to edit the selected record.

Displaying an Input Forms

The following code shows a possible implementation for the *Edit* method on the *Customer* controller:

```
// The parameter listCustomers is automatically resolved if you have a posting
// HTML element with the same name in the form. In this case, it is the drop-down
```

```
                                                                     // list of customers.
public ActionResult Edit(string listCustomers)
{
    // Get information about the customer to edit
    string customerId = listCustomers;
    Customer customer = _service.GetCustomer(customerId);

    // Get the data to populate the list of customers. (Data is obtained
    // from the service layer as discussed in Chapter 4)
    var list = _service.GetCustomerListItems();

    var data = new CustomerEditViewModel();
    data.Customers = new SelectList(list, "CustomerID", "CompanyName");
    data.CustomerBeingEdited = customer;

    return View("Edit", data);
}
```

You might have noticed that the drop-down list has to be repopulated. This is a consequence of not having the view state around. In the following code, I just place another call to the service layer; a more serious application would use a registry approach (as you saw in Chapter 6) and use the ASP.NET cache to store data upon loading. In any case, this is one instance of the classic scenario where the same block of data is shared among multiple views.

Here's the code for the view:

```
<table>
    <tr>
        <td valign="top">
            <% Html.BeginForm("Edit", "Customer"); %>
            <%= Html.DropDownList("listCustomers", ViewData.Model.Customers) %>
            <input type="submit" id="btnEdit" name="btnEdit" value="Edit" />
            <% Html.EndForm(); %>
        </td>
        <td valign="top">
            <% Html.RenderPartial("CustomerEdit",
                                ViewData.Model.CustomerBeingEdited); %>
        </td>
    </tr>
</table>
```

CustomerEdit is a user control that contains the HTML form to edit the selected customer.

As you can see, having multiple forms in the same view is not a problem in ASP.NET MVC because it has never been a problem in plain HTML. Only Web Forms considered it to be a problem, thus limiting us for years to just one (server-side) form. Note also that you still haven't done anything serious to ensure that the URL displays the ID of the customer being edited.

Synchronizing the View and the URL

You execute the preceding code when the user posts to the page to edit customer information. Imagine that a user types the following URL in the address bar of the browser:

```
http://yourserver/customer/edit/alfki
```

The application receives an HTTP GET request and maps it to the *Edit* method of the *Customer* controller. Unfortunately, though, the parameter is not matched this time. There's no *listCustomers* value in the body of the request or in the collection of routed values. This is the situation assuming you take the standard route; if you rename the *id* parameter of the standard route or add another route, the match might even work. However, the problem here is clearly not the route.

The point is that to keep the view and URL in sync you need to have two distinct *Edit* methods—one for an HTTP POST request and one for any HTTP GET request. This scenario is fully supported by ASP.NET MVC through the *AcceptVerbs* and *ActionName* attributes you met in Chapter 4. Here's a possible way to rewrite the *Edit* method:

```
[ActionName("Edit"), AcceptVerbs(HttpVerbs.Post)]
public ActionResult EditViaPost(string listCustomers)
{
    // Same code as shown before for Edit
       :
       :
}

[ActionName("Edit"), AcceptVerbs(HttpVerbs.Get)]
public ActionResult EditViaGet(string id)
{
    // Same code as shown before for Edit
       :
       :
}
```

You create two methods with different names and bind both *Edit* actions using the *ActionName* attribute. In addition, you use *AcceptVerbs* to restrict each method to one particular HTTP verb. In this way, if the user types a full URL in the address bar, the URL obtains the specified customer in edit mode; if the user posts from the displayed form to do the same, on the other hand, she can edit the customer but the URL is not updated.

To add insult to injury, you still have two methods with the same body, fully ignoring the common principle of "Once And Only Once" (OAOO). You need to do further refactoring, and you need to introduce a new pattern—the Post-Redirect-Get (PRG) pattern.

> **Note** Regarding repeated code, you might be surprised to see that I mentioned the OAOO principle instead of the most popular "Don't Repeat Yourself" (DRY). Both come from the world of Extreme Programming (XP) and are two of the 12 common XP practices. What's the difference between the two? DRY refers to storing data in one place and with one unambiguous representation. OAOO refers to implementing a given behavior once and only once. It turns out that OAOO is more difficult to achieve and often only a driving vector. OAOO is the ideal goal of any refactoring attempt, and it's similar to *normalization*, as you might know it from the theory of relational databases.

The Post-Redirect-Get Pattern

The purpose of the pattern is self-explanatory. It essentially teaches you a way to reuse the same code to serve both GET and POST requests for the same resource or, as in ASP.NET MVC, for the same action. You start by fully writing your code for the GET scenario, as shown here:

```
[ActionName("Edit"), AcceptVerbs(HttpVerbs.Get)]
public ActionResult EditViaGet(string id)
{
    var data = new CustomerViewModel();
    data.Customers = ...;
    data.CustomerBeingEdited = ...;

    return View("Edit", data);
}
```

Next, you refactor the POST method so that it first does its own things (if any) and then redirects to the GET action. Here's the new version of the POST action:

```
[ActionName("Edit"), AcceptVerbs(HttpVerbs.Post)]
public ActionResult EditViaPost(string listCustomers)
{
    string customerId = listCustomers;
    return RedirectToAction("Edit",
                      new RouteValueDictionary(new { id = customerId }));
}
```

If the user types the URL directly in the address bar, the selected customer is edited and the view and URL are in full sync. If the user picks up a customer from the drop-down list and then posts to edit it, a redirection occurs and the *Edit* action receives an HTTP GET request.

The PRG pattern is helpful in keeping the URL and view in sync, but it's even more useful for keeping update code and the view neatly separated, as you'll see in a moment. In this regard, the PRG pattern saves you from the nasty F5 problem (page refresh requests from the client). If the user refreshes the currently displayed page (that is, he hits the F5 button) after an update, no POST is repeated and no message pops up to announce your intent to resend data. In fact, when F5 is pressed the browser repeats its latest action. When using PRG, the browser repeats a GET action, not a POST action, when from the user's perspective, their last action was a POST.

Saving Data

After the input form is displayed, the user enters any valid data and then presses the button that posts the current content of the form. Here's a typical form that posts changes:

```
<% Html.BeginForm("Update", "Customer", new {id = ViewData.Model.CustomerID}); %>
    ⋮
<% Html.EndForm() %>
```

The resulting URL for a customer ID of ALFKI is the following:

```
http://yourserver/customer/update/alfki
```

The content of the form is uploaded with the request and packaged into the *Request* object. However, as you saw in Chapter 6 a controller's method has various options for binding posted data to its own parameters.

Binding Input Data

Let's examine a few possible signatures for the *Update* action that is ultimately responsible for saving changes on the edited customer:

```
public ActionResult Update(string id,
                           string companyName,
                           string contactName,
                           string country,
                           string city,
                           string address);
```

The *id* parameter is resolved through route data, whereas all the other parameters are resolved in the presence of input elements with matching IDs. This signature also allows you to pass in fixed data for testing purposes. Another signature is the following:

```
public ActionResult Update(string id);
```

In this case, the remaining input data is resolved using the *TryUpdateModel* on the controller class that uses model binders internally.

Validation

Most of the time, you have a client-side validation mechanism that prevents the user from posting patently invalid data. However, having a client-side validation layer—no matter how effective it might be—is never a good reason to skip server-side data validation.

After you have gathered all the information about the record to update, you might want to validate it to see whether it is safe to store its content to the database. Server-side validation depends on the structure of your domain model and on the technology you might use to add validation.

Persistence

Updating the object in the database is a task that belongs to the Object/Relational Mapper (O/RM) you have chosen or, more generally, to the Data Access Layer. If you use an O/RM such as LINQ-to-SQL or Entity Framework, you might need to reload the record and update it against any posted data:

```
var customer = _service.GetCustomer(id);
TryUpdateModel(customer);
```

The *TryUpdateModel* method is defined on the controller class and updates the properties of the provided object with any matching value found in the posted data. Finally, the freshly modified domain object is persisted to the database using the persistence tools of the O/RM of choice. The following code shows how it works with LINQ-to-SQL:

```
public ActionResult Update(string id)
{
    using (var context = new NorthwindDataContext())
    {
        try
        {
            var customer = (from c in context.Customers
                            where c.CustomerID == id
                            select c).FirstOrDefault<Customer>();
            TryUpdateModel(customer);
            context.SubmitChanges();
        }
        catch(Exception ex) { ... }
    }
    return RedirectToAction("Edit",
            new RouteValueDictionary(new { id = id }));
}
```

Note the call to *RedirectToAction* at the end of the update procedure to ensure that the next view is the Edit view. The Edit view, in particular, will be opened on the same record just updated. The PRG pattern guarantees that if the user refreshes the page no second attempt is made to apply changes, as shown in Figure 7-3. With the PRG pattern, the latest action, in fact, is now a GET action.

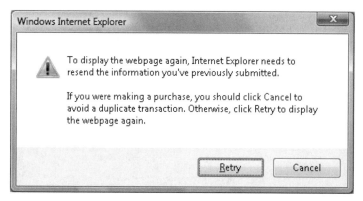

FIGURE 7-3 The user pressed F5, and the browser is about to repeat the latest action.

Data Validation

In Chapter 6, I discussed various ways to add validation capabilities to a server-side domain model. Abstractly speaking, a validation layer is the portion of code designed to guarantee the correctness, integrity, and coherence of any significant aggregation of data you manage. In other words, the validation layer exists to ensure that business rules apply to the data you work with.

Validation is essential on the server side, where you typically manage the persistence of the data. Validation is also extremely useful on the client side, where you might want to employ it to stop incorrect or inconsistent data at the gate.

Validation on the Server Side

The way in which you add validation depends on the specific technology you might employ to create the model and to persist it. Attribute-based validation blocks, such as data annotations in the Microsoft .NET Framework 4, are popular. However, they aren't always as effective as one might expect when you have to deal with extremely dynamic rules, or even rules that some users can enter or modify on the fly.

A much more flexible approach is to write your own infrastructure that can get input data preferably from outside of the code (for example, from configuration files). In any case, you need to have, or to offer, an API for checking whether a given object is in a valid state. In addition, the validation block must be able to report why a given object is not valid.

Let's go through an example of a custom server-side validation layer similar to what I discussed in Chapter 6.

Designing a Validation Layer with Enterprise Library

The public API for a custom validation layer is typically incorporated in all objects in the domain. This can be done by defining an interface and implementing that in a base class. As you did in Chapter 6, you can have an interface like this:

```
interface ISupportValidation
{
    bool IsValid{get;}
    ValidationResults Validate();
}
```

The *ValidationResults* type is a collection of objects that contains a report about the detected error. The report typically includes the object that was validated, any error message, perhaps a tag for the purpose of categorization, and a reference to the object that validated the instance of the domain object. If you create your own library, the details of the class are up to you. If you opt for Enterprise Library as the infrastructure for defining and checking business rules, you find such a class there and ready to use. The following code shows a possible custom implementation:

```
public class ValidationResults : List<ValidationResult>
{
}
public class ValidationResult
{
    public string ErrorMessage {get; set;}
    public object Target {get; set;}
    public string PropertyName {get; set;}
    public string Tag {get; set;}
}
```

You also need to define a base class that implements the validation API. The following code shows a class you can use as the root of your model:

```
public class MyRootDomainObject : ISupportValidation
{
    public virtual bool IsValid
    {
        get
        {
            try
            {
                return Validate().IsValid;
            }
            catch
            {
                return false;
            }
        }
    }
```

```
ValidationResults ISupportValidation.Validate()
{
    Validator validator = ValidationFactory.CreateValidator(this.GetType());
    var results = validator.Validate(this);
    return results;
}
}
```

The preceding code is based on Enterprise Library.

When you derive a new type from *MyRootDomainObject*, the type automatically inherits the validation capabilities built into the parent class. How do you specify your business rules?

The approach based on attributes is easy to implement and effective while you have static rules that do not change regularly:

```
public class Customer : MyRootDomainObject
{
    public Customer()
    {
        Id = string.Empty;
        PostalCode = String.Empty;
        :
        :
        :
    }

    [NotNullValidator(MessageTemplate="The customer ID cannot be null")]
    [StringLengthValidator(5, 5, MessageTemplate="ID must be 5 characters long")]
    public virtual string Id { get; set; }
    :
    :
    :
}
```

If you can't afford to recompile the code when business rules change, an attribute-based approach is not really the best choice. Attributes, in fact, are hard coded in the deployed binaries.

Saving Business Rules to a Configuration File

As mentioned in Chapter 6, Enterprise Library offers you the possibility of defining business rules in a configuration file that can be updated offline without requiring a new compilation. At the same time, you can also modify rules on the fly through an ad hoc user interface by simply updating the configuration file programmatically. Last but not least, when business rules are kept offline and the validation block of Enterprise Library is used, you are free of validating any objects regardless of the technology employed in the creation of the model. Figure 7-4 shows the configuration dialog box for Enterprise Library 4.x.

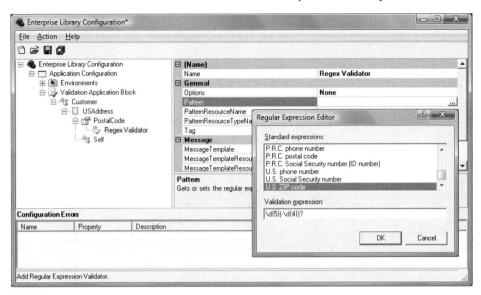

FIGURE 7-4 Using a configuration dialog box to define a sample validation rule set

The dialog box shows how you visually proceed to define a rule that expects the typical U.S. ZIP code format in the *PostalCode* property of the *Customer* type. The output of the dialog box of Figure 7-4 is the following XML content:

```xml
<configuration>
    <configSections>
        <section name="validation"
            type="Microsoft.EnterpriseLibrary.Validation, ..." />
    </configSections>
    <validation>
        <type assemblyName="MyDataModel" name="MyDataModel.Customer">
            <ruleset name="USAddress">
                <properties>
                    <property name="PostalCode">
                        <validator pattern="\d{5}(-\d{4})?"
                                   options="None"
                                   patternResourceName=""
                                   patternResourceType=""
                                   messageTemplate=""
                                   messageTemplateResourceName=""
                                   messageTemplateResourceType=""
                                   tag=""
                                   type="RegexValidator,
                                         Microsoft.EnterpriseLibrary.Validation"
                                   name="Regex Validator" />
                    </property>
                </properties>
            </ruleset>
        </type>
    </validation>
</configuration>
```

Embedded in the application's configuration file, this setting will be processed by the *Validate* method of the root class, resulting in a response for the validity of the tested object.

If new rules are to be added, or if some parameters of an existing rule are to be modified, all you have to do is edit a small segment of the configuration file. This happens regardless of what object model you have, and whether it's created by you or generated through a designer such as the LINQ-to-SQL or Entity Framework designer.

> **Important** Because Microsoft is integrating Data Annotations in the .NET Framework 4, it might seem that attribute-based validation is the way to go. Attribute-based validation certainly works and is a relatively simple approach both to understand and to code. However, attributes are hard-coded once they are compiled and are simply meant to statically decorate properties. XML-based rule sets in Enterprise Library offer an unprecedented level of flexibility. An alternative to using Enterprise Library to support dynamic business rules is to create a new set of attributes that expose a query interface to callers. This is in no way different from writing your own validation layer from scratch. Attribute-based validation is an excellent feature to have, but it mostly works for view models and client-side scenarios.

Checking the Validity of an Object

After you have a validation layer in place, checking the validity of an object takes you only a couple of lines of code. This code can consist of a simple short sequence of *if* statements or rely on an entire validation layer. From the perspective of an input form, here's the type of code you might have in a controller:

```
public ActionResult Update(CustomerViewModel model)
{
    // Invoke the service layer to update the customer
    try {
        _service.UpdateCustomer(model);
    }
    catch(BusinessRuleException ex)
    {
        ModelState.AddModelError("Business Rule Violation", e.ValidationResults);
    }
}
```

A slim controller simply delegates any action to the service layer and receives a response from it about the success or failure of the operation. The service layer might throw an exception or swallow the exception and return a composite response object. Let's tackle the first scenario assuming that the target object inherits from the aforementioned *MyRootDomainObject* class and that Enterprise Library is used in the implementation of the validation layer.

The method *UpdateCustomer* checks the validity of the object and throws a custom exception if it fails:

```
public void UpdateCustomer(Customer customer)
{
    // Check against the validation layer (assume the domain
    // object inherits from MyRootDomainObject)
```

```
    ValidationResults results = customer.Validate();
    if (!results.IsValid)
    {
        throw new BusinessRuleException(results);
    }

    // Proceed with the operation
    .
    .
    .
}

public class BusinessRuleException : Exception
{
    public BusinessRuleException : base() {}
    public BusinessRuleException(ValidationResults results) : base()
    {
        ValidationResults = results;
    }

    public ValidationResults ValidationResults { get; private set; }
}
```

The method throws a custom exception that encapsulates all validation information stored in the *ValidationResults* type.

Exceptions are more expensive than plain code. For this reason, it is preferable to avoid exceptions to handle validation. Here's a possible alternative for the *UpdateCustomer* method:

```
public UpdateCustomerResult UpdateCustomer(Customer customer)
{
    // Check against the validation layer (assume the domain
    // object inherits from MyRootDomainObject)
    ValidationResults results = customer.Validate();
    if (!results.IsValid)
    {
        return new UpdateCustomerResult(results);
    }

    // Proceed with the operation
    .
    .
    .
    return new UpdateCustomerResult();
}

public class UpdateCustomerResult
{
    public UpdateCustomerResult()
    {
        ValidationResults = new ValidationResults();
        IsValid = true;
    }
    public UpdateCustomerResult(ValidationResults results)
    {
        ValidationResults = results;
        IsValid = false;
    }
```

```
    public bool IsValid { get; private set; }
    public ValidationResults ValidationResults { get; private set; }
}
```

You define an ad hoc, data transfer object to contain the response of the method, which includes any return value plus any error information. The controller's code changes as follows:

```
public ActionResult Update(CustomerViewModel model)
{
    // Invoke the service layer to update the customer
    var result = _service.UpdateCustomer(model);
    if (!result.IsValid)
    {
        // AddModelError can accept only a string or an exception. Let's loop
        // through the validation results and add them individually. Alternately,
        // use an extension method.
        foreach(var r in result.ValidationResults)
            ModelState.AddModelError(r.PropertyName, r.ErrorMessage);
        return View();
    }
}
```

As you can see, the business layer returns any validation results and the presentation logic then processes it further to decide whether this is going to have an impact on the user interface. The *ModelState* property on the *Controller* class is the missing link between the presentation logic and user interface.

> **Important** In Chapter 4, I discussed the role of the controller and identified two possible stereotypes for it: controller and coordinator. These stereotypes nearly match two adjectives—fat and skinny—that are often used in the development community to describe the expected structure of the controller class. A fat controller is the controller that takes care of all operations, including the validation and execution of data access tasks. A skinny controller is the controller that delegates most of the work to the business layer and is limited to getting results and preparing the next view. The code discussed earlier addresses a scenario in which the controller class acts as the *coordinator* or, if you prefer, is particularly skinny.

The Model State

The *ModelState* property on the *Controller* class is designed to express the state of an object that belongs to the application's model. Strictly speaking, the definition is correct, but it is a bit obscure. The *ModelState* property is part of the *ViewData* collection and is an instance of the *ModelStateDictionary* class. Here's its implementation in the *Controller* class:

```
public ModelStateDictionary ModelState
{
    get { return base.ViewData.ModelState; }
}
```

At the end of the day, the class *ModelStateDictionary* is a helper class that contains information about the results of two possible operations: model binding and model validation.

When you perform a model binding operation via a model binder, you expect to find errors added to the model state dictionary to report the state of the operation if any binding failed. Likewise, when you validate the state of an object, you can put your error messages into the model state dictionary. From here, you can draw the conclusion that the *ModelState* property on the controller class is the container of error messages resulting from binding, validation, or both.

The model state dictionary is a collection of *ModelState* objects:

```
public class ModelState
{
    private ModelErrorCollection _errors;

    public ModelState();
    public ModelErrorCollection Errors { get; }
    public ValueProviderResult Value { get; set; }
}
```

You can add a model state through the *Add* method, as follows:

```
public void Add(string key, ModelState value);
public void Add(KeyValuePair<string, ModelState> item);
```

Alternately, you can use a more direct and simpler syntax based on the *AddModelError* methods:

```
public void AddModelError(string key, string errorMessage);
public void AddModelError(string key, Exception exception);
```

The *AddModelError* method adds the specified error message or exception to the *Errors* collection of the model state entry with a matching key name. If no such entry is found, a new one is automatically created.

In ASP.NET MVC, the *ModelState* property on the controller class is the preferred way of collecting binding and validation errors for the purpose of giving feedback to the user. You are not strictly required to always use *ModelState*; however, there are benefits in doing so. Some HTML helpers, in fact, are smart enough to read the content of the dictionary and display appropriate messages. By reporting error messages to *ModelState*, you gain some free user interface assistance.

In a preceding code snippet, I used a loop to add all errors reported by the service layer to the model state dictionary. Alternately, you could also define an extension method, as demonstrated here:

```
public static class ModelStateExtensions
{
    public static void AddModelError(
        this ModelStateDictionary modelStateDictionary,
        ValidationResults validationResults)
    {
        foreach (var r in validationResults)
            modelStateDictionary.AddModelError(r.PropertyName, r.ErrorMessage);
    }
}
```

Some applications at times might decide to swallow exceptions and hide the details of certain errors from their users. There are errors, however, that can't be ignored and must be communicated to the user. Validation errors are among these.

Giving Feedback to the User

In a typical scenario, the service layer method invoked by the controller validates any data and reports any error to the controller by either throwing an exception or storing details in a data transfer object. The controller then loads the invalid model state into the model state dictionary and renders the view. Let's see how this can happen.

Direct Rendering of the View

The following code shows a simple scenario for rendering error messages to the view and giving feedback to the user when an update fails:

```
<!-- Excerpt from the Edit.aspx view  -->

<form method="post" action="/customer/update">
    <input type="text" id="name" name="name" />
    <%= Html.ValidationMessage("name")%>


    ⋮


    <input type="submit" value="Save" />
</form>
```

The form lists a few input fields. Each input field is characterized by a code block displaying a validation message, if there is any. When the form posts, the controller method forwards the call to the service layer, receives a response, and then renders the view, as follows:

```
public ActionResult Update(CustomerViewModel model)
{
    // Invoke the service layer to update the customer
    var result = _service.UpdateCustomer(model);
    if (!result.IsValid)
    {
        ModelState.AddModelError(result.ValidationResults);
        return View();
    }
    ⋮

}
```

In the case of errors, the *ValidationMessage* automatically filters the content of the model state to display any error message that relates to the specified input field. By convention, the ASP.NET MVC machinery can also automatically style input fields with pending errors using a default cascading style sheet (CSS) style named *input-validation-error*. Such a CSS class is defined in the default style sheet added to the standard project template:

```
.input-validation-error
{
    border: 1px solid #ff0000;
    background-color: #ffeeee;
}
```

The CSS style can, of course, be customized. (See Figure 7-5.)

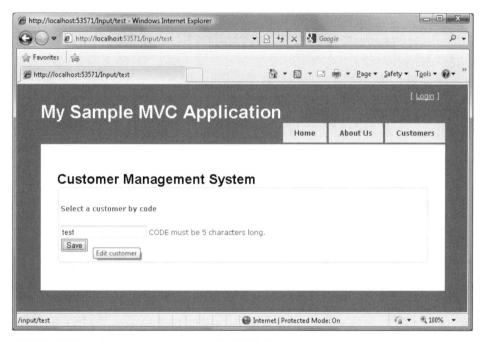

FIGURE 7-5 Displaying an error message via the *ValidationMessage* helper

In the list of standard HTML helpers, you find two methods that can be useful for displaying feedback to the user about incorrect input data. One of these helpers is *ValidationMessage*.

You use *ValidationMessage* in a code block and initialize it with the name of the model state entry to investigate. The model state name is the key the service layer (or in a simpler scenario, the controller itself) used to add a model error to the dictionary. Most of the time, the key matches the name of an input field. The helper displays a message if the specified field contains an error in the model state dictionary associated with the current view.

In addition to or as an alternative to *ValidationMessage*, you can use *ValidationSummary*. As the name suggests, the *ValidationSummary* helper renders the list of all detected errors by means of a bulleted list. (See Figure 7-6.)

FIGURE 7-6 The *ValidationSummary* helper in action

By default, validation messages and the validation summary work independently of one another; if both are used in a view, both display their messages, which in the end are duplicated. In ASP.NET MVC 2, you can use a special overload of the *ValidationSummary* helper that displays only messages not already rendered by a specific *ValidationMessage* helper.

Finally, an ad hoc CSS style also exists for the validation summary. The CSS class is defined as follows:

```
.validation-summary-errors
{
    font-weight: bold;
    color: #ff0000;
}
```

So far we've considered a relatively simple scenario where any detected error is directly rendered through the view. Earlier in the chapter, though, I discussed the PRG pattern, which advocates the use of a redirect to render the view after a POST action. Because model state errors are part of the view data, what happens if a redirect is performed instead of simply rendering the view?

The *TempData* Collection

The PRG pattern is an old pattern of Web applications that has been revamped by ASP.NET MVC. The reason is that ASP.NET MVC takes you closer to the metal and then provides you with more control over the life cycle of a request. The primary purpose of the PRG pattern is to avoid duplicate form submissions; the trick used for this purpose is redirecting to a page that just renders rather than having the posted command render the new form directly.

The PRG pattern is not specific to ASP.NET MVC and can easily be used with Web Forms, too. The problem is that with Web Forms, the postback mechanism is so natural and fully integrated in the rendering cycle that nobody would even think of using a redirect. If you want to update a Web Forms page, you simply bind server controls to fresh data and go. In ASP.NET MVC, conversely, you work at a lower abstraction level and can get full control of the rendering process.

So when the PRG pattern is used, the entire content of the *ModelState* object is lost, including any validation messages. Consider the following code snippet:

```
public ActionResult Update(CustomerViewModel model)
{
    // Invoke the service layer to update the customer
    var result = _service.UpdateCustomer(model);
    if (!result.IsValid)
    {
        ModelState.AddModelError(result.ValidationResults);
        return RedirectToAction("Edit", new RouteValueDictionary(new { id = model.Id });
    }

        .
        .
        .

}
```

In the case of invalid input, the controller redirects to the *Edit* action so that the user can fix the values. A redirect is just another action suggested to the browser. It turns out that the request that actually displays the view to the user is a new GET action that is distinct from the original POST. Any content prepared by the controller for the view is then lost. The content of the *ModelState* collection is no exception.

How can you preserve view-specific information across a redirect? You copy any information you intend to use in the view in a persistent data container—the *TempData* dictionary.

The *TempData* dictionary is a property of the *ViewPage* class and is defined as follows:

```
public TempDataDictionary TempData
{
    get
    {
        return this.ViewContext.TempData;
    }
}
```

The *TempDataDictionary* is a plain dictionary class that, in addition to the typical dictionary interfaces, also implements the *ISerializable* interface. It represents a set of data that needs to be persisted across successive requests.

Any content stored in the dictionary is processed by an ad hoc, temporary data provider object that takes care of persistence. The temporary data provider object belongs to the controller and is used within the *ExecuteCore* method of the *Controller* class, as I briefly hinted at in Chapter 4:

```
// Defined in the Controller class
protected override void ExecuteCore()
{
    base.TempData.Load(base.ControllerContext, this.TempDataProvider);
    try
    {
        string requiredString = this.RouteData.GetRequiredString("action");
        if (!this.ActionInvoker.InvokeAction(base.ControllerContext, requiredString))
        {
            this.HandleUnknownAction(requiredString);
        }
    }
    finally
    {
        base.TempData.Save(base.ControllerContext, this.TempDataProvider);
    }
}
```

The *TempDataProvider* property of the *Controller* class is defined as follows:

```
public ITempDataProvider TempDataProvider
{
    get
    {
        if (this._tempDataProvider == null)
        {
            this._tempDataProvider = new SessionStateTempDataProvider();
        }
        return this._tempDataProvider;
    }
    set
    {
        this._tempDataProvider = value;
    }
}
```

As you can see, by default the content of the *TempData* dictionary is saved in the session state. A unique entry is created in the session state where all the dictionary content is copied (if an in-process session provider is used) or serialized (if an out-of-process session provider is used).

The temporary data dictionary is loaded before any controller's method is executed. When this happens, however, the default provider tracks any element that is initially part of the dictionary. Every time a new item is added to the dictionary or an item in the dictionary is updated, the change is tracked too. At save time, items initially loaded but not further used during the request are removed. As a result, most of the time items stored in *TempData* last for two consecutive requests and then are gone.

> **Note** Tailor-made to support PRG scenarios, the behavior of *TempData* is subject to a few race conditions in ASP.NET MVC version 1. In particular, when you have interleaved or multiple consecutive redirects, it might happen that a new request kicks in and gets executed before one of the redirects. This usually happens when the user opens a new tab or window in the browser (where session state is shared) or when an AJAX request is made. In any of these cases, the content of *TempData* might be deleted before it is actually used by the target method.
>
> To avoid that result, in ASP.NET MVC 2 a few changes were made. In particular, items are now removed from the dictionary only if they have been read. Reading an item marks it for deletion; ignoring an item leaves it in the dictionary with the understanding that if you don't read it, you are not interested in it and the item is there for the purpose of a successive request. A new method—the *Keep* method—has been added to give you a chance to undelete a previously read item and keep it in the dictionary for later use. Finally, anytime you redirect, all items in the dictionary are undeleted. Overall, the new behavior keeps data in the dictionary longer, but it gives you more flexibility and reduces the risk of weird race conditions.

Persisting Validation Messages

How can you leverage *TempData* to persist your validation message in the case of a redirect? You have to manually copy the content of the dictionary into the *TempData* dictionary. In the controller's method that holds the results of the validation, you do as follows:

```
public ActionResult Update(CustomerViewModel model)
{
    // Invoke the service layer to update the customer
    var result = _service.UpdateCustomer(model);
    if (!result.IsValid)
    {
        ModelState.AddModelError(result.ValidationResults);

        // Persist validation messages
        TempData["ModelState"] = ViewData.ModelState;
        return RedirectToAction("Edit", new RouteValueDictionary(new { id = model.Id }));
    }

    :
    :
}
```

The name of the item you add to *TempData* is arbitrary, but *ModelState* is a commonly used name. Next, you must ensure that the redirected action method knows about any model state–related content it has to process. Any action method will load data into the *TempData* dictionary, but in this case an extra step is required—loading model state information into the *ModelState* collection:

```
[ActionName("Edit"), AcceptVerbs(HttpVerbs.Get)]
public ActionResult EditViaGet(string id)
{
    // Reload the model state if any
    var modelState = TempData["ModelState"] as ModelStateDictionary;
```

```
    if (modelState != null)
        ViewData.ModelState.Merge(modelState);

    // Prepare the view
    :
    :

    return View("Edit");
}
```

An interesting extension to this solution is making it an action filter. In this way, you can save yourself from the extra code just shown and reduce it to just an attribute of the controller's method, as shown here:

```
[ActionName("Edit"), AcceptVerbs(HttpVerbs.Get), ModelState(Entry="ModelState"]
public ActionResult EditViaGet(string id)
{
    :
    :
}
```

The name and syntax of the attribute *ModelState* are arbitrary. I'll return to action filters in Chapter 11, "Customizing ASP.NET MVC."

Redisplaying Attempted Values

The screen following a failed validation should display all attempted values so that the user can fix the faulty ones. Doing this has never been a problem in Web Forms thanks to the view state. In ASP.NET MVC, though, you should ideally take care of that yourself in much the same way you used to in classic Active Server Pages (ASP). HTML helpers such as *TextBox*, however, can retrieve attempted values from the model state. But who writes attempted values to the model state, and when? Consider the following code in a controller's method:

```
// Filling the model manually (not using automatic model binding...)
customer.Country = Request.Form["Country"];
:
:

// Validating
if (!customer.IsValid)
{
    ModelState.AddModelError("Country", "Invalid country.");
    :
    :
}
```

This code works just fine in ASP.NET MVC 2, but it might give you problems in an ASP.NET MVC 1 application. In particular, combined with the controller's snippet just shown, the following code will get a null reference exception in ASP.NET MVC 1:

```
<%= Html.TextBox("Country", ViewData.Model.Country,
        new Dictionary<string, object>() { { "class", "textBox" } })%>
```

The *TextBox* helper, in fact, assumes that if an error is found for the field "Country", the attempted value entered by the user also should be available somewhere. If this is not the case, it throws an exception.

Nothing that bad would happen if you used model binding either through the *TryUpdateModel* method of the controller class or the method's signature. If you don't go through model binding, you have to explicitly create a wrapper object that contains attempted values. Here's the code you need:

```
// Filling the model manually...
customer.Country = Request.Form["Country"];
  :
  :

// Validating
if (!customer.IsValid)
{
    ModelState.AddModelError("Country", "Invalid country.");
    ModelState.SetModelValue("Country", ValueProvider["Country"]);
      :
      :

}
```

The *SetModelValue* method adds information to the model state by reading the matching entry in the controller's value provider. The *ValueProvider* object of the controller is a component that groups all posted values regardless of their origin.

> **Note** If you don't use a stock HTML helper such as *TextBox*, you might not need the extra call to *SetModelValue*. You can use plain HTML literals and ensure the invalid value is retrieved and displayed in some way through your own algorithm.

Temporary Messages

Although error messages should stay up until the user fixes them, success messages are desirable on one end and boring on the other. Upon completion of an update operation, for instance, you want to notify the user of the successful operation. At the same time, though, you don't want the message to be either a pop-up message box or a static message. With a bit of help from JavaScript, you can create temporary messages. I use temporary messages mostly for success messages, but nothing prevents you from using them in other situations.

```
// Validating  `
if (!customer.IsValid)
{
      :
      :

}
```

```
else
{
   TempData["OutputMessage"] = "Successfully updated!";
     ⋮
}
```

You can store the message either in *ViewData* or *TempData*, depending on how you are rendering the view. You should opt for *TempData* if you are making use of the PRG pattern.

In the view, you proceed as follows:

```
<% String msg = TempData["OutputMessage"] as String; %>
  ⋮
<span id="UpdateMsg"> <%= msg %></span>
```

To hide the message at some point, you need some script code; nothing special, just a client-side timer:

```
<script type="text/javascript">
  var timer;
  $(document).ready(function() {
      timer = window.setInterval("clearMsg()", 2000);
  });

  function clearMsg() {
      $("#UpdateMsg").text("");
      window.clearInterval(timer);
  }
</script>
```

The preceding code uses the jQuery library to activate a two-second timer upon document loading. Upon expiration, the message is cleared.

Data Annotations and Validators

ASP.NET MVC 2 includes full support for data annotations, which are a complete set of attributes for annotating a class from a variety of angles, including validation. In Chapter 6, I covered data annotation validation attributes. In this chapter, you'll see a demonstration of how to use annotations to validate on the server and then on the client.

Preliminary Considerations Regarding Data Annotations

Data annotations are easy to use and quite effective. However, they're designed to be used essentially from within the controller's code. As you'll see in a moment, you use data annotations to decorate view model objects and rely on model binders to check metadata and detect errors.

Is checking view model objects within the presentation layer where the controller code runs adequate from a security and data-consistency perspective?

In general, the answer is no, but using data annotations might be acceptable in relatively simple cases where you don't have complex and data-driven business rules. The point here tracks back to the distinction I made in Chapter 6 between the view model and domain model. If they nearly coincide in your application—and it happens more often than you might think—then using a single layer of validation on the server side in the controller methods makes sense and turns out to be effective. Otherwise, you have the following options:

Implement a double layer of validation   Basically, you map view model objects to the controller's methods and use data annotations to filter out incorrect input values. Next, you copy data into domain objects and validate within the boundaries of the business layer. This second layer of validation should occur in a service layer class to preserve separation of concerns. The service layer, in fact, is technically part of the business layer and, in this regard, it's acceptable that it runs queries against databases to implement business-specific rules.

Don't use data annotation facilities   To avoid having a double layer of validation (which easily becomes three if you add JavaScript validation on the browser), the most sensible option is dropping data annotation facilities completely. You pass your view model object as is to the service layer and have the business logic perform all required checks, against input and against business rules. As discussed in Chapter 6, you can still use data annotations to express validation rules, but you won't be leveraging the user interface facilities of ASP.NET MVC model binders. In complex scenarios, though, where the business layer is located on a physically separated tier, you might find that a double layer (one on the presentation tier and one on the business tier) is still beneficial. Using this approach, some errors might be caught on the presentation, thus saving you some costly roundtrips to another server.

Validation is a delicate part of the business logic, but it's also an aspect that applies to input data and then to the presentation layer. In the end, there's no fixed rule to tell you where to have validation and how to code it. I strongly recommend you go beyond the facilities of data annotation metadata built around ASP.NET MVC controllers and don't blindly consider it the way to go just because Microsoft built it, it works great, and it is easy to use—because it may not provide enough validation control for all situations.

 Note Data annotation facilities like those I'll be describing in the remainder of the chapter are available only in ASP.NET MVC 2.

Metadata and Display

Data annotations are attributes defined in the *System.ComponentModel.DataAnnotations* namespace. They can be used to attach metadata information to a class and its members. Metadata can be of two main types: display and validation. Metadata is not executable code per se; however, it provides information to specific pieces of executable code designed to read and process metadata information.

When it comes to data annotations in ASP.NET MVC 2, display metadata is consumed primarily by templated helpers that create an ad hoc user interface for editing or displaying objects. Validation metadata, on the other hand, is used by model binders to perform a quick but effective check on the validity of the object by applying the rules set in the metadata.

Table 7-1 shows most popular metadata attributes for decorating the user interface when classes are rendered or edited.

TABLE 7-1 Quick list of display attributes in data annotations

Attribute	Description
DataType	Indicates the real type of the data, which might not be reflected by the .NET Framework type system. Special types are from the *DataType* enumeration and include *EmailAddress*, *PhoneNumber*, and *Date*.
Display	Indicates the text for the label to use (if required) when displaying and editing the property.
HiddenInput	Indicates that the property is rendered to a hidden field. The property can optionally be hidden from view, too.
UIHint	Indicates the user control to be used for displaying or editing the value of the property.
Scaffold	Indicates whether the property has to be added to the scaffolding that some UI tools might automatically create for display or editing purposes.

Combined with the validation attributes you already met in Chapter 6, display attributes form an extremely powerful duo that makes creating input forms extremely quick and effective.

Important Without meaning to become a proverbial pain in the neck, I want to emphasize again that although using data annotations to build display and validation functionality couldn't be faster or more effective, from an architectural perspective this is not necessarily what you want in your application—especially when you have to deal with dynamic and database-driven business rules. They can be helpful and provide a start, but they are by no means a complete solution.

Evolution of Model Binding in ASP.NET MVC 2

A few changes occurred in ASP.NET MVC 2 regarding the internal architecture of the model binding. These changes mostly made up for the data annotation support, but there's also some room left for custom extensions, including the possibility of plugging in other types of metadata.

First, model binding still occurs through the *DefaultModelBinder* class. An instance of this class is created whenever the *DefaultBinder* property of the *ModelBinderDictionary* class is invoked:

```
public IModelBinder DefaultBinder
{
    get
    {
        if (this._defaultBinder == null)
            this._defaultBinder = new DefaultModelBinder();
        return this._defaultBinder;
    }
```

```
    set
    {
        this._defaultBinder = value;
    }
}
```

As usual, you can change the default binder programmatically in *global.asax* or on a per-type basis using attributes. (See Chapter 6.)

One of the most common reasons for writing a custom model binder is to add a validation layer in it. In ASP.NET MVC 1, you had some support for it only if your class was implementing the *IDataErrorInfo* interface from the *System.ComponentModel* assembly.

```
public interface IDataErrorInfo
{
    string Error { get; }
    string this[string columnName] { get; }
}
```

In ASP.NET MVC 1, the *DefaultModelBinder* first checks whether the class implements the *IDataErrorInfo* interface. If so, the indexer property is invoked for each property in the class and any error messages are reported to the model state automatically. In addition, the default binder checks for the global *Error* property on any bindable class that implements *IDataErrorInfo*. If a general-purpose, non-property-specific validation message is present, it is added to the model state.

In ASP.NET MVC 2, this behavior remains the first option; however, a second and much more flexible option is offered if your class doesn't implement *IDataErrorInfo* or if no error was detected through *IDataErrorInfo*. The default binder will look for registered validators and metadata providers. Let's have a look at the source code of the *OnModelUpdated* method on the default binder class:

```
protected virtual void OnModelUpdated(
        ControllerContext controllerContext,
        ModelBindingContext bindingContext)
{
    // This code is nearly the same as in ASP.NET MVC 1
    var model = bindingContext.Model as IDataErrorInfo;
    if (model != null)
    {
        string error = model.Error;
        if (!string.IsNullOrEmpty(error))
            bindingContext.ModelState.AddModelError(bindingContext.ModelName, error);
    }

    // Here's the second option in ASP.NET MVC 2
    if (IsModelValid(bindingContext))
    {
        foreach (var validator in
                bindingContext.ModelMetadata.GetValidators(controllerContext))
        {
            foreach (var result in validator.Validate(null))
                bindingContext.ModelState.AddModelError( ... );
        }
    }
}
```

As you can see, a bunch of validators can be registered with ASP.NET MVC, and they will be called in sequence to validate the model. A validator is a class that inherits from *ModelValidator*.

```
public abstract class ModelValidator
{
    public virtual IEnumerable<ModelClientValidationRule> GetClientValidationRules();
    public abstract IEnumerable<ModelValidationResult> Validate(object container);

    protected internal ControllerContext ControllerContext { get; private  set; }
    protected internal ModelMetadata Metadata { get; private set; }
}
```

A validator has two methods—one for validating the state of a server-side object and one for validating input available within the browser. A validator works by checking real values stored in the object against provided metadata. In ASP.NET MVC 2, model metadata is a set of information defined in the public class *ModelMetadata*. Only one metadata provider is registered by default, and it is the *DataAnnotationsModelMetadataProvider* class. Metadata information based on data annotations are then processed by up to three default validators: *DataAnnotationsModelValidatorProvider*, *ClientDataTypeModelValidatorProvider*, and *DataErrorInfoModelValidatorProvider*.

As far as model binding is concerned, the default behavior in ASP.NET MVC 2 is that data annotation attributes are used to express display and validation metadata for a type. These annotations are validated by the default validators (on both the browser and the server side) and any errors are reported to the model state.

Validating Annotated Objects

Let's experience the combined power of data annotation metadata, templated helpers, and model binders in ASP.NET MVC 2. The following class is a typical view model class used to gather data being posted by an input form. The class is expected to add a new memo into a system. The memo includes an automatically generated ID, a title, the owner's name, the priority level, the due date, an e-mail address to use to follow up, and a flag indicating whether or not the memo has to show up in the calendar.

```
public class MemoViewModel
{
    [HiddenInput(DisplayValue = false)]
    public int Id { get; set; }

    [Required]
    [DisplayName("Title")]
    [StringLength(20, ErrorMessage = "Too long, cut your text.")]
    public String Title { get; set; }

    [Required]
    [DisplayName("Owner")]
```

```
    [RegularExpression(@"^[a-zA-Z''-'\s]{1,10}$")]
    public String OwnerName { get; set; }

    [Required]
    [Range(1,5)]
    [DisplayName("Priority")]
    public int Priority { get; set; }

    [Required]
    [DisplayName("Due by")]
    [DataType(DataType.Date)]
    public DateTime DueBy { get; set; }

    [DisplayName("Show on calendar")]
    public bool ShowOnCalendar { get; set; }

    [RegularExpression(@"\w+([-+.']\w+)*@\w+([-.]\w+)*\.\w+([-.]\w+)*")]
    [DataType(DataType.EmailAddress)]
    [DisplayName("Follow up")]
    public String FollowupEmail { get; set; }
}
```

To arrange an input form around this class, here's what you can do:

```
<h2>Create a new memo</h2>
<hr />
<% using (Html.BeginForm()) { %>
    <%= Html.ValidationSummary(true) %>
    <div>
        <fieldset>
            <legend>Memo</legend>
            <p>
                <%= Html.EditorForModel() %>
            </p>
            <p>
                <input type="submit" value="Save" />
            </p>
        </fieldset>
    </div>
<% } %>
```

The *EditorForModel* HTML helper is a shortcut for editing the entire object being passed as the model in the view page:

```
<%@ Page ... Inherits="System.Web.Mvc.ViewPage<MemoViewModel>" %>
```

From a controller action, you ask to render the form just shown and what you get looks like Figure 7-7.

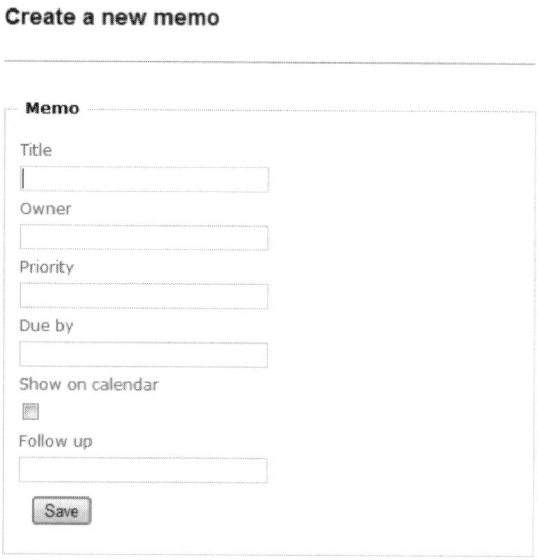

Create a new memo

Memo

Title

Owner

Priority

Due by

Show on calendar

☐

Follow up

[Save]

FIGURE 7-7 An input form automatically created by the editor templates

When you submit the form, any content will be bound to an HTTP POST–enabled action, as shown here:

```
[HttpPost]
public ActionResult Index(MemoViewModel model)
{
    return View();
}
```

Note In ASP.NET MVC 2, a new set of attributes has been introduced to make it simpler for you to restrict the controller's action method to certain HTTP verbs. The *AcceptVerbs* attribute introduced in ASP.NET MVC is still the repository of any code that selects a method for execution. However, its use is now simplified by more direct and parameterless wrapper attributes such as *HttpPost*, *HttpGet*, *HttpPut*, and *HttpDelete*. Which approach you use is purely a matter of preference because *HttpPost* and the others are implemented in terms of the underlying *AcceptVerbs* attribute. See Chapter 4, "Inside Controllers," for more information.

During the binding process, the actual content of the data being mapped to the model is checked carefully against the metadata in the class definition. Errors are reported as shown in Figure 7-8.

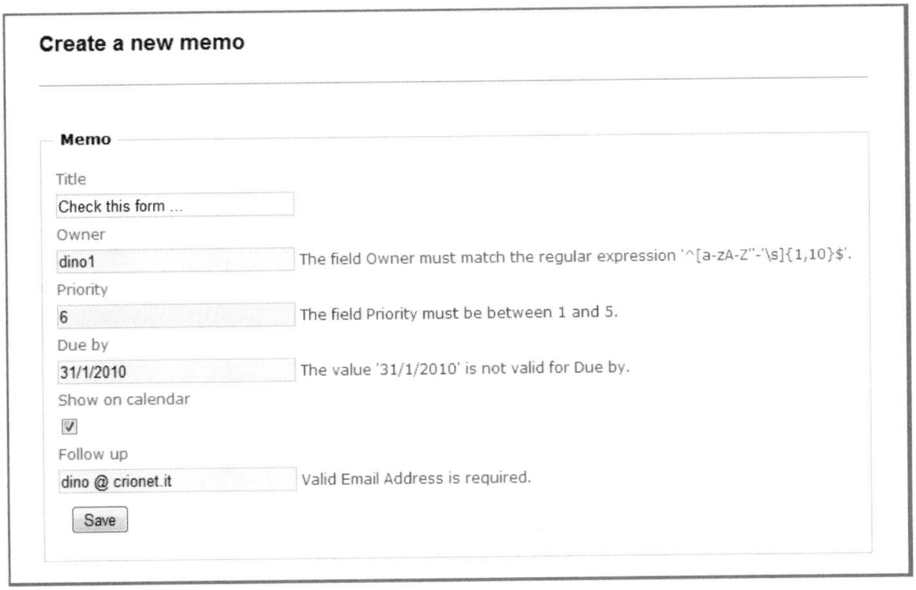

Create a new memo

Memo

Title
Check this form ...

Owner
dino1   The field Owner must match the regular expression '^[a-zA-Z"-'\s]{1,10}$'.

Priority
6   The field Priority must be between 1 and 5.

Due by
31/1/2010   The value '31/1/2010' is not valid for Due by.

Show on calendar
☑

Follow up
dino @ crionet.it   Valid Email Address is required.

Save

FIGURE 7-8 Posting invalid input data according to specified metadata

Regular expressions and range validators work just fine when a comment is required to explain the behavior of the *DataType* attribute. When *DataType* refers to a value of a non-*String* type such as *DateTime*, validation is included. When *DataType* refers to a special meaning of a *String* type, no validation is taken into account; in this regard, the *DataType* attribute works as a plain display attribute. For example, using *DataType[DataType. EmailAddress]* ensures that any content is rendered as a hyperlink, but not that the content is checked against the typical e-mail address format. If you want validation, you have to add a regular expression, as in the code snippet shown earlier.

Adding Custom Attributes

In Chapter 6, I briefly talked about using a custom attribute. Let's resume that discussion and see how easy it can be to integrate a new attribute with the data annotation infrastructure. Consider the *EvenNumber* attribute:

```
[AttributeUsage(AttributeTargets.Property, AllowMultiple = true, Inherited = true)]
public class EvenNumberAttribute : ValidationAttribute
{
    public EvenNumberAttribute()
        : base(_defaultErrorMessage)
    { }

    private const string _errorMessage = "The value must be an exact multiple of {0}.";

    public bool MultipleOf4 { get; set; }
```

```
    public override bool IsValid(object value)
    {
        if (value == null)
            return false;

        // If here, it is a number (otherwise, it would have been trapped
        // by the model binder)
        var number = (double) value;

        if (MultipleOf4)
            return (number % 4) == 0;

        return (number % 2) == 0;
    }

    public override string FormatErrorMessage(string name)
    {
        return String.Format(CultureInfo.CurrentUICulture,
                ErrorMessageString, (MultipleOf4 ?4 :2));
    }
}
```

The attribute checks whether the value associated with the property is an even number. Note that the model binder performs a preliminary check on the type before invoking the attribute:

```
[EvenNumber]
[DisplayName("Maximum number of days to wait")]
public double MaxNumberOfDays { get; set; }
```

If the value being passed cannot be converted to the declared type of the property—in this case, *double*—the attribute is not invoked and the user receives a default message stating that the value is invalid for the field. Otherwise, the control is passed on to the attribute and the error message, if any, can be more specific, as in Figure 7-9.

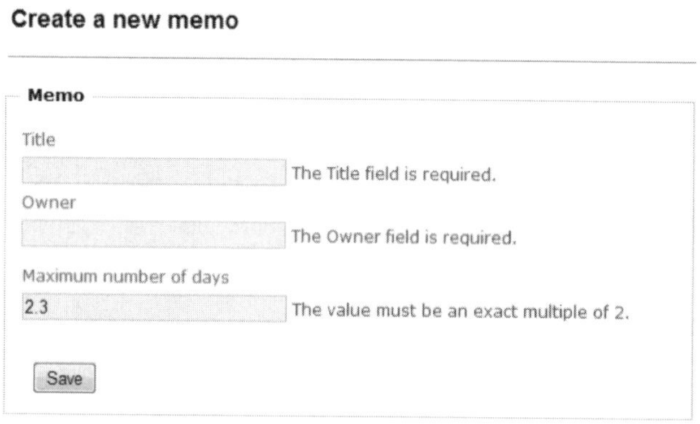

FIGURE 7-9 A custom validation attribute in action

All the code we've considered so far runs on the server side in the context of a controller action method. It would be nice if some work could be done directly on the browser side to save some network roundtrips at least for the most common (and easy-to-fix) mistakes.

Client-Side Validation

Web applications these days can't get by without a bit of script code in every page that makes the interaction with the user seamless. Validation is an excellent fit for some scripting. The good news is that the same set of annotations you use for server-side validation can be used to emit some ad hoc script that runs in the browser.

Enabling Client Validation

To enable client validation, you need a bunch of JavaScript files in the page to bring in all the dynamic validation capabilities:

```
<script src="/Scripts/jquery-1.3.2.min.js" type="text/javascript"></script>
<script src="/Scripts/jquery.validate.min.js" type="text/javascript"></script>
<script src="/Scripts/MicrosoftMvcValidation.js" type="text/javascript"></script>
```

Next, you need to ensure that you invoke the *EnableClientValidation* method from the HTML helper class right before the form tag:

```
<%= Html.ValidationSummary(true) %>
<% Html.EnableClientValidation(); %>

<% using (Html.BeginForm()) { %>
    <%=Html.EditorForModel() %>
    <p>
      <input type="submit" value="Save" />
    </p>
<% } %>
```

The final page served to the user will contain some JSON metadata—a faithful copy of the annotations in the object being edited—and registers a few handlers for user events such as blur, click, and submit. As a result, your form will never post if a required field is left empty.

Validators for Custom Attributes

Client validation doesn't work for custom attributes. The reason is that the custom attribute lacks a client-side validator module. A client validator currently exists for the following attributes: *StringLength*, *Range*, *Required*, and *RegularExpression*. For any other attribute you intend to use on the client, a new class is expected.

```
public class EvenNumberValidator : DataAnnotationsModelValidator<EvenNumberAttribute>
{
  bool _multipleOf4;
  string _message;

  public EvenNumberValidator(ModelMetadata metadata,
                ControllerContext context, PriceAttribute attribute)
    : base(metadata, context, attribute)
  {
    _multipleOf4 = attribute.MultipleOf4;
    _message = attribute.ErrorMessage;
  }
```

```
public override IEnumerable<ModelClientValidationRule> GetClientValidationRules()
{
    var rule = new ModelClientValidationRule {
        ErrorMessage = _message,
        ValidationType = "evenNumber"
    };

    rule.ValidationParameters.Add("multipleOf4", _multipleOf4);
    return new[] { rule };
}
}
```

At a minimum, the validator class will override the method *GetClientValidationRules* to emit metadata for a validation rule that will be checked on the client. Note that the validator just emits metadata that describes which fields to validate using which parameters. Metadata is converted to a JSON string and injected in the page. The script that consumes the metadata can be plugged in at will. By default, it is the jQuery Validate library. For a custom validation attribute, you also are responsible for writing the script code that will do the actual validation.

```
<script type="text/javascript">
    Sys.Mvc.ValidatorRegistry.validators["evenNumber"] = function(rule) {
        ⋮
        ⋮

        return function(value, context) {
            // Logic goes here
            ⋮
            ⋮

        }
    }
}
</script>
```

Finally, you must register the validator for the custom validation attribute. You can do that in *global.asax*, as shown here:

```
DataAnnotationsModelValidatorProvider.RegisterAdapter(
        typeof(EvenNumberAttribute), typeof(EvenNumberValidator));
```

In the end, ASP.NET MVC 2 brings to the table the same idea that is the basis of another popular open-source validation framework that many developers use—the *xVal* framework. The idea is to use the same set of annotations to decorate classes and have the framework use the same metadata to validate objects both on the server and the client.

ASP.NET MVC 2 uses data annotations for server-side validation and the jQuery Validator plug-in for client validation. This is only the default choice, though.

A Word or Two About xVal

As mentioned, xVal is an open-source validation framework for ASP.NET MVC that you can download from *http://xval.codeplex.com*. The overall idea is nearly the same as what you get natively from ASP.NET MVC, with the significant consideration that xVal came first.

In xVal, you decorate your classes using data annotations and use an ad hoc validation runner to validate object instances. (A method for validating an object against annotations is being added to data annotations in the .NET Framework 4.)

The xVal library operates on the server side in the context of the service layer. Any errors reported by the runner are packaged into a custom exception object that the controller will catch.

```
public ActionResult Edit(Customer customer)
{
    try
    {
        _service.Update(customer);
    }
    catch(RulesException exception)
    {
        exception.AddModelStateErrors(ModelState, "update");
        return View();
    }
    return RedirectToAction("Index")
}
```

The *RulesException* type is defined within the library and features the *AddModelStateErrors* helper method to copy reported errors to the model state.

To get client-side validation, you link jQuery, jQuery Validate, and the xVal-specific wrapper library.

```
<head>
    <script src="/Scripts/jquery-1.3.2.js"></script>
    <script src="/Scripts/jquery.validate.js"></script>
    <script src="/Scripts/xVal.jquery.validate.js"></script>
</head>
```

You also need to bring into the project the xVal HTML helpers and invoke them to emit proper script code in the page:

```
<%= Html.ClientSideValidation<Customer>("update") %>
```

If you don't like jQuery Validate, you can create (or reuse) an xVal plug-in for any other validation library you want to use. For more information, see the documentation at *http://xval.codeplex.com.*

As a final point, consider that with both xVal and ASP.NET MVC 2 client validation you get automatic fallback to server-side validation if JavaScript is not available on the user's machine.

Note Should you use xVal or should you go for native client-side validation in ASP.NET MVC 2? In terms of functionality, xVal is probably slightly richer and more consolidated. (Consider that xVal was announced before the first official release of ASP.NET MVC 1.) However, for the core part the libraries are equivalent. In many organizations, developers are forced to pick up products with active support and open-source products are deliberately avoided. In such scenarios, the client-validation capabilities of ASP.NET MVC 2 are not likely to disappoint you.

Summary

Input forms are common in any Web application, and ASP.NET MVC applications are no exception. In Web Forms, though, writing input forms was far easier because of server controls and automatic data binding. ASP.NET MVC uses much less abstraction and requires you to write view pages using more HTML and JavaScript. This inevitably has an impact on input forms, making it harder and more boring to create them.

For a while, there was a sentiment in the industry that ASP.NET MVC was not well suited to support data-driven applications because it required a lot of data entry and validation to do so. Ultimately, ASP.NET MVC measures up nicely to the task. It does use a different set of tools than Web Forms, but it is still effective and to the point.

ASP.NET MVC 2 improves the infrastructure for input forms by adding templated helpers and client-side validation. By combining view model objects, templated editors, and validators, you can build effective data entry pages in a fraction of the time it would have taken you in ASP.NET MVC 1.

Chapter 8
The ASP.NET MVC Infrastructure

A multitude of rulers is not a good thing. Let there be one ruler, one king.

—Homer

ASP.NET MVC works and thrives on top of the classic ASP.NET infrastructure. Typically, the infrastructure of ASP.NET includes a few built-in HTTP handlers and HTTP modules, such as those for authentication, output caching, session state, and a bunch of container or service classes such as *HttpContext* and *HttpRuntime*. To a large extent, ASP.NET MVC can be considered as a specialization of the classic ASP.NET runtime environment that just supports a different application and programming model.

ASP.NET MVC applications have full access to any built-in components that populate the ecosystem of ASP.NET, including *Cache*, *Session*, *OutputCache*, and the authentication layer. Nothing is different in ASP.NET MVC in the way in which these components can be used. So what's really the purpose of this chapter?

Because ASP.NET MVC is essentially an extension of the ASP.NET runtime, it comes with its own runtime shell—inside of which, you'll find that your perception of things is a bit different and features are more coarse-grained. Where traditional ASP.NET controls abstract much of the underlying markup, ASP.NET MVC encourages you to work with the markup nuts and bolts directly. From this perspective, the infrastructure of an ASP.NET MVC application is made of aspects that can be considered to be system oriented, such as authentication and routing as well as aspects that were originally catalogued as programming features, such as error handling and localization. Among other things, error handling is related to forms of Search Engine Optimization (SEO), and localization is a feature that is becoming so important and widely used as to justify a full discussion about the options and the tools you have available to make it happen.

Finally, the .NET developer of the next decade—whether that person is a Web, Windows, or WPF developer—can't avoid getting at least a working knowledge of dependency injection and related Inversion of Control (IoC) container frameworks. From the perspective of ASP.NET MVC applications, therefore, exposing a global object factory that can traverse an offline catalog of dependencies and resolve them to a graph of objects is a definite plus, if not a must-have capability.

In a nutshell, this chapter is a collection of distinct and, to some extent, self-contained topics—each touching on a feature that many ASP.NET MVC applications out there already have or are likely to have in the future.

Routing

In Chapter 2, "The Runtime Environment," I covered the basics of URL routing and ASP.NET MVC routes. In this chapter, I delve deeper into some specific aspects of using and defining routes, such as ordering, constraints, SEO, testing, and—more importantly—design of URLs.

Dealing with Routes

Ultimately, a route is a pattern that the URL-routing HTTP module attempts to recognize in the URL of the request being processed. If the URL-routing HTTP module finds a match, the selected route is picked up and processed in some way. At a minimum, a route comes with a schema for the URL and a route handler that decides which HTTP handler for the associated action is required.

Let's start by reviewing how a route is formally defined in the *system.web.routing* namespace, which is now part of the ASP.NET framework and no longer a feature specific to ASP.NET MVC.

Processing a Route

A route is defined as an instance of the type *Route*, defined as follows. Note that the base class *RouteBase* simply provides an abstract definition of the two overridden methods you find in the following code:

```
public class Route : RouteBase
{
    // Constructors
    public Route(string url,
            IRouteHandler routeHandler);
    public Route(string url,
            RouteValueDictionary defaults,
            IRouteHandler routeHandler);
    :
    :

    // Methods
    public override RouteData GetRouteData(
            HttpContextBase httpContext);
    public override VirtualPathData GetVirtualPath(
            RequestContext requestContext,
            RouteValueDictionary values);
    protected virtual bool ProcessConstraint(
            HttpContextBase httpContext,
            object constraint,
            string parameterName,
            RouteValueDictionary values,
            RouteDirection routeDirection);
```

```
// Properties
public RouteValueDictionary Constraints { get; set; }
public RouteValueDictionary DataTokens { get; set; }
public RouteValueDictionary Defaults { get; set; }
public IRouteHandler RouteHandler { get; set; }
public string Url { get; set; }
}
```

In summary, a route defines a list of URLs that are acceptable to an ASP.NET MVC application. If a requested URL matches any of the patterns represented by existing routes, the URL is further processed to extract information and control is yielded to the route handler object.

When you define a route in the *global.asax* file, you specify the expected layout of any matching URL as well as required strings (such as *{controller}* and *{action}* in the default route), default values, constraints, and data tokens. Most of the time, you use the predefined *MapRoute* extension of the *RouteCollection* class to define your routes. Here's an alternative way that lets you address any possible member of the *Route* class. Note that the following code is similar to the code used by *MapRoute* internally:

```
var stdRoute = new Route("{controller}/{action}/{id}", new MvcRouteHandler());
stdRoute.Defaults = new RouteValueDictionary
                        {
                            { "controller", "Home" },
                            { "action", "Index" },
                            { "id", ""}
                        };
stdRoute.DataTokens = new RouteValueDictionary
                        {
                            { "format", "short" }
                        };
routes.Add("Default", stdRoute);
```

As you might have guessed, the code has nearly the same effect as the default *MapRoute* call shown next:

```
routes.MapRoute("Default",
                "{controller}/{action}/{id}",
                new { controller = "Home", action = "Index", id = "" } );
```

The only difference is that you can't assign any content to *DataTokens* via *MapRoute*. The content of the *DataTokens* collection is values that get passed to the route handler and optionally are used to process the request. The default route handler just ignores data tokens; a custom route handler, however, might use them to make decisions about the HTTP handler to use to serve the request. Data tokens are not used to determine whether or not an incoming URL matches a given route. Along with constraints and route values, data tokens are packaged in the *RouteData* structure and belong to the *RequestContext* object.

Route Handlers

Each route is associated with a route handler. A route handler is a class that implements *IRouteHandler*.

```
public interface IRouteHandler
{
    IHttpHandler GetHttpHandler(RequestContext requestContext);
}
```

Any route that is added through the *MapRoute* extension method is bound to the default *MvcRouteHandler* class. This class doesn't do anything special and is limited to returning a reference to the default ASP.NET MVC HTTP handler:

```
public class MvcRouteHandler : IRouteHandler
{
    // Methods
    protected virtual IHttpHandler GetHttpHandler(RequestContext requestContext)
    {
        return new MvcHandler(requestContext);
    }

    IHttpHandler IRouteHandler.GetHttpHandler(RequestContext requestContext)
    {
        return this.GetHttpHandler(requestContext);
    }
}
```

A route handler is a sort of factory and is responsible for determining the HTTP handler that will serve the request. Any requests that match a given route will be mapped to the handler selected by the route handler looking at the information passed through *RequestContext*, including data tokens.

The ASP.NET MVC framework doesn't offer many route handlers, and this is probably a sign that the need to use a custom route handler is not that common. Yet, the extensibility point exists and, in case of need, you can take advantage of it.

StopRoutingHandler is an alternative route handler associated with any routes created through the *IgnoreRoute* extension method. All it does is throw a *NotSupported* exception when its *GetHttpHandler* method is invoked.

Another route handler available is *PageRouteHandler*, which defines how a URL maps to a physical file. Note that this class is defined in the *system.web* assembly for the .NET Framework 4 and is not available to applications compiled for any earlier version of the framework. You typically use the *PageRouteHandler* via the *MapPageRoute* extension method:

```
var pageRoute = new Route("SalesReport/{locale}/{year}",
                          new PageRouteHandler("~/sales.aspx"));
routes.Add("Sales", pageRoute);
```

The *PageRouteHandler* object specifies the virtual path of the physical file and optionally determines whether authorization rules for the physical URL have to be checked. To deal with authorization, you use one of the constructor's overloads.

The *PageRouteHandler* has been added primarily for making routing support easier in ASP.NET Web Forms 4. However, you can use it also from within ASP.NET MVC to bind a route to some legacy URL.

Using Route Constraints

Most of the time, the pattern defined by the route is sufficient to decide whether or not a given URL matches. However, this is not always the case. Consider, for example, the situation in which you are defining a route for recognizing requests for product details. You want to confirm the following two aspects:

- First, you want to be sure that the incoming URL is of the type *http://server/{controller}/ {productId}*, where *{controller}* identifies the ASP.NET MVC controller to invoke and *{productId}* indicates the ID of the product to retrieve.

- Second, you also want to be sure that no invalid product ID is processed. You probably don't want to trigger a database call right from the URL routing module; however, at the very least, you want to rule out as early as possible any requests that propose a product ID in an incompatible format.

Regular expressions are a simple way to filter requests to see if any segment of the URL is acceptable. Here's a sample route that keeps URLs with a string product ID off the application:

```
routes.MapRoute(
    "ProductInfo",
    "{controller}/{productId}/{locale}",
    new { controller = "Product", action = "Index", locale="en-us" },
    new { productId = @"\d{8}",
          locale = ""[a-z]{2}-[a-z]{2}" }
);
```

The fourth parameter to the *MapRoute* extension method is a dictionary object that sets regular expressions for *productId* and *locale*. In particular, the product ID must be a numeric sequence of exactly eight digits, whereas the locale must be a pair of two-letter strings separated by a dash. The filter doesn't ensure that all invalid product IDs and locale codes are stopped at the gate, but at least it cuts off a good deal of work.

An invalid URL is presented as an HTTP 404 failure and is subject to application-specific handling of HTTP errors. Figure 8-1, however, shows the effect of a customized way of handling some HTTP errors that you can implement in ASP.NET MVC on top of routes. (I'll get into the related details in the "Error Handling" section.)

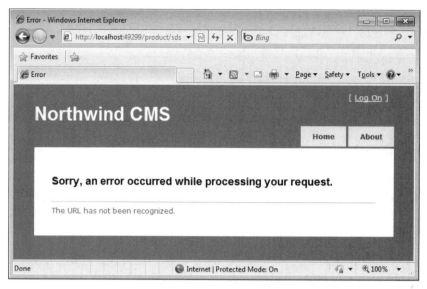

FIGURE 8-1 The URL matches the route pattern but fails on constraints.

In addition to using *MapRoute*, you can also use the *Constraints* property on the *Route* class to set a constraint, as shown here:

```
myRoute.Constraints = new RouteValueDictionary {
        { "productId", @"\d{8}" },
        { "locale", "[a-z]{2}-[a-z]{2}" }
};
```

If a regular expression is not enough to express the logic you need for deciding if an incoming URL is valid, you resort to constraint objects. As you saw in Chapter 2, a route constraint is a class that implements the *IRouteConstraint* interface. The interface includes just one method—*Match*—which returns a Boolean.

The following example shows a constraint that checks whether a parameter of the URL matches a set of predefined values. In particular, the constraint makes requests bounce back for customers that are not in the predefined list of countries.

```
public class CountryConstraint : IRouteConstraint
{
    public CountryConstraint(IList<String> cachedCountries)
    {
        _cachedCountries = cachedCountries;
    }

    private readonly IList<String> _cachedCountries = null;

    public bool Match(HttpContextBase httpContext,
                      Route route,
                      string parameterName,
```

```
                RouteValueDictionary values,
                RouteDirection routeDirection)
{
    bool result = true;

    // Adding logic here might have an impact on testing.
    var countries = (IList<string>) (_cachedCountries ??
            httpContext.Cache[Registry.CountryListCacheEntry]);
    if (countries == null)
        return false;

    if ((routeDirection == RouteDirection.IncomingRequest) &&
        (parameterName.ToLower(CultureInfo.InvariantCulture) == "countryname"))
    {
        var countryName = (string)values["countryName"];
        if (!countries.Contains(countryName))
            result = false;
    }
    return result;
    }
}
```

The list of countries can be provided as an argument to a constraint constructor, which is good for testability. By default, it is retrieved via a registry object that caches it at application startup. Here's how to declare the constraint:

```
routes.MapRoute(
    "CustomersForCountry",
    "{controller}/{countryName}",
     new { controller = "Customer", action = "Index" },
     new { countryName = new CountryConstraint(cachedCountries) }
     );
```

The *cachedCountries* parameter is passed as an argument to the caller of *MapRoute*:

```
public static void RegisterRoutes(RouteCollection routes, IList<String> cachedCountries)
{
     .
     .
     .
}
```

A URL that doesn't map to any routes originates an HTTP 404 error; a URL that maps to a route, but contains invalid values, will be handled by the controller.

Testing Routes

Like any other part of an ASP.NET MVC application, routes can be the subject of some unit testing. In particular, you might want to check whether a given URL is matched to the right route and if route data is extracted properly.

To test routes, you must reproduce the *global.asax* environment and begin by invoking the *RegisterRoutes* method. The *RegisterRoutes* method populates the collection with available routes.

```
[TestMethod]
public void TestIfProductRoutesWork()
{
    var routes = new RouteCollection();
    MvcApplication.RegisterRoutes(routes);

    RouteData routeData = null;
    routeData = GetRouteDataForUrl("~/product/sds", routes);

    // Test whether the right route was found
    Assert.AreEqual(((Route) routeData.Route).Url, "{controller}/{action}/{id}");
}
```

The *GetRouteDataForUrl* method in the test is a local helper defined as follows:

```
private static RouteData GetRouteDataForUrl(string url, RouteCollection routes)
{
    var httpContextMock = MockRepository.GenerateMock<HttpContextBase>();
    httpContextMock.Expect(c => c.Request.AppRelativeCurrentExecutionFilePath).Return(url);

    RouteData routeData = routes.GetRouteData(httpContextMock);
    Assert.IsNotNull(routeData, "Should have found the route");
    return routeData;
}
```

The method is expected to invoke *GetRouteData* to get information about the requested route. Unfortunately, *GetRouteData* needs a reference to *HttpContextBase*, where it places all inquiries about the request. In particular, *GetRouteData* needs to invoke *AppRelativeCurrentExecutionFilePath* to know about the virtual path to process.

By mocking *HttpContextBase* to provide an ad hoc URL, you completely decouple the route from the runtime environment and can proceed with assertions.

The sample code shown earlier uses Rhino Mocks to create mocks of objects. (See *http://www.ayende.com/projects/rhino-mocks.aspx*.) I'll return to the topic of mocking frameworks in Chapter 10, "Testability and Unit Testing."

Keeping an Eye on SEO

One of the reasons to pay more attention to routes is to enforce a set of rules that can increase the appeal of your site to search engines and end users. Search Engine Optimization, or SEO for short, has become a precise goal of most Web projects.

At its root, SEO consists of adding metadata to pages, reviewing URLs, and restructuring content with a particular focus on cross-page links, error pages, use of JavaScript, redirects, and images. SEO considers how search engines work and what people search for. The idea is to make it easier for popular search engines to find your pages and rank your pages higher with reference to specific keywords. All in all, URL design, unique content, and a wise redirection strategy are all key achievements on the way to getting the most out of search engines. Let's see how to accomplish this in ASP.NET MVC.

Devising Routes and URLs

I still remember very well when Microsoft Windows 95 introduced long file names and, with that, the ability to give files and directories names up to 255 characters. It's hard to believe if you never programmed in the era of 16-bit applications, but there really was a time when you had to express disk resources using an 8+3 notation—that is, only 8 characters for the name plus 3 for the extension. All developers welcomed long file names in Windows 95 as the long-awaited way to give files more readable and sensible names.

In the beginning of the Web era, URL names were chosen much like file names, with the goal of representing the intended resource in a sensible way. Then Content Management Systems (CMS) started mechanizing the process of URL creation. To generalize the management of some content over the Web, CMS applications began using a base URL plus some variable parameters appended to the query string. URLs like the following one were common:

```
http://code.yourserver.com/bin/10day-ITXX0067
    ?cm_ven=myapp_it&cm_cat=citypage&cm_ite=weather&cm_pla=10day&cm_fmt=metrics
```

These URLs perfectly fulfill their mission, but they can't really be understood, let alone remembered. Are URLs something that users should care about? Ideally, they should not. However, just as for files and directories, URLs are visible and, to some extent, they do matter. In the end, URLs can even be created and managed by the application in any way that suits the tool and developers as long as they can be exposed to the user in a more sensible way. This is just what routes ultimately do.

A URL scheme must enforce a few characteristics, such as readability and uniqueness. A readable URL is a URL that is clear about what it points to. In addition, a readable URL results from a *breadcrumb*. Breadcrumb navigation refers to presenting the URL as a sequence of segments much like directories in a file system path. However, each segment points to a page that is meaningful for the system and is not simply showing the content of a virtual directory. Here's an example:

```
http://yourserver.com/weather/italy/lazio/north/today/afternoon/
```

If you visit the preceding URL, you'll be shown forecasts for the afternoon, but if you remove two trailing segments, you'll get forecasts for the north of the specified region for a default period. If you stop at the country level, instead, you'll get an overview of the situation for the whole country and for the default period.

Another key principle of URL design and organization is that each URL must be unique. Having the need to reference the same URL many times is fine, but you manage to resolve the reference via a permanent redirect. Uniqueness has a significant impact on SEO, and I'll return to that point in a moment.

The Trailing Slash

For a long time, I wondered whether using or not using a trailing slash in an ASP.NET URL that doesn't directly refer to a page would make any difference. For the Web server, it actually does make a small difference. If the URL ends with a slash, the Web server understands you're requesting a directory. If the URL doesn't end with the slash, ASP.NET Web Forms performs an automatic HTTP 301 permanent redirect to the same URL but with a trailing slash. So in ASP.NET, whether you're using the trailing slash or not, it always results in a single URL being used. And if you keep the slash, you also save yourself a redirect.

There are some SEO concerns related to the trailing slash. In particular, a search engine incorporates a filter that detects and penalizes duplicate content in search results. Duplicate content is any page (that is, any distinct URL) in the search results that actually is reckoned to serve the same content as others. To serve the most relevant content possible to the user, a search engine tries to rank lower the pages that seem nearly the same as others. But this process can accidentally reduce the rank of good pages. Permanent redirects, such as those occurring for non-file URLs without a trailing slash, are a way to share more information about pages with a search engine.

What about ASP.NET MVC and the routing system? Should you force a trailing slash?

Ultimately, an ASP.NET MVC application is entirely responsible for its URLs and, subsequently, for what a search engine will ask for. In a new application, it's ultimately up to you because your routes determine how the request is processed. Helpers used to generate URL in the markup tend to avoid trailing slashes, so let's say that not having trailing slashes is a more common solution in ASP.NET MVC. But keep in mind that the other approach is equally valid. In ASP.NET MVC, it's up to you to resolve (or not resolve) URLs with and without the trailing slash in the same way. You ultimately decide about your page rank.

If you're porting an existing site to ASP.NET MVC, you might have many legacy URLs to maintain. You can install a custom route handler and permanently redirect (HTTP 301) from legacy URLs to new URLs. This approach works, but in practice it might take weeks for the search engine to physically update the internal tables of links to reflect all of your permanent redirects. Meanwhile, you might lose quite a bit of income because of that.

The search engine always likes to deal with the existing URLs. In this case, you might want to install a rewrite module in Microsoft Internet Information Services (IIS) to map an ASP.NET MVC URL to a legacy one. The following post provides some details: *http://www.hanselman .com/blog/ASPNETMVCAndTheNewIIS7RewriteModule.aspx*.

Same Content, Multiple URLs

In general, you might want to apply the principle of "Once And Only Once" (OAOO) to URL design as well as to the rest of your system. At the foundation of Agile programming, OAOO says that it would be ideal to have the same content exposed through one and only one URL.

One of the primary purposes of a search engine is determining how relevant the content pointed to by a given URL is. Of course, a given piece of information is much more relevant if it can be found only in one place and through a unique URL. Sometimes, however, even if the content is unique, it can be reached through multiple, subtly different, URLs. The risk is that you get a lower rank from search engines or, worse yet, a portion of your site is blacked out because the same content can be retrieved elsewhere.

The problem here does not have much to do with storage and page content, but with the shape and format of URLs. Even though the W3C suggests you consider using case-sensitive URLs, from a SEO perspective single-case (and lowercase at that) URLs are a better choice. If you can manage to keep all of your URLs lowercase, that would add consistency to the site while reducing duplicate URLs. What about inbound links?

Well, there's not much you can do to avoid having external sites link to pages in your site using the case they prefer. Most likely, they will just copy your URLs, thus repeating the same case you might have chosen. If this is not the case, you can always force a permanent redirect via an HTTP module that intercepts the *BeginRequest* event. Forcing all inbound links to use the same case saves you from splitting traffic across multiple URLs instead of concentrating all of it on a single URL with a higher rank. (We can call this strategy "Unite and Conquer," as opposed to the "Divide and Conquer" strategy that is so popular in other software scenarios.)

To address this problem, the *canonical URL* format also has been defined. The canonical URL describes your idea of a URL in the form of a preferred URL scheme. All you do is add a *<link>* tag to the *<head>* section, as shown here:

```
<link rel="canonical" href="http://yourserver.com/" />
```

If your site has a significant amount of content that can be accessed through multiple URLs, the canonical URL gives more information to search engines so that they can treat similar URLs as a single one and come to a more appropriate ranking of the content of the resource. A possible effect of the canonical URL feature (zero costs on your side) is that it can clear up the controversy between having or not having the trailing slash. With a canonical URL that defaults to either choice, it makes no difference to a search engine which one is actually linked.

Permanent Redirection

Permanent redirection is another aspect of URL design and implementation that is strictly related to SEO.

In ASP.NET, when you invoke *Response.Redirect* you return to the browser an HTTP 302 code indicating that the requested content is now available from another specified location. Based on that, the browser makes a second request to the specified address and gets any content. A search engine that visits your page, however, takes the HTTP 302 code literally. The actual meaning of the HTTP 302 status code is that the requested page has been *temporarily* moved to a new address. As a result, search engines don't update their internal tables, and when someone later clicks to see your page, the engine returns the original address. As a result, the browser receives an HTTP 302 code and needs to make a second request to finally get to display the desired page.

If the redirection is used to convey requests to a given URL, permanent redirection is a better option because it represents a juicier piece of information for a search engine. To set up a permanent redirection, you return the HTTP 301 response code. This code tells user agents that the location has been permanently moved. Search engines know how to process an HTTP 301 code and use that information to update the page URL reference. The next time they display search results that involve the page, the linked URL is the new one. In this way, users can get to the page quickly and a second roundtrip is saved. Here's how to arrange a permanent redirection programmatically:

```
void PermanentRedirect(string url, bool endRequest)
{
    Response.Clear();
    Response.StatusCode = 301;
    Response.AddHeader("Location", url);

    // Optionally end the request
    if (endRequest)
        Response.End();
}
```

In ASP.NET 4, the *HttpResponse* class features a new method for such a thing. It is named *RedirectPermanent*. You use the method in the same way you used the classic *Response. Redirect*, except that this time the caller receives an HTTP 301 status code. For the browser, it makes no big difference, but it is a key difference for search engines.

If you compile against the .NET Framework 4, the method is also exposed by the *HttpResponseBase* class. Therefore, it is also available to the ASP.NET MVC runtime shell, and you don't have to fear introducing undesired dependencies to the ASP.NET runtime that could hinder testability.

In Chapter 11, "Customizing ASP.NET MVC," I'll show how to create a custom action result object for permanent redirects.

Error Handling

Because ASP.NET MVC works on top of the classic ASP.NET runtime environment, you can't expect to find a radically different infrastructure to handle runtime errors. Error handling still depends on the settings you configure through the *<customErrors>* section of the *web.config* file. Even so, however, ASP.NET MVC does offer a bunch of new and more specific facilities. In particular, it is interesting to review the whole error-handling strategy in light of search engine optimization.

Foundations of ASP.NET Error Handling

Overall, error handling in ASP.NET MVC spans two main areas: the handling of logical exceptions and route exceptions. The former is concerned with catching errors in controllers and views; the latter is more about redirection and HTTP errors.

Handling Program Exceptions

Most of the code you write in ASP.NET MVC applications resides in controller classes. In a controller class, you can deal with possible exceptions in a number of equivalent ways. In the first place, you can use local *try/catch* blocks to protect yourself against a possible exception in a specific section of the code. This is the approach that gives you maximum flexibility. In this context, ASP.NET MVC offers an interesting facility—the *HandleError* attribute for controller methods and classes.

The default action invoker executes controller methods within a *try/catch* block and catches any resulting exceptions, as shown here:

```
try
{
    // Try to invoke the action method
    :
    :
}
catch(ThreadAbortException)
{
    throw;
}
catch(Exception exception)
{
    // Execute exception filters
    var exceptionContext = InvokeExceptionFilters(
            controllerContext, filters.ExceptionFilters, exception);

    // Re-throw if not completely handled
    if (!exceptionContext.ExceptionHandled)
    {
        throw;
    }

    // Generates the view following the exception
    InvokeActionResult(controllerContext, exceptionContext.Result);
}
```

If an exception is thrown at some point during the method's execution or during the rendering of the view, the control passes to the code in the *catch* block as long as the exception is not a *ThreadAbortException*. Handling the exception entails looping through the list of registered exception filters and giving each its own chance to fix things.

Defined, an exception filter is a class that implements the *IExceptionFilter* interface. The base *Controller* class is the world's simplest exception filter because it implements the interface but doesn't really perform any action. You transform your own controller class into a true exception filter by overriding the *OnException* method:

```
protected virtual void OnException(ExceptionContext filterContext)
{
}
```

As an alternative to overriding the *OnException* method, you can decorate the class (or just individual methods) with the *HandleError* attribute or any custom class that derives from it:

```
[HandleError]
public class ProductController
{
    .
    .
    .
}
```

As you saw in Chapter 4, "Inside Controllers," the *HandleError* attribute traps any exceptions unless you specify the list of exception types it has to look for. The attribute also lets you indicate the view to render next:

```
[HandleError(ExceptionType=typeof(NullReferenceException), View="SyntaxError")]
```

Note that for *HandleError* to produce visible results in debug mode you need to enable custom errors at the application level, as shown here:

```
<customErrors mode="On">
</customErrors>
```

If you leave on the default settings for the *<customErrors>* section of the configuration file, only remote users will get the selected error page. Local users (for example, developers doing some debugging) will receive the classic error page with detailed information about the stack trace as produced by the normal ASP.NET exception handler.

Inside the *HandleError* Attribute

The *HandleError* attribute provides an out-of-the-box implementation of an exception filter. It checks whether the HTTP status code associated with the inner exception is 500 (internal error). Next, it propagates the error code to the output stream along with the content generated by the selected view.

HandleError is an attribute used to decorate controller classes and methods. How does it make it to the list of registered exception filters that the action invoker awakes when an exception is thrown?

Before executing a method, the action invoker gets the list of action filters attached to it and creates type-specific collections. Action filters are attributes (for example, *HandleError*, *Authorize*, and *OutputCache*, plus your own ones) used to decorate methods. When an action is caught, the invoker picks up the list of exception handlers and runs them. During the building of the filters list, a bit of reflection is used to detect whether *HandleError* is defined for the method. If it is, the attribute instance is added to the list. The *HandleError* class, in fact, implements *IExceptionFilter*.

Figure 8-2 shows the effect of running the following code with a breakpoint set on the return line (note the exception filters collection):

```
public class MyActionInvoker : ControllerActionInvoker
{
    protected override FilterInfo GetFilters(
            ControllerContext controllerContext, ActionDescriptor actionDescriptor)
    {
        var filters = base.GetFilters(controllerContext, actionDescriptor);

        // Place a breakpoint on the next line
        return filters;
    }
}

[HandleError]
public partial class ProductController : Controller
{
    public ProductController()
    {
        // Sets a custom action invoker only to override GetFilters
        this.ActionInvoker = new MyActionInvoker();
    }

    public virtual ActionResult Index(int? productId)
    {
        throw new ArgumentException();
    }
}
```

The filters collection available to the action invoker shows two objects in the *ExceptionFilters* member: the controller itself and the *HandleError* attribute.

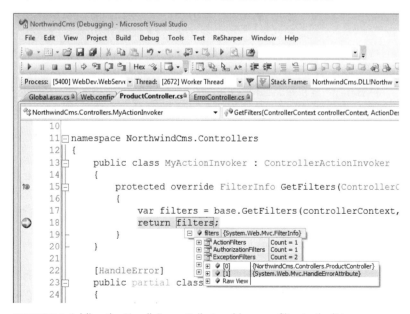

FIGURE 8-2 Adding the *HandleError* attribute adds a new filter to the list.

Note that when you use the *HandleError* attribute and an exception is caught, you lose all the content currently stored in the *ViewData* dictionary. In fact, the *OnException* method on the filter class doesn't simply copy the controller's *ViewData* in the view result. It instead creates a brand-new dictionary that contains error information packaged in an instance of the *HandleErrorInfo* class. The net effect is that anything you put in the *ViewData* disappears. Here's an excerpt of the code run by the *OnException* method in the *HandleError* filter:

```
public virtual void OnException(ExceptionContext filterContext)
{
    if (filterContext == null)
        throw new ArgumentNullException("filterContext");
    if (!filterContext.IsChildAction &&
        (!filterContext.ExceptionHandled &&
         filterContext.HttpContext.IsCustomErrorEnabled))
    {
        Exception innerException = filterContext.Exception;
        if ((new HttpException(null, innerException).GetHttpCode() == 500))
        {
            string controllerName = (string) filterContext.RouteData.Values["controller"];
            string actionName = (string) filterContext.RouteData.Values["action"];
            HandleErrorInfo model = new HandleErrorInfo(
                    filterContext.Exception, controllerName, actionName);

            ViewResult result = new ViewResult();
            result.ViewName = this.View;
            result.MasterName = this.Master;
            result.ViewData = new ViewDataDictionary<HandleErrorInfo>(model);
            result.TempData = filterContext.Controller.TempData;
            filterContext.Result = result;
            filterContext.ExceptionHandled = true;
            filterContext.HttpContext.Response.Clear();
            filterContext.HttpContext.Response.StatusCode = 500;
            filterContext.HttpContext.Response.TrySkipIisCustomErrors = true;
        }
    }
}
```

If the default behavior of the *HandleError* filter is too much trouble for you, the only option is creating a custom error-handling filter that deals with this scenario differently.

Handling Route Exceptions

In addition to any detected program errors, your application might be throwing exceptions because the URL of the incoming request doesn't match any of the mapped routes—whether because of an invalid URL pattern or a violated constraint. In this case, your users get an HTTP 404 error. Letting users receive the default 404 ASP.NET page is something you might want to avoid for a number of reasons—primarily, to be friendlier to end users.

The typical solution enforced by the ASP.NET framework consists of defining custom pages (or routes in ASP.NET MVC) for common HTTP codes such as 404 and 403. Whenever the user types or follows an invalid URL, she is redirected to another page where some hopefully nice and useful information is provided. Here's how to register ad hoc routes in ASP.NET MVC:

```
<customErrors mode="On">
    <error statusCode="404" redirect="/error/show" />
    .
    .
    .
</customErrors>
```

This trick works just fine, and there's no reason to question it from a purely functional perspective. So where's the problem, then?

However, imagine a search engine requesting a URL that doesn't exist in an application that implements custom error routing. The application first issues an HTTP 302 code and tells the caller that the resource has been temporarily moved to another location. At this point, the caller makes another attempt and finally lands on the error page. This approach is great for humans, who ultimately get a pretty message; it is less than optimal from an SEO perspective because it leads search engines to conclude the content is not missing at all—just harder than usual to retrieve. And an error page is catalogued as regular content and related to similar content.

On the other hand, route exceptions are a special type of error and deserve a special strategy distinct from program errors. Ultimately, route exceptions refer to some missing content.

Dealing with Missing Content

The routing subsystem is the front end of your application and the door at which request URLs knock to get some content. In ASP.NET MVC, it is easy to treat requests for missing content in the same way as valid requests. No redirection and additional configuration are required if you create a dedicated controller that catches all requests that would go unhandled.

Catch-All Route

A common practice to handle this situation consists of completing the route collection in *global.asax* with a catch-all route that traps any URLs sent to your application that haven't been captured by any of the existing routes:

```
public static void RegisterRoutes(RouteCollection routes)
{
    // Main routes
    .
    .
    .
    // Catch-all route
    routes.MapRoute(
```

```
    "ErrorHandling",
    "{*anything}",
    new { controller = "Error", action = "Missing" }
);
}
```

Obviously, the catch-all rule needs to go at the very bottom of the routes list. This is necessary because routes are evaluated from top to bottom and parsing stops at the first match found. The catch-all route will map the request to your application-specific *Error* controller. The controller, in turn, will look at content and headers and decide which HTTP code to return. Here's an example of such an *Error* controller:

```
public class ErrorController : Controller
{
    public ActionResult Missing()
    {
        HttpContext.Response.StatusCode = 404;
        HttpContext.Response.TrySkipIisCustomErrors = true;

        // Log the error
        :
        :

        // Pass some optional information to the view
        var model = ErrorViewModel();
        model.Message = ...;
        :
        :

        // Render the view
        return View(model);
    }
}
```

The *ErrorViewModel* class in the example is any view-model class you intend to use to pass data to the underlying view in a strongly typed manner. Using the *ViewData* dictionary is fine as well, and overall it's an acceptable compromise in this specific and relatively simple context.

By using an error controller, you can improve the friendliness of the application and optimize it for search engines. In fact, you actually serve a pretty user interface to users while returning a direct (that is, not redirected) error code to any callers.

Skipping IIS Error-Handling Policies

In the preceding code snippet, the *Missing* method on the *ErrorController* class at some point sets to *true* the *TrySkipIisCustomErrors* property on the *Response* object. It is a new property introduced with ASP.NET 3.5 that specifically addresses a feature of the IIS 7 integrated pipeline.

As you saw in Chapter 2, when an ASP.NET application (both Web Forms and ASP.NET MVC) runs under IIS 7 within an integrated pipeline, some of the ASP.NET configuration settings will be merged with the settings defined at the IIS level. (See Figure 8-3.)

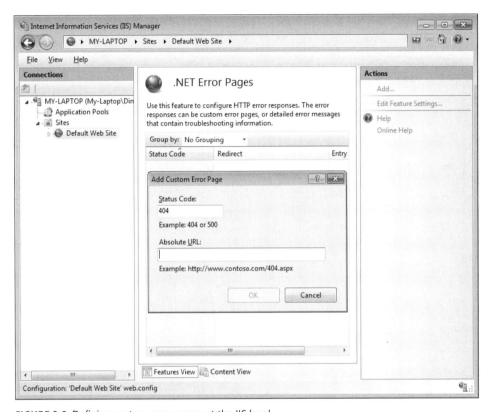

FIGURE 8-3 Defining custom error pages at the IIS level

In particular, if error pages are defined in IIS for common HTTP status codes, in the default case these pages will take precedence over the ASP.NET-generated content. As a result, your application might trap an HTTP 404 error and serve a nice-looking ad hoc page to the user. Like it or not, your page will never make it to the end user because it will be replaced by another page that might be set at the IIS level.

To make sure that the IIS error handling is always bypassed, you set the *TrySkipIisCustomErrors* property to *true*. The property is useful only for applications that run under IIS 7 in integrated pipeline mode. In integrated pipeline mode, the default value of the property is *false*. The implementation of the *HandleError* exception filter, for example, takes this aspect into careful consideration and sets the property to *true*.

Localization

The whole theme of localization is nothing new in the .NET Framework, and ASP.NET is no exception. You have had tools to write culture-specific pages since the very first version of ASP.NET. The beauty is that nothing has changed, so adding localization capabilities to ASP.NET MVC applications is neither more difficult nor different than in classic ASP.NET.

Considering localization from the perspective of an entire application with a not-so-short expectation of life, there are three aspects of it that need to be addressed: how to make resources localizable, how to add support for a new culture, and how to use (or whether to use) databases as a storage place for localized information.

Making Resources Localizable

A localizable ASP.NET MVC view, as well as an ASP.NET Web Form, uses resources instead of hard-coded text to flesh out the user interface. After a resource assembly is linked to the application, the ASP.NET runtime selects the correct value at run time according to the user's language and culture. In ASP.NET, you create resource assemblies by simply creating ad hoc resource files in appropriate folders: *App_LocalResources* for resources local to the views, and *App_GlobalResources* for resources visible from within all views. Figure 8-4 shows the local resource folder for the views of a particular controller.

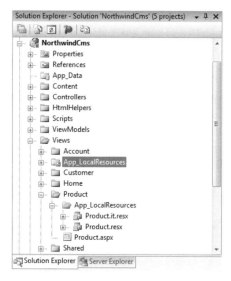

FIGURE 8-4 Local resources for the views related to the *Product* controller

Let's find out more about global and local resources.

Overall Strategy for Global and Local Resources

In general terms, a local resource file is a resource file specific to a page or a bunch of pages located in the same folder. The visibility of the resource strings doesn't overcome the boundaries of the folder. A simple naming convention binds the file to the page. If the page is named *sample.aspx*, its corresponding resource file will be *sample.aspx.resx*. To be precise, this resource file is language neutral and has no culture defined. To create a resource assembly for a specific culture—say, Italian—you need to name the resource file as follows: *sample.aspx.it.resx*. The *it* string should be replaced with any other equivalent string that identifies a culture, such as *fr* for French or *en* for English.

A global resource file is a resource file that is available to all pages of the application. It is placed in the *App_GlobalResources* ASP.NET folder and can be named at will. Multiple files can be placed in the same folder.

Global and local resource files can happily coexist in the same application. Finding the right balance between what's global and what's local is ultimately up to you. From what I have learned on the battlefield, having a single global file to hold all localizable resources turns into a not-so-pleasant experience even for a moderately complex Web application. One issue is the size of the file, which grows significantly; another issue, which is even more painful, is the possible concurrent editing that multiple developers might be doing on the same file with the subsequent need for a continuous merge. However, I encourage you not to overlook the naming issue. When you have hundreds of strings that cover the entire application scope, how do you name them? Many strings look the same or differ only on subtle points. Many strings are not entire strings with some sensible meaning; they often are bits and pieces of some text to be completed with dynamically generated content. Trust me: naming a few of them in the restricted context of only some pages is doable; handling hundreds of them for the entire application is really painful.

Overall, the best approach seems to be having multiple resource files—either local or global. You might start with a local resource file for each page, and then merge strings and other resources into a global resource file as you find them referenced from multiple pages.

Dealing with Resources in ASP.NET

In classic ASP.NET, local resources are strictly page-specific in the sense that if properly named after the ASPX source file, the content of a resource file can be referenced using direct syntax from the markup, as shown here:

```
<asp:Label runat="server" ID="Label1"
          meta:resourcekey="Label1_ResourceID" />
```

The *resourcekey* meta attribute indicates that property values for the *Label1* control are to be taken from a page-specific resource file. If the resource file for the page contains an entry such as *Label1_ResourceID.Text*, the *Text* property of *Label1* will be set to the stored value. The same can be done for any other properties.

This feature is specific to server controls and can be used in ASP.NET MVC only if you populate your views with server-control references.

Global resources—that is, content placed in a resource file within *App_GlobalResources*—can be referenced in one of two ways. You can do it programmatically via the *GetGlobalResourceObject* method of the *HttpContext* object:

```
var msg = HttpContext.GetGlobalResourceObject("globals.resx", "WelcomeMessage");
```

Alternately, you can reference global resources declaratively from the markup through the *$Resources* expression as shown here:

```
<asp:Literal runat="server" Text="<% $Resources:Globals, WelcomeMessage %>" />
```

As you can see, many of the built-in features of ASP.NET are aimed at server controls, which might not be the way you build views in ASP.NET MVC. For this reason, the distinction between *App_GlobalResources* and *App_LocalResources* is blurred in ASP.NET MVC.

Dealing with Resources in ASP.NET MVC

I deliberately used the term *page* earlier to force the idea that this is how it works in ASP.NET. Let's now see what sort of an ad hoc strategy you can come up with in ASP.NET MVC.

In ASP.NET MVC, you don't really need the facilities specifically built by the framework for declarative server controls programming. My suggestion, therefore, is to ignore that difference and just be ready to manage resource files as individual project items, making yourself responsible for the partition in multiple assemblies.

You might start by adding a Resource item to the project. When you do so, an RESX file is added to the root of the project. (See Figure 8-5.)

Any string you place in such a file is global and can be referenced from any view. You can also scope resources to one view or to a few views. However, you do that using naming conventions such as ad hoc file names and different namespaces.

All RESX files that use the default language are compiled to the same assembly as the application. This is the case for files whose name doesn't include a culture reference, such as *errors.resx*, *global.resx*, *product.resx*, and so forth. Culture-specific resources are compiled in separate assemblies, one per culture. I also suggest you consider keeping even default resources in their own assembly. All you need to do is create a new class library project, drop all RESX files in it (including localized versions), and reference the library from the main application.

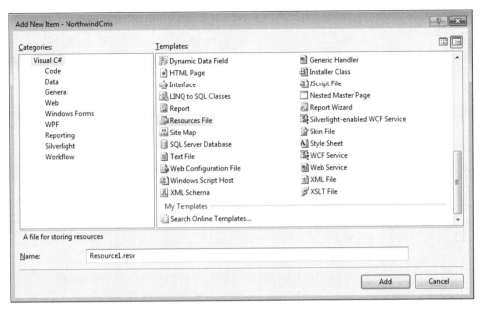

FIGURE 8-5 Adding a new resource file

Consuming Localized Resources

An RESX file is ultimately an XML file that gets compiled on the fly by the Microsoft Visual Studio designer. It originates a C# class like the one shown here:

```
namespace NorthwindCms {
  using System.Resources;
  using System.Globalization;

  internal class MyGlobals
  {
      private static ResourceManager resourceMan;
      private static CultureInfo resourceCulture;
      internal static ResourceManager ResourceManager
      {
        get {
           if (resourceMan == null) {
               var temp = new ResourceManager("NorthwindCms.MyGlobals",
                               typeof(MyGlobals).Assembly);
               resourceMan = temp;
           }
           return resourceMan;
        }
      }
      internal static global::System.Globalization.CultureInfo Culture {
          get { return resourceCulture; }
          set { resourceCulture = value; }
      }
```

```
internal static string WelcomeMessage {
    get {
        return ResourceManager.GetString("WelcomeMessage", resourceCulture);
    }
}
```

⋮

}

As a developer, you have some control over the namespace and the access modifier of the class members. In other words, when you add a resource to the project you can choose whether to make all the properties public or internal (the default) and decide which namespace will group them. A *public* modifier is necessary if you're compiling resources in their own assembly. (See Figure 8-6.)

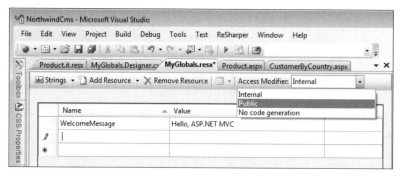

FIGURE 8-6 Selecting the access modifier for resource strings

Also make sure that in the project the resource file is associated with the Embedded Resource build action. (See Figure 8-7.)

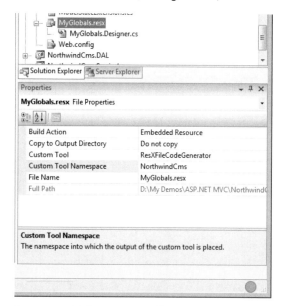

FIGURE 8-7 Adding a resource file as an embedded resource

You set the global namespace through the Custom Tool Namespace property shown in Figure 8-7. The access modifier and namespace are important because they contribute to determining the expression you use in your views to reference a localized string or resource. Here's what you need:

```
<%= NorhtwindCms.MyGlobals.WelcomeMessage %>
```

The preceding expression guarantees that either the language-neutral value or the localized value is retrieved and displayed. The resource manager will pick up the right assembly resource for the current culture.

> **Note** There are various options for referencing localizable resources. The approach presented here is strongly typed and causes compile-time errors if you happen to use invalid object names. Another popular approach you find described in a number of posts entails using a made-to-measure HTML helper that gets the resource file and item name and returns localized content. Finally, you can still directly call the resource-specific methods on *HttpContext*. All these techniques are functionally equivalent; picking one is mostly a matter of preference, with strong typing being the only core reason for choosing one over the other.

Setting the Current Culture

In the .NET Framework, the culture is set on the current thread through the *CurrentCulture* and *CurrentUICulture* properties. In general, both properties are necessary when you want to support multiple languages in a page or view. In fact, the two properties refer to distinct capabilities and have an impact on different areas of the user interface.

The *CurrentCulture* property affects the results of functions, such as the date, the number, and currency formatting. The *CurrentUICulture* property, on the other hand, determines the localized resource file from which page resources are loaded. The following code snippet shows a possible way to arrange a unit test aimed at testing whether culture-specific items are correctly retrieved. If you intend to test only whether resource files are being used as expected, you can comment out the setting of *CurrentCulture*.

```
const string culture = "it-IT";
var cultureInfo = CultureInfo.CreateSpecificCulture(culture);
Thread.CurrentThread.CurrentCulture = cultureInfo;
Thread.CurrentThread.CurrentUICulture = cultureInfo;
```

Note that the two culture properties might or might not have the same value. For example, you can switch the language of text and messages according to the browser's configuration while leaving globalization settings (such as dates and currency) constant.

In ASP.NET, you use similar properties on the *Page* class to set the current culture: *Culture* and *UICulture*. The value of *Auto* assigned to *UICulture* automatically selects the browser's language for the thread in charge of the request. In this way, the user is responsible for the language of the pages.

You can also employ a global setting for the culture by using the <*globalization*> section of the *web.config* file:

```
<globalization uiculture="it" culture="it-IT" / >
```

Most of the time, though, what you really want is the ability to set the culture programmatically and the ability to change it on the fly as the user switches to a different culture by clicking an icon or using a culture-specific URL.

Changing Culture on the Fly

To change the culture programmatically, you need to satisfy two key requirements. First, define the policies you'll be using to retrieve the culture to set. The policy can be a value you read from some database table or perhaps from the ASP.NET cache. It can also be a value you retrieve from the URL. Finally, it can even be a parameter you get via geolocation—that is, by looking at the IP address the user is using for connecting.

After you have the culture to set, you have to set it by acting on the current thread, as shown earlier. Note that the culture must be set for each request because each request runs on its own thread. In ASP.NET MVC, an easy way to achieve this is by using a custom action invoker. As mentioned, the action invoker is the component that takes care of executing each controller method. By overriding the *InvokeAction* method, you can set the desired culture on the current thread and make sure that this setting is automatically applied for every request.

```
public class MyActionInvoker : ControllerActionInvoker
{
    public override bool InvokeAction(
            ControllerContext controllerContext, string actionName)
    {
        string lang = DetermineLocaleToEnforce(controllerContext);
        Thread.CurrentThread.CurrentUICulture = CultureInfo.CreateSpecificCulture(lang);
        return base.InvokeAction(controllerContext, actionName);
    }

    private string DetermineLocaleToEnforce(ControllerContext context)
    {
        // Current language assumed to be in a specific location of the Cache
        string lang = "en-us";
        object o = controllerContext.HttpContext.Cache["Lang"];
        if (o != null)
            lang = o as string;

        return lang;
    }
}
```

With this infrastructure in place, you can add links to your pages (typically, the master page) to switch languages on the fly:

```
<%= Html.ActionLink("Italian", "SwitchLang", "Home", new { lang = "it" }, null) %
<%= Html.ActionLink("English", "SwitchLang", "Home", new { lang = "en" }, null)%>
```

The action method simply stores the newly selected language in the store you selected—the ASP.NET cache in the example—and redirects:

```
public virtual void SwitchLang(string lang)
{
    if (String.Equals(lang, "it", StringComparison.InvariantCultureIgnoreCase))
        SetCulture("it-it");
    else
        SetCulture("en-us");

    // Return to the calling URL (or go to the site's home page)
    HttpContext.Response.Redirect(HttpContext.Request.UrlReferrer.AbsolutePath);
}

private void SetCulture(string lang)
{
    HttpContext.Cache["Lang"] = lang;
}
```

All you need to do is ensure that the current culture identifier is stored somewhere. Next, for each request, the modified invoker will do the job.

Finally, how do you replace the action invoker? Here's some sample code:

```
public BaseController()
{
    this.ActionInvoker = new MyActionInvoker();
}
```

For a site that supports language switches, you can use a base controller class that exposes the preceding constructor. Otherwise, you can set the custom invoker only for the controllers for which you intend to support localization.

> **Note** More and more Web sites check the location from where a user is connected and suggest a language and a culture. This feature requires an API that looks up the IP address and maps that to a country and then a culture. Some browsers (for example, Firefox 3.5, Safari, iPhone, and Opera) have built-in geolocation capabilities that work according to the W3C API. (See *http://www.mozilla.com/firefox/geolocation.*)
>
> To support other browsers (including Internet Explorer), you can resort to third-party services such as Google Gears. Google Gears is a plug-in that extends your browser in various ways, including adding a geolocation API that returns the country of the user from the current geographical location. Note that Google returns the ISO 3166 code of the country (for example, *GB* for the United Kingdom) and its full name. From here, you have to determine the language to use. The country code doesn't always match the language. For the United Kingdom, the language is *en*. To install Google Gears, pay a visit to *http://gears.google.com.*

Storing Localized Resources in a Database

While discussing localization, it seems inevitable that you have to talk about databases as a possible store for localized data. Is this an option? You bet. However, there are some pros and cons to consider.

In the first place, using a database adds latency even though you will not be making a database call for each segment of a view to be localized. Most likely, instead, you'll read a bunch of records and probably cache them for a long time. The performance hit represented by using the database in this way is therefore less devastating than one might think at first.

Storing localization data inside a database requires a custom localization layer, whereas going through the classic XML-based approach of resource files doesn't lead you to writing much extra code and offers you excellent support from the Visual Studio designers.

When the number of views become significant (for example, in the order of hundreds), the number of resource items will be at least in the order of thousands. At this point, managing them can be problematic. You can have too many assemblies loaded in the AppDomain consuming runtime memory, and that will have an impact on the overall performance of the site. Hence, a database is probably the best way to go for a large share of localizable content.

Data stored within a relational database is easier to manage, query, and cache, and the size is not an issue. In addition, with a database and a custom localization layer you gain more flexibility in the overall retrieval process of local resources. In fact, you can ask the layer for a group of strings—or, better yet, for raw data—to then be formatted for the needs of UI. In other words, a custom localization layer decouples you from maintaining a direct binding between resource item and specific pieces of the user interface.

Dependency Injection

ASP.NET MVC is a deeply stratified framework where a great number of native components are designed to be easily replaced with custom components that implement the same interface. In this regard, you can say that ASP.NET MVC is a natural habitat for implementing extensibility patterns such as the Dependency Injection (DI) pattern.

Dependency injection is a relatively recent term introduced by Martin Fowler to replace, and further specialize, another popular term that was in use for many years (especially in the Java space)—Inversion of Control (IoC). Today, *DI* tends to indicate the general pattern, whereas

IoC is a term that describes a family of powerful productivity tools widely employed in the implementation of the DI pattern—IoC containers.

ASP.NET MVC lends itself very well to DI and IoC containers, which are ideal tools to leverage the natural extensibility of the ASP.NET MVC framework. As a result, implementing forms of dependency injection is a necessary step in nearly any ASP.NET MVC—whether for gaining the benefits of customizing certain areas (for example, the controller factory or the action invoker) or to achieve more testability. A reference to an IoC container is therefore a common presence in most ASP.NET MVC projects.

Before taking a closer look at an IoC container, let's briefly review the theory of dependency injection and focus on a key principle in today's software design—the Dependency Inversion Principle (DIP).

> **Note** Dependency inversion is one of the design principles at the foundation of software development that are today summarized under the umbrella term *SOLID* (along with Single Responsibility, Open/Closed, Liskov's Substitutability, and Interface Segregation).

Dependency Inversion in Action

Defined, the Dependency Inversion Principle states that high-level classes should not depend on lower-level classes. High-level classes, instead, should always depend on abstractions of their required lower-level classes. In a way, this principle is a specialization of one of the pillars of object-oriented design—program to an interface, not to an implementation.

DIP is the formalization of a top-down approach to defining the behavior of any significant class method. In using this top-down approach, you focus on the work flow that happens at the method level rather than focusing on the implementation of its particular dependencies. At some point, though, lower-level classes should be linked to the mainstream code. DIP suggests that this should happen via injection.

In a way, DIP indicates an inversion of the control flow whenever a dependency is met— the main flow doesn't care about details of the dependency as long as it has access to an abstraction of it. The dependency is then resolved in some way. Figure 8-8 shows the classic DIP diagram for the canonical example of DIP as originally presented by Robert Martin in the paper you can find at the following URL: *http://www.objectmentor.com/resources/ articles/dip.pdf*.

The paper describes a sample Copy function that reads from a source and writes to a target stream. The Copy function ideally doesn't care about the details of the reader and writer components. It should care only about the interface of the reader and writer. Reader and writer are then injected or resolved in some way around the implementation of the

Copy function. How this point is approached depends on the actual pattern you intend to use.

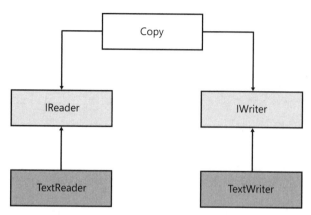

FIGURE 8-8 The DIP diagram

To address DIP, you commonly use either of two patterns: the Service Locator pattern or the Dependency Injection pattern.

The Service Locator Pattern

The Service Locator pattern defines a component that knows how to retrieve the services an application might need. The caller has no need to specify the concrete type; the caller normally indicates an interface, a base type, or even a nickname of the service in the form of a string or a numeric code.

The implementation of a Service Locator pattern is typically based on an instance of the Factory pattern plus any additional logic that is needed to figure out the components to instantiate. The Service Locator pattern hides the complexity of component lookup, handles caching or pooling of instances and, in general, offers a common façade for component lookup and creation. Here's the typical implementation of a service locator:

```
public class ServiceLocator
{
    private static const string SERVICE_QUOTEPROVIDER = "quoteprovider";

    // You might also want to have a generic method GetService<T>()...
    public static object GetService(Type t)
    {
      if (t == typeof(IQuoteProvider))
      {
        return new SomeQuoteProvider();
      }
```

```
       ⋮

    }

    public static object GetService(string serviceName)
    {
        switch(serviceName)
        {
            case SERVICE_QUOTEPROVIDER:
                return new SomeQuoteProvider();
                ⋮


        }
    }
}
```

As you can see, the locator is merely a wrapper around a *Factory* object that knows how to get an instance of a given (or indirectly referenced) type. Let's have a look now at the code that calls the locator. The following code illustrates a class that first gets quotes for the specified list of symbols and then renders values out to an HTML string:

```
public class FinanceInfoService
{
  public string GetQuotesAsHtml(string symbols)
  {
    // Get the Finder component
    IQuoteProvider provider = ServiceLocator.GetService("quoteprovider");
    StockInfo[] stocks = provider.FindQuoteInfo(symbols);

    // Get the Renderer component
    IRenderer renderer = ServiceLocator.GetService("quoterenderer");
    string html = renderer.RenderQuoteInfo(stocks);

    return html;
  }
}
```

The locator code lives inside the method that manages the abstraction, and the factory is part of the deal. By simply looking at the signature of the *FinanceInfoService* class, you can't say whether or not it has dependencies on external components. You have to inspect the code of the *GetQuotesAsHtml* method to find it out.

The main Service Locator focus is to achieve the lowest possible amount of coupling between components. The locator represents a centralized console that an application uses to obtain all the external dependencies it needs. In doing so, the Service Locator pattern also produces the pleasant side effect of making your code more flexible and extensible.

Using the Service Locator pattern is not a bad thing from a purely functional perspective. However, in more practical terms a likely better option exists: the DI pattern.

The Dependency Injection Pattern

The biggest difference between Service Locator and DI is that with dependency injection the factory code lives outside of the class being worked on. The pattern suggests that you design the class in such a way that it receives all of its dependencies from the outside. Here's how to rewrite the *FinanceInfoService* class for making use of DI:

```
public class FinanceInfoService
{
    private IQuoteProvider _provider;
    private IRenderer _renderer;

    public FinanceInfoService(IQuoteProvider provider, IRenderer renderer)
    {
        _provider = provider;
        _renderer = renderer;
    }

    public string GetQuotesAsHtml(string symbols)
    {
        StockInfo[] stocks = _provider.FindQuoteInfo(symbols);
        string html = _renderer.RenderQuoteInfo(stocks);
        return html;
    }
}
```

When it comes to using DI in classes, a critical decision for the developer is about how and where to allow for code injection. There are three ways to inject dependencies into a class— using the constructor, a settable property, or the parameters of a method. All techniques are valid, and the choice is ultimately up to you. In general terms, the consensus is for using constructors for necessary dependencies and setters for optional dependencies. However, some considerations apply.

Injection Mechanisms

Using the constructor seems to be the default approach to tackle. In the first place, it is always desirable to have valid objects from the beginning. In light of this, when a class needs a dependency, the dependency has to be injected at construction time. However, what if you have many dependencies? In this case, your constructor would look dangerously messy.

Even though a long list of parameters in the constructor is often the sign of some design issues, this isn't a hard-and-fast rule. You might encounter situations where you have complex constructors with many parameters. In this case, grouping dependencies in a compound object is a solution. In ASP.NET MVC, you see this pattern frequently used in the implementation of the controller logic. Any *XxxContext* class you run across in ASP.NET MVC is ultimately a way to group multiple dependencies together.

In a nutshell, your goal should be to reveal dependencies and intentions right at construction time. This can be done in two ways: via a set of classic constructors you manage to keep as simple as possible or via factories.

Factories are the preferred approach in the Domain-Driven Design (DDD) methodology. Using a factory, you can express more clearly the context in which you need an instance of the type. You can also deal with dependencies inside the factory code and ensure you return valid objects from the beginning. In addition, your classes end up having only the default constructor (probably implemented as a protected member).

Using constructors also hinders inheritance because derived classes might have the need to receive dependencies as well. When you add a new dependency, this design scheme might require more refactoring work.

When the dependency is optional, however, there's no strict need to make it show up at the constructor level. In this case, using a setter property is fine and probably the recommended approach that helps keeping the constructor (or factory code) leaner and cleaner.

In summary, there are good reasons for using the constructor and good reasons for going with setter properties. As with many other architectural questions, the right answer is, "*It depends.*" And it depends also on your personal taste.

> **Note** The complexity and duration of the solution you are developing is another important parameter you need to consider. In an enterprise scenario when discussing large domain models, as an architect I mostly recommend using factories rather than constructors, and passing factories whatever dependencies they need to create instances of the valid type for the specific context. Anything else that is optional can go through setter properties.
>
> Admittedly, I'm mixing two different aspects of class design: the injection mechanism (constructors vs. setters) and instantiation mechanism (constructors vs. factories). They are related, however. In fact, one argument you might hear against using injection via constructors is to avoid spoiling constructors by using too many parameters for the sake of inheritance. In relatively simpler scenarios, any injection mechanism is probably fine, and you get just the one you feel most comfortable with.

A Simple and Highly Testable Solution

Dependency injection is a great solution because it decouples your mainstream code and its dependencies. Subsequently, dependencies are to be created and then injected. On the other hand, the work required to create instances is certainly repetitive; it is also error prone, especially if you're dealing with complex and nested hierarchies of dependencies. This is exactly the driving force that brought about IoC containers.

Before I get to IoC containers, however, let me refine the code shown earlier for the *FinanceInfoService* class to make it more effective in both testing and implementing use-cases:

```
public class FinanceInfoService
{
   private IQuoteProvider _provider;
   private IRenderer _renderer;

   public FinanceInfoService()
   {
      _provider = _provider ?? new DefaultQuoteProvider();
      _renderer = _renderer ?? new DefaultHtmlRenderer();
   }

   public FinanceInfoService(IQuoteProvider provider, IRenderer renderer)
   {
      _provider = provider;
      _renderer = renderer;
   }
   .
   .
   .
}
```

In this version, the *FinanceInfoService* class features a default constructor that resolves all necessary dependencies in a default way—that is, by directly using an implementation of a type or, if you prefer, using the world's simplest embedded locator. The second constructor, instead, accepts all dependencies explicitly and is great for testability. In situations where factories are overkill, this solution offers a good balance between testability, good design, and programming comfort.

IoC Containers

An IoC container is a framework specifically created to support DI. It can be considered a productivity tool for implementing DI quickly and effectively. From the perspective of an application, a container is a rich factory that provides access to external objects to be retrieved and consumed later.

All IoC frameworks are built around a container object that, when bound to some configuration information, resolves dependencies. The caller code instantiates the container and passes the desired interface as an argument. In response, the IoC framework returns a concrete object that implements that interface. An IoC container holds a dictionary of type mappings where typically an abstract type (for example, an interface) is mapped to a concrete type or an instance of a given concrete type. Table 8-1 lists some of the most popular IoC frameworks available today.

TABLE 8-1 **Popular IoC frameworks**

Framework	URL
Autofac	*http://code.google.com/p/autofac*
Castle Windsor	*http://www.castleproject.org/container/index.html*
NInject	*http://www.ninject.org*
Spring.NET	*http://www.springframework.net*
StructureMap	*http://structuremap.sourceforge.net/Default.htm*
Unity	*http://codeplex.com/unity*

After it is configured, an IoC container gives you the ability to resolve the whole chain of dependencies between your types with a single call. And you save yourself all the intricacies of inner dependencies. For example, if you have some *ISomeService* parameter in a class constructor or property, you can be sure you'll get it at run time as long as you tell the IoC container to resolve it. The beauty of this approach is that if the constructor of the concrete type mapped to *ISomeService* has its own dependencies, these are resolved as well and automatically.

Take this further and you see the point: with an IoC container, you stop caring about the cloud of dependencies. Furthermore, all you do is design the graph of dependencies using the syntax supported by the IoC of choice. Everything else happens free of charge.

Advanced Features of IoC Containers

As mentioned, an IoC container is born to be a smart factory. If you don't give it any other responsibilities, you can reasonably write a fully functional (yet simple) IoC container with very few lines of code. (See *http://ayende.com/Blog/archive/2007/10/20/Building-an-IoC-container-in-15-lines-of-code.aspx* for a nice proof of concept.) So what's the difference between a simple IoC that takes 15 lines to work and an IoC library of several thousands of lines? The answer is fairly obvious: features.

Table 8-1 lists six different IoC containers. IoC containers differ in terms of the syntax they support (for example, lambda expressions), the configuration policies (for example, the external XML scheme), plus additional features. Two features are gaining a lot of importance today: aspect-orientation capabilities and specialized modules that facilitate integration with specific Web or Windows technologies. In particular, I feel that aspect-oriented programming (AOP) is an excellent source of some IoC tools, and it's even better if coupled with integration modules. As a quick example, consider the aspect-oriented capabilities of Spring.NET with regard to WCF services.

Spring.NET comes with its own service host factory that takes care of creating proxies for a given WCF service. Here's the code you need to put in a *.svc* service endpoint file to enable the Spring's WCF factory:

```
<%@ ServiceHost Service="calculator"
                Factory="Spring.ServiceModel.Activation.ServiceHostFactory" %>
```

At this point, the service delegates its instantiation process to the library, meaning that the library can automatically resolve some dependencies and surround the execution of each method with pre- and post-interceptors. Note that by using an AOP-enabled framework you don't change anything in the code of the WCF service. All you might need to change to add AOP to an existing service is the *Factory* attribute in the *.svc* file. Next, you need the following in the application's configuration file:

```
<objects xmlns="http://www.springframework.net"
         xmlns:aop="http://www.springframework.net/aop">

    <!-- Define the service to be customized -->
    <object id="someService" singleton="false" type="YourApp.Services.SomeService">
        <property name="SampleProperty" value="..." />
    </object>

    <!-- Define the services to be intercepted: all found in the specified namespace -->
    <object id="interceptedServices"
            type="Spring.Aop.Support.SdkRegularExpressionMethodPointcut, Spring.Aop">
        <property name="pattern" value=" YourApp.Services.*" />
    </object>

    <!-- Define interceptors to be added -->
    <object id="newBehavior" type="YourApp.Extensions.SomeInterceptor">
        <property name="..." value="..." />
        .
        .
        .
    </object>

    <!-- Configure AOP -->
    <aop:config>
        <aop:advisor pointcut-ref="interceptedServices" advice-ref="newBehavior" />
    </aop:config>
</objects>
```

First you register the WCF service with the Spring.NET framework. At this time, you specify any required properties to be injected. Next, you define a point-cut and advice as in a classic AOP framework. A point-cut identifies the classes to be added to some new behavior (or an *aspect* or advice if you use the AOP jargon).

IoC containers are primarily a productivity tool because they retrieve object instances for you. However, some of them offer advanced features that can be used to implement an extremely powerful extensibility layer on top of your application. I'll return to the topic of scenarios for using IoC containers within ASP.NET MVC in a moment. For now let's get acquainted with a particular IoC container—Unity, the IoC container available from Microsoft.

> **Note** In the .NET Framework 4, a new subsystem makes its debut, and it is closely related
> to dependency injection. The framework is the Managed Extensibility Framework (MEF).
> Dependency injection is only part of the work that MEF tries to do. In brief, MEF provides
> a programming model for classes to declare which properties they intend to import and which
> properties they intend to publicly export.

A Brief Tour of Unity

Unity is an open-source project from Microsoft aimed at creating a classic IoC framework for
developers to build object instances in a smart and highly configurable way. In this chapter,
I'll focus on version 1.2; however, be aware that version 2.0 ships in the same time frame of
Visual Studio 2010.

To add Unity to a project, you add a reference to the *Microsoft.Practices.Unity* and
Microsoft.Practices.ObjectBuilder2 assemblies, plus a third one—the *Microsoft.Practices
.Unity.Configuration* assembly—if you configure the container using the application's
configuration file.

Let's see how to accomplish some key IoC operations with Unity, such as registering types
both programmatically and declaratively.

Registering Types and Instances

In Unity, the container type is *UnityContainer* and you use it to register types and instances,
as shown here:

```
var container = new UnityContainer();
container
      .RegisterType<IServiceLayer,
                     DefaultServiceLayer>()
      .RegisterType<ICustomerRepository,
                     CustomerRepository>();
var serviceLayer = container.Resolve<IServiceLayer>();
```

You use the *RegisterType* method to establish a mapping between an abstract type and
a concrete type. If the same abstract type should be mapped to different types in different
contexts of the same application, you can use the following overload:

```
container
   .RegisterType<ILogger, DefaultLogger>()
   .RegisterType<ILogger, FileLogger>("Tracing");
```

The additional string parameter disambiguates the request and gives Unity enough
information about which concrete type to pick up. You use *RegisterInstance* instead of
RegisterType to supply a prebuilt instance of a type to the container.

Does it really make sense for an application to pass to a factory the instance it will get back later? The purpose is to preserve the benefits of an IoC also in situations in which you can't annotate a class to be automatically resolved by Unity.

To see an example of this, let's first introduce the syntax required to annotate constructors and properties for injection. When requested to create an instance of a given type, Unity gets information about the constructors of the type. If multiple constructors are found, Unity picks up the one with the longest signature. If multiple options are available, an exception is thrown. It might be the case, however, that you want a particular constructor to be used. This requires that an attribute be attached to the selected constructor:

```
[InjectionConstructor]
public MyClass()
{
    .
    .
    .
}
```

If you have no access to the source code, you might want to consider *RegisterInstance*. Similarly, if injection happens through the setter of a property, you need to decorate the property accordingly, as shown here:

```
private ILogger _logger;

[Dependency]
public ILogger Logger
{
    get { return _logger; }
    set { _logger = value; }
}
```

RegisterType and *RegisterInstance* are the methods you work with if you opt for configuring the Unity framework programmatically. However, offline configuration is also supported via an ad hoc section in the application's configuration file. In any case, programmatic and declarative configuration is totally equivalent.

Resolving Dependencies

In Unity, you invoke the method *Resolve* on the container to trigger the process that returns an instance of the type at the root of the dependency chain:

```
container.Resolve(registeredType);
```

The resolver can be passed any additional information it might need to figure out the correct type to return:

```
var logger = container.Resolve<ILogger>("Tracing");
```

The *ResolveAll* method is used instead to resolve in a single step all objects registered with the specified abstract type.

Declarative Configuration

The Unity framework comes with a custom configuration section that can be merged with the *web.config* file of a Web application. Here's the script you need to register types:

```
<unity>
   <containers>
      <container name="MyApp">
         <types>
            <type type="ILogger" mapTo="DefaultLogger">
               <lifetime type="singleton"/>
               <typeConfig>
                  <constructor>
                     <param name="sourceName" parameterType="string">
                        <value value="default"/>
                     </param>
                  </constructor>
               </typeConfig>
            </type>
         </types>
      </container>
   </containers>
</unity>
```

Under the *<types>* section, you list the abstract types mapped to some concrete implementation. The following code shows how to map *ILogger* to *DefaultLogger*:

```
<type type="ILogger" mapTo="DefaultLogger">
```

Taking the declarative approach, you can also select the constructor to be used and set up the lifetime of the instance. To configure the Unity container with the information in the *web.config* file, you need the following code:

```
var container = new UnityContainer();

// Retrieve the <unity> section
var section = ConfigurationManager.GetSection("unity") as UnityConfigurationSection;
if (section != null)
{
    // Retrieve the specified container by name
    UnityContainerElement containerElement = section.Containers["MyApp"];

    // Load information into the specified instance of the container
    if (containerElement != null)
        containerElement.Configure(container);
}
```

As it turns out, Unity allows you to have multiple containers with different settings to load as appropriate.

Lifetime Managers

Just like any other IoC framework, Unity allows you to assign a fixed lifetime to any managed instance of mapped types. By default, Unity doesn't apply any special policy to control the lifetime of the object returned for a registered type. It simply creates a new instance of the type each time you call the *Resolve* or *ResolveAll* method. However, the reference to the object is not stored so that a new one is required to serve a successive call.

The default behavior can be modified by using any of the predefined lifetime managers you find in Unity. Table 8-2 lists them.

TABLE 8-2 Lifetime managers

Class	Description
ContainerControlledLifetimeManager	Singleton
ExternallyControlledLifetimeManager	Singleton, but one that holds a weak reference so that the garbage can clear it if it's out of scope
PerThreadControlledLifetimeManager	Per-thread singleton

You can also create custom managers by inheriting the *LifetimeManager* base class.

Here's how you set a lifetime manager in code:

```
container
    .RegisterType<ILogger, DefaultLogger>(
        "Tracing",
        new ContainerControlledLifetimeManager());
```

Here's what you need instead to set a lifetime manager declaratively:

```
<type type="ILogger" mapTo="DefaultLogger">
    <lifetime type="singleton" />
</type>
```

Note, however, that the word *singleton* you assign to the *type* attribute is not a keyword or a phrase with a special meaning. More simply, it is intended to be an alias for a type that must be declared explicitly:

```
<typeAliases>

    <!-- Lifetime manager types -->
    <typeAlias alias="singleton"
        type="Microsoft.Practices.Unity.ContainerControlledLifetimeManager,
            Microsoft.Practices.Unity" />
    <typeAlias alias="perThread"
        type="Microsoft.Practices.Unity.PerThreadLifetimeManager,
            Microsoft.Practices.Unity" />
    <typeAlias alias="external"
        type="Microsoft.Practices.Unity.ExternallyControlledLifetimeManager,
            Microsoft.Practices.Unity" />
```

```
<!-User-defined aliases -->
<typeAlias alias="IMyInterface"
    type="MyApplication.MyTypes.MyInterface, MyApplication.MyTypes" />
    ⋮
</typeAliases>
```

After you have the aliases all set, you can use alias names in the section where you register types.

Creating a Global Container

Let's consider now the steps required to integrate Unity with an ASP.NET MVC application. ASP.NET MVC pushes you toward the creation of layered applications where you have an overall architecture like the one shown in Figure 8-9.

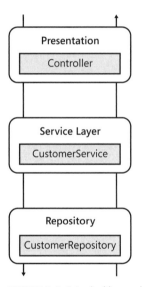

FIGURE 8-9 A typical layered architecture for an ASP.NET MVC application

This model implies that the controller needs to instantiate a class that implements the use-cases for a given context—the customer operations. Next, the *CustomerService* class will likely need to perform some data access. All classes might have dependencies on some cross-cutting module such as a logger. How would you handle this?

In Chapter 4, I discussed controllers with at least a couple of constructors—one bound to the expected behavior and one accepting dependencies. The second constructor mostly serves the need of unit tests and lets you test the controller (and the service layer classes) in isolation, as dependencies can be easily mocked up. This is an effective, yet manual, implementation of raw dependency injection.

Let's reconsider the same scenario in light of IoC tools and see how Unity (or another IoC framework) works. The final effect is the same, but with IoC, you have in place a much more extensible and flexible solution. So an IoC will give you more than just dependency injection. The real question to answer is whether you need all of it. So don't be too surprised if you realize that in your relatively simple scenario IoC is overkill.

> **Tip** Adding an extra constructor to a class for the sole purpose of testability might not be acceptable in some cases. In this case, the .NET Framework offers an elegant and effective solution through partial classes. If the class is marked as partial, in the test project you can add a twin partial class that completes the base one by adding the extra constructor. In this way, you preserve testability without spoiling your design.

Custom Controller Factory

In ASP.NET MVC, the instantiation of the controller class is automated (even though sometimes you might like control over this automation process, which is something Chapter 11 discusses). The execution of the request determines the response for the user and any impact on the middle tier. The ASP.NET MVC infrastructure includes a factory that uses the default constructor of the selected controller class. What if you have parameterized constructors on your controller class and need to pass in some data?

This scenario is not supported out of the box, but the extremely extensible design of ASP.NET MVC offers a hook for you to replace the default controller factory with your own. A common way to replace the default controller factory is to integrate an IoC container in it so that any parameter can be resolved brilliantly by looking at the table of registered types. Here's how to do it.

It all starts in *Application_Start*, where you register your own controller factory. A controller factory is a class that implements the *IControllerFactory* interface. To register the factory, you pass an instance of the *SetControllerFactory* method to the current instance of the controller builder:

```
protected void Application_Start()
{
    RegisterRoutes(RouteTable.Routes);
    :
    :

    // Register a custom controller factory
    RegisterControllerFactory();
}
public static void RegisterControllerFactory()
{
    // Create and configure the container to pass as an argument to the factory
    var container = new UnityContainer();
    :
    :
```

```
    // Create and register the factory
    IControllerFactory factory = new MyAppControllerFactory(container);
    ControllerBuilder.Current.SetControllerFactory(factory);
}
```

Another method on the controller builder—*GetControllerFactory*—is used by the
ASP.NET MVC infrastructure to obtain a reference to the object actually responsible for
getting a controller instance. Let's see a controller factory from the inside:

```
public class MyAppControllerFactory : DefaultControllerFactory
{
    private IUnityContainer _container;
    public MyAppControllerFactory(IUnityContainer container)
    {
        _container = container;
    }

    protected override IController GetControllerInstance(Type controllerType)
    {
        if (controllerType == null)
            return null;
        return _container.Resolve(controllerType) as IController;
    }
}
```

As you can see, the controller is resolved via Unity instead of directly using the *new* operator.
This guarantees that further dependencies are identified and resolved.

Managing Dependencies

With a Unity-based factory in place, the following controller class can be safely instantiated:

```
public class CustomerController : Controller
{
    [InjectionConstructor]
    public CustomerController(ICustomerService service)
    {
        _service = service;
    }

    private readonly ICustomerService _service;

        :
        :
        :
}
```

Note that the *InjectionConstructor* is not strictly necessary unless you have additional
(and longer) constructors.

You can list as many dependencies as you need in the controller's constructor, and you
can even group them in a context object. Furthermore, you can add public properties to
your controller and have the factory resolve them (thus injecting logic into the controller

class) as long as the properties are decorated as dependencies and their types are properly registered with Unity.

This approach can be taken regardless of the IoC framework you choose. In this regard, a point to be further analyzed is the level of coupling you want between the constructor and the IoC framework. The *InjectionConstructor* attribute we employed in the preceding code snippet sets up a relationship between Unity and the controller class. In general, you might want to resort to the Unity's programmatic API to configure the controller:

```
container.RegisterType<CustomerController>(
        new InjectionConstructor(new ResolvedParameter<ICustomerService>()));
```

The code indicates that the constructor with a single parameter of type *ICustomerService* must be used to resolve *CustomerController*.

Some degree of coupling between your application and the IoC container is unavoidable; managing to keep coupling off the controllers is a great result. Code in *global.asax* and code in the controller's factory are inevitably bound to the IoC you're using.

Injecting a Custom Action Invoker

Earlier in this chapter, while discussing the localization features we ran into the need to replace the action invoker of some controllers. In particular, we found out that a specialized invoker is required to set the right culture on the current thread. You need to set the custom invoker on each controller interested in the localization features—nearly all controllers in the application. How do you do that?

The most obvious, but least enticing, option is that you modify the constructor of each controller as follows:

```
public class CustomerController()
{
    this.ActionInvoker = new MySpecialInvoker();
}
```

A slightly better solution is deriving all controllers from a base class—an approach you would probably take anyway—that provides a made-to-measure base constructor. Having a custom controller factory, however, makes it nifty and unobtrusive. Here's how to rewrite the controller factory:

```
public class MyAppControllerFactory : DefaultControllerFactory
{
    private IUnityContainer _container;
    public MyAppControllerFactory(IUnityContainer container)
    {
        _container = container;
    }
```

```
protected override IController GetControllerInstance(Type controllerType)
{
    if (controllerType == null)
        return null;

    var controller = container.Resolve(controllerType) as Controller;
    if (controller == null)
        return controller;

    // Set the action invoker that fully supports localization
    controller.ActionInvoker = new MyActionInvoker();

    return controller;
}
}
```

With this code in the project, when the user switches to a different language, all views and controllers are aware of it because the invoker ensures that the proper culture is set on the thread. As long as you have code and resource-aware markup, it just works.

Having a customer controller factory doesn't necessarily mean you have an IoC container around. If you don't have one, however, you can further improve the previous solution by resolving the action invoker type, as shown here:

```
controller.ActionInvoker = container.Resolve<IActionInvoker>();
```

In this case, you also need to add some configuration settings either in the *web.config* file or programmatically to let Unity know about the mapping between *IActionInvoker* and the actual type you intend to use. Here it is with the fluent API of Unity:

```
container.RegisterType<IActionInvoker, MyActionInvoker>();
```

The customization of the action invoker component is an important aspect of the extensibility model of ASP.NET MVC. I'll return to the topic of action invokers in Chapter 11.

Summary

An application built with ASP.NET MVC is primarily a Web application. Modern Web applications have more numerous requirements than only a few years ago. For example, a Web application today has to be SEO-friendly and must likely support full localization to be able to drive the user's actions using the user's specific language and culture. Finally, serving a notorious yellow-screen-of-death (namely, one of those default error pages of ASP.NET) is hardly acceptable; it still happens, but it is really a bad statement about the site. (An unhandled error has always been a bad thing, but the level of default forgiveness that users were according only a few years ago today is definitely a thing of the past.)

For all these reasons, the infrastructure of any Web applications (and, in this context, the infrastructure of ASP.NET MVC applications) need to be stronger and richer. In particular, you need to pay more attention to the URLs you recognize and design both for SEO and error handling. You need to design views and controllers to check the current locale and adjust graphics and messages automatically. You also need to detect the culture and let users switch among the languages you support.

To achieve many of these goals, you need to design your site for extensibility and separation of concerns. In practical terms this means applying the principle of Dependency Inversion extensively and systematically. In summary, a realistic site can hardly do without an IoC container today.

This chapter missed another key change that has characterized Web applications in the past five years—AJAX. How would you do AJAX in an ASP.NET MVC application? That's just what I'm going to cover in the next chapter.

Chapter 9
AJAX Capabilities

It matters not what someone is born, but what they grow to be.

—J. K. Rowling

As disappointing as it might sound, the term *AJAX* (Asynchronous JavaScript and XML) was coined around 2005 primarily as a concise and cool way to sell a set of technologies, and a new approach to Web development, to a customer. What initially was simply a clever approach to craft nice features inside a Web page eventually became the incarnation of a new paradigm for writing a new generation of Web applications. The AJAX approach is destined to last for the foreseeable future or until conditions exist to rebuild the Web from scratch.

AJAX is no longer a plus for the Web; AJAX is a native part of the Web. When you discuss use-cases and requirements with a customer, as long as a Web front end is involved, AJAX capabilities are an obvious part of the deal.

I foresee in the near future a scenario where we have two approaches to Web development: an evolved ASP.NET-based platform for server-side development using a classic programming language, and an ad hoc platform for JavaScript-intensive applications. In both cases, the client has to be rich and capable of placing requests asynchronously.

While waiting for such an exciting future, let's focus on what we have today for building a rich user interface for the Web. If AJAX is possible in Web Forms, it has to be possible in ASP.NET MVC too—and in a similar way. All solutions for AJAX that work in an ASP.NET Web Forms application can be successfully employed in an ASP.NET MVC application. In addition, ASP.NET MVC offers a bunch of HTML helpers optimized for offering certain AJAX functions at a very low cost for the developer.

Overall, the best service that ASP.NET MVC offers in an AJAX context is the total control over HTML (and subsequently, JavaScript) that it provides regardless of the view engine of choice. In this chapter, I'll first review the theme of AJAX programming in ASP.NET as a platform. Then I'll focus on the specific AJAX capabilities of the ASP.NET MVC framework.

AJAX in ASP.NET

The AJAX development model revolves around one common software element—the *XMLHttpRequest* object. The availability of this object in most browsers' object models is the key to the current ubiquity and success of AJAX applications. The *XMLHttpRequest* object allows script code to send HTTP requests and handle their responses. With *XMLHttpRequest*, developers directly control the placement and outcome of the request. The actual mechanics of the request/response activity doesn't make any difference to the user. However, the possibility of using *XMLHttpRequest* enables Web developers to build features that ultimately deliver a much better user experience.

So adding AJAX capabilities to a page requires only a bit of script code, and you can add AJAX capabilities to any page regardless of the underlying programming platform—be it classic ASP, ASP.NET, ASP.NET MVC, Java Server Pages, or PHP and so forth.

The use of *XMLHttpRequest* is hidden in a variety of APIs and exposed at various levels of abstraction. In ASP.NET, we can sum it up by mentioning two APIs: *partial rendering* and *direct scripting*.

Partial Rendering

Partial rendering is an interesting form of compromise between a pure AJAX approach and the existing code base of an ASP.NET application. The idea behind partial rendering is that you wrap any portions of the page that might be updated by some user in an ad hoc panel control. When a postback that refreshes that panel is requested, some "special" code executes that hooks up the postback process and returns only the delta of the page that has changed. That same *special code* then will take care of updating the current DOM tree with the fresh content just downloaded.

The Implementation

ASP.NET partial rendering is centered on a special container control—the *UpdatePanel* control—that you use to surround portions of existing pages or portions of new pages developed with the usual programming model of ASP.NET. A postback request that originates within any of these updatable regions is captured by the *UpdatePanel* control and resolved asynchronously using *XMLHttpRequest*. In this way, fresh HTML is downloaded for the selected region, bypassing the browser and reducing page flickering. Here's how you use the *UpdatePanel* control:

```
<asp:UpdatePanel runat="server" ID="UpdatePanel1">
    <ContentTemplate>
        <%--
            This region of the page can be updated separately from the rest.
            You only have to configure how and when.
        --%>
    </ContentTemplate>
    <Triggers>
        <%--
            List here server-side events that will cause the content
            of this panel to update asynchronously.
        --%>
    </Triggers>
</asp:UpdatePanel>
```

The *UpdatePanel* control goes hand in hand with the *ScriptManager* control. After you have enabled partial rendering through the script manager, an event handler for the form's *submit* event is registered with the DOM. The handler intercepts any outbound requests and swallows them. In return, the event handler places a new, and nearly identical, request that runs asynchronously. Figure 9-1 compares a classic ASP.NET request with a partial rendering request.

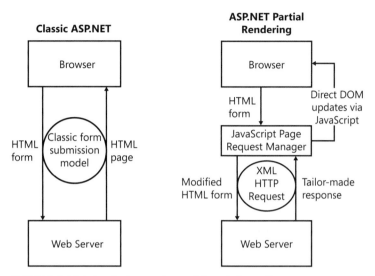

FIGURE 9-1 High-level schema of a partial rendering call

The ASP.NET runtime doesn't treat an asynchronous postback request differently from a standard one. It finds a proper HTTP handler and sets it to work. The page life cycle continues as usual until rendering time approaches. This means that your code-behind class will receive regular *Init* and *Load* events, the view state is properly deserialized, and the state on controls is restored and updated with posted data. The postback event is then executed, and controls are further updated according to the results. At this point, you need to render out some response for the caller.

The normal rendering algorithm for an ASP.NET page consists of a recursive visit of the tree of controls, starting from the root of the page. In a partial rendering scenario, the modified algorithm begins its recursive visit from the root of the *UpdatePanel* to refresh. Post-rendering steps (that is, serializing the new view state) are accomplished as usual and are in no way different from a standard postback.

The markup produced is serialized as text into a buffer using an internal, record-based representation format. This string is the response written to the output stream and received by the calling instance of *XMLHttpRequest*.

After the generated response is served back to the page request manager in the browser's context (as shown in Figure 9-1), another block of JavaScript code takes care of parsing it up. The response looks like an array of records where each record might refer to an *UpdatePanel* section, a hidden field, or perhaps a block of server-generated data to share with the JavaScript environment.

Any *UpdatePanel* record is resolved by extracting the markup and attaching that to the *<div>* or *<span>* tag in the DOM with a matching ID. The DOM update occurs through the *innerHTML* property, as shown here:

```
document.getElementById("UpdatePanel1").innerHTML = markup;
```

Similarly, hidden fields are resolved by loading the new content into the matching DOM elements. Finally, server-generated data (referred to as *data items*) that needs to be loaded into the JavaScript engine is made available to JavaScript functions and page event handlers.

You can use any number of *UpdatePanel* controls in your page. The only limitation might be the total number of controls you end up having in the page if you add too many updatable panels. Likewise, *UpdatePanel* controls can be freely nested.

Because a partial rendering page doesn't interfere much with the standard page life cycle, any security barrier you might have in your application remains functional. The timing of an asynchronous postback, in fact, is like that of a postback and occurs after all authentication and authorization steps have been taken.

The Good and the Bad

Partial rendering is definitely the easiest way to add AJAX capabilities to an ASP.NET Web site. The impact on existing code is close to zero. It doesn't require significant new skills, doesn't require exposure to JavaScript, and leaves the application model intact. All that you need to learn is how to use a small set of new server controls—*UpdatePanel*, *ScriptManager*, and *UpdateProgress*. No new application architecture is required, and no code refactoring needs to be done.

Advocates of a pure AJAX approach might say that partial rendering completely misses the whole point of AJAX. And such a statement is not a false one.

Overall, partial rendering is only *one* possible way to approach AJAX. It preserves most of your current investments and is relatively cheap to implement. Partial rendering just makes your pages refresh in a smarter way, thus delivering the same pleasant effect of a canonical AJAX feature.

Partial rendering doesn't turn your existing application into a true AJAX application. There's no new architectural point in partial rendering. It's a great technique to quickly update legacy applications, and it's an excellent choice when you lack the time, skills, or budget to move on and redesign the application. But in a good number of cases, an improved user interface and optimized rendering are all that your users demand. So partial rendering would perfectly fit in. And, as if we needed more reasons to use it, partial rendering is actually tremendously effective.

In any case, you should also be aware of the structural limitations of partial rendering. You might want to start with partial rendering to improve your pages and then move on to other, more purely AJAX, solutions to fix particular bottlenecks that still remain.

JavaScript will never make you productive; a server-side application model will never give you the responsiveness and interactivity users loudly demand. Finding the right balance and making the correct trade-offs is entirely up to you and your creativity. AJAX is cool, but AJAX is structurally a tough trade-off to make.

Let's see the other side of the coin: scripting functionalities directly from within the browser.

> **Note** Why is it so darned hard to write pure AJAX applications? AJAX applications are all about the client, and the client is JavaScript and HTML. Both JavaScript and HTML have significant limitations in light of the complexity of today's applications.
>
> JavaScript is an interpreted language, and it does not have a particularly modern syntax. Additionally, JavaScript is subject to the implementation that browsers provide. So a feature might be flaky in one browser and super-optimized in another.
>
> Originally born as a document format, HTML is used more as an application delivery format. But for this purpose, HTML is simply inadequate because it lacks strong, built-in graphics and layout capabilities. Silverlight with its embedded Common Language Runtime (CLR), support for managed languages and full support for Windows Presentation Foundation (WPF), tries to address both issues.

Direct Scripting

At the highest level of abstraction, Web applications are client/server applications that require an Internet connection between the two layers. Before AJAX, this connection was incorporated in the special client application—the browser. The browser opens the connection, clears the user interface, and then updates the screen with the response received. With AJAX, the client code gains the ability to bypass the browser and enter user interface updates without fully refreshing the displayed page—a great step forward toward usability and rich user experiences.

To make the usability of Web applications grow as close as possible to that of desktop applications, the overall software platform must fulfill two key requirements. One is a client-side infrastructure that can manage the Internet connection with the server. The other requirement is to have available a public and known programming interface on the server—an AJAX-specific service layer.

The Overall Idea

Direct scripting refers to the idea of having JavaScript code that calls into a publicly exposed endpoint, gets transferred data, and uses client logic for binding and rendering. Figure 9-2 gives an overview of the architecture.

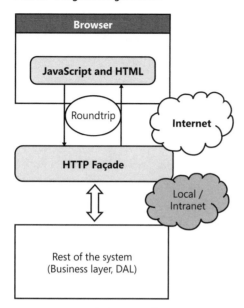

FIGURE 9-2 A typical AJAX architecture

The presentation layer is hosted in the browser and communicates via HTTP with an ad hoc façade made of URLs. Behind the URLs, you have server code at work. The server code can be exposed in a number of ways, and the approach used is determined by the programming API you choose. For example, you can choose to expose server code as a WCF service. At the same time, you can expose client-callable functionality using the controller of an ASP.NET MVC application that returns JSON data. (I'll take a deeper look at this specific scenario in the rest of the chapter.)

The data being exchanged between the presentation layer and the HTTP façade depends on the client and server APIs and their capabilities. However, most of the time (albeit not always and not necessarily), the serialization format of choice is JSON.

Invoking the HTTP Façade

Behind an HTTP façade, you can find a classic Web service (one not specifically hosted on a .NET platform, although it could be) or various flavors of a WCF service, including REST and WCF Data services (formerly known as ADO.NET Data Services). You can also find a handmade HTTP handler, which consists of a public URL with some ASP.NET code behind. This is the case with ASP.NET MVC controller actions and ASP.NET page methods.

The biggest difference between using a service backed by a technology (such as WCF) and using handmade HTTP handlers is in how easy it is to get a proxy object to use on the client. When you add a server-side reference to Web service, you go through a Microsoft Visual Studio wizard, indicate the URL of the service, specify the desired namespace, and have the wizard generate a proxy class and add it in the folds of the project solution.

When you intend to add a reference to Web service to be consumed from within a client page, there's no Visual Studio wizard to help you. Instead, you programmatically add the service reference to the page either using the *ScriptManager* control or via a tailor-made URL. The following code snippet shows how to use the *ScriptManager* control:

```
<asp:ScriptManager ID="ScriptManager1" runat="server">
    <Services>
        <asp:ServiceReference Path="northwind.svc" />
        :
        :
    </Services>
</asp:ScriptManager>
```

The script manager emits the following markup:

```
<script src="northwind.svc/js" type="text/javascript"></script>
```

Obviously, you can insert the same *<script>* tag yourself, skipping a control reference. The */js* suffix is the magic word that instructs the service infrastructure to generate a JavaScript proxy class for the page code to call into the service. A proxy renders in JavaScript any aspects of the service contract, including service operations and data contracts. Here's some code that shows how to call a service method from JavaScript:

```
// Making an async call to method GetCustomerById with a callback
MyApp.Services.NorthwindService.GetCustomerById("ALFKI", onDataAvailable);
```

The response is being processed by the specified callback, as shown here:

```
function onDataAvailable(results, context, methodName)
{
    // results is the response obtained from the HTTP façade mapped to a JS object
    // context is any optional data the caller may have passed to the callback
    // methodName indicates the name of the service method invoked
    :
    :
}
```

Not binding to a Web service requires that you parse the response literally to make any further decision and update the user interface.

Parsing the raw response is only half the job. The second half consists of updating the user interface. Most of the time it requires data-binding capabilities and, ideally, an AJAX framework with specific capabilities, such as the newest ASP.NET AJAX 4 framework from Microsoft.

The Good and the Bad

Placing direct calls to some remote endpoint gives you the greatest flexibility as you receive raw data completely devoid of any layout information. This is the gist of AJAX, after all. On the down side of it, though, you find the JavaScript language and the DOM environment.

You can program your presentation logic only by using lines and lines of JavaScript code; you can make updates only by setting properties on the browser's DOM. Most of the time, you can reach a good compromise between complexity and the quantity of code to write and performance. However, that has to be verified each and every time.

For now, a better and richer JavaScript is possible only through libraries that cover parts of client-side programming that the language doesn't natively cover. Classes, networking, static type checking, and a common and cross-browser model for managing events and exploring the document are all features required in modern JavaScript code. Popular libraries, such as the Microsoft AJAX library, provide just this.

The key trait of the Microsoft AJAX library is the set of extensions to transform JavaScript into an object-oriented language. JavaScript is not a true object-oriented programming (OOP) language even though it always has supported objects and also provides a rudimentary mechanism for prototyping classes and derived classes. The Microsoft AJAX library builds on top of this basic functionality to add namespace and interface support in addition to a number of helpful facilities.

In addition to extending the core of the language, for effective scripting you need rich libraries that provide higher-level tools for UI tasks. The jQuery library is the de facto standard, and the jQuery UI library has become one of the coolest plugins around.

Direct scripting takes you toward JavaScript-intensive applications and a new set of programming tools, such as the one coming out of the ASP.NET AJAX 4 development. If you're familiar with and feel comfortable with JavaScript today, you can even consider JavaScript-only sections for a Web application.

AJAX in ASP.NET MVC

Discussing the AJAX capabilities of a given ASP.NET framework entails discussing the way in which that particular framework hides its own calls to the underlying *XMLHttpRequest* object.

In the context of ASP.NET MVC, you typically use three types of wrappers for low-level *XMLHttpRequest* calls: the jQuery API for AJAX, the JavaScript proxy classes for Web services, and some native HTML helpers that use a specific, AJAX-oriented JavaScript library that comes with ASP.NET MVC.

The JavaScript API

ASP.NET MVC owes a large share of its popularity to the full control it yields to developers when it comes to generating HTML. Full control over HTML also means full control over the script code being included in the page. The default project template you get in Visual Studio 2010 for ASP.NET MVC stores in the *Scripts* folder a bunch of JavaScript files, including the latest jQuery library, as shown in Figure 9-3.

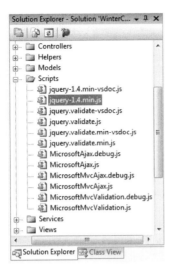

FIGURE 9-3 Default script files inserted in the standard ASP.NET MVC project template

This means that the AJAX API available in jQuery is an effective starting point for implementing AJAX functionalities in ASP.NET MVC. As you can also see in Figure 9-3, the Microsoft AJAX library, and its native support for Web service proxy classes, is another good option. Let's start with jQuery, then.

Using jQuery to Perform AJAX Calls

In jQuery, you can have a few shorthand methods to quickly arrange asynchronous calls to a remote endpoint. All methods, however, leverage the services of a single function—the *ajax* function. You use the *ajax* function, as shown next:

```
$.ajax(
  {
    type: "POST",
    url: "getOrder.aspx",
    data: "id=1234&year=2007",
    success: function(response) {
      alert( response );
    }
  }
);
```

The *ajax* function gets a list of parameters, such as *type, url, data, dataType, cache, async,* and *success*. The *dataType* parameter indicates the type of the expected response, whereas *success* indicates the completion callback. The callback function receives the URL response as its sole argument.

In addition to *ajax*, a number of helper methods exist to simplify common operations such as downloading a script. Table 9-1 lists such helpers.

TABLE 9-1 Shorthand methods in jQuery for AJAX functionalities

Method	Description
jQuery.get()	Gets a URL, and performs an HTTP GET request that loads data from the server.
jQuery.getJSON()	Gets a URL, and loads JSON-encoded data from the server through a GET HTTP request. After the request is received, the response is transformed into a JavaScript object.
jQuery.getScript()	Gets a URL, and loads a JavaScript file from the server using a GET HTTP request. After the request is received, the script is automatically executed.
jQuery.load()	Gets a URL, and loads data and markup from the server. After the data is received, the response is inserted into the DOM at a specified position.
jQuery.post()	Gets a URL, and performs an HTTP POST request against the server.

As you can see, all the methods in Table 9-1 perform basic HTTP operations (a GET or POST request) and differ with regard to the additional tasks they perform and the expected format of the response.

For example, the *getJSON* method expects a JSON string as a result. If a syntax error is detected in the downloaded string, the request fails. Note also that if the URL points to a remote server, the request is converted to a JSONP request. (See the following note for more details about *JSON with Padding*, or JSONP for short.)

> **Note** For security reasons, modern browsers require that any calls that go through *XMLHttpRequest* and frames don't trespass the boundaries of the local server. Therefore, no cross-domain calls are allowed via script.
>
> Honestly, for years this was not perceived as a terrible limitation, but it started being viewed as such with the advent of AJAX. By default, you can't download data of any kind via script from a remote location. However, you can create a *<script>* tag on the fly and make it point to any URL you know, regardless of the location.
>
> JSONP is a special convention through which you request a server that supports it to give you the response (be it data or script) of a given call. If simply pointed from a *<script>* tag, however, the response is simply downloaded but not necessarily processed. Here's where the JSONP convention kicks in. The JSONP convention suggests you append a *?callback=xxx* segment to the URL. The *xxx* placeholder is a local script function you want to be invoked to process the response. For example, if *getOrder.aspx* returns the JSON representation of an order, the related JSONP call might look like *getOrder.aspx?callback=showIt*, where *showIt* is a local JavaScript function that processes the information about the order. The *getJSON* method in jQuery is smart enough to detect whether the URL passed in is local or not. If it is not, it automatically turns the JSON call into a JSONP call using the provided callback function to pad the URL.

Using the jQuery AJAX API requires that you provide a callback to handle the response. Here's an example that shows how to get a list of customers after a button click:

```
<script type="text/javascript">
    $(document).ready(function() {
```

```
    $('#Button1').click(function() {
        $.getJSON("/Home/GetCustomers",
                null,
                function(data) { showCustomers(data); });
    });
});
</script>
```

The URL invoked by *getJSON* is related to the action *GetCustomers* on the Home controller. The method is expected to return a JSON object that the provided callback processes to refresh the user interface. In the section "The Controller Façade," I'll return to this example to discuss the structure of a controller action that returns JSON data.

Invoking Web Services from ASP.NET MVC

Any ASP.NET Web Forms developer will probably tell you that the *ScriptManager* control is necessary in order to have free JavaScript proxy classes for a referenced Web service. In reality, this is not strictly necessary because you can simply reference the service URL with the */js* suffix from within a *<script>* tag:

```
<script src="northwind.svc/js" type="text/javascript"></script>
```

In this way, you have an easy-to-use JavaScript proxy available without the burden of dealing with server controls. And it is not a secondary point that you can switch to a custom view engine (such as, say, Spark) while being able to leverage a JavaScript proxy for Web services. In Spark and other custom view engines, in fact, you might not be allowed to use ASP.NET server controls in the source code of a view.

The ASP.NET AJAX 4 Library

The total control over HTML and JavaScript that ASP.NET MVC offers also makes smooth integration between an ASP.NET MVC view and the ASP.NET AJAX 4 library possible. The ASP.NET AJAX 4 library comes with strong support for client-side data binding and conditional template rendering.

The library supplies a formal syntax for you to define an HTML template that will be populated with data during a binding operation. The library also makes available a rich client control—the *DataView* component—to link a remote data source to an HTML template and populate it entirely from the client.

In ASP.NET AJAX, an HTML template is essentially a *<div>* tag that contains fixed and repeatable parts. A fixed part is a fragment of HTML that is emitted only once—such as a header or footer. A repeatable part is an HTML fragment that is linked to data and repeated for each bound element.

An HTML template is initially hidden from view, and the framework takes care of turning on the visibility attribute of interested parts as appropriate. A common way to control visibility is by defining in the page a *sys-template* cascading style sheet (CSS) style, as shown here:

```
<style type="text/css">
    .sys-template { display:none; visibility:hidden; }
</style>
```

The *sys-template* style is the discriminating element that determines whether a fragment of HTML will be emitted once or repeated. Let's consider the following template:

```
<div>
  <table>
    <tr>
       <th>SYMBOL</th>
       <th>LAST</th>
       <th>CHANGE</th>
    </tr>
    <tbody id="grid" class="sys-template">
      <tr>
        <td align="left">{{ Symbol }}</td>
        <td align="right">{{ Quote }}</td>
        <td align="right">{{ Change }}</td>
      </tr>
    </tbody>
  </table>
</div>
```

The table contains a *<tbody>* element styled as a *sys-template*. That part will be repeated for each bound item. To identify a repeatable part, you use a unique ID. In this case, the ID is *grid*. Names within {{ … }} identify public properties on the data source whose content has to be displayed.

To attach data to this template, you can use a *DataView* component. The following code snippet shows how to create a *DataView* programmatically upon page loading:

```
<script type="text/javascript">
function pageLoad() {
   $create(
       Sys.UI.DataView,
       {},
       {},
       {},
       $get("grid")
   );
}
</script>
```

After creation, the *DataView* is attached to the specified DOM element—the *grid* element in the example. As a result, any data associated with the *data* property of the *DataView* is bound to the template. The *DataView* can receive data programmatically or via a Web service. The following code snippet shows how to configure a *DataView* declaratively:

```
<div>
  <table>
    <tr>
      <th>SYMBOL</th>
      <th>LAST</th>
      <th>CHANGE</th>
    </tr>
    <tbody id="grid" class="sys-template"
           sys:attach="dataview"
           dataview:data="{{ stockQuotes }}">
      <tr>
        <td align="left">{{ Symbol }}</td>
        <td align="right">{{ Quote }}</td>
        <td align="right">{{ Change }}</td>
      </tr>
    </tbody>
  </table>
</div>
```

In this case, it is assumed that *stockQuotes* is a JavaScript expression that produces a non-empty result.

In summary, ASP.NET MVC supports a wide range of JavaScript APIs through which you can code any presentation and rendering logic in pure JavaScript so that many user actions are handled directly within the realm of the Web browser. Server data is provided by ad hoc HTTP endpoints. These endpoints can be generalized, Web-based services—in the widest possible scope you can give to this term—as well as plain controller actions exposed by the same ASP.NET MVC application. Let's see how to tweak a controller action method to properly support a JavaScript call.

The Controller Façade

In Chapter 4, "Inside Controllers," we thoroughly discussed the structure and expected behavior of ASP.NET MVC controllers. Any public method on a controller class that is not decorated with the *NonAction* attribute can be invoked from a client using any JavaScript API.

The response a client receives depends on the return value of the controller method. In Chapter 4, we reviewed the various results a caller can get from a controller. The most common result is expressed via an instance of the *ViewResult* class, which essentially wraps an HTML string. However, other result types can be returned, such as *JsonResult*.

Returning JSON Content

Earlier in the chapter, I presented a short JavaScript code snippet using the *getJSON* function from the jQuery library to grab some JSON data from a URL. For completeness, the code snippet is reproduced here:

```
<script type="text/javascript">
    $(document).ready(function() {
        $('#Button1').click(function() {
            $.getJSON("/Home/GetCustomers",
                    null,
                    function(data) { showCustomers(data); });
        });
    });
</script>
```

When the document is fully loaded, a handler is registered for the *click* event of the specified button, named *Button1*. The handler uses the *getJSON* function to connect to the */Home/GetCustomers* URL. The sample call doesn't pass any parameters to the URL—the second parameter is null—and it sets a callback to process the response.

Here's a possible definition for the invoked action method:

```
public JsonResult GetCustomers()
{
    // Grab some data to return
    var customers = CustomerRepository.GetAll();

    // Serialize to JSON and return
    return this.Json(customers);
}
```

Defined on the *Controller* class, the *Json* method creates a *JsonResult* object. The purpose of the *JsonResult* object is to serialize the specified .NET object—a customer list in the example—to the JSON format. The *Json* method has a few overloads through which you can specify the desired content type string (with the default being *application/json*) and request behavior. The request behavior consists of allowing or denying JSON content over an HTTP GET request.

In ASP.NET MVC 2, by default JSON content is not delivered through an HTTP GET request. This means that the previous code using *getJSON* will fail in ASP.NET MVC 2 unless the controller's method is modified to allow JSON content to be served over HTTP GET requests:

```
public JsonResult GetCustomers()
{
    // Grab some data to return
    var customers = CustomerRepository.GetAll();

    // Serialize to JSON and return
    return this.Json(customers, JsonRequestBehavior.AllowGet);
}
```

Obviously, the reason why ASP.NET MVC 2 prevents controllers from returning JSON data from HTTP GET requests is security. However, enabling JSON over HTTP GET requests is not problematic as long as you don't return sensitive data packed in arrays.

You can use the *getJSON* method to pass parameters to the controller action. In this case, you use the second parameter of the *getJSON* method as shown here:

```
$.getJSON("/Home/GetCustomers", {country:"USA"},
          function(data) { showCustomers(data); });
```

You can use the parameter of *getJSON* to compose a dictionary of name/value pairs to pass to the endpoint. The content of the dictionary is serialized to the query string of the URL. The preceding code, for instance, generates the following URL:

```
http://yourserver/Home/GetCustomers?country=USA
```

The default model binder will catch any URL parameters and pass them to the method:

```
public JsonResult GetCustomers(string country)
{
    // Grab some data to return
    var customers = CustomerRepository.GetAll(country);

    // Serialize to JSON and return
    return this.Json(customers, JsonRequestBehavior.AllowGet);
}
```

Let's see now how you can process JSON data from JavaScript. According to *getJSON*, the response from the URL is passed to the specified callback and can be parsed and used to update the user interface.

```
function showCustomers(data)
{
    // Get the reference to the drop-down list
    var list = $("#ddCustomerList")[0];

    // Fill the list
    for (var i = 0; i < data.length; i++)
    {
        var customer = data[i];
        var option = new Option(customer.CompanyName, customer.CustomerID);
        list.add(option);
    };
};
```

The preceding sample code populates a drop-down list with the names of customers.

Returning JSONP Content

As mentioned, JSONP is a convention used by some sites to expose their JSON content in a way that makes it easier for callers to consume data via script even from an external domain. The trick is recognizing an additional parameter in the URL that contains the name of the JavaScript function to invoke around the JSON content to be returned. In other words, an HTTP endpoint that supports JSONP is capable of returning the following instead of the plain content of the *jsonData* string:

```
yourFunction(jsonData)
```

In the example, *yourFunction* is a user-defined JavaScript function whose name is passed through a conventional URL parameter. For example, consider the following URL that gets you a few pictures of cats from Flickr:

```
http://api.flickr.com/services/feeds/photos_public.gne?tags=cat&format=json&jsoncallback=?
```

As you can see, the last piece of the URL is a parameter named *jsoncallback*. The value assigned to the parameter indicates the name of the JavaScript function to place around the JSON string to return. As far as Flickr is concerned, *jsoncallback* is the conventional name of the JSONP extra parameter. If you define your own JSONP data provider, you are responsible for supporting and documenting an analogous parameter. Let's briefly consider an example:

```
public JsonpResult GetCustomers()
{
    // Grab some data to return
    var customers = CustomerRepository.GetAll();

    // Serialize to JSON and return
    return this.Jsonp(customers, JsonRequestBehavior.AllowGet);
}
```

The *GetCustomers* method now returns a *JsonpResult* object obtained through a call made to a new *Jsonp* method. No *Jsonp* method and no *JsonpResult* objects exist in ASP.NET MVC 2, however. Let's define the *JsonpResult* class:

```
public class JsonpResult : JsonResult
{
    private const string JsonpCallbackName = "callback";

    public override void ExecuteResult(ControllerContext context)
    {
        if (context == null)
            throw new ArgumentNullException("context");

        if ((JsonRequestBehavior == JsonRequestBehavior.DenyGet) &&
            String.Equals(context.HttpContext.Request.HttpMethod, "GET"))
            throw new InvalidOperationException();

        HttpResponseBase response = context.HttpContext.Response;
        if (!String.IsNullOrEmpty(this.ContentType))
            response.ContentType = this.ContentType;
        else
            response.ContentType = "application/json";
        if (this.ContentEncoding != null)
            response.ContentEncoding = this.ContentEncoding;
```

```
            if (this.Data != null)
            {
                string buffer;
                HttpRequestBase request = context.HttpContext.Request;
                var serializer = new JavaScriptSerializer();
                if (request[JsonpCallbackName] != null)
                    buffer = String.Format("{0}({1})", request[JsonpCallbackName],
                                                        serializer.Serialize(Data));
                else
                    buffer = serializer.Serialize(Data);

                response.Write(buffer);
            }
        }
    }
}
```

The class is nearly the same as *JsonResult* except for a small change in the *ExecuteResult* method. Before serializing to JavaScript, the code checks whether the conventional JSONP parameter has been passed with the request and fixes the JSON string accordingly.

At this point, the implementation of the *Jsonp* method is straightforward:

```
protected JsonpResult Jsonp(object data, JsonRequestBehavior behavior)
{
    return new JsonpResult
    {
        Data = data,
        JsonRequestBehavior = behavior
    };
}
```

The *Jsonp* method will be added to the controller classes in cases where you intend to support JSONP, or it will be added to a base class if you want to have JSONP available throughout the whole application.

Returning JavaScript Content

The *$.getScript* method in the jQuery library is dedicated to downloading script files. When you invoke the method, you pass it a URL that just returns JavaScript. The downloaded code is then executed, and execution takes place before the callback is invoked:

```
$.getScript("/Home/About");
```

To return JavaScript code as a string, here's what you need to do in your controller:

```
public JavaScriptResult SayHello()
{
    return new JavaScriptResult() { Script = "alert('Hello');" };
}
```

The implementation of the *JavaScriptResult* class is simple, as the following code snippet shows:

```
public override void ExecuteResult(ControllerContext context)
{
    if (context == null)
        throw new ArgumentNullException("context");

    HttpResponseBase response = context.HttpContext.Response;
    response.ContentType = "application/x-javascript";
    if (this.Script != null)
        response.Write(this.Script);
}
```

The *ExecuteResult* method of the *JavaScriptResult* class simply sets the content type and writes out the script as a string.

What about sending out an entire JavaScript file selected by the controller? You can write an enhanced action result class:

```
public class JavaScriptFileResult : JavaScriptResult
{
    public JavaScriptFileResult(string filename)
    {
        FileName = fileName;
    }

    public String FileName {get; set;}

    public override void ExecuteResult(ControllerContext context)
    {
        if (context == null)
            throw new ArgumentNullException("context");

        HttpResponseBase response = context.HttpContext.Response;
        response.ContentType = "application/x-javascript";
        response.WriteFile(FileName);
    }
}
```

And finally, you invoke the *JavaScriptFileResult* class as follows:

```
public JavaScriptResult GetFile(string file)
{
    // Run your own logic here
    :
    :

    // Return the selected JavaScript file
    return new JavaScriptResult() { FileName = file };
}
```

The logic you need to run before downloading a JavaScript file can range from selecting a localized version of the script to versioning, and even versioning with ad hoc debug and tracing information.

> **Note** If you have a link in your view that points to a controller action defined to return a *JavaScriptResult* object, expect the browser to attempt a download of the content. This is because the *Accept* header in the request is not set to *text/javascript*, *application/javascript*, or both.

Returning Markup

When it comes to AJAX, service methods that return plain HTML have never been particularly popular. The reason is that the returned markup inevitably contains both data and the layout, thus consuming more bandwidth than a classic AJAX request that returns only raw data.

The idea of a service method that returns some markup is not a far-fetched one, however. The HTML Message pattern describes it as an approach that is worth considering, especially in situations where you need to compose the user interface by assembling various relatively static pieces, such as subviews and user controls.

In jQuery, you have the *load* function to connect to a given URL and download markup. Nicely enough, though, the *load* function also appends the markup to the DOM subtree you specify:

```
$('.grid').load("/Home/GetCustomers",
    function() {
        alert("Refresh the view now.");
    }
);
```

The preceding example uses the *load* function to populate a DOM element named *grid* with the results returned by the specified ASP.NET MVC route. The granularity of the *load* function can be even finer because it allows you to select only a fraction of the view and always through a CSS-based query syntax:

```
$('.grid').load("/Home/DataGrid #body",
    function() {
        alert("Refresh the view now.");
    }
);
```

In this case, the *load* method downloads any content returned by the URL—the */Home/ DataGrid* URL in the example. However, the jQuery library then parses the entire response and filters it based on the additional information. As a result, only the elements that match the subquery—the *#body* expression in the example—will be processed as usual and attached to the current page DOM.

To fully support the jQuery *load* function, you might want to have methods that return a *ViewResult* object or, better yet, a *PartialViewResult* object.

AJAX Helpers in ASP.NET MVC

Because ASP.NET MVC is mostly focused on giving developers total control over the HTML being output, probably the most natural way of incorporating AJAX capabilities into a view is using direct scripting and jQuery functions. In ASP.NET MVC, you are never going to face issues with element IDs, as is too often the case with Web Forms. You might know exactly the ID used to reference a given HTML element and be able to address that via script in a safe way. (Total control over the IDs of HTML elements even when HTML is generated from a server control is a feature you gain in ASP.NET 4.)

At any rate, if you feel a bit uncomfortable going through an intensive JavaScript experience, you might wonder what else exists in ASP.NET MVC to code some good AJAX functions. As an example of what's available, you have a few AJAX-enabled HTML helpers, such as action links.

The *AjaxHelper* Class

ASP.NET MVC comes with the *AjaxHelper* class, which is responsible for emitting script and markup for asynchronous requests. An instance of the *AjaxHelper* class is exposed out of the *ViewPage* class through the *Ajax* property, which is defined as follows:

```
public class ViewPage : Page, IViewDataContainer
{
    :
    :
    public AjaxHelper Ajax { get; set; }
}
```

The *AjaxHelper* class adds any necessary support that is required for implementing AJAX features within an ASO.NET MVC view. The class is defined as shown here:

```
public class AjaxHelper
{
    public AjaxHelper(ViewContext context, IViewDataContainer container);
    public AjaxHelper(ViewContext context, IViewDataContainer container,
                      RouteCollection routeCollection);

    // Methods
    public string JavaScriptStringEncode(string message);

    // Properties
    public static string GlobalizationScriptPath { get; set; }
    public RouteCollection RouteCollection { get; private set; }
    public ViewContext ViewContext { get; private set; }
    public ViewDataDictionary ViewData { get; }
    public IViewDataContainer ViewDataContainer { get; private set; }
}
```

Table 9-2 describes each of the public members of the class.

TABLE 9-2 Members of the *AjaxHelper* class

Member	Description
JavaScriptStringEncode	The method formats the specified string as a JSON string. The method uses *JavaScriptSerializer* internally.
GlobalizationScriptPath	The property gets and sets the path for localized scripts to be used by the extension methods of the class. The default path for localized scripts is *~/Scripts/Globalization*.
RouteCollection	The property gets the collection of URL routes for the application.
ViewContext	The property gets the context information about the view.
ViewData	The property gets the current view data dictionary. The property is implemented as a plain accessor for the *ViewData* property of the *ViewDataContainer* object.
ViewDataContainer	The property gets the view data container—that is, a container class that currently includes only the *ViewData* dictionary.

The *AjaxHelper* class also has a generic version—*AjaxHelper<TModel>*—used for rendering HTML in AJAX scenarios within a strongly typed view. The generic version just implements the *ViewData* property differently to expose it as a *ViewDataDictionary<TModel>* object.

More important than the source code of the *AjaxHelper* class itself is the list of the extension methods defined for it by the ASP.NET MVC framework.

Extension Methods for the *AjaxHelper* Class

There are not too many extension methods defined for the *AjaxHelper* class, even though the ones defined are important. The extension methods are outlined in Table 9-3.

TABLE 9-3 Extension Methods for the *AjaxHelper* class

Method	Description
ActionLink	Emits an anchor tag pointing to the URL for the specified action.
BeginForm	Emits a form tag using some ad hoc JavaScript code to submit any content. The URL of the action is expressed in the form of an action link.
BeginRouteForm	Emits a form tag using some ad hoc JavaScript code to submit any content. The URL of the action is expressed in the form of a route link.
RouteLink	Emits an anchor tag pointing to the URL for the specified route.

Each extension method comes with a long list of overloads to give developers a chance to specify an AJAX request with or without route parameters, HTML attributes, and so forth. As an example, here's the full list of overloads defined for the *ActionLink* method:

```
public static MvcHtmlString ActionLink(this AjaxHelper ajaxHelper,
                         string linkText,
                         string actionName,
                         AjaxOptions ajaxOptions);
```

```
public static MvcHtmlString ActionLink(this AjaxHelper ajaxHelper,
                                       string linkText,
                                       string actionName,
                                       object routeValues,
                                       AjaxOptions ajaxOptions);
public static MvcHtmlString ActionLink(this AjaxHelper ajaxHelper,
                                       string linkText,
                                       string actionName,
                                       string controllerName,
                                       AjaxOptions ajaxOptions);
public static MvcHtmlString ActionLink(this AjaxHelper ajaxHelper,
                                       string linkText,
                                       string actionName,
                                       RouteValueDictionary routeValues,
                                       AjaxOptions ajaxOptions);
public static MvcHtmlString ActionLink(this AjaxHelper ajaxHelper,
                                       string linkText,
                                       string actionName,
                                       object routeValues,
                                       AjaxOptions ajaxOptions,
                                       object htmlAttributes);
public static MvcHtmlString ActionLink(this AjaxHelper ajaxHelper,
                                       string linkText,
                                       string actionName,
                                       string controllerName,
                                       object routeValues,
                                       AjaxOptions ajaxOptions);
public static MvcHtmlString ActionLink(this AjaxHelper ajaxHelper,
                                       string linkText,
                                       string actionName,
                                       string controllerName,
                                       RouteValueDictionary routeValues,
                                       AjaxOptions ajaxOptions);
public static MvcHtmlString ActionLink(this AjaxHelper ajaxHelper,
                                       string linkText,
                                       string actionName,
                                       RouteValueDictionary routeValues,
                                       AjaxOptions ajaxOptions,
                                       IDictionary<string, object> htmlAttributes);
public static MvcHtmlString ActionLink(this AjaxHelper ajaxHelper,
                                       string linkText,
                                       string actionName,
                                       string controllerName,
                                       object routeValues,
                                       AjaxOptions ajaxOptions,
                                       object htmlAttributes);
public static MvcHtmlString ActionLink(this AjaxHelper ajaxHelper,
                                       string linkText,
                                       string actionName,
                                       string controllerName,
                                       RouteValueDictionary routeValues,
                                       AjaxOptions ajaxOptions,
                                       IDictionary<string, object> htmlAttributes);
```

```
public static MvcHtmlString ActionLink(this AjaxHelper ajaxHelper,
                                 string linkText,
                                 string actionName,
                                 string controllerName,
                                 string protocol,
                                 string hostName,
                                 string fragment,
                                 object routeValues,
                                 AjaxOptions ajaxOptions,
                                 object htmlAttributes);
public static MvcHtmlString ActionLink(this AjaxHelper ajaxHelper,
                                 string linkText,
                                 string actionName,
                                 string controllerName,
                                 string protocol,
                                 string hostName,
                                 string fragment,
                                 RouteValueDictionary routeValues,
                                 AjaxOptions ajaxOptions,
                                 IDictionary<string, object> htmlAttributes);
```

As you can see, all extension methods return a special flavor of a string type—the *MvcHtmlString* type—that you briefly met in Chapter 5, "Inside Views." *MvcHtmlString* indicates that the string it represents has to be considered as a sanitized piece of HTML that should not be further encoded.

You might want to be aware of some interesting aspects of *MvcHtmlString* that touch on the actual integration between ASP.NET MVC 2 and the underlying ASP.NET platform. Discussing such internal aspects of *MvcHtmlString* would probably be a digression from the current topic, so you can find out more in the sidebar "Inside the *MvcHtmlString* Class."

Getting back to the extension methods on the *AjaxHelper* class, the essential fact is that all extension methods in Table 9-3 emit a link that when clicked triggers an asynchronous request to the specified URL. Let's then delve deeper into action links.

Inside the *MvcHtmlString* Class

ASP.NET 4 comes with a new subsystem for auto-encoding HTML text. When you have a code block, by simply using the colon symbol (:) you instruct the runtime to HTML-encode any text being displayed. Here's an example:

```
<%: "<script>alert('Hello');</script>" %>
```

The net result of the expression is outputting the script command as plain text. What if you emit text in the code block from an existing utility that already provides sanitized HTML? You might end up in a situation like the one illustrated next:

```
<%: Server.HtmlEncode("<script>alert('Hello');</script>") %>
```

In this case, the original text will be encoded twice—once because of the explicit call to *HtmlEncode* and once because of the : symbol in the code block. To prevent this nasty situation, the auto-encoding subsystem has been designed to recognize special strings that don't have to be further encoded. Note that the subsystem doesn't really check whether the string is already encoded; it simply looks at whether or not the string belongs to a special new class and exposes a special interface—the *IHtmlString* interface. Put another way, the auto-encoding subsystem is not really idempotent, but it knows when it has to stop.

You should also be aware that *IHtmlString* is known to the new auto-encoding subsystem of ASP.NET 4 and is supported by *HttpUtility.HtmlEncode*, but it is blissfully ignored by the *HtmlEncode* method on the *Server* object. As a result, the following code would work as expected and avoid double encoding. It won't work that way, however, if you replace *HttpUtility.HtmlEncode* with *Server.HtmlEncode*.

```
<%=
    HttpUtility.HtmlEncode(
        new HtmlString(
            HttpUtility.HtmlEncode("<script>alert('Hello');</script>")
        )
    )
%>
```

So what about ASP.NET MVC?

ASP.NET MVC 2 is not compiled for each .NET platform. Instead, the *system.web.mvc* assembly is built only for ASP.NET 3.5 SP1 and then is included with both Visual Studio 2008 SP1 and Visual Studio 2010 with product-specific tooling. So it's just one assembly taking advantage of the .NET platform's backward compatibility. How can you take advantage of *IHtmlString* and the auto-encoding feature that is defined for ASP.NET 4 and requires the .NET 4 platform?

As mentioned, ASP.NET MVC 2 comes with the *MvcHtmlString* type defined as follows:

```
public class MvcHtmlString
{
    private static readonly MvcHtmlStringCreator _creator;
    static MvcHtmlString()
    {
        _creator = GetCreator();
        :
        :
    }

    private static MvcHtmlStringCreator GetCreator()
    {
        :
        :
    }

    :
    :
}
```

The first consideration to make is that the class doesn't implement *IHtmlString*. The reason is fairly obvious—there's no such interface in .NET 3.5 SP1. Subsequently, any instances of the *MvcHtmlString* class are created via a factory—the *MvcHtmlString.Create* method. The factory checks whether the *IHtmlString* interface is available; if it is not available, the factory proceeds with the dynamic generation of a type that implements the interface.

In the end, the auto-encoding subsystem of ASP.NET 4 will be able to handle objects of type *MvcHtmlString* because they actually will get a proxy that offers the proper interface. Finally, let me clarify something that could be the source of trouble and misunderstandings: neither *HtmlString* in ASP.NET 4 nor *MvcHtmlString* in ASP.NET MVC 2 perform any internal HTML encoding. They are simple string wrappers that, by exposing an interface, tell the ASP.NET 4 auto-encoding infrastructure not to *further* encode their content.

AJAX Action Links

An action link is an HTML helper that emits a hyperlink bound to a piece of JavaScript code. As a result, when you click on the hyperlink the URL is invoked asynchronously and a JavaScript callback runs when the response is ready. Here's an example:

```
<%= Ajax.ActionLink("Show catalog", "Index",
        new AjaxOptions
        {
            OnSuccess="fillProductList"
        })
%>
```

In this case, the *ActionLink* method generates a hyperlink that points to the *Index* action and displays the "Show catalog" text.

What about the controller? When the *ActionLink* code block is processed, the name of the controller is resolved to the controller that is processing the view, if no other controller is specified. As you saw earlier, if the controller is different you simply pick up another overload of the method.

The *ActionLink* method emits the following JavaScript call for the previous code block:

```
<a href="/Products/Index"
    onclick="Sys.Mvc.AsyncHyperlink.handleClick(
        this,
        new Sys.UI.DomEvent(event),
        {
            insertionMode: Sys.Mvc.InsertionMode.replace,
            onSuccess: Function.createDelegate(this, fillProductList)
        }
    );">
    Show catalog
</a>
```

To use the *ActionLink* method successfully, you must link both *MicrosoftAjax.js* and *MicrosoftMvcAjax.js* from your application. Both files can be linked from your site or from the Microsoft content delivery network (CDN). These files are also automatically added to the project you create via Visual Studio and are available from the *Scripts* folder. The following listing shows how to link ASP.NET MVC script files from the Microsoft CDN if you don't want to host them on your site:

```
<script type="text/javascript"
    src="http://ajax.microsoft.com/ajax/4.0/MicrosoftAjax.js">
</script>
<script type="text/javascript"
    src="http://ajax.microsoft.com/ajax/mvc/MicrosoftMvcAjax.js">
</script>
```

You use the *AjaxOptions* class to indicate additional parameters for an AJAX action link.

AJAX Options

The *AjaxOptions* class groups a few settings you can use to customize an AJAX request. An instance of the *AjaxOptions* class is required by all overloads of the *ActionLink* method. Not all of the properties are to be set, however. As mentioned, though, at the very minimum, you might want to specify the *OnSuccess* callback to decide what to do if the request completes successfully and some data is made available to the client. Note, however, that *OnSuccess* is not a mandatory parameter, as you might have a fire-and-forget sort of call (for example, an update) that has no response for the user.

The signature of the class *AjaxOptions* is listed here:

```
public class AjaxOptions
{
    public string Confirm { get; set; }
    public string HttpMethod { get; set; }
    public InsertionMode InsertionMode { get; set; }
    public string LoadingElementId { get; set; }
    public string OnBegin { get; set; }
    public string OnComplete { get; set; }
    public string OnFailure { get; set; }
    public string OnSuccess { get; set; }
    public string UpdateTargetId { get; set; }
    public string Url { get; set; }
}
```

Table 9-4 summarizes the role that each property of *AjaxOptions* plays.

TABLE 9-4 Members of the *AjaxOptions* class

Property	Description
Confirm	Indicates the JavaScript function to call to have a confirmation before the request executes.
HttpMethod	Indicates the HTTP method to use for the request.

Property	Description
InsertionMode	Indicates the insertion mode for any content downloaded that has to be injected in the current DOM.
LoadingElementId	Indicates the ID of the DOM element to be displayed while the request is ongoing.
OnBegin	Indicates the JavaScript function to call before the request executes.
OnComplete	Indicates the JavaScript function to call when the request has completed.
OnFailure	Indicates the JavaScript function to call when the request completes with a failure.
OnSuccess	Indicates the JavaScript function to call when the request completes successfully.
UpdateTargetId	Indicates the ID of the DOM element to be updated with any HTML content downloaded.
Url	Indicates the target URL of the request if it is not already specified in the markup, such as when a link or a form are used.

During the execution of an AJAX request, three JavaScript callbacks might be involved. The first is *OnBegin*, which fires just before the request is placed. Next, you receive *OnComplete* followed by either *OnSuccess* or *OnFailure*.

AJAX action links provide a ready-made infrastructure for displaying progress information and performing DOM updates on the fly. In particular, the properties of *LoadingElementId* and *UpdateTargetId* lend themselves well to displaying a quick progress message and then updating a piece of the user interface.

Dealing with the Client-Side Events

Let's consider an example of an AJAX action link where you need a callback function to process the response. An action link callback takes the following form:

```
function fillProductList(callContext)
{
    var response = callContext.get_data();
    .
    .
    .
};
```

The parameter *callContext* is a JavaScript object of type *AjaxContext*. The members are listed in Table 9-5.

TABLE 9-5 Members of the *AjaxOptions* class for JavaScript

Property	Description
data	Indicates the response being returned.
insertionMode	Indicates the insertion mode for the response.

Property	Description
loadingElement	Indicates the DOM element used to show feedback during the request.
request	Indicates the library object that incorporates the Web request.
response	Indicates the internal object used to execute the request.
updateTargetId	Indicates the DOM element used to update the user interface.

The member named *data* contains the response. Note that *data* is implemented as a string. If it is a JSON string, you must use the *eval* function to transform it into a usable JavaScript object.

```
// Assuming that the AJAX call returned an array of
// products as a JSON string
function fillProductList(callContext)
{
    var response = callContext.get_data();
    var products = eval(response);

    // Process the list of products
    :
    :
};
```

The JavaScript *AjaxContext* object contains members such as *request* and *response*, which are useful in preliminary events such as *OnBegin* rather than when a request has completed successfully. Note that *request* is an object of type *Sys.Net.WebRequest*, whereas *response* is an object of type *Sys.Net.WebRequestExecutor*. Both types are defined in the *MicrosoftAjax.js* library.

Another feature that the AJAX support in ASP.NET MVC makes easy to implement is updating the user interface with the results downloaded from the server.

Partial Rendering in ASP.NET MVC

If you look at it in a technology-agnostic way, *partial rendering* simply refers to the application's ability to refresh only a fragment of the current view in response to specific user actions. You can use the more neutral term of *selective update* if partial rendering makes you think inevitably of Web Forms.

AJAX action links can be used to trigger asynchronous calls, grab some HTML content, and use that content to refresh a specific section of the existing view.

Updating the User Interface

Let's consider an example where an AJAX action link is used to get details about a customer. Here's the code you need:

```
<%= Ajax.ActionLink("Details", "/Customer/GetCustomerDetails", new { id = "ALFKI" },
        new AjaxOptions { HttpMethod="GET",
                         LoadingElementId="lblWait",
                         UpdateTargetId="pnlDetails"
                     })
%>
```

The link calls into the *GetCustomerDetails* method on the *Customer* controller and passes an ID of ALFKI. The following action method runs and produces some response:

```
public string GetCustomerDetails(string id)
{
    var customer = CustomerRepository.Find(id);
    if (customer != null)
        return FormatAsMarkup(customer);
    return "<b>No data found.</b>";
}
```

The action method returns an HTML string that is ready to be incorporated in the client page. In this case, I'm assuming that you'll build the HTML programmatically. If you have a user control for this purpose, you can return a *PartialViewResult* as well.

During the request, ASP.NET MVC temporarily displays the content of the panel named *lblWait* to indicate that an operation is in progress. When the operation finishes, the panel is automatically hidden and the response is appended to the DOM as the new content of the element named after the *UpdateTargetId* parameter. Figure 9-4 shows the request in action.

FIGURE 9-4 An AJAX request waiting for a response and updating the view

When you set the *UpdateTargetId* member of the JavaScript *AjaxContext* object, you assume that the response you are going to get will come in a format suitable for browser rendering. It is important to clarify that no check is made by the framework in this regard.

Furthermore, you can control the way in which such a response is incorporated in the existing document object model. The *InsertionMode* member does just that. Its default value is *Replace*, meaning that the entire subtree rooted in the element will be wiped out and replaced with the new content. Possible values for the *InsertionMode* member come from the following object:

```
Sys.Mvc.InsertionMode.prototype = {
    replace: 0,
    insertBefore: 1,
    insertAfter: 2
}
```

As you can see, in addition to replacing the existing content, other options exist—such as inserting the new markup before or after the existing content.

Posting Forms the AJAX Way

In addition to using hyperlinks, you might want to post the content of an entire input form, trigger some server-side processing, and then refresh the user interface accordingly. In ASP.NET MVC, a specific AJAX helper also exists to enhance the *<form>* element.

The following code posts the content of the form to the *Update* method of the current controller. The AJAX request executes according to the specified options. The user will see an update progress indicator, and the user interface is updated at the end.

```
<% using (Ajax.BeginForm("Update",
          new AjaxOptions {
                  LoadingElementId = "panelPleaseWait",
                  InsertionMode = InsertionMode.Replace,
                  UpdateTargetId = "panelResults" }))
   { %>
     <% Html.TextBox("Name", ViewData.Model.Name); %>
     <% Html.TextBox("Date", ViewData.Model.Date); %>
     <input type="submit" value="Save" />
<% } %>
:
<div id="panelResults"> ... </div>
<div id="panelPleaseWait">Please wait ...</div>
```

Here's the markup generated for the previous code:

```
<form action="/Home/GetCustomerDetails"
      method="post"
      onclick="Sys.Mvc.AsyncForm.handleClick(this, new Sys.UI.DomEvent(event));"
```

```
         onsubmit="Sys.Mvc.AsyncForm.handleSubmit(this, new Sys.UI.DomEvent(event), {
                        insertionMode: Sys.Mvc.InsertionMode.replace,
                        loadingElementId: 'lblWait',
                        updateTargetId: 'pnlDetails' });">
    <input type="text" id="Name" ... />
    <input type="text" id="Date" ... />
    <input type="submit" value="Save" />
</form>
```

A JavaScript function—*handleSubmit*—hooks up the form submission and, as its first step, prevents the default event handler from triggering. In this way, the classic browser-led form submission process is stopped and replaced with a custom one that works asynchronously. The same *handleSubmit* function then proceeds with a classic AJAX request that mimics the typical behavior of a form submission.

Adjusting the URL on the Fly

There might be situations in which you need to adjust the URL on the fly to reflect the data being entered or selected by the user. The *OnBegin* member of the *AjaxOptions* object serves this purpose:

```
<%= Ajax.ActionLink("Details", "/GetCustomerDetails", new { id = "12345" },
        new AjaxOptions { HttpMethod="GET",
                          LoadingElementId="lblWait",
                          UpdateTargetId="pnlDetails",
                          OnBegin="adjustURL" })%>
```

Here's a piece of code that adjusts the URL of a hyperlink to reflect the customer currently selected in a list box:

```
function adjustURL(context)
{
    // Get the selected item
    var listBox = document.getElementById("listOfCustomers");
    var id = listBox.options[listBox.selectedIndex].value;

    // Get the current request object
    var request = context.get_request();

    // Get the target URL
    var url = request.get_url();

    // Modify as appropriate. (Assuming the URL
    // has a 12345 placeholder to replace.)
    url = url.replace(/12345/, id);
    request.set_url(url);
}
```

Attached to the *OnBegin* event, the code retrieves the request object, gets the target URL, and modifies the URL as appropriate.

Reflecting on Partial Rendering in ASP.NET MVC

At first sight, the ASP.NET MVC ability to update portions of the view asynchronously looks similar to the classic partial rendering you know from Web Forms. However, some relevant differences exist.

In Web Forms, partial rendering executes as a regular postback, except that it occurs asynchronously. In the mechanics of Web Forms, a postback is a one-at-a-time operation and two postbacks are not allowed to run concurrently. The reason for this is the dependency of the postback event on the page's view state.

If two postbacks run asynchronously and simultaneously, two copies of the view state are being sent to the server. Hence, two differently updated copies of the view state will be sent back at different times. Neither of them, though, is representative of the state resulting from the two distinct operations.

In ASP.NET MVC, you have no view state, at least if you avoid using server controls in the view. This fact removes a key impediment to having asynchronous operations that can be run concurrently and safely. AJAX helpers in ASP.NET MVC delivers a feature that is reminiscent of Web Forms partial rendering, but it doesn't have all the restrictions you encounter in classic ASP.NET.

Summary

AJAX is not simply one or two particular features you can add to a page or a view. Although you can certainly consider AJAX to be the implementation of a JavaScript-based trick in a page, it should be clear that AJAX is much more than an asynchronous call.

It is relatively easy to change the paradigm for a single feature in a single page. It might be quite difficult to extend the paradigm to the whole application. AJAX represents a complete change of paradigm for Web development, and in this regard the world of AJAX programming has not been wrapped into one nice, neat, easy-to-use package. Or at least not yet.

I expect to see in a few years a unified Web platform where at least some basic AJAX capabilities are offered out of the box. In this ideal world, you build your page or view and all of the requests it fires are processed asynchronously. This could be achieved through a new generation of client browsers or perhaps via a new software platform.

Looking at the current landscape, however, the emerging fact is that each framework has its own set of facilities for AJAX. In ASP.NET MVC, the total control over HTML you can gain makes it easy to choose any AJAX strategy. You can go with jQuery and craft your asynchronous requests, or you can go with the Microsoft AJAX library and the new data-binding features in ASP.NET AJAX 4. Alternately, you can pick up any other JavaScript library out there and resort to the old, faithful ASP.NET partial-rendering scheme.

Is there anything really tailor-made for ASP.NET MVC developers? You bet.

You have a few ad hoc AJAX helpers to output asynchronous action links and forms. In the end, you still keep writing your controller methods and you can invoke them from links and forms that work asynchronously. The refresh of the view is commanded from within JavaScript callbacks, but some facilities exist to make it look similar to partial rendering overall. But the partial rendering you get in ASP.NET MVC is not dependent on the postback model; it is lightweight and supports concurrent calls. In a way, it is a truly AJAX strategy for updating views partially.

Chapter 10
Testability and Unit Testing

In preparing for battle I have always found that plans are useless, but planning is indispensable.

—Dwight D. Eisenhower

I confess I never paid much attention to unit testing until 2004. I was sitting in the audience of an ASP.NET conference session and I heard "unit testing" mentioned in the Q&A period. I think it was a comment regarding the provider model being introduced in ASP.NET 2.0 and the concept of separation of concerns (SoC) it was pushing. The comment was something like "Yes, that's really great for unit testing." All of a sudden, I found myself wondering how it was that I, as well as thousands of other developers in the community, had overlooked and even neglected unit testing for years.

It turns out that the ISO/IEC 9126 paper—an international standard document issued back in 1991—lists testability as one of the key quality characteristics for any software architecture. The necessity of testing software, therefore, is an old one and can be traced back to the very early days of software engineering.

The question I asked myself on that day in 2004 went unanswered for a couple more years. Since its beginning, the .NET platform made a point of taking us toward the rapid application development (RAD) paradigm and, maybe inadvertently, we ended up sacrificing to RAD some core concepts of good software design. The message of RAD was often perceived as "You don't need principles and good design practices to be productive." Productivity means doing your job more quickly and using tools that, to the extent that it is possible, do it for you.

The success of .NET as a platform resulted in many companies over the full spectrum of the industry needing to acquire new line-of-business applications. In doing so, they dumped an incredible amount of complexity and business rules on the various development teams. High productivity remained a primary objective, but being *really* productive became harder and harder with the sole support of the RAD paradigm.

It was ultimately a complete change of priorities: In addition to having to be concerned with time to market, we had to pay much more attention to maintainability and extensibility. And maintainability brought with it the need to write readable code that could deal with a growing requirement churn.

What's the role of testing in this context? The ability to test software, and in particular to test software automatically, is an aspect of extraordinary importance because automated tests give you a mechanical way to figure out quickly and reliably whether certain features that worked at some point still work after you make some required changes. In addition, tests allow you to calculate metrics and take the pulse of a project as well. In the end, the big change that has come about is that we can no longer spend money on software projects that do not complete successfully. Testing is an important part of the change.

We've all learned a hard lesson lately. Productivity is still important, but focusing on productivity alone costs us too much because it can lead to low-quality code that is difficult and expensive to maintain. And if it's hard to maintain, where's the benefit?

The necessity of testing software in an automated way—we could call it the necessity of applying the RAD paradigm to tests—raised another key point: the need to have software that is easy to test. In fact, the ISO/IEC 9126 paper since 1991 has recognized testability as one of the fundamental qualities of software.

In this chapter, I'll first try to nail down the technical characteristics that a piece of software needs to have to be testable. Next, I'll briefly introduce the basics of unit testing—fixtures, assertions, test doubles, and code coverage—and finish up with some ASP.NET MVC–specific examples of unit tests.

Testability and Design

In the context of software architecture, a broadly accepted definition for testability presents it as "the ease of performing testing." Testing, of course, is the process of checking software to ensure that it behaves as expected, contains no errors, and satisfies its requirements.

Testing software is conceptually simple: just force the program to work on correct, incorrect, missing, or incomplete data and see whether the results you get are in line with any set expectations. How would you force the program to work on your input data? How would you measure the correctness of results? In cases of failure, how would you track the specific module that failed?

These questions are the foundation of a paradigm known as Design for Testability (DfT). Any software built in full respect of DfT principles is inherently testable and, as a very pleasant side effect, it is also easy to read, understand and, subsequently, maintain.

Design for Testability

Design for Testability was developed as a general concept a few decades ago in a field that was not software. The goal of DfT, in fact, was to improve the process of building low-level circuits within boards and chips.

DfT pioneers employed a number of design techniques and practices with the purpose of enabling effective testing in an automated way. What pioneers called "automated testing equipment" was nothing more than a collection of ad hoc software programs written to test some well-known functions of a board and report results for diagnostic purposes.

DfT was adapted to software engineering and applied to test units of code through tailor-made programs. Ultimately, writing unit tests is like writing software. When you write regular code, you call classes and functions, but you focus more on the overall behavior of the program and the actual implementation of use-cases. When you write unit tests, on the other hand, you need to focus on the input and output of individual methods and classes—a different level of granularity.

DfT defines three attributes that any unit of software must have in order to be easily testable: control, visibility, and simplicity. You will be surprised to see that these attributes address exactly the questions I outlined earlier when discussing the foundation of DfT.

The Attribute of *Control*

The attribute of *control* refers to the degree to which the code allows testers to apply fixed input data to the software under test. Any piece of software should be written in a way that makes it clear what parameters are required and what return values are generated. More, any piece of software should abstract its dependencies—both parameters and low-level modules—and provide a way for external callers to inject them at will.

The canonical example of the control attribute applied to software is a method that requires a parameter instead of using its knowledge of the system to figure out the parameter's value from another publicly accessible component. In DfT, control is all about defining a virtual contract for a software component that includes preconditions. The easier you can configure preconditions, the easier you can write effective tests.

The Attribute of *Visibility*

The attribute of *visibility* is defined as the ability to observe the current state of the software under test and any output it can produce. Once you've implemented the ability to impose ad hoc input values on a method, the next step is being able to verify whether the method behaved as expected. Visibility is all about this aspect—postconditions to be verified past the execution of a method.

The sense of visibility is that if testers have a way to programmatically observe a given behavior, they can easily test it against expected or incorrect values. Postconditions are a way to formalize the expected behavior of a software module.

The Attribute of *Simplicity*

Simplicity is always a positive attribute for any system and in every context. Testing is clearly no exception. Simple and extremely cohesive components are preferable because the less you have to test, the more reliably and quickly you can do that.

In the end, design for testability is a driving factor when writing the source code—preferably right from the beginning of the project—so that attributes such as visibility, control, and simplicity are maximized. When design for testability accomplishes this, writing unit tests is highly effective and overall easier. DfT also offers some pleasant side benefits. Overall, a better design, which primarily maximizes maintainability, also helps with code regression and leads to producing code that is easier to read.

> **Note** Many would agree that maintainability is the aspect of software to focus upon because of the long-term benefits it can deliver. However, readability is strictly related to and, to a good extent, also part of any maintainability effort. Readability is concerned with writing code that is easy to read and, subsequently, easy to understand and safer to update and evolve. Readability passes through company-wide naming and coding conventions and, better yet, implements ways to effectively convey these conventions to the development teams. In this regard, custom policies in Microsoft Visual Studio Team Foundation Server are a great help.

Loosen Up Your Design

Testable software is inherently better software from a design perspective. When you apply control, visibility, and simplicity to the software development process, you end up with relatively small building blocks that interact only via contracted interfaces. Testable software is software written for someone else to use it programmatically. The typical programmatic user of testable software is the test harness—the program used to run unit tests. In any case, we are talking about software that uses other software. Low coupling, therefore, is the universal principle to apply systematically, and interface-based programming is the best practice to follow for software that's easier to test.

Interface-Based Programming

Tight coupling makes software development much simpler and faster. Tight coupling results from an obvious point: if you need to use a component, just get an instance of it. This leads to code like that in the following listing:

```
public class MyComponent
{
    private MyDefaultLogger _logger;
    public MyComponent()
    {
        _logger = new MyDefaultLogger();
    }
    public bool PerformTask()
    {
        // Some work here
        bool success = true;
        :
        :
```

```
        // Log activity
        _logger.Log(...);

        // Return success or failure
        return success;
    }
}
```

The *MyComponent* class is strictly dependent on *MyDefaultLogger*. You can't reuse the *MyComponent* class in an environment where *MyDefaultLogger* isn't available. Moreover, you can't reuse *MyComponent* in a runtime environment that prevents *MyDefaultLogger* from working properly. This is an example of where tight coupling between classes can take you. From a testing perspective, the *MyComponent* class can't be tested without reproducing a runtime environment that is perfectly compatible with the production environment. For example, if *MyDefaultLogger* logs to Microsoft Internet Information Services (IIS), your test environment must have IIS properly configured and working.

The beauty of unit testing, on the other hand, is that you run your tests quickly and punctually, focusing on the behavior of a small piece of software and ignoring or controlling dependencies. This is clearly impossible when you program your classes to use a concrete implementation of a dependency. Here's how to rewrite the *MyComponent* class so that it depends on an interface, thus resulting in more maintainable and testable code:

```
public class MyComponent
{
    private ILogger _logger;
    public MyComponent()
    {
        _logger = new MyDefaultLogger();
    }
    public MyComponent(ILogger logger)
    {
        _logger = logger;
    }
    public bool PerformTask()
    {
        // Some work here
        bool success = true;
        :
        :

        // Log activity
        _logger.Log(...);

        // Return success or failure
        return success;
    }
}
```

The class *MyComponent* is now dependent on the *ILogger* interface that abstracts the dependency on the logging module. The *MyComponent* class now knows how to deal with any objects that implement the *ILogger* interface, including any objects you might inject programmatically.

The solution just shown is acceptable from a testing perspective, even though it is far from perfect. In the preceding implementation, the class is still dependent on *MyDefaultLogger* and you can't really reuse it without having available the assembly where *MyDefaultLogger* is defined. At a minimum, however, it allows you to test the behavior of the class in isolation, bypassing the default logger, as shown here:

```
// Arrange the call
var fakeLogger = new FakeLogger();
var component = new MyComponent(fakeLogger);

// Perform the call and check against expectations
Assert(component.PerformTask());
```

Instructing your classes to work against interfaces rather than implementations is one of five pillars of modern software development. The five principles of development are often summarized with the acronym SOLID, formed from the initials of the five principles:

- Single Responsibility Principle
- Open/Closed Principle
- Liskov's Substitution Principle
- Interface Segregation Principle
- Dependency Inversion Principle

For more information on these principles, check out my book *Microsoft .NET: Architecting Applications for the Enterprise* (Microsoft Press, 2008).

Dependency Injection

In modern software, the idea of writing code against interfaces rather than implementations is widely accepted and applied, but it is also often shadowed by another, more specific, concept—*dependency injection*.

We could say that the whole concept of interface-based programming is hard-coded in the Dependency Inversion Principle and that dependency injection is a popular design pattern used to apply the principle. As Robert Martin formulated it, the Dependency Inversion Principle reads like this:

High-level modules should not depend upon low-level modules. Both should depend upon abstractions.

Each method in a class is expected to perform a number of actions. As you specify these actions, you proceed in a top-down way, going from high-level abstractions down the stack to more and more precise and specific functionalities. In a top-down approach, you are interested in recognizing these functionalities, but you don't need to specify details for these components in the first place. All that you need to do is hide details behind a stable interface. Next, you program your methods against the interface.

That's what the Dependency Inversion Principle says. What about the practice, instead? Because an interface simply represents a contract, you need to provide a concrete object that adheres to that contract. To apply the Dependency Inversion Principle, you need a factory that returns a valid implementation of the dependency.

There are two main patterns that help in this regard: Service Locator and Dependency Injection. Both were covered in Chapter 8, "The ASP.NET MVC Infrastructure."

There are several possible implementations of the Service Locator pattern, but the main fact remains that, with it, the factory is embedded in the method that uses the interface. To figure out dependencies, you have to snoop into the source code of the method. Another downside of the Service Locator pattern is that you cannot change its behavior on the fly to switch from a runtime scenario to a testing scenario. You can get that if you code the locator to read about type mappings from an external configuration file or a database. This approach significantly raises the testing-friendliness of the pattern.

A much more helpful pattern from a testing viewpoint is Dependency Injection. In this case, the factory is moved out of the class that uses the dependencies. In some way, external dependencies are to be injected dynamically. This has two benefits. First, by simply looking at the signature of a method you can spot all of its dependencies, which greatly helps readability. Second, you can explicitly instantiate a fake dependency and pass it on programmatically, which is ideal for effective testing.

Dependency Injection, whether coded manually as shown here or implemented through productivity tools such as IoC containers (which are discussed in Chapter 8), is a much more useful pattern when testability is a primary concern.

Relativity of Software Testability

Is design for testability important because it leads to software that is easy to test? Or rather, is it so important because it leads to inherently better designed software? I definitely favor the second option (even though a strong argument can be made for the first option too).

You probably won't go to a customer and use the argument of testability to sell a product of yours. You would likely use other arguments such as features, overall quality, user-friendliness, and ease of use. Testability is important only to developers, because it is an excellent barometer of the quality of design and coding. From the user's perspective there's no difference between "testable code that works" and "untestable code that works."

On the other hand, a piece of software that is easy to test is necessarily loosely coupled, provides a great separation of concerns between core parts, and is easy to maintain because it can have a battery of tests to promptly catch any regression. In addition, it is inherently simpler in its structure and lends itself well to future extensions.

In the end, pursuing testability is a great excuse to have well-designed software. And once you get it, you can also easily test it!

Testability and Coupling

There's a strict relationship between coupling and testability. A class that can't be easily instantiated in a test has some serious coupling problems. This doesn't mean you can't test it automatically, but you will probably have to configure some database or external connection also in a test environment, which will definitely produce slower tests and higher maintenance costs.

To be effective, a test has to be quick and execute in memory. A project that has good test coverage will likely have a few simple tests per class, which likely amount to a few thousand test calls. It is a manageable problem if each test is quick enough and has no latency due to synchronization and connections. It is a serious issue otherwise.

If the problem of coupling between components is not properly addressed in the design, you end up testing components that interact with others, producing something that looks more like an integration test than a unit test. Integration tests are still necessary, but they ideally should run on individual units of code (for example, classes) that already have been thoroughly tested in isolation. Integration tests are not run as often as unit tests because of their slow speed and higher setup costs.

In addition, if you end up using integration tests to test a class and a failure occurs, how easily can you identify the problem? Was it in the class you intended to test, or was it due to a problem in some of the dependencies? Finding the right problem gets significantly more expensive. And even when you've found it, fixing it can have an impact on components in the upper layers.

By keeping coupling under control at the design level (for example, by systematically applying the SOLID principles and Dependency Injection in particular), you enforce testability. On the other hand, by pursuing testability you keep coupling under control and get a better design for your software.

Testability and Object Orientation

A largely debated point is whether or not it is acceptable (and if it is, to what degree) to sacrifice some design principles (specifically, object-oriented principles) to testability. As mentioned, testability is a driver for better design, but you can have a great design without unit tests and also have great software that is almost impossible to test automatically.

The point here is slightly different. If you pursue good object-oriented design, you probably have a policy that limits the use of virtual members and inheritable classes to situations where it is only strictly necessary. Nonvirtual methods and sealed classes, however, can be hard to test because most test environments need to mock up classes and override members. Furthermore, why should you have an additional constructor that you won't use other than for testing? What should you do?

It is clearly mostly a matter of considering the trade-offs.

However, consider that commercial tools exist that let you mock and test classes regardless of their design, including sealed classes and nonvirtual methods. An excellent example is TypeMock. (See *http://site.typemock.com.*)

In .NET, the mechanism of partial classes offers a great solution for adding to an existing class some extra members provided solely for the purpose of unit testing. Using partial classes gives you the chance to have highly testable classes without spoiling the overall design with test-specific additions.

Basics of Unit Testing

Unit testing verifies that individual units of code are working properly according to their expected behavior. A *unit* is the smallest part of an application that is testable—typically, a method on a class.

Unit testing consists of writing and running a small program (referred to as a *test harness*) that instantiates classes and invokes methods in an automatic way. In the end, running a battery of tests is much like compiling. You click a button in the programming environment of choice (for example, Visual Studio), you run the test harness and, at the end of it, you know what went wrong, if anything. (See Figure 10-1.)

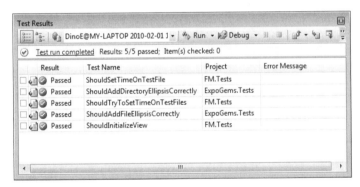

FIGURE 10-1 The results of a running a test project in Visual Studio

Working with a Test Harness

In its simplest form, a test harness is a manually written program that reads test-case input values and the corresponding expected results from some external files. Then the test harness calls methods using input values and compares the results with the expected values. Needless to say, writing such a test harness entirely from scratch is, at a minimum, time consuming and error prone. More importantly, it is restrictive in terms of taking advantage of the testing capabilities.

The most effective and common way to conduct unit testing entails using an automated test framework. An automated test framework is a developer tool that normally includes a runtime engine and a framework of classes for simplifying the creation of test programs.

MSTest and NUnit

Two of the most popular tools are MSTest and NUnit. MSTest is the testing tool incorporated into all versions of Visual Studio 2010. It is also available with some earlier versions, starting with Visual Studio 2005 Team Tester and Team Developer. Figure 10-1 shows the user interface of MSTest within Visual Studio.

NUnit (which you can find at *http://www.nunit.org*) is an open-source product that has been around for quite a few years. NUnit is created to be a stand-alone tool and doesn't *natively* integrate with Visual Studio, which can be either good or bad news—it depends on your perspective of things and your needs and expectations. However, a few tricks exist that enable you to use NUnit from inside Visual Studio. You can configure it as an external executable or, better yet, you can get a plug-in such as ReSharper or TestDriven.NET.

At the end of the day, picking a testing framework is really a matter of preference. Regardless of which one you choose, you are hardly *objectively* losing anything really important. The testing matters much more than the framework you use. In my opinion, as of Visual Studio 2010 no significant technical differences exist between MSTest and NUnit. This doesn't mean you can't make an argument for preferring one over the other, but the argument would likely be more about personal preference than the capabilities of the tools themselves. Both are very good.

I'll use MSTest in this book.

Text Fixtures

You start by grouping related tests in a *text fixture*. Text fixtures are just test-specific classes where methods typically represent tests to run. In a text fixture, you might also have code that executes at the start and end of the test run. Here's the skeleton of a text fixture with MSTest:

```
using Microsoft.VisualStudio.TestTools.UnitTesting;
  :
  :

[TestClass]
public class CustomerTestCase
{
  private Customer customer;

  [TestInitialize]
  public void SetUp()
  {
    customer = new Customer();
  }
```

```
[TestCleanup]
public void TearDown()
{
  customer = null;
}

// Your tests go here
[TestMethod]
public void ShouldComplainInCaseOfInvalidId()
{
    .
    .
    .
}
    .
    .
    .
}
```

Text fixtures are grouped in an ad hoc Visual Studio project. When you create a new ASP.NET MVC project, Visual Studio offers to create a test project for you.

You transform a plain .NET class into a test fixture by simply adding the *TestClass* attribute. You turn a method of this class into a test method by using the *TestMethod* attribute instead. Attributes such as *TestInitialize* and *TestCleanup* have special meanings and indicate code that runs before and after, respectively, each test in that class. By using attributes such as *ClassInitialize* and *ClassCleanup*, you can define, instead, code that runs only once before and after all tests you have in a class.

Arrange, Act, Assert

The typical layout of a test method is summarized by the triple "A" acronym: arrange, act, assert. You start arranging the execution context in which you will test the class by initializing the state of the class and providing any necessary dependencies.

Next, you put in the code that acts on the class under test and performs any required work. Finally, you deal with results and verify that the received output is correct. You do this by verifying assertions based on your expectations.

You write your assertions using the ad hoc assertion API provided by the test harness. At a minimum, the test framework will let you check whether the result equals an expected value:

```
[TestMethod]
public void AssignPropertyId()
{
    // Define the input data for the test
    Customer customer = new Customer();
    string id = "IDS";
    string expected = id;

    // Execute the action to test.
    customer.ID = id;
```

```
   // Test the results
   Assert.AreEqual(expected, customer.ID);
}
```

A test doesn't necessarily have to check whether results are correct. A valid test is also the test aimed at verifying whether under certain conditions a method throws an exception. Here's an example where the setter of the *Id* property in the *Customer* class is expected to raise an *ArgumentException* if the empty string is assigned:

```
[TestMethod]
[ExpectedException(typeof(ArgumentException))]
public void AssignPropertyId()
{
    // Define the input data for the test
    Customer customer = new Customer();
    string id = String.Empty";
    string expected = id;

    // Execute the action to test.
    customer.ID = id;

    // Test the results
    Assert.AreEqual(expected, customer.ID);
}
```

When writing tests, you can decide to temporarily ignore one because you know it doesn't work but you have no time to fix it at present. You use the *Ignore* attribute for this:

```
[Ignore]
[TestMethod]
public void AssignPropertyId()
{
    .
    .
    .
}
```

Likewise, you can decide to mark the test as temporarily inconclusive because you are currently unable to determine under which conditions the test will succeed or fail:

```
[TestMethod]
public void AssignPropertyId()
{
    .
    .
    .
    Assert.Inconclusive("Unable to determine success or failure");
}
```

You might think that ignoring a test, or marking it as inconclusive, are unnecessary tasks because you could more simply comment out tests that for some reason just don't work. This is certainly true, but experience teaches that testing is a delicate task that is always on the borderline between normal and low priority. And it is so easy to forget about a test after it has been commented out. It's not by chance that all test frameworks offer a programmatic way to ignore tests while keeping the code active in the project. Test harness authors know project schedules and budgets are always tight, but they also know maintaining tests in an executable state is important. Whenever you run the tests, you'll be reminded that some tests were ignored or inconclusive rather than encouraged to forget you commented out one or several.

Data-Driven Tests

When you arrange a test for a class method, you might sometimes need to try it with a range of possible values, including correct and incorrect values and values that represent edge conditions. In this case, a data-driven test is a great help.

MSTest supports two possible data sources: a Microsoft Office Excel *.csv* file or any valid ADO. NET data source. The test must be bound to the data source using the *DataSource* attribute, and an instance of the test will be run for each value in the data source. The data source will contain input values and expected values:

```
string id = TestContext.DataRow["ID"].ToString();
string expected = TestContext.DataRow["Result"].ToString();
:
:
Assert.AreEqual(id, expected);
```

You use the *TestContext* variable to read input values. In MSTest, the *TestContext* variable is automatically defined when you add a new unit test:

```
private TestContext testContextInstance;
public TestContext TestContext
{
    get { return testContextInstance; }
    set { testContextInstance = value; }
}
```

Among other things, the *DataSource* attribute also lets you specify whether test input values are to be processed randomly or sequentially.

Aspects of Testing

Writing unit tests is still a form of programming and has the same need for good practices and techniques as software programming aimed at production code. Writing unit tests, however, has its own set of patterns and characteristics that you might want to keep an eye on.

Very Limited Scope

When introducing DfT at the beginning of the chapter, I wrote it quite clearly: Simplicity is a fundamental aspect of software that is key in enabling testability. When applied to unit testing, simplicity is related to giving a very limited scope to the code under test.

A limited scope makes the test self-explanatory and reveals its purpose clearly. This is beneficial for at least two reasons. First, any developers looking into it, including the same author a few weeks later, can quickly and unambiguously understand what the expected behavior of the method under test is.

Second, a test that fails poses the additional problem of you needing to figure out why it failed in order to fix the class under test. The simpler the test method is, the simpler it will be to isolate problems within the class being tested. Furthermore, the more layered the class under test is, the easier it will be to apply changes without the risk of breaking the code somewhere else. Finally, writing tests with a very limited scope is significantly easier for classes that control their dependencies on other components.

Unit testing is like a circle: making it virtuous or vicious is up to you, and it mostly depends on the quality of your design.

Testing in Isolation

An aspect of unit tests that is tightly related to having a limited scope is testing in isolation. When you test a method, you want to focus only on the code within *that* method. All that you want to know is whether *that* code provides the expected results in the tested scenarios. To get this, you need to get rid of all dependencies the method might have.

If the method, say, invokes another class, you assume that the invoked class will *always* return correct results. In this way, you eliminate at the root the risk that the method fails under test because a failure occurred down the call stack. If you test method A and it fails, the reason has to be found *exclusively* in the source code of method A and not in any of its dependencies.

It is highly recommended that the class being tested be *isolated* from its dependencies. Note, though, that this can happen only if the class is designed in a loosely coupled manner. In an object-oriented scenario, class A depends on class B when any of the following conditions are verified:

- Class A derives from class B.

- Class A includes a member of class B.

- One of the methods of class A invokes a method of class B.

- One of the methods of class A receives or returns a parameter of class B.

- Class A depends on a class that, in turn, depends on class B.

How can you neutralize dependencies when testing a method? You use *test doubles*.

Fakes and Mocks

A test double is an object that you use in lieu of another. A test double is an object that pretends to be the real one expected in a given scenario. A class written to consume an object that implements the *ILogger* interface can accept a real logger object that logs to IIS or some database table. At the same time, it also can accept an object that pretends to be a logger but just does nothing. There are two main types of test doubles: fakes and mocks.

The simplest option is to use *fake* objects. A fake object is a relatively simple clone of an object that offers the same interface as the original object, but returns hard-coded or programmatically determined values. Here's a sample fake object for the *ILogger* type:

```
public class FakeLogger : ILogger
{
    public void Log(string message)
    {
        return;
    }
}
```

As you can see, the behavior of a fake object is hard-coded; the fake object has no state and no significant behavior. From the fake object's perspective, it makes no difference how many times you invoke a fake method and when in the flow the call occurs. You use fakes when you just want to ignore a dependency.

A more sophisticated option is using *mock* objects. A mock object does all that a fake does, plus something more. In a way, a mock is an object with its own personality that mimics the behavior and interface of another object. What more does a mock provide to testers?

Essentially, a mock allows for verification of the context of the method call. With a mock, you can verify that a method call happens with the right preconditions and in the correct order with respect to other methods in the class.

Writing a fake manually is not usually a big issue—all the logic you need is for the most part simple and doesn't need to change frequently. When you use fakes, you're mostly interested in the state that a fake object might represent; you are not interested in interacting with it.

You use a mock instead when you need to interact with dependent objects during tests. For example, you might want to know whether the mock has been invoked or not, and you might decide within the test what the mock object has to return for a given method.

Writing mocks manually is certainly a possibility, but it is rarely an option you want to consider. For the level of flexibility you expect from a mock, you need an ad hoc mocking framework. Table 10-1 lists a few popular mocking frameworks.

TABLE 10-1 Some popular mocking frameworks

Product	URL
Moq	*http://code.google.com/p/moq*
NMock2	*http://sourceforge.net/projects/nmock2*
TypeMock	*http://www.typemock.com*
Rhino Mocks	*http://www.ayende.com/projects/rhino-mocks.aspx*

Note that no mocking framework is currently incorporated in Visual Studio 2010 and earlier versions.

With the notable exception of TypeMock, all frameworks in the table are open-source software. TypeMock is a commercial product with unique capabilities that basically don't require you to (re)design your code for testability. TypeMock enables testing code that was previously considered untestable, such as static methods, nonvirtual methods, and sealed classes. Here's a quick example of how to use a mocking framework such as Rhino Mocks:

```
[TestMethod]
public void Test_If_Method_Works()
{
    // Arrange
    var logger = MockRepository.GenerateMock<ILogger>();
    logger.Expect(l => l.Log(Arg<String>.Is.Anything));
    var controller = new HomeController(logger);

    // Act
    :
    :


    // Assert
    :
    :

}
```

The class under test—the *HomeController* class—has a dependency on an object that implements the *ILogger* interface:

```
public interface ILogger
{
    void Log(string msg);
}
```

The mock repository supplies a dynamically created object that mocks up the interface for what the test is going to use. The mock object implements the method *Log* in such a way that it does nothing for whatever string argument it receives. You are not really testing the logger here; you are focusing on the controller class and providing a quick and functional mock for the logger component the controller uses internally.

There's no need for you to create an entire fake class; you just specify the code you need a given method to run when invoked. That's the power of mocks compared to fakes.

Assertions per Test

This is a controversial point. How many assertions should you have per test? Should you force yourself to have just one assertion per test in full homage to the principle of narrowly scoped tests?

Many people in the industry seem to think so. Arguments used in support of this opinion are good ones, indeed. One assertion per test leads you to write more focused tests and keep your scope limited. One assertion per test makes it obvious what each test is testing.

The need for multiple assertions often hides the fact that you are testing many features within a single test. And this is clearly a thing to avoid. Counting the number of assertions is not necessarily the rule to follow in any case; even though if you need just one rule, one assertion per test is probably the best compromise you can make.

If you're testing the state of an object after a given operation, you probably need to check multiple values and need multiple assertions. Now, you can certainly find a way to express this through a bunch of tests, each with a single assertion. In my opinion, though, that would be a lot of refactoring for little gain.

I don't mind having multiple assertions per test as long as the code in the test is testing just one very specific behavior. Most frameworks stop at the first failed assertion, so you theoretically risk that other assertions in the same test will fail on the next run. If you hold to the principle that you test just one behavior and use multiple assertions to verify multiple aspects of the class related to that behavior, all assertions are related and if the first one fails, the chances are great that by fixing it you won't get more failures in that test.

Testing Inner Members

In some situations, a protected method or property needs to be accessed within a test. In general, a class member doesn't have to be public to deserve some tests. However, testing a nonpublic member raises some additional issues.

A common approach to testing a nonpublic member consists of creating a new class that extends the class under test. The derived class then adds a public method that calls the protected method. This class is added only to the test project, without spoiling the class design.

As mentioned earlier, in the .NET Framework an even better approach consists of adding a partial class to the class under test. For this to happen, though, the original class needs to be marked as partial itself. However, this is not a big deal design-wise.

In .NET, you can also easily make internal members of a class visible to another assembly (for example, the test assembly) by using the *InternalsVisibleTo* attribute:

```
[assembly: InternalsVisibleTo("MyTests")]
```

You can add the preceding line to the *assemblyinfo.cs* file of the project that contains the class with *internal* members to make available. Note that you can use the attribute multiple times so that you make visible internal members of classes to multiple external executables.

As I see things, using this attribute is a little more obtrusive than using partial classes. To take advantage of the attribute, in fact, you must mark as *internal* any members that you want to recall from tests. Internal members are still not publicly available, but the level of visibility they have is higher than private or protected. In other words, you should use *internal* and *InternalsToVisible* sparingly and only where a specific need justifies its use.

Finally, MSTest also offers a nice programming feature that offers to call nonpublic members via reflection—the *PrivateObject* class:

```
var resourceId = "WelcomeMessage";
var resourceFile = "MyRes.it.resx";
var expected = "...";
var po = new PrivateObject(controller);
var text = po.Invoke("GetLocalizedText", new object[] { resourceId, resourceFile });
Assert.AreEqual(text, expected);
```

You wrap the object that contains the hidden member in a new instance of the *PrivateObject* class. Next, you call the *Invoke* method to indirectly invoke the method with an array of objects as its parameter list. The method *Invoke* returns an object that represents the return value of the private member.

Code Coverage

The primary purpose of unit and integration tests is to make the development team confident about the quality of the software. Basically, unit testing tells the team whether they are doing well and are on the right track. How reliable are the results of unit tests?

Any measure of reliability you want to consider certainly depends on the number of unit tests and the related code coverage. On the other hand, no realistic correlation exists between code coverage and the quality of the software.

Typically, unit tests cover only a subset of the code base, but no common agreement has ever been reached on what is a "good" percentage of code coverage. Some say 80 percent is good; some do not even instruct the testing tool to calculate it. For sure, forms of full code coverage are actually impractical or impossible. Visual Studio 2008 Team System and all versions of Visual Studio 2010 have code-coverage tools. (See Figure 10-2.)

There are a number of code coverage criteria, such as function, statement, decision, and path coverage. *Function* coverage measures whether each function in the program has been executed in some tests. *Statement* coverage looks more granularly at individual lines of the source code. *Decision* coverage measures the branches (such as an *if* statement) evaluated, whereas *path* coverage checks whether every possible route through a given part of the code has been executed.

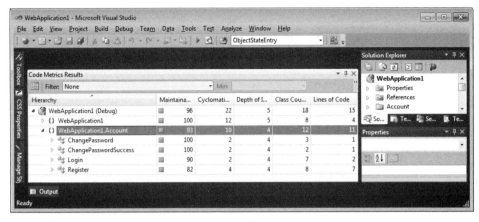

FIGURE 10-2 Code coverage tools in Visual Studio 2010

Each criterion provides a viewpoint into the code, but what you get back are only numbers to be interpreted. So it might seem that testing all the lines of code (that is, getting 100 percent statement coverage) is a great thing; however, a higher value for path coverage is probably more desirable. Code coverage is certainly useful because it helps you identify which code hasn't been touched by tests. However, code coverage doesn't tell you much about how well tests have exercised the code. Want a nice example?

Imagine a method that processes an integer. You can have 100 percent statement coverage for it, but if you lack a test in which the method gets an out-of-range, invalid value you might get an exception at run time in spite of all the successful tests you have run.

In the end, code coverage is a number subject to specific measurement. Focusing on behavior is the best way to approach testing.

Important Testability is often presented as an inalienable feature that makes ASP.NET MVC the first option to consider when it comes to Web development for the Microsoft platform. For sure, ASP.NET MVC helps developers write more solid and well-designed software with due separation of concerns between view and behavior. The ASP.NET MVC runtime also offers an API that abstracts away any dependencies your code can have on ASP.NET intrinsic objects. This change marks a huge difference from Web Forms as far as testing is concerned. This fact increases the feeling that ASP.NET MVC encourages test-driven development.

Is ease of testing a good reason to push the use of ASP.NET MVC over Web Forms? Does this alone translate to concrete and tangible benefits for the customer? As you saw in Chapter 1, "Goals of ASP.NET and Motivations for Its Development," ASP.NET MVC clearly has an architecture that is superior to Web Forms. But, again, is this a sufficient reason for saying that you should go with ASP.NET MVC all the time and forget about Web Forms? My answer is no. As I see things, the architecture of the tool you use to write an application is not necessarily a valid metric to measure the quality of the final product.

In the end, testability is a fundamental aspect of software, as the ISO/IEC 9126 paper recognized back in 1991. With ASP.NET MVC, designing your code for testability is easier and encouraged. (It is not guaranteed, however.) But you also can write testable code in ASP.NET Web Forms and test it to a good extent. Testability is an excellent excuse to pursue good design. And design makes a difference under the hood.

Unit Testing in ASP.NET MVC

Any environment that provides a good separation of concerns between its parts is inherently more testable. ASP.NET Web Forms was not designed with the principle of interface-based programming in mind. At the same time, though, if you code it properly you can add a great deal of SoC and make some significant portion of your code inherently testable.

By implementing the Model-View-Presenter (MVP) pattern (which was discussed in Chapter 1 and Chapter 3, "The MVC Pattern and Beyond"), you can add a presenter class to Web Forms and keep it separate from the view represented by the system's *Page* class. In this way, you can test the presenter class in isolation much like you can with a controller class in ASP.NET MVC.

Testing-wise, the aspect most characteristic of ASP.NET MVC is the set of abstractions it provides over the ASP.NET intrinsic objects that populate the HTTP context of a request: *Response*, *Request*, *User*, and the like. In the ASP.NET runtime that both Web Forms and ASP.NET MVC share, these objects are treated as concrete objects and are not manipulated via an interface. In the ASP.NET MVC runtime shell, you find the new *HttpContextBase* class, which provides an abstraction layer over the physical implementation of objects. This little detail makes a huge difference because it enables you to take advantage of a number of new testing scenarios.

Testing Controller Actions

You need an ad hoc test project to start writing your unit tests. Whenever you create a new ASP.NET MVC project, Visual Studio offers to create a sample test project. Figure 10-3 shows a realistic configuration of a test project in Visual Studio.

A test project is just a project, and its ultimate purpose is executing code correctly. Building a test project is like building an application with no user interface of its own. Your purpose is to write code that places calls to existing classes and methods. The test project can be shaped up to reference ad hoc assemblies, test-specific classes, or its own configuration file, and tricks of any sort are allowed and welcome just as in any other type of project.

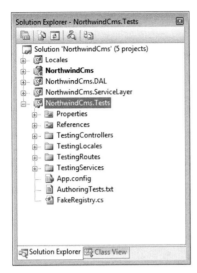

FIGURE 10-3 A sample ASP.NET MVC test project

Testing Controller Actions

The most common and effective type of test you want to perform is on a controller's action methods. The controller class is loosely coupled to the rest of the application. It gets called by the invoker, receives context information through the abstract interface of the *HttpContextBase* class, does its job, and passes an in-memory object down to the rendering engine.

Testing a controller action couldn't be smoother. (Also, note that this is the same level of testability you can achieve in Web Forms by implementing the MVP pattern.)

```
[TestClass]
public class HomeControllerTest
{
    [TestMethod]
    public void Try_Invoking_Action_Index()
    {
        // Arrange
        var controller = new HomeController();

        // Act
        var result = controller.Index() as ViewResult;

        // Assert
        var viewData = result.ViewData;
        Assert.AreEqual(Locales.HomeController.WelcomeMessage, viewData["Message"]);
    }
}
```

The test method first gets a new instance of the controller class and then acts on it by calling the method under test—the method *Index* in the preceding code snippet.

Because the controller is essentially a class that retains no hidden dependencies on the runtime environment, testing one of its methods is as simple as invoking a method on a class. A controller action method typically returns an *ActionResult* object, and that is the class you have to deal with to verify the correctness of the response.

As you saw in Chapter 4, "Inside Controllers," *ActionResult* is only the base type and a controller method will likely return a more specific type, such as *JsonResult* or *ViewResult*. You can use any information you hold in this regard to cast the response and check its content.

Let's assume the *Index* method has the following code:

```
public virtual ActionResult Index()
{
    ViewData["Message"] = Locales.HomeController.WelcomeMessage;
    return View();
}
```

The method returns an object that references an HTML view. More important than this, the view is based on the data stored in the *ViewData* dictionary (or in the model object if the view is strongly typed).

In ASP.NET MVC, the view is mostly passive and is limited to hosting in specific placeholders the data it receives from the controller through *ViewData*, *ViewData.Model*, or both. You don't need to automatically test the HTML for the view; it is sufficient that you ensure that correct data is being passed to the view.

Subsequently, in the Assert section of the test you check whether the expected value is found in the *ViewData* dictionary.

Note In Web Forms, you can achieve nearly the same result by implementing the MVP pattern manually or perhaps by using some of the facilities in the Web Client Software Factory. This applies to the way in which you call the controller and also to the approach you take to check the response of a controller action.

Passing Parameters to a Controller Action

The model-binding mechanism we reviewed in Chapter 6, "Inside Models," greatly simplifies the scenario in which you want to test a controller method that requires input parameters. A model binder makes it possible to define a controller method with its own signature, as shown here:

```
// From a ProductController class
public virtual ActionResult Index(int productId)
{
    :
    :
}
```

The ID of the product is excerpted from the request, but that code doesn't belong to the controller itself. The action invoker and the model binder do the trick, and the controller action just gets the value. In testing, this translates to fairly simple code:

```
var controller = new ProductController();
var result = controller.Index(42) as ViewResult;
var model = result.ViewData.Model as ProductViewModel;
if (model == null)
    Assert.Fail("ViewData.Model is null");
Assert.IsNotNull(model.Product);
Assert.AreEqual(model.Product.ProductID, 42);
```

As you can see, the test contains multiple assertions. However, all the assertions refer to just one action—getting the details of the specified product.

Testing Different Views

There might be situations in which the controller decides on the fly about the view to render. This happens when the view to render is based on some conditions known only at run time. An example is a controller method that has to switch view templates based on the locale, user account, day of the week, or anything else your users might ask you. The structure of the controller action looks like the code shown here:

```
public virtual ViewResult Index(int productId)
{
    var cultureInfo = Thread.CurrentThread.CurrentUICulture;
    if (cultureInfo == "it-IT")
        return View("Index_it");
    return View();
}
```

In a test, you can catch the view being rendered using the *ViewName* property of the *ActionResult* object:

```
[TestMethod]
public void Should_Render_Italian_View()
{
    // Set the it-IT culture
    :
    :

    // Act
    var controller = new ProductController();
    var result = controller.Index(42) as ViewResult;
    if (result == null)
        Assert.Fail("Invalid result");
    Assert.AreEqual(result.ViewName, "Index_it", true);
}
```

By checking the public properties of the specific *ActionResult* object returned by the controller method, you can perform ad hoc checks when a particular response is generated such as JSON, JavaScript, binaries, files, and so forth.

Testing Redirections

A controller action might also redirect to another URL or route. Testing a redirection, however, is no harder than testing a context-specific view. A controller method that redirects will return a *RedirectResult* object if it redirects to a specific URL; it will instead return a *RedirectToRouteResult* object if it redirects to a named route.

The *RedirectResult* class has a familiar *Url* property you can check to verify whether the action completed successfully. The *RedirectToRouteResult* class has properties such as *RouteName* and *RouteValues* that you can check to ensure the redirection worked correctly.

Injecting Mocks and Fakes

Even in a moderately complex application, you might have the need to pass some dependencies to a controller. In Chapter 4, we discussed two possible stereotypes for a controller. It can be devised to play the role of the *controller* or the role of the *coordinator*.

In spite of the naming conflict, a controller that follows the *controller* stereotype contains methods that direct activities and make most of the important decisions regarding the assigned task. In this case, you probably end up doing the entire job from within the controller without the need of having external dependencies on services and data repositories. However, when you make a point of building a layered solution, a typical method in the controller delegates work to other components such as services and components for data access. In this case, it's coordinating the work. Here's the layout of a controller designed to operate as a coordinator:

```
public class CustomerController : Controller
{
    public CustomerController(ICustomerService service, IRegistry registry)
    {
        _service = service;
        _registry = registry;
    }

    private readonly ICustomerService _service;
    private readonly IRegistry _registry;

    :
    :
    :
}
```

The *CustomerController* class depends on two external components being properly abstracted by interfaces. The *IRegistry* interface identifies a container of global data shared across the application. For example, the *IRegistry* object can cache the list of menu items, or the list of countries to use in a variety of places. The *ICustomerService* interface identifies the component that takes care of executing tasks that involve the entity *Customer.*

In a controller that behaves like a coordinator, what kind of behavior are you going to test? Certainly not the behavior coded in the registry or in the customer service. Here's a sample method:

```
// From CustomerController class
public virtual ActionResult Index(string country)
{
    // Action
    var customers = _service.LoadCustomersByCountry(country);

    // Rendering
    var model = new CustomerViewModel();
    model.CurrentCountry = country;
    model.Customers = customers;
    model.Countries = _registry.GetCountriesFromCache();
    return View("CustomerByCountry", model);
}
```

The controller invokes the service to get the list of customers from a given country and then packages the data for the view. In doing so, the controller also accesses the registry to grab the list of countries to be placed in the view. With this implementation, the controller is clearly acting as a coordinator. From a testing viewpoint, you're not interested in testing dependencies. More precisely, you will test dependencies separately; when it comes to testing the controller, you need to mock up (or fake) dependencies and just ensure that the controller does its coordination job well.

Ignoring Dependencies

As far as testing is concerned, we could say that there are two main types of dependencies: those you want to ignore, and those you want to interact with but in a controlled way. The rule of thumb is to use fakes when you want to ignore a dependency and use mocks when you need more interaction. How do you decide?

A fake is a class you write and add to the test project. It makes sense to have a fake if you don't need multiple versions of it for multiple tests. If one implementation fits all the needs you have for it, go for a fake. For a registry, you probably want to use a fake:

```
public class FakeRegistry : IRegistry
{
    #region IRegistry Members
    public void LoadCountriesIntoCache()
    {
        // No op
    }
```

```
public IList<String> GetCountriesFromCache()
{
    var testData = new List<String>(new string[]
                            {
                                "Austria",
                                "Italy",
                                "Germany"
                            });

    return testData;
}
#endregion
}
```

In this example, the *IRegistry* interface has only two members: one for storing data into the cache, and one for reading. The fake object doesn't do anything when loading and returns canned values when a caller attempts to read. This implementation works throughout the application. Here's how to use the *FakeRegistry* class in a test:

```
[TestClass]
public class CustomersControllerTests
{
    [TestMethod]
    public void Test_If_Service_Returns_Customers_From_Given_Country()
    {
        // Arrange
        var service = ...;
        var controller = new CustomerController(service, new FakeRegistry());

        // Act
        var result = controller.Index("Italy");

        // Assert that member Countries in the model is filled as expected
        Assert.IsTrue(model.Countries.Contains("Italy"));
    }
}
```

The assertion verifies that the specified country (Italy, in the example) is one of the countries known to the registry—namely, one of the countries that can be selected from the user interface. Figure 10-4 provides a glimpse of the user interface for such a scenario.

The user interface lists customers and orders, but the drop-down list of countries also needs the entire list of known countries. That list doesn't have to be reloaded every time and can stay cached for the session, and often for the entire application. The registry object provides a common interface to access that data from wherever it stays—typically, from the ASP.NET *Cache*.

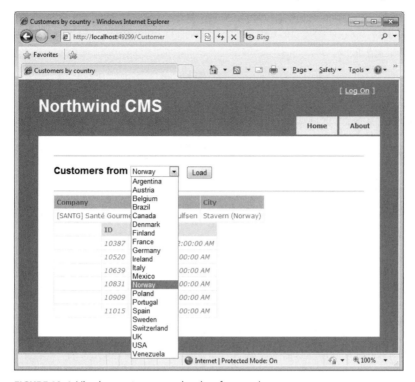

FIGURE 10-4 Viewing customers and orders from a given country

Interacting with Dependencies

The *CustomerController* class we considered in the previous example is also dependent on a service that performs most of the searches and updates. It is an inherently more interactive object that can hardly be ignored. More likely, you need a different version of it for each test. If you opt for a fake, you must be ready to write several small and similar classes. A mocking framework (for example, Rhino Mocks) can help you define, in the scope of the test, just the dynamic object that behaves as you need. Here's how to mock up the customer service that retrieves customers and orders, as shown in Figure 10-4:

```
// Arrange
var service = MockRepository.GenerateMock<ICustomerService>();
service.Expect(s => s.LoadCustomersByCountry("Italy")).Return(
        new List<Customer>()
                {
                    new Customer() {Country = "Italy"},
                    new Customer() {Country = "Italy"}
                });

// Act
var controller = new CustomerController(serv, new FakeRegistry());
```

The *GenerateMock* method returns a dynamically created object that implements the specified interface. Figure 10-5 shows what you see if you place a breakpoint right after the call to *GenerateMock*.

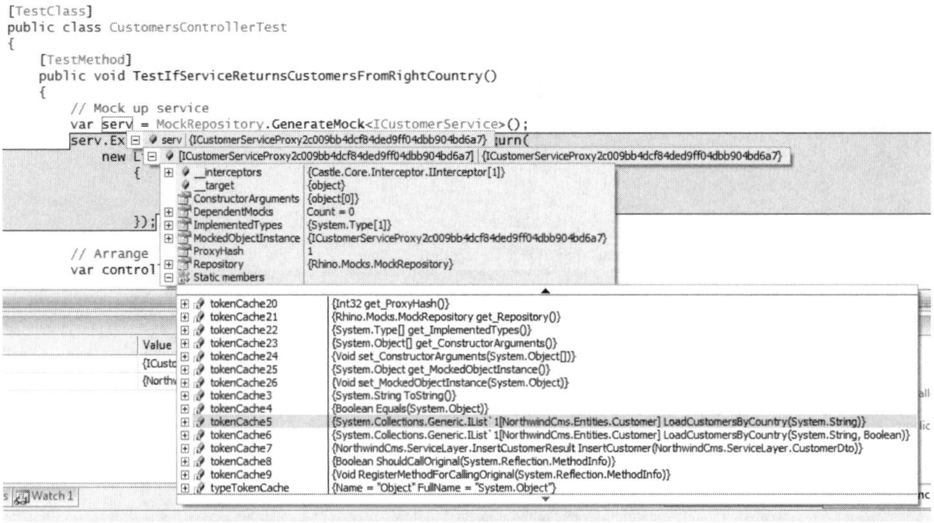

FIGURE 10-5 Snooping the internals of *GenerateMock*

The actual type is *ICustomerServiceProxyXxx*, where *Xxx* is a GUID. The type exposes methods as appropriate for the interface it represents. The *Expect* method that follows the mock factory dynamically defines the expected return value for the method when *Italy* is passed as an argument:

```
service.Expect(s => s.LoadCustomersByCountry("Italy")).Return(
        new List<Customer>()
            {
                new Customer() {Country = "Italy"},
                new Customer() {Country = "Italy"}
            });
```

In this case, the mocked method returns a list of stubs for the *Customer* type where only the *Country* property is set to a default value. For the scope of the test, you don't really need to know about other details: the service method is expected to return customers from Italy, and that's all that matters. Here are some possible assertions:

```
// Assert
Assert.AreEqual(model.CurrentCountry, "Italy");
foreach (Customer c in model.Customers)
{
  Assert.AreEqual(c.Country, model.CurrentCountry);
}
```

The controller's job in the example we are considering is limited to packaging data for the view. In particular, it sets the *CurrentCountry* property on the model object to the country being processed and fills the *Customers* property with the list of retrieved customers.

Subsequently, an assertion is required to check whether each customer in the *Customers* collection is based in the specified country.

Mocking the HTTP Context

As mentioned, a big selling point of ASP.NET MVC is its ability to mock up ASP.NET intrinsic objects such as *Session*, *Request*, and *Cache*. You saw in Chapter 1 that all the objects that populate the ASP.NET runtime have been abstracted to base classes and interfaces with the precise purpose of making it easier to test.

It's fairly obvious that in a Web application at some point you need to access *Session* or *Cache*, and because the vast majority of an ASP.NET MVC application logic lives in controllers, it's from within controllers that you need to abstract those dependencies. Without abstractions such as the *HttpContextBase* class, using ASP.NET MVC would not be much different than using Web Forms with the MVP pattern.

With that said, you are not supposed to access *Session* or *Cache* from the view; it's the controller that needs to access those containers and pass any data down to the view. How would you test such a controller mocking intrinsic objects? Let's see a few examples.

Mocking the Session State

Imagine you have a controller method that, at some point, writes some data to the *Session* container:

```
public virtual ActionResult SetColor()
{
    // Do some work using Session
    Session["PreferredColor"] = "Green";

    // Prepare the view
    ViewData["Color"] = "Green";
    return View("Color");
}
```

The *Session* object used in the preceding code is a property defined on the *Controller* class, as shown here:

```
public abstract class Controller : ControllerBase, ...
{
    public HttpSessionStateBase Session
    {
        get
        {
            if (this.HttpContext != null)
              return this.HttpContext.Session;
            return null;
        }
    }
    :
    :
}
```

As you can see, the property *Session* is of type *HttpSessionStateBase*, one of the abstractions for ASP.NET intrinsic objects. This is the lever that makes it possible to get a fully mocked session state.

In a test method, you need a couple of things. First, you need a mock for the *HttpContext* object, which is for the container of the *Session* object. Second, you need a fake for *Session* object.

Why a mock for *HttpContext* and a fake for *Session*? Functionally speaking, fakes and mocks are equivalent because both are test doubles. Which one is preferable depends on the context and tests you need to write. A mock is easier to use, but sometimes it requires you to assign a behavior to the various methods. This is easy to do when the behavior is as simple as returning a given value. To effectively test whether the method correctly updates the session state, you need to provide an in-memory object that simulates the behavior of the original object and has the ability to store information—not exactly an easy task to mock. Using a fake session class, instead, makes it straightforward. Here's a minimal yet effective fake for the session state:

```
public class FakeSession : HttpSessionStateBase
{
    private Dictionary<String, Object> _sessionItems =
                                    new Dictionary<String, Object>();

    public override void Add(String name, Object value)
    {
        _sessionItems.Add(name, value);
    }

    public override object this[String name]
    {
        get {
                if(_sessionItems.ContainsKey(name))
                    return _sessionItems[name];
                else
                    return null;}
        set { _sessionItems[name] = value; }
    }
}
```

And here's how to arrange a test:

```
[TestMethod]
public void Should_Write_To_Session_State()
{
    // Arrange
    var contextBase = MockRepository.GenerateMock<HttpContextBase>();
    contextBase.Expect(s => s.Session).Return(new FakeSession());
    var controller = new HomeController();
    controller.ControllerContext = new ControllerContext(
                    contextBase, new RouteData(), controller);
```

```
    // Act
    controller.SetColor();
    var test = controller.HttpContext.Session["PreferredColor"];

    // Assert
    Assert.AreEqual(test, "Green");
}
```

Using Rhino Mocks, you first get a mock for the HTTP context object and next instruct it to return a new instance of *FakeSession* whenever it is asked to return the value associated with the *Session* property. The final step entails configuring the controller invoker to use a controller context based on the fake context you just created.

If your controller method only reads from *Session*, your test can be even simpler and you can avoid faking the *Session* entirely. Here's a sample controller action:

```
public ActionResult GetColor()
{
    object o = Session["PreferredColor"];
    if (o == null)
        ViewData["Color"] = "No preferred color";
    else
        ViewData["Color"] = o as String;

    return View("Color");
}
```

The following code snippet shows a possible way to test the method just shown:

```
// Arrange
var contextBase = MockRepository.GenerateMock<HttpContextBase>();
contextBase.Expect(s => s.Session["PreferredColor"]).Return("Blue");
var controller = new HomeController();
controller.ControllerContext = new ControllerContext(
                               contextBase, new RouteData(), controller);

// Act
var result = controller.GetColor() as ViewResult;
if (result == null)
    Assert.Fail("Result is null");

// Assert
Assert.AreEqual(result.ViewData["Color"].ToString(), "Blue");
```

In this case, you instruct the HTTP context mock to return the string "Blue" when its *Session* property is requested to provide a value for the entry "PreferredColor."

In what is likely the much more common scenario where a controller method needs to read *and* write the session state, you need to use the test solution based on *FakeSession*.

Building a Fake HTTP Context

The same approach discussed for *Session* can be applied to any other intrinsic object, including *Request, Server, Response,* and *User.* Here's a utility that attempts to build a fake HTTP context for the given controller where a few intrinsic objects are mocked up:

```
public void FakeHttpContextForController(Controller controller)
{
    var contextBase = MockRepository.GenerateMock<HttpContextBase>();
    var request = MockRepository.GenerateMock<HttpRequestBase>();
    var response = MockRepository.GenerateMock<HttpResponseBase>();
    var server = MockRepository.GenerateMock<HttpServerUtilityBase>();

    contextBase.Expect(c => c.Request).Return(request);
    contextBase.Expect(c => c.Response).Return(response);
    contextBase.Expect(c => c.Server).Return(server);

    var context = new ControllerContext(
                new RequestContext(contextBase, new RouteData()), controller);
    controller.ControllerContext = context;
    return;
}
```

Consider that many similar pieces of code are available from several blog posts, including a few from popular Microsoft bloggers such as Scott Hanselman. This is an interesting one: *http://www.hanselman.com/blog/ASPNETMVCSessionAtMix08TDDAndMvcMockHelpers.aspx.*

Also notice that MVCContrib—the portal for community contributions to ASP.NET MVC—has several facilities built for the purpose, in particular the *TestHelpers* class. You can learn more about MVCContrib at *http://www.codeplex.com/MVCContrib.*

Mocking the *Request* Object

Note that the code shown earlier is necessary, but it will likely be insufficient to pay your unit testing bills. You probably want to extend it with expectations regarding some specific members of the various intrinsic objects. For example, here's how to simulate a GET or POST request in a test:

```
public void SetHttpMethodForRequest(HttpContextBase contextBase, string method)
{
    contextBase.Expect(c => Request.HttpMethod).Return(method);
}
```

When discussing the testing of routes you will commonly also run into code much like the following:

```
public void SetUrlForRequest(HttpContextBase contextBase, string url)
{
    contextBase.Expect(c => Request.AppRelativeCurrentExecutionFilePath).Return(url);
}
```

You probably don't want to use the *Request.Form* object to read about posted data from within a controller because you might find model binders to be more effective. However, if you have a call to *Request.Form["MyParam"]* in one of your controller's methods, how would you test it?

```
// Prepare the fake Form collection
var formCollection = new NameValueCollection();
formCollection["MyParam"] = ...;

// Fake the HTTP context and bind Request.Form to the fake collection
var contextBase = MockRepository.GenerateMock<HttpContextBase>();
contextBase.Expect(c => c.Request.Form).Return(formCollection);
// Assert
    :
    :
```

Clearly, in addition to configuring the *Request* object you also have to set the fake context on the controller instance you're going to test. In this way, every time your code reads anything through *Request.Form* it actually ends up reading from the name/value collection provided for testing purposes.

Mocking the *Response* Object

Let's see a few examples that touch on the *Response* object. For example, you might want to mock up *Response.Write* calls by forcing a fake *HttpResponse* object to write to a text writer object:

```
var writer = new StringWriter();
var contextBase = MockRepository.GenerateMock<HttpContextBase>();
contextBase.Expect(c => c.Response).Return(new FakeResponse(writer));
```

In this case, the *FakeResponse* class is used as shown here:

```
public class FakeResponse : HttpResponseBase
{
    private readonly TextWriter _writer;
    public FakeResponse(TextWriter writer)
    {
        _writer = writer;
    }

    public override void Write(string msg)
    {
        _writer.Write(msg);
    }
}
```

This code will let you test a controller method that has calls to *Response.Write* like the one shown here:

```
public ActionResult Output()
{
    HttpContext.Response.Write("Hello");
    return View();
}
```

Here's the test:

```
[TestMethod]
public void Should_Response_Write()
{
    // Arrange
    var writer = new StringWriter();
    var contextBase = MockRepository.GenerateMock<HttpContextBase>();
    contextBase.Expect(c => c.Response).Return(new FakeResponse(writer));
    var controller = new HomeController();
    controller.ControllerContext = new ControllerContext(
                contextBase, new RouteData(), controller);

    // Act
    var result = controller.Output() as ViewResult;
    if (result == null)
        Assert.Fail("Result is null");

    // Assert
    Assert.AreEqual("Hello", writer.ToString());
}
```

Similarly, you can configure a dynamically generated mock if you need to make certain properties or methods to just return a specific value. Here are a couple of examples:

```
var contextBase = MockRepository.GenerateMock<HttpContextBase>();

// Mock up the Output property
contextBase.Expect(c => Response.Output).Return(new StringWriter());

// Mock up the Content type of the response
contextBase.Expect(c => Response.ContentType).Return("application/json");
```

For cookies, instead, you might want to mock the *Cookies* collection on both *Request* and *Response* to return a new instance of the *HttpCookieCollection* class, which will act as your cookie container for the scope of the unit test.

Mocking the ASP.NET *Cache*

Mocking the ASP.NET *Cache* is a task that deserves a bit more attention, even though mocking the cache doesn't require a new approach. The *HttpContextBase* class has a *Cache* property, but you can't mock it up because the property doesn't represent an abstraction of the ASP.NET cache; instead, it is a concrete implementation. Here's how the *Cache* property is declared on the *HttpContextBase* class:

```
public abstract class HttpContextBase : IServiceProvider
{
    public virtual Cache Cache { get; }
    :
    :
}
```

The type of the *Cache* property is actually *System.Web.Caching.Cache*—the real cache object, not an abstraction. Even more unfortunately, the *Cache* type is sealed and therefore is not mockable and is unusable in unit tests. As an example, the following Rhino Mocks code won't work:

```
// Fails with an error that says "Can't create mocks of sealed classes"
var cacheBase = MockRepository.GenerateMock<Cache>();
```

Likewise, the following approach fails also:

```
// FakeCache should be usable wherever Cache is expected, but this is impossible because
// FakeCache should derive from Cache, which is sealed instead.
contextBase.Expect(c => c.Cache).Return(new FakeCache());
```

What can you do? There are two options. One entails using the TypeMock Isolator tool, which is designed to mock any class, including sealed classes. (As mentioned, unlike most mocking frameworks, TypeMock is a commercial tool.)

The other possibility is using a wrapper class to perform any access to the cache from within any code you intend to test. You start by creating the interface of this wrapper object. At a minimum, a cache wrapper will have an indexer property:

```
public interface ICacheProvider
{
    object this[String name] { get; set; }
}
```

You can add more members here to support, add, or remove dependencies and other facilities of the real ASP.NET *Cache* object. Next, you implement the cache wrapper you would use from within your controllers:

```
public class MyCache : ICacheProvider
{
    private readonly Cache _aspnetCache;
    public MyCache()
    {
        if (HttpContext.Current != null)
            _aspnetCache = HttpContext.Current.Cache;
    }

    public object this[string name]
    {
        get { return _aspnetCache[name]; }
        set { _aspnetCache[name] = value; }
    }
}
```

Finally, you remove any calls to *HttpContext.Cache* from your controllers. Your controller will have the following layout:

```
public partial class HomeController : Controller
{
    private readonly ICacheProvider _cache;

    public HomeController()
    {
        _cache = new MyCache();
    }

    public HomeController(ICacheProvider cacheProvider)
    {
        _cache = cacheProvider;
    }

    public ActionResult SetCache()
    {
        // HttpContext.Cache["PreferredColor"] = "Blue";
        _cache["PreferredColor"] = "Blue";
        return View();
    }
    .
    .
    .
}
```

Of course, you could also consider moving the initialization of the cache wrapper in some custom base class to avoid rewriting the same code over and over again.

How would you test this? Here's an example:

```
[TestMethod]
public void Should_Write_To_Cache()
{
    // Arrange
    var fakeCache = new FakeCache();
    var controller = new HomeController(fakeCache);

    // Act
    controller.SetCache();

    // Assert
    Assert.AreEqual("Blue", fakeCache["PreferredColor"].ToString());
}
```

The *FakeCache* class can be something like this:

```
public class FakeCache : ICacheProvider
{
    private readonly Dictionary<String, Object> _cacheItems =
                new Dictionary<String, Object>();
```

```
public object this[String name]
{
    get
    {
        if (_cacheItems.ContainsKey(name))
            return _cacheItems[name];
        else
            return null;
    }
    set { _cacheItems[name] = value; }
}
}
```

As you might have noticed, the default constructor of *MyCache* has an *if* statement that checks whether *HttpContext.Current* is null. Is this really necessary?

```
if (HttpContext.Current != null)
    _aspnetCache = HttpContext.Current.Cache;
```

It is not strictly necessary when the code runs in the Web application. In that case, the *Current* property is never null. However, if you run that code in the context of a unit test, *HttpContext.Current* is always *null*. This is not a problem for the fixture where you test the cache because, in this case, you don't use the default constructor. It is a problem for all other tests you perform for the same controller where you use the default constructor. Without the *if*, you will get a null reference exception.

> **Note** In this regard, many posts suggest you use *HttpRuntime.Cache* instead of *HttpContext*
> *.Cache* everywhere. In doing so, it seems you could save yourself the burden of writing a cache
> wrapper.
>
> *HttpContext* uses *HttpRuntime.Cache* internally to initialize the object returned by its *Cache*
> property. If necessary, *HttpRuntime.Cache* can properly and silently initialize the cache container
> to be used by the Web application. For this reason, by simply linking the *System.Web.Caching*
> assembly (in ASP.NET 4) you have the cache object available even in unit tests. This configures
> a third solution to the problem of mocking the ASP.NET cache: you just don't mock it up; you use
> *HttpRuntime.Cache* instead of *HttpContext.Cache*, and it's always there. In ASP.NET 4, that moves
> the caching API to a separate assembly, with the precise purpose of making it available outside
> ASP.NET. This seems to be more of a supported solution than a hack.
>
> We'll see what the trend is in the months ahead. As of today, however, using wrappers remains
> my favorite solution.

More Specific Tests

The heart of an ASP.NET MVC application is the controller, and testing the results and effectiveness of controller actions is the primary goal of unit testing. Testing controller actions means testing the response generated for a given input, but also it means isolating the controller logic from dependencies such as the service layer, data repositories, the file system, and especially the ASP.NET HTTP context.

Testing, however, doesn't end with the controller actions and routes that we examined earlier in this chapter and in Chapter 8. Let's then review a few other, more specific aspects of an ASP.NET MVC application that you want to test.

Testing HTML Helpers

In ASP.NET MVC, a view is usually humble and passive, and often it doesn't require any automated test. However, if you have custom HTML helpers—that is, custom extension methods you use to render HTML into a view—you might want to consider writing a few unit tests to ensure they produce the markup you expect.

Making assertions for an HTML helper method is not a task that requires a lot of imagination. There are not too many ways to make it other than asserting that the response you get matches a given fixed HTML string. Let's briefly examine one of the Microsoft unit tests for one of the standard HTML helpers—the *CheckBox* helper:

```
[TestMethod]
public void CheckBox_With_Only_Name()
{
    // Arrange
    HtmlHelper helper = HtmlHelperTest.GetHtmlHelper();

    // Act
    MvcHtmlString html = helper.CheckBox("foo");

    // Assert
    Assert.AreEqual(@"<input checked=""checked"" id=""foo"" name=""foo"" " +
                @"type=""checkbox"" value=""true"" />" +
                @"<input name=""foo"" type=""hidden"" value=""false"" />",
                html.ToHtmlString());
}
```

The most critical part of the test is hidden in the *GetHtmlHelper* method. A possible implementation of the method is shown here:

```
public static HtmlHelper<object> GetHtmlHelper()
{
    var contextBase = MockRepository.GenerateMock<HttpContextBase>();
    var viewData = new ViewDataDictionary();
    var viewContext = new ViewContext() {
        HttpContext = httpcontext,
        RouteData = new RouteData(),
        ViewData = viewData
    };

    var viewDataContainer = MockRepository.GenerateMock<IViewDataContainer>();
    viewDataContainer.Expect(v => v.ViewData).Returns(viewData);
    var htmlHelper = new HtmlHelper<object>(
                viewContext, viewDataContainer, new RouteCollection());
    return htmlHelper;
}
```

Most of the work is related to arranging the call; after the call has been made, all that remains to be done is literally check the HTML returned against expectations.

Testing Localized Resources

In Chapter 8, we discussed the theme of localization. Sometimes, it is useful to have some tests that quickly check whether certain parts of the user interface are going to receive proper localized resources when a given language is selected. Here's how to proceed with a unit test:

```
[TestMethod]
public void Test_If_Localized_Strings_Are_Used()
{
    // Arrange
    const string culture = "it-IT";
    var cultureInfo = CultureInfo.CreateSpecificCulture(culture);
    Thread.CurrentThread.CurrentCulture = cultureInfo;
    Thread.CurrentThread.CurrentUICulture = cultureInfo;

    // Act
    string showMeMoreDetails = MyText.Product.ShowMeDetails;

    // Assert
    Assert.AreEqual(showMeMoreDetails, "Maggiori informazioni");
}
```

In the unit test, you first set the culture on the current thread, and then you attempt to retrieve the value for the resource and assert against expected values.

Testing Asynchronous Methods

As you saw in Chapter 4, methods on asynchronous controllers are executed in two distinct steps. The first step triggers the long-running operation and yields to an operating system thread outside of the ASP.NET thread pool for any subsequent wait for results. The second step uses computed results to prepare the view.

An asynchronous method is made of two actual methods, as shown in the following example:

```
// From MyAsyncController
public void PerformTaskAsync(SomeData data)
{
    .
    .
    .
}
public ActionResult PerformTaskCompleted(SomeResponse data)
{
    .
    .
    .
}
```

How about testing? Methods are to be tested separately. Let's tackle the completed method first. You test it as you would with any other controller method:

```
[TestMethod]
public void Should_Complete_The_View()
{
    var controller = new MyAsyncController();
    var data = new SomeResponse() { Data="hello" };
    var result = controller.PerformTaskCompleted(data) as ViewResult;

    Assert.IsNotNull(result);
    Assert.AreEqual(result.ViewData["d.Data"], "hello");
}
```

A bit more interesting is the unit test for the *Async* method:

```
[TestMethod]
public void Should_Run_Async()
{
    var controller = new MyAsyncController();
    var waitHandle = new AutoResetEvent(false);

    // Create and attach event handler for the "Finished" event
    EventHandler eventHandler = delegate(object sender, EventArgs e)
                                {
                                    // Signal that the finished event was raised
                                    waitHandle.Set();
                                };
    controller.AsyncManager.Finished += eventHandler;
    string expected = ...;

    var data = new SomeData() {Id = 1};
    controller.PerformTaskAsync(data);
    if (!waitHandle.WaitOne(5000, false))
    {
        // Wait until the event handler is invoked or times out
        Assert.Fail("Test timed out.");
    }

    // data is the entry name used by PerformTaskAsync to forward information
    var response = controller.AsyncManager.Parameters["data"] as SomeResponse;
    Assert.IsNotNull(response);
    Assert.AreEqual(response.Data, expected);
}
```

The test consists of invoking the *Async* method using a synchronization tool to prevent the method from terminating. The *waitHandle* synchronization object waits at most for five seconds until it fails. If the method completes before the timeout, an event handler associated with the *Finished* event on the *AsyncManager* object fires so that you can signal the lock. The programming paradigm of asynchronous controllers requires that an *Async* method use the *Parameters* dictionary on the *AsyncManager* object to pass information to the *completed* method. The same dictionary can be used in testing to assert expectations.

Note In a layered system, controllers belong to the presentation layer and contain the logic that triggers the service layer, which in turn scripts the business and data access logic. Controllers, services, and business components are therefore the primary targets of software testing.

In addition, testing routes is critical for an application that makes a point of using its own URL scheme. You might also want to ensure via tests whether the correct result and view are generated for each controller action.

Summary

In the .NET space, topics such as software testing, unit testing, and testability have been overlooked for too many years. Only in the past few years have these topics started gaining more attention, and only recently have we been able to have a serious test environment in Visual Studio.

The key point is that you should take the view that your code works only if you can provide evidence for that. A piece of software can gain the status of *working* not when someone (end users, the project manager, the customer, or the chief architect) simply states that it works, but only when its correctness is proven beyond any reasonable doubt. The final stage of any project is the acceptance test performed on the system as a whole in its production environment. On the way to that, though, unit tests and integration tests make the team confident about the work being done and provide evidence of regression at the end of tough refactoring sessions.

Testability is an attribute of software systems that was recognized some 20 years ago in the ISO/IEC 9126 paper. Testability refers to aspects of the software design that make the software itself easy to test. The fact is, to be easily testable, any piece of software has to be well designed; separation of concerns, abstractions, and talking to immediate objects are key assets of any well-designed and testable software.

ASP.NET MVC is well designed itself and makes it easier for a developer to write good quality code that is easy to test. There's no magic involved, however. I like to say that ASP.NET MVC shows you the way to go, and sometimes it takes you to the beginning of the road and gently gives you a pat on the shoulder before sending you on your way. You're alone, however, from that moment onward.

In this chapter, I discussed principles, frameworks, and practices of testing. I hope that I transmitted the sense that ASP.NET MVC is an extremely flexible and extensible platform. The next chapter—which is also the final chapter—is all about aspects of ASP.NET MVC that you can customize to unplug certain subsystems and how to roll your own.

Chapter 11
Customizing ASP.NET MVC

We need men who can dream of things that never were.

—John F. Kennedy

ASP.NET MVC was built with extensibility in mind and in full respect of many good design principles, such as Dependency Inversion, Open/Closed, and Single Responsibility. As obvious as it might sound, the net effect is just what these principles claim you will get if you apply them systematically. You can extend the application without changing the source code, without painful refactoring, and without heavy regression. If properly designed, your application is then open for extensions but closed for modifications.

Because the Open/Closed principle is mostly a driver for architects and developers, the other two principles provide concrete guidance on how to design classes that favor the injection of custom components to replace built-in functionalities. The simpler and more well-defined a class is, the easier it is for developers to customize and replace built-in functionalities. In this regard, ASP.NET MVC is an excellent example of application design.

Because ASP.NET MVC is ultimately a framework, the benefits of its design will ripple across any applications built on top of it. In this chapter, my goal is to help you discover the points of extensibility you find in ASP.NET MVC and to illustrate them with a few examples. I organized the extensibility points of ASP.NET into three main categories: execution of actions, filters, and view rendering.

 Note For more information about the aforementioned design principles, often summarized with the acronym *SOLID*, you can have a look at a recent book I wrote with Andrea Saltarello, *Microsoft .NET: Architecting Applications for the Enterprise* (Microsoft Press, 2008). You might find it curious that we don't use the acronym SOLID anywhere in the text; however, the acronym is a more recent (and nice) invention of some industry gurus. We do, though, cover exactly the principles that contribute their initials to the acronym: Single Responsibility, Open/Closed, Liskov Substitution, Interface Segregation, and Dependency Inversion.

The Controller Factory

I spent a lot of time and effort studying the internal implementation of ASP.NET Web Forms. At the end of the day, any request that hits an ASP.NET Web Forms application is processed by a class that derives from *System.Web.UI.Page*. This class implements the *IHttpHandler* interface and does its work through the *ProcessRequest* method on the *IHttpHandler* interface. Have you ever run across the implementation of this method?

ProcessRequest is a rather intricate mishmash of different programming styles, and it forms a natural habitat for a number of common code smells: long method calls, endless branches, switch statements, data clumps.

In ASP.NET MVC, any intercepted requests are routed to a new HTTP handler—the *MvcHandler* class that you met already in Chapter 2, "The Runtime Environment." This class is designed to contain code functionally equivalent to the code in the *ProcessRequest* method of the Web Forms' *Page* class. The quality of the code in *MvcHandler* is significantly better— it's more readable, far easier to maintain and, in particular, extensible.

To understand the extensibility points of ASP.NET MVC, you have to start from controllers and their factory. (And possibly also follow the example they provide in your own code.)

ASP.NET MVC Request Processing

On the way to controllers, the first stop is the *MvcHandler* class, where each ASP.NET MVC request eventually lands. In Chapter 2, we briefly examined the source code of the *MvcHandler* class with the purpose of explaining how an MVC request is processed. In this context, we'll get back to that source code with a different aim: to gain an understanding of the mechanics and identify points of extensibility.

For simplicity, I'll focus on the synchronous way of processing requests that is coded in *MvcHandler*. For asynchronous calls, the same steps occur, but they are split in two distinct phases—before and after the async point. (See Chapter 4, "Inside Controllers," for more details on asynchronous controllers and asynchronous request processing.)

Inside the *MvcHandler* Class

The core of an ASP.NET MVC request processing lies in the following code, which is invoked directly by the ASP.NET runtime:

```
protected virtual void ProcessRequest(HttpContext httpContext)
{
    HttpContextBase contextBase = new HttpContextWrapper(httpContext);
    this.ProcessRequest(contextBase);
}
```

In the first place, the original HTTP context is encapsulated in an *HttpContextBase* class to decouple the rest of the code from the details of the HTTP runtime environment. These lines of code are the key for mocking and testability, as discussed in Chapter 10, "Testability and Unit Testing."

The second call to *ProcessRequest* results in the following behavior:

```
protected virtual void ProcessRequest(HttpContextBase httpContext)
{
    IController controller;
```

```
    IControllerFactory factory;
    this.ProcessRequestInit(httpContext, out controller, out factory);
    try
    {
        controller.Execute(this.RequestContext);
    }
    finally
    {
        factory.ReleaseController(controller);
    }
}
```

The controller in charge of the request is instantiated and configured in *ProcessRequestInit*. Then it is given control over the request and released.

The Controller Builder

A first point of extensibility can be found in the *ProcessRequestInit* method, where the process of instantiating the controller is abstracted to a factory. Here are some more details:

```
private void ProcessRequestInit(
     HttpContextBase context, out IController controller, out IControllerFactory factory)
{
    this.AddVersionHeader(httpContext);
    string requiredString = this.RequestContext.RouteData.GetRequiredString("controller");

    // Get the factory object for the controller
    factory = this.ControllerBuilder.GetControllerFactory();

    // Create the controller
    controller = factory.CreateController(this.RequestContext, requiredString);
    if (controller == null)
    {
        throw new InvalidOperationException();
    }
}
```

The key thing that is going on in the *ProcessRequestInit* method occurs in the invocation of the controller builder. *ControllerBuilder* is a singleton class that holds the default instance of the factory component in charge of creating controller instances:

```
public ControllerBuilder()
{
    :
    :
    DefaultControllerFactory controllerFactory = new DefaultControllerFactory();
    controllerFactory.ControllerBuilder = this;
    this.SetControllerFactory(controllerFactory);
}
```

The default factory for controllers is the *DefaultControllerFactory* class. This class gets the type of the controller class to instantiate and uses .NET reflection to activate it. In doing so, it assumes a default constructor on the controller class and defaults to that.

The Default Controller Factory

As you can see in the preceding code snippets, the *ControllerBuilder* class encapsulates an instance of the controller factory and makes it available through a pair of getter and setter methods. In particular, the *SetControllerFactory* method is the tool you can use to unplug the default controller factory and roll your own.

In Chapter 8, "The ASP.NET MVC Infrastructure," I demonstrated how to leverage the *SetControllerFactory* method to introduce an Inversion of Control (IoC)–based controller factory that can automatically resolve the chain of dependencies rooted in the controller class.

You register your custom controller factory in *Application_Start* and have it kick in every time a request is made:

```
protected void Application_Start()
{
    :
    :

    // Create and register an IoC-based factory (using the Unity framework)
    var container = new UnityContainer();
    IControllerFactory factory = new MyAppControllerFactory(container);
    ControllerBuilder.Current.SetControllerFactory(factory);
}
```

At this point, the logic of the controller factory is up to you.

Even though a controller factory is abstracted to a specific interface—the *IControllerFactory* interface—you probably want to start from the *DefaultControllerFactory* class to create your own factory. At any rate, the *IControllerFactory* interface is shown here:

```
public interface IControllerFactory
{
    IController CreateController(RequestContext requestContext, string controllerName);
    void ReleaseController(IController controller);
}
```

The *DefaultControllerFactory* class implements the interface, but it also exposes overridable methods at a slightly more granular level than the raw interface.

Extending the Default Controller Factory

In the *DefaultControllerFactory* class, the *CreateController* method is a two-step operation: getting the controller's type and getting an instance of that type. For both of these actions, the *DefaultControllerFactory* class offers a ready-made virtual method. As a result, there are three aspects of a controller factory that you might want to customize: getting the type for the controller in charge of the current request, getting the controller instance, and releasing the controller instance.

Here's the list of methods on the *DefaultControllerFactory* class that you might want to override:

```
protected virtual IController GetControllerInstance(Type controllerType);
protected virtual Type GetControllerType(string controllerName);
public virtual void ReleaseController(IController controller);
```

Let's examine each scenario in more detail.

Getting the Controller Type

You override the *GetControllerType* method if you want to change the naming convention applied to resolve the controller type. The default convention entails that the controller type name be whatever strings result from appending the word "Controller" to the controller name. The controller name is the string passed as an argument to the method and obtained from the route processing.

When the default URL scheme is used, the controller name is the first token of the URL that follows the server name. For example, it will be *Home* for a URL such as *http://yourserver/home/index*. The *GetControllerType* method on the default factory just returns a *Type* object for the name *HomeController*:

You can change the default naming algorithm by using the following code:

```
protected override Type GetControllerType(string controllerName)
{
    string defaultNamespace = "NorthwindCms.Controllers";
    string suffix = "MyController";

    // Prepare the type name
    string typeName = String.Format("{0}.{1}.{2}",
                        defaultNamespace, controllerName, suffix);

    // Build and return a Type object.
    // This is NOT an instance of the controller; the assembly with the type
    // definition must be loaded in the AppDomain.
    return Type.GetType(typeName);
}
```

Note that the method returns a *Type* object that describes the class to instantiate later, not one that is already an instance of the controller type. In addition, the assembly where the type is defined must be available in the current *AppDomain*. Figure 11-1 shows the exception you get if the type can't be found.

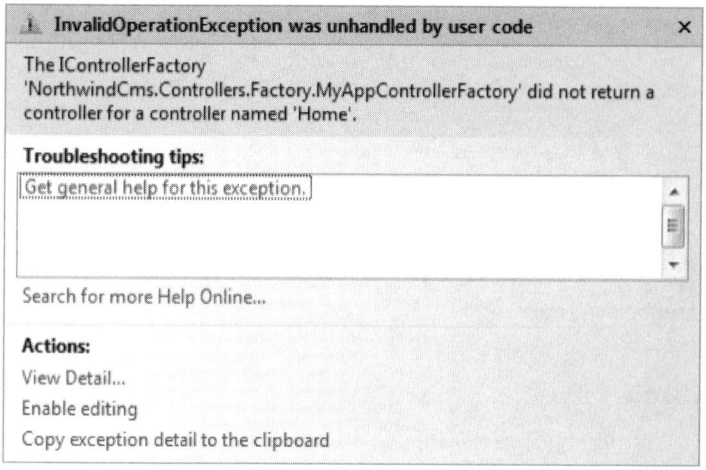

FIGURE 11-1 The method couldn't find a type for the specified controller name.

The Controller Type Cache

It's interesting to find out more about the way in which the default controller factory gets the type for a controller name. For performance reasons, the default factory uses a type cache. The type cache is implemented in the *ControllerTypeCache* class. During its initialization, this class enumerates all the referenced assemblies and explores them, looking for publicly exposed controller types. A controller type is recognized by the following code:

```
static bool IsControllerType(Type t)
{
    return
        t != null &&
        t.IsPublic &&
        t.Name.EndsWith("Controller", StringComparison.OrdinalIgnoreCase) &&
        !t.IsAbstract &&
        typeof(IController).IsAssignableFrom(t);
}
```

The controller type has to be public and nonabstract; its name must terminate with the suffix *Controller*, and it must be assignable to an *IController* variable.

The controller type cache uses a dictionary to store controller types and keep them mapped to controller names. The key in the dictionary is the controller name (for example, *Home* when the type is *HomeController*), and the value in the dictionary is a LINQ lookup table. A LINQ lookup table is a dictionary object with additional capabilities. Nested dictionaries are required in ASP.NET MVC version 2 to take into proper account areas and situations in which the same controller name is used in different namespaces.

The controller type cache is fully identified by the declaration shown here:

```
var _typeCache = new Dictionary<string, ILookup<string, Type>>();
```

Figure 11-2 provides a graphical view of the controller type cache.

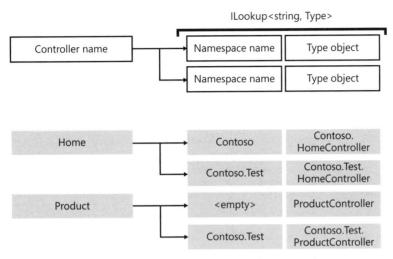

FIGURE 11-2 A graphical representation of the controller type cache

The topmost part of the figure shows the layout of the dictionary, whereas the bottom part illustrates some sample content.

Customizing the Controller Name

When the default URL scheme is used, the controller name is the first token of the URL that follows the server name. If you opt for a custom URL routing scheme, identifying the controller name is up to you. The controller name can be one of the segments in the URL, it can be a fixed class, or it can even be determined algorithmically.

What matters is that the name of the controller needs to be stored in the route dictionary so that the ASP.NET MVC infrastructure can get it using the following code:

```
// From any context where you have access to a valid instance of RequestContext
string controllerName = requestContext.RouteData.GetRequiredString("controller");
```

The following example demonstrates a custom route where the *controller* token is not specified explicitly, but it results from the composition of two other tokens:

```
routes.Add(
    "CompositeRoute",
    new Route("{app}/{context}/{action}/{id}",
            new RouteValueDictionary(new { context="home", action = "Index", id = ""}),
            new CompositeRouteHandler())
);
```

For example, a valid URL could be *http://yourserver/blogs/home*. The logic to determine the name of the controller class to serve a request belongs to the route handler. For a custom route, you clearly need a custom route handler. In the sample code, the resolved controller name is something like *Blogs_Home_* for a resulting controller type of *Blogs_Home_Controller*—at least if you stick to the default algorithm for getting the controller type. Here's the custom route handler:

```
public class CompositeRouteHandler: IRouteHandler
{
    public IHttpHandler GetHttpHandler(RequestContext requestContext)
    {
        // Get route data as extracted from the URL definition
        var routeData = requestContext.RouteData;

        // Complete route data with a programmatically created "controller" entry
        string controllerName = String.Format("{0}_{1}_",
                requestContext.RouteData.GetRequiredString("app"),
                requestContext.RouteData.GetRequiredString("context"));
        routeData.Values.Add("controller", controllerName);

        // Return the default MVC HTTP handler for the configured request
        return new MvcHandler(requestContext);
    }
}
```

A route handler is a class that implements the *IRouteHandler* interface. In the *GetHttpHandler* member, it first reads any route data that's available and then algorithmically determines the controller name and adds it to the route data dictionary of the current request context. Finally, the updated request context is passed to the default ASP.NET MVC HTTP handler to serve the request.

> **Note** Just as for the controller name, the action name also can be programmatically configured in a custom URL scheme. All you do is figure out the name of the action by applying any necessary logic and then store it in the *RouteData* collection under the key of "action."

Getting the Controller Instance

The *GetControllerInstance* method on the controller factory class is responsible for returning a concrete instance of the controller type that was found by *GetControllerType*. The two methods are bound together in the implementation of *CreateController* in the default controller factory class:

```
public virtual IController CreateController(
        RequestContext requestContext, string controllerName)
{
    // Check preconditions
    :
    :

    //
    Type controllerType = this.GetControllerType(requestContext, controllerName);
    return this.GetControllerInstance(requestContext, controllerType);
}
```

You override this method when you need to change something in the way in which
a controller is instantiated. Here's the implementation of the method in the default factory:

```
protected virtual IController GetControllerInstance(
        RequestContext requestContext, Type controllerType)
{
    // Check preconditions
    IController controller;
    if (controllerType == null)
        throw new HttpException();
    if (!typeof(IController).IsAssignableFrom(controllerType))
        throw new ArgumentException();

    // Get the instance
    try
    {
        controller = (IController) Activator.CreateInstance(controllerType);
    }
    catch (Exception exception)
    {
        throw new InvalidOperationException();
    }
    return controller;
}
```

Here's a common implementation based on an IoC container. (This is the same
implementation we considered in Chapter 8.)

```
protected override IController GetControllerInstance(
        RequestContext requestContext, Type controllerType)
{
    // Note: the signature of this method has changed in the transition
    //       from ASP.NET MVC 1 to ASP.NET MVC 2. In the latest version,
    //       the RequestContext argument has been added.

    if (controllerType == null)
        return null;

    // Container is a property on the factory class that exposes the IoC container
    var controller = Container.Resolve(controllerType) as Controller;
    if (controller == null)
        return null;

    // Further customize the newly created controller instance
    :
    :
    :

    return controller;
}
```

A common reason for replacing the controller factory is to enable dependency injection
and enable scenarios where the controller class receives a reference to the service layer class,
the data access repository, or whatever other cross-cutting dependencies it might need.

The IoC-based approach is also helpful when you have to distinguish between various types and initialize each in a different way. However, if for whatever reason the controller type is not configurable through the IoC, the following code will still work:

```
protected override IController GetControllerInstance(Type controllerType)
{
    if (controllerType == null)
        return null;

    if(controllerType == typeof(HomeController))
    {
        .
        .
        .
    }
    if(controllerType == typeof(ProductController))
    {
        .
        .
        .
    }

    // More code here
    .
    .
    .
}
```

The factory is also the place where you can add the code that configures any instance of a controller. This typically happens when you have a base controller class with custom properties. Another scenario is when you need to customize the action invoker. I'll return to this in a moment.

Releasing the Controller Instance

The controller factory also exposes a method that provides for the disposal of the controller instance. Most of the time, you don't need code significantly different from the following, which is the default implementation of the method in *DefaultControllerFactory*:

```
public virtual void ReleaseController(IController controller)
{
    IDisposable disposable = controller as IDisposable;
    if (disposable != null)
    {
        disposable.Dispose();
    }
}
```

However, if your controller instantiates its own resources, that is a good place to get rid of them. When you employ an IoC container to create the controller instance, you might also want to tear the instance down in the container; so here's the code for Unity:

```
public override void ReleaseController(IController controller)
{
    // Container is the reference to the Unity container
    Container.Teardown(controller);
}
```

Similar code probably will be needed for any IoC container you happen to use, including the newest Managed Extensibility Framework (MEF) that Microsoft ships with the .NET Framework 4.

Note When you use an IoC container to instantiate a controller, you probably don't need more than a transient instance created intentionally for the request and disposed of at the end of the request life cycle. However, a custom controller class might have injected via IoC a number of external objects—for example, proxies for WCF services. Objects injected via IoC in the context of a controller might be configured with a different lifetime (for example, singletons). It turns out that disposing of them in *ReleaseController* might be way too early to dispose of them and cause trouble. This is not necessarily a problem, but just take it into account when overriding *ReleaseController*.

Invoking Actions

After it has the controller instance, the *MvcHandler* class proceeds and tasks the controller with the execution of the current request. This is done via a call to the *Execute* method on the controller class. The *Execute* method is defined in the *IController* interface that any controller class is called to implement.

As you saw in Chapter 4, the core functionality of a controller is split among a few classes, including *ControllerBase*, *Controller*, and then your specific controller class. The *Execute* method, in particular, is implemented on the *ControllerBase* class and the very core of it is re-exposed through a protected abstract method named *ExecuteCore*:

```
protected abstract void ExecuteCore()
```

You might find it interesting to take a second glance at the source code of *ExecuteCore* in the class *Controller* to identify new points of extensibility:

```
// From class Controller
protected override void ExecuteCore()
{
    this.PossiblyLoadTempData();
    try
    {
        string requiredString = this.RouteData.GetRequiredString("action");
        if (!this.ActionInvoker.InvokeAction(base.ControllerContext, requiredString))
        {
            this.HandleUnknownAction(requiredString);
        }
    }
    finally
    {
        this.PossiblySaveTempData();
    }
}
```

Regardless of the code at the beginning and end that deals with the loading and unloading of the *TempData* collection, the key things to note about the *ExecuteCore* method are going on in the *try* block. The action associated with the request is invoked through the services of an ad hoc component—the action invoker. The action invoker controls a number of aspects related to the execution of each action and, more importantly, it is exposed as a public property out of the *Controller* class.

Role of the Action Invoker

The invoker represents the class responsible for invoking the action methods of a controller. It implements the internal life cycle of each ASP.NET MVC request. The action invoker is an object that implements the *IActionInvoker* interface. A default invoker is provided through the *ActionInvoker* property of the controller class. As you can see, the property is a plain *get/set* property:

```
public IActionInvoker ActionInvoker
{
    get
    {
        if (this._actionInvoker == null)
        {
            this._actionInvoker = this.CreateActionInvoker();
        }
        return this._actionInvoker;
    }
    set
    {
        this._actionInvoker = value;
    }
}
```

From the property implementation, it turns out that that the action invoker can be changed at will for any controller. However, because the invoker is involved at quite an early stage of the request life cycle, you probably need a controller factory to replace the default invoker with your own. Alternately, you can define a custom controller base class and override the *CreateActionInvoker* method to return the invoker you need. This is the approach that the ASP.NET MVC framework employs to support the asynchronous execution of controller actions:

```
public abstract class AsyncController : Controller, ...
{
    :
    :
    protected override IActionInvoker CreateActionInvoker()
    {
        return new AsyncControllerActionInvoker();
    }
}
```

The action invoker is built around the *IActionInvoker* interface. The interface is fairly simple—it exposes just one method:

```
public interface IActionInvoker
{
    bool InvokeAction(ControllerContext controllerContext, string actionName);
}
```

Although the overall behavior of an action is clear, the specific steps it performs depend on the implementation and context. A few tasks, however, are common to any implementation.

The Default Action Invoker

The task list of an action invoker includes at least the following steps:

- Getting the controller descriptor

- Getting the action descriptor

- Getting the list of action filters

- Checking the authorization permissions of the user

- Validating the request against potentially dangerous posted data

- Invoking the action while taking into account any registered filters

- Taking care of any unhandled exceptions

These are also the tasks accomplished by the default action invoker. The default action invoker class is *ControllerActionInvoker*. Let's look at some more details.

Controller Descriptors

A controller descriptor is a class that encapsulates information that collectively describes a controller, such as its name, type, attributes, and actions. The invoker builds its own cache of descriptors using .NET reflection. The default invoker gets the descriptor for a particular controller context using the following method:

```
protected virtual ControllerDescriptor GetControllerDescriptor(
        ControllerContext controllerContext)
{
    // Get the type of the controller class
    Type controllerType = controllerContext.Controller.GetType();

    Func<ControllerDescriptor> creator = delegate {
            return new ReflectedControllerDescriptor(controllerType);
        };

    // Retrieve the descriptor from the cache or create a new one on the fly
    return this.DescriptorCache.GetDescriptor(controllerType, creator);
}
```

By overriding the *GetControllerDescriptor* method in your custom action invoker class, you can modify the way in which controller information is retrieved and cached. Note, though, that the *DescriptorCache* member is marked as internal and, as such, it is *not* available in a derived class. This means that you can still override the way in which a controller descriptor is retrieved, but in doing so you also make yourself responsible for implementing a descriptor cache. Of course, having a descriptor cache is not mandatory; it is merely a way to improve performance on a very frequent operation that occurs for each ASP.NET MVC request.

A possible scenario in which you might want to delve this deep into the internal architecture of an action invoker and controller descriptors is when you decide to keep the configuration of controllers (attributes and actions) out of the controller classes—for example, in an external file that can be updated without recompiling and redeploying the application. Here's the code you need in this case:

```
protected virtual ControllerDescriptor GetControllerDescriptor(
        ControllerContext controllerContext)
{
    // Get the type of the controller class
    Type controllerType = controllerContext.Controller.GetType();

    Func<ControllerDescriptor> creator = delegate {
            return new DynamicControllerDescriptor(controllerType);
        };

    // Retrieve the descriptor from the cache or create a new one on the fly
    return this.MyDescriptorCache.GetDescriptor(controllerType, creator);
}
```

You provide a custom *DynamicControllerDescriptor* class that will probably inherit from *ControllerDescriptor* and override some of the methods listed here:

```
public abstract class ControllerDescriptor : ICustomAttributeProvider
{
    // Properties
    public virtual string ControllerName { get; }
    public abstract Type ControllerType { get; }

    // Method
    public abstract ActionDescriptor[] GetCanonicalActions();
    public virtual object[] GetCustomAttributes(bool inherit);
    public abstract ActionDescriptor FindAction(
            ControllerContext controllerContext, string actionName);
    public virtual object[] GetCustomAttributes(
            Type attributeType, bool inherit);
    public virtual bool IsDefined(
            Type attributeType, bool inherit);
}
```

The method *GetCanonicalActions* in particular returns a list of action descriptors for all the methods that are available on a controller. For example, you can find this feature useful to enable or disable certain features of your application for certain users or in certain time frames.

The Controller Descriptor Cache

In the preceding code snippet, where I showed a possible override of the *GetControllerDescriptor* method on the action invoker, at some point you see a member named *MyDescriptionCache*. What's that?

As mentioned, for some reason ASP.NET MVC doesn't give you access to either the internal descriptor cache or the class used to implement it. At this point, in the case of a custom controller descriptor engine, either you create your own cache or you do without caching.

In the default action invoker, the descriptor cache is a static type/descriptor dictionary that has just one peculiarity: it is a cache built around the *ReaderWriterLockSlim* class from *System. Threading*. The name of the cache class is *ControllerDescriptorCache*. As a result, the cache class manages read/write access to the descriptors in a multithreaded environment, allowing multiple threads for reading and exclusive access for writing.

Because a cache is always a great thing for frequent operations, you definitely need one. So you can't reuse the descriptor cache as implemented in ASP.NET MVC, but you can borrow its source code and bring it into your applications. No hidden dependencies prevent that from happening in a process that overall is seamless and smooth. (And this is definitely a great statement in support of the quality of the ASP.NET MVC source code.)

Here's a piece of the resulting custom action invoker that overrides the controller descriptor cache:

```
public class MyActionInvoker : ControllerActionInvoker
{
    private static readonly ControllerDescriptorCache _staticDescriptorCache;
    private ControllerDescriptorCache _instanceDescriptorCache;

    static MyActionInvoker()
    {
        _staticDescriptorCache = new ControllerDescriptorCache();
    }

    internal ControllerDescriptorCache MyDescriptorCache
    {
        get
        {
            if (this._instanceDescriptorCache == null)
                this._instanceDescriptorCache = _staticDescriptorCache;
            return this._instanceDescriptorCache;
        }
        set
        {
            this._instanceDescriptorCache = value;
        }
    }
}
```

```
    protected override ControllerDescriptor GetControllerDescriptor(
            ControllerContext controllerContext)
    {
        // Get the type of the controller class
        Type controllerType = controllerContext.Controller.GetType();

        Func<ControllerDescriptor> creator = delegate {
            return new DynamicControllerDescriptor(controllerType);
        };

        // Retrieve the descriptor from the cache or
        return this.MyDescriptorCache.GetDescriptor(controllerType, creator);
    }

        :
        :
}
```

The implementation of the sample *DynamicControllerDescriptor* cache can be as simple
as in the following code snippet:

```
public class DynamicControllerDescriptor : ReflectedControllerDescriptor
{
    public DynamicControllerDescriptor(Type controllerType) : base(controllerType)
    {
    }

    public override ActionDescriptor FindAction(
            ControllerContext controllerContext, string actionName)
    {
        var disabledMethods = GetDisabledActionMethods(controllerContext);
        if (disabledMethods.Contains(actionName))
            return null;

        return base.FindAction(controllerContext, actionName);
    }

    private string[] GetDisabledActionMethods(ControllerContext context)
    {
        string controllerName = context.RouteData.GetRequiredString("controller");

        // Disable action Index on Home controller. This content can be easily
        // read from a file
        if (String.Equals(controllerName, "Home"))
            return new string[] { "Index" };

        return new string[] { };
    }
}
```

When an action is invoked, the *FindAction* method on the descriptor class is invoked to find
related information. At this point, a custom descriptor that reads its input from an offline file
can decide about which method to eventually execute. The code snippet shows how to deny
execution of an otherwise well-defined method. As a result, the user receives the message
in Figure 11-3.

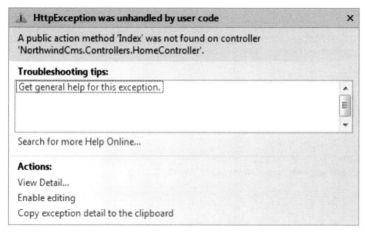

FIGURE 11-3 The action *Index* cannot be executed.

Action Descriptors

The power of custom descriptors doesn't end here. You can leverage the same mechanism to enable actions that correspond to nonpublic methods or even enable actions that are defined on classes different from the controller class. In this case, though, you need to deal with action descriptors:

```
public class DynamicControllerDescriptor : ReflectedControllerDescriptor
{
    public DynamicControllerDescriptor(Type controllerType) : base(controllerType)
    {
    }
    public override ActionDescriptor FindAction(
            ControllerContext controllerContext, string actionName)
    {
        var enabledMethods = GetEnabledActionMethods(controllerContext);
        if (enabledMethods.Contains(actionName))
        {
            var methodInfo = GetMethodInfo(this.ControllerType, actionName);
            return new DynamicActionDescriptor(methodInfo, actionName, this);
        }

        return base.FindAction(controllerContext, actionName);
    }

    protected virtual string[] GetEnabledActionMethods(ControllerContext context)
    {
        string controllerName = context.RouteData.GetRequiredString("controller");

        // Enable Index on Home controller regardless of the settings on HomeController
        if (String.Equals(controllerName, "Home"))
            return new string[] { "Index" };

        return new string[] { };
    }
```

```
    private MethodInfo GetMethodInfo(Type type, string actionName)
    {
        var flags = BindingFlags.Public | BindingFlags.NonPublic | BindingFlags.Instance;
        return type.GetMethod(actionName, flags);
    }
}


public class DynamicActionDescriptor : ReflectedActionDescriptor
{
    public DynamicActionDescriptor(
        MethodInfo methodInfo, string actionName, ControllerDescriptor controllerDescriptor)
        : base(methodInfo, actionName, controllerDescriptor)
    {
    }
}
```

This time, the method *FindAction* reads the list of valid actions from an external source. In the source code, the variable *enabledMethods*—an array of strings—contains the name of the method to be executed when a given action string is specified through the route.

If the code finds a match between the required action and the list of enabled methods, it creates an action descriptor on the fly and plugs it into the existing ASP.NET MVC machinery.

As in the listing, a new action descriptor is required that wraps method information. The example assumes that the method to execute still belongs to the controller type and uses .NET reflection to get some dynamic information:

```
private MethodInfo GetMethodInfo(Type type, string actionName)
{
    var flags = BindingFlags.Public | BindingFlags.NonPublic | BindingFlags.Instance;
    return type.GetMethod(actionName, flags);
}
```

The implementation just shown also enables you to invoke a private member on the controller class. In this way, you can have all private or *NonAction* members on the controller class and still be able to execute them.

More in general, the real power of action and controller descriptors is that they provide a way to decouple the name of the requested action from the method that actually executes it. This link defaults to some conventions that are established via reflection and coded in the classes *ReflectedControllerDescriptor* and *ReflectedActionDescriptor*.

The code shown here demonstrates that, in some cases, you can take control of even this aspect of ASP.NET MVC. It's not a feature you want to use in every application, but it is useful for making the application more resilient and capable of supporting dynamic addition (or subtraction) of features based on temporary situations, such as advertisement campaigns, reward systems, and special working modes such as maintenance.

> **Important** Let me state it once more and as a stand-alone statement. In ASP.NET MVC, the
> action requested is not necessarily a segment of the URL, and the method that runs in response
> is not necessarily a public method on the matching controller class. This is only the default
> behavior, and it is fully customizable.

Custom Invokers

Controller and action descriptors are governed by a custom action invoker. As mentioned,
you can set a custom invoker either in the constructor of a common base controller class
or using a controller factory. The effect is the same; the choice is up to you.

If you already have a base controller class, you can just instantiate the invoker in the
controller class constructor. Of course, inheriting from the base class is a necessary condition
to take advantage of the new invoker. Alternately, you can set up a controller factory and set
the invoker there. In this case, you get the benefits of the new invoker with no further effort
of your own.

Here's what you need when you opt for a custom factory:

```
protected override IController GetControllerInstance(
    RequestContext requestContext, Type controllerType)
{
    if (controllerType == null)
        return null;

    // Instantiate the controller via IoC
    var controller = AppContext.Container.Resolve(controllerType) as IController;
    if (controller == null)
        return null;

    // Attach the new invoker via IoC
    controller.ActionInvoker = AppContext.Container.Resolve<IActionInvoker>();
    return controller;
}
```

You are not forced, of course, to use an IoC container. In Chapter 8, I walked you through
an interesting scenario where a custom invoker was the perfect solution: switching the
language of a view.

```
public class MyActionInvoker : ControllerActionInvoker
{
    public override bool InvokeAction(
        ControllerContext controllerContext, string actionName)
    {
        // Set the language as read out of the cache (or other source)
        string lang = GetLocale(controllerContext);
        Thread.CurrentThread.CurrentUICulture = CultureInfo.CreateSpecificCulture(lang);
```

```
        // Business as usual. . .except that any invoked view detects the new locale
        return base.InvokeAction(controllerContext, actionName);
    }

    protected virtual string GetLocale(ControllerContext context)
    {
        string language = ...;
        return language;
    }
}
```

The action invoker gives you control over the entire process behind the execution of a request. You need a custom invoker only in a small number of circumstances. Most of the ASP.NET controller customization occurs through just one of the specific aspects that an invoker makes customizable: action filters.

Action Filters

An action filter is a piece of code that runs around the execution of an action method. An action filter, though, has nothing to do with the way in which the code for an action method is resolved. If you let ASP.NET MVC resolve an action method via reflection, an action filter is likely a custom attribute you use to decorate the method on the controller class. If you use your own action resolver, the action filter is simply an instance of a dynamically loaded class whose name can be read from any source, including a configuration file.

You already met action filters in Chapter 4. Let's now go through a short gallery of examples.

Gallery of Action Filters

An action filter is an attribute that provides a declarative means to attach some behavior to a controller's action method. By writing an action filter, you can hook up the execution pipeline of an action method and adapt it to your needs. In this way, you can take out of the controller class any logic that doesn't strictly belong to the controller. In doing so, you make this particular behavior reusable and, more importantly, optional. Action filters are ideal for implementing cross-cutting concerns that affect the life of your controllers.

ASP.NET MVC comes with a few predefined filters, such those you met in Chapter 4: *HandleError*, *Authorize*, and *OutputCache* to name just a few. Action filters are classified in different types depending on the tasks they actually accomplish. An action filter is characterized by an interface; you have a different interface for each type of filter. Special action filters are exception filters, authorization filters, and result filters. Table 11-1 lists the types of action filters in ASP.NET MVC. (For more details on these interfaces, refer back to Chapter 4.)

TABLE 11-1 Types of action filters in ASP.NET MVC

Filter Interfaces	Description
IActionFilter	Defines two methods that execute before and after the controller action
IAuthorizationFilter	Defines a method that executes early in the action pipeline, giving you a chance to verify whether the user is authorized to perform the action
IExceptionFilter	Defines a method that runs whenever an exception is thrown during the execution of the controller action
IResultFilter	Defines two methods that execute before and after the processing of the action result

When it comes to writing an action filter, you typically inherit from *FilterAttribute* and then implement one or more of the interfaces defined in Table 11-1.

The *FilterAttribute* class is an abstract class that defines only one property, as shown here:

```
public abstract class FilterAttribute : Attribute
{
    // Fields
    private int _order;

    // Methods
    protected FilterAttribute();

    // Properties
    public int Order { get; set; }
}
```

The *Order* property refers to the order in which the filter will be executed. No order is defined by default on action filters. Unless explicitly set, the *Order* property is assumed to be –1, which means the filter will be run in no particular order. Note that if you explicitly set the same order on two or more action filters on a method, an exception will be thrown. The *ActionFilterAttribute* class is another, richer, base class for creating your custom action filters. It inherits from *FilterAttribute* and provides a default implementation for all the interfaces listed in Table 11-1.

Let's take a closer look at some sample action filters.

Browser-Specific Views

Offering the same view and user experience across different browsers is an old problem of Web developers. ASP.NET Web Forms supports browser-specific master pages and also allows you to assign browser-specific values to control properties. By creating an HTTP module, you can also redirect the original request made to a given URL to another URL that offers the same content but that is optimized for the current browser.

In ASP.NET MVC, a similar solution is perhaps too much of a hack, because a simpler and neater approach exists that is based on action filters. The idea is to write a custom action filter that kicks in just before the action invoker begins processing the action result. According to the classification introduced earlier in the chapter, this technically is a *result filter*. Let's have a look at the source code:

```
public class BrowserSpecificAttribute : ActionFilterAttribute
{
    public override void OnResultExecuting(ResultExecutingContext filterContext)
    {
        :
        :
    }
}
```

The filter inherits from *ActionFilterAttribute* and overrides the method *OnResultExecuting*. The method is invoked after the execution of the action method but before the result of the action is processed to generate the response for the browser:

```
public override void OnResultExecuting(ResultExecutingContext filterContext)
{
    // Get the action result based on which the view will be generated
    var viewResult = filterContext.Result as ViewResult;
    if (viewResult == null)
        return;

    // You never reach this point if the method returned anything different
    // from ViewResult such as JsonResult or FileResult.

    // Get the name of the view as requested by the action method
    string viewName = viewResult.ViewName;

    // Retrieve the name of the browser that placed the request
    var controllerContext = filterContext.Controller.ControllerContext;
    string browserName = controllerContext.HttpContext.Request.Browser.Browser;

    // Based on the browser name, sets the name of the new view to use.
    string newViewName = GetViewNameForBrowser(viewName, browserName);

    // Check whether the current view engine supports such a view
    ViewEngineResult result = ViewEngines.Engines.FindView(
                                controllerContext, newViewName, viewResult.MasterName);

    // If the view is supported, then set it as the view to use for rendering
    if (result.View != null)
        viewResult.ViewName = newViewName;
}
```

The algorithm employed is simple. Using the *ControllerContext* object, the filter retrieves the *Request* object from the request context; from there, it gets to know the capabilities of the current browser. The browser name is used as a discriminator to decide about the next view to select. The following listing shows a possible implementation of the algorithm that maps a view name to a browser-specific version of that view:

```
public string GetViewNameForBrowser(string viewName, string browserName)
{
    // Assume views named like Index_IE or Index_Firefox
    return String.Format("{0}_{1}", viewName, browserName);
}
```

The code assumes that given a view named *Index*, an Internet Explorer–specific version of the view is named *Index_IE*, a version for Firefox is named *Index_Firefox*, and so forth.

After the filter has determined the name of the candidate view to show, it also checks with the current view engine to see whether such a view is supported. If so, the *ViewName* property of the *ViewResult* to render is set to the browser-specific view. If no browser-specific view is found, you need to do nothing else because the generic view invoked by the action method remains in place.

As you can see, this is a rather generic solution that assumes a fixed naming convention for browser-specific views. You can further refine this solution by defining a bunch of public properties on the *BrowserSpecificAttribute* class, through which you can control the name of the view for a particular browser:

```
public class BrowserSpecificAttribute : ActionFilterAttribute
{
    public string Firefox {get; set;}
    public string InternetExplorer {get; set;}
    :
    :
    public override void OnResultExecuting(ResultExecutingContext filterContext)
    {
        :
        :
    }
}
```

Using the attribute couldn't be easier. All you need to do is decorate the controller method with the attribute, as shown here:

```
[BrowserSpecific]
public virtual ActionResult Index()
{
    :
    :
}
```

An action filter like this will save you from adding a bunch of *if* statements to each controller method to return a different *ViewResult* object for each supported browser.

```
public virtual ActionResult Index()
{
    if(GetCurrentBrowser() == "IE")
        return View("Index_IE");

        .
        .
        .

}
```

That code is still necessary if you intend to provide optimized views, but an action filter takes it from the controller class, thus simplifying the entire design.

Linking Data Shared Across Views

In Chapter 6, "Inside Models," we ran across an interesting point while discussing how data should be passed from the controller down to the view. It is not unlikely that a view needs more data than can be managed by the controller method that invokes the view. This typically happens when the view incorporates some fixed data that is shared with other views (for example, menus and breadcrumbs) but for some reason was not stored in a master page.

In Chapter 6, I discussed the use of a registry object to store any data that is global so that the controller can simply reference the registry to populate the view model object the view is based on. However, I also hinted at another solution that many members in the community employed or at least discussed. This alternate solution is based on an action filter.

To put the solution in context, imagine that you find yourself needing to pass data to the view that is not strictly dependent on what the current action method does. That is not data calculated by the method; rather, it is global data stored somewhere that you don't want the view to retrieve on its own so that you can avoid having (too much?) logic and complexity leak into the view.

The logic of the action filter is simple: it accesses the data and loads it into the *ViewData* collection for the view to retrieve it. Let's start with the controller code:

```
[AddGlobalData]
public virtual ActionResult Find(string id)
{
    // Find a particular customer

        .
        .
        .

    // Prepare the view-model object
    var model = new CustomerViewModel();
    model.Customer = ...;

    // Return the view
    return View("Find", model);
}
```

The view-model object (or the *ViewData* collection if you opt for a generic data container) contains just the data that the controller method manipulates directly. Any other data required by the view, but unrelated to the current operation, will be added by the action filter, named *AddGlobalData* in the example. Here's some code for the filter:

```
public class AddGlobalDataAttribute : ActionFilterAttribute
{
    public override void OnActionExecuted(ActionExecutedContext filterContext)
    {
        // Retrieve global data
        var data = "Global data";

        // Add global data to the ViewData dictionary to make it
        // available to the view
        filterContext.Controller.ViewData.Add("GlobalData", data);
    }
}
```

The trick works just fine and suffers from just one little bug. It forces you to use *ViewData* to pass data from the controller to the view. You might have a strongly typed view at the controller level but still need to resort to a weakly typed *ViewData* for global data.

To sum it up, nothing prevents you from writing the code shown here:

```
var model = filterContext.ViewData.Model as CustomerViewModel;
if (model == null)
    return;
model.GlobalData = data;
```

However, in this case you are forced to link your code to a specific type. *CustomerViewModel*, which is used in the example, might work in one scenario, but it won't necessarily work for any views that need global data. A possible solution is to derive any view-model class that needs global data from a common base class that exposes members to get and set that data. As long as all view models employed within action methods decorated with *AddGlobalData* inherit from *GlobalContainerViewModel*, the following code works:

```
// Segregating the view model type to a section works in this case,
// as in the current context you're interested only in the segment of
// the view model that contains global data
var model = filterContext.ViewData.Model as GlobalContainerViewModel;
if (model == null)
    return;
model.GlobalData = data;
```

If your application is compiled with Microsoft Visual Studio 2010 against the Microsoft .NET Framework 4, you can take advantage of the new features of C# 4, such as the *dynamic* keyword. The following code compiles and works just fine:

```
// Tells the compiler the variable model will be resolved at run time
dynamic model = filterContext.Controller.ViewData.Model;
model.GlobalData = data;
```

Using the *dynamic* keyword saves you from creating the base class that would otherwise be required in .NET 3.5. However, in my opinion, using the base class instead eliminates some run-time burden and keeps the code cleaner and easier to read.

Compressing the Response

These days, HTTP compression is a feature that nearly every Web site can afford because the number of browsers having trouble with that is approaching zero. (Any browser released in the past ten years recognizes most popular compression schemes.)

In ASP.NET Web Forms, compression is commonly achieved through HTTP modules that intercept any request and compress the response. You can also enable compression at the Microsoft Internet Information Services (IIS) level. Both options work well in ASP.NET MVC, so the decision is up to you. You typically make your decision based on the parameters you need to control, including the MIME type of the resource to compress, level of compression, files to compress, and so forth.

ASP.NET MVC makes it particularly easy to implement a third option—an action-specific filter that sets things up for compression. In this way, you can control a specific URL without the need to write an HTTP module. Let's go through another example of an action filter that will add compression to the response stream for a particular method.

In general, HTTP compression is controlled by two parameters: the *Accept-Encoding* header sent by the browser with each request, and the *Content-Encoding* header sent by the Web server with each response. The *Accept-Encoding* header indicates that the browser is able to handle only the specified encodings—typically, *gzip* and *deflate*. The *Content-Encoding* header indicates the compression format of the response. Note that the *Accept-Encoding* header is just a request sent by the browser; in no way should the server feel obliged to return compressed content, but neither should the server return content the browser has not specifically identified it can handle.

When it comes to writing a compression filter, the hardest part is fully understanding what the browser is requesting. Here's some code that works:

```
public class CompressAttribute : ActionFilterAttribute
{
    public override void OnActionExecuting(ActionExecutingContext filterContext)
    {
        // Analyze the list of acceptable encodings
        var preferredEncoding = GetPreferredEncoding(filterContext.HttpContext.Request);

        // Compress the response accordingly
        var response = filterContext.HttpContext.Response;
        response.AppendHeader("Content-encoding", preferredEncoding.ToString());
```

```
        if (preferredEncoding == CompressionScheme.Gzip)
            response.Filter = new GZipStream(response.Filter, CompressionMode.Compress);
        if (preferredEncoding == CompressionScheme.Deflate)
            response.Filter = new DeflateStream(response.Filter, CompressionMode.Compress);

        return;
    }
    private CompressionScheme GetPreferredEncoding(HttpRequest request)
    {
        string acceptableEncoding = request.Headers["Accept-Encoding"].ToLower();

        if (acceptableEncoding.Contains("gzip"))
            return CompressionScheme.Gzip;
        if (acceptableEncoding.Contains("deflate"))
            return CompressionScheme.Deflate;

        return CompressionScheme.Identity;
    }

    enum CompressionScheme
    {
        Gzip = 0,
        Deflate = 1,
        Identity = 2
    }
}
```

You apply the *Compress* attribute to the method as follows:

```
[Compress]
public ActionResult Index()
{
    .
    .
    .
}
```

Figure 11-4 demonstrates that the content-encoding response header is set correctly and the response is understood and decompressed within the browser.

Almost any browser sets the *Accept-Encoding* header to the string "gzip, deflate," which is not the only possibility. As you can read in RFC 2616 (see *http://www.w3.org/Protocols/ rfc2616/rfc2616-sec14.html*), an *Accept* header field supports the *q* parameter as a way to assign a priority to an acceptable value. The following strings are acceptable values for an encoding:

```
gzip, deflate
gzip;q=.7,deflate
gzip;q=.5,deflate;q=.5,identity
```

FIGURE 11-4 FireBug shows the content-encoding response header.

Even though *gzip* appears in all strings, only in the first one is it the preferred choice. If a value is not specified, the *q* parameter is set to 1; this assigns to *deflate* in the second string and to *identity* in the third string a higher rank than *gzip*. So simply checking whether *gzip* appears in the encoding string still sends back something the browser can accept, but it doesn't take the browser's preference into full account. To write a *Compress* attribute that takes into account the priority (if any) expressed through the *q* parameter, you need to refine the *GetPreferredEncoding* method, as shown here:

```
private CompressionScheme GetPreferredEncoding(HttpRequest request)
{
    string acceptableEncoding = request.Headers["Accept-Encoding"].ToLower();
    acceptableEncoding = SortEncodings(acceptableEncoding);

    if (acceptableEncoding.Contains("gzip"))
        return CompressionScheme.Gzip;
    if (acceptableEncoding.Contains("deflate"))
        return CompressionScheme.Deflate;

    return CompressionScheme.Identity;
}
```

The *SortEncodings* method will parse the header string and extract the segment of it that corresponds to the choice with the highest priority.

Loading Action Filters Dynamically

Action filters are therefore a powerful mechanism for developers to use to decide exactly how a given action method executes. From what we have seen so far, however, action filters are also a static mechanism that requires a new compile-and-deploy step to be modified. Let's explore an approach to loading filters dynamically from an external source.

Interception Points for Filters

Filters are resolved for each action method within the action invoker. There are two main points of interception: the *GetFilters* and *InvokeActionMethodWithFilters* methods. Both methods are marked as protected and virtual. The signature of both methods is shown here:

```
protected virtual ActionExecutedContext InvokeActionMethodWithFilters(
    ControllerContext controllerContext,
    IList<IActionFilter> filters,
    ActionDescriptor actionDescriptor,
    IDictionary<string, object> parameters);

protected virtual FilterInfo GetFilters(
    ControllerContext controllerContext,
    ActionDescriptor actionDescriptor)
```

The *GetFilters* method is invoked earlier and is expected to return the list of all filters for a given action. After invoking the base method of *GetFilters* in your custom invoker, you have available the full list of filters for each category—that is, a list including exception, result, authorization, and action filters. Note that the *FilterInfo* class—a public class in *System.Web.Mvc*—offers specific collections of filters for each category:

```
public class FilterInfo
{
    // Private members
    :
    :

    public IList<IActionFilter> ActionFilters { get; }
    public IList<IAuthorizationFilter> AuthorizationFilters { get; }
    public IList<IExceptionFilter> ExceptionFilters { get; }
    public IList<IResultFilter> ResultFilters { get; }
}
```

The *InvokeActionMethodWithFilters* method is invoked during the process related to the performance of the action method. In this case, the method receives only the list of action filters—that is, those filters that are to execute before or after the code for the method.

Adding an Action Filter Using Fluent Code

By overriding the *InvokeActionMethodWithFilters* method, you can use fluent code to configure controllers and controller methods with action filters. (For information about fluent code, see *http://en.wikipedia.org/wiki/Fluent_interface*.) The following code shows how to add the *Compress* attribute on the fly to the *Index* method of the *Home* controller:

```
protected override ActionExecutedContext InvokeActionMethodWithFilters(
    ControllerContext controllerContext,
    IList<IActionFilter> filters,
    ActionDescriptor actionDescriptor,
    IDictionary<string, object> parameters)
{
    // Add the Compress action filter to the Index method of the Home controller
    if (actionDescriptor.ControllerDescriptor.ControllerName == "Home" &&
        actionDescriptor.ActionName == "Index")
    {
        // Configure the filter and add to the list
        var compressFilter = new CompressAttribute();
        filters.Add(compressFilter);
    }

    // Go with the usual behavior and execute the action
    return base.InvokeActionMethodWithFilters(
        controllerContext, filters, actionDescriptor, parameters);
}
```

This code can be refined in a number of aspects. For example, you can support areas and check the controller type rather than the name. In addition, you can read the filters to add from a configuration file and also use an IoC container to resolve them all.

More in general, this approach gives you a chance to dynamically configure the filters, and it also lets you keep attributes out of the controller code. This piece of code has the same value as the *RegisterInstance* methods of Unity (and similar IoC frameworks) or the fluent API of NHibernate and Entity Framework.

Building Up Filters via an IoC Container

Another aspect of filter attributes you can customize is their ultimate behavior. This feature is kind of orthogonal to the previous one because it can be applied regardless of the way in which you register your filters—whether declaratively through attributes or via fluent code.

Suppose you have a *Logging* filter. The purpose of such a filter is pretty clear: you want it to log some information. But where? The logger component might or might not be integrated into the filter. You might want to have a scheme like that shown here:

```
public class LoggingAttribute : ActionFilterAttribute
{
    public ILogger Logger {get; set;}

    public override void OnActionExecuting(ActionExecutingContext filterContext)
    {
        // Use the Logger component here
        :
        :
    }
}
```

How can you inject the logger component into the filter? The easiest (and also most natural) way of achieving that is using an IoC container. Let's work out an example where we use an IoC container, but we'll base the example on the *BrowserSpecific* filter we created earlier. (Tailoring the example to logging is trivial.)

The *BrowserSpecific* filter changes the name of the view based on the current browser agent. In our previous implementation, the logic to decide about the new view name was hard-coded. Let's make it pluggable through Unity:

```
public class BrowserSpecificAttribute : ActionFilterAttribute
{
    [Dependency]
    public IBrowserViewMapper Mapper { get; set; }

    public override void OnResultExecuting(ResultExecutingContext filterContext)
    {
        var viewResult = filterContext.Result as ViewResult;
        if (viewResult == null)
            return;

        string viewName = viewResult.ViewName;
        ControllerContext context = filterContext.Controller.ControllerContext;
        string browserName = context.HttpContext.Request.Browser.Browser;

        // Get the name of the browser-specific view to use
        string newViewName = string.Empty;
        if (Mapper == null)
            newViewName = GetViewNameForBrowserInternal(viewName, browserName);
        else
            newViewName = Mapper.GetViewName(viewName, browserName);

        if (!String.IsNullOrEmpty(newViewName))
        {
            ViewEngineResult result = ViewEngines.Engines.FindView(
                        context, newViewName, viewResult.MasterName);
            if (result.View != null)
                viewResult.ViewName = newViewName;
        }
    }

    // Hard-coded logic for picking up the browser-specific view name
    private string GetViewNameForBrowserInternal(string viewName, string browserName)
    {
        return String.Format("{0}_{1}", viewName, browserName);
    }
}
```

The filter now includes an injectable property that corresponds to a component of type *IBrowserViewMapper*:

```
public interface IBrowserViewMapper
{
    string GetViewName(string viewName, string browserName);
}
```

The next challenge to take is resolving the dependency. If you opt for a fluent syntax, your code creates the instance of the filter. You can use the IoC resolver to ensure that all dependencies are properly injected into the filter.

What if, instead, you attach filters using attributes? In this case, you need to override the *GetFilters* method on the action invoker class:

```
protected override FilterInfo GetFilters(
      ControllerContext controllerContext, ActionDescriptor actionDescriptor)
{
    var filters = base.GetFilters(controllerContext, actionDescriptor);

    foreach (var filter in filters.ActionFilters)
    {
        if (filter is ActionFilterAttribute)
        {
            // If no mapping is defined for the filter
            // you get an exception
            try
            {
                AppContext.Container.BuildUp(filter.GetType(), filter);
            }
            catch(ResolutionFailedException)
            {
            }
        }
    }
    return filters;
}
```

Note that the *ActionFilters* collection also includes the controller type. You normally don't have dependencies to build up at this time, so you check the type in order to skip controller types.

If you registered filters via attributes, ASP.NET MVC has already instantiated them. You use the *BuildUp* method of the Unity container to inject dependencies on existing objects. (This feature is supported by all IoC frameworks.)

> **Note** The *try/catch* block in the preceding code is not strictly necessary. To avoid using it, you simply define a mapping for any pending dependencies the filter might have. Note that Unity throws a *ResolutionFailedException* if the object has pending dependencies that can't be resolved. The implementation of *BrowserSpecific*, shown earlier, assumes a default hard-coded behavior for the property *Mapper*. The expected behavior, therefore, is that the dependency, if any, is loaded and the default behavior is adhered to otherwise. For this to happen, a *try/catch* block is required.

Action Selectors

Another special category of filters are action selectors. Action selectors come in two distinct flavors: action method selectors and action name selectors. Selectors kick in before the process that leads to executing the action code starts. In a way, the selector is responsible for validating the action method being executed and determines whether it is a valid action or not. Action method selectors validate the request against some runtime conditions. Action name selectors, on the other hand, check whether the action requested has a valid name. Both attributes are applied to action methods in a controller class.

Selecting an Action by Name

The base class for action name selectors is *ActionNameSelectorAttribute*. The class has a simple structure, as the code here demonstrates:

```
public abstract class ActionNameSelectorAttribute : Attribute
{
    public abstract bool IsValidName(
        ControllerContext controllerContext, string actionName, MethodInfo methodInfo);
}
```

The purpose of the selector is simple: checking whether the action name is valid or not. In ASP.NET MVC, there's just one action name selector: the *ActionName* attribute that you can use to alias a controller method. You encountered the *ActionName* attribute in Chapter 7, "Data Entry in ASP.NET MVC," in the discussion about the Post-Redirect-Get pattern for input forms.

```
[ActionName("Edit"), AcceptVerbs(HttpVerbs.Post)]
public ActionResult EditViaPost(string listCustomers)
{
    string customerId = listCustomers;
    return RedirectToAction("Edit",
                            new RouteValueDictionary(new { id = customerId }));
}
```

The implementation of the *ActionName* attribute is trivial, as the following code demonstrates:

```
public sealed class ActionNameAttribute : ActionNameSelectorAttribute
{
    public ActionNameAttribute(string name)
    {
        if (string.IsNullOrEmpty(name))
            throw new ArgumentException(MvcResources.Common_NullOrEmpty, "name");
        this.Name = name;
    }
```

```
public override bool IsValidName(
        ControllerContext controllerContext, string actionName, MethodInfo methodInfo)
{
    // Check that the action name matches the specified name
    return string.Equals(actionName, this.Name, StringComparison.OrdinalIgnoreCase);
}

public string Name { get; set; }
}
```

The net effect of the attribute is that it logically renames the controller method it is applied to. For example, in the previous example the method is named *EditViaPost*, but it won't be invoked unless the action name that results from the routing process is *Edit*.

Action Method Selectors

Action method selectors are a more powerful and interesting tool for developers. Such a selector is specifically designed to skip requests when certain runtime conditions hold. Here's the definition of the base class:

```
public abstract class ActionMethodSelectorAttribute : Attribute
{
    public abstract bool IsValidForRequest(
        ControllerContext controllerContext, MethodInfo methodInfo);
}
```

Also, in this case, the role of the class is straightforward. In ASP.NET MVC, quite a few predefined method selectors exist. They are *AcceptVerbs*, *NonAction*, plus a bunch of HTTP-specific selectors introduced with ASP.NET MVC 2 to simplify coding (*HttpDelete*, *HttpGet*, *HttpPost*, and *HttpPut*). Let's have a look at some of them.

The *NonAction* attribute just prevents the processing of the current action. Here's how it's implemented:

```
public override bool IsValidForRequest(
    ControllerContext controllerContext, MethodInfo methodInfo)
{
    return false;
}
```

The *AcceptVerbs* attribute receives the list of supported HTTP verbs as an argument and checks the current verb against the list. Here are some details:

```
public override bool IsValidForRequest(
    ControllerContext controllerContext, MethodInfo methodInfo)
{
    if (controllerContext == null)
        throw new ArgumentNullException("controllerContext");

    // Get the (overridden) HTTP method
    string method = controllerContext.HttpContext.Request.GetHttpMethodOverride();
```

```
    // Verbs is an internal member of the AcceptVerbsAttribute class
    return Verbs.Contains<string>(method, StringComparer.OrdinalIgnoreCase);
}
```

Note the use of the *GetHttpMethodOverride* method to retrieve the actual verb intended by the client. The method reads the value in a header field or parameter named *X-HTTP-Method-Override*. (See *http://code.google.com/apis/gdata/docs/2.0/basics.html#UpdatingEntry* for more information about *X-HTTP-Method-Override*). This is a common protocol for letting browsers place any HTTP verbs even though the physical request is either GET or POST. The method is not defined natively on the *HttpRequest* object, but it was added in ASP.NET MVC only as an extension method on *HttpRequestBase*.

The other selectors are simply implemented in terms of *AcceptVerbs*, as shown here for *HttpPost*:

```
public sealed class HttpPostAttribute : ActionMethodSelectorAttribute
{
    private static readonly AcceptVerbsAttribute _innerAttribute;

    public override bool IsValidForRequest(
        ControllerContext controllerContext, MethodInfo methodInfo)
    {
        return _innerAttribute.IsValidForRequest(controllerContext, methodInfo);
    }
}
```

Let's see how to write a custom method selector. All you need is a class that inherits from *ActionMethodSelectorAttribute* and overrides the *IsValidForRequest* method. The code here is a refinement of a selector available with the ASP.NET MVC Futures. (See *http://aspnet.codeplex.com/releases/view/39978*.)

```
[AttributeUsage(AttributeTargets.Method, AllowMultiple = false, Inherited = true)]
public sealed class AcceptAjaxAttribute : ActionMethodSelectorAttribute
{
    private bool _shouldAcceptAjaxRequest;
    public AcceptAjaxAttribute()
    {
        _shouldAcceptAjaxRequests = true;
    }

    public AcceptAjaxAttribute(bool shouldAcceptAjaxRequests)
    {
        _shouldAcceptAjaxRequests = shouldAcceptAjaxRequests;
    }

    public override bool IsValidForRequest(
        ControllerContext controllerContext, MethodInfo methodInfo)
    {
        if (controllerContext == null)
            throw new ArgumentNullException("controllerContext");
```

```
        // Figure out whether this is an AJAX request or not
        bool isAjaxRequest = controllerContext.HttpContext.Request.IsAjaxRequest();
        if (!isAjaxRequest)
            return true;

        return (isAjaxRequest == _shouldAcceptAjaxRequests);
    }
}
```

The *AcceptAjax* attribute accepts a Boolean parameter to decide whether AJAX requests are valid or not. Next, the selector figures out the type of the current request and matches it to the input received. A variation of this selector could be one that accepts only AJAX calls.

Action Results and Rendering

As you have read thus far, there are many ways to control the process of performing the requested action. Let's move to the next stage now and consider the tools you have to customize the production and presentation of the action result.

Processing the Result of the Action

The actual return value of any controller action is an object that inherits from *ActionResult*. As the name suggests, this object represents the result of the action. It embeds data and knows how to process it in order to generate the response for the browser.

This is an important point to note: the *ActionResult* object is not what the client browser is going to receive. Getting an *ActionResult* object is only the first step to finalizing the request.

Generating the Response for the Browser

The response for the browser is generated and written to the output stream when the *ActionResult* object, as returned by the controller action method, is further processed by the action invoker. In this regard, you can consider the *ActionResult* class as a way to encapsulate a particular type of response you want to send to the browser. The response certainly comprehends the actual data, but it also includes the content type, the status code, and any cookies and headers you intend to send. All of these things are aspects of the response you might want to control through a tailor-made *ActionResult* class.

As you saw already in Chapter 5, "Inside Views," the method that governs the processing of the action result is *InvokeActionResult*, which is defined on the default action invoker:

```
protected virtual void InvokeActionResult(
    ControllerContext controllerContext, ActionResult actionResult)
{
    actionResult.ExecuteResult(controllerContext);
}
```

The *ActionResult* object is defined as follows:

```
public abstract class ActionResult
{
    protected ActionResult()
    {
    }

    public abstract void ExecuteResult(ControllerContext context);
}
```

The actual action result classes that you use in your applications, including the numerous action result classes defined by ASP.NET MVC, extend the base class with a few public properties to store the concrete data that *ExecuteResult* will eventually render to the browser.

Dissecting Some Built-in Action Result Classes

To understand the mechanics of an action result object, it is useful to look at a couple of action result classes built into ASP.NET MVC. One of the simplest is the *HttpUnauthorizedResult* class:

```
public class HttpUnauthorizedResult : ActionResult
{
    public override void ExecuteResult(ControllerContext context)
    {
        if (context == null)
            throw new ArgumentNullException("context");

        // Prepare the response for the browser
        context.HttpContext.Response.StatusCode = 0x191;
    }
}
```

As you can see, all it does is set the status code of the response object. This class is used by the *Authorize* action filter when it turns out that the user behind the current request is not authorized. Here's a code snippet from the source code of the *Authorize* filter:

```
public virtual void OnAuthorization(AuthorizationContext filterContext)
{
    :
    :
    if (this.AuthorizeCore(filterContext.HttpContext))
    {
        :
        :
    }
    else
    {
        // If authorization failed, then the response for the request
        // is determined by the Response object as configured by the
        // HttpUnauthorizedResult class
        filterContext.Result = new HttpUnauthorizedResult();
    }
}
```

A slightly more sophisticated example is the *JavaScriptResult* class. This class supplies a public property—the *Script* property—that contains the script code to write to the output stream:

```
public class JavaScriptResult : ActionResult
{
    public string Script { get; set; }

    public override void ExecuteResult(ControllerContext context)
    {
        if (context == null)
            throw new ArgumentNullException("context");

        // Prepare the response
        HttpResponseBase response = context.HttpContext.Response;
        response.ContentType = "application/x-javascript";
        if (Script != null)
            response.Write(Script);
    }
}
```

You use the *JavaScriptResult* class from the action method, as shown here:

```
public JavaScriptResult GetScript()
{
    string script = ...;
    return JavaScriptResult(script);
}
```

Note that, strictly speaking, a controller action method is not forced to return an *ActionResult* object. However, be aware that whatever type you return will be wrapped up in a *ContentResult* object by the ASP.NET MVC framework. If the method is void, on the other hand, the action result will be an *EmptyResult* object. By using action filters, you can modify the result object, and its parameters, at will. So in the end, you can still have a controller method declared to return nothing, but tailor that to return a value with an action filter attached that programmatically returns a given result object.

Custom *ActionResult* Objects

Ultimately, the action result object is a way to encapsulate all the tasks you need to accomplish in particular situations, such as when a requested resource is missing or redirected or when some special response must be served to the browser. Let's examine a few interesting scenarios for having custom action result objects.

The *PermanentRedirectResult* Object

In Chapter 8, we discussed permanent redirection as an aspect of a Web application that can have a nontrivial impact on Search Engine Optimization (SEO). Suppose that at some point you decide to expose a given feature of your application through another URL but still need to support the old URL. To increase your SEO ratio, you might want to implement a permanent redirect instead of a classic (temporary) HTTP 302 redirect.

ASP.NET MVC supplies a *RedirectResult* class, but it lacks a *PermanentRedirectResult* class. Here's a possible implementation that follows closely that of *RedirectResult* in ASP.NET MVC 2:

```
public class PermanentRedirectResult : ActionResult
{
    public string Url { get; set; }
    public bool ShouldEndResponse { get; set; }

    public PermanentRedirectResult(string url)
    {
        if (String.IsNullOrEmpty(url))
            throw new ArgumentException("url");

        Url = url;
        ShouldEndResponse = false;
    }

    public override void ExecuteResult(ControllerContext context)
    {
        // Preconditions
        if (context == null)
            throw new ArgumentNullException("context");
        if (context.IsChildAction)
            throw new InvalidOperationException();

        // Mark all keys in the TempData dictionary for retention
        context.Controller.TempData.Keep();

        // Prepare the response
        string url = UrlHelper.GenerateContentUrl(Url, context.HttpContext);
        HttpResponseBase response = context.HttpContext.Response;
        response.Clear();
        response.StatusCode = 301;
        response.AddHeader("Location", url);

        // Optionally end the request
        if (ShouldEndResponse)
            response.End();
    }
}
```

By having this class available, you can easily move your features around without affecting the SEO level of your application:

```
public ActionResult Old()
{
    string newUrl = "/Home/Index";
    return new PermanentRedirectResult(newUrl);
}
```

Figure 11-5 shows the results in FireBug.

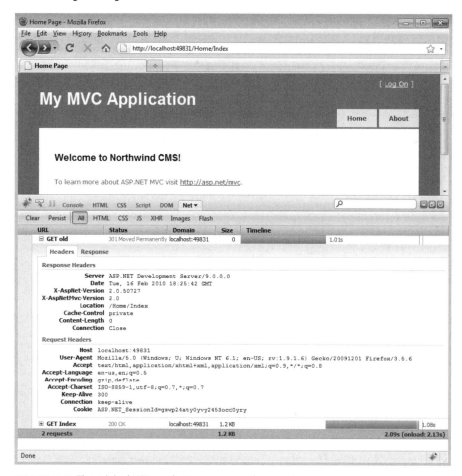

FIGURE 11-5 The original URL results are permanently moved.

A Syndication Result Object

If you search the Web for a nontrivial example of an action result, you likely find a syndication action result object at the top of the list. Let's briefly go through this popular example.

The class *SyndicationResult* supports both RSS 2.0 and ATOM 1.0 and offers a handy property for you to choose programmatically. By default, the class produces an RSS 2.0 feed. To compile this example, you need to reference the *System.ServiceModel.Web* assembly and import the *System.ServiceModel.Syndication* namespace:

```
public class SyndicationResult : ActionResult
{
    public SyndicationFeed Feed { get; set; }
    public FeedType Type { get; set; }

    public SyndicationResult()
    {
        Type = FeedType.Rss;
    }
```

```
    public SyndicationResult(
        string title, string description, Uri uri, IEnumerable<SyndicationItem> items)
    {
        Type = FeedType.Rss;
        Feed = new SyndicationFeed(title, description, uri, items);
    }
    public SyndicationResult(SyndicationFeed feed)
    {
        Type = FeedType.Rss;
        Feed = feed;
    }


    public override void ExecuteResult(ControllerContext context)
    {
        // Set the content type
        context.HttpContext.Response.ContentType = GetContentType();

        // Create the feed and write it to the output stream
        var feedFormatter = GetFeedFormatter();
        var writer = XmlWriter.Create(context.HttpContext.Response.Output);
        if (writer == null)
            return;
        feedFormatter.WriteTo(writer);
        writer.Close();
    }

    private string GetContentType()
    {
        if(Type == FeedType.Atom)
            return "application/atom+xml";
        return "application/rss+xml";
    }

    private SyndicationFeedFormatter GetFeedFormatter()
    {
        if (Type == FeedType.Atom)
            return new Atom10FeedFormatter(Feed);
        return new Rss20FeedFormatter(Feed);
    }
}

public enum FeedType
{
    Rss = 0,
    Atom = 1
}
```

The class gets a syndication feed and just serializes it to the client using either the
RSS 2.0 or ATOM 1.0 format. Creating a consumable feed is another story; but it is also
a concern that belongs to the controller rather than to the infrastructure. Here's how to write
a controller method that returns a feed:

```
public SyndicationResult Blog()
{
    var items = new List<SyndicationItem>();
    items.Add(new SyndicationItem(
        "Controller descriptors",
```

```
            "This post shows how to customize controller descriptors",
            null));
    items.Add(new SyndicationItem(
        "Action filters",
        "Using a fluent API to define action filters",
        null));
    items.Add(new SyndicationItem(
        "Custom action results",
        "Create a custom action result for syndication data",
        null));
    var result = new SyndicationResult(
        "Programming ASP.NET MVC 2",
        "Dino's latest book",
         Request.Url,
         items);

    result.Type = FeedType.Atom;
    return result;
}
```

You create a list of *SyndicationItem* objects and provide for each a title, some content, and
an alternate link (*null* in the code snippet). You typically retrieve these items from some
repository you might have in your application. Finally, you pass items to the *SyndicationResult*
object along with a title and description for the feed to be created and serialized. Figure 11-6
shows an ATOM feed in Internet Explorer.

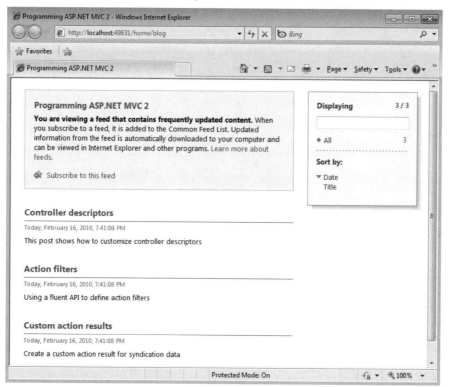

FIGURE 11-6 An ATOM feed displayed in Internet Explorer

Returning Binary Data

A common developer need is returning binary data from a request. Under the umbrella of binary data fall many different types of data, such as the pixels of an image, the content of a PDF file, or even a Silverlight package.

You don't really need an ad hoc action result object to deal with binary data. Among the built-in action result objects, you can certainly find one that helps you when working with binary data. If the content you want to transfer is stored within a disk file, you can use the *FilePathResult* object. If the content is available through a stream, you use *FileStreamResult* and opt for *FileContentResult* if you have it available as a byte array. All these objects derive from *FileResult* and differ from one another only in how they write out data to the response stream. Let's briefly review how *ExecuteResult* works within *FileResult*:

```
public override void ExecuteResult(ControllerContext context)
{
    if (context == null)
        throw new ArgumentNullException("context");

    HttpResponseBase response = context.HttpContext.Response;
    response.ContentType = this.ContentType;
    if (!String.IsNullOrEmpty(this.FileDownloadName))
    {
        string headerValue = ContentDispositionUtil.GetHeaderValue(FileDownloadName);
        context.HttpContext.Response.AddHeader("Content-Disposition", headerValue);
    }

    // Write content to the output stream
    WriteFile(response);
}
```

The class has a public property named *ContentType* through which you communicate the MIME type of the response and which does all of its work via an abstract method—*WriteFile*—that derived classes must necessarily override.

The base class *FileResult* also supports the Save As dialog box within the client browser through the *Content-Disposition* header. The property *FileDownloadName* specifies the default name the file will be given in the browser's Save As dialog. The *Content-Disposition* header has the following format, where *XXX* stands for the value of the *FileDownloadName* property:

```
Content-Disposition: attachment; filename=XXX
```

Note that the file name should be in the US-ASCII character set and no directory path information is allowed. Finally, the MIME type must be unknown to the browser; otherwise, the registered handler will be used to process the content.

Inside Built-in Binary Action Result Classes

The delta between the base class *FileResult* and derived classes is mostly related to the implementation of the *WriteFile* method. In particular, *FileContentResult* writes an array of bytes straight to the output stream, as shown here:

```
// FileContents is a property on FileContentResults that points to the bytes
protected override void WriteFile(HttpResponseBase response)
{
    response.OutputStream.Write(FileContents, 0, FileContents.Length);
}
```

FileStreamResult offers a different implementation. It has a *FileStream* property that provides the data to read, and the code in *WriteFile* reads and writes in a buffered way:

```
protected override void WriteFile(HttpResponseBase response)
{
    Stream outputStream = response.OutputStream;
    using (FileStream)
    {
        byte[] buffer = new byte[0x1000];
        while (true)
        {
            int count = FileStream.Read(buffer, 0, 0x1000);
            if (count == 0)
                return;
            outputStream.Write(buffer, 0, count);
        }
    }
}
```

Finally, *FilePathResult* copies an existing file to the output stream. The implementation of *WriteFile* is quite minimal in this case:

```
// FileName is the name of the file to read and transmit
protected override void WriteFile(HttpResponseBase response)
{
    response.TransmitFile(FileName);
}
```

With these classes available, you can deal with any sort of binary data that you need to serve programmatically from a URL.

Important Speaking of binary data, I must note that an ASP.NET MVC endpoint is not necessarily the fastest way to serve this kind of data. Using a plain HTTP handler as the endpoint results in leaner processing and, likely, in a faster response. Using an HTTP handler to serve, say, an image stored into a database is significantly more efficient than using an ASP.NET Web Forms page. With ASP.NETMVC, the gap is reduced but still remains favorable to HTTP handlers. In summary, I definitely invite you to consider HTTP handlers when it comes to serving binary data to Web clients.

View Engines

In ASP.NET MVC, generating the view is a process completely separated from the calculation of the data to be displayed. In Chapter 5, we discussed the mechanism behind the rendering of the view. The most important aspect of the rendering engine in ASP.NET MVC is that it is replaceable.

The view engine is the part of ASP.NET MVC that parses a template file to produce an HTML response when the action method is expected to serve HTML to the user. By default, ASP.NET MVC requires you to write the view file using an ASPX-compatible markup that will be processed through the same internal machinery used by ASP.NET Web Forms. In this way, you can use server controls, user controls, master pages, and themes, as well as code blocks interspersed with HTML literals and markup elements.

As mentioned, the view engine is abstracted by the *IViewEngine* interface, making it possible for third-party companies and the community to develop alternate engines based on a different syntax. Many view engines have been proposed over the past couple of years, but the only serious alternative to the default view engine seems to be the Spark view engine.

Providing full coverage of Spark probably deserves an entire chapter, if not a book, of its own. In this chapter, my goal is simply to discuss the pluggability mechanism of ASP.NET MVC views that makes it possible to use Spark today. In doing so, I'll also take a quick look at some of the samples that come with the package. For further documentation and even the source code, you can start from *http://sparkviewengine.com*.

Adding an Alternate View Engine

In ASP.NET MVC, the static class *ViewEngines* represents the collection of view engines that are currently available to the application. The class is coded as follows:

```
public static class ViewEngines
{
    // Fields
    private static readonly ViewEngineCollection _engines;

    // Methods
    static ViewEngines()
    {
        ViewEngineCollection engines = new ViewEngineCollection();
        engines.Add(new WebFormViewEngine());
        _engines = engines;
    }

    // Properties
    public static ViewEngineCollection Engines
    {
        get { return _engines; }
    }
}
```

It turns out that each and every ASP.NET MVC application has at least one view engine registered, and that view engine understands the Web Forms ASPX markup. To add your own view engine—whether it is a new engine or simply a customized version of the standard engine that just supports different locations for templates—you write some code to *global.asax*. The following code registers the Spark view engine:

```
protected void Application_Start(object sender, EventArgs e)
{
    // Your own default stuff here
    RegisterRoutes(RouteTable.Routes);
    :
    :


    // Register the Spark view engine (as long as the Spark
    // assemblies are properly referenced)
    SparkEngineStarter.RegisterViewEngine();
}
```

If you're wondering where the code is that adds a new *IViewEngine* object to the *Engines* collection, here is a code snippet taken from the source code of the Spark library:

```
public static void RegisterViewEngine()
{
    ViewEngines.Engines.Add(CreateViewEngine());
}
public static IViewEngine CreateViewEngine()
{
    return CreateContainer().GetService<IViewEngine>();
}
```

With this code in place, your application actually runs with two view engines—the default one plus the Spark engine. The default view engine always takes precedence over Spark. You can, of course, remove the default view engine and run your application with just the Spark engine (or whatever else you intend to use). Here's what you need to do in this case:

```
protected void Application_Start(object sender, EventArgs e)
{
    // Your own default stuff here
    RegisterRoutes(RouteTable.Routes);
    :
    :


    // Remove the default view engine
    ViewEngines.Engines.Clear();

    // Register the Spark view engine (as long as the Spark
    // assemblies are properly referenced)
    SparkEngineStarter.RegisterViewEngine();

    // You can re-add the default engine here after the Spark engine
    // to (try to) give it a lower priority. As we'll see later, this is not what
    // will happen in all cases, though.
    ViewEngines.Engines.Add(new WebFormViewEngine());
}
```

When multiple engines are registered, normally they are resolved in the order of registration. However, there's a caveat to consider. The search through the list of registered view engines is conducted by the *FindView* method on *ViewEngineCollection* using the following algorithm:

```
ViewEngineResult result;

// Check whether the view engine has a cached view that matches the name
foreach (IViewEngine engine in ViewEngines.Engines)
{
    if (engine != null)
    {
        // Final Boolean parameter indicates use-cache (if any)
        result = engine.FindView(controllerContext, viewName, masterName, true);
        if (result.View != null)
            ...
    }
}

// Check whether the view engine can produce a view that matches the name
foreach (IViewEngine engine in ViewEngines.Engines)
{
    if (engine != null)
    {
        // Final Boolean parameter indicates NOT to use the cache
        result = engine.FindView(controllerContext, viewName, masterName, false);
        if (result.View != null)
            ...
    }
}
```

As you can see, the view engine first gets an inquiry to see if it has a cached view with a matching name. At least with the default configuration, Spark doesn't cache views. Because the default engine always caches views, conversely, it is picked up even if you added it to the list after the Spark engine.

> **Note** The default view engine and Spark can be used at the same time, which would make the transition gradual. Ultimately, you can begin by simply changing the extension of an *.aspx* template file to *.spark* and removing the top @ directives. You can even have Spark views rendered as partial views in the Web Forms engine.

Overview of the Spark View Engine

To use the Spark view engine, you start by referencing a couple of assemblies: *Spark* and *Spark.Web.Mvc*. Next, you register the engine with ASP.NET MVC in *global.asax* and proceed with the definition of the templates.

Obviously, Spark supports many levels of configuration and the precompilation of views. For more information, refer to *http://sparkviewengine.com/documentation*.

The big difference between Spark and the Web Forms engines is in the syntax. Spark was designed around the idea of having HTML (or a tag-based, HTML-like syntax) all the way through. You won't have code blocks in Spark, and there's no mix of code and markup whatsoever. HTML markup dominates the flow, and the code just fits into it smoothly.

Spark still supplies constructs that match the master pages and user controls that you find in the Web Forms engine. Spark extends the classic HTML syntax with a bunch of new tags to address specific needs, such as linking to the view-model object, executing a test or a loop, or importing a pregenerated chunk of HTML. Here's a taste of the Spark syntax right from the site:

```
<var versions="new [] {'Preview', 'Beta', 'RC', 'RTM'}"/>
<for each="var productVersion in versions">
  <test if="productVersion == 'RTM'">
    <p>Enjoy the product!</p>
    <else/>
    <p>${productVersion} is here. Just wait for RTM...
  </test>
</for>
```

The snippet shows off a few specific tags, such as *var, for, test*, and *else*. The *var* tag defines a variable named *versions* and assigns it a few fixed values. Next, the *for* tag loops over the array, checks the value, and emits markup accordingly. The *${ . . . }* expression emits the value of an expression that has a return value. The output you get might or might not be encoded automatically, depending on the current settings. If you have the following in the configuration file, the result of any *${...}* expression will be silently encoded:

```
<spark>
    ⋮

    <pages automaticEncoding="true" />
<spark>
```

However, note that you can always force unescaped strings by using the *!{ . . . }* macro instead. A nice feature of Spark is that null exceptions are caught and swallowed automatically if only you use the following syntax:

```
$!{ expression }
```

In this case, any *null* values and *NullReferenceException* that result from the expression are ignored and produce no output at all.

Defining a Layout with Spark

Spark is a view engine that can be successfully used with both ASP.NET MVC and Castle MonoRail—two ASP.NET frameworks that follow the same pattern. The core rendering engine is then customized by a second assembly that adapts the engine to the needs of the host framework and plugs it in.

When used with ASP.NET MVC, Spark requires you to define view files and place them in the same folders as the default view engine. View files are retrieved and invoked by name. Let's briefly consider the following action method:

```
public ActionResult Index()
{
    return View();
}
```

It invokes the view named *Index* on the current controller. When the default engine is employed, the view file is expected to be *index.aspx* and it's expected to be located in the controller-specific folder under *Views* or in the *Shared* folder. If you switch to the Spark engine, the view file the framework will look for is *index.spark*. The locations where it is searched are the same as with the default engine.

It is not uncommon that the template of a page requires a master layout or a master page just to use the Web Forms expression. With Spark, you can define a master layout in a number of ways. You typically choose to have a single *application.spark* file in the *Views/Shared* folder when you use just one template for all your views. Alternately, you can have a *.spark* file named after the controller. A controller-specific template takes precedence over the *application.spark* file. Note also that if you specifically indicate a particular *.spark* file as the master name in the call to *View()*, that will be used regardless of other settings you might have in place. Here's a sample application layout file:

```
<html>
  :
  :
  <body>
    <div id="main">
      <div id="content">
        <use content="MainContent" />
      </div>
      <div id="footer">
        <use content="FooterContent" />
      </div>
    </div>
  </body>
</html>
```

The *use* element indicates a placeholder for content generated by the template file.

Finally, you can have reusable blocks of markup in Spark similar to user controls in the Web Forms view engine of ASP.NET MVC. All you do is create *.spark* files in the *Views/Shared* folder and reference them in other templates using an element that matches the name. It is key to note that the file name must be prefixed with an underscore. So suppose you have a *_Footer.spark* file defined, as shown here:

```
<p>
    Courtesy of "Programming ASP.NET MVC 2" &copy; Copyright 2010 Dino Esposito
</p>
```

You can insert it into a master layout or a template, as shown here:

```
<div id="main">
    <div id="content">
        <use content="MainContent" />
    </div>
    <div id="footer">
        <Footer />
    </div>
</div>
```

Note that the tag is case-sensitive in the sense it has to match perfectly the case of the *.spark* file name in the *Shared* folder.

Importing the View Model with Spark

The *viewdata* element in Spark is a declarative wrapper around the *ViewData* object of ASP.NET MVC. Note that a similar object also exists in Castle MonoRail—the other MVC Web framework that Spark works well with. You can use the *viewdata* element in your template file in a variety of ways. Here's the layout of the element first:

```
<viewdata property="type" />
```

You can have as many distinct properties as you like in a single element and as many *viewdata* elements as you want. The *property* attribute indicates the name of the property you can use in your expressions to retrieve data from the *ViewData* object. The value of the attribute, on the other hand, describes the type of the property. Here's a simple example:

```
<viewdata Message="string" />
```

In this way, you are defining a strongly typed accessor for any *string* value in *ViewData* that can be reached through the expression *Message*. This can be any value that the controller has stored through the following expressions:

```
// Create an entry in the dictionary named Message and of type String
ViewData["Message"] = ...;

// ViewData.Model references an object with a Message property of type String
ViewData.Model.Message = ...;
```

If both expressions are used, the value in the dictionary is used. Internally, the *viewdata* element is resolved using the *ViewData.Eval* method, which attempts first to resolve through the dictionary and then looks into what's possibly referenced by the property *Model*.

Note that in your *.spark* templates, you can also freely use any of the following expressions:

```
ViewData["Message"]
ViewData.Model.Message
ViewData.Eval("Message")
```

In other words, using the *viewdata* element adds one more possibility and doesn't limit you in any way.

Let's consider another example. In this case, the *viewdata* element is used to reference a complex type, such as *MyContainer*:

```
namespace MyBook.Samples
{
    public class MyContainer
    {
        public string Message { get; set; }
    }
}
```

The controller stores an instance of *MyContainer* into the *ViewData* dictionary:

```
var myContainer = new MyContainer();
myContainer.Message = "...";
ViewData["MyModel"] = myContainer;
```

You retrieve this data via the *viewdata* element as follows:

```
<use namespace="MyBook.Samples" />
<viewdata MyModel="MyContainer" />
    .
    .
    .
${MyModel.Message}
```

And finally, if your view-model object is stored in the *Model* property of the *ViewData* collection, here's what you can do:

```
<use namespace="MyBook.Samples" />
<viewdata model="MyContainer" />
    .
    .
    .
${Model.Message}
```

The case of property names in the *viewdata* element doesn't matter. To finish off, here's a complete demo that renders a data-driven user interface. The view model is a collection of *Category* object. Note the special *[[type]]* syntax used in the *viewdata* element for generics:

```
<content name="MainContent">
    <viewdata model="IEnumerable[[Category]]"/>

    <h2>Browse Products
        <span class="action">
            !{Html.ActionLink("[add]", "NewCategory")}
        </span>
    </h2>
    <ul>
        <li each="var category in ViewData.Model"
            id="!{Html.AttributeEncode(category.CategoryName)}">
```

```
        !{Html.ActionLink(category.CategoryName,
                          "List",
                          new { id=category.CategoryName })}
      </li>
    </ul>
</content>
```

Figure 11-7 shows the output produced by this template.

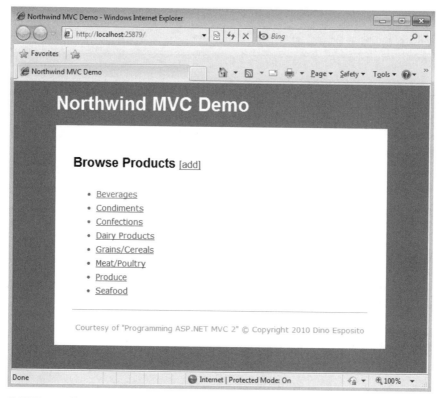

FIGURE 11-7 The output of the view as designed with Spark

Note What makes Spark so attractive to so many people in the relatively small (but growing) ASP.NET MVC community? The reason is essentially this: Spark gives you a clean syntax to describe the view you want. Your final result will probably be much cleaner and more readable than the tag soup you are likely to produce with the default Web Forms view engine. This increases readability which, in turn, helps maintenance because Spark makes it inherently easier to spot what's wrong at some point. Spark makes it harder for you to produce a tag soup, but a readable syntax with the default engine is definitely possible. The reality is that Spark brings with it a new syntax and binds you to a community-driven project.

In my opinion, it couldn't be farther from the truth that community-driven and open-source projects are lesser software. However, I've seen too many customers who are just not willing to use any software without "a clear vendor behind it" to yield to the sincere geek enthusiasm for something that—like Spark—is inherently cool.

Ultimately, using Spark or sticking to the default view engine doesn't generally make a big difference in the economy of a project. Although I won't deny that Spark is really cool and effective, I won't list it as one of the must-have features that could make your project a success. This said, I welcome any improvement to the view syntax that Microsoft could deliver in the near future. Compile-time checking, ordered mix-up of HTML and code, and optional declarative components for when you need more abstraction—these are, in my opinion, the pillars of the ideal ASP.NET MVC view engine.

HTML Helpers

Many developers go through the same experience when they approach ASP.NET MVC. The initial enthusiasm for the technology and the attraction to the overall high quality of the design are soon softened by the consideration that, when it comes to the view, you seem to go 10 years back to the tag soup of old-fashioned ASP. Spark (as well as other engines such as NVelocity) can certainly contribute to making a view template more readable and cleaner, but it doesn't change a basic fact: ASP.NET MVC today lacks a component model to give you the level of productivity you can achieve in Web Forms through server controls.

ASP.NET MVC and a Component Model

ASP.NET MVC pushes simplicity and, as a result, it is designed to stay really close to the metal. Because the URL of a Web application typically returns HTML, staying close to the metal means staying close to the machinery that produces HTML and granting developers total control over it. This is a good point and fulfills a real demand.

The point is: should the quest for simplicity and control preclude adding a more abstract component model conceptually similar to server controls, but technically different? If we could get to this, in my opinion, we would be more than halfway toward the unification of the various ASP.NET frameworks (Web Forms, ASP.NET MVC, and also Dynamic Data).

You might recall from Chapter 1, "Goals of ASP.NET MVC and Motivation for Its Development," the success of Web Forms is largely due to the abstraction it provides over the production of HTML and script code. This abstraction is mostly achieved through server controls. You can certainly use Web Forms server controls in ASP.NET MVC, but server controls follow their own paradigm, which is tightly integrated with the Page Controller pattern of Web Forms. A component model that is analogous to server controls just doesn't exist for ASP.NET MVC. This fact definitely cuts down to some extent the potential of the framework and makes the choice between Web Forms and ASP.NET MVC more difficult (and, in a way, pointless) for architects and project managers.

The fundamental question—should we use ASP.NET Web Forms or ASP.NET MVC—too often ends up being an endless and pointless religious discussion where all parties are just pushing their own vision and screaming louder with the gathering force of their conviction.

ASP.NET MVC is an excellent choice from the perspective of developers, but that doesn't necessarily translate to a tangible benefit for the customer and the project. As a result, many developers—probably the largest share—stick to Web Forms and lack the great opportunity to upgrade to an inherently superior platform. As of today, it looks like the classic egg vs. chicken dilemma.

I envision a near future in which ASP.NET MVC shows off a set of declarative components supported at least by the default view engine that could boost the productivity of the average developer, without requiring the developer to learn an entirely new model. It could be a new family of server components that are not bound to postbacks and view state but still offer a rich and declarative programming model.

Emitting Common HTML Elements

HTML helpers are the closest you get in ASP.NET MVC to the server controls of Web Forms. As you saw in Chapter 5, an HTML helper is an extension method on the *HtmlHelper* class that returns a common chunk of HTML markup.

At the core, there's no difference between a server control and an HTML helper. Both just take some input arguments and prepare some markup for the output stream. The difference is in the programming interface they offer and in their internal behavior. An HTML helper is a simple markup generator with no logic whatsoever; a server control has a much more sophisticated life cycle, and rendering is only one of its responsibilities. In addition, an HTML helper offers only an imperative syntax, whereas a server control is mostly used declaratively. You won't stray too far from the truth by saying that an HTML helper is a very simple server control.

As the name suggests, an HTML helper helps you when it comes to producing a common (and reusable) piece of HTML. ASP.NET MVC supplies a number of helpers to help you with many of the basic HTML elements. In ASP.NET MVC 2, you won't have helpers for submit buttons, even though such helpers exist in the MVC Futures library. Here's how to create one:

```
public static class ButtonHelpers
{
    public static MvcHtmlString SubmitButton(this HtmlHelper helper,
            string name, string caption)
    {
       return SubmitButton(helper, name, caption, null);
    }

    public static MvcHtmlString SubmitButton(this HtmlHelper helper,
            string name, string caption, object htmlAttributes)
    {
        // Convert from object to dictionary
        var dict = (IDictionary<string, object>) new RouteValueDictionary(htmlAttributes);

        // Build the button
        var submit = new TagBuilder("input");
        submit.MergeAttribute("type", "submit");
        submit.MergeAttribute("value", caption);
        submit.MergeAttribute("name", name, true);
```

```
        return MvcHtmlString.Create(
               submit.ToString(TagRenderMode.SelfClosing));
    }
}
```

As mentioned, an HTML helper is an extension method for the *HtmlHelper* class in *System. Web.Mvc*. You are entirely responsible for the programming interface of the method. It is a good practice to offer several overloads and make the helper return an *MvcHtmlString* object instead of a plain string. (In ASP.NET MVC 2, an *MvcHtmlString* is a special wrapper for a string that indicates the string should not be encoded further.)

Overloads of an HTML helper typically list a growing number of parameters, including a dictionary of cross-cutting HTML attributes such as *class* or perhaps *disabled*. The logic of the helper is entirely focused on producing HTML. You can manually accumulate markup in a text buffer, or you can use the specialized *TagBuilder* class that ASP.NET MVC gently offers. The *MergeAttribute* method attaches to the in-memory structure created by *TagBuilder* information about an attribute to emit and its value. *MergeAttribute* comes in various forms:

```
public void MergeAttribute(string key, string value);
public void MergeAttribute(string key, string value, bool replaceExisting);
public void MergeAttributes<TKey, TValue>(
        IDictionary<TKey, TValue> attributes);
public void MergeAttributes<TKey, TValue>(
        IDictionary<TKey, TValue> attributes, bool replaceExisting);
```

Other useful methods on the *TagBuilder* class are *SetInnerText*, *GenerateId*, and *AddCssClass*. Finally, the class also supplies a public *InnerHtml* property if you just need to get or set the inner HTML explicitly.

The *ToString* method of *TagBuilder* can optionally render the closing or self-closing tag as well as the initial tag. A bit surprisingly, the *TagBuilder* doesn't have a public *ToMvcHtmlString* method. The method exists, but it is marked as internal. For this reason, you resort to *MvcHtmlString.Create* when it comes to emitting the markup.

Emitting Common HTML Blocks

You can use HTML helpers not just to emit functional elements such as buttons or drop-down lists, but also to emit meta and link tags, include tags, script code, and so forth.

Some developers also argue that whenever you feel the need to have an *if* in your rendering logic, you have to create an HTML helper. Frankly, the suggestion is not far-fetched, but it probably doesn't address the real problem. Having a lot of highly specialized HTML helpers will make the whole view syntax cleaner and HTML-like because it would save you from too many <% . . . %> code blocks, especially code blocks used to create a control flow logic. If you strongly agree with this vision, probably you'd be better off dropping the default engine to embrace Spark. With Spark, you can still use HTML helpers, but at least you save yourself from creating many generic helpers that are already built into the Spark engine.

Let's see how to create an HTML helper to emit some meta information, such as the Web site icon—the favicon:

```
public static class FavIconHelpers
{
    public static MvcHtmlString Favicon(this HtmlHelper helper)
    {
        return Favicon(helper, "", "", false);
    }
    public static MvcHtmlString Favicon(this HtmlHelper helper, string iconPath)
    {
        return Favicon(helper, iconPath, "", false);
    }
    public static MvcHtmlString Favicon(this HtmlHelper helper,
            string iconPath, bool animated)
    {
        return Favicon(helper, iconPath, "", animated);
    }
    public static MvcHtmlString Favicon(this HtmlHelper helper,
            string iconPath, string iconName, bool animated)
    {
        var urlHelper = new UrlHelper(helper.ViewContext.RequestContext);
        var builder = new StringBuilder();

        // Fix the icon path
        string path = iconPath;
        if (!String.IsNullOrEmpty(path))
        {
            path = urlHelper.Content(iconPath);
            if (!path.EndsWith("/"))
                path += "/";
        }

        // Fix the icon name
        string icon = "favicon.ico";
        if (!String.IsNullOrEmpty(iconName))
            icon = iconName;
        icon = path + icon;

        // Add the favicon tag
        builder.AppendFormat("<link rel=\"shortcut icon\"
                                href=\"{0}\"
                                type=\"image/x-icon\" />\n", icon);

        // In this case, an animated favicon was requested
        if (animated)
        {
            string animatedIcon = "animated_favicon.gif";
            animatedIcon = path + animatedIcon;
            builder.AppendFormat("<link rel=\"icon\"
                                    type=\"image/gif\"
                                    href=\"{0}\" />\n", animatedIcon);
        }

        return MvcHtmlString.Create(builder.ToString());
    }
}
```

The *FavIconHelpers* class has a few overloads to simplify the usage from within views and master pages. It accepts the path and icon name as well as a Boolean argument for when an animated icon is required. The code works to emit a chunk of HTML, as shown here:

```
<link rel="shortcut icon" href="favicon.ico" type="image/x-icon" />
```

The favicon usually resides in the home directory, but nothing prevents you from moving it elsewhere. Likewise, the name of the icon defaults to *favicon.ico*, but it can be changed at will. If anything is changed, it will then be reflected by the *href* attribute. Some browsers (including the latest versions of Opera and Firefox, but noticeably not Internet Explorer 8) support animated favicons. You get that by simply adding the following:

```
<link rel="icon" href="animated_favicon.gif" type="image/gif" />
```

Of course, the content of the *href* attribute can be changed at will. The type of the file, though, has to be GIF and the actual content must be an animated GIF. For simplicity, the *FavIconHelpers* class shown here doesn't let you choose a name for the animated icon but defaults to *animated_favicon.gif*. You use the following code to emit a favicon in a master page:

```
<head runat="server">
    <%= Html.Favicon("/images", true) %>
    <title><asp:ContentPlaceHolder ID="TitleContent" runat="server" /></title>
        .
        .
        .
</head>
```

Figure 11-8 shows an animated favicon in Firefox.

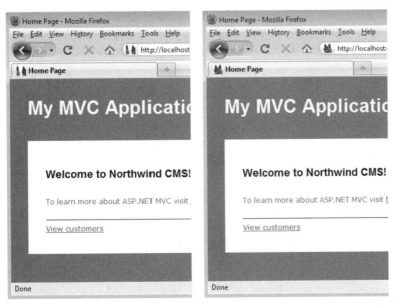

FIGURE 11-8 An animated favicon iterates for a few seconds and then remains still.

Emitting Common Blocks of jQuery UI Script

HTML helpers can also be used to speed up the creation of boilerplate script code. An excellent example is the use of the jQuery UI library. (See *http://jqueryui.com*.) The library extends the popular *jquery* library with nice user interface features such as effects, transitions, animations and, more interesting in this context, rich widgets such as tabstrips, accordions, dialog boxes, and a calendar component.

All of these widgets require a fixed HTML layout in the page and then some ad hoc script code to perform dynamic transformation and styling. As an example, consider the following rather scanty markup:

```
<h2> Some static content </h2>
<hr />
<div id="accCustomers">
    <h3><a href="#"> ALFKI </a></h3>
        <div>
            Customer ALFKI
        </div>
    <h3><a href="#">BOTTM</a></h3>
        <div>
            Customer BOTTM
        </div>
    <h3><a href="#">CACTU</a></h3>
        <div>
            Customer CACTU
        </div>
</div>
```

After it is processed by the jQuery *accordion* function, it shows up as illustrated in Figure 11-9.

To set up a jQuery UI widget, you need some ad hoc script code that can be placed in the script block you run upon loading. Most commonly, the code goes within the *ready* function of jQuery or in an analogous handler if you're using, say, ASP.NET AJAX:

```
<script type="text/javascript">
    $(document).ready(
        function() {
            .
            .
            .
        }
    );
</script>
```

The script code you need might be as simple as a parameterless function call or it might be more sophisticated, depending on the parameters you need to pass and the level of customization you want to achieve. HTML helpers can simplify the declaration of your intents as far as jQuery UI widgets are concerned. As an example, let's see how to define an HTML helper to attach a date picker to a plain *input* tag like the one shown here:

```
<input type="text" id="FavoriteDay" />
```

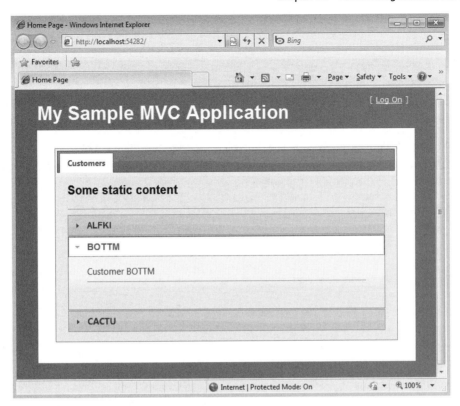

FIGURE 11-9 An accordion created with jQuery UI

To attach a date picker, you need the following script code:

```
$("#FavoriteDay").datepicker();
```

This code will get more complex the more features you want to use. Here's a less trivial example:

```
$("#FavoriteDay").datepicker(
    {
        dateFormat: 'yy-mm-dd',
        numberOfMonths: 3,
        showCurrentAtPos: 1,
        changeMonth: true,
        showOn: 'both',
        showOtherMonths: true,
        beforeShowDay: function(date) {
            if (date.getMonth() == 1 && (date.getDate() >5 && date.getDate() <10))
                    return [false, 'selected-day'];
            return [true, 'selected-day a'];
        },
        buttonText: 'Choose'
    }
);
```

Using an HTML helper, you can hide most of these details behind a simpler syntax, like the following:

```
<script type="text/javascript">
  $(document).ready(function() {
      <%= Html.jQueryUI().Calendar().Setup("FavoriteDay", "dd MM yy", true) %>
  });
</script>
```

The result of the preceding code is a date picker that shows the days of the other months (preceding and successive) and defaults to the *day Month year* format for selection. Let's dig out the source code of the HTML helper:

```
public class jquiContainer
{
    . .
    .
}
public class jquiCalendarHelpers
{
    . .
    .
}

public static class MyHelpers
{
    public static jquiContainer jQueryUI(this HtmlHelper helper)
    {
        return new jquiContainer();
    }

    public static jquiCalendarHelpers Calendar(this jquiContainer helper)
    {
        return new jquiCalendarHelpers();
    }

    public static MvcHtmlString Setup(this jquiCalendarHelpers helper, string id)
    {
        var builder = new StringBuilder();
        builder.AppendFormat("$(\"#{0}\").datepicker();", id);
        return MvcHtmlString.Create(builder.ToString());
    }
    public static MvcHtmlString Setup(this jquiCalendarHelpers helper,
            string id, string dateFormat, bool showOtherMonths)
    {
        var builder = new StringBuilder();
        var config = BuildConfig(dateFormat, showOtherMonths);
        builder.AppendFormat("$(\"#{0}\").datepicker({1}{2}{3});", id, "{", config, "}");
        return MvcHtmlString.Create(builder.ToString());
    }

    private static string BuildConfig(string dateFormat, bool showOtherMonths)
    {
        var builder = new StringBuilder();
```

```
        builder.AppendFormat("dateFormat:\"{0}\",showOtherMonths:{1}",
                dateFormat, showOtherMonths.ToString().ToLower());
        return builder.ToString();
    }
}
```

The helper is a bit more structured than in other examples. The *HtmlHelper* class is not extended directly by the method you would use in your code. Instead, a *jQueryUI* extension method is defined that returns a custom container object. The container, in turn, is extended with one container method for each category of widget. In the example, we have only one: the *Calendar* container, which represents the *datepicker* widget. Finally, the *Calendar* method is extended with the *Setup* method where you define the script you want. The *Setup* helper method on the *Calendar* container manages to emit the right script to customize the date picker the way you want. (See Figure 11-10.)

FIGURE 11-10 The jQuery UI date-picker widget configured using an HTML helper

Note If you find the default set of HTML helpers in ASP.NET MVC 2 a bit limiting, you might want to look at the ASP.NET MVC Futures assembly or, better yet, to its source code. You get ASP.NET MVC 2 Futures with the source code of the ASP.NET MVC 2 framework from the official site. Examples of HTML helpers in the Futures library include facilities for linking script files, style sheets, and images, and also buttons, radio-button lists, and mail-to links.

Summary

My gut feeling is that ASP.NET MVC was not designed to be as extensible and customizable as it turned out to be. However, I do believe it was *simply* written, adhering to sane design principles and accommodating current best practices. The net result is a framework that is highly extensible and easy to test. The two things go hand in hand because in order to test things effectively you need to isolate and abstract all dependencies. And once you have achieved this, you also have the tools to unplug a component and roll your own.

In ASP.NET MVC, you can take control over the execution of the action and intervene before and/or after the request has been processed. Likewise, you can gain control over nearly all aspects of the process that emits the response for the client browser. In this final chapter of the book, I mostly focused on customizing controllers and views. In past chapters, however, I touched on routes and custom routes, validation and custom validators, and model binders and custom model binders.

Even though nearly all aspects of ASP.NET MVC are customizable, you don't want to rewrite all of them all the time. The aspects of customization discussed in this chapter are those I feel are more frequently customized and, more importantly, those that, if properly customized, deliver the greatest benefits.

ReSharper and the Power of Tools

Pleasure in the job puts perfection in the work.

—Aristotle

Do you remember what it meant dealing with Web applications back in the '90s? Very much of it was a manual process. If you wanted a table, you had to render it out yourself. If you needed forms, you had to type in each HTML element manually. And it was just ordinary business at the time. When ASP.NET MVC came along in late 2007 and proposed a similar model for arranging the response to a request, well, to many people it was like déjà-vu— an unpleasant and bitter déjà-vu.

In fact, during initial talks and workshops I gave on ASP.NET MVC, there was some negativity in the air. After all, we were moving away from the productivity that frameworks such as Web Forms guaranteed. I could see the benefit of testability and cleaner design coming, but I was unable to balance those benefits with the quirkiness of manual view rendering. However, as newer builds of the ASP.NET MVC framework shipped, this view I had of ASP.NET MVC faded, and it largely disappeared with the release of version 1 (and now version 2).

The main reason behind this shift in my perception of the technology was because of the helpers and tooling that started shipping out of the box. Scaffolding, T4 support, and an extensive offering of HTML helpers have made a world of difference when developing in ASP.NET MVC. The tooling around ASP.NET MVC is what will make it or break it in terms of productivity. I often refer to the role of tools in development as a form of *sustainable development*. Think about it, and let me know if I completely missed the point here.

In this appendix, I'm going to take you for a tour around some ASP.NET MVC–specific capabilities of ReSharper (R# for short). R# is a popular plug-in for Microsoft Visual Studio developed by JetBrains. In the latest version—version 5.0—R# offers first-class support for the ASP.NET MVC framework. In the rest of the appendix, I'll go through some of these features to show how they can make your everyday development efforts more productive and pleasant.

For more information about R# 5.0, pay a visit to *http://www.jetbrains.com/resharper*.

IntelliSense Extensions

Microsoft IntelliSense has undoubtedly provided .NET developers with a great productivity boost. Not only has it made typing more efficient, but it also has enhanced accuracy. IntelliSense helps us by preventing spelling mistakes while invoking method names and by giving us information about parameters, quick documentation, and so forth. Combine IntelliSense with a strongly typed language, and you can have instant feedback on the syntactical accuracy of your code.

Choose the Right View Name with IntelliSense Tips

ASP.NET MVC relies heavily on strings. Many of the HTML helpers use strings to denote properties, actions, controllers, or views, among other things. Take for instance the action method shown here:

```
public ActionResult About()
{
    return View("Company");
}
```

If the view subsequent to a method takes the same name of the method, you can save parameters in the call to the *View* method. More often than not, however, a view with a different name is required. This is not a problem per se; however, suppose for a moment that you typed the string *Company* incorrectly. ASP.NET MVC will detect your error only at run time and serve you a nasty invalid operation exception. This is not just counterproductive, but it could also lead to quite embarrassing situations during deployment!

In similar situations, R# helps by providing IntelliSense tips when it comes to view names. To access this functionality, just press Ctrl+Space while writing the call to the *View* method, as shown in Figure A-1.

```
public ActionResult About()
{
    return View("|");
}
```

FIGURE A-1 R# helps you to pick up the right view name.

R# explores the current project and discovers the possible view names you might want to call at that point. The list of available views is easy to prepare: all files under *Views/Shared* and *Views/Xxx*, where *Xxx* is the current controller name. Note also that R# provides IntelliSense from inside a string—a not-so-obvious thing.

A clear benefit deriving from this feature is that if you reference a view that does not exist, you receive immediate visual feedback, as shown in Figure A-2. As such, you have substantially reduced your chances of deploying an application with a missing view.

```
public ActionResult About()
{
    return View("AboutCompany");
}
```

FIGURE A-2 R# detects that a missing view is being used.

Views with tree structures such as *Views/Home/Private/Login* are also supported. Further on in this appendix, you will see some more possibilities that R# offers in this regard.

Action Links and URLs

Action links have always been a painful feature to use in ASP.NET MVC because they force developers to use plain strings:

```
<li><%= Html.ActionLink("Home", "Index", "Home") %></li>
```

Similar to what happens when you pass an incorrect view name, mistyped strings resulting in broken links are not discovered until run time. One solution to this problem has been to use the expression-based *ActionLink* helpers that ship with the ASP.NET MVC Futures library. They make use of lambda expressions to provide strongly typed references to actions. The markup just shown could be written as it appears here:

```
<li><%= Html.ActionLink<HomeController>(actionName => actionName.Index(), "Home") %></li>
```

You still have a string, but that string now is only the text for the hyperlink. Note that ASP.NET MVC Futures is still a Microsoft library, but the features there are not considered to be ready for prime time yet. If you feel confident with a given feature, however, you are free to use the Futures library. Expression-based action links provide some good compile-time benefits but are known to have some impact on performance because of the heavy usage of expression trees.

A tool such as R# can help you write the correct code at the right time without any performance hit. Thanks to its firsthand knowledge of the ASP.NET MVC framework, R# can intelligently pop up a list of actions and controllers when you are editing an action link. (See Figure A-3.)

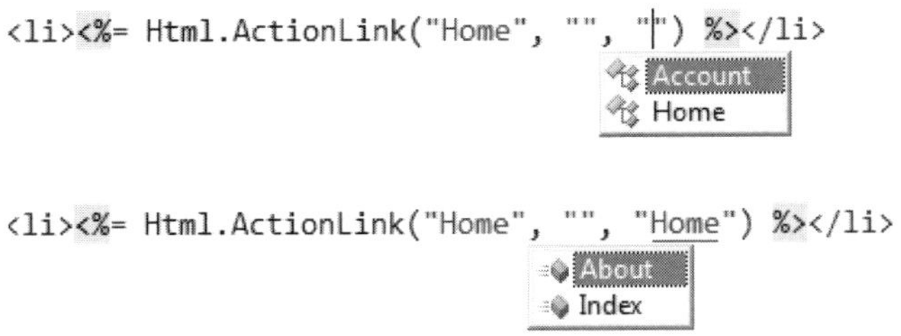

```
<li><%= Html.ActionLink("Home", "", "|") %></li>
                              Account
                              Home
```

```
<li><%= Html.ActionLink("Home", "", "Home") %></li>
                                     About
                                     Index
```

FIGURE A-3 R# gives you suggestions about controller and action names to use.

User Controls

R# provides the same support you've seen for views and action links for user controls and the corresponding *RenderPartial* method. Figure A-4 shows an example of it.

```
<% Html.RenderPartial(""); %>
```

FIGURE A-4 R# gives you suggestions about user controls.

More importantly, R# not only displays the list of user controls, but also includes any view that qualifies. The screen shot in Figure A-4 was taken while editing one of the master pages. Intelligently, R# lists only views and user controls located in the Views/Shared folder. If you try to do the same from inside the view of a specific controller, R# instead provides the list of views and user controls related to that controller, plus all those located in the Views/Shared folder.

Static Analysis to Detect Missing Views and Actions

In addition to providing editing facilities, R# can also perform a static analysis of your solution to detect any compile-time errors. The static analysis runs in the background and informs you promptly about what's wrong so that you can save yourself some full compile steps.

You can configure R# to determine what should be considered an error, a warning, or simply a hint. By default, R# reports as errors whatever would lead the compiler to fail. However, as you've seen, a missing view or an invalid action name will still produce an error—though probably not a compile error. When properly instructed, R# can detect these potential errors too.

The static analysis is a cross-project feature and detects errors in any files within the solution. You are notified of pending errors in your solution by an icon placed at the bottom-right corner of Visual Studio, as shown in Figure A-5.

FIGURE A-5 You have pending errors in your solution.

By clicking on the icon, you can navigate to the errors and solve them without hitting the compiler and with no unpleasant and time-consuming run-time experience.

Coding Assistants

As you saw in Chapter 10, "Testability and Unit Testing," ASP.NET MVC is a framework open to test-driven development (TDD). In a classic TDD cycle, you first create a test (more precisely, you write a specification to define the expected behavior of the class) and then proceed to implement the class. When using TDD, you frequently write code that references other code that doesn't exist yet. Visual Studio 2010 includes a number of enhancements to better support TDD scenarios, but it still lacks quite a few features that would make the overall experience significantly richer.

R# works to minimize the hassle associated with TDD by providing a collection of coding assistants. Coding assistants help particularly in TDD scenarios, but they are helpful regardless of the methodology in use. Let's find out more.

Creating Views by Usage

In Figure A-2, R# signals that a missing view is being used. A view might be missing for essentially two reasons: the name was mistyped or the view has not been created yet. You can create a new view in a number of ways. You can, for example, right-click in the solution and choose the Add View option from the Visual Studio context menu. Or you can just navigate to the appropriate location and create a new file.

With R#, you can create a view *by usage*. When R# detects an error, it provides a list of possible actions you can take at that point. When R# detects a missing view, it offers to create a new view. The list of actions is associated with the familiar red light bulb that appears next to the left margin. (See Figure A-6.)

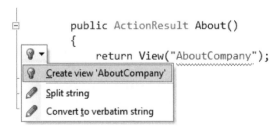

FIGURE A-6 R# suggests possible actions to take at this point.

After pressing the Enter key, you are prompted with the dialog box shown in Figure A-7, which is ready to collect information about the new view to be created. By default, the new view takes the name of the view referenced in code.

FIGURE A-7 R# offers to create a new view.

After you click OK, the view is created and placed in the appropriate folder.

Creating Action Links by Usage

Similar to its helpfulness with creating views, R# offers a usage menu when you're trying to create an action link and use incorrect strings. (See Figure A-8.)

FIGURE A-8 R# offers a quick-fix menu for broken action links.

The newly created controller contains code like that shown here:

```
public CustomerController : Controller
{
    public ActionResult Details()
    {
        throw new NotImplementedException();
    }
}
```

Surround with Tags

When writing code, you often encounter the need to wrap some blocks inside a statement, be it a *try/catch*, *using*, or *if* statement. This also can occur when you're working with ASP.NET markup. In this case, you likely want the existing markup to go inside a *div* or *span* or maybe in a *foreach* code block. R# 5.0 adds this new capability.

By selecting one or more lines of markup and pressing Ctrl+E,U (Ctrl+Alt+J if you're using the IntelliJ keyboard layout), you are prompted with a menu like the one shown in Figure A-9.

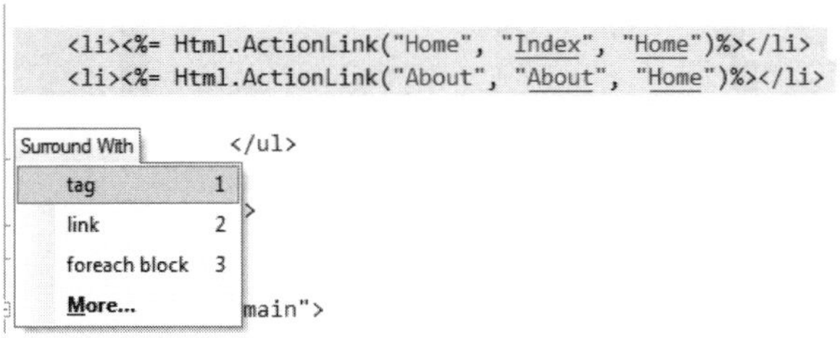

```
<li><%= Html.ActionLink("Home", "Index", "Home")%></li>
<li><%= Html.ActionLink("About", "About", "Home")%></li>

Surround With        </ul>
   tag          1
   link         2
   foreach block 3
   More...          main">
```

FIGURE A-9   R# is ready to surround the highlighted markup with your selection.

The first option is surrounding with a tag. By selecting it, you get another menu that allows you to choose the desired tag to wrap the code in.

Navigation

As solutions grow in size, it becomes harder to locate items. We tend to spend quite a bit of time with Solution Explorer searching for a specific class or file. This is a clear waste of time. R# adds many features when it comes to code navigation, and in this section you will see how it can help you when you're working with ASP.NET MVC solutions.

Controller and View Navigation

Both Visual Studio 2008 and Visual Studio 2010 offer to go from an action to the corresponding view and vice versa. However, navigation is limited to actions and views, and it doesn't work when the view name doesn't match the action method name.

R# provides a more generic way to navigate between controllers and views by means of its Type And File Navigation feature. By using the Go To Type feature, which is accessible by pressing Ctrl+T (or Ctrl+N in the IntelliJ scheme), you can quickly jump to a type by either entering a series of matching characters or typing the uppercase characters if the name is in CamelCase. For instance, to locate the *CustomerController* type, you can just type **CC**, as shown in Figure A-10.

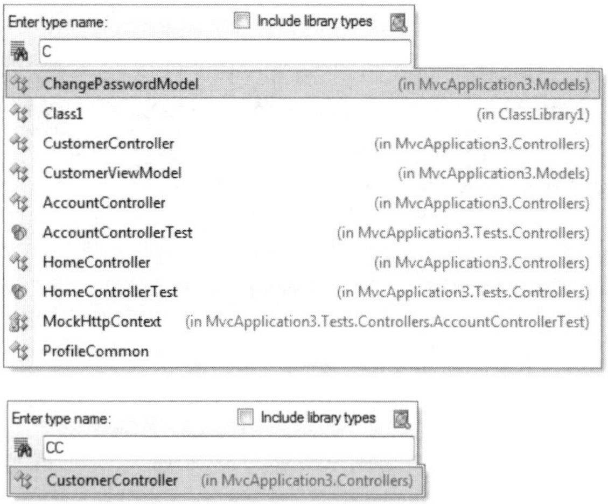

FIGURE A-10 The Go To Type navigation feature of R#

There is also a Go To File feature, through which you can locate a specific view by pressing Ctrl+Shift+T and entering the name of a view, as shown in Figure A-11.

FIGURE A-11 The Go To File navigation feature of R#

R# 5.0 also adds an ASP.NET MVC–specific feature known as View Navigation. Figure A-12 shows two distinct action methods. The first returns a view with the default name, whereas the second uses a custom name. Notice also that when the default view name is used, the *View* method is underlined; where a custom view name is used, instead, the string is underlined. This indicates where to click to navigate to the actual view template file.

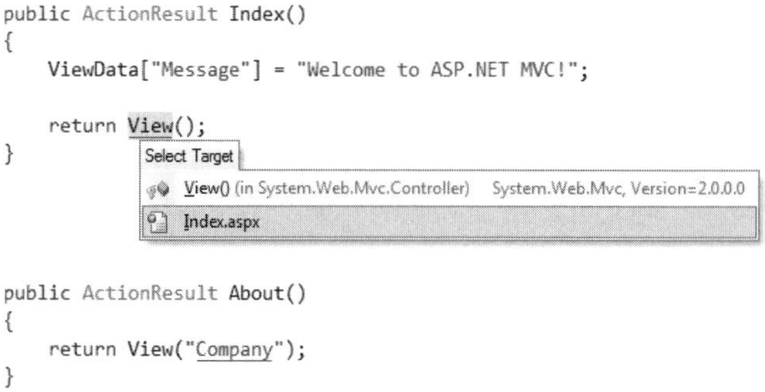

```
public ActionResult Index()
{
    ViewData["Message"] = "Welcome to ASP.NET MVC!";

    return View();
}
```

Select Target
View() (in System.Web.Mvc.Controller)   System.Web.Mvc, Version=2.0.0.0
Index.aspx

```
public ActionResult About()
{
    return View("Company");
}
```

FIGURE A-12 The View Navigation feature of R#

Finally, with R# 5.0 and permission from Microsoft to access the source code of the framework for browsing, the Go To Declaration feature has been extended to also reach types defined outside of the project, including the ASP.NET MVC native classes. This comes in very handy when you become willing to delve into the inner workings of ASP.NET MVC.

Similarly, R# allows navigating from the controller and view names within the syntax of an action link. Both strings appear underlined, meaning that by holding down the Ctrl key and pressing the left mouse button, you are taken directly to the required location.

Locating Symbols

The Go To Member feature has been extended in R# 5.0 to include support for Web files. So you can easily locate a specific element in a view file, as demonstrated in Figure A-13.

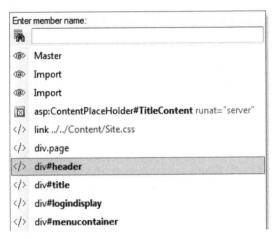

FIGURE A-13 The Go To Member feature of R#

Navigating Inside Master and Content Pages

In ASP.NET, you use master and content pages to give a homogenous look and feel to views. A master page defines placeholders for which a content page provides actual content. Master and content files are related but distinct, with no easy way to navigate inside of them. R# fills the gap through the Navigate To menu invoked by pressing Alt+[. (See Figure A-14.)

FIGURE A-14 The Navigate To menu for master/content navigation

Of particular interest is the Related Files menu item. It lists all files that are related to the current view—whether they are script files, style sheets, user controls, or even controllers. Here's a view of the menu:

FIGURE A-15 Navigating related files

Refactoring for ASP.NET MVC

Refactoring has always been the core business of R#. With 40 solution-wide automatic refactorings, plus time-saving features such as safe deletion and moving of types and files, R# is the de facto standard for cleaning up .NET code. Covering the many features of R# related to refactoring would take a chapter of its own. So let's just have a quick look at items in the refactoring menu specific to ASP.NET MVC.

Like it or not, ASP.NET MVC is dependent on strings. Renaming an action method, for example, is a critical action in ASP.NET MVC. Suppose you want to rename an action named *LogOn* to *LogIn*. If you do it via R#, you are prompted with the dialog box shown in Figure A-16.

FIGURE A-16 Renaming an action method

Just finding and renaming all occurrences of the string is not enough in ASP.MVC if the string is actually the name of an action method. When the method to rename is an ASP.NET MVC action method, R# will in fact also rename the view with the same name (if any), making sure that your change won't originate a 404 exception at run time. In addition, R# looks for any places where the action method is used in links and renames that too. This behavior is the result of the combined effect of selecting the first two check boxes you see in Figure A-16.

When, instead, you rename a view, R# ensures that no action methods that invoke the view are broken.

Conclusion

Web Forms was successful 10 years ago because it offered a thick abstraction layer over the actual mechanics of the Web and HTTP. Today, ASP.NET MVC is a new framework that answers the growing demand for control over HTML, JavaScript, cascading style sheets (CSS), and the like.

Thick abstraction and closeness-to-the-metal are opposite concepts.

The thick abstraction of Web Forms boosts the productivity of developers; the *closeness-to-the-metal* that characterizes ASP.NET MVC, instead, maximizes the control that developers can exercise over the markup. More control, however, means more work and at a lower level of abstraction.

How does this improve productivity, then?

One way is to increase the dose of Convention-over-Configuration in the framework so that many aspects of your code work automatically, in a given way, and without requiring additional effort on your part. Another way is to leverage smart tools like R#.

If you intend to use ASP.NET MVC in your next project, I definitely recommend you consider R# as well. Visual Studio 2010 comes with a lot of improvements over previous versions, especially in the area of refactoring, IntelliSense extensions, coding assistance, and navigation. Although this is much better than the little bit offered in Visual Studio 2008, made-to-measure tools such as R# offer a ton of extra features. It won't take you more than a week to become addicted to a tool like R#.

ASP.NET MVC has you working at a low level of abstraction. R# raises the abstraction level at which you work, reduces the amount of time wasted searching for and fixing bugs, and promotes better code and effective techniques. And, most importantly, you end up writing much better code through simple mechanical operations.

Index

Symbols and Numbers

A

I

Dino Esposito

Dino Esposito is an architect and a trainer based in Rome, Italy. Dino specializes in Microsoft Web technologies, including ASP.NET, AJAX, and Silverlight, and spends most of his time teaching and consulting across Europe, Australia, and the United States.

Over the years, Dino developed hands-on experience and skills in architecting and building distributed systems in industry contexts where the demand for maintainability, extensibility, scalability, and interoperability is dramatically high. Every month, a variety of magazines and Web sites throughout the world publish Dino's articles covering topics ranging from Web development to data access and from software best practices to design principles. A prolific author, Dino writes the monthly "Cutting Edge" column for *MSDN Magazine* and the "CoreCoder" column for *DevProConnections* magazine.

As a widely acknowledged expert in Web applications built with .NET technologies, Dino often works with emerging companies, helping them realize their potential with passion and pleasure. In particular, Dino is directly involved in the Ibrii project (*http://www.ibrii.com*). Ibrii is a cool, new social network application for sharing everything you see on Web pages and was built entirely with the Microsoft Web stack.

Dino has written an array of books, most of which are considered state of the art in their respective areas. His more recent books are *Microsoft .NET: Architecting Applications for the Enterprise* (co-authored by Andrea Saltarello; Microsoft Press, 2008) and *ASP.NET and AJAX: Architecting Web Applications* (Microsoft Press, 2009). Dino regularly speaks at industry conferences all over the world (including Microsoft TechEd, Microsoft TechDays, DevConnections, DevWeek, Software Architect, and Basta) and at local technical conferences and meetings in Europe and the United States.

Dino lives near Rome and keeps in shape playing tennis at least twice a week at CT Monterotondo.

Best Practices for Software Engineering

Software Estimation: Demystifying the Black Art
Steve McConnell
ISBN 9780735605350

Code Complete, Second Edition
Steve McConnell
ISBN 9780735619678

Amazon.com's pick for "Best Computer Book of 2006"! Generating accurate software estimates is fairly straight-forward—once you understand the art of creating them. Acclaimed author Steve McConnell demystifies the process—illuminating the practical procedures, formulas, and heuristics you can apply right away.

Widely considered one of the best practical guides to programming—fully updated. Drawing from research, academia, and everyday commercial practice, McConnell synthesizes must-know principles and techniques into clear, pragmatic guidance. Rethink your approach—and deliver the highest quality code.

Agile Portfolio Management
Jochen Krebs
ISBN 9780735625679

Simple Architectures for Complex Enterprises
Roger Sessions
ISBN 9780735625785

Agile processes foster better collaboration, innovation, and results. So why limit their use to software projects—when you can transform your entire business? This book illuminates the opportunities—and rewards—of applying agile processes to your overall IT portfolio, with best practices for optimizing results.

Why do so many IT projects fail? Enterprise consultant Roger Sessions believes complex problems require simple solutions. And in this book, he shows how to make simplicity a core architectural requirement—as critical as performance, reliability, or security—to achieve better, more reliable results for your organization.

The Enterprise and Scrum
Ken Schwaber
ISBN 9780735623378

ALSO SEE

Software Requirements, Second Edition
Karl E. Wiegers
ISBN 9780735618794

More About Software Requirements: Thorny Issues and Practical Advice
Karl E. Wiegers
ISBN 9780735622678

Software Requirement Patterns
Stephen Withall
ISBN 9780735623989

Extend Scrum's benefits—greater agility, higher-quality products, and lower costs—beyond individual teams to the entire enterprise. Scrum cofounder Ken Schwaber describes proven practices for adopting Scrum principles across your organization, including that all-critical component—managing change.

Agile Project Management with Scrum
Ken Schwaber
ISBN 9780735619937

Solid Code
Donis Marshall, John Bruno
ISBN 9780735625921

microsoft.com/mspress

What do you think of this book?

We want to hear from you!

To participate in a brief online survey, please visit:

microsoft.com/learning/booksurvey

Tell us how well this book meets your needs—what works effectively, and what we can do better. Your feedback will help us continually improve our books and learning resources for you.

Thank you in advance for your input!

Microsoft® *Press*

Stay in touch!

To subscribe to the *Microsoft Press*® *Book Connection Newsletter*—for news on upcoming books, events, and special offers—please visit:

microsoft.com/learning/books/newsletter